# Modeling Applications and Theoretical Innovations in Interdisciplinary Evolutionary Computation

Wei-Chiang Samuelson Hong
*Oriental Institute of Technology, Taiwan*

**Information Science**
**REFERENCE**

| | |
|---|---|
| Managing Director: | Lindsay Johnston |
| Editorial Director: | Joel Gamon |
| Book Production Manager: | Jennifer Yoder |
| Publishing Systems Analyst: | Adrienne Freeland |
| Development Editor: | Joel Gamon |
| Assistant Acquisitions Editor: | Kayla Wolfe |
| Typesetter: | Lisandro Gonzalez |
| Cover Design: | Jason Mull |

Published in the United States of America by
Information Science Reference (an imprint of IGI Global)
701 E. Chocolate Avenue
Hershey PA 17033
Tel: 717-533-8845
Fax: 717-533-8661
E-mail: cust@igi-global.com
Web site: http://www.igi-global.com

Library of Congress Cataloging-in-Publication Data

Modeling applications and theoretical innovations in interdisciplinary
evolutionary computation / Wei-Chiang Samuelson Hong, Editor.
       pages cm
   "This book contains articles from the four issues of volume 2 of the International Journal of Applied Evolutionary Computation (IJAEC)."
   Includes bibliographical references and index.
   ISBN 978-1-4666-3628-6 (hardcover) -- ISBN 978-1-4666-3629-3 (ebook) -- ISBN 978-1-4666-3630-9 (print & perpetual access) 1. Evolutionary programming (Computer science) 2. Evolutionary computation. 3. Genetic algorithms. I. Hong, Wei-Chiang Samuelson, 1972- editor. II. International journal of applied evolutionary computation.
   QA76.618.M63 2013
   005.1--dc23
                            2012046679

British Cataloguing in Publication Data
A Cataloguing in Publication record for this book is available from the British Library.

All work contributed to this book is new, previously-unpublished material. The views expressed in this book are those of the authors, but not necessarily of the publisher.

# Table of Contents

# Detailed Table of Contents

**Chapter 1**

    *Alice Yalaoui, University of Technology of Troyes, France*
    *Farah Belmecheri, University of Technology of Troyes, France*
    *Eric Châtelet, University of Technology of Troyes, France*
    *Farouk Yalaoui, University of Technology of Troyes, France*

Reliability optimization is an important step in industrial systems design. In order to develop a reliable system, designers may introduce different redundant technologies with the same functionality in parallel. In this paper, each technology is assumed to be composed of series components. The obtained configuration belongs to the series-parallel systems. The presented tool is for the design or the improvement of such systems, in order to minimize the system cost with a reliability constraint. The aim is to find the reliability to allocate to each component in order to minimize the total cost, such that the global system reliability verifies a minimal level constraint. This problem is known to be NP-hard. In this paper, a metaheuristic approach, based on the Ant Colony Optimization technics (ACO), is used in order to improve an existing approach. The experimental results, based on randomly generated instances, outperform the one of previous method dedicated to this problem.

**Chapter 2**

    *Liau Heng Fui, University of Nottingham Malaysia, Malaysia*
    *Dino Isa, University of Nottingham Malaysia, Malaysia*

Feature selection is crucial to select an "optimized" subset of features from the original feature set based on a certain objective function. In general, feature selection removes redundant or irrelevant data while retaining classification accuracy. This paper proposes a feature selection algorithm that aims to minimize the area under the curve of detection error trade-off (DET) curve. Particle swarm optimization (PSO) is employed to search for the optimal feature subset. The proposed method is implemented in face recognition and iris recognition systems. The result shows that the proposed method is able to find an optimal subset of features that sufficiently describes iris and face images by removing unwanted and redundant features and at the same time improving the classification accuracy in terms of total error rate (TER).

*Julliany Sales Brandão, Centro Federal de Educação Tecnológica Celso S. da*
*Fonseca – CEFET/RJ, Brasil*
*Alessandra Martins Coelho, Instituto Politécnico do Rio de Janeiro – UERJ, Brasil*
*João Flávio V. Vasconcellos, Instituto Politécnico do Rio de Janeiro – UERJ, Brasil*
*Luiz Leduíno de Salles Neto, Universidade Federal de São Paulo – UNIFESP, Brasil*
*André Vieira Pinto, Universidade Federal do Estado do Rio de Janeiro – UNIRIO, Brasil*

This paper presents the application of the one new approach using Genetic Algorithm in solving One-Dimensional Cutting Stock Problems in order to minimize two objectives, usually conflicting, i.e., the number of processed objects and setup while simultaneously treating them as a single goal. The model problem, the objective function, the method denominated SingleGA10 and the steps used to solve the problem are also presented. The obtained results of the SingleGA10 are compared to the following methods: SHP, Kombi234, ANLCP300 and Symbio10, found in literature, verifying its capacity to find feasible and competitive solutions. The computational results show that the proposed method, which only uses a genetic algorithm to solve these two objectives inversely related, provides good results.

*Periasamy Vivekanandan, Park College of Engineering and Technology, India*
*Raju Nedunchezhian, Kalaignar Karunanidhi Institute of Technology, India*

Genetic algorithm is a search technique purely based on natural evolution process. It is widely used by the data mining community for classification rule discovery in complex domains. During the learning process it makes several passes over the data set for determining the accuracy of the potential rules. Due to this characteristic it becomes an extremely I/O intensive slow process. It is particularly difficult to apply GA when the training data set becomes too large and not fully available. An incremental Genetic algorithm based on boosting phenomenon is proposed in this paper which constructs a weak ensemble of classifiers in a fast incremental manner and thus tries to reduce the learning cost considerably.

*Y. S. Rao, Sri Veeravenkata Satyanarayana (SVVSN) Engineering College, India*
*C. S. P. Rao, National Institute of Technology, India*
*G. Ranga Janardhana, Jawaharlal Nehru Technological University, India*
*Pandu R. Vundavilli, DVR & Dr. HS MIC College of Technology, India*

Tolerance plays a major role in the manufacturing industry, as it affects product design, manufacturing, and quality of the product. This paper considers product design, manufacturing, and quality simultaneously, and introduces a concurrent approach for tolerance allocation using evolutionary algorithms. A non-linear model that minimizes the combination of manufacturing cost and quality loss simultaneously, in a single objective function has been considered. In the proposed work, evolutionary algorithms (that is, Genetic Algorithms (GA), Differential Evolution (DE), and Particle Swarm Optimization (PSO)) have been used to determine the optimal tolerances at the minimum manufacturing and quality loss cost. The application of the proposed methodology has been demonstrated on a simple mechanical assembly.

This paper critically reviews the reported research on parallel single and multi-objective genetic algorithms. Many early efforts on single and multi-objective genetic algorithms were introduced to reduce the processing time needed to reach an acceptable solution. However, some parallel single and multi-objective genetic algorithms converged to better solutions as compared to comparable sequential single and multiple objective genetic algorithms. The authors review several representative models for parallelizing single and multi-objective genetic algorithms. Further, some of the issues that have not yet been studied systematically are identified in the context of parallel single and parallel multi-objective genetic algorithms. Finally, some of the potential applications of parallel multi-objective GAs are discussed.

The Differential Evolution (DE) is a well known Evolutionary Algorithm (EA), and is popular for its simplicity. Several novelties have been proposed in research to enhance the performance of DE. This paper focuses on demonstrating the performance enhancement of DE by implementing some of the recent ideas in DE's research viz. Dynamic Differential Evolution (dDE), Multiple Trial Vector Differential Evolution (mtvDE), Mixed Variant Differential Evolution (mvDE), Best Trial Vector Differential Evolution (btvDE), Distributed Differential Evolution (diDE) and their combinations. The authors have chosen fourteen variants of DE and six benchmark functions with different modality viz. Unimodal Separable, Unimodal Nonseparable, Multimodal Separable, and Multimodal Nonseparable. On analyzing distributed DE and mixed variant DE, a novel mixed-variant distributed DE is proposed whereby the subpopulations (islands) employ different DE variants to cooperatively solve the given problem. The competitive performance of mixed-variant distributed DE on the chosen problem is also demonstrated. The variants are well compared by their mean objective function values and probability of convergence.

The asymmetric volatility, temporary volatility, and permanent volatility of financial asset returns have attracted much interest in recent years. However, a consensus has not yet been reached on the causes of them for both the stocks and markets. This paper researched asymmetric volatility and short-run and long-run volatility through global financial crisis for eight Asian markets. EGARCH and CGARCH models are employed to deal with the daily return to examine the degree of asymmetric volatility (temporary volatility and permanent volatility). The authors find that after global financial crisis asymmetric volatility is lower (expect Hong Kong), and the long-run effect is more than the short-run effect. The empirical results for the short-run show that, after global financial crisis, there is significant decreasing in China and Taiwan but not in Japan; the others are significantly increasing. For the long-run, there is significant decreasing (except Thailand and Korea).

*Tarun Kumar Sharma, Indian Institute of Technology Roorkee, India*
*Millie Pant, Indian Institute of Technology Roorkee, India*

Artificial Bee Colony (ABC) is one of the most recent nature inspired (NIA) algorithms based on swarming metaphor. Proposed by Karaboga in 2005, ABC has proven to be a robust and efficient algorithm for solving global optimization problems over continuous space. However, it has been observed that the structure of ABC is such that it supports exploration more in comparison to exploitation. In order to maintain a balance between these two antagonist factors, this paper suggests incorporation of differential evolution (DE) operators in the structure of basic ABC algorithm. The proposed algorithm called DE-ABC is validated on a set of 10 benchmark problems and the numerical results are compared with basic DE and basic ABC algorithm. The numerical results indicate that the presence of DE operators help in a significant improvement in the performance of ABC algorithm.

*B. B. Choudhury, IGIT Sarang, India*
*B. B. Biswal, NIT Rourkela, India*
*D. Mishra, VSS University of Technology, India*
*R. N. Mahapatra, Institute of Technical Education and Research, India*

The diffusion of flexible manufacturing systems (FMS) has not only invigorated production systems, but has also given considerable impetus to relevant analytical fields like scheduling theory and adaptive controls. Depending on the demand of the job there can be variation in batch size. The change in the jobs depends upon the renewal rate. But this does not involve much change in the FMS setup. This paper obtains an optimal schedule of operations to minimize the total processing time in a modular FMS. The FMS setup considered here consists of four numbers of machines to accomplish the desired machining operations. The scheduling deals with optimizing the cost function in terms of machining time. The powers Evolutionary Algorithms, like genetic algorithm (GA) and simulated annealing (SA), can be beneficially utilized for optimization of scheduling FMS. The present work utilizes these powerful approaches and finds out their appropriateness for planning and scheduling of FMS producing variety of parts in batch mode.

*Archana Sarangi, Siksha O Anusandhan University, India*
*Sasmita Kumari Padhy, Siksha O Anusandhan University, India*
*Siba Prasada Panigrahi, Konark Institute of Science & Technology, India*
*Shubhendu Kumar Sarangi, Siksha O Anusandhan University, India*

This paper proposes a neuro-fuzzy filter for equalization of time-varying channels. Additionally, it proposes to tune the equalizer with a hybrid algorithm between Genetic Algorithms (GA) and Bacteria Foraging (BFO), termed as GBF. The major advantage of the method developed in this paper is that all parameters of the neuro-fuzzy network, including the rule base, are tuned simultaneously through the proposed hybrid algorithm of genetic Algorithm and bacteria foraging. The performance of the Neuro-Fuzzy equalizer designed using the proposed approach is compared with Genetic algorithm based equalizers. The results confirm that the methodology used in the paper is much better than existing approaches. The proposed hybrid algorithm also eliminates the limitations of GA based equalizer, i.e. the inherent characteristic of GA, i.e. GAs risk finding a sub-optimal solution.

## Chapter 12

*S. Chakravarty, Regional College of Management Autonomous, India*

*P. K. Dash, Siksha O Anusandhan University, India*

*V. Ravikumar Pandi, Indian Institute of Technology Delhi, India*

*B. K. Panigrahi, Indian Institute of Technology Delhi, India*

This paper proposes a hybrid model, evolutionary functional link neural fuzzy model (EFLNF), to forecast financial time series where the parameters are optimized by two most efficient evolutionary algorithms: (a) genetic algorithm (GA) and (b) particle swarm optimization (PSO). When the periodicity is just one day, PSO produces a better result than that of GA. But the gap in the performance between them increases as periodicity increases. The convergence speed is also better in case of PSO for one week and one month a head prediction. To testify the superiority of the EFLNF, a number of comparative studies have been made. First, functional link artificial neural network (FLANN) and functional link neural fuzzy (FLNF) were combined with back propagation (BP) learning algorithm. The result shows that FLNF performs better than FLANN. Again, FLNF is compared with EFLNF where the latter outperforms the former irrespective of the periodicity or the learning algorithms with which it has been combined. All models are used to predict the most chaotic financial time series data; BSE Sensex and S&P CNX Nifty stock indices one day, one week and one month in advance.

## Chapter 13

*Shih-Yung Wei, National Yunlin University of Science & Technology, Taiwan*

*Wei-Chiang Hong, Oriental Institute of Technology, Taiwan*

*Kai Wang, China University of Technology, Taiwan*

Investors attend importance to forecast the price of financial assets, thus, the factors affecting the stock price are usually the focus of financial research in the field, in which the most important factors to scholars are firm size transmission effect and price-volume relationship. In this study, the analysis of these two items in the Taiwan stock market is conducted. The results indicate that the firm size transmission effect is almost significant, and the reversal phenomenon also exists. However, before the financial tsunami, the firm size transmission effect does not significantly exist; this result also indirectly proves the directional asymmetry of the market returns, proposed by McQueen, Pinegar, and Thorley (1996). For price and volume relationship, big cap index reveals that volume leads to price before the financial tsunami, and small cap index appears that price leads to volume in 2010.

## Chapter 14

*Lei Fang, Xi'an Jiaotong-Liverpool University, China*

*Sheng-Uei Guan, Xi'an Jiaotong-Liverpool University, China*

*Haofan Zhang, Xi'an Jiaotong-Liverpool University, China*

Rule-based Genetic Algorithms (GAs) have been used in the application of pattern classification (Corcoran & Sen, 1994), but conventional GAs have weaknesses. First, the time spent on learning is long. Moreover, the classification accuracy achieved by a GA is not satisfactory. These drawbacks are due to existing undesirable features embedded in conventional GAs. The number of rules within the chromosome of a GA classifier is usually set and fixed before training and is not problem-dependent. Secondly, conventional approaches train the data in batch without considering whether decomposition solves the problem. Thirdly, when facing large-scale real-world problems, GAs cannot utilise resources efficiently, leading to premature convergence. Based on these observations, this paper develops a novel algorithmic framework that features automatic domain and task decomposition and problem-dependent chromosome length (rule number) selection to resolve these undesirable features. The proposed Recursive Learning of Genetic Algorithm with Task Decomposition and Varied Rule Set (RLGA) method is recursive and trains and evolves a team of learners using the concept of local fitness to decompose the original problem into sub-problems. RLGA performs better than GAs and other related solutions regarding training duration and generalization accuracy according to the experimental results.

## Chapter 15

*Worasait Suwannik, Kasetsart University, Thailand*

To solve a problem using Genetic Algorithms (GAs), a solution must be encoded into a binary string. The length of the binary string represents the size of the problem. As the length of the binary string increases, the size of the search space also increases at an exponential rate. To reduce the search space, one approach is to use a compressed encoding chromosome. This paper presents a genetic algorithm, called LZWGA, that uses compressed chromosomes. An LZWGA chromosome must be decompressed using an LZW decompression algorithm before its fitness can be evaluated. By using compressed encoding, the search space is reduced dramatically. For one-million-bit problem, the search space of the original problem is 21000000 or about 9.90x10301029 points. When using a compressed encoding, the search space was reduced to 8.37x10166717 points. LZWGA can solve one-million-bit OneMax, RoyalRoad, and Trap functions.

## Chapter 16

*R. Rathipriya, Periyar University, India*
*K. Thangavel, Periyar University, India*
*J. Bagyamani, Government Arts College, Dharmapuri, India*

Biclustering has the potential to make significant contributions in the fields of information retrieval, web mining, and so forth. In this paper, the authors analyze the complex association between users and pages of a web site by using a biclustering algorithm. This method automatically identifies the groups of users that show similar browsing patterns under a specific subset of the pages. In this paper, mutation operator from Genetic Algorithms is incorporated into the Binary Particle Swarm Optimization (BPSO) for biclustering of web usage data. This hybridization can increase the diversity of the population and help the particles effectively escape from the local optimum. It detects optimized user profile group according to coherent browsing behavior. Experiments are performed on a benchmark clickstream dataset to test the effectiveness of the proposed algorithm. The results show that the proposed algorithm has higher performance than existing PSO methods. The interpretation of this biclustering results are useful for marketing and sales strategies.

**Chapter 17**

*Jiansheng Wu, Wuhan University of Technology, China & Liuzhou Teachers College, China*

Rainfall forecasting is an important research topic in disaster prevention and reduction. The characteristic of rainfall involves a rather complex systematic dynamics under the influence of different meteorological factors, including linear and nonlinear pattern. Recently, many approaches to improve forecasting accuracy have been introduced. Artificial neural network (ANN), which performs a nonlinear mapping between inputs and outputs, has played a crucial role in forecasting rainfall data. In this paper, an effective hybrid semi-parametric regression ensemble (SRE) model is presented for rainfall forecasting. In this model, three linear regression models are used to capture rainfall linear characteristics and three nonlinear regression models based on ANN are able to capture rainfall nonlinear characteristics. The semi-parametric regression is used for ensemble model based on the principal component analysis technique. Empirical results reveal that the prediction using the SRE model is generally better than those obtained using other models in terms of the same evaluation measurements. The SRE model proposed in this paper can be used as a promising alternative forecasting tool for rainfall to achieve greater forecasting accuracy and improve prediction quality.

# Preface

This book contains articles from the four issues of Volume 2 of the *International Journal of Applied Evolutionary Computation* (IJAEC). As mentioned in journal's description, this book reflects the journal's mission of publishing high-quality comprehensive interdisciplinary academic and practitioner research, and surveys that provide a reference channel for disseminating all experimental, theoretical and application emerging aspects of intelligent computation (IC) and its applications, with particular focus on breaking trends in evolutionary computation, evolutionary algorithms, evolutionary programming, fuzzy computation, neural computation, traditional probabilistic computation, and their industrial applications. Over the last years, EC in its various forms has emerged as one of the major topics in the scientific community and many EC techniques have been successfully applied to solve problems in a wide variety of fields. These articles also reflect the journal's objective of dedicating to provide a exchangeable forum academically and high quality results for innovative topics, trends and research in the field of EC, to succeed in expanding the fields and depths the most principal and critical concepts that will form the applications from EC more matured in the future.

*IJAEC* is intended to serve and support scientists, professionals, entrepreneurs, government employees, policy and decision makers, educators, students and all people who are working in this scientific field or who are interested in considering and using EC techniques for their specific applications. This academic resource dedicates to provide international audiences with the highest quality research manuscripts in emphasizing computational results which have been are ideally put in the context of algorithm design; in addition, purely theoretical papers will also be encouraged. Researchers, academicians, practitioners and students will find this journal as a critical source of reference for all advanced intelligent computational applications and developments. On the other hand, along with the tremendous development in complicated public economic and business operations, EC has also been viewed as a great application and a solution to solve in a variety of business modelling. *IJAEC* is also devoted to data analysis and applications and tools used for business modelling, including all areas of pattern recognition, forecasting, classification, optimization cluster, bio-inspired systems and novel applications. A summary of the scope of IJAEC includes: (1) *Intelligent techniques.* Fuzzy computing, neural computing, and evolutionary computing; evolutionary algorithms (genetic algorithms, simulated annealing algorithms,...); evolutionary programming; probabilistic computing; immunological computing; grid computing; natural computing; expert and hybrid systems (methods); Chaos theory; and other intelligent techniques (interactive computational models); (2) *Data analysis.* Classification, regression, and optimization cluster; decision support system; statistical pattern recognition; signal or image processing; (3) *Applications and tools.* Vision or pattern recognition, time series forecasting; biomedical engineering; manufacturing systems; power and energy; data mining; data visualization; bio-inspired systems and tools and applications.

The first article in the first issue, volume 2 of IJAEC, titled "Reliability Allocation Problem in Series-Parallel Systems: Ant Colony Optimization" by Yalaoui, Belmecheri, Châtelet, and Yalaoui from University of Technology of Troyes (France), applies ant colony optimization (ACO) algorithm to minimize the cost of the series-parallel system with a reliability constraint. Reliability optimization is an important step in industrial systems design. Different technologies with the same functionality in parallel are introduced to develop a reliable system. Authors propose a two-stage algorithm, namely ACO-SS algorithm (Ant Colony Optimization- Sub-System) for the first step and ACO-SG algorithm (Ant Colony Optimization-General System) for the global system, to optimally solve problems. Their experiments outperform the one of previous method dedicated to this problem.

The second article of this issue, titled "Feature Selection Based on Minimizing the Area Under the Detection Error Tradeoff Curve" by Liau and Isa from the University of Nottingham (Malaysia Campus), employs particle swarm optimization (PSO) to search for the optimal feature subset in face recognition and iris recognition systems to minimize the area under the curve of detection error trade-off (DET) curve. Their experimental results show that the proposed method is able to find an optimal subset of features that sufficiently describes iris and face images by removing unwanted and redundant features and at the same time improving the classification accuracy in terms of total error rate (TER).

The third article of the issue, titled "Application of Genetic Algorithm to Minimize the Number of Objects Processed and Setup in a One-Dimensional Cutting Stock Problem" by Brandão from Universidade Federal Fluminense (Brazil), Coelho, Vasconcellos, Pinto from Rio de Janeiro State University (Brazil), and Neto from Federal University of São Paulo (Brazil), applies genetic algorithm (GA) to solve one-dimensional cutting stock problems. The model problem, the objective function, the method denominated SingleGA10 and the steps used to solve the problem are also presented. The computational results show that the proposed method, which only uses a genetic algorithm to solve these two objectives inversely related, provides good results.

The final article of this issue, titled "A Fast Boosting Based Incremental Genetic Algorithm for Mining Classification Rules in Large Datasets" by Nedunchezhian from Park College of Engineering and Technology (India) and Vivekanandan from Kalaignar Karunanidhi Institute of Technology (India), presents an incremental genetic algorithm (IGA) based on boosting phenomenon to construct a weak ensemble of classifiers in a fast incremental manner and thus to try to reduce the learning cost considerably. During the learning process it makes several passes over the data set for determining the accuracy of the potential rules. Due to this characteristic it becomes an extremely I/O intensive slow process. It is particularly difficult to apply GA when the training data set becomes too large and not fully available. The proposed IGA could successfully to overcome this kind of drawback.

The first article of Volume 2, Issue 2, titled "Simultaneous Tolerance Synthesis for Manufacturing and Quality using Evolutionary Algorithms" by Rao from S. V. V. S. N. Engineering College (India), Rao from National Institute of Technology (India), Rangajanardhan from J. N. T. University (India), and Vundavilli from DVR & Dr. HS MIC College of Technology (India), applies evolutionary algorithms (e.g., genetic algorithms, differential evolution and particle swarm optimization) to determine the optimal tolerances at the minimum manufacturing and quality loss cost. A non-linear model that minimizes the combination of manufacturing cost and quality loss simultaneously, in a single objective function has been considered. Their experiments obtained by these algorithms are found to be comparable with those obtained by other alternative methods.

The second article of the issue, titled "Parallel Single and Multiple Objectives Genetic Algorithms: A Survey" by Mishra from KIIT University (India), Dehuri from Fakir Mohan University (India), Mall from Indian Institute of Technology Kharagpur (India), and Ghosh from Indian Statistical Institute (India), provides a thorough review on parallel single and multi-objective genetic algorithms. They indicate that many early efforts on single and multi-objective genetic algorithms were proposed to reduce the processing time needed to reach an acceptable solution. Finally, some of the potential applications of parallel multi-objective GAs are discussed.

The third article, titled "Experimental Study on Recent Advances in Differential Evolution Algorithm" by Jeyakumar and Shanmugavelayutham from Amrita School of Engineering (India), is focusing on demonstrating the performance enhancement of dynamic differential evolution (dDE), multiple trial vector differential evolution (mtvDE), mixed variant differential evolution (mvDE), best trial vector differential evolution (btvDE), distributed differential evolution (diDE) and their combinations. The chapter applies genetic algorithm (GA) to solve one-dimensional cutting stock problems. The computational results show that the variants are well compared by their mean objective function values and probability of convergence.

The final article of the second issue of 2011 is titled "The Volatility for Pre and Post Global Financial Crisis: An Application of Computational Finance" and is written by Wei and Yang from National Yunlin University of Science & Technology (Taiwan), Chen from TransWorld University (Taiwan), and Hong from Oriental Institute of Technology (Taiwan), presents an application of computational finance by employing EGARCH and CGARCH models to deal with the daily return to examine the degree of asymmetric volatility (temporary volatility and permanent volatility). They find that after global financial crisis asymmetric volatility is lower (expect Hong Kong), and the long-run effect is more than the short-run effect. In addition, the empirical results for the short-run show that, after Global Financial Crisis, there are significantly decreasing in China and Taiwan but not in Japan, the others are significantly increasing. For the long-run, there are significantly decreasing (except Thailand and Korea). It is valuable to enable policy makers to design new market mechanisms.

The first article of Volume 2, Issue 3, "Differential Operators Embedded Artificial Bee Colony Algorithm" by Sharma and Pant from Indian Institute of Technology, Roorkee (India), employs the differential evolution (DE) as a mechanism to balance two antagonist factors, i.e., exploration and exploitation, in the artificial bee colony algorithm (ABC). Their experiments obtained by the improved algorithm (DE-ABC) are found that the presence of DE operators help in a significant improvement in the performance of ABC algorithm.

In "Appropriate Evolutionary Algorithm for Scheduling in FMS," the second article in Volume 2, Issue 3, Choudhury from IGIT Sarang (India), Biswal from NIT Rourkela (India), Mishra from VSS University (India), and Mahapatra from ITER (India) consider the optimal schedule of operations to minimize the total processing time in a modular flexible manufacturing system (FMS). However, the scheduling deals with optimizing the cost function in terms of machining time. Thus, they apply the genetic algorithm (GA) and simulated annealing algorithm (SA) to beneficially utilize the scheduling to obtain an optimal schedule of operations and to minimize the total processing time in a modular FMS. They conclude that GA and SA are appropriate for planning & scheduling of FMS producing variety of parts in batch mode.

In the third article in Volume 2, Issue 3, "GBF Trained Neuro-fuzzy Equalizer for Time Varying Channels," Sarangi, Padhy, and Sarangi from Siksha O Anusandhan University (India), and Panigrahi from Konark Institute of Science & Technology (India) employ the hybrid genetic algorithms with bacteria foraging, namely GBF to tune the neuro fuzzy filter for equalization of time-varying channels. In the proposed GBF, all parameters of the neuro fuzzy network including the rule base are tuned simultaneously. The performance of the neuro fuzzy equalizer with GBF, compared with genetic algorithm based equalizers, is much better than existing approaches.

In "An Evolutionary Functional Link Neural Fuzzy Model for Financial Time Series Forecasting," the fourth paper in Volume 2, Issue 3, Chakravarty from Regional College of Management Autonomous (India), Dash from Siksha O Anusandhan University (India), and Pandi and Panigrahi from Indian Institute of Technology (India) present a comparison between GA and SA in parameters optimization, in terms of forecasting accuracy improvement, by an evolutionary functional link neural fuzzy model (EFLNF) in financial time series (one day, one week, one month ahead) forecasting. Their results indicate that when the periodicity is just one day, PSO produces a little better result than that of GA, however, when the gap in the performance between them increases as periodicity increases, the convergence speed is also better in case of PSO for one week and one month a head prediction. In addition, to further verify the superiority of the EFLNF, authors also provide a number of comparative studies. Another two models, functional link artificial neural network (FLANN) and functional link neural fuzzy (FLNF), have been taken into account by combining both with back propagation (BP) learning algorithm. The result shows that FLNF performs better than that of FLANN, and EFLNF performs better than that of FLNF irrespective of the periodicity or the learning algorithms it has been combined with.

In "Firm Size Transmission Effect and Price-Volume Relationship Analysis During Financial Tsunami Periods," the last paper in Volume 2, Issue 3, Wei from National Yunlin University of Science & Technology (Taiwan), Hong from Oriental Institute of Technology (Taiwan), and Wang from China University of Technology (Taiwan) present an application of firm size transmission effect and price-volume relationship analysis in Taiwan stock market to conclude that how small size enterprise leads large enterprises during the financial tsunami periods. They find that the firm size transmission effect is almost significant and the reversal phenomenon is also existed. Before the financial tsunami, firm size transmission effect does not significantly exist, this result also indirectly approves that the directional asymmetry of the market returns, proposed by McQueen, Pinegar and Thorley (1996), is really existed. It is valuable to enable policy makers to answer the lead-lag effects in financial crisis periods.

In "Recursive Learning of Genetic Algorithms with Task Decomposition and Varied Rule Set," the first paper in Volume 2, Issue 4, Fang, Guan, and Zhang from Xi'an Jiaotong-Liverpool University (China) proposes the recursive learning of genetic algorithm (RLGA), by using recursive learning mechanism to decompose the original problem into sub-problems, to overcome time consuming and improve classification accuracy in pattern classification problem. Their experiments indicate that RLGA performs better than GA and other related solutions regarding training duration and generalization accuracy according to our experimental results.

The second article of Volume 2, Issue 4, "LZW Encoding in Genetic Algorithm," by Suwannik from Kasetsart University (Thailand), presents an approach that uses compressed chromosomes (namely LZWGA) instead of binary ones while employing genetic algorithm (GA), to reduce the exponential increasing computing time when the problem is complicate to require more size of the search space. His experiments conclude that, by using LZWGA, the search space is reduced dramatically, and in the case of one-million-bit problem, the search space of the original problem is $2^{1000000}$ or about $9.90 \times 10^{301029}$ points, when using a compressed encoding (LZWGA), the search space was reduced to $8.37 \times 10^{166717}$ points.

The third article in Volume 2, Issue 4 is "Usage Profile Generation from Web Usage Data Using Hybrid Biclustering Algorithm" by Rathipriya and Thangavel from Periyar University (India), and Bagyamani from Government Arts College (India), proposes biclustering algorithm to analyze the complex association between users and pages of a web site. In the proposed biclustering algorithm, mutation operator from Genetic Algorithms is incorporated into the Binary Particle Swarm Optimization (BPSO) for biclustering of web usage data, this method can automatically identify the groups of users that show similar browsing patterns under a specific subset of the pages. The results manifest that the proposed algorithm has the higher performance than the existing PSO methods.

Presenting hybrid semi-parametric regression ensemble (SRE) model was presented for rainfall forecasting, the fourth paper in Volume 2, Issue 4, titled "An Effective Hybrid Semi-Parametric Regression Strategy for Rainfall Forecasting Combining Linear and Nonlinear Regression," by Wu from Wuhan University of Technology (China) and Liuzhou Teachers College (China). In this model, three linear regression models are used to capture rainfall linear characteristics and three nonlinear regression model based on ANN are able to capture rainfall nonlinear characteristics. The semi-parametric regression is used for ensemble model based on the principal component analysis technique. Empirical results obtained reveal that the prediction using the SRE model is generally better than those obtained using the other models presented in this study in terms of the same evaluation measurements.

The articles in this compendium display a broad range of cutting edge topics in evolutionary algorithms, evolutionary programming, and neural fuzzy computation. The preface author believes that modeling applications and theoretical innovations will play more important role in the evolutionary computation fields, such as hybrid different evolutionary algorithms/models to overcome some critical shortcoming of a single evolutionary algorithm/model or directly improve the shortcoming by theoretical innovative arrangements.

For hybridizing different evolutionary algorithms/models,

1. **Hybrid Different Evolutionary Algorithms:** As known that evolutionary algorithms almost have their theoretical drawbacks, such as lack of knowledge memory or storage functions, time consuming in training, and being trapped in local optimum, therefore, by hybridizing some novel search technique to adjust their internal parameters (e.g., mutation rate, crossover rate, annealing temperature, etc.) to overcome those mentioned shortcomings. For example, in genetic algorithm (GA), new individuals are generated by the following operators, selection, crossover, and mutation. For all types of objective functions, the generation begins with a binary coding for the parameter set. Based on this special binary coding process, GA is able to solve some specified problems which are not easily to be solved by traditional algorithms. GA can empirically provide a few best fitted off-springs from the whole population, however, after some generations, due to low diversity of the population, it might lead to a premature convergence. Similarly, simulated annealing (SA) is a generic probabilistic search technique that simulates the material physical process of heating and controlled cooling. Each step of SA attempts to replace the current state by a random move. The new state may then be accepted with a probability that depends both on the difference between the corresponding function values and also on a global parameter, temperature. Thus, SA has some institution to reach more ideal solutions. However, SA costs lots of computation time in annealing process. To improve premature convergence and to receive more suitable objective function values, it is necessary to find some effective approach to overcome these drawbacks from GA and SA. Hybridization of genetic algorithm with simulated annealing (GA-SA) algorithm is an innovative trial by applying the superior capability of SA algorithm to reach more ideal solutions, and by employing the mutation process of GA to enhance searching process. GA-SA algorithm has been applied to the fields of system design (Shieh & Peralta, 2005), system and network optimization (Zhao & Zheng, 2006), continuous-time production planning (Ganesh, 2005), and electrical power districting problem (Bergey, Ragsdale, & Hoskote, 2003).

2. **Hybrid Different Models:** Each single model may have its drawback, such as Box-Jenkins' ARIMA model, the worst disadvantage is inability to predict changes that are not clear in historical data, particularly for the nonlinearity of data patterns; such as support vector regression (SVR) model, it can not provide accurate forecasting performance particularly while data set reveals cyclic (seasonal)

tendency, which is caused by cyclic economic activities or seasonal nature hour to hour, day to day, week to week, month to month, and season to season, such as hourly peak in a working day, weekly peak in a business week, and monthly peak in a demand planned year. Figure 1 illustrates that the original SVR model can not deal well the cyclic tendency. Therefore, the concepts of combined or hybrid models are deserved to be considered. Please notice that the so-called hybrid model means that some process of the former model is integrated into the process of the later one, for example, hybrid A and B implies some process of A are controlled by A, some are by B. On the other hand, for the so-called combined model, it only indicated that the output of the former model is then the input of the later one, therefore, the classification results from combined models will be superior to single model. The combined models can be employed to further capture more data pattern information from the analyzed data series. For the mentioned shortcoming of the original SVR model, it is necessary to estimate this seasonal component, i.e., applying the seasonal mechanism (Azdeh & Ghaderi, 2008; Deo & Hurvich, 2006) to accomplish the goal of high accurate forecasting performance. The seasonal mechanism (see Figure 2), the preface author proposes two-step mechanism for convenience to be implemented: the first step is calculating the seasonal index ($SI$) for each cyclic point in a cycle length peak period by Eqs.(1) and (2),

$$cyclicpont_t = \frac{actual_t}{forecasting_t} \tag{1}$$

*Figure 1. Original SVR model cannot keep the cyclic tendency (Hong, 2011)*

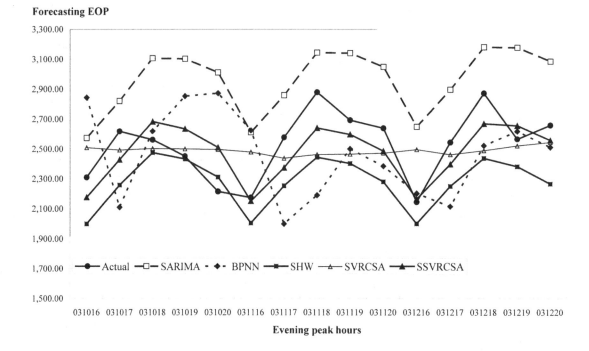

*: "031016" denotes the 16 o'clock on 10 March 2005, and so on.

*Figure 2. The process of seasonal mechanism*

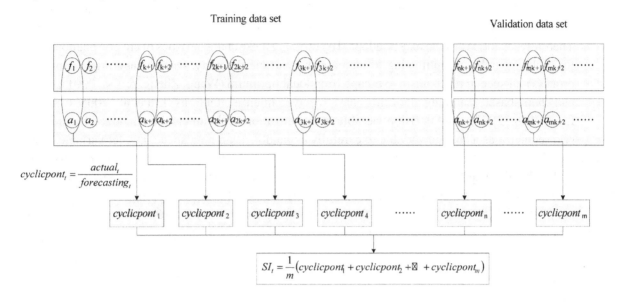

$$SI_t = \frac{1}{m}\begin{pmatrix} cyclicpont_1 + cyclicpont_2 \\ + \cdots + cyclicpont_m \end{pmatrix} \tag{2}$$

where *actual*$_t$ is the actual value at time $t$; *forecasting*$_t$ in the forecasting value at time $t$; *cyclicpont*$_t$ is the ratio between actual value and forecasting value at time $t$; $SI_t$ is the seasonal index for each cyclic point in a cycle length. The second step is computing the forecasting value by Eq.(3),

$$\hat{f}_{t+1} = forecasting_{t+1} \times SI_t \tag{3}$$

where $\hat{f}_{t+1}$ is the forecasting value adjusted by seasonal mechanism.

Another model-hybridization example can be found in artificial neural network models. Inspired by the concept of recurrent neural networks (RNNs) that every unit is considered as an output of the network and the provision of adjusted information as input in a training process (Kechriotis, Zervasd, & Manolakos, 1994), the recurrent learning mechanism framework is also combined into the original analyzed model. For a feed-forward neural network, links may be established within layers of a neural network. These types of networks are called recurrent neural networks. RNNs include an additional information source from the output layer or the hidden layer, therefore, they use mainly past information to capture detailed information, then improve their performances.

For improving by theoretical innovative arrangements,

Several disadvantages embedded in these evolutionary algorithms, such as trapped in local optimization and evolutionary mechanism failure can be improved by theoretical innovative arrangements to get more satisfied performance.

1. **Chaotization of Decision Variables:** Chaos is a ubiquitous phenomenon in the nonlinear system, chaotic behaviors has such characteristics as high sensitivity for initial value, ergodicity, and randomness of motion trail and it can traverse each trail within a certain range according to its rule. Therefore, chaotic variable may be adopted by utilizing these characteristics of chaotic phenomenon for global search and optimizing to increase the particle diversity. Due to easy implementation process and special mechanism to escape from local optimum (Wang, Zheng, & Lin, 2001), chaos and chaos-based searching algorithms have received intense attentions (Liu et al., 2005; Cai, Ma, Li, & Peng, 2007). Any decision variable in optimization problem can be chaotized by the chaotic sequence as a chaotic variable to carefully expand its searching space, i.e., let variable travel ergodically over the searching space. The critical factor influenced the performance improvement is the chaotic mapping function. There are several mostly adopting chaotic mapping functions, such as the Logistic mapping function (May, 1976) (Eq.(4)), the Tent mapping function (Sheng et al., 2010) (Eq.(5)), the An mapping function (Dong & Guo, 2011) (Eq.(6)), and the cat mapping function (Kao & Zahara, 2008) (Eq.(7)) as the chaotic sequence generator.

$$x_{n+1} = \mu \cdot x_n (1 - x_n) \tag{4}$$

where $x_n$ is the iteration value of the variable $x$ in the $n^{th}$ time; $\mu$ is a control parameter; when $\mu=4$, the system will be completely in a chaos state, and $x_0$ may take any initial value in (0,1) except 0.25, 0.5 and 0.75.

$$x_{n+1} = \begin{cases} 2x_n & x \in [0,0.5] \\ 2(1-x_n) & x \in (0.5,1] \end{cases} \tag{5}$$

where $x_n$ is the iteration value of the variable $x$ in the $n^{th}$ time and $n$ is the iteration times.

$$x_{n+1} = \begin{cases} \dfrac{3}{2}x_n + \dfrac{1}{4} & x \in [0,0.5) \\ \dfrac{1}{2}x_n - \dfrac{1}{4} & x \in [0.5,1] \end{cases} \tag{6}$$

where $x_n$ is the iteration value of the variable $x$ in the $n^{th}$ time and $n$ is the iteration times.

$$\begin{cases} x_{n+1} = (x_n + y_n)\bmod 1 \\ y_{n+1} = (x_n + 2y_n)\bmod 1 \end{cases} \tag{7}$$

where $x\bmod 1 = x-[x]$.

To Analyze the chaotic characteristics of these four mapping functions, set the initial value of these four mapping functions as 0.1, respectively, and set the iteration times as 50,000; the occurrence number of the obtained chaotic variable for each mapping function are recorded. The statistical results for each mapping function are as shown in Figure 3. in which the value of the probability density for the

*Figure 3. Iterative distribution of four mapping (Li, Hong, & Kang, 2013)*

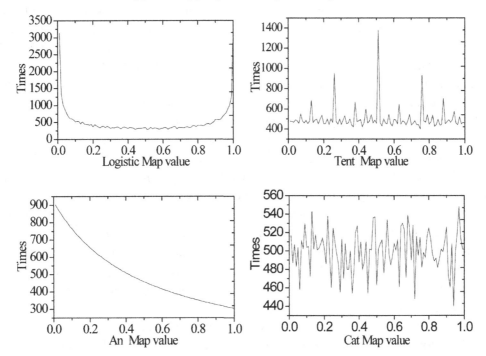

chaotic sequence generated by the Logistic mapping function is mostly distributed at both ends due to complying with Chebyshev distribution of more at both ends and less in middle; the chaotic sequence generated by the Tent mapping function is affected by limited word length and limited precision of the computer and is rapid to fall into a minor cycle or a fixed point; the number of variables generated by the An mapping function gradually reduces along with variable values changing from small to large; however, different from above three mapping functions, the distribution of the cat mapping function is relatively uniform in the interval [0,1], and has no cyclic phenomenon during its iteration process. Therefore, the cat mapping function has better chaotic distribution characteristic than other alternatives. More and more papers are tended to test the superiority of different chaotic mapping functions to improve their optimization performance.

2.   **Adjustments by Cloud Theory:** For example, based on the operation procedure of SA, subtle and skillful adjustment in the annealing schedule is required, such as the size of the temperature steps during annealing. Particularly, the temperature of each state is discrete and unchangeable, which does not meet the requirement of continuous decrease in temperature in actual physical annealing processes. In addition, SA is easy to accept deteriorate solution with high temperature, and it is hard to escape from local minimum trap with low temperature (Pin, Lin, & Zhang, 2009). To overcome these drawbacks of SA, the cloud theory is considered. Cloud theory is a model of the uncertainty transformation between quantitative representation and qualitative concept using language value (Pin, Lin, & Zhang, 2009). Based on the operation procedure of SA, subtle and skillful adjustment in the annealing schedule is required, such as the size of the temperature steps during annealing, the temperature range, the number of re-starts and re-direction of the search, the annealing process is like a fuzzy system in which the molecules move from large scale to small scale randomly as the temperature decreases. In addition, due to its Monte Carlo scheme and lacking of

knowledge memory functions, time consuming is also an another boring problem. Author has tried to employ chaotic simulated annealing (CSA) algorithm, to overcome these shortcomings. In which, the transiently chaotic dynamics are temporarily generated for foraging and self-organizing, then, gradually vanished with autonomous decreasing of the temperature, and are accompanied by successive bifurcations and converged to a stable equilibrium. Therefore, CSA has significantly improved the randomization of Monte Carlo scheme, and, has controlled the convergent process by bifurcation structures instead of stochastic "thermal" fluctuations, eventually, performed efficient searching including a global optimum state. However, as mentioned that the temperature of each state is discrete and unchangeable, which does not meet the requirement of continuous decrease in temperature in actual physical annealing processes. Even some temperature annealing function is exponential in general, the temperature is gradually falling with a fixed value in every annealing step and the changing process of temperature between two neighbor steps is not continuous. This phenomenon also appears while other types of temperature update functions are implemented, such as arithmetical, geometrical or logarithmic one. In the cloud theory, by introducing the $Y$ condition normal cloud generator (see Figure 4) to the temperature generation process, it can randomly generate a group of new values that distribute around the given value like "cloud". Let the fixed temperature point of each step become a changeable temperature zone in which the temperature of each state generation in every annealing step is chosen randomly, the course of temperature changing in the whole annealing process is nearly continuous and fits the physical annealing process better. Therefore, based on chaotic sequence and cloud theory, the CCSA is employed to replace the stochastic "thermal" fluctuations control from traditional SA, to enhance the continuously physical temperature annealing process from CSA. The cloud theory can realize the transformation between a qualitative concept in words and its numerical representation. It is able to be employed to avoid problems mentioned above.

Based on the discussions above, it will also become another research tendency in evolutionary computation, that is, evolutionary algorithms support systems to guide researchers how to use proper evolutionary algorithms in parameters determination for their analysis models. This is because that for any analysis models (including classification model, forecasting model, and so on), the most important problem is how to catch the data pattern, and applied the learned patterns or rules to receive satisfied performance, i.e., the key successful factor is how to suitably look for data pattern. However, each model itself has excelled ability to catch specific data pattern. For example, exponential smoothing and ARIMA models focus on strict increasing (or decreasing) time series data, i.e., linear pattern, even they have seasonal modification mechanism to analyze seasonal (cyclic) change; due to artificial learning

*Figure 4. Schematic of the normal cloud model (Li, Hong, & Kang, 2013)*

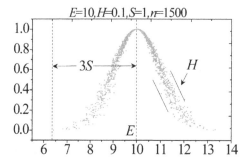

function to adjust the suitable training rules, ANN model is excelled only if historical data pattern has been learned, it is lacks of systematic explanation how the accurate forecasting results are obtained; support vector regression (SVR) model could acquire superior performance only if proper parameters determination search algorithms. Therefore, it is essential to construct an inference system to collect the characteristic rules to determine the data pattern category. Secondly, it should assign appropriate approach to implement forecasting: for (1) ARIMA or exponential smoothing approaches, the only work is to adjust their differential or seasonal parameters; (2) ANN or SVR models, the forthcoming problem is how to determine best parameters combination (e.g., numbers of hidden layer, units of each layer, learning rate; or hyper-parameters) to acquire superior forecasting performance. Particularly, for the focus of this discussion, in order to determine the most proper parameter combination, a series of evolutionary algorithms should be employed to test which data pattern is familiar with. Based on experimental findings, those evolutionary algorithms themselves also have merits and drawbacks, for example, GA and IA could handle excellently in regular trend data pattern (real number) (Pai & Hong, 2005a), SA excelled in fluctuation or noise data pattern (real number) (Pai & Hong, 2006; 2005b), TA is good in regular cyclic data pattern (real number) (Hong, Pai, Yang, & Theng, 2006), and ACO is well done in integer number searching.

As aforementioned, it is possible to build an intelligent support system to improve the efficiency of hybrid evolutionary algorithms/models or improving by theoretical innovative arrangements (chaotization and cloud theory) in all forecasting/prediction/classification applications, namely general hybridization chaotization cloudization support system (GHCCSS). The main flow chart of the GHCCSS suggested in this conclusion is given in Figure 5. Firstly, filter the original data by the data base with well defined

*Figure 5. The general hybridization chaotization cloudization support system (GHCCSS)*

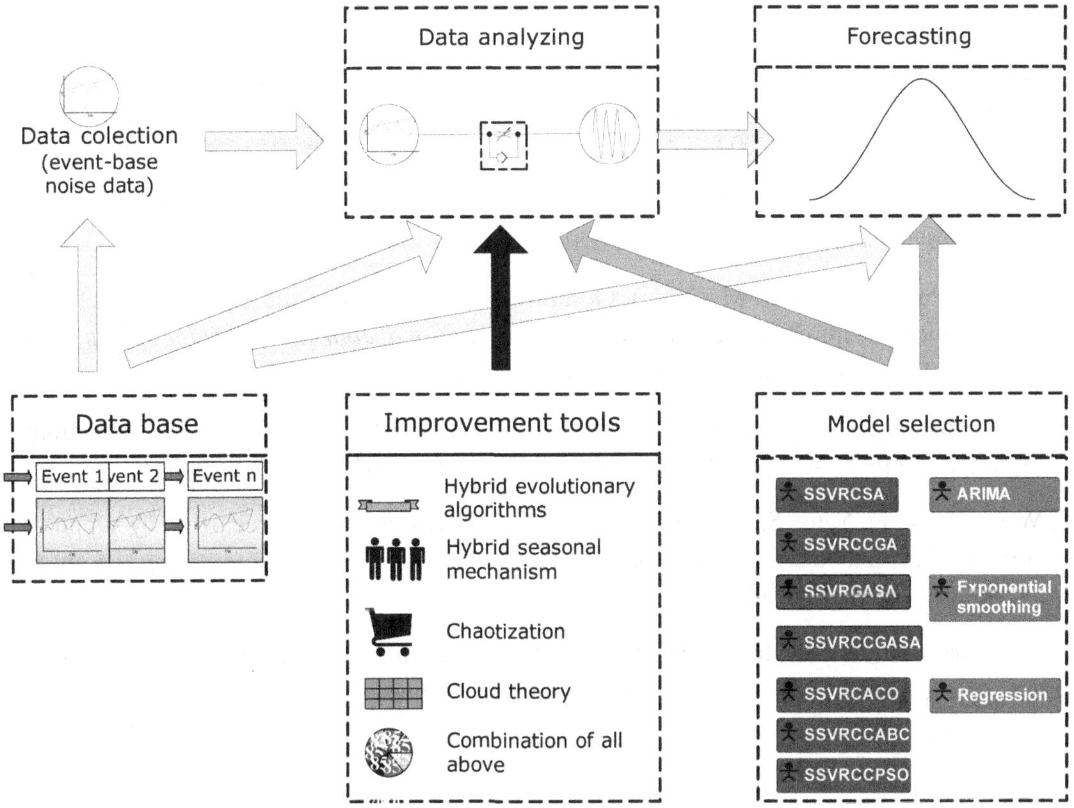

characteristic rules set of data pattern, such as linear, logarithmic, inverse, quadratic, cubic, compound, power, growth, exponential, etc, to recognize the appropriate data pattern (fluctuation, regular, or noise). The recognition decision rules should include two principles: (1) the change rate of two continuous data; and (2) the decreasing or increasing trend of the change rate, i.e., behavior of the approached curve. Secondly, select adequate improvement tools (hybrid evolutionary algorithms, hybrid seasonal mechanism, chaotization of decision variables, cloud theory, and any combination of all tolls) to avoid trapping in local optimum, improvement tools could be employed into these optimization problems to obtain an improved, satisfied solution.

This discussion of the work by the author of this preface highlights work in the modeling applications and theoretical innovations for interdisciplinary evolutionary computation that has come to the forefront over the past decade. These articles in this text span a great deal more of cutting edge areas that are truly interdisciplinary in nature.

## REFERENCES

Azadeh, A., & Ghaderi, S. F. (2008). Annual electricity consumption forecasting by neural network in high energy consuming industrial sectors. *Energy Conversion and Management*, *49*, 2272–2278. doi:10.1016/j.enconman.2008.01.035

Bergey, P. K., Ragsdale, C. T., & Hoskote, M. (2003). A simulated annealing genetic algorithm for the electrical power districting problem. *Annals of Operations Research*, *121*, 33–55. doi:10.1023/A:1023347000978

Cai, J., Ma, X., Li, L., & Peng, H. (2007). Chaotic particle swarm optimization for economic dispatch considering the generator constraints. *Energy Conversion and Management*, *48*, 645–653. doi:10.1016/j.enconman.2006.05.020

Deo, R., & Hurvich, C. (2006). Forecasting realized volatility using a long- memory stochastic volatility model: estimation, prediction and seasonal adjustment. *Journal of Econometrics*, *131*, 29–58. doi:10.1016/j.jeconom.2005.01.003

Dong, Y., & Guo, H. (2011). Adaptive chaos particle swarm optimization based on colony fitness variance. *Application Research of Computers*, *28*, 855–859.

Ganesh, K., & Punniyamoorthy, M. (2005). Optimization of continuous-time production planning using hybrid genetic algorithms-simulated annealing. *International Journal of Advanced Manufacturing Technology*, *26*, 148–154. doi:10.1007/s00170-003-1976-4

Hong, W. C. (2011). Traffic flow forecasting by seasonal SVR with chaotic simulated annealing algorithm. *Neurocomputing*, *74*, 2096–2107. doi:10.1016/j.neucom.2010.12.032

Hong, W. C., Pai, P. F., Yang, S. L., & Theng, R. (2006). Highway traffic forecasting by support vector regression model with tabu search algorithms. In *Proceedings of the IEEE International Joint Conference on Neural Networks*, (pp. 1617-21).

Kao, Y., & Zahara, E. (2008). A hybrid genetic algorithm and particle swarm optimization for multimodal functions. *Applied Soft Computing*, *8*, 849–857. doi:10.1016/j.asoc.2007.07.002

Kechriotis, G., Zervas, E., & Manolakos, E. S. (1994). Using recurrent neural networks for adaptive communication channel equalization. *IEEE Transactions on Neural Networks, 5*, 267–278. doi:10.1109/72.279190

Li, M., Hong, W. C., & Kang, H. (2013). Urban traffic flow forecasting using Gauss-SVR with cat mapping, cloud model and PSO hybrid algorithm. *Neurocomputing, 99*, 230–240. doi:10.1016/j.neucom.2012.08.002

Liu, B., Wang, L., Jin, Y. H., Tang, F., & Huang, D. X. (2005). Improved particle swarm optimization combined with chaos. *Chaos, Solitons, and Fractals, 25*, 1261–1271. doi:10.1016/j.chaos.2004.11.095

May, R. M. (1976). Simple mathematical models with very complicated dynamics. *Nature, 261*, 459–467. doi:10.1038/261459a0

Pai, P. F., & Hong, W. C. (2005a). Forecasting regional electric load based on recurrent support vector machines with genetic algorithms. *Electric Power Systems Research, 74*, 417–425. doi:10.1016/j.epsr.2005.01.006

Pai, P. F., & Hong, W. C. (2005b). Support vector machines with simulated annealing algorithms in electricity load forecasting. *Energy Conversion and Management, 46*, 2669–2688. doi:10.1016/j.enconman.2005.02.004

Pai, P. F., & Hong, W. C. (2006). Software reliability forecasting by support vector machines with simulated annealing algorithms. *Journal of Systems and Software, 79*, 747–755. doi:10.1016/j.jss.2005.02.025

Pin, L., Lin, Y., & Zhang, J. (2009). Cloud theory-based simulated annealing algorithm and application. *Engineering Applications of Artificial Intelligence, 22*, 742–749. doi:10.1016/j.engappai.2009.03.003

Sheng, Y., Pan, H., Xia, L., Cai, Y., & Sun, X. (2010). Hybrid chaos particle swarm optimization algorithm and application in benzene-toluene flash vaporization. *Journal of Zhejiang University of Technology, 38*, 319–322.

Shieh, H. J., & Peralta, R. C. (2005). Optimal in situ bioremediation design by hybrid genetic algorithm-simulated annealing. *Journal of Water Resources Planning and Management, 131*, 67–78. doi:10.1061/(ASCE)0733-9496(2005)131:1(67)

Wang, L., Zheng, D. Z., & Lin, Q. S. (2001). Survey on chaotic optimization methods. *Computing Technology and Automation, 20*, 1–5.

Zhao, F., & Zeng, X. (2006). Simulated annealing—Genetic algorithm for transit network optimization. *Journal of Computing in Civil Engineering, 20*, 57–68. doi:10.1061/(ASCE)0887-3801(2006)20:1(57)

# Chapter 1
# Reliability Allocation Problem in Series–Parallel Systems:
## Ant Colony Optimization

**Alice Yalaoui**
*University of Technology of Troyes, France*

**Eric Châtelet**
*University of Technology of Troyes, France*

**Farah Belmecheri**
*University of Technology of Troyes, France*

**Farouk Yalaoui**
*University of Technology of Troyes, France*

## ABSTRACT

*Reliability optimization is an important step in industrial systems design. In order to develop a reliable system, designers may introduce different redundant technologies with the same functionality in parallel. In this paper, each technology is assumed to be composed of series components. The obtained configuration belongs to the series-parallel systems. The presented tool is for the design or the improvement of such systems, in order to minimize the system cost with a reliability constraint. The aim is to find the reliability to allocate to each component in order to minimize the total cost, such that the global system reliability verifies a minimal level constraint. This problem is known to be NP-hard. In this paper, a metaheuristic approach, based on the Ant Colony Optimization technics (ACO), is used in order to improve an existing approach. The experimental results, based on randomly generated instances, outperform the one of previous method dedicated to this problem.*

## INTRODUCTION

Quality and safety management of production tools is a great challenge for industries. This leads them to develop cost management policies adapted to the encountered problems. For example, let consider the case of a hospital which must change its electrical power system. It is obvious that, in

case of electricity breakdown, it must have one or two other reliable electricity systems. Its aim is to have electrical power systems (in redundancy, i.e., in parallel) which are reliable and not expensive. The hospital must study the reliability and the cost of the technological solutions in order to choose the less expensive combination which guarantees the minimum reliability level required for such

DOI: 10.4018/978-1-4666-3628-6.ch001

system. Generally, this cost management approach arises at the system design step, for any system: a product, a production tool, a detection system or a safety one for example (Zeblah et al., 2009). A system is competitive if it answers to the requirements of its user and at the slightest expense. It means that at the design step, we have not only to answer to the functionalities requirements, but also to consider reliability and expense criteria.

The issue of this paper is a reliability allocation problem. A lot of authors as (Tzafesta, 1980), (Tillman et al., 1980; Misra, 1986; Kuo & Prasad, 2000; Kuo et al., 2001) have proposed classifications according to several criteria, as the system type (repairable, not repairable, series, parallel...) for example. The reliability optimization problems are *NP-hard* (Chern, 1992), which means we cannot compute the optimal solution in polynomial time. (Yalaoui et al., 2005b) compute the time complexity of the enumeration of all the solutions of such a problem and show that it is better to use an approximation method for real life problems.

In reliability allocation studies, two different approaches can be distinguished according to the values nature of components reliability (Yalaoui et al., 2004). In the continuous case, components reliability values may be any real value between 0 and 1 (Elegebede et al., 2003; Yalaoui et al., 2005a). In the discrete case, components reliability values may only take their value in a finite set of values between 0 and 1 (Yalaoui et al., 2005b; Aneja et al., 2004; Yalaoui et al., 2005c). In this paper, we are interested in the discrete case, which corresponds to the availability market constraint. As far as the use of ant colony optimization (ACO) for the design problem with reliability, (Nahas & Nourelfath, 2005) developed a specific method used for series systems. They studied this system, maximizing its reliability under cost constraints. They considered a system composed of several components in series. For each component, it exits different available technologies with different costs, weights, and reliabilities. The design problem studied in Nahas and Nourelfath (2005)

is to choose the best components combination in order to maximize the reliability for a given cost.

As far as the parallel-series systems are concerned, Liang and Smith (2004) used Ant Colony optimization for redundancy allocation problems to maximize the system reliability. Meziane et al. (2005) adopted the UMGF approach (Universal Moment generating Function) with Ant Colony Algorithm for the reliability maximization. Nahas et al. (2007) presented Ant Colony Optimization for redundancy and reliability allocation in parallel-series systems, to maximize the system reliability. Their study consists in random choice of a redundancy level in each subsystem. Then, they assigned randomly among the available technologies, the type to each component. At each probabilistic choice, the ACO verified if it respects the cost constraint. Zhao et al. (2007) improved the work of (Liang and Smith, 2004). They used Ant System Colony to solve the allocation problem in parallel-series systems, maximizing the system reliability. The authors compared their results with Ant Colony Optimization - Redundancy Allocation Problem and Genetic Algorithm - Redundancy Allocation Problem (Liang & Smith, 2004). They improved the reliability with a smaller cost and less iterations. Let note that Ant Colony Optimization is also used for the minimization of preventive maintenance cost for example (Samrout et al., 2005).

Series-parallel systems have been less studied than the other types of systems. There are two studies for continuous and discrete reliabilities cases (Yalaoui et al., 2005a; Yalaoui et al., 2005c). For this second one, (Yalaoui et al., 2005c) developed a heuristic method called YCC-SP algorithm. Their two-stage approach used dynamic programming and the analogy between the reliability allocation problem and the knapsack one. As explained by (Yalaoui et al., 2005c), the performances (in terms of computation time and average gaps to the optimum) of YCC-SP are limited by the problem size, due to the use of dynamic programming which implies to use variable changes and to lose precisions (Yalaoui et al., 2005c). In order to improve the performances of this approach, it may be interesting to use another resolution method instead of Dynamic Programming. That is why, in this paper, a new two-stage approach, inspired from YCC-SP, is proposed using Ant Colony Optimization. This method has never been applied to this type of system before.

This article is composed of six sections. The following one presents shortly principles and expressions of ant colony optimization. The third section presents the assumptions and definitions of this work. In this section, the YCC-SP algorithm (Yalaoui et al., 2005c) is also presented. The following section is dedicated to the application of Ant Colony Optimization to the reliability allocation. The obtained results are compared to the results of the YCC-SP method in the last section. The paper ends with the conclusions and perspectives.

## ANT COLONY OPTIMIZATION

(Dorigo et al., 1996) introduced Ant Colony Optimization for the Travelling Salesman Problem (TSP). It draws inspiration from the collective behavior of the ants that objective is to find the ants that objective is to find the shortest path from their nest to the source of food. It was also applied to several other problems as maintenance optimization for example (Samrout et al., 2005, 2007).

(Dréo et al., 2003) presented the basic algorithm of ant colonies "Ant System" for the Travelling Salesman Problem which may be describe as follow. Let consider a population of $m$ ants and a graph constituted by $n$ nodes to visit. At each iteration $t$, $(1 \leq t \leq t_{max})$, each ant $k$ $(k=1,...m)$ builds a complete path visiting the $n$ nodes. When ant $k$ is at the node $i$, it chooses the next node $j$ to visit among the set $J_i^k$ of unvisited nodes. The choice of node $j$ is made taking into account the inverse of the distance between the nodes $n_{ij} = 1/d_{ij}$, also called the visibility. The heuristic information is used to choose the nearest nodes and avoid the furthest ones. The pheromone quantity $\tau_{ij}(t)$ is deposited on the edges between the nodes $(i,j)$ and is also called intensity of the path. The parameter defines the attraction of the path between $i$ and $j$ and it varies at each time an ant uses the edge between $i$ and $j$. With these notations, the probabilities associated to the choices of the different paths are as follows:

$$p_{ij}^k = \begin{cases} \dfrac{(\tau_{ij}(t))^\alpha \times (n_{ij})^\beta}{\sum_{l \in J_i^k} (\tau_{il}(t))^\alpha \times (n_{il})^\beta} & \text{if } j \in J_i^k \\ 0 & \text{otherwise} \end{cases}$$

(1)

with $\alpha$ and $\beta$, two parameters allowing to control the intensity importance on the edge $\tau_{ij}(t)$, and the heuristic information $n_{ij}$. Once an ant has constructed a complete path, it deposits a certain quantity of pheromone $\Delta \tau_{ij}(t)$ between nodes $i$ and

*Box 1. Ant colony algorithm*

```
This article is composed of six sections. The following one presents shortly principles and expressions of ant colony t_max
        for each ant k=1,...m
                choose randomly the first node
                while J^k ≠ Ø
                        choose a node j in J^k with the probabilities (Equation (1))
                                C^k_i
                end while
                update the pheromones with Equations (3) and (4).
        end for
end
```

*j* (Equations (2) and (3)). The quantity depends on the quality of the obtained solution by the ant.

$$\Delta\tau_{ij}(t) = \sum_{k=1}^{m}\Delta\tau_{ij}^{k}(t) \tag{2}$$

$$\Delta t_{ij}^{k}(t) = \begin{cases} \dfrac{Q}{L^{k}(t)} & if(i,j) \in T^{k}(t) \\ 0 & \text{otherwise} \end{cases} \tag{3}$$

with $T^k(t)$ the path constructed by ant $k$ at iteration $t$, $L^k(t)$ the length of the path and $Q$ a fixed parameter of the pheromone quantity. In order to avoid suboptimal solutions, it exists an evaporation process which allows penalizing unfeasible solutions. This means that, at each iteration, a path which gives unfeasible solutions will have less probability to be chosen at the following iteration. The formula to update the pheromones is described by Equation (2):

$$\tau_{ij}(t+1) = \rho\tau_{ij}(t) + \Delta\tau_{ij}(t) \tag{4}$$

with $\rho$ the evaporation speed ($0<\rho<1$). The algoritm in Box 1 summarizes Ant System for the TSP.

## PROBLEM DESCRIPTION

The studied system is a set of parallel subsystems. Each subsystem is composed by a set of series blocks. Figure 1 shows a series-parallel system.

Each block may be, for example, a facility, or a component or a function of the studied system. In each block, several articles may be able to be used in order to fill the function. Each article is characterized by its reliability and its cost. The goal is to find the article to assign to each block, according to the cost and reliability objectives for the system. Some assumptions are considered such as: the system components are not repairable, or, if they are, we are interested in their reliability at the end of a given horizon, the system components are independent, which means that the failure of a component does not have an influence on other components of the system, the system components can have only two states: functioning or failed.

## Notations

A series-parallel system is composed of $K$ subsystems in parallel (active redundancy), where each subsystem $i$ ($i=1,...,K$) is composed of $n_i$ components (blocks) in series (Figure 1). The reliability of the system is:

$$R_S = 1 - \Pi_{i=1}^{K}(1 - \Pi_{j=1}^{n_i}r_{ij}) \tag{5}$$

with $r_{ij}$ the reliability of the $j^{th}$ component of subsystem i (i=1,...,K and j=1,...,$n_i$). These reliabilities must be any value in set:

$$\Omega_{ij} = \left\{ \tilde{p}_{ij1}, \tilde{p}_{ij2}, ..., \tilde{p}_{ijm_{ij}} \right\}$$

*Figure 1. Series-parallel system*

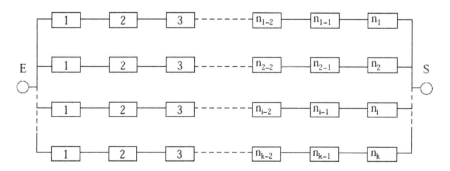

of the $n_{ij}$ different technologies available in the market. We also assume that $\tilde{p}_{ijt} < \tilde{p}_{ijl}$ for $1 \leq t \leq m_{ij}$. $c_{ij}$ is the cost associated to $r_{ij}$ with $c_{ij} = f_{ij}(r_{ij})$. Then, the total cost of the system is:

$$Cs = \sum_{i=1}^{K} \sum_{j=1}^{n_i} f_{ij}(r_{ij}) \tag{6}$$

## Models

(Yalaoui et al., 2005c) proposed different models for this allocation problem. With the components reliabilities as decision variables, the problem may be modeled as follow:

$$(M1) \quad \min \sum_{i=1}^{K} \sum_{j=1}^{n_i} f_{ij}(r_{ij}) \tag{7}$$

$$1 - \Pi_{i=1}^{K}(1 - \Pi_{j=1}^{n_i} r_{ij}) \geq R_{\min} \tag{8}$$

$$r_{ij} \in \Omega_{ij} \forall i = 1,...K \text{ and } \forall j = 1,...n_i \tag{9}$$

with $R_{min}$ the minimum reliability objective for the system. Let define $x_{ijl}$ a new decision variable which is equal to 1 if the component of reliability $\tilde{p}_{ijl}$ is used, and is equal to 0 otherwise ($i=1,...K$, $j=1,...n_i$, $l=1,...m_{ij}$). With this notation, the obtained model M2 is as follows:

$$(M2) \min \sum_{i=1}^{K} \sum_{j=1}^{n_i} \sum_{l=1}^{m_{ij}} c_{ijl}(x_{ijl}) \tag{10}$$

$$1 - \Pi_{i=1}^{K}(1 - \Pi_{j=1}^{n_i} \Pi_{l=1}^{m_{ij}}(\tilde{p}_{ijl})x_{ijl}) \geq R_{\min} \tag{11}$$

$$\sum_{l=1}^{m_{ij}} x_{ijl} = 1$$
$$i = 1...K, j = 1...n_i, l = 1,...m_{ij} \tag{12}$$

$$x_{ijl} \in \{0,1\}$$
$$i = 1...K, j = 1...n\_i, l = 1,...m\_ij \tag{13}$$

with

$$c_{ijl} = f_{ij}(\tilde{p}_{ijl})$$

## THE YCC-SP METHOD

This method introduced by (Yalaoui et al., 2005c) is composed of two steps. At the first one, for each series subsystem, the reliability allocation solutions ($N_i$) which give a subsystem reliability $R_i$, ($i=1,...K$) between two bounds $\underline{R_i}$ and $\overline{R_i}$ are computed and saved. This is done using Dynamic Programming, and based on the analogy between the allocation problem and the knapsack one. At the second step, the reliability allocation of the global system is realized using the results of the first step, with Dynamic programming. This approach may be summarized in Box 2.

The YCC-SP algorithm is based on variables changes. These changes allow the authors to make an analogy between the allocation problem and the knapsack one and consequently to use Dynamic Programming. These changes of variable generate a lot of precision in the computations. This pseudo-polynomial method converges through the optimum, but the optimality is not guaranteed, especially for large problems ( $\sum_{i=1}^{K} \sum_{j=1}^{n_i} m_{ij} > 50$ ) (Yalaoui et al., 2005c). In this work, we keep the same two-steps approach as in the YCC-SP algorithm, but Dynamic Pro-

*Box 2. YCC-SP algorithm*

```
Begin
    for t=1,...t_max
        for each ant k=1,...m
            choose randomly the first node
    while J_i^k ≠ ∅
    choose a node j in J_i^k with the probabilities (Equation (1))
                    J_i^K = J_i^K − {j}
            end while
            update the pheromones with Equations (3) and (4).
        end for
end
```

gramming is replaced by Ant Colony Optimization in order to be able to study large problems and to improve the results.

## ANT COLONY FOR RELIABILITY OPTIMIZATION

The steps decomposition used to solve the reliability allocation in series-parallel system is the same as the YCC-SP method. The first stage solves problems relating to subsystems and finds all the solutions ($N_i$) such that $\underline{R_i} \leq R_i \leq \overline{R_i}$ . The second stage solves the global problem. Unlike to YCC-SP, Dynamic Programming is replaced by Ant colony optimization. The ACO-SS algorithm (Ant Colony Optimization-Sub-Systems) is used for the first step and the ACO-SG algorithm (Ant Colony Optimization-General System) is applied to the global system. In the following subsections, these two algorithms are presented.

### Sub-Systems Resolution: ACO-SS Algorithm

In this part, the application of Ant Colony Optimization to the subproblems resolution is explained.

## Subproblem Decomposition

The aim of the subproblems resolution is to find all the configurations such that, for each subsystem $i$ ($i=1,...K$) the reliability $R_i$ is between $\underline{R_i}$ and $\overline{R_i}$ (Yalaoui et al., 2005c). For each subsystem $i$ ($i=1,...K$), let consider a population of $m$ ants. Each ant $k$ ($k=1,...m$) has to construct a solution for the reliability allocation of subsystem $i$. This solution construction is composed of $n_i$ steps (Figure 2). At step $j$ ($j=1,...n_i$), the ant chooses a node $l$ to visit among the $m_{ij}$ available ($l=1,...m_{ij}$). The choice of the node corresponds to the choice of article $l$ for the component $j$ ($j=1,... n_i$) of subsystem $i$ ($i=1,...K$). These choices are calculated using the probabilities associated to each edge between two nodes.

### Probabilities

At each edge between nodes, we consider a probability $p_{ijl}$ to choose an article $l$ ($l=1,...m_{ij}$) for the component $j$ ($j=1,... n_i$) of subsystem $i$ ($i=1,...K$). These probabilities are such that:

$$\sum_{l=1}^{mij} p_{ijl} = 1 \tag{14}$$

*Figure 2. Subsystems decomposition*

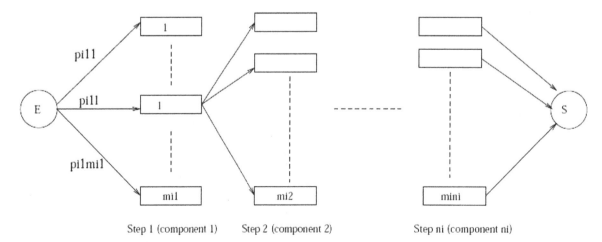

$$p_{ijl} = \frac{(\tau_{ijl}(t))^{a_{ss}} \times (n_{ijl})^{\beta_{ss}}}{\sum_{f=1}^{m_{ij}} ((\tau_{ilf}(t))^{a_{ss}} \times (n_{ilf})^{\beta_{ss}})} \qquad (15)$$

with $a_{ss}$ and $\beta_{ss}$ the parameters of the pheromone information and the heuristic information relative importance respectively. The heuristic information $n_{ijl}$ which guides the ants is given by:

$$n_{ijl} = \frac{\tilde{p}_{ijl}}{c_{ijl}} \qquad (16)$$

Figure 2 shows the subproblem decomposition, with the different choices for each steps, and the associated probabilities.

## Update of the Pheromones

Once the $m$ ants have constructed a solution, at iteration $t$, the pheromones are updated. The new pheromones rates are the result of the evaporation of the old one and the addition of the new deposited quantities.

$$\tau_{ijl}(t) = \rho_{SS} \times \tau_{ijl}(t-1) + \sum_{k=1}^{m} \Delta \tau_{ijl}^{k} \qquad (17)$$

$$\Delta \tau_{ijl}^{k} = \begin{cases} Q_{SS} penalty_k \times \frac{y}{C_{i}^{K}} & \text{if ant } k \text{ has visited } (j,l) \\ 0 & \text{otherwise} \end{cases} \qquad (18)$$

$$penalty_k = \begin{cases} \left[ \frac{(C_i^*)}{C_i^k} \right]^{A_{SS}} & \text{if } \underline{R}_i \leq R_i^k \leq \overline{R}_i \\ \left[ \frac{R_i^k}{\underline{R}_i} \right]^{B_{SS}} & \text{if } R_i^K \leq \underline{R}_i \end{cases} \qquad (19)$$

In order to update the pheromone rate, we add to $\tau_{ijl}(t-1)$ a quantity which depends on the quality of the obtained solutions at iteration $t$. The quality of the solution comes from the choice of article $l$ ($l=1,... m_{ij}$) for component $j$ ($j=1,...n_i$) of subsystem $i$ ($i = 1,...K$). The increase of the

pheromones (Equation 16) is inversely proportional to the cost of the solution (because the aim is to minimize the cost), and is affected by the parameter $Q$. The penalty (Equation 17) allows to favor solutions of ants $k$ which respect the constraint $\underline{R}_i \leq R_i^k \leq \overline{R}_i$, where $R_i^k$ represents the reliability of subsystem $i$ for ant $k$. For these solutions, the more the cost $C_i^k$ is low, the more the deposited pheromone is important, where $C_i^*$ represents the best known cost at iteration $t$. In the case where the reliability $R_i^k$ is less than $\underline{R}_i$, pheromone rates is increased to avoid a local minimum. These updates are affected by the two parameters $A_{ss}$ and $B_{ss}$.

## Global System Resolution: ACO-SG Algorithm

Let $N_i$ the number of solutions obtained for subsystem $i$ ($i=1,...K$) such that $\underline{R}_i \leq R_i \leq \overline{R}_i$. These solutions are used for the global problem resolution. The approach used for the global resolution is the same as the subsystems one. Only the update of the pheromones is different. Each ant $k$ ($k=1,...m$) constructs a solution for the system reliability allocation. The allocation problem is a $K$ steps decision problem (Figure 3).

At step $i$ ($i=1,...K$), we choose a solution $n$ ($n=1,... N_i$) obtained by ACO-SS for subsystem $i$ ($i=1,...K$). This construction uses probabilities $P_{in}$:

$$P_{in} = \frac{(\tau_{in}(t))^{\alpha} \times (\eta_{in})^{\beta}}{\sum_{n=1}^{N_i} ((\tau_{in}(t))^{\alpha} \times (\eta_{in})^{\beta})} \qquad (20)$$

where $P_{in}$ denotes the probability to choose the solution $n$ ($n=1,...N_i$) for subsystem $i$ ($i=1,...K$). $\tau_{in}(t)$ is the intensity of the pheromone associated to choose solution $n$ ($n=1,...N_i$), from step $i-1$. Figure 3 shows the problem decomposition with the different choices for each step and the associated probabilities. The heuristic information

*Figure 3. Systems decomposition*

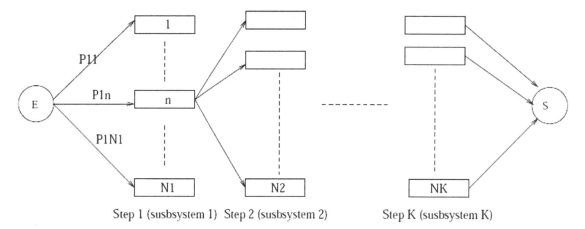

Step 1 (susbsystem 1)  Step 2 (susbsystem 2)     Step K (susbsystem K)

$\eta_{in}$ guides the ant to choose solution $n$ ($n=1,...N_i$) of subsystem $i$ ($i=1,...K$) which have a good reliability with a low cost (Equation 19). $\alpha$ and $\beta$ are respectively the pheromone intensity parameter and the heuristic information of the global problem.

$$\eta_{in} = \frac{R_{in}}{C_{in}} \qquad (21)$$

After the construction of the solutions, the pheromone rates are updated with the following Equation:

$$\tau_{in}(t) = \rho \tau_{in}(t-1) + \sum_{k=1}^{m} \Delta \tau_{in}^{k} \qquad (22)$$

where $\rho$ is the evaporation speed. As for the subsystem resolution, a parameter $Q$ allows to penalize the paths:

$$\Delta \tau_{in}^{k}(t) = \begin{cases} Q \times penality_k \times \mathcal{Y}_{C^K} & \text{if ant } k \text{ has visited } (i,n) \\ 0 & \text{otherwise} \end{cases} \qquad (23)$$

$$penality_k = \begin{cases} \left[ \left(C^*\right) \middle/ C^k \right]^{A} & \text{if } R_{min} \leq R^k \\ \left[ R^k \middle/ R_{min} \right]^{B} & \text{if } R^K \leq R_{min} \end{cases} \qquad (24)$$

If the solution obtained by ant $k$ is such that $R_{min} \leq R^k$, the corresponding pheromone rate is increased with the parameter $A$. The more the cost is minimized, the more this path will be interesting for ants of the next population. If the solution does not satisfy the reliability condition, the pheromone rate is increased (with parameter $B$). This penalization guaranties to avoid a local optimum.

## Global ACO Algorithm

In this section, the global approach developed using Ant Colony Optimization is summarized. The algorithm is composed, as the YCC-SP algorithm, of two steps: the $K$ subproblems resolution and the global resolution of the problem.

## RESULTS

In this section, the obtained results with the Ant Colony Optimization (ACO) are presented. First, we present the adopted approach for obtaining the best parameters for the ACO. The algorithms have been encoded in C++ 6.0, on a RAM 512 Mo Pentium 4. Then, the results are compared to the one given by the YCC-SP method, encoded like the ACO.

*Box 3. Global ACO algorithm*

---

**begin**

    **for** $i=1,...K$

evaluate $\underline{R}_i = \max\left\{1 - \dfrac{1 - R\min}{\Pi_{Q=1\neq i}^{K}(1 - \bar{R}_Q)} ; \prod_{j=1}^{n_i} \tilde{p}_{ijl}\right\}$

$\underline{R}_i = \max\left\{1 - \dfrac{1 - R_{\min}}{\Pi_{Q=1\neq i}^{K}(1 - \bar{R}_q)} ; \Pi_{j=1}^{n_i}\tilde{p}_{ijl}\right\}$

$and \ \bar{R}_i = \Pi_{j=1}^{n_i}\tilde{p}_{ijm_{ij}}$

    **for** $t=1,... \ t_{\max}^{SS}$

            **for** each ant $k=1,...m_{ss}$

                **for** each component $j$ from 1 to $n_i$ choose randomly (with the probabilities $p_{ijl}$ (Equation 15) among the $m_{ij}$

available.

                **end for**

                Evaluate the $m$ solutions

                Update the pheromones with Equation (17)

            **end for**

  **end for**

Save the solutions such that $\underline{R}_i \leq R_i \leq \overline{R}_i$ . Let $N_i$ the number of found solutions.

    **end for**

    **for** $t=1,...t_{max}$

        **for** each ant $k=1,...m$

            **for** each subsystem $i$ from 1 to $K$ choose randomly (with the probabilities $P_{in}$ ($n=1,...N_i$) (Equation 20) among the $N_i$

available.

            **end for**

            Evaluate the $m$ solutions

            update the pheromones with Equation (22)

        **end for**

    **end for**

**end**

---

## The Parameters Setting

Tests have been made in order to find the best values for the parameters of the ACO. We used the same instances generations scheme as (Yalaoui et al., 2005c). As far as the subsystems parameters are concerned, the number of components $n\_i$ is generated randomly between 1 and 7, as the number of articles $m_{ij}$ for each component. The problems are generated with sizes $K=2, 3, 4, 6$.

As the ACO approach uses different parameters as the number of ants or $\alpha$ and $\beta$, for example, in the probabilities computation, we realized different tests in order to find the best parameters setting.

## Parameters Setting for the Subsystems

In order to realize the parameters (Table 1) setting of the ACO for subsystems, we decided to look for the values maximizing the number $N_i$ of found solutions for each subsystem $i$ ($i=1,...K$).

For each size of subsystem, the $a_{ss}$ value has varied with fixed values for the other parameters. Then, the value of $a_{ss}$ which gives the maximum number of solutions ($N_i$) between the reliability bounds has been saved. The same approach has been applied for obtaining the best value of $\beta_{ss}$, fixing the other values, for different values of $n_i$ and $m_{ij}$.

*Table 1. Subsystems parameters*

| $m_{ss}$ | number of ants |
|---|---|
| $t_{max}^{SS}$ | number of iterations |
| $a_{ss}$ | pheromone importance in probabilities computation |
| $\beta_{ss}$ | heuristic importance in probabilities computation |
| $\rho_{SS}$ | pheromone conservation rate |
| $Q_{ss}, A_{ss}, B_{ss}$ | sensibility parameters for the penalties |

We observed that the parameter setting of the subproblems depends on the total number of articles $\sum_{j=1}^{n_i} m_{ij}$, which define the global size of the considered instance. The best values are given, in function of the number of components, in Table 2.

Let note that $a_{ss}$ and $\beta_{ss}$ increase when the total number of components increases also. Parameters $\rho_{SS}$, $Q_{ss}$ also vary with the number of components. As far as parameters $A_{ss}$ and $B_{ss}$ are concerned, the best values do not depend on the problem size. The number of ants $m_{ss}$ has an impact on the quality of the solutions too. The more the $\sum_{j=1}^{n_i} m_{ij}$ increases, the more $m_{ss}$ increases too.

## Parameters Setting for the Global System

Test problems of each sizes $K=2$, 3, 4, 6 have been generated in order to find the best values for the parameters of the global resolution. Once the $N_i$ solutions are obtained for each subsystem $i$ ($i=1,...K$) of each test problems (using the parameter values obtained previously), they are used for obtaining the best parameters (Table 3) setting for the global problem ACO.

The same approach as for the subsystems is adopted. For $K=3$ for example, the parameters are fixed to $\beta = 0.04$, $\rho = 0.95$, $Q=0.1$, $A=1$, $B=0.1$, $m=10$ and $t_{max}=200$. $a$ has varied from 0.01 to 1. This was done for several systems. The value $a = 0.04$ has been saved because this value allows to obtain the best solution for the global problem, with a few number of iterations.

*Table 2. Best parameters values in function of the subsystem size*

| size | $a_{ss}$ | $\beta_{ss}$ | $\rho_{SS}$ | $Q_{ss}$ | $A_{ss}$ | $B_{ss}$ | $m_{ss}$ | $t_{max}^{SS}$ |
|---|---|---|---|---|---|---|---|---|
| $1 \le \sum_{j=1}^{n_i} m_{ij} \le 10$ | 0.0009 | 0.0009 | 0.95 | 0.1 | 1 | 0.1 | 5 | 200 |
| $10 \le \sum_{j=1}^{n_i} m_{ij} \le 15$ | 0.55 | 0.005 | 0.95 | 0.01 | 1 | 0.1 | 5 | 200 |
| $15 \le \sum_{j=1}^{n_i} m_{ij} \le 25$ | 0.55 | 0.01 | 0.99 | 0.1 | 1 | 0.1 | 10 | 200 |
| $25 \le \sum_{j=1}^{n_i} m_{ij} \le 35$ | 0.65 | 0.01 | 0.97 | 0.1 | 1 | 0.1 | 10 | 200 |
| $35 < \sum_{j=1}^{n_i} m_{ij} \le 40$ | 0.8 | 0.01 | 0.95 | 0.1 | 1 | 0.1 | 20 | 200 |
| $40 < \sum_{j=1}^{n_i} m_{ij}$ | 0.8 | 0.01 | 0.95 | 0.1 | 1 | 0.1 | 30 | 200 |

*Table 3. System parameters*

| | |
|---|---|
| $m$ | number of ants |
| $t_{max}$ | number of iterations |
| $a$ | pheromone importance in probabilities computation |
| $\beta$ | heuristic importance in probabilities computation |
| $\rho$ | pheromone conservation rate |
| $Q, A, B$ | sensibility parameters for the penalties |

Then, for this fixed value of $a$ and the same values for $\rho$, $Q$, $A$, $B$, $m$, $t_{max}$, $\beta$ has varied from 0.01 to 1. The value $\beta = 0.07$ has been obtained because it gives the best solutions with few iterations. The obtained results are in Table 4.

We did not observe an influence of the problem size (number of components and values available for each one) on the parameters setting.

## The Method Performances

### Experimental Protocol

The evaluation process consists in testing the ACO approach on 50 problems randomly generated of each size $K$=2, 3, 4, 6. At each subsystem $i$ ($i$=1,...$K$), the number of components $n_i$ and the number of articles $m_{ij}$ are generated randomly between 1 and 7. The reliabilities of the available components are generated between [0.5, 1] and the cost are evaluated with classical cost functions as Misra, Truelove or Tillman's one (Yalaoui et al., 2005c).

### Example

First, we present an example with 2 subsystems in parallel. The first one is composed of two components in series and the second one is composed of 3 components.

The components available on the market for the different components are presented in the following table. Each couple of values represents a component characterized by its reliability and its cost. For example, for the first component C1, there are 4 components available with reliabilities 0.55, 0.58, 0.63, 0.70. The minimum reliability constraint is $R_{min}$=65 (Table 5).

The following table presents the solution obtained by the YCC-SP method and the one obtained by the ACO. The optimal solution, founded by enumeration has a cost $C^*$=282. The ACO gives the same solution (Table 6).

### Results

On the 50 problems generated, we obtained results with the enumeration (optimal solution) for only 34 problems, and results by the YCC-SP for only 37 problems. For the 13 other one, these two methods do not give solution in acceptable computational, especially for $K$=6. We present

*Table 4. Best parameters values in function of the system size*

| size | $a$ | $\beta$ | $\rho$ | Q | A | B | m | $t_{max}$ |
|---|---|---|---|---|---|---|---|---|
| $K = 2$ | 0.04 | 0.07 | 0.7 | 0.1 | 1 | 0.1 | 10 | 200 |
| $K = 3$ | 0.04 | 0.07 | 0.7 | 0.1 | 1 | 0.1 | 20 | 400 |
| $K = 4$ | 0.004 | 1.95 | 0.95 | 0.01 | 1 | 0.1 | 20 | 800 |
| $K = 6$ | 0.004 | 2.95 | 0.95 | 0.1 | 1 | 0.1 | 20 | 800 |

*Table 5. Data example*

| C1 | (0.55;15), (0.58;18), (0.63;24), (0.70;44) |
|---|---|
| C2 | (0.52;14), (0.60;20), (0.64;26), (0.68;35), (0.68;37) |
| C3 | (0.54;16), (0.59;22), (0.75;127), (0.76;142) |
| C4 | (0.62;22), (0.70;42), (0.74;68), (0.77;118) |
| C5 | (0.58;18), (0.67;34), (0.82;286) |

*Table 6. YCC-SP and ACO solutions for the example*

| Component | ACO | YCC-SP |
|---|---|---|
| C1 | (0.70;44) | (0.63;24) |
| C2 | (0.68;35) | (0.68;35) |
| C3 | (0.75;127) | (0.75;127) |
| C4 | (0.70;42) | (0.74;68) |
| C5 | (0.67;34) | (0.67;34) |
| Cost | 282 | 288 |
| reliability | 0.66 | 0.65 |

the set of 37 problems for which we have at least results for YCC-SP and the ACO in order to compare. For each problem, we indicate the number $K$ of subsystems, $\Sigma_{i \in k} n_i$, $\Sigma_{i \in k} \Sigma_{j \in ni} m_{ij}$, the optimal value $C^*$ once it is known, the reliability constraint $R_{min}$, the solution obtained by YCC-SP (cost and computational time) and the solution given by the ACO (cost and computational time) (Table 7).

For all the 10 problems with $K=2$, the ACO gives the optimal solution with a mean computational time of 0.428 second CPU. For three of these problems, the YCC-SP do not find the optimum, but has a mean computational time of 0.02 second CPU. We did not observe a real influence of the values of $\Sigma_{i \in k} n_i$ and $\Sigma_{i \in k} \Sigma_{j \in ni} m_{ij}$ on the ACO computation time (Table 8).

For all the 5 problems with $K=3$, the ACO gives the optimal solution with a mean computational time of 2.588 second CPU. For two of these

*Table 7. Results K=2*

| | $\Sigma_{i \in k} n_i$ | $\Sigma_{i \in k} \Sigma_{j \in ni} m_{ij}$ | $C^*$ | R | $COST_{YCC\text{-}SP}$ | $Time_{YCC\text{-}SP}$ | $COST_{ACO}$ | $Time_{ACO}$ |
|---|---|---|---|---|---|---|---|---|
| PB1 | 6 | 26 | 325 | 0,6 | 325 | 0,01 | 325 | 0,6 |
| PB2 | 6 | 21 | 516 | 0,62 | 528 | 0,01 | 516 | 0,62 |
| PB3 | 5 | 22 | 282 | 0,66 | 282 | 0,03 | 282 | 0,66 |
| PB4 | 6 | 26 | 284 | 0,85 | 284 | 0,03 | 284 | 0,4 |
| PB5 | 10 | 34 | 540 | 0,52 | 542 | 0,02 | 540 | 0,64 |
| PB6 | 6 | 21 | 272 | 0,65 | 272 | 0,03 | 272 | 0,23 |
| PB7 | 8 | 27 | 384 | 0,71 | 384 | 0,03 | 384 | 0,43 |
| PB8 | 6 | 21 | 157 | 0,7 | 157 | 0,01 | 157 | 0,15 |
| PB9 | 8 | 27 | 239 | 0,7 | 239 | 0,02 | 239 | 0,37 |
| PB10 | 5 | 22 | 84 | 0,71 | 97 | 0,01 | 84 | 0,18 |

*Table 8. Results K=3*

| | $\Sigma_{i \in k} n_i$ | $\Sigma_{i \in k} \Sigma_{j \in ni} m_{ij}$ | $C^*$ | R | $COST_{YCC\text{-}SP}$ | $Time_{YCC\text{-}SP}$ | $COST_{ACO}$ | $Time_{ACO}$ |
|---|---|---|---|---|---|---|---|---|
| PB12 | 9 | 45 | 203 | 0,55 | 213 | 0,55 | 203 | 0,56 |
| PB13 | 6 | 34 | 135 | 0,8 | 135 | 0,06 | 135 | 8,56 |
| PB14 | 6 | 21 | 260 | 0,88 | 260 | 0,05 | 260 | 0,85 |
| PB15 | 6 | 34 | 55 | 0,8 | 60 | 0,08 | 55 | 1,74 |
| PB16 | 6 | 21 | 59 | 0,78 | 59 | 0,03 | 59 | 1,23 |

problems, the YCC-SP does not find the optimum, but has a mean computational time of 0.154 second CPU.

The computational time of the ACO is more important than the one of YCC-SP, but it gives the optimal solution 100% of the instances for $K=2$ and $K=3$ (Table 9).

For 10 of the 16 problems with $K=4$, the ACO gives the optimal solution with a mean computational time of 1.77 second CPU. The mean distance from the optimal solution on the 16 instances is 0.41%. For two of these 16 problems, the ACO improve the solution of YCC-SP for 8 instances (Table 10).

For these 3 problems, ACO improves the results of YCC-SP of 18.63%.

The ACO outperforms the YCC-SP method in 43% of the instances. The more the problem size increase, the more the performances of ACO are greater than the one of YCC-SP. In spite of the fact that ACO computational time is greater than the one of YCC-SP (which can be explained by the metaheuristic nature of the ACO and the generation of different population), this is acceptable as it corresponds as a few seconds.

Based on the results presented above we can claim that ACO proposed algorithm successes to deal with the problem considered and gives more interesting performances on a hard problem. The method is effective and not much time consumer. We notice also that this allow us to be optimistic because as it is well known, the meta-heuristics

*Table 9. Results for K=4*

| | $\Sigma_{i \in k} n_i$ | $\Sigma_{i \in k} \Sigma_{j \in ni} m_{ij}$ | $C^*$ | $R$ | $COST_{YCC-SP}$ | $Time_{YCC-SP}$ | $COST_{ACO}$ | $Time_{ACO}$ |
|---|---|---|---|---|---|---|---|---|
| PB17 | 15 | 48 | 511 | 0,65 | 511 | 0,03 | 511 | 0,92 |
| PB18 | 14 | 49 | 615 | 0,82 | 624 | 0,03 | 615 | 1,37 |
| PB19 | 16 | 68 | 900 | 0,63 | 910 | 0,06 | 905 | 3,29 |
| PB20 | 14 | 50 | 513 | 0,82 | 522 | 0,09 | 520 | 1,48 |
| PB21 | 22 | 81 | 3483 | 0,55 | 3497 | 0,06 | 3490 | 2,5 |
| PB22 | 8 | 32 | 1019 | 0,94 | 1019 | 0,05 | 1019 | 4,4 |
| PB23 | 14 | 49 | 607 | 0,73 | 607 | 0,08 | 607 | 1,69 |
| PB24 | 16 | 68 | 802 | 0,87 | 809 | 0,26 | 805 | 1,4 |
| PB25 | 22 | 81 | 1157 | 0,92 | 1197 | 0,11 | 1174 | 1,01 |
| PB26 | 8 | 32 | 335 | 0,99 | 335 | 0,08 | 335 | 0,61 |
| PB27 | 15 | 48 | 423 | 0,85 | 493 | 0,03 | 434 | 0,73 |
| PB28 | 12 | 46 | 113 | 0,87 | 113 | 0,08 | 113 | 1,78 |
| PB29 | 14 | 49 | 262 | 0,88 | 262 | 0,06 | 262 | 1,15 |
| PB30 | 16 | 68 | 576 | 0,85 | 595 | 0,06 | 576 | 2,8 |
| PB31 | 14 | 50 | 220 | 0,88 | 220 | 0,13 | 220 | 1,17 |
| PB32 | 8 | 32 | 232 | 0,97 | 232 | 0,13 | 232 | 1,97 |

*Table 10. Results for K=6*

| | $\Sigma_{i \in k} n_i$ | $\Sigma_{i \in k} \Sigma_{j \in ni} m_{ij}$ | $C^*$ | $R$ | $COST_{YCC-SP}$ | $Time_{YCC-SP}$ | $COST_{ACO}$ | $Time_{ACO}$ |
|---|---|---|---|---|---|---|---|---|
| PB33 | 27 | 100 | - | 0,62 | 1205 | 0,41 | 1126 | 5 |
| PB34 | 15 | 57 | - | 0,55 | 663 | 1,26 | 508 | 4,7 |
| PB37 | 15 | 57 | - | 0,7 | 374 | 0,45 | 316 | 3,58 |

resolution may be improve as using some tests we can obtain more interesting parameters tuning and then improve the performances.

## CONCLUSION

This paper addresses series-parallel system reliability optimization. The problem considers the discrete case, when the reliability of the components has to be chosen among a finite set. This assumption takes into account the market availability. For the cost minimization of the system, the proposed approach is an Ant Colony Optimization. This resolution is divided in two steps: the resolution of the allocation problem in the subsystems and the global resolution of the problem.

This ACO approach improves the best known results given by the YCC-SP method for this hard design problem. Add to this, many ways of improvement are possible using fine-tuning technics but also using a hybridization scheme. We could consider for example the ACO with a local search method called at some specific moment of the resolution steps. In future works, we plan to improve the proposed method using a local search. Then, the performances of the ACO approach on larger instances should be studied and an optimal resolution approach using the results of the ACO as an upper bound on the optimal solution should be developed. A similar approach should be applied to hybrid structures or multistate systems (MSS).

## REFERENCES

Aneja, Y. P., Chandrasekaran, R., & Nair, K. P. K. (2004). Minimal - cost system reliability with discrete choice sets for components. *IEEE Transactions on Reliability, 53*, 71–76. doi:10.1109/TR.2004.824829

Chern. (1992). On the computational complexity of the reliability redundancy allocation in a series system. *Operations Research Letters, 11*, 309-315.

Dorigo, M., Maniezzo, V., & Colorni, A. (1996). The Ant: System Optimization by colony of co-operating Agents. *IEEE Transactions on Systems, man and cybernetics, part B, 26*, 1-13.

Dréo, J., Petrowski, A., Siarry, P., & Taillard, E. (2003). Métaheuristiques pour l'optimisation difficile, *Eyrolles*, 356.

Elegbede, A. O. C., Chu, C., Adjallah, K. H., & Yalaoui, F. (2003). Reliability Allocation through cost minimization. *IEEE Transactions on Reliability, 52*(1), 106–111. doi:10.1109/TR.2002.807242

Kuo, W., & Prasad, V. R. (2000). An annotated overview of system reliability optimization. *IEEE Transactions on Reliability, 49*, 176–187. doi:10.1109/24.877336

Kuo, W., Prasad, V. R., Tilman, F. A., & Hwang, C. L. (2001). *Optimal Reliability Design: Fundamentals and Applications*. Cambridge, UK: Cambridge University Press.

Liang, Y.-C., & Smith, A. E. (2004). Ant colony optimization algorithm for the redundancy allocation problem (RAP). *IEEE Transactions on Reliability, 53*(3), 471–23. doi:10.1109/TR.2004.832816

Meziane, R., Massim, Y., Zeblah, A., Ghoraf, A., & Rahli, R. (2005). Reliability optimization using ant colony algorithm under performance and cost constraints. *Electric Power Systems Research, 76*(1-3), 1–6. doi:10.1016/j.epsr.2005.02.008

Misra, K. (1986). On optimal reliability design: a review. *System Science, 12*, 5–30.

Nahas, N., & Nourelfath, M. (2005). Ant system for reliability optimization of series system with multiple choice and budget constraints. *Reliability Engineering & System Safety, 87*(1), 1–12. doi:10.1016/j.ress.2004.02.007

Nahas, N., Nourelfath, M., & Ait-Kadi, D. (2007). Coupling ant colony and the degraded ceiling algorithm for the redundancy allocation problem of series parallel systems. *Reliability Engineering & System Safety, 92*(2), 211–222. doi:10.1016/j. ress.2005.12.002

Samrout, M., Kouta, R., Yalaoui, F., Châtelet, E., & Chebbo, N. (2007). Parameters setting of the ant colony algorithm applied in preventive maintenance optimization. *Journal of Intelligent Manufacturing, 18*(6), 663–677. doi:10.1007/s10845-007-0039-3

Samrout, M., Yalaoui, F., Châtelet, E., & Chebbo, N. (2005). New methods to minimize the preventive maintenance cost of series-parallel systems using ant colony optimization. *Reliability Engineering & System Safety, 89*(3), 346–354. doi:10.1016/j.ress.2004.09.005

Tillman, F. A., Hwang, C. L., & Kuo, W. (1980). *Optimization of systems reliability*. New York: Marcel Dekker.

Tzafestas, S. G. (1980). Optimization of system reliability: A survey of problems and techniques. *International Journal of Systems Science, 11*, 455–486. doi:10.1080/00207728008967030

Yalaoui, A., Châtelet, E., & Chu, C. (2005b). A new dynamic programming method for reliability and redundancy allocation in parallel-series system. *IEEE Transactions on Reliability*, (2): 254–261. doi:10.1109/TR.2005.847270

Yalaoui, A., Chu, C., & Châtelet, E. (2004). Allocation de fiabilité et de redondance. *Journal européen des systèmes automatisés, 38*(1-2), 85-102.

Yalaoui, A., Chu, C., & Châtelet, E. (2005a). Reliability allocation problem in a series-parallel system. *Reliability Engineering & System Safety, 90*, 55–61. doi:10.1016/j.ress.2004.10.007

Yalaoui, A., Chu, C., & Châtelet, E. (2005c). Series-parallel systems design: Reliability Allocation. *Journal of Decision Systems, 14*(4), 473–487. doi:10.3166/jds.14.473-487

Zeblah, A., Châtelet, E., Samrout, M., Yalaoui, F., & Massim, Y. (2009). Series-parallel power system optimization using a harmony search algorithm. *International Journal Power Energy Conversion, 1*, 15–30. doi:10.1504/IJPEC.2009.023474

Zhao, J. H., Liu, Z., & Daou, M. T. (2007). Reliability optimization using multiobjective ant colony system approaches. *Reliability Engineering & System Safety, 92*(1), 109–222. doi:10.1016/j.ress.2005.12.001

*This work was previously published in the International Journal of Applied Evolutionary Computation, Volume 2, Issue 1, edited by Wei-Chiang Samuelson Hong, pp. 1-17, copyright 2011 by IGI Publishing (an imprint of IGI Global).*

# Chapter 2
# Feature Selection Based on Minimizing the Area Under the Detection Error Tradeoff Curve

**Liau Heng Fui**
*University of Nottingham Malaysia, Malaysia*

**Dino Isa**
*University of Nottingham Malaysia, Malaysia*

## ABSTRACT

*Feature selection is crucial to select an "optimized" subset of features from the original feature set based on a certain objective function. In general, feature selection removes redundant or irrelevant data while retaining classification accuracy. This paper proposes a feature selection algorithm that aims to minimize the area under the curve of detection error trade-off (DET) curve. Particle swarm optimization (PSO) is employed to search for the optimal feature subset. The proposed method is implemented in face recognition and iris recognition systems. The result shows that the proposed method is able to find an optimal subset of features that sufficiently describes iris and face images by removing unwanted and redundant features and at the same time improving the classification accuracy in terms of total error rate (TER).*

## 1. INTRODUCTION

In real world application, the feature set is generally large in term of dimensionality. The features may be noisy and may contain irrelevant or redundant information about the target concept. This may cause performance degradation on classifiers. Besides that, large feature set also increases the storage cost and require more computation time to process. Feature selection is crucial to select an "optimized" subset of features from the original feature set based on certain objective function. In general, feature selection removes redundant or irrelevant data while retaining classification accuracy. Although there has been a great deal of work in different areas to address this issue (Guyon & Elissee, 2003), these results have not been fully explored or exploited in emerging computer vision applications. Only recently, there has been an increased interest in implementing feature

DOI: 10.4018/978-1-4666-3628-6.ch002

selection for applications such as face detection (Sun, Bebis & Miller, 2003; Viola & Jones, 2001), face recognition (Shen & JI, 2009; Kanan & Faez, 2008a, 2008b), auditory brainstem responses tracking (Acir, Ozdamar & Guzelisc, 2005), gene expression data (Chuang et al., 2008) etc.

Sequential forward selection (SFS) and sequential backward selection (SBS) are the two well-known feature selection methods. SFS starts with an empty feature set; the feature that benefits the performance is added iteratively. In contrast, SBS starts with the full feature set and at each step, feature whose absence causes least decreases in terms of classification performance is dropped. Combining SFS and SBS gives birth to the "plus *l*-take away *r*" feature selection method (Stearns, 1976), which first enlarges the feature subset by adding *l* using SFS and then deletes r features using SBS. Sequential forward floating search (SFFS) and sequential backward floating search (SBFS) (Pudil, Novovicova & Kittler, 1994) are generalizations of the Stearn's method since they make decisions based on single feature iteratively. Hence, they cannot be expected to find globally optimal solutions. Another famous feature selection method is the relief algorithm (Kira & Rendell, 1992) and extension of it (Wiskott et al., 1994). Features are ranked according to the hypothesis margin. Features that give large hypothesis margin are selected.

Recently, evolutionary computing methods, such as genetic algorithms (GA) (Siedlecki & Sklansky, 1989), ant colony optimization (ACO) (Dorigo & Caro, 1999) and particle swarm optimization (PSO) (Kennedy & Eberhart, 1995, 1997) have gained more popularity in the feature selection area. Genetic algorithms (GA's) are optimization techniques based on the mechanism of natural selection. They try to mimic the operations found in natural genetics to guide itself through the paths in the search space (Siedlecki & Sklansky, 1989). Sun, Bebis, & Miller (2003) employed GA to select a subset of principal components analysis (PCA) features for vehicle and face detection. The fitness evaluation is based on accuracy and number of principle components. The subset that consists of fewer numbers of features and gives comparable result is favored. Kanan & Faez (2008a) proposed a scale, rotation and translation invariant face recognition system using Pseudo Zernike moment invariant (PZMI). PZMI feature set is very large and an optimal subset of PZMI features subset is selected using GAs. ACO algorithm was inspired by ant's social behavior. Ants are capable of finding the shortest route between a food source and their nest by chemical materials called pheromone that they release when moving. Kanan & Faez (2008b) employed ACO to perform feature selection on a PZMI and discrete wavelet transform (DWT) features that represent facial image. PSO was inspired by the graceful but unpredictable movements of a flock of birds and a school of fishes. Inertia weight was later introduced into the particle swarm optimizer to produce the standard PSO (Shi & Eberhart, 1998). Huang and Dun (2008) employed PSO to performed feature selection and at the same time tuning the parameter of SVM classifier. The binary PSO is incorporated to select the features sets while a common PSO is used to tune SVM's parameter and the kernel's parameter. PSO has been used to perform feature selection for gene expression data (Chuang et al, 2008).

Receiver operation characteristic (ROC) curve has been widely used in measuring the performance of binary classifiers. The performance of a classifier can be evaluated based on a single terms, which is the area under the ROC curve. Greater the area under the curve (AUC) implies better robustness of the classifier. Several methods have been proposed based on the idea of maximizing the area under the ROC curve. Toh, Kim and Lee (2008a) proposed a parameter selection method similar to that of the classifiers that maximized the AUC of TOC curve. Zhang et al (2006) perform feature selection based the AUC of ROC curve for each features. The AUC of ROC features below certain threshold value will be discarded. Features with high AUC is assigned with greater weighting. However, note that most existing algorithms for feature selection rank features according to their weights/scores that are computed independently from the number of selected features. As argued by Guyon and Elisseeff (2003), variables that are less informative individually can be informative collectively. However, most of the feature selection algorithms only consider single feature each time, possibly only giving suboptimal results in identifying the set of the most informative features.

While most the previous works are based on maximizing the AUC of the ROC curve, this paper proposes a feature selection method based on minimizing the AUC of Detection Error trade-off curve (DET) curve (Martin et al., 1997). Unlike ROC curve, the DET curve shows the relationship between the false acceptance rate (FAR) and false rejection rate (FRR) directly. Minimizing the AUC of the DET curve is equivalent to minimizing the FAR and FRR. The binary PSO is employed to search for an optimal subset of features that gives the lowest area under the DET curve. Several features may be removed or included in the feature subset by the sigmoid-limiting transformation for each feature set iteratively. Rather that calculating the fitness value for each feature independently, the PSO search for an optimal subset of feature or combination of feature that gives the best fitness value. In this case, the fitness function is the AUC of the DET curve. The fitness function is evaluated based on different combinations of features set. Therefore, the proposed method is able to overcome the problem of giving suboptimal output by algorithms which evaluate each feature independently. The performance of the system is evaluated in terms of total error rate (TER) (Toh, Kim & Lee, 2008b), which is the sum of FAR and FRR. The proposed method is implemented in the two most popular biometric methods, iris recognition and face recognition. The widely-used feature selection method based on cross-validation is selected to compare with proposed method.

The paper is organized as follows. The ideal of DET and important parameters such as FAR and FRR are briefly discussed in section 2. The computation of the AUC of DET is also presented is section 2. The PSO algorithm is presented in Section 3. The simulation result and the discussion are presented in Section 4. The simulation result of PSO is discussed first, followed by the simulation result of face recognition system based on the discrete cosine transform (DCT) features and PCA feature. Lastly, simulation results for iris recognition is discussed.

## 2. DETECTION ERROR TRADEOFF CURVE

The output of a biometric system can only be either genuine user or imposter. Figure 1 shows the distributions of imposters and genuine users under different similarity scores. Suppose a classifier produces an output based on certain similarity measurements such as Hamming distance and Euclidean distance. In order for a probed biometric template to be classified as a genuine user, its similarity scores must exceed certain pre-defined threshold value. By increasing the threshold value, the chances that an imposter is mistreated as a genuine user would decrease. However, the chances of a genuine user being misclassified as an imposter would also increase. This trend can be characterized by FAR and FRR curves. By varying the threshold value from 0 to 1 in normalized case, the FRR shows an increasing trend while the FAR shows a decreasing trend, as in Figure 2. Along the variation in the threshold value, there is one point where the FAR curve meets the FRR curve. This point is called the EER point and the corresponding threshold value is denoted as $\tau$'. Total error rate (TER) is the sum of FAR and FRR. In other words, the value of TER is equals to twice the value of EER. From Figure 2, TER is frequently found to be at its minimum at $\tau$'.

*Figure 1. Imposter and genuine-user distributions*

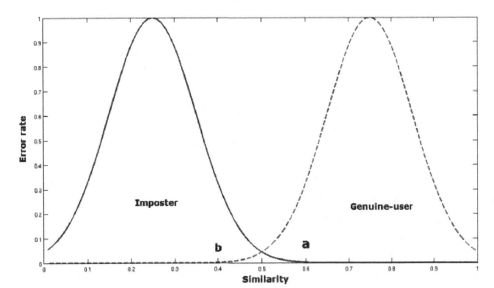

*Figure 2. FAR and FRR curves*

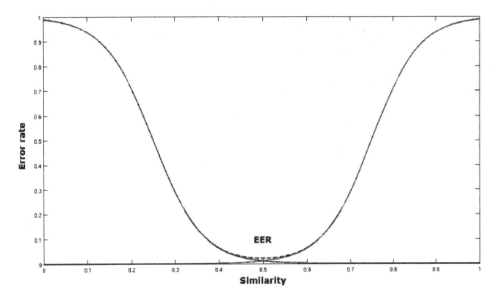

The ROC curve has been widely used in signal detection to measure the performance of a system. The ROC curve plots the True positive rate (TPR=1-FRR) at the vertical axis and FAR at the horizontal axis. Each point of the ROC curve is an operation point at certain threshold value of similarity score that produces a set of TPR and FAR values. In practical, we prefer to use a single-value index to indicate the performance of a classifier. Larger AUC of ROC curve indicates that the classifier has better overall performance. Therefore, the AUC of ROC is widely used to measure the performance of a biometric system.

For DET curve, the vertical axis is replaced by FRR, uniform treatment is given to both types of error, and a scale for both axes which spreads out the plot and better distinguishes different well-performing systems is used. The DET curve shows the performance trade-off between FAR and FRR directly at each operating point. Our optimization is to select an optimal feature subset that minimizes the TER. The AUC of DET curve is proportional to the product of FAR and FRR. Minimizing the AUC of DET is equivalent to reducing either one of the error types or both. In contrast to DET, maximizing the AUC of ROC curve only focuses on improving the TPR over the operating range. In other words, the AUC of DET curve is directly related to FRR and FAR, both of which are important performance indicators of biometric system. More discussion on the advantage of using DET curve can be found in (Martin et al., 1997). In this paper, Figure 3 and Figure 4 show the ROC and DET curves of the face recognition system. The AUC of the DET curve is equivalent to the product of FAR and FRR across the entire the operating region which ranges between the threshold value that gives FAR =0 and FAR=1. Although the AUC is corresponding to the product of FRR and FAR instead of the sum

of FAR and FRR, nevertheless, it still provides good indication of the performance of the system.

## 2.1 Direct Computation of the Area Under the DET Curve

In order to compute the area under the DET curve, one must compute the FAR and FRR for the threshold value ranging from 0 to 1. Consider a biometric system, the output of the system can only be either genuine user, corresponding to "1," or imposter, corresponding to "0". From Figure 1, it is clearly shown that the mean similarity scores of genuine-users is normally higher than the imposters. Let m+ denote the total number of genuine user's biometric samples and m- denote the total number of imposter's biometric samples (do you have different genuine users/imposters as the samples or just one with different samples?). The FAR and FRR values at certain threshold value of similarity score, $\tau$ can be found as follows:

$$FAR = \frac{1}{m^-} \int_{i=1}^{m^-} 1_{g(x_i^-) \geq \tau} \qquad (1)$$

*Figure 3. ROC curve of face recognition system using DCT*

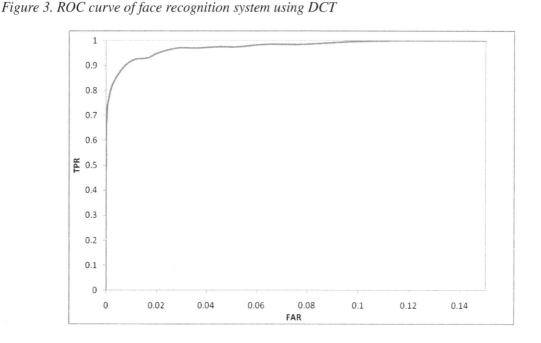

*Figure 4. DET curve of face recognition system using DCT*

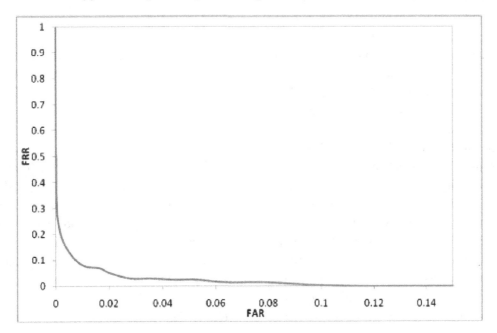

$$FRR = \frac{1}{m^+} \int_{i=1}^{m^+} 1_{g(x_i^+) \geq \tau} \qquad (2)$$

where g(x) is the decision function of a biometric system. $x^+$ represents genuine user's biometric sample while $x^-$ represents imposter's biometric sample. The area under the DET curve can be found by the following Equation:

$$AUC \, of \, DET = \int_{\tau_{FAR=0}}^{\tau_{FAR=1}} f(\tau) \, d\tau \qquad (3)$$

However, the Equation that describes the relationship between FAR and FRR is unknown. Therefore, the area under the DET curve is approximated using trapezium rule, as in Equation 4. The Equation 4 serves as the fitness function that evaluates the performance of each particle of the PSO algorithm.

$$AUC \, of \, DET \approx \sum_{\tau_{FAR=0}}^{\tau_{FAR=1}} \frac{1}{2} \times (FAR(\tau+1) - FAR(\tau))$$
$$\times (FRR(\tau) + FRR(\tau+1))$$
$$(4)$$

## 3. PARTICLE SWARM OPTIMIZATION

PSO is initialized with a swarm which is a population of random solutions called 'particles'. Each particle is treated as a point in an n-dimensional feature space. The $i$th particle is represented as Xi = (xi1,xi2, . . ., xin). Each particle has memory and is capable of memorizing the best previous position (pbest, the position giving the best fitness value) of any particle that is recorded and represented as Pi = (pi1,pi2, . . ., piP), where P is size of the population. The position of the best particle among the entire swarm is represented by the symbol 'gbest'. The velocity for $i$th particle is represented as Vi = (vi1, vi2...vin). The position and velocity of the particles are updated according to Equation 5 and Equation 6 rspectively.

$$v_{id} = wv_{id} + c1 \times rand(\ )(p_{id} - x_{id})$$
$$+c2 \times rand(\ )(p_{gd} - x_{id}) \qquad (5)$$

$$x_{id} = \begin{cases} 1 \, if \, \dfrac{1}{1+e^{-vid}} > rand() \\ 0 \qquad\qquad\qquad otherwise \end{cases} \qquad (6)$$

Where d = 1, 2, n, *w* is the inertia weight. The inertia weight is set to 1 to provide a balance between global and local exploration. The acceleration constants, c1 and c2 in Equation5, represent the weighting of the stochastic acceleration terms that pull each particle towards their previous best position and the global best positions. Both values are set as 2. rand() is a random number selected from a uniform distribution in [0.0, 1.0]. Particles' velocities on each dimension are limited to a maximum velocity, Vmax, and minimum velocity, Vmin. The value of Vmax has to be set carefully. If Vmax is too small, the particles may be trapped in local optimal. If Vmax is too large, the particles may fly pass the global optimal and never reach it. Equation 5 is used to calculate the particle's new velocity according to its previous velocity and the distances of its current position from its own best experience (position) and from the group's best experience. The experience is evaluated using the fitness function. In this paper, the fitness function is the area under the DET curve which can be found using Equation 4. The smaller the value indicates the better the robustness of the feature subset. The selection of feature is based on Equation 6. Equation 6 is a sigmoid limiting transformation and rnd() is a random number selected from a uniform distribution in [0.0, 1.0]. The value of one implies that the feature is selected for the next iteration.

## PSO Algorithm

```
while (k<maximum iteration or termi-
nation criteria is meet)
for i=1: P, the population of the
swarm
Fitness=Fitnessfunction(Xi);
if Fitness < FitnessBest of ith par-
ticles
Update FitnessBest of ith particles;
Pi=Xi;
if Fitness <GlobalFitnessBest
```

```
Update GlobalFitnessBest;
Pg=Xi;
for j=1:d,
Update Vid based on Equation 5
Update Xid based on Equation 6
j++
i++
k++
```

In this work, the data sets for iris and face recognition are divided into two groups, the training set and testing set. The training set is used to select the optimal features and testing set is used to evaluate the performance. For each dataset group, the detailed experimental procedure for training and testing is as follows:

**Step 1:** PSO parameter setting: The maximum number of generation, number of swarm particle, velocity limitation, inertia weight and the acceleration constants are set. The particle position is actually a multi-dimension discrete-valued feature mask. The feature mask is Boolean that "1" represents the feature is selected and "0" indicates that feature is not selected.

**Step 2:** For each particle, the estimated AUC of DET curve based on the selected the feature is computed using Equation 4.

**Step 3:** If the fitness value is lower (since we try to minimize the AUC of DET) than the previous best value of the particle itself, update the previous best of the particle itself with the new one. If the fitness value is lower than the global best, update the global best with the new one.

**Step 4:** For each dimension of the particle which each dimension corresponding to one feature, update the velocity and position of the particle using Equation 5 and Equation 6 respectively.

**Step 5:** For each iteration, repeat step 2-4 until it reaches maximum number of iteration or termination criteria.

## 4. SIMULATION RESULTS

The performance of the PSO for different inertia weight is investigated and the result is presented in the first part. To evaluate the performance of the proposed method, it was implemented in the two most popular biometric method, iris recognition and face recognition. The performance of the system was evaluated using TER instead of using recognition rate. Evaluation based on recognition rate only concerns the gallery sample that gives highest similarity score. It does not show how well a system rejects the imposters and accepts the genuine users. TER is the sum of FAR and FRR. It is a single-value index that gives the total number of errors that a system has made given a set of samples. Besides that, TER gives uniform treat-

ment for FAR and FRR, which better distinguishes different well-performing system. The common cross-validation method result is included for comparison purpose. Our implementation was carried out on Matlab 2008a development environment. The empirical evaluation was run on Intel Core 2 Duo E6750 CPU and 2GB RAM. The details of the experiment and results are presented in the next two sections.

### 4.1 Simulation Result of PSO

The performance of PSO with varying inertia weight is investigated. The value of the inertia weight in Equation 5 is set to 0.5, 1 and 2. The acceleration constants, c1 and c2 are both set to 2 so that the particles treat the previous best position and global best position equally important. Besides, the varying inertia weight method also included in the study as shown in Equation 7. The inertia weight has the highest value which is 2 at the first iteration. As the iteration goes on,

*Figure 5. Simulation result of PSO*

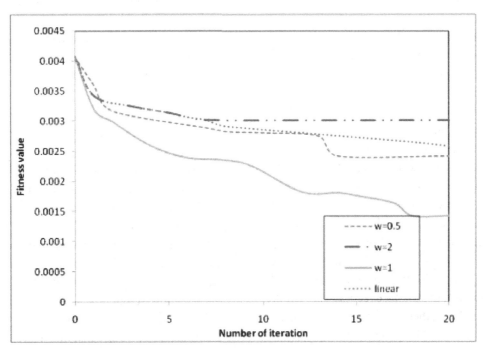

the inertia weight decreases and become zero toward the end. It is designed in such a way that it promotes the particles to search for boarder area at the beginning and decreases the searching area and fine tuning the global best position toward the end.

$$w = \frac{2 \times (\max iteration - iteration - 1)}{maxiteration}$$

(7)

Figure 5 shows the result of different PSO algorithm. The lower the fitness value indicates better performance since we are looking for the features set that gives lowest AUC of DET. The classic PSO Equation with inertia weight equal to 1 gives the best result. The result shows that the selection of inertia weight value has big impact on the performance. One should carefully set the influence of the current particle direction and the influence of the previous best and global best (Shi & Eberhart, 1998). The rest of the simulation results in this paper are based on the same setting.

## 4.2 Face Recognition

Face recognition has gained much attention in the past two decades, particularly for its potential role in information and forensic security. 'Eigenface' method based on principal component analysis (PCA) (Turk & Pentland, 1991) and 'Fisherface' method based on linear discriminant analysis (LDA) (Belhumeur, Hespanha, & Kriegman, 1997) are the two most well-known and widely-used appearance-based methods. More recently, frequency domain analysis methods such as discrete cosine transform (DCT) (Er, Chen, & Wu, 2005), Fourier transforms (FT) (Jing, Wong, & Zhang, 2006a, 2006b) and discrete wavelet transforms (DWT) (Delac, Grgis, & Grgic, 2007) have been widely used in face recognition. Unlike subspace methods, these transformation methods extract the features of an image based on the frequency domain information. Any arbitrary image can then be approximately represented by a set of coefficients and their corresponding frequencies. DCT has lower computation complexity than DWT and fast algorithms are also available for the ease of hardware implementation. In this paper, DCT and PCA are employed as a feature extractor and PSO is used to obtain an "optimized" subset of those features. The Olivetti Research Laboratory (ORL) database (ORL face database,http://www. cl.cam.ac.uk/research/dtg/attarchive/facedatabase.html) was chosen to evaluate the performance of our proposed system. ORL database contains 400 pictures from 40 persons with 10 different face pictures of each person. For each person, 5 pictures were randomly selected as training images and the remaining images served as test images. The similarity between two images is measured using Euclidean Distance. Shorter distance implies higher similarity between two face images. Since 144 DCT features or 144 principal components are selected to represent facial image, the population of the swarm is set as 144 and the maximum number of generation is set as 15 and 20 for face recognition using DCT and Eigenface method respectively to avoid over-training.

## 4.2.1 Simulation Result for Face Recognition Using Discrete Cosine Transform

Discrete cosine transform (DCT) has been widely used in modern imaging and video compression. According to the JPEG image compression standard, an image is first divided into 8×8 blocks for the purpose of computation efficiency. DCT coefficients with larger magnitude are mainly concentrated at the upper-left corner. The DCT coefficients at the upper-left corner are selected and converted to a 1D vector. As a matter of fact, human visual system is more sensitive to variation in the low-frequency band (Er, Chen, & Wu, 2005). Nine coefficients at the top-left corner of each block are chosen. Each image is represented by 144 features.

Besides that, the performance of the proposed method for a fixed number of selected feature is investigated. Take for example, one would like to select only 50 features out of 144 features. This can be done by forcing all the new global best and previous best of particle must have 50 features. Hence, the algorithm only updates the values when the particle has the amount of features. The result is recorded in Table 2.

From Table 1, the proposed method reduced the number of features that needed to sufficiently described face image for recognition purpose by half. On top of that, the TER is reduced by 14.7%. It shows that the proposed system is robust enough to handle the certain degree of pose and expression variation for face recognition. In term of recognition rate, for Set 1, the recognition rate increases to 96.5% from 94%. The size of the feature selected by cross-validation method is 68, one lesser compared to proposed method. The difference is negligible. In terms of TER and recognition rate, the proposed method outperforms the cross-validation method. The result also shows that cross-validation method only concerns the recognition rate rather than the more important TER. The recognition rate is improved by 1.5%

*Table 1. Simulation result for face recognition using DCT*

| Method | Number of Features | TER | Recognition Rate (%) |
|---|---|---|---|
| Full feature set | 144 | 0.150 | 94 |
| 5 fold cross-validation method | 69 | 0.148 | 95.5 |
| Selected feature subset | 68 | 0.128 | 96.5 |

*Table 2. Simulation result for face recognition using DCT for fixed number of feature*

| Number of features | TER (before) | TER (After) |
|---|---|---|
| 50 | 0.200 | 0.143 |
| 70 | 0.151 | 0.142 |

compared the full feature set. However, the TER only improved by 0.002.

TER value in the second column is the TER value of the random chosen fixed number of features. It was recorded in the as the global best in the first iteration. As the number of iteration increases, the TER slowly decreased. The TER value in the third the column the global best at iteration=20. The result shows that proposed algorithm capable to looks for optimal feature set for fixed number of feature.

## 4.2.2 Simulation Result for Eigenface Method

PCA is a classical face recognition method. PCA seeks for a set of projection vectors which projects the input data in such a way that the covariance matrix of the training images is maximized. Let us consider a set of $n$ training images, $\{x_1, x_2, \ldots, x_n\}$ with $N \times N$ dimension. The covariance matrix is computed as follows:

$$S = \sum_{i=1}^{N} (x_i - \mu)(x_i - \mu)^T \quad (8)$$

where $\mu$ is the mean of the $n$ training images. The dimension reduction is realized by solving the problem of eigenvalues as shown below through singular value decomposition.

$$S\varnothing = \forall\varnothing \quad (9)$$

where $\forall$ is a $N \times N$ matrix whose diagonal elements are the eigenvalues of $S$ in descending order. The $\varnothing$ matrix is a set of eigenvectors. The magnitude of the $i$th of column of $\varnothing$ is the $i$th diagonal element of $\forall$. Generally, the eigenvectors with large eigenvalues contain useful information while eigenvectors with small eigenvalues are regarded as noise components. $m$ number of eigenvector corresponding to $m$ largest eigenvalue are chosen as the projection matrix. The resulting vector is not only smaller in terms of dimensionality

*Table 3. Simulation result for face recognition using PCA*

| Method | Number of Features | TER | Recognition Rate (%) |
|---|---|---|---|
| Full feature set | 144 | 0.181 | 94 |
| 87 largest principal components | 87 | 0.152 | 94 |
| 5 fold cross-validation method | 78 | 0.157 | 94 |
| Selected feature subset | 87 | 0.142 | 93.5 |

( $m \ll N$ ), but it also removes some noise of the image. The Euclidean distance metric is employed as classifiers. The nearest-neighbor rule is then used to classify the face images.

From Table 3, the original feature sets in which the projection matrix was formed by the 144 largest principal components contained a lot of irrelevant information and degraded the classification accuracy. As mentioned earlier, PCA aims to seek for low dimensional data that is best to represent the image and does not take into account classification purpose. Some of the large to principal components correspond to illumination variations which do not contribute to the classification accuracy (Belhumeur, Hespanha, & Kriegman, 1997). The feature set containing 87 largest principal components was selected to compare the performance under the same number of features. The result shows that our method outperforms the other two feature sets in terms of TER. The DET curve treated both FAR and FRR as equally important. Therefore, in terms of recognition rate, the proposed method only achieved 93.5% recognition rate, which is 0.5% less than the other two because the selected feature subset has higher FAR. But the proposed method had much lower FRR, leading to lower TER compared to the other two feature sets. For the cross-validation method, similar result as in the DCT case is obtained. The cross-validation method select less feature and gives better recognition rate. In

term of TER, the proposed method outperforms cross-validation method.

## 4.3 Iris Recognition

Iris recognition has a higher accuracy rate than other biometric recognition methods such as face recognition, fingerprint recognition, voice recognition and vein recognition because the iris has rich pattern information and is stable through a lifetime (Daugman, 1993, 2004; Ma et al., 1997; Wildes, 1997). A typical iris recognition method consists of five steps: image acquisition, segmentation, normalization, feature encoding, and feature matching.

Iris image is captured using near-infrared sensor. The iris region is located in between pupil and sclera region. The iris region is segmented by locating the boundaries between the pupil and iris regions and between sclera and iris regions. There are two well-known iris segmentation methods; including Daugman's integro-differential operator (Daugman, 1993, 2004) and edge detection using the circular Hough transform (Wildes, 1997). In normalization step, for reliable feature matching, the segmented iris region is re-sampled to the fixed-size rectangular image to counter the dilation problem of iris input image. A typical normalization method uses a Daugman's rubber sheet model (Daugman, 1993, 2004). During the segmnetation stage, iris regions that are occluded by eyelid or eyelash are marked so that they will not be taken into account in the comparing stage. Masek (2003) separated the eyelid and iris region by a horizontal line which is constructed using combination of Radon transform and Hough transform techniques. Kang and Park (2007) isolated the eyelid region using parabolic Hough Transform. The eyelid boundary is parabolic in shape. Using such method, less information may be lost compared to Hough Transform and resulting in higher classification accuracy. However, the computation of parabolic Hough Transform is expensive because it has greater number of parameters to be determined. Min and Park (2009) reduced the computation of the parabolic Hough Transform by searching eyelid on the normalized image instead of on the original eye image. Hence, the searching space is greatly reduced. The eyelashes are further located using Otsu's thresholding method. All of the above mentioned methods generate a mask in order to mask out corrupted regions within the iris. Besides that, the global information that is contained in each 1D iris track may be corrupted due to eyelids and eyelashes removing process which breaks the 1D iris track to multiple small regions. In the normalization stage, the detected circular iris region is normalized as a rectangular shape image.

In a feature encoding step, a template representing iris pattern information is created using a Gabor filter (Daugman, 2004) or zero-crossing of the wavelet transform (Boles & Boashash, 1998). Daugman demodulated the output of the Gabor filters in order to compress the data. This was done by quantizing the phase information into four levels, for each possible quadrant in the complex plane, because the phase information provides the most

significant information within an image. Taking only the phase will allow encoding of discriminating information in the iris, while discarding the illumination, which is represented by the amplitude component. Hence, the iris recognition based on phase information is illumination invariant. Ma et al., (1997) proposed multichannel Gabor filter to capture both the local and global information of the iris pattern. Yao et al., (2006) proposed log-Gabor filter which is able to extract compact information from the iris pattern. Other than using Gabor filter, wavelet analysis also received substation attention. Boles and Boashash (1998) first porposed wavelet transform method based on zero-crossing information. Abhyankar, Hornal and Schukers (2005) presented bi-orthogonal wavelet encoding scheme. The authors claimed that bi-orthogonal wavelet anaysis has good local resolution in both frequency and spatial domains. Hence, it is capable to capture the local information of iris. This method is further enhanced using directional bi-orthogonal filter (Abhyankar & Schukers, 2009). The created templates are compared using the Hamming distance (Daugman,

*Figure 6. Normalized iris pattern*

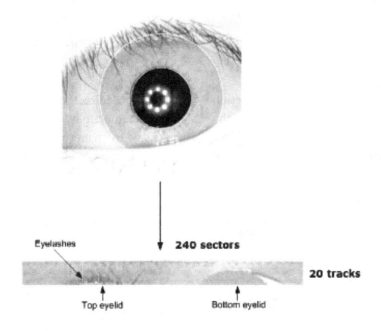

2004) or Euclidean distance (Zhu et al., 2000), and then the similarity values are evaluated.

In this paper, the implementation of the iris recognition is mainly based on the Matlab source code provided by Libor Masek (Masek, 2003). The iris region was normalized to a 20 X 240 rectangular image as shown in Figure 6. The inner and outer iris boundaries were adjusted to 240 pixels by linear interpolation. Then, the normalized iris was divided into 20 tracks. Each track consists of 240 sectors and is regarded as 1D iris signal. For each pixel of the normalized image, a log-Gabor filter was employed to encode the pattern and quantized the phase information into four levels, for each possible quadrant in the complex plane, as described by Daugman (2004). These four levels are represented using two bits of data, so each pixel in the normalized iris pattern corresponds to two bits of data in the iris template. A total of 9,600 bits were calculated for the template, and an equal number of masking bits were generated in order to mask out corrupted regions within the iris. Hence, each iris template was represented by 19200 bits or 2.4k bytes. For a large iris database, it may require an amount of space to store the iris template. The noise mask may degrade the performance of the system by breaking the 1D iris signal track into multiple different small regions, where some global information may be lost. Furthermore, the process of locating the eyelids and eyelashes is complex and has high computation load.

This paper proposes the use of feature selection to select the useful 1D iris tracks to contain the most discriminant information that leads to low TER without locating the eyelid and eyelashes.

The proposed method has several advantages. First, it has lower computation time. The detection of eyelids and eyelashes is complex and has high computation load, (especially eyelid detection method based on parabolic Hough transform). Second, the proposed method improved the classification accuracy in terms of TER. As mentioned above, some of the tracks were close to eyelid region or pupil region were badly corrupted. They might not have contained any useful information and might also degrade the performance. Third, the resulting iris template is much smaller in terms of size compared to conventional method. The final iris template does not have the noise mask that marks the location of the eyelids and eyelashes. The iris template is also smaller because not all of the 1D iris tracks are selected.

The CAISA database (CASIA, http://www. cbsr.ia.ac.cn/IrisDatabase.htm) was chosen to evaluate the performance of the proposed method. Iris images belonging to 40 different randomly chosen persons were selected. For each person, 3 iris images were selected as training images and the remaining three iris images served as testing images. The iris features were extracted using log-Gabor filter. The similarity measurement was based on Hamming distance and was normalized ranging from 0 to1.

### 4.3.1 Simulation Result for Iris Recognition

The proposed method reduced the size of the of the iris template by 30% by removing 6 useless tracks of iris pattern which contains mostly corrupted data due to eyelid, eyelashes and pupil. By

*Table 4. Iris recognition result*

|  | Number of tracks | Size of template | TER | Recognition rate |
|---|---|---|---|---|
| Full feature set | 20 | 2.4KB | 0.131 | 94.2% |
| Full feature set with noise mask | 20 | 4.8KB | 0.125 | 95% |
| 3 fold cross-validation method | 14 | 1.68 KB | 0.131 | 92.5% |
| Selected feature subset | 14 | 1.68 KB | 0.113 | 95% |

removing the unwanted tracks of iris pattern, the computation time for encoding the iris feature and comparing the iris template will be reduced. At the same data, by removing the unwanted the data, the performance of the system improved by 8.3%. The cross-validation method also selected 14 tracks. However, it does not improve the TER and the recognition rate decreases. It shows the proposed method is better than cross-validation method in this case.

## 5. CONCLUSION

This paper proposed a feature selection algorithm based on minimizing the area under the DET curve. The DET curve has advantage over ROC because it gives uniform treatment for FAR and FRR. PSO is employed to search for an optimal subset of features that gives the smallest area under the DET curve. The PSO algorithm evaluates the fitness based on different subset of feature rather than each feature independently. Thus, it can avoid from trapping in local optimal solution. The proposed method is implemented in face recognition and iris recognition system. The results show that the proposed method is able to find an optimal subset of feature that sufficiently describes iris and face images by removing unwanted and redundant features and at the same time improving the classification accuracy.

## REFERENCES

Abhyankar, A., Hornak, L. A., & Schuckers, S. (2005). Biorthogonal-wavelets-based iris recognition. *Proceedings of the SPIE Society of Photo Optical Instrumentation Engineers Conference, 5779*, 59–67.

Abhyankar, A., & Schuckers, S. (2009). Iris quality assessment and bi-orthogonal wavelet based encoding for recognition. *Pattern Recognition, 42*, 1878–1894. doi:10.1016/j.patcog.2009.01.004

Acir, N., Özdamar, O., & Güzeliş, C. (2006). Automatic classification of auditory brainstem responses using SVM-based feature selection algorithm for threshold detection. *Engineering Applications of Artificial Intelligence, 19*, 209–218. doi:10.1016/j.engappai.2005.08.004

Belhumeur, P., Hespanha, J., & Kriegman, D. (1997). Eigenfaces vs. fisherfaces: Recognition using class specific linear projection. *IEEE Transactions on Pattern Analysis and Machine Intelligence, 19*(7), 711–720. doi:10.1109/34.598228

Boles, W. W., & Boashash, B. (1998). A human identification technique using images of the iris and wavelet transform. *IEEE Transactions on Signal Processing, 46*(4), 1185–1188. doi:10.1109/78.668573

CASIA iris database version 3.0, http://www.cbsr.ia.ac.cn/IrisDatabase.htm, (downloaded at 11-December-2008).

Chuang, L. Y., Chang, H. W., Tu, C. J., & Yang, C. H. (2008). Improved binary PSO for feature selection using gene expression data. *Computational Biology and Chemistry, 32*, 29–38. doi:10.1016/j.compbiolchem.2007.09.005

Daugman, J. G. (1993). High confidence visual recognition of persons by a test of statistical independence. *IEEE Transactions on Pattern Analysis and Machine Intelligence, 15*(11), 1148–1161. doi:10.1109/34.244676

Daugman, J. G. (2004). How iris recognition works. *IEEE Transaction on Circuits Systems and Video Technology, 14*(1), 21–30. doi:10.1109/TCSVT.2003.818350

Delac, K., Grgis, M., & Grgic, S. (2007). Image compression effect in face recognition systems. *Face Recognition, 75-92.*

Dorigo, M., & Caro, G. D. (1999). Ant colony optimization: a new meta-heuristic. *Congress on Evolutionary Computation* (pp. 1470-1477).

Er, M., Chen, W., & Wu, S. (2005). High-speed face recognition based on discrete cosine transform and RBF neural networks. *IEEE Transactions on Neural Networks, 16,* 679–691. doi:10.1109/TNN.2005.844909

Guyon, I., & Elissee, A. (2003). An introduction to variable and feature selection. *Journal of Machine Learning Research, 3,* 1157–1182. doi:10.1162/153244303322753616

Huang, C., & Dun, J. (2008). A distributed PSO–SVM hybrid system with feature selection and parameter optimization. *Applied Soft Computing, 8,* 1381–1391. doi:10.1016/j.asoc.2007.10.007

Jing, X., & Wong, H., & Zhang, David. (2006). Face recognition based on discriminant fractional Fourier feature extraction. *Pattern Recognition Letters, 27,* 1465–1471. doi:10.1016/j.patrec.2006.02.020

Jing, X., & Wong, H., & Zhang, David. (2005). A Fourier-LDA approach for image recognition. *Pattern Recognition, 38,* 453–457. doi:10.1016/j.patcog.2003.09.020

Kanan, H. R., & Faez, K. (2008a). GA-based optimal selection of PZMI features for face recognition. *Applied Mathematics and Computation, 205,* 706–715. doi:10.1016/j.amc.2008.05.114

Kanan, H. R., & Faez, K. (2008b). An improved feature selection method based on ant colony optimization (ACO) evaluated on face recognition system. *Applied Mathematics and Computation, 205,* 716–725. doi:10.1016/j.amc.2008.05.115

Kennedy, J., & Eberhart, R. C. (1995). Particles swarm optimization. *IEEE International Conference on Neural Network: Vol. 4.* (pp. 1942-1948).

Kennedy, J., & Eberhart, R. C. (1997). A discrete binary version of the particle swarm algorithm. *IEEE International Conference on Computational Cybernatics and Simulation: Vol. 5* (pp. 4104-4108).

Kira, K., & Rendell, L. (1992). A practical approach to feature selection. *Proceedings of Ninth International Conference on Machine Learning* (pp. 249–256).

Ma, L., Tan, T., Wang, Y., & Zhang, D. (1997). Personal identification based on iris texture analysis. *IEEE Transactions on Pattern Analysis and Machine Intelligence, 25*(12), 1519–1533.

Martin, A., Doddington, G., Kamm, T., Ordowski, M., & Przybocki, M. (1997) The DET curve in assessment of detection task performance. *In Proceedings of the European Conference on Speech Communication and Technology* (pp. 1895–1898).

Masek, L. (2003). Recognition of human iris patterns for biometric identification. Bachelor of Engineering Thesis, University of Western Australia, Perth, Australia.

Min, T.-H., & Park, R.-H. (2009). Eyelid and eyelash detection method in the normalized iris image using the parabolic Hough model and Otsu;s thresholding method. *Pattern Recognition Letters, 30,* 1138–1143. doi:10.1016/j.patrec.2009.03.017

Pudil, P., Novovicova, J., & Kittler, J. (1994). Floating search methods in feature selection. *Pattern Recognition Letters, 15,* 1119–1125. doi:10.1016/0167-8655(94)90127-9

Shen, l., & Zhen, J. (2009). Gabor wavelet selection and SVM classification for object recognition, *ACTA Automatica Sinica, 35(4), 350-355.*

Shi, Y., & Eberhart, R. C. (1998). A modified particle swarm optimizer. *IEEE International Conference on Evolutionary Computation* (pp. 69-73).

Siedlecki, W., & Sklansky, J. (1989). A note on genetic algorithm for large-scale feature selection. *Pattern Recognition Letters, 10*, 335–347. doi:10.1016/0167-8655(89)90037-8

Stearns, S. (1976). On selecting features for pattern classifiers. *Proceedings of Third International Conference of Pattern Recognition* (pp. 71–75).

Sun, Z., Bebis, G., & Miller, R. (2003) Boosting object detection using feature selection, *IEEE International Conference on Advanced Video and Signal Based Surveillance* (pp. 290–296).

Toh, K. A., Kim, J., & Lee, S. (2008b). Biometric scores fusion based on total error rate minimization. *Pattern Recognition, 41*, 1066–1082. doi:10.1016/j.patcog.2007.07.020

Toh, K. A., Kim, J., & Lee, S. (2008a). Maximizing area under ROC curve for biometric scores fusion. *Pattern Recognition, 41*(11), 3373–3392. doi:10.1016/j.patcog.2008.04.002

Turk, M., & Pentland, A. (1991). Eigenfaces for recognition. *Journal of Cognitive Neuroscience, 3*(1), 71–86. doi:10.1162/jocn.1991.3.1.71

Viola, P., & Jones, M. (2001). Rapid object detection using a boosted cascade of simple features. *Proceedings of IEEE Computer Society Conference on Computer Vision and Pattern Recognition, 1*, 511–518.

Wiskott, L., Fellous, J., Kruger, N., & Malsburg, C. (1994). Estimating attributes: analysis and extension of relief. *Proceedings of European Conference on Machine Learning* (pp. 171–182).

Yao, P. Li, Jun., Ye, X., Zhuang, Z., & Li, B. (2006). Iris recognition using modified log-gabor filters. *Proceedings of the 18th International Conference on Pattern Recognition Vol. 4* (pp. 461-464).

Zhang, S., & Maruf Hossain, M. Rafiul Hassan, Md., Bailey, J., & Ramamohanarao, K. (2006). Feature weighted SVMs using receiver operating characteristics. *Proceedings of the Sixth SIAM International Conference on Data Mining* (pp. 487-508).

*This work was previously published in the International Journal of Applied Evolutionary Computation, Volume 2, Issue 1, edited by Wei-Chiang Samuelson Hong, pp. 18-33, copyright 2011 by IGI Publishing (an imprint of IGI Global).*

# Chapter 3
# Application of Genetic Algorithm to Minimize the Number of Objects Processed and Setup in a One-Dimensional Cutting Stock Problem

**Julliany Sales Brandão**
*Centro Federal de Educação Tecnológica Celso S. da Fonseca – CEFET/RJ, Brasil*

**João Flávio V. Vasconcellos**
*Instituto Politécnico do Rio de Janeiro – UERJ, Brasil*

**Alessandra Martins Coelho**
*Instituto Politécnico do Rio de Janeiro – UERJ, Brasil*

**Luiz Leduíno de Salles Neto**
*Universidade Federal de São Paulo – UNIFESP, Brasil*

**André Vieira Pinto**
*Universidade Federal do Estado do Rio de Janeiro – UNIRIO, Brasil*

## ABSTRACT

*This paper presents the application of the one new approach using Genetic Algorithm in solving One-Dimensional Cutting Stock Problems in order to minimize two objectives, usually conflicting, i.e., the number of processed objects and setup while simultaneously treating them as a single goal. The model problem, the objective function, the method denominated SingleGA10 and the steps used to solve the problem are also presented. The obtained results of the SingleGA10 are compared to the following methods: SHP, Kombi234, ANLCP300 and Symbio10, found in literature, verifying its capacity to find feasible and competitive solutions. The computational results show that the proposed method, which only uses a genetic algorithm to solve these two objectives inversely related, provides good results.*

DOI: 10.4018/978-1-4666-3628-6.ch003

## INTRODUCTION

With recent advances in computing, it has become important and valuable to study the problems of cutting and packing, as well as optimization models for the control and planning of production systems, which have been stimulated by various industries such as glass, paper, textile, chemical, among others, aimed at making their processes more efficient due to competition between companies in search of lower costs, reducing waste and efficiency in delivery.

The cutting stock problem consists in finding the best way to get parts of different sizes (items) from the cutting of larger pieces (objects) in order to minimize any kind of cost or maximize profit. The items are arranged on the object to perform cuts along the production. On the disposition of items is given the default name of cutting. It is important to highlight the importance of geometry on cutting stock problems, since the shapes and dimensions of items and objects determine their possible standards.

Kantorovick (1960) was a pioneer in the field of cutting stock problems. However, the breakthrough of the area was the work of Gilmore and Gomory (1961, 1963) studying the cutting stock problem through the process of column generation.

To solve a cutting stock problem you need the cutting patterns and the frequency of the patterns, ie the number of times that the standards will be implemented.

Although the overall objective is to minimize losses, there are several modelings of the problem, as the maximization of profits, the reduction of objects used, the production time and/or a combination of these.

The cost of preparing the machine is a relevant factor in some cutting processes. Thus, it is interesting to evaluate the effect of minimizing the number of processed objects (input minimization) and the minimizing of the number of cutting patterns (setup), goals which are partially conflicting, for a more general assessment of the

cost. Haessler (1975) was the first to address the non-linear one-dimensional cutting stock problem this way. The objectives are considered inversely related or partially conflicting, because, as the setup, is reduced, the number of processed objects is increased.

For most formulations of the cutting problem there is no knowledge, until now, of a method that produces a solution in polynomial time. According to Salles Neto (2005), the large number of applications and the difficulty of solving the cutting problems, mostly NP-Complete, have led many researchers around the world to focus efforts on developing new and efficient methods of resolution, most of them heuristic. The problem discussed here belongs to the class NP-Complete. In this case the use of heuristics or metaheuristics is justified, generating, for these, good solutions in a short period of time.

According to Ribeiro et al. (2007), Metaheuristics are high-level procedures that coordinate simple heuristics and rules to find good (often optimal) approximate solutions to computationally difficult combinatorial optimization problems.

This work was conducted via the implementation of object-oriented programming for a new approach using a single genetic algorithm in order to solve the same problem initially treated by Haessler (1975), inspired by a recent approach presented by Golfeto et al. (2007, 2009b), in which two genetic algorithms, which interact themselves in a mutualistic relationship, aim to minimize the number of processed objects and setup. The approach here presented, aimed at achieving the same goals as Golfeto et al. (2007, 2009b) described, uses only a simple single genetic algorithm. Not known in the literature so far, the implementation of a single genetic algorithm to minimize these two goals simultaneously treated in a single objective version. In this paper, we will analyze the behavior of the proposed method, SingleGA10, to meet these goals and compare it with other methods.

The paper is organized by formally dealing with the cutting problem in order to reduce the number of processed objects and the setup. The basic concepts of genetic algorithms are presented after this. The next section presents the computational implementation and finally the computational results and conclusions are illustrated.

## ONE-DIMENSIONAL CUTTING STOCK PROBLEM

The cutting stock problem consists in deciding how to cut a set of rectangular pieces with pre-set demands, from a standard rectangular plate, in order to minimize the cost, time and material loss involved in manufacturing, or a combination of these (Carneiro, 1994). More specifically there is a number $m$ of different items, with width $w_i$, $i = 1, ..., m$ that need to be produced to meet each demand $d$, starting with a master piece of width $W > w_i$ for every $i$, by cutting along its length. This problem is classified as 1/V/I/R, according to the typology of Dyckoff (1990) and SSSCSP (Single Stock Size Cutting Stock Problem) in the typology of Wascher et al. (2007).

To the disposition of the items in the master piece is given the name of cutting pattern, and the reconfiguration time of the cutting machine, at each change of pattern, is called a setup.

In industry, minimizing the number of objects processed and/or waste, in most cases, may not be enough. Other factors such as cost reduction and efficiency in the delivery of orders have been stimulating research in this area. When a demand must be met within a short time, the cost of changing patterns becomes important as they require an adjustment on the machines (knives for cutting) and therefore, time and labor. Thus, minimizing the setup cost becomes one more goal in the industry production process and, being inversely related goals, it is necessary to find the balance between them.

A formal mathematical model that represents these goals is described below:

$$\text{Minimize} \quad c_1 \sum_{j=1}^{n} x_j + c_2 \sum_{j=1}^{n} \delta(x_j) \qquad (1)$$

$$\text{Subject to :} \quad \sum_{j=1}^{n} a_{ij} x_j \geq d_i \quad i = 1, ..., m$$

$$x_j \in N \; \text{j=1,...,n}$$

where:

- 1, if $x_j > 0$
- $\delta(x_j) = 0$, if $x_j = 0$
- $n$ = number of possible cutting patterns;
- $m$ = number of different items;
- $c_1$ = cost of each coil;
- $c_2$ = cost of replacement of standard cutting;
- $x_j$ = number of coils processed with the standard cut $j$;
- $a_{ij}$ = number of items of type $i$ in pattern $j$;
- $d_i$ = number of items $i$ demanded;

## Genetic Algorithms

Genetic algorithms are search and optimization of solutions algorithms, based on genetic and evolutionary mechanisms of living beings, as natural selection and the survival of the fittest, introduced by Charles Darwin in his classic "The Origin of Species" (1859) whose first published work known date from the late 50's and early 60's.

The Genetic Algorithms, rigorously introduced by John Holland (Holland, 1975), work with a population of individuals, in which each one represents a possible solution to a given problem. Each individual is given a fitness, that is, a value that quantifies the individual's adaptability to the environment (treated problem). Individuals with higher fitness have higher chances of being selected for reproduction through the intersection, and thereby spread their characteristics for future generations, allowing the most promising areas of search to be explored, taking the genetic algorithm, in most cases, to the convergence to the optimal solution of the problem.

The Genetic Algorithms use an adaptive and parallel process of search for solutions in complex problems. It is adaptive, because the current solutions influence the search for future solutions. The parallelism comes from the fact that every time a set of solutions is considered.

Some important and necessary concepts to the understanding of Genetic Algorithms are presented below:

- **Gene:** The representation of each parameter according to the alphabet used (binary, integer or real);
- **Genome:** Sets of genes to form an individual;
- **Phenotype:** Genome coding;
- **Population:** All individuals in the search space;
- **Selection:** Choice of individuals that favors the most likely to remain and multiply the population. Selection methods most used are: elitism, diversity and tournament;
- **Recombination (Crossover):** Responsible for recombining the characteristics of the parents, during reproduction, allowing their offspring inherit these characteristics. The best known are: point(s) of cutting and uniform;
- **Mutation:** The possibility of any gene of the individual has to present different characteristics from those in the parents, after an operation of recombination.

## Computing Construction

The modeling of the cutting problem is quite simple, however, the its resolution is complex and, as mentioned earlier, there is no knowledge so far of any method that solves it in polynomial time.

To assess and solve a cutting problem it is necessary to generate the cutting patterns and methods to manipulate them so that the final disposition of the items is a good solution, ie, with less waste and setup reduction.

The SingleGA10 is a genetic algorithm composed of two kinds of population: the solutions and the patterns, ie, has the ability to build cutting patterns, regardless of the solution. The population patterns, generated randomly, is static, ie not suffering from any kind of evolution. This method was based on Symbio10 from Golfeto et al. (2007, 2009b). However, the Symbio10 makes use of concepts of symbiosis (Allaby, 1998), more specifically, in a mutualistic relationship between two genetic algorithms (Pianka, 1994) that evolve in a beneficial way, while the method of the present study makes use of only a genetic algorithm to solve the same goal.

The gene of the solution population was represented by two elements. The first one refers to the amount of times (frequency) that the standard indicated by the second element was processed. The second element of the solution population only served as a pointer to the patterns population.

The patterns population gene was represented by a real number that indicates the length of the item from the list of requests made by the client. Figure 1 shows a representation of the patterns population gene and the solutions population gene.

*Figure 1. Representation of the genes*

Solutions Population Gene:

Pattens Population Gene:

The maximum amount of genes from the solution individual (maximum size of the genome) used was equal to the number of setups (number of different items). However, if the largest item to be cut presented a length less than or equal to 50% of the length of the coil, the following procedure would be adopted, experimentally determined and presented in Figure 2.

The genome size of the pattern adopted was equal to the greatest integer, less than or equal to the result of the division between the size of the default coil and the smaller item of the pattern.

The items were added to the pattern from left to right, if and only if, the pattern had sufficient free space to accommodate it (approach based on the work of Golfeto et al., 2009a, 2009b).

The solutions population (individuals formed by genes from the solutions population) was formed by 600 individuals and the patterns population (individuals formed by genes from the patterns population) by 400, in both cases, all individuals were generated randomly, with no direction. Population sizes were defined experimentally, after simulations with different values.

The selection structure adopted was the elitism with steady state. It was chosen because of the fact that this feature increases the performance of genetic algorithm, since it ensures that the best solution found so far is maintained in future generations. The steady state used is available in the package GALib (Wall, 1996) form the

*Figure 2. Number of genes of the solution individual*

```
if (number of items> 30) then
        SolutionGenes = 16
else
        if (Number of items> 15) then
                SolutionGenes = 12
        else
                SolutionGenes = 8
        end if;
end if
```

class of genetic algorithms GASteadyStateGA. According to the GALib's tutorial (Wall, 1996), the method generates, in each generation, a temporary population of individuals by cloning, and they are inserted in the population of the current generation, removing the worst individuals. The replacement rate, found experimentally, was 25%, which is to say that 75% of the best individuals in the population of solutions will be selected and remain in the population.

The calculation of fitness (*Fs*) of the solution individual to meet the objective of minimizing both the number of processed objects and *setup,* based and described on Golfeto et al. (2007, 2009b), was performed as follows:

$$F_s = c_1\sum\nolimits_{j=1}^{n} x_j + \alpha\sum\nolimits_{j=1}^{n} \delta(x_j) + \sum\nolimits_{j=1}^{n} \tau(x_j) + \rho \tag{2}$$

where:

- $\tau$ : Is the relative loss and can be calculated by $\tau(x_j) = \dfrac{t_j}{w\sum\nolimits_{j=1}^{n} x_j}$, being $t_j$ the waste of standard j.

- $\rho$ : Are penalties if the solution is not feasible. Is proportional to the sum of the infeasibilities, i.e., the value remaining to meet the demand of the item, multiplied by 1000 (value experimentally chosen).

Values $c_1$ and $\alpha$ , respectively, are the costs of processed objects and setup, treated explicitly in the objective function, not requiring any other modifications to achieve different objectives, i.e., the cost is already involved directly in the minimization of the objective function.

To calculate the objective function an interpretation of the patterns was performed, i.e., it was determined which were the active genes of the pattern. The active genes are those that fit in the master-piece without blowing its size.

The recombination operator (crossover) used was the uniform, which consists on randomly choose a value between 0 and 1. If the number drawn was less than or equal to 0.7 the recombination was carried out with the individual who owned the greatest fitness, otherwise, it was carried out with the worst individual. The recombination rate, found experimentally, was 30%.

The mutation operator adopted consisted on randomly choosing a position in the genome of the gene to be mutated and then randomly determining which of its elements (frequency or default_index) would suffer mutation. If the chosen element of the gene were the frequency, a value between the minimum and maximum limits were drawn, otherwise, one individual was randomly chosen in the pattern population and a pointer would be created. For the standard index, component of the solution population's gene, the limits were between zero and the maximum number of setups and for the frequency, the limits were between zero and the value of the highest demand (Golfeto et al., 2009a, 2009b). The mutation rate was given by the ratio between 1 and different number of items (*1/m*).

Regarding the stopping criteria, three were used:

- **Maximum Number of Generations:** 1000;
- **Maximum Execution Time:** 500s;
- **Convergence:** 500 generations, i.e., if the algorithm does not improve the solution by 500 generations, it stops.

Here is presented, the pseudo code of the proposed method called SingleGA10:

## Procedure SingleGA10

1. Generate the individuals of the patterns population randomly;
2. Generate the individuals of the solutions population randomly;
3. Calculate the objective function of the solutions individuals;
4. Select the solutions individuals parents;
5. Use recombination and mutation operators to generate new solutions;
6. Evolve the population;
7. **if** some stopping criterion is satisfied STOP the execution of the algorithm;
8. **else** return to step 3.
   End-Procedure SingleGA10

The similarity with the Symbio10 consists on the objective function, in the way patterns are added and some limits cited. However, besides using only one genetic algorithm, the other procedures, genetic operators, rates and values adopted are different, as presented in pseudocode and stopping criteria described above.

## Computational Tests

The proposed method, SingleGA10 was implemented in C++, compiler Bloodshed DevC++, on a Pentium Dual Core 1.73 533MHz, 2G RAM.

The problems used for the computational tests with the SingleGA10 were generated randomly by CUTGEN1, a one-dimensional cutting problems generator developed by Gau and Wascher (1995). We generated 18 classes characterized by different values of input parameters, presented in Table 1 and Table 2, below, each class containing 100 problems, totaling 1800 tests for evaluating the quality of the proposed method.

The parameters and the seed used to generate the 1800 problems in CUTGEN1 were the same used by Foerster and Wascher (2000), Salles Neto and Moretti (2005) and Golfeto et al. (2009a, 2009b).

Table 1 and Table 2 describe the parameters used for each class. Parameters $v_1$ and $v_2$ represent the upper and lower length limits of the items. $m$ represents the number of demanded items and $d$

*Table 1. Input parameters to generate the classes from 1 to 9*

| Class | 1 | 2 | 3 | 4 | 5 | 6 | 7 | 8 | 9 |
|---|---|---|---|---|---|---|---|---|---|
| $v_1$ | 0,01 | 0,01 | 0,01 | 0,01 | 0,01 | 0,01 | 0,01 | 0,01 | 0,01 |
| $v_2$ | 0,2 | 0,2 | 0,2 | 0,2 | 0,2 | 0,2 | 0,8 | 0,8 | 0,8 |
| $m$ | 10 | 10 | 20 | 20 | 40 | 40 | 10 | 10 | 20 |
| $d$ | 10 | 100 | 10 | 100 | 10 | 100 | 10 | 100 | 10 |

*Table 2. Input parameters to generate the classes from 10 to 18*

| Class | 10 | 11 | 12 | 13 | 14 | 15 | 16 | 17 | 18 |
|---|---|---|---|---|---|---|---|---|---|
| $v_1$ | 0.01 | 0.01 | 0.01 | 0.2 | 0.2 | 0.2 | 0.2 | 0.2 | 0.2 |
| $v_2$ | 0.8 | 0.8 | 0.8 | 0.8 | 0.8 | 0.8 | 0.8 | 0.8 | 0.8 |
| $m$ | 20 | 40 | 40 | 10 | 10 | 20 | 20 | 40 | 40 |
| $d$ | 100 | 10 | 100 | 10 | 100 | 10 | 100 | 10 | 100 |

indicates the average demand (Gau & Wascher, 1995). The following were generated: six classes with small items (classes 1-6), six classes with different items (classes 7-12) and six classes with large items (classes 13-18).

For purposes of assessing the quality of the proposed method in solving the cutting problem it was compared with four different methods, found in the literature and described below, which have the same goals being treated under the same vision of a single-objective problem:

1.  **SHP:** programmed in FORTRAN, using the g77 compiler for Linux on an AMD AthlonXP 1800 MHz with 512 RAM PC. Method based on a comprehensive technique, in which, in each iteration it is calculated some aspiration parameters, making a search for cutting patterns that satisfy these parameters until they meet all the demand (Haessler, (1975);

2.  **Kombi234:** Code in Modula-2 in MS-DOS 6.0 using an IBM 486/66. Method based on pattern matching to decrease the setup of an initial solution. It is based on the fact that the sums of the frequencies of the resulting

patterns are the same of the frequencies of default patterns, thus keeping constant the number of processed objects, with a possible reduction of setup, i.e., the number of standards is reduced for making the same original demand (Foerster & Wascher, 2000).

3.  **ANLCP300:** Programmed in FORTRAN, using the g77 compiler for Linux on an AMD AthlonXP 1800 MHz with 512 RAM PC. Method proposed by Salles Neto and Moretti (2005), which seeks to minimize the number of processed objects and the setup by applying the Lagrangian method, increasing in a problem with objective function, proposed by Haessler (1975), smoothed. The ANLCP300 adapts the method of column generation of Gilmore and Gomory (1961, 1963) and to obtain a viable solution uses a simple heuristic rounding.

4.  **Symbio10:** Implemented in FORTRAN, using Microsoft FORTRAN Power Station compiler in a AMD Sempron 2300+ 1533MHz PC with 640 MB of RAM. It is a method which consists of two genetic algorithms that, based on a symbiotic process between two populations of different species,

generates its own standards in conjunction with solutions to the problem (Golfeto et al., 2007, 2009b).

## Computational Results

To differentiate from other tests that can be undertaken in the future with the proposed method, it was used the name SingleGA10 to the results presented here, which used the parameters $c_1 = 1$ and *setup* cost $\alpha = 10$.

The proposed method, SingleGA10 managed to converge in all the 1800 problems tested, ie, the algorithm terminated before reaching the 100 generations or 500 seconds.

For best viewing of the performance of the proposed method, on the table of percentage changes we used color schemes whose meaning is described in Table 3.

Table 4 and Table 5 respectively show, for comparison, the average results of processed objects and setup for the 18 classes tested with SingleGA10 and methods SHP, ANLCP300, and Kombi234 Symbio10.

Aiming at a more detailed analysis, it was calculated the change of the setup and the number of objects processed in SingleGA10 compared to other methods through the expression represented by the equation (3).

$$100 \times \left( \frac{setup_{SingleGA} - setup_{comparedmethod}}{setup_{SingleGA}} \right) \quad (3)$$

*Table 3. Meanings of the colors*

| COLOR | MEANING |
|---|---|
| | The proposed method is better |
| | The percentage differences are small |
| | The difference is null or practically null |
| | The proposed method is worse |
| | Number of classes in which the method was better |
| | The value of the percentage differences |

Similarly, the expression to determine the percentage change of the number of processed objects is equal to:

$$100 \times \left( \frac{\Pr ocObj_{SingleGA} - \Pr ocObj_{comparedmethod}}{\Pr ocObj_{SingleGA}} \right) \quad (4)$$

Table 6 and Table 7 show respectively the percentage change in setup and number of processed objects. Analyzing these tables, looking the setup, the SingleGA10 was better than all other methods in most classes, except for the ANLCP300 with which tied on the number of classes; exceeded the SHP in 16 classes, got better results in all classes when compared with the Kombi234; was superior than the ANLCP300 than in 9 classes, and was better in 12 classes by comparing it with the Symbio10.

The negative results obtained by equations (3) and (4), indicate that, in that class, the SingleGA10 showed better results than the method compared.

The variations in Table 5 and Table 6 are considered valid, because even examining each goal separately, they were treated simultaneously (Table 3 and Table 4) allowing an analysis of the performance of each part of the method as well as it as a whole.

Regarding the number of processed objects, the performance of SingleGA10 was reduced when compared with the average of the setups. This result is justified because inversely related goals are treated. However, the SingleGA10 was greater than 4 classes when compared with the SHP and another 4 the percent difference was about 3.7%. It surpassed ANLCP300 in three classes and in two more classes differed by 2.8%. In others methods SingleGA didn't present better results than any class, however, compared with Symbio10, very small differences were obtained showing a difference in five classes below 1%. The percentage change in the number of processed objects showed that, despite the performance of

*Table 4. Average number of processed objects*

| Class | SHP | Kombi234 | ANLCP300 | Symbio10 | SingleGA10 |
|---|---|---|---|---|---|
| 1 | 14.17 | 11.49 | 14.30 | 14.84 | 15.56 |
| 2 | 116.47 | 110.25 | 121.48 | 117.80 | 127.36 |
| 3 | 25.29 | 22.13 | 25.14 | 28.23 | 32.50 |
| 4 | 255.33 | 215.93 | 224.86 | 239.72 | 269.73 |
| 5 | 46.89 | 42.96 | 45.66 | 61.42 | 71.14 |
| 6 | 433.59 | 424.71 | 432.72 | 518.85 | 623.58 |
| 7 | 55.84 | 50.21 | 51.54 | 53.75 | 54.23 |
| 8 | 515.76 | 499.52 | 495.94 | 514.65 | 518.21 |
| 9 | 108.54 | 93.67 | 114.52 | 101.62 | 104.63 |
| 10 | 1001.59 | 932.32 | 969.20 | 975.72 | 1031.98 |
| 11 | 202.80 | 176.97 | 231.84 | 201.44 | 249.01 |
| 12 | 1873.05 | 1766.20 | 1861.20 | 1917.40 | 2462.56 |
| 13 | 69.97 | 63.27 | 70.54 | 67.32 | 67.63 |
| 14 | 643.55 | 632.12 | 634.02 | 650.52 | 652.43 |
| 15 | 136.05 | 119.43 | 127.38 | 128.87 | 130.16 |
| 16 | 1253.55 | 1191.80 | 1194.74 | 1251.90 | 1301.94 |
| 17 | 256.01 | 224.68 | 297.58 | 247.62 | 270.00 |
| 18 | 2381.54 | 2342.4 | 2430.04 | 2422.41 | 2751.49 |

*Table 5. Average of the numbers of setup*

| Class | SHP | Kombi234 | ANLCP300 | Symbio10 | SingleGA10 |
|---|---|---|---|---|---|
| 1 | 3.95 | 3.40 | 3.02 | 1.85 | 1.97 |
| 2 | 5.94 | 7.81 | 4.50 | 4.68 | 3.78 |
| 3 | 5.00 | 4.84 | 4.84 | 4.47 | 4.18 |
| 4 | 7.31 | 7.28 | 7.28 | 9.36 | 7.10 |
| 5 | 6.87 | 10.75 | 7.02 | 8.23 | 7.79 |
| 6 | 10.81 | 25.44 | 10.92 | 14.08 | 12.36 |
| 7 | 8.84 | 7.90 | 5.54 | 5.21 | 5.35 |
| 8 | 9.76 | 9.96 | 8.00 | 7.76 | 6.07 |
| 9 | 17.19 | 15.03 | 10.58 | 10.01 | 9.39 |
| 10 | 19.37 | 19.28 | 13.96 | 16.04 | 13.34 |
| 11 | 32.20 | 28.74 | 20.00 | 21.56 | 24.02 |
| 12 | 37.25 | 37.31 | 23.68 | 31.52 | 34.58 |
| 13 | 9.38 | 8.97 | 5.64 | 6.68 | 6.56 |
| 14 | 9.85 | 10.32 | 7.92 | 8.21 | 7.22 |
| 15 | 18.03 | 16.88 | 9.92 | 12.99 | 12.90 |
| 16 | 19.63 | 19.91 | 13.88 | 16.34 | 15.33 |
| 17 | 34.39 | 31.46 | 22.60 | 25.62 | 25.86 |
| 18 | 38.23 | 38.28 | 27.44 | 32.18 | 33.76 |

*Table 6. Percentage change of setup in relation to SingleGA10 with the other methods*

| Class | %SHP | %Kombi234 | %ANLCP300 | %Symbio10 |
|-------|------|-----------|-----------|-----------|
| 1 | -100.508 | -72.5888 | -53.2995 | 6.091370558 |
| 2 | -57.1429 | -106.614 | -19.0476 | -23.8095238 |
| 3 | -19.6172 | -15.7895 | -15.7895 | -6.93779904 |
| 4 | -2.95775 | -2.53521 | -2.53521 | -31.8309859 |
| 5 | 11.81 | -37.9974 | 9.884467 | -5.64826701 |
| 6 | 12.5405 | -105.825 | 11.65049 | -13.9158576 |
| 7 | -65.2336 | -47.6636 | -3.5514 | 2.61682243 |
| 8 | -60.7908 | -64.0857 | -31.7957 | -27.8418451 |
| 9 | -83.0671 | -60.0639 | -12.6731 | -6.6027689 |
| 10 | -45.2024 | -44.5277 | -4.64768 | -20.2398801 |
| 11 | -34.055 | -19.6503 | 16.73605 | 10.24146545 |
| 12 | -7.72123 | -7.89474 | 31.52111 | 8.849045691 |
| 13 | -42.9878 | -36.7378 | 14.02439 | -1.82926829 |
| 14 | -36.4266 | -42.9363 | -9.69529 | -13.7119114 |
| 15 | -39.7674 | -30.8527 | 23.10078 | -0.69767442 |
| 16 | -28.0496 | -29.8761 | 9.458578 | -6.58838878 |
| 17 | -32.9853 | -21.6551 | 12.60634 | 0.928074246 |
| 18 | -13.2405 | -13.3886 | 18.72038 | 4.680094787 |
| Better in: | 16 | 18 | 9 | 12 |

SingleGA10 has been lower than the others, these percentage differences, in most of the middle classes of SingleGA10 when compared with other methods, was quite small.

The total cost is the cost of the objective function and its calculation was performed by the following formula represented below (Table 7)

$$\cos t_{total} = c_1 \times obj_{average} + \alpha \times setup_{average}$$
(5)

where:

- $obj_{average}$ is the average number of objects processed in the 100 problems in each class;
- $setup_{average}$ is the average of the number of setup among the 100 problems of each class.

The average total cost was calculated to assess the quality and performance of the proposed method, at the same time, the two goals for comparison of the value of the objective function with the other methods. Table 8 brings the average of the total cost and for a better understanding of the results, in Table 9, it is presented the percentage change of the total cost of the proposed method, SingleGA10, in relation with other methods compared, making it easier to analyze the performance of the method.

The results obtained by SingleGA10 were better than the SHP in 12 classes and in one more, in class 16, showed a difference of only 0.4%. Overcame Kombi234 in 10 classes, the ANLCP300 in 3 classes, and in the latter, in more than 5 classes showed a difference of less than 2%. It performed better in 4 classes when compared with the Symbio10 and in 7 classes the difference presented was less than 3%.

*Table 7. Percentage change in the number of processed objects in relation to SingleGA10 with other methods*

| Class | %SHP | %Kombi234 | %ANLCP300 | %Symbio10 |
|---|---|---|---|---|
| 1 | 8.93316 | 26.15681 | 8.097686 | 4.62724936 |
| 2 | 8.55057 | 13.43436 | 4.616834 | 7.50628141 |
| 3 | 22.1846 | 31.90769 | 22.64615 | 13.1384615 |
| 4 | 5.33867 | 19.94587 | 16.63515 | 11.1259408 |
| 5 | 34.0877 | 39.61203 | 35.8167 | 13.6631993 |
| 6 | 30.4676 | 31.89166 | 30.60714 | 16.7949581 |
| 7 | -2.9688 | 7.412871 | 4.960354 | 0.88511894 |
| 8 | 0.47278 | 3.606646 | 4.297486 | 0.68698018 |
| 9 | -3.737 | 10.47501 | -9.45236 | 2.87680398 |
| 10 | 2.94483 | 9.657164 | 6.083451 | 5.45165604 |
| 11 | 18.5575 | 28.93057 | 6.895305 | 19.1036505 |
| 12 | 23.9389 | 28.27789 | 24.42012 | 22.1379378 |
| 13 | -3.46 | 6.446843 | -4.30282 | 0.45837646 |
| 14 | 1.36107 | 3.112978 | 2.821759 | 0.29275171 |
| 15 | -4.5252 | 8.2437 | 2.135833 | 0.99108789 |
| 16 | 3.71676 | 8.459683 | 8.233866 | 3.84349509 |
| 17 | 5.18148 | 16.78519 | -10.2148 | 8.28888889 |
| 18 | 13.4454 | 14.86794 | 11.68276 | 11.9600653 |
| Better in: | 4 | 0 | 3 | 0 |
| Dif % = | (4) 3.7% | | (2) 2.8% | (5) 1% |

The SingleGA10 was better than Kombi234 and SHP in most classes, a fact that in relation to ANLCP300 and Symbio10 has not occurred. However, due to small differences in percentage changes, the behavior of SingleGA10 with ANLCP300 and Symbio10 (Figure 3) was graphically analyzed, and it can be noticed that the performance is almost matched in 15 classes with ANLCP and in 16 when compared to Symbio10. The major differences presented by SingleGA10, for all the methods compared, are in classes 12 and 18.

The choice of the value of the setup, also discussed and exemplified by Salles Neto and Moretti (2005), as well as the cost of the number of processed objects take into account, several variables such as delivery time, demand required, cost of labor, among other factors.

The computational time was not considered in this work, since each method has been implemented in different languages and machines, making it impossible to compare them.

## CONCLUSIONS AND PERSPECTIVES

This work conducted a study on the problem of one-dimensional cutting in order to minimize the number of processed objects and the setup, and implemented it by the application of a new genetic algorithm that, alone, was able to resolve these objectives, usually conflicting.

The contribution of this work was the development of a new method capable of solving the

*Table 8. Averages of the total cost*

| Class | SHP | Kombi234 | ANLCP300 | Symbio10 | SingleGA10 |
|---|---|---|---|---|---|
| 1 | 53.67 | 45.49 | 44.5 | 33.34 | 35.26 |
| 2 | 175.87 | 188.35 | 166.48 | 164.6 | 165.16 |
| 3 | 75.29 | 70.53 | 73.54 | 72.93 | 74.3 |
| 4 | 328.43 | 288.73 | 297.66 | 333.32 | 340.73 |
| 5 | 115.59 | 150.46 | 115.86 | 143.72 | 149.04 |
| 6 | 541.69 | 679.11 | 541.92 | 659.65 | 747.18 |
| 7 | 144.24 | 129.21 | 106.94 | 105.85 | 107.73 |
| 8 | 613.36 | 599.12 | 575.94 | 592.25 | 578.91 |
| 9 | 280.44 | 243.97 | 220.32 | 201.72 | 198.53 |
| 10 | 1195.29 | 1125.12 | 1108.8 | 1136.12 | 1165.38 |
| 11 | 524.8 | 464.37 | 431.84 | 417.04 | 489.21 |
| 12 | 2245.55 | 2139.3 | 2098 | 2232.6 | 2808.36 |
| 13 | 163.77 | 152.97 | 126.94 | 134.12 | 133.23 |
| 14 | 742.05 | 735.32 | 713.22 | 732.62 | 724.63 |
| 15 | 316.35 | 288.23 | 226.58 | 258.77 | 259.16 |
| 16 | 1449.85 | 1390.9 | 1333.54 | 1415.3 | 1455.24 |
| 17 | 599.91 | 539.28 | 523.58 | 503.82 | 528.6 |
| 18 | 2763.84 | 2725.2 | 2704.44 | 2744.21 | 3089.09 |

minimization problem proposed, called Single-GA10, as well as to provide a comparative study of its performance with the methods SHP, Kombi234, ANLCP300 and Symbio10, and the opportunity to work with the two costs ($c_1$ and $\alpha$), directly in the objective function, which is an advantage of the method over Kombi234 and SHP.

To validate the proposed method 1800 test problems, randomly generated by the generator of one-dimensional cutting stock problems, CUTGEN1, were used. It was found that the SingleGA10 was superior than Kombi234 and SHP in most classes tested, and obtained good results in some classes when compared with the ANLCP300 and Symbio10.

Once the setup was the main goal, SingleGA10 performed better in relation to its minimization, in virtually all classes of all methods, except when compared with ANLCP300 which tied in the number of classes.

It was observed that the excellent performance in minimizing the number of setups, reduces the efficiency in minimizing the number of objects processed in most classes, which may be explained as they are inversely related goals.

The graphical analysis carried out showed the good performance of the method and made more noticeable that the percentual variations are small for most classes, when SingleGA10 is compared with other methods. However, the major disadvantage of SingleGA10 in comparison with other methods compared regards computational time. It is believed that the choice of parameters and genetic operators adopted may be responsible for the high computational cost, especially the selection operator that selects only the fittest and thus damaging the diversity of the population.

And, based on the computational results presented, it can be said that the new method is promising and competitive in the environment of one-dimensional cutting stock problems.

As future works, it is aimed to study other setup costs and the behavior of other genetic operators, especially the selection and recombination

*Table 9. Percentage change in the total cost of SingleGA10, in comparison with other methods*

| Class | %SHP | %Kombi234 | %ANLCP300 | %Symbio10 |
|-------|------|-----------|-----------|-----------|
| 1 | -52.2121 | -29.013046 | -26.2053318 | 5.44526376 |
| 2 | -6.48462 | -14.04093 | -0.79922499 | 0.33906515 |
| 3 | -1.33244 | 5.07402423 | 1.022880215 | 1.84387618 |
| 4 | 3.609896 | 15.2613506 | 12.64050715 | 2.17474247 |
| 5 | 22.44364 | -0.9527644 | 22.26247987 | 3.56951154 |
| 6 | 27.50207 | 9.11025456 | 27.47129206 | 11.714714 |
| 7 | -33.8903 | -19.938736 | 0.733314768 | 1.7451035 |
| 8 | -5.95084 | -3.4910435 | 0.513033114 | -2.3043306 |
| 9 | -41.2582 | -22.888228 | -10.9756712 | -1.6068101 |
| 10 | -2.56654 | 3.45466715 | 4.855068733 | 2.51076902 |
| 11 | -7.27499 | 5.07757405 | 11.72707017 | 14.7523558 |
| 12 | 20.04052 | 23.8238687 | 25.29447792 | 20.5016451 |
| 13 | -22.9228 | -14.816483 | 4.721158898 | -0.6680177 |
| 14 | -2.40399 | -1.4752356 | 1.574596691 | -1.1026317 |
| 15 | -22.0674 | -11.217009 | 12.57138447 | 0.15048619 |
| 16 | 0.370386 | 4.42126385 | 8.362881724 | 2.74456447 |
| 17 | -13.4904 | -2.0204313 | 0.949678396 | 4.68785471 |
| 18 | 10.52899 | 11.7798446 | 12.45188713 | 11.164453 |
| Better in: | 12 | 10 | 3 | 4 |
| Dif % = | (1) 0.4% | | (5) 2% | (6) 2.8% 1= |

*Figure 3. Graphic of the averages of the total cost of SingleGA10 with ANLCP300 (a) and Symbio10 (b)*

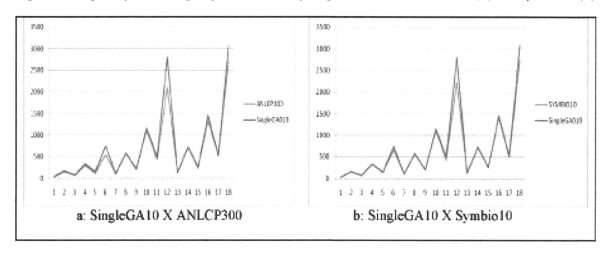

a: SingleGA10 X ANLCP300    b: SingleGA10 X Symbio10

to achieve better results in the shortest space of time, and add a constraint to the demand to keep the numbers of objects processed from being very high. After that, we seek to adapt the new method to treat the one-dimensional cutting problem proposed, as a multiobjective problem, also using the concepts and techniques of parallelization in order to make them more efficient.

# REFERENCES

Allaby, M. (1998). *Dictionary of ecology*. New York: Oxford University Press.

Carneiro, S. A. (1994). *Problema de Corte via Algoritmo Genético. Dissertação (Mestrado), Universidade Federal do Espírito Santo*. Brasil: UFES.

Dyckhoff, H. (1990). A typology of cutting and packing problems. *European Journal of Operational Research, 44*, 145–159. doi:10.1016/0377-2217(90)90350-K

Foerster, H., & Wascher, G. (2000). Pattern reduction in one-dimensional cutting-stock problems. *International Journal of Production Research, 38*, 1657–1676. doi:10.1080/002075400188780

Gau, T., & Wascher, G. (1995). CUTGEN1: A Problem Generator for the Standard One-dimensional Cutting Stock Problem. *European Journal of Operational Research, 84*, 572–579. doi:10.1016/0377-2217(95)00023-J

Gilmore, P. C., & Gomory, R. E. (1961). A linear programming approach to the cutting stock problem. *Operations Research, 9*, 849–859. doi:10.1287/opre.9.6.849

Gilmore, P. C., & Gomory, R. E. (1963). A linear programming approach to the cutting stock problem. *Operations Research, 11*, 863–888. doi:10.1287/opre.11.6.863

Golfeto, R. R., Moretti, A. C., & SallesNeto, L. L. (2007). Algoritmo genético simbiótico aplicado ao problema de corte unidimensional. In *Anais do XXXIX Simpósio Brasileiro de Pesquisa Operacional*.

Golfeto, R. R., Moretti, A. C., & Salles Neto, L. L. (2009a). A Genetic Symbiotic Algorithm Applied to the Cutting Stock Problem with Multiple Objectives. *Advanced Modeling and Optimization, 11*, 473–501.

Golfeto, R. R., Moretti, A. C., & Salles Neto, L. L. (2009b). *A Genetic Symbiotic Algorithm Applied To The One-Dimensional Cutting Stock Problem*. Pesquisa Operacional.

Haessler, R. (1975). Controlling cutting pattern changes in one-dimensional trim problems. *Operations Research, 23*, 483–493. doi:10.1287/opre.23.3.483

Holland, J. H. (1962). Outline for a logical theory of adaptive systems. *Journal of the ACM, 3*, 297–314. doi:10.1145/321127.321128

Kantorovich, L. V. (1960). Mathematical Methods of Organizing and Planning Production. *Management Science, 6*, 366–422. doi:10.1287/mnsc.6.4.366

Ribeiro, C. C., Martins, S. L., & Rosseti, I. (2007). Metaheuristics for optimization problems in computer communications. *Computer Communications, 30*, 656–669. doi:10.1016/j.comcom.2006.08.027

Salles Neto, L. L., & Moretti, A. C. (2005). Modelo não-linear para minimizar o número de objetos processados e o setup num problema de corte unidimensional. In *Anais do XXXVII Simpósio Brasileiro de Pesquisa Operacional* (pp. 1679-1688).

Wall, M. (1996). *A C++ Library of Genetic Algorithm Components*. Boston: Mechanical Engineering Department Massachusetts Institute of Technology.

Wäscher, G., Haubner, H., & Schumann, H. (2007). An improved typology of cutting and packing problems. *European Journal of Operational Research, 183*, 1109–1130. doi:10.1016/j.ejor.2005.12.047

*This work was previously published in the International Journal of Applied Evolutionary Computation, Volume 2, Issue 1, edited by Wei-Chiang Samuelson Hong, pp. 34-48, copyright 2011 by IGI Publishing (an imprint of IGI Global).*

# Chapter 4
# A Fast Boosting Based Incremental Genetic Algorithm for Mining Classification Rules in Large Datasets

**Periasamy Vivekanandan**
*Park College of Engineering and Technology, India*

**Raju Nedunchezhian**
*Kalaignar Karunanidhi Institute of Technology, India*

## ABSTRACT

*Genetic algorithm is a search technique purely based on natural evolution process. It is widely used by the data mining community for classification rule discovery in complex domains. During the learning process it makes several passes over the data set for determining the accuracy of the potential rules. Due to this characteristic it becomes an extremely I/O intensive slow process. It is particularly difficult to apply GA when the training data set becomes too large and not fully available. An incremental Genetic algorithm based on boosting phenomenon is proposed in this paper which constructs a weak ensemble of classifiers in a fast incremental manner and thus tries to reduce the learning cost considerably.*

## INTRODUCTION

Genetic Algorithm (GA) based classification procedure (Spears & Gordon, 1993; Janikow, 1993; Greene & Smith, 1993; Yu, Goldberg, & Sastry, 2003; Rivera, 2004) is a stochastic search method which uses natural selection and reproduction techniques for examining and fine tuning a random population of candidate rules into a suitable, accurate solution for the given prob-lem. The accuracy of the rules that GA finds are comparable and some times even more accurate than the rules obtained by other classification algorithms (Yang, Dwi, Widyantoro, Ioerger, & Yen, 2001) and it also performs well in complex domains where other methods fails . This is due to the ability of GA to build the model based only on natural evolution process and not based on the Domain knowledge. But when the size of the example data set increases, GA becomes unacceptable because of its high learning cost.

DOI: 10.4018/978-1-4666-3628-6.ch004

This is due to the repeated access of the data set by the Algorithm for evaluating its candidate rule set accuracy. This behavior should be minimized in order to make it scalable to large data sets.

## PREVIOUS WORK

Boosting is one of the commonly used classifier learning approach (Treptow & Zell, 2004; Freund & Schapire, 1995; Freund & Schapire, 1996; Schapire & Singer, 1998). According to Schapire and Singer (1998) boosting is a method of finding a highly accurate hypothesis by combining many "weak" hypotheses, each of which is only moderately accurate. It manipulates the training examples to generate multiple hypotheses. In each iteration, the learning algorithm uses different weights on the training examples, and it returns a hypothesis ht. The weighted error of ht is computed and applied to update the weights on the training examples. The result of the change in weights is to place more weight on training examples that were misclassified by ht, and less weight on examples that were correctly classified. The final classifier is constructed by weighted vote of the individual classifiers. In the proposed method many weak GA based classifiers are built iteratively. When combined, the weak classifiers form an accurate strong model because ensemble classifiers outperform single classifiers (Chandra & Yao, 2006).

In the GA literature Complexity arising due to Scalability is mainly addressed by parallel processing.( *Wilson Rivera, 2004*; Lopes & Freitas, 1999) For example parallel genetic algorithm proposed by Lopes and Freitas (1999), addresses the scalability issue with respect to GA. It involves multiple processors and the data set is divided into multiple parts (data sets). The multiple data sets are distributed to multiple processors and each processor generates rules for each data set. The rules generated by each processor are again shared by all processors for fitness calculation.

Incremental learning is very popular in making the classification methodologies (Domingos & Hulten, 2000; Spencer & Domingos, 2001; Polikar, Upda, Upda, & Honavar, 2001; Gao, Ding, Fan, Han, & Yu, 2008) scalable and they try to build the model by scanning the data set only once. Only very few methods in the data mining literature employs GA as base algorithm for incremental learning. An incremental GA was proposed by Guan and ZhuCollard (2005), for a dynamic environment which updates the rules based on the new data. Due to the arrival of new data or new attribute or class, the classification model may change. So to deal with this the author proposes an incremental based GA.

## PROPOSED METHOD

### Overview

In genetic algorithm the potential solution is represented by individuals called candidate rules (Dehuri & Mall, 2006) and are of the form

A1$_\wedge$ A2…An THEN C.

The antecedent part of the rule is the conjunction of conditions say A (conjunction of attribute value pairs A1, A2…An) and the consequent part C is the class label.

These candidates are initially generated randomly and are processed in Sequential steps, such that an accurate solution gradually emerges. The Sequential Steps are called generations. Each generation goes through the selection (or testing) phase and the reproduction phase. During the selection phase, candidate rules accuracy (fitness) is evaluated using the example data set. The Fitness of the rules is calculated based on a function containing two terms namely predictive accuracy and comprehensibility (Dehuri & Mall, 2006). A very simple way to measure the predictive accuracy is

Predictive accuracy (PA) = (|A&C|-1/2)/|A|

$$(1)$$

where |A| is the number of examples satisfying all the conditions in the antecedent A and |A&C| is the number of examples that satisfy both the antecedent A and the consequent C. Intuitively, this metric measures predictive accuracy in terms of how many cases both antecedent and consequent hold out of all cases where the antecedent holds. The term ½ is subtracted to penalize the rules covering few training examples (Dehuri & Mall, 2006). The standard way of measuring Comprehensibility is to count the number of condition in the rule. If a rule has at most $L$ condition, the comprehensibility of the rule (or individual) $p$ can be defined as

Comprehensibility(CM)= $(L-n)/(L-1)$. $\quad$ (2)

Where $n$ is the length of the rule (or individual) $p$.

The fitness function is computed as the arithmetic weighted mean of comprehensibility and predictive accuracy.

Fitness= $W1*PA+W2*CM$ $\quad$ (3)

After every generation to calculate the fitness of the rules the data set should be repeatedly accessed. This process increases the learning cost. To make GA scalable this learning cost must be reduced.

## Boosting Incremental GA

A new Boosting Incremental GA is proposed in this paper which builds the model in an incremental iterative fashion by dividing the training data set into blocks and building a weak classification model sequentially for each block in a fast manner. The classifiers collectively form an ensemble of classifiers.

In each iteration of the learning process more importance is given to the misclassified record

(definition 1). For this purpose a weight is assigned to each of the training set record of the current block for which rules are to be mined and is used during the fitness calculation. The A&C term defined in predictive accuracy definition (equation 1) is modified as described in equation 4.

A&C= $\sum Wi$ $\qquad$ (4)

Where Wi is the weight of all the examples that satisfy both antecedent A and the class C

**Definition 1:** (Misclassified Records). A Record is called as a misclassified record if it has no matching rule in the given rule set.

To calculate Wi of each example first it is classified using the ensemble of classifier generated in the previous iterations.

If a record is classified correctly its weight $W_i$ =1 If it is misclassified then its weight Wi is calculated as described in equation 5.

$W_i$=Initial Wt+ (Total number of records/ Total number of misclassified records)*number of iterations *$(\gamma)$ $\qquad$ (5)

The weight value depends on two quantities:

1. **Based on the Number of Misclassified Records:** Wi value will inversely proportionate to the number of misclassified records. The first term in the above equation corresponds to it. Initial Wt term in the equation is normally set to 1 and can be varied based on the distribution of the class. For rare class it will be fixed higher.

2. **Based on the Number of Iterations:** As iteration increases Number of classifiers in the ensemble increases and so the chance of classification also increases. If a record is still not classified then its weight should be increased proportionately with respect to the number of iteration to mine rules to classify it. The second term in the equation

corresponds to it and the quantity $\lambda$ is a user defined value $(0.1, 0.15, 0.2$ etc) and is based on the size of the data set.

The number of generation (n) for which GA is executed depends on the number of blocks. If GA is not partitioned then it is executed maximum m times and depending on the number of blocks it is proportionately reduced. Even though the algorithm is executed less number of generations it tries to mine rules for misclassified records preferentially since they have more weight assigned to them.

## Proposed Method

In the proposed method, the data set is divided into equal sized blocks. GA is applied for each block and rules set is formed for each block of data separately by applying only less number of generations. The rule sets collectively form an ensemble of classifier which can be used for future prediction.

## IGA Algorithm

The algorithm for the proposed method find_rule() is described below:-

## Algorithm Find_Rule()

1.  **Input:** Example data set containing records D1,D2 ---Dm
2.  **Output:** Comprehensible Antecedents sets R=R1...Ri...Rn for all the classes 1 to n initially empty
3.  **Variables:** IRi...IRn intermediate antecedent sets for all the classes 1 to n
4.  Wi.....Wn Windows for classes 1 to n
5.  for i=1 to m
6.  c=Class(Di)
7.  Add(Di,Wc)
8.  if Wc is full
9.  begin
10. Wt= Weight(wc)
11. IRc= Simple_Genetic_Algorthim(Wc,Wt)
12. Wc=Empty(Wc)
13. Rc=Rc U IRc
14. end if
15. end loop i
16. Post_process(R)
17. return Rule set R

Class() function call in the above algorithm determines the class of a record and Add() function call adds the record to the corresponding window of the class. If a window of a class i has data then weights are assigned to each example of the window as discussed. This is done by the function Weight() .GA is called and applied only for fixed number of generations(n). The rules generated are the intermediate rule set $IR_i$ and the rule set is added to the final rule set $R_i$ as an ensemble rule set for that particular class. All records are removed from the window $W_c$ by the Empty() function. The process is repeated for the entire data set.

Simple_Genetic_algorithm() call in the find_rule() generates the potential rules for the particular class for the Data set in the window of that class by applying GA. The Encoding used in the GA is a fixed length encoding containing one bit for each value of the attribute. By an extra flag bit for each attribute it is made to represent variable length rule [7, 15]. The potential solutions are encoded as chromosomes and this is called population. The population is processed in loop using selection, crossover, mutation, insert and remove operations such that the best solution gradually emerges. Two best chromosomes are selected by Rowlett wheel selection method and Crossover is performed by exchanging the genes including flag bit with a probability called crossover probability (P*c*). The fitness of the chromosomes is calculated based on the method described. The child chromosomes thus created forms the population for the next generation. The Mutation operator changes the value of an attribute to another random value selected from the same domain with a probability called mutation Probability (Pm*)*. Insert and remove operators (Dehuri & Mall, 2006) control the size of the rule. Insert operator activates the gene by setting its flag bits and remove operator deactivate a gene by resetting the flag bit with a varying probability (Pi and Pr). The probabilities range from 0 to 30% based on number of genes that take part in the rule. Best Elite_percent of chromosomes are considered as elite and they are copied to the next generation unaltered. The rules generated by GA are stored in the set IRc for a class c and best rules of support above certain threshold are copied to the set Rc. The process is repeated for n number of generations. The value of n depends upon the number of blocks.

In the second phase the final ensemble classifier is built separately for all the classes by pruning unwanted and overlapping rules. The final ensemble classifier forms the classification model. A meta classifer can also be built by applying GA over all the ensemble classifier.

## SIMULATION

### Description of the Dataset

The simulation was performed using the Car Evolution and Balance Scale datasets. They are obtained from the UCI machine repository (http://www.ics.uci.edu/). These data sets are normally used as a benchmark for evaluating algorithms performing classification task.

### Car Evolution Data Set

Car evaluation data set contains 1728 records and 6 attributes. All attributes are categorical and are listed in Table 1. The target class attribute has four values namely 'unacc', 'acc', 'good', 'vgood'. To generate larger data sets of size 10000, 20000, 30000 etc the records are duplicated and randomly arranged such that the data distribution is proportionately similar to the original data set.

### Balance Scale Data Set

Balance Scale data set contains 626 records and 4 attributes. All attributes are categorical and are listed in Table 2. The target class attribute has three values namely L, B, R. As before the records are duplicated without altering their distribution to form larger data sets.

### Results

The experiments have been performed on windows XP System and the algorithm was developed using java. For each of the dataset, the simple genetic algorithm had 100 individuals in the population and was executed for 100 generations. Some related parameters are set as follows: $Pc=0.8$, $Pm=0.05$, $Pi= [0, 0.3]$, $Pr= [0, 0.3]$, $W1=0.7$, and $W2= 0.3$. For the proposed method the number of blocks is five and the number of generations is 25. The experiment is performed for different sizes of data set ranging from 5000 to 40000 records for both simple genetic algorithm (SGA) (Dehuri & Mall, 2006) and for the proposed incremental method

*Table 1. Car Evaluation attributes*

| Attributes | Values |
|------------|--------|
| Buying | Vhigh, high, med, low. |
| Maintenance | Vhigh, high, med, low. |
| Doors | 2, 3, 4, 5more. |
| Persons | 2, 4, more. |
| Lug boot: | Small, med, big |
| Safety | Low, med, high. |

*Table 2. Balance Scale attributes*

| Attributes | Values |
|------------|--------|
| Left-Weight | 1,2,3,4,5 |
| Left-Distance | 1,2,3,4,5 |
| Right-Weight | 1,2,3,4,5 |
| Right-Distance | 1,2,3,4,5 |

(IGA). The Execution time and the accuracy of the overall rules were monitored. Figure 1 and Figure 2 depicts the comparison of the performance of both methods with respect to time. Figure 3 and Figure 4 depict the accuracy for both the data sets.

*Figure 1. Comparison of time with size of car evolution data set*

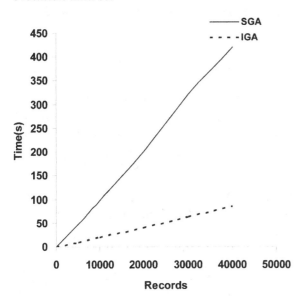

*Figure 2. Comparison of time with size of the Balance Scale data set*

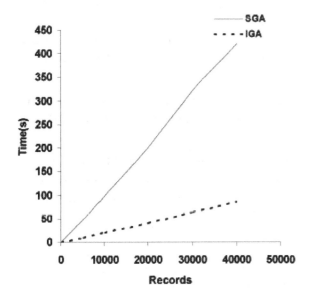

## Execution Time

Let us assume that for a classification problem GA takes 200 generations to converge. Let there be 10000 records in the training data set. Suppose if the data set is divided into tow blocks of 5000 each and two weak classifiers are built by running proposed GA for only 100 generations on each of the blocks almost the running time is reduced by half. If GA is applied only after checking if there are any misclassified records above certain thresh-

*Figure 3. Comparison of accuracy for car evolution data set*

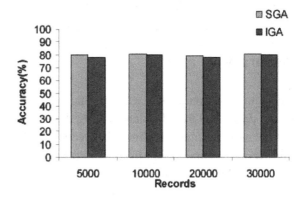

*Figure 4. Comparison of accuracy for balance scale data set*

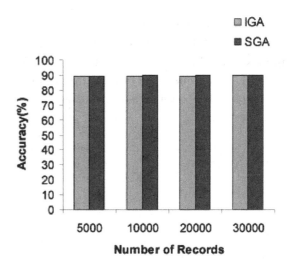

*Table 3. Comparison of Classification accuracy in percentage with C4.5 and NB*

| Data set | IGA | VFDT | NB |
|---|---|---|---|
| Car | 79% | 75.5% | 79% |
| Balance Scale | 90% | 86% | 89% |

old then execution time can be further reduced. So if the proposed method is used to mine very large data sets with multiple blocks the run time will be reduced considerably.

It can be noticed from Figure 1 and Figure 2 that the proposed methods execution time is five times lower when compared to Simple Genetic algorithm. The difference in execution time is due to the reduction in time related to reading the records again and again and processing them.

## Accuracy

The data set is divided into ten parts and one part of the data set is used for determining the accuracy. The experiment is repeated several times and average accuracy of the process is considered. The accuracy of rules of the proposed method is comparable with the accuracy of simple genetic algorithm (Figure 3 and Figure 4).

The accuracy is also compared with decision tree VFDT (Domingos & Hulten, 2000) classifier a fast tree building algorithm and naive bayes classifier(NB) (John & Langley, 1995) for 5000 records example data set and the results are described in Table 3. The result shows that the proposed algorithm performs better than VFDT and NB. This is due to the fact that the proposed method builds rule set for each class separately.

## CONCLUSION

To make Genetic algorithm applicable for generating rules for large data sets it should be made scalable and for this purpose a boosting based incremental genetic algorithm is discussed in this paper. It uses the e concept of boosting to build an ensemble of classifiers in a fast manner. The efficiency of the algorithm is proved by using bench marked data sets. In future the effect of concept drifts on the evolving rule set will be studied.

## REFERENCES

Araujo, D. L. A., Lopes, H. S., & Freitas, A. A. (1999). A parallel genetic algorithm for rule discovery in large databases. In *Proceedings of the IEEE Systems, Man and Cybernetics Conference*, Tokyo, (Vol. 3, pp. 940-945).

Chandra, A., & Yao, X. (2006). Evolving hybrid ensembles of learning machines for better generalization. *Neurocomputing*, *69*, 686–700. doi:10.1016/j.neucom.2005.12.014

De Jong, K. A., Spears, W. M., & Gordon, D. F. (1993). Using genetic algorithms for concept learning. *Machine Learning*, *13*, 161–188. doi:10.1023/A:1022617912649

Dehuri, S., & Mall, R. (2006). Predictive and Comprehensible Rule Discovery Using A Multi-Objective Genetic Algorithm. *Knowledge-Based Systems*, *19*, 413–421. doi:.doi:10.1016/j.knosys.2006.03.004

Domingos, P., & Hulten, G. (2000). Mining high-speed data streams. In *Proceedings of KDD* (pp. 71-80).

Freund, Y., & Schapire, R. E. (1995). *A Decision-theoretic Generalization of On-line Learning and an Application to Boosting (Tech. Rep.)*. Murray Hill, NJ: AT&T Bell Laboratories.

Freund, Y., & Schapire, R. E. (1996). Experiments with a New Boosting Algorithm. In *Proceeding of 13th international Conference on Machine Learning* (pp. 148-156).

Gao, J., Ding, B., Fan, W., Han, J., & Yu, P. S. (2008). *Classifying Data Streams with Skewed Class Distributions and Concept Drifts. IEEE Internet Computing, Special Issue on Data Stream Management* (pp. 37–49). IEEEIC.

Greene, D. P., & Smith, S. F. (1993). Competition-based induction of decision models from examples. *Machine Learning, 13*, 229–257. doi:10.1023/A:1022622013558

Guan, S. U., & ZhuCollard, F. (2005). An incremental approach to genetic-algorithms based classification. Systems. *Man and Cybernetics, Part B, IEEE Transactions, 35*(2), 227-239.

Hulten, G., Spencer, L., & Domingos, P. (2001). Mining time-changing data streams. In *Proceedings of KDD* (pp. 97-106). New York: ACM.

Janikow, C. J. (1993). A knowledge-intensive genetic algorithm for supervised learning. *Machine Learning, 13*, 189–228. doi:10.1023/A:1022669929488

John, G. H., & Langley, P. (1995). Estimating continuous distributions in Bayesian classifiers. In *Proceedings of the Eleventh Conference on Uncertainty in Artificial Intelligence* (pp. 338-345). San Francisco: Morgan Kaufmann Publishers.

Kenneth, A. D. J., & Spears, W. M. (1991). Learning concept classification rules using genetic algorithms. In *Proceedings of the 12th international joint conference on Artificial intelligence*, Sydney, New South Wales, Australia (pp. 651-656).

Kwedlo, W., & Kretowski, M. (1998). Discovery of Decision Rules from Databases: An Evolutionary Approach Principles of Data Mining and Knowledge Discovery. In *Proceedings of the Second European Symposium (PKDD '98)*, Nantes, France.

Polikar, R., Upda, L., Upda, S. S., & Honavar, V. (2001). Learn++: an incremental learning algorithm for supervised neural networks. *IEEE Transactions on Systems, Man, and Cybernetics, 31*(4), 497–508. doi:10.1109/5326.983933

Rivera, R. (2004). Scalable Parallel Genetic Algorithms. *Artificial Intelligence Review, 16*, 153–168. doi:10.1023/A:1011614231837

Schapire, R. E., & Singer, Y. (1998). Improved Boosting Algorithms Using Confidence-rated Predictions. In *Proceedings of the 11th Annual Conference on Computational Learning Theory* (pp. 80-91).

Shi, X.-J., & Lei, H. (2008). A Genetic Algorithm-Based Approach for Classification Rule Discovery. *International Conference on Information Management, Innovation Management and Industrial Engineering, 1*, 175-178.

Treptow, A., & Zell, A. (2004). Combining adaboost learning and evolutionary search to select features for real-time object detection. *IEEE congress on Evolutionary Computation, 2*, 2107-2113.

Kwedlo, W., & Kretowski, M. (1998). Discovery of Decision Rules from Databases: An Evolutionary Approach Principles of Data Mining and Knowledge Discovery, *Second European Symposium*, PKDD '98, Nantes, France, September 23-26, 1998.

Yang, L., Dwi, H. W., Ioerger, T., & Yen, J. (2001). An Entropy-based Adaptive Genetic Algorithm for Learning Classification Rules. In *Proceedings of the 2001 Congress on Evolutionary Computation* (pp. 790-796).

Yu, T. L., Goldberg, D. E., & Sastry, K. (2003). Optimal sampling and speed-up for genetic algorithms on the sampled onemax problem. In *Proceedings of the Genetic and Evolutionary Computation Conference (GECCO 2003)* (pp. 1554-1565).

*This work was previously published in the International Journal of Applied Evolutionary Computation, Volume 2, Issue 1, edited by Wei-Chiang Samuelson Hong, pp. 49-58, copyright 2011 by IGI Publishing (an imprint of IGI Global).*

# Chapter 5

# Simultaneous Tolerance Synthesis for Manufacturing and Quality using Evolutionary Algorithms

**Y. S. Rao**
*Sri Veeravenkata Satyanarayana (SVVSN) Engineering College, India*

**G. Ranga Janardhana**
*Jawaharlal Nehru Technological University, India*

**C. S. P. Rao**
*National Institute of Technology, India*

**Pandu R. Vundavilli**
*DVR & Dr. HS MIC College of Technology, India*

## ABSTRACT

*Tolerance plays a major role in the manufacturing industry, as it affects product design, manufacturing, and quality of the product. This paper considers product design, manufacturing, and quality simultaneously, and introduces a concurrent approach for tolerance allocation using evolutionary algorithms. A non-linear model that minimizes the combination of manufacturing cost and quality loss simultaneously, in a single objective function has been considered. In the proposed work, evolutionary algorithms (that is, Genetic Algorithms (GA), Differential Evolution (DE), and Particle Swarm Optimization (PSO)) have been used to determine the optimal tolerances at the minimum manufacturing and quality loss cost. The application of the proposed methodology has been demonstrated on a simple mechanical assembly.*

## INTRODUCTION

The functional performance and manufacturing cost of a product is majorly affected by tolerance design, which is one of the key aspects of mechanical design. By keeping this fact in mind dimensional tolerances are classified as design tolerances

DOI: 10.4018/978-1-4666-3628-6.ch005

and manufacturing tolerances. Moreover, the functional requirements of a mechanical assembly are taken care by design tolerances, whereas the process plan of manufacturing a part is dealt by manufacturing tolerances. It is important to note that tolerance plays a major role in the design and manufacturing of a part. For example, tight tolerances will lead to high manufacturing cost, while loose tolerances will lead to malfunctioning of the product. Preferably, one can imagine that for achieving the goal of minimal total cost and reduced lead time, the best technique for tolerance synthesis is to take into account the coupling between design, manufacturing, and quality.

Conventionally, tolerance synthesis is being carried out in two stages namely design and process planning stages, respectively. However, design engineers allocating design tolerances are often unaware of manufacturing processes and their production capabilities. This may be due to either a lack of communication between design engineers and process engineers, or a lack of knowledge of the manufacturing processes by the design engineers. The resulting process plans often cannot be executed effectively, or can only be executed at undesirably high manufacturing cost. When this happens, process engineers must modify the design tolerances. Furthermore, manufacturing engineers who allocate processes must typically work within the tolerance limits set by design engineers, which results in longer lead times. But in accepting tolerances set by design engineers, the process planners also limit the range within which they can set process tolerances. This, in turn, leads to tight process tolerances and higher manufacturing cost.

While considering total manufacturing cost, it is also important to take the quality loss also into account. In order to find the effect of quality, Taguchi had introduced quality loss function (Taguchi, 1989). In order to compare this important factor with the others that affect the design process, the quality loss can be translated in a hypothetical financial loss or a cost for quality loss. For reducing the quality loss tight tolerances are to be allocated, which leads to higher manufacturing cost. Therefore, it is essential to allocate tolerances simultaneously to balance manufacturing cost and quality loss that optimize cost of the product over life. The following paragraphs discuss some of the analytical methods developed for solving the tolerance allocation problems.

Non-linear optimization problem formulations of tolerance assignment were first introduced by Speckhart (1972), Spotts (1973), and Sutherland and Roth (1975). They proposed an exponential cost model, reciprocal squared cost model, reciprocal power model respectively, based on the production cost–tolerance data curve. Further the researchers focused on the mathematical modeling and optimization of tolerance related issues using conventional approaches. Later on, Ostwald and Huang (1977) formulated a technique for optimal tolerance allocation choosing one process variable at a time. Linear integer programming, with cost as the objective function and design requirements as constraints was considered in their approach. This technique is suitable where sequences and tolerances of operations are fixed. A different approach was proposed by Lee and Woo (1989) after considering process specific tolerances and optimized using integer programming. Chase et al. (1990), presented three methods such as exhaustive search, univariate search and sequential quadratic programming to solve the tolerance related problems. It is important to note that the limitation of the above methods is that the models assume the components were produced utilizing a single process, where as the present research focuses on the components that require more than one processes to complete a component. Few researches had tried to develop models for the components that require more than one process to complete the component. Some of the literature related to non-traditional optimization methods is explained below.

Chase and Greenwood (1988) introduced the reciprocal model with better empirical data fitting capability, considering both the continuous as well as discrete cost functions. Later on Zhang and Wang (1993) proposed mathematical models with the consideration of manufacturing process for continuous cost function and solved it utilizing non-traditional optimization technique called simulated annealing. In addition to this, Zhang

(1996) approached the problem in a totally different manner after introducing a new concept of interim tolerances, which help to determine appropriate manufacturing process and solved the problem using a non-linear programming technique (mixed penalty function approach). Al-Ansary and Deiab (1997) adopted a model similar to that proposed by Zhang and Wang (1993) and solved the model by considering worst-case stack-up criteria using a genetic algorithm. Singh et al. (2003) solved the same model for four different stack-up conditions using a genetic algorithm. It is important to note that the manufacturing cost only was considered in the approaches discussed so far. It was observed from the literature that quality loss is also an important factor while considering the total cost. The approaches that utilized both the manufacturing and quality costs in considering the total cost are discussed in the preceding paragraph.

Taguchi (1989) proposed a quality loss function which estimates the cost of quality value versus target value and the variability of the product characteristic in terms of the monetary loss due to product failure in the eyes of consumer. The quality loss function is used to determine the reduction in value due to an off target product, which is then balanced against reductions in manufacturing cost. Moreover, Soderberg (1993) developed a quality loss function based on component lifetime, which represents the customer's objective. The function is developed from physical relations between critical dimensions and lifetime. In Jeang (1997), a trade-off analysis between manufacturing cost and quality loss had been considered in tolerance design for product improvement and cost reduction. Later on, Feng and Kusiak (1997) considered quality loss in addition to manufacturing cost in a discrete cost function. Ye and Salustri (2003) developed a simultaneous tolerance synthesis (STS) model with quality loss after considering continuous cost function.

In the present work, STS optimization method has been extended to minimize manufacturing

cost with quality loss function in a continuous cost function to achieve near optimal tolerance allocation using total cost minimization as the criteria. The nonlinear multivariable optimization problem formulated in this manner can be solved effectively with the help of global optimization techniques. The solution methodology for the optimization of the above problem has been solved using most popular evolutionary algorithms, such as GA (Goldberg, 1989; Deb, 1995, 1999), DE (Storn & Price, 1997), and PSO (Kennedy & Eberhart, 1995). In the recent part, evolutionary algorithms are used for solving many complex real-world problems. A brief review and applications of evolutionary algorithms are mentioned in Sarker, Kamruzzaman, and Newton (2003). In the present study, a case study involving piston cylinder assembly for concurrent allocation of design and machining tolerances with quality loss function is presented to demonstrate the effectiveness of the methods.

The rest of the manuscript is organized as follows: First, mathematical formulation of the problem is explained. Introduction to evolutionary algorithms is described and a case study is presented. Results are presented and described and concluding remarks of the present study are provided.

## MATHEMATICAL FORMULATIONS: THE STS METHOD

The existing literature shows that manufacturing costs have been increased due to the allocation of tight tolerances after employing traditional tolerance synthesis methods, and methods based on quality loss. The STS method simultaneously allocates tolerances to balance manufacturing cost and quality loss and thus optimize cost over the product's life. In the present study, tolerance synthesis can be formulated as a simultaneous optimization problem. In this model, the objective function is chosen as a combination of manufacturing cost and quality loss. By combining these two measures, this method seeks to balance them and achieve an overall minimum total cost over the product's lifetime. In the present model, design and process tolerance are taken as the decision variables. Moreover, manufacturing cost and quality loss are considered as function of process tolerances and design tolerances, respectively. For simultaneous selection of design and manufacturing tolerances, an optimization problem based on minimization of assembly manufacturing cost is formulated as follows.

## Formulation as Optimization Problem

The objective function considered in the present study minimizes the total cost (that is, manufacturing cost and quality loss) of the assembly. The weights $W_1$ and $W_2$ are introduced in the objective function to represent the relative importance of the two components of the objective function. The formulation of the problem as optimization problem is given below.

$$\text{Min. } C_T = \sum_{i=1}^{n} \sum_{j=1}^{pi} W_1 C(tpij) + W_2 K \sigma_y^2 \tag{1}$$

Subjected to:

$$\sum_{i=1}^{n} t_{id} \leq T_f, \text{ worst case criteria} \tag{2}$$

or

$$\sqrt{\sum_{i=1}^{n} t_{id}^2} \leq T_f, \text{ RSS criteria} \tag{3}$$

or

$$\frac{1}{2} \left[ \sum_{i=1}^{n} t_{id} + \sqrt{\sum_{i=1}^{n} t_{id}^2} \right] \leq T_f \text{ Spotts criteria} \tag{4}$$

or

$$\sum_{i=1}^{n} m_i t_{id} + \frac{Z}{3} \sqrt{\sum_{i=1}^{n} (1 - m_i)^2 t_{id}^2} \leq T_f \tag{5}$$

Estimated mean shift criteria

and

$$t_{ij} + t_{i(j-1)} \leq Tp_{ij} \tag{6}$$

and

$$tp_{ij}^{\min} \leq tp_{ij} \leq tp_{ij}^{\max} \tag{7}$$

and

$$tp_{ipi} = t_{id} \tag{8}$$

where the constraints equations (2), (3), (4), (5) represents the design tolerance constraints for different cases, where as equation (6) represents the manufacturing tolerance constraint and the equations (7) and (8) represents the process tolerance constraints, respectively. The significance of various terms used in the above equations are given below.

The total manufacturing cost is then the sum of the manufacturing costs of each machining process of each component's dimension

$$C_m(tp_{ij}) = \sum_{i=1}^{n} \sum_{j=1}^{p_i} C(tp_{ij}) \tag{9}$$

where $n$ is the number of dimensions in the dimension chain, $p_i$ is the number of processes to produce dimension $i$, and *C(tpij)* is the cost–tolerance function of the machining process. In this study, an exponential function is used to model cost–process tolerances. For a particular manufacturing process, we have

$$C_m(tp_{ij}) = A_{ij}e^{-B_{ij}(tp_{ij}-C_{ij})} + D_{ij} \qquad (10)$$

where the constant parameters $A$, $C$ and $D$ control the position, while $B$ covers the curvature of the cost function.

Quality loss is quantified, as a quadratic expression relating the loss to the variation of a product characteristic

$$L(Y) = k(y\text{-}m)^2 \qquad (11)$$

where $k=A/T_f$, $A$ is the cost of replacement or repair if the dimension does not meet the tolerance requirements, $T_f$ is the functional tolerance requirement, $m$ is the target value of the functional dimension, and $y$ is the design characteristic.

The functional dimension has been assumed as a normal distribution and a mean at the target value. The quality loss can then be represented by the standard deviation of the functional dimension. Then, the expected value of the loss function can be written as:

$$QL = E(L(Y)) = k((\mu - m)^2 + \sigma_y^2) \qquad (12)$$

where $\mu$ and $\sigma_y^2$ are the mean and the variance of $Y$, respectively. The equation combines linearly the variance of Y and distance of the mean of Y, that is, $\mu$, from the target value m. To lower the quality loss (and hence its associated cost), a quality engineer adjusts $\mu$ during parameter design. These adjustments do not affect the value of process variability $\sigma_y$. From this point of view, then, the quality loss can be written as:

$$QL = E(L(Y)) = k \, \sigma_y^2 \qquad (13)$$

Based on the design function, a set of individual quality characteristics can be used to estimate the overall quality characteristic. It is to be noted that Taylor's series expressions can be used to found these approximate functions. The resultant variance can then be expressed in terms of the variances $\sigma_{xi}^2$, of the individual quality characteristics

$$\sigma_y^2 = \sum_{i=1}^{n} \left( \frac{\partial f}{\partial x_i} \right)^2 \sigma_{xi}^2 \qquad (14)$$

Moreover, tolerances are always related and designed in conjunction with the application of a specific manufacturing process. One way to express this relationship is with the help of a process capability index $Cp$, which is the ratio of design tolerance boundaries to the measured variability of the output response of a manufacturing process, and is defined by:

$$Cp = \frac{t_d}{3\sigma} \qquad (15)$$

we can now write

$$\sigma_{xi} = \frac{t_{id}}{3C_{pi}} \qquad (16)$$

substituting into above (Eq.7) gives

$$\sigma_y^2 = \sum_{i=1}^{n} \left( \frac{\partial f}{\partial x_i} \right)^2 \left( \frac{t_{id}}{3C_p} \right)^2 \qquad (17)$$

and the total quality loss is

$$QL\left(t_d\right) = k\sigma_y^2 \qquad (18)$$

## Constraints

The above mentioned optimization problem has been subjected to the constraints related to both the design and manufacturing tolerances.

## Design Tolerance Constraints

The fundamental considerations of the assembly of various dimensions are based on the design tolerance. It is to be noted that the design tolerance constraint is formulated in such a way that the accumulated tolerance in the dimensional chain should not exceed the specified tolerance on the assembly dimension. Several approaches had been proposed to estimate the accumulated tolerances, which are applicable under different conditions. Apart from the commonly used worst case and RSS stack up approaches, a few non-traditional tolerance accumulation formulae like Spotts criteria and EMS have also been used. The equations related to these cases are given in equations (2), (3), (4) and (5). Where $t_{id}$ are the design tolerances on the constituent dimensions and $n$ is the number of constituent dimensions associated with the dimensional chain, $m_i$ are the mean shift factors of process distribution, $Z =$ 3.00 corresponds to 99.73% yield and $T_f$ is the permissible variation in the assembly dimension.

## Manufacturing Tolerance Constraints

In allocating machining tolerances, consideration should be given not only to process capability, but also to the amount of machining allowance for each operation. It is important to note that the amount of machining allowance is the difference between the machining dimension obtained from the preceding operation and that in the current operation. Because of operation errors, the actual amount of material removed varies within some range; this variation is a cumulative sum of manufacturing tolerances. In practice, typical levels of material removal are set on a per-process basis and are defined in various handbooks.

The manufacturing tolerance constraints can be formulated in equation (6). Where $t_{ij}$ and $t_{i(j-1)}$ are the manufacturing tolerance obtainable in the $j^{th}$ and $j$-$1^{th}$ operations respectively, in production of the $i^{th}$ dimension. $Tp_{ij}$ is the difference between the nominal and the minimum stock removal/deformation allowance for manufacturing operation j.

## Process Tolerance Constraint

It is important to note that every process operation has its own accuracy (again, usually available from reference handbooks) and must be performed within its process capability. The process tolerance constraints are formulated in equation (7).

In the STS model, manufacturing cost is a function of process tolerances, while quality loss is a function of design tolerances, acting in combination. It is to be noted that no quality loss is associated with the intermediate process tolerances as they are not the final tolerances. It is instead the tolerances of last processes (i.e. design tolerances) that constitute the final tolerances for a manufactured dimension. Moreover, quality loss is associated with design tolerances, which are the tolerances of the last processes. Therefore, the last process tolerances equal the design tolerances, and link the manufacturing cost and the quality loss. The design tolerance constraints are formulated in equation (8).

## OVERVIEW OF EVOLUTIONARY ALGORITHMS

In the present work some prominent evolutionary algorithms have been employed to investigate their performance in the simultaneous tolerance synthesis optimization. Three famous evolutionary algorithms, namely Genetic Algorithms (GA), Differential Evolution (DE) and Particle Swarm Optimization (PSO) are chosen for performance analysis in tolerance synthesis optimization. The explanation for GA, DE and PSO are elaborated in the sub-sections below.

## Genetic Algorithms

GA is simple and powerful optimization procedures that are motivated by the principles of natural genetics and natural selection used for optimization of multimodal functions. The working principle of GA is shown in the Figure 1. The GA uses four main stages: *evaluation*, *selection*, *crossover* and *mutation* to evolve the optimal solution. The GA begins its search by randomly creating a number of solutions (equals to the population size). Each solution in the population is then evaluated to assign a fitness value. Thereafter, each population is modified by using three operators – reproduction scheme or selection procedure, crossover and mutation. The *selection* procedure randomly selects individuals of the current population for development of the next generation. The *crossover* procedure takes two selected individuals and combines them about a crossover point thereby creating two new individuals.

The *mutation* procedure randomly modifies the genes of an individual subject to a small mutation factor, introducing further randomness into the population. This iterative process continues until one of the possible termination criteria is

*Figure 1. A flow chart showing the working principle of Genetic Algorithm*

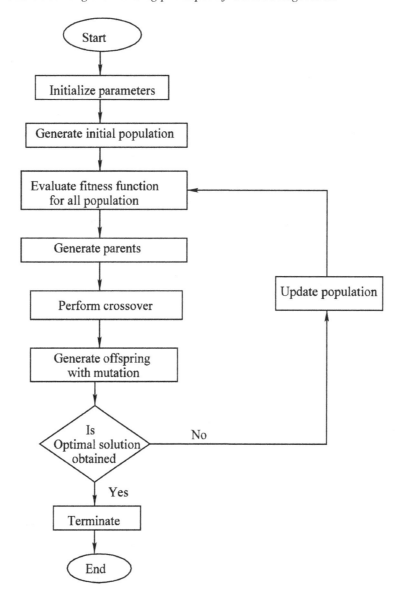

met: if a known optimal or acceptable solution level is attained: or if a maximum number of generations have been performed:

## Differential Evolution

DE is an exceptionally simple, fast and robust evolutionary computation method proposed by Storn and Price (1997) for solving continuous space optimization problems and is more likely to find the true optimum of a problem. This method has been applied to several diverse fields: digital filter design (Storn, 1995), neural network learning (Slowik & Bialko, 2008), fuzzy-decision-making problems of fuel ethanol production (Feng-Sheng, Wang, & Jing, 1998), multi-sensor fusion (Joshi & Sanderson, 1999), dynamic optimization of continuous polymer reactor (Lee, Han, & Chang, 1999), and optimization of heat transfer parameters in trickle-bed reactors (Babu & Sastry, 1999).

The operation of DE (Figure 2) also starts with an initial population of individuals generated at random, and finds the global best solution by utilizing the distance and direction information according to the differentiation among the population. The optimization problem consisting of $D$ parameters can be represented by a $D$-dimensional vector. DE starts with an initial population size of $NP$ vectors generated at random as shown below.

$$X_{i,G} = X_{1,i} ......X_{D,I} \qquad (19)$$

where $i = 1$ to $NP$ (that is, population size), $D$ represents number of parameters and $G$ indicates the current population. The initial solution vectors are generated randomly utilizing the following formula:

$$X_{D,G} = X_{D,G}^{min} + (X_{D,G}^{max} - X_{D,G}^{min}) \times r \qquad (20)$$

where $X$ is the variable, $X^{max}$ the upper bound, $X^{min}$ the lower bound of the variable, and $r$ is the uniformly distributed random number in the range

*Figure 2. A flow chart showing working principle of differential evolution*

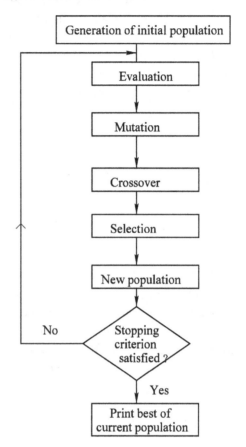

[0, 1]. The objective function value is calculated after substituting the values of the variables generated using Eqn. (5). The new parameter vectors in the next generation are obtained after extracting the distance and direction information from the current vectors. Considering $X_{i,G}$ as the target vector in the $G^{th}$ generation, a corresponding donor vector $V_{i,G+1}$ is obtained. In the present study, "DE/rand/1" mutation scheme has been employed to generate the donor vector or mutant vector. The expression for generating the donor vector for the said mutation scheme is as follows:

$$\nu_{i,G+1} = x_{r1,G} + F(x_{r2,G} - x_{r3,G}) \qquad (21)$$

where $F$ is mutation constant or scaling factor in [0, 2], which controls the amplification of difference between two individuals, and $i$, $r1$, $r2$, $r3$ are the index of individuals selected randomly and are distinct. The crossover operator has been introduced to increase the diversity of the mutant vectors. The trail vector $U_{ji, G+1}$ is developed from the elements of target vector, $X_{i, G}$ and the elements of the donor vector, $V_{i, G}$ as follows:

$$\{u_{ji,G+1} = \begin{matrix} v_{ji, G+1,} & \text{if } rn_j \leq C_r \\ \\ x_{ji,G,} & \text{otherwise} \end{matrix} \quad (22)$$

where j=1,2 ….. D

To determine the member for the next generation, the trail vector produced by the crossover operator has been compared with the target vector. If the trail vector produces a smaller objective functional value, it is passed to the next generation otherwise target vector is copied in to the next generation.

If $f(u_{i,G+1}) \leq f(x_{i,G})$, set $x_{i,G+1} = u_{i,G+1}$

Otherwise $x_{i,G+1} = x_{i,G}$ (23)

Mutation, recombination and selection continue until some stopping criterion is met. Here, the criterion is the number of generations is equal to the predefined maximum value.

## Particle Swarm Optimization

The PSO, first introduced by Kennedy and Eberhart (1995) is a stochastic, population-based optimization method modeled on swarm intelligence. PSO algorithm is a model that mimics the movement of the individuals within a group. PSO is inspired by models of flocking behavior. In the present study, MOPSO-CD (Raquel & Naval, 2005), a variant of PSO has been utilized for the simultaneous tolerance synthesis process.

The working procedure of the PSO is summarized in Figure 3.

At each generation, the adjustment of the flight of each particle is based on the subdivision of the swarm. The velocity and position vectors changes are done like the following.

The new velocity "V[i]"

$$V[i] = W \times V[i] + R_1 [P_{best}[i] - P[i]] + R_2 \times [A(G_{best}) - p[i]] \quad (24)$$

where W is the inertia weight, which is equal to 0.4, R1 and R2 are the random numbers in the range of [0–1], Pbest (i) is the best position that the particle i reached and, A (Gbest) is the global best guide for each dominated solution

The new position of "P[i]"

$$P[i] = P[i] + V[i] \quad (25)$$

The parameters, namely, swarm size, number of generations, inertia weight (W), social components R1 and R2, and repository size, play an important role in the present approach.

## CASE STUDY

The proposed methodologies have been explained with the help of an example case study of a simple mechanical assembly as shown in Figure 4.

## Problem Description

The details of the cylinder-piston assembly (Al-Ansary & Deiab, 1997) for near optimal design and manufacturing tolerances are taken as follows: The given diameter of the piston is 50.8 mm, the cylinder bore diameter is 50.856 mm, and the clearance is 0.056 ± 0.0005 mm. In the present study, the machining process plan for the piston and cylinder contains four operations each. The sequence of operations for piston and cylinder are {rough turning, finish turning, rough grind-

*Figure 3. A Flow chart showing working principle of Particle Swarm Optimization*

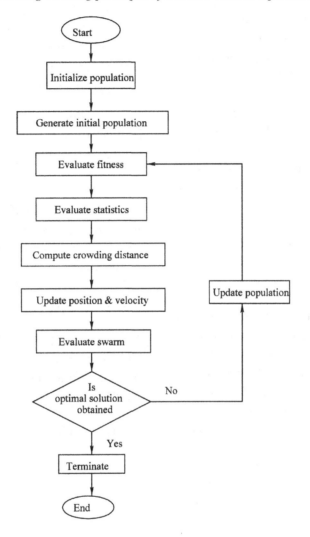

*Figure 4. A piston-cylinder bore assembly*

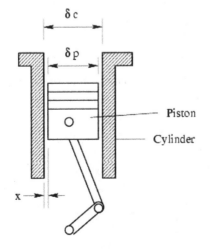

ing, finish grinding} and {drilling, boring, finish boring, grinding}, respectively.

Table 1 shows the ranges of machining tolerances for the piston and cylinder bore from Al-Ansary and Deiab (1997). It is important to note that there are 10 tolerances values or design variables (four machining tolerance parameters for each of the piston and cylinder, piston diameter and cylinder bore diameter) for the assembly. The design and machining tolerance parameters are represented as $t_{id}$ and $t_{ij}$, respectively. Where i=1 for piston and 2 for cylinder bore, j = 1 to 4 for the machining processes for the piston and cylinder bore. Moreover, the design and final machining tolerances for a given feature are equal. This condition leads to $t_{id} = t_{14}$ for piston and $t_{2d} = t_{24}$ for the cylinder. It is also important to note that the quality loss coefficient A is set at \$100 (Taguchi, 1989).

In the piston–cylinder bore assembly, there is only one resultant dimension (the clearance between the two parts) and two dimensions that form the chain (the diameters of the piston and cylinder bore). So, the design function is

$$x = \delta c - \delta p \qquad (26)$$

## Formulation as Optimization Problem

In the present study, simultaneous minimization of manufacturing cost and quality loss has been considered as the objective function. It is to be noted that the manufacturing cost of an individual process is represented as a monotonically decreasing function between tolerance and associated manufacturing cost. Several researchers (Spekhart, 1972; Spotts, 1973; Sutherland & Roth, 1975) studied and evaluated the relationship between cost and tolerances. Although, different non-traditional cost function models available in the literature, exponential cost function given in equation (3) has been used in the present study. Thus, the total cost of the assembly can be expressed as a minimization problem as given in the expression (1)

The values of the constant parameters for the cost functions of different manufacturing processes are given in Table 2 (Al-Ansary & Deiab, 1997).

Since we are only interested in determining the near optimal tolerances for these parts with respect to the clearance between them, for representing the possible cases:

$$W_1 = W_2 = 1; \quad Cp_1 = Cp_2 = 1;$$

*Table 1. Ranges of the principal machining tolerances for the piston and cylinder bore diameter*

| Piston diameter (mm) Cylinder bore diameter (mm) | | |
|---|---|---|
| Notation Lower limit Upper limit Notation Lower limit Upper limit | | |
| $t_{11}$ 0.005 0.02 $t_{21}$ 0.007 0.02 | | |
| $t_{12}$ 0.002 0.012 $t_{22}$ 0.003 0.012 | | |
| $t_{13}$ 0.0005 0.003 $t_{23}$ 0.0006 0.005 | | |
| $t_{14}$ 0.0002 0.001 $t_{24}$ 0.0003 0.002 | | |

In this case, manufacturing cost and quality loss have the same weight that is, they are equally important and Cp=1 in accordance with typical North American practice for quality standards.

## Constraints

In the present paper, four stack up conditions, namely worst case (WC), RSS, Spotts' (1973) modified method and estimated mean shift criteria (EMS), have been used to formulate the constraints on the design tolerance. These stack up conditions yield a set of design constraints as follows:

$$t_{14} + t_{24} \leq 0.001 \text{ worst case criteria,} \qquad (27)$$

$$t_{14}^2 + t_{24}^2 \leq (0.001)^2 \text{ RSS criteria,} \qquad (28)$$

$$\frac{1}{2}\left[(t_{14} + t_{24}) + \sqrt{[t_{14}^2 + t_{24}^2]}\right] \qquad (29)$$
$$\leq 0.001 \text{ Spotts criteria,}$$

*Table 2. Values of the constant parameters for the cost functions of different manufacturing processes*

| $C_{11}(t_{11})$ $C_{12}(t_{12})$ $C_{13}(t_{13})$ $C_{14}(t_{14})$ $C_{21}(t_{21})$ $C_{22}(t_{22})$ $C_{23}(t_{23})$ $C_{24}(t_{24})$ | | |
|---|---|---|
| A 5 9 13 18 4 8 10 2 | | |
| B 309 790 3196 8353 299 986 3206 9428 | | |
| C $5\times10^{-3}$ $2.04\times10^{-3}$ $5.3\times10^{-4}$ $2.19\times10^{-4}$ $7.02\times10^{-3}$ $2.97\times10^{-3}$ $6\times10^{-4}$ $3.6\times10^{-4}$ | | |
| D 1.51 4.36 7.48 11.99 2.35 5.29 9.67 13.12 | | |

$$(m_1 t_{14} + m_2 t_{24})$$

$$+ \frac{Z}{3} \sqrt{\left[(1 - m_1)^2 t_{14}^2 + (1 - m_2)^2 t_{24}^2 \right]} \qquad (30)$$

$$\leq 0.001 \text{EMS criteria,}$$

It is to be noted that the nominal and minimal machining allowances are available in machining manuals or hand books. Moreover, the difference of the nominal and minimum machining allowances for the process is greater than or equal to the sum of the machining tolerances for a process and its preceding process.

For piston : $t_{11} + t_{12} \leq 0.02, t_{12}$

$$+ t_{13} \leq 0.005, t_{13} + t_{14} \leq 0.0018 \qquad (31)$$

For cylinder bore : $t_{21} + t_{22} \leq 0.02, t_{22}$

$$+ t_{23} \leq 0.005, t_{23} + t_{24} \leq 0.0018 \qquad (32)$$

Each process operation has its own accuracy and must be performed within its process capability. Thus
For piston

$$0.005 \leq t11 \leq 0.02, 0.002 \leq t12 \leq 0.012,$$
$$0.0005 \leq t13 \leq 0.003, 0.0002 \leq t14 \leq 0.001 \qquad (33)$$

For Cylinder bore

$$0.005 \leq t_{21} \leq 0.02, 0.0002 \leq t_{24} \leq 0.001, 0.0005$$
$$\leq t_{23} \leq 0.003, 0.002 \leq t_{22} \leq 0.012 \qquad (34)$$

The last process tolerances equal the design tolerances links the manufacturing cost and the quality loss; that is,

$$t_{1d} = t_{14}, t_{2d} = t_{24,} \qquad (35)$$

## Optimization

Finally the total cost of the assembly as represented by equation (1) is optimized subject to the constraints and ranges of the tolerances (process limits). The scheme of GA, DE and PSO as explained above are used as the optimization strategies. All the three evolutionary algorithms, such as GA, DE and PSO are being implemented with the help of real variables. Moreover, all eight variables representing process tolerances are generated in their ranges (Table 2) to represent one population of GA, DE and PSO. The standard codes available for the three evolutionary algorithms are customized to implement inequality constraints on the tolerances. The code is implemented in C – language and is being executed in Linux environment on a P – IV personal computer.

## RESULTS AND DISCUSSION

The near-optimal piston and cylinder tolerances and corresponding manufacturing and quality costs, for different approaches and for the four stack-up conditions, namely RSS, WC, Spotts' and EMS.

A systematic study (that is, varying one parameter at a time) conducted to determine the near-optimal GA-parameters are shown in Figure 5. Figure 5(a) shows the variation of fitness (that is, objective function value for RSS condition) value with the change in probability of crossover ($p_c$), after keeping the other parameters of GA (that is, probability of mutation ($p_m$), population size (*pop*) and maximum number of generations (*gen*)) at the fixed level. It is to be noted that the minimum value of fitness is obtained for a $p_c$ of 0.7 (Figure 5(a)). Later on, the variation of objective function value with the variation of probability of mutation ($p_m$) has been studied (Figure 5(b)). Here, $p_c$ is kept at 0.7 and, *pop* and *gen* levels are kept at the same levels used in the $p_c$ study. It is found that the minimum value of objective function is obtained for the probability of mutation ($p_m$) of 0.01. Moreover, the variation of fitness value with change in population size is shown in Figure 5(c). In this case the other parameters, such as maximum number of generations are kept same as the one used in the $p_c$ and $p_m$ study, and they are kept fixed at the previous minimum value of fitness (that is, obtained in Figure 5(a) and 5(b), respectively). It is found that the minimum value of fitness is obtained for the population size of 100 (Figure 5(c)). Similarly, the variation of fitness value with the number of generations is shown in Figure 5(d). In this study the other parameters, such as probability of crossover, probability of mutation and population size are kept fixed at the values obtained in Figures 5(a), (b) and (c), respectively. It is interesting to note that the fitness value converges to a minimum value at 100 generations and then stabilized (that is, no further improvement in the solutions) (Figure 5(d)). The

GA parameters responsible for the optimal value of the objection function (for RSS criterion) are as follows:

Crossover probability ($p_c$) = 0.7 (uniform crossover)

Mutation probability ($p_m$) = 0.01

Population size (pop) = 100

Maximum number of generations (gen) = 100.

Moreover, the GA parameters (that is, $p_c$, $p_m$, *pop* and *gen*) that are responsible for the near-optimal solution for the piston and cylinder tolerance allocation problem for other criterion, such as WC, Spotts and EMS are found to be equal to (0.7, 0.01, 90,100), (0.7, 0.01, 100,100) and (0.7, 0.01, 90, 90), respectively.

*Figure 5. Results of parametric study of GA, (a) Crossover probability vs. fitness, (b) mutation probability vs. fitness, (c) population size vs. fitness, (d) maximum number of generations vs. fitness*

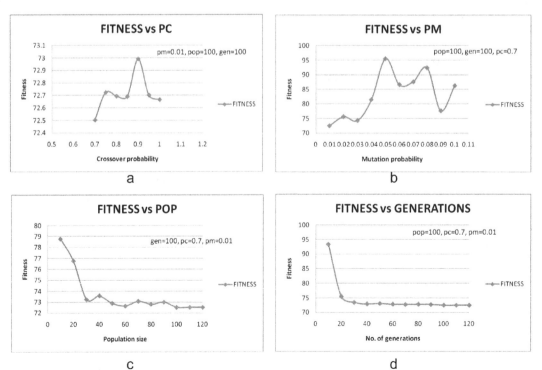

The optimization of tolerance allocation has also been carried out with the help of DE. The objective function and constraints used are the same as the one mentioned above. Selection of the four important controlling parameters of DE, namely number of population members (*NP*), crossover operator (*CR*), scaling factor or mutation constant (*F*) and maximum number of generations is an important aspect in solving the problems using DE. Therefore, a careful study has been conducted to identify the values of CR and F, after varying one parameter at a time, and keeping the other parameters at a fixed level. The plots that show the variation of objective functions with the change in the DE parameters are not shown here. The DE parameters that are responsible for the better performance of the tolerance allocation problem (that is, RSS criteria) are as follows:

Number of population members (NP) = 100

Crossover operator (CR) = 0.2

Scaling factor (F) = 0.1

Maximum number of generations = 80.

The optimal DE parameters (NP, CR, F and generations) for other criterion, such as WC, Spotts and EMS are seen to be equal to (90, 0.3, 0.1, 80), (100, 0.2, 0.2, 80) and (100, 0.2, 0.1, 90), respectively.

PSO has also been utilized to solve the assembly tolerance synthesis of the piston-cylinder problem. Here also a systematic study has been performed to obtain the optimal parameters of PSO. It is important to note that the values of number of particles (NP) and Generations that produced the minimum value of objective function for various criterion, such as RSS, WC, Spotts and EMS are found to be equal to (100, 60), (90, 60), (100, 70) and (100, 80), respectively. The variation of the fitness value (that is, the minimum of the assembly manufacturing cost) with the number of generations, have been plotted, for four stack-up conditions and different approaches (Figures 6 through 8). The trend of the plots indicates that the rate of reduction in cost is faster for the first 20 generations and slows down after that point. The reduction is nominal beyond 30 generations, and hence the curves become almost flat. This flat portion is significant from the optimal design point of view. The optimal costs obtained for various

*Figure 6. Minimum manufacturing cost among the feasible population in a given number of generations for GA*

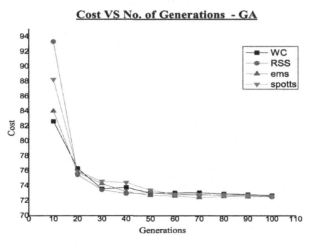

*Figure 7. Minimum manufacturing cost among the feasible population in a given number of generations for DE*

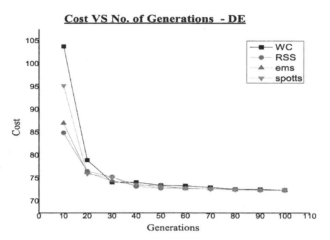

stack up conditions using different evolutionary algorithms are given in Tables 3 through 6.

The flat portions of the curves indicate that the minimum total cost of the assembly is lowest with RSS criteria and highest with the worst case criteria. It is observed that the solutions obtained by PSO are superior to those of using GA and DE. The minimum costs obtained by PSO with different criteria are 72.315613 (worst-case criterion), 72.240024 (RSS criterion), 72.271168 (Spotts' criterion), and 72.246396 (estimated mean shift criterion) units. The minimum manufacturing cost of the assembly is lowest with the RSS criterion (whose cost is comparable with the cost obtained with the STS method (Ye & Salustri, 2003) and highest with the worst-case criterion. The minimum manufacturing cost for the other two stack-up conditions lie in between the above two extreme cases.

*Figure 8. Minimum manufacturing cost among the feasible population in a given number of generations for PSO*

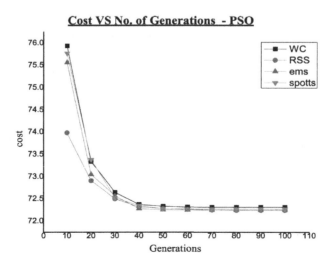

*Table 3. Near-optimal tolerances & costs for example (based on the RSS criteria)*

| GA | | | | |
|---|---|---|---|---|
| Piston tolerances | Cylinder tolerances | Manufacturing cost | Quality cost | *Total cost* |
| $t_{11}$ 0.015330 | $t_{21}$ 0.015616 | **67.593944** | **4.909378** | **72.503322** |
| $t_{12}$ 0.00374 | $t_{22}$ 0.003783 | | | |
| $t_{13}$ 0.00126 | $t_{23}$ 0.001206 | | | |
| $t_{14}$ 0.0005 | $t_{24}$ 0.000438 | | | |
| DE | | | | |
| Piston tolerances | Cylinder tolerances | Manufacturing cost | Quality cost | *Total cost* |
| $t_{11}$ 0.015440696 | $t_{21}$ 0.016086051 | **67.389248** | **5.034973** | **72.424221** |
| $t_{12}$ 0.003709833 | $t_{22}$ 0.003744351 | | | |
| $t_{13}$ 0.001262933 | $t_{23}$ 0.001247237 | | | |
| $t_{14}$ 0.000518273 | $t_{24}$ 0.000429582 | | | |
| PSO | | | | |
| Piston tolerances | Cylinder tolerances | Manufacturing cost | Quality cost | *Total cost* |
| $t_{11}$ 0.016283 | $t_{21}$ 0.016282 | **67.225247** | **5.014777** | **72.240024** |
| $t_{12}$ 0.003717 | $t_{22}$ 0.003715 | | | |
| $t_{13}$ 0.001283 | $t_{23}$ 0.001285 | | | |
| $t_{14}$ 0.000517 | $t_{24}$ 0.000429 | | | |

*Table 4. Near-optimal tolerances & costs for example (based on the WC criteria)*

| GA | | | | |
|---|---|---|---|---|
| Piston tolerances | Cylinder tolerances | Manufacturing cost | Quality cost | *Total cost* |
| $t_{11}$ 0.015936 | $t_{21}$ 0.016113 | **67.539665** | **5.156489** | **72.696154** |
| $t_{12}$ 0.003774 | $t_{22}$ 0.003827 | | | |
| $t_{13}$ 0.001218 | $t_{23}$ 0.001139 | | | |
| $t_{14}$ 0.000530 | $t_{24}$ 0.000428 | | | |
| DE | | | | |
| Piston tolerances | Cylinder tolerances | Manufacturing cost | Quality cost | *Total cost* |
| $t_{11}$ 0.015821166 | $t_{21}$ 0.016012715 | **67.305328** | **5.153929** | **72.459257** |
| $t_{12}$ 0.003754871 | $t_{22}$ 0.003725206 | | | |
| $t_{13}$ 0.001238129 | $t_{23}$ 0.001258012 | | | |
| $t_{14}$ 0.000519094 | $t_{24}$ 0.000440902 | | | |
| PSO | | | | |
| Piston tolerances | Cylinder tolerances | Manufacturing cost | Quality cost | *Total cost* |
| $t_{11}$ 0.016294 | $t_{21}$ 0.016181 | **67.369825** | **4.945788** | **72.315613** |
| $t_{12}$ 0.003706 | $t_{22}$ 0.003819 | | | |
| $t_{13}$ 0.001294 | $t_{23}$ 0.001181 | | | |
| $t_{14}$ 0.000505 | $t_{24}$ 0.000436 | | | |

*Table 5. Near-optimal tolerances & costs for example (based on the SPOTT's criteria)*

| GA | | | | |
|---|---|---|---|---|
| Piston tolerances | Cylinder tolerances | Manufacturing cost | Quality cost | *Total cost* |
| $t_{11}$ 0.016051 | $t_{21}$ 0.015400 | **67.824916** | **4.802056** | **72.626972** |
| $t_{12}$ 0.003727 | $t_{22}$ 0.003834 | | | |
| $t_{13}$ 0.001271 | $t_{23}$ 0.001140 | | | |
| $t_{14}$ 0.000499 | $t_{24}$ 0.000428 | | | |
| DE | | | | |
| Piston tolerances | Cylinder tolerances | Manufacturing cost | Quality cost | *Total cost* |
| $t_{11}$ 0.016097359 | $t_{21}$ 0.016179927 | **67.616938** | **4.840313** | **72.457251** |
| $t_{12}$ 0.003698989 | $t_{22}$ 0.00372994 | | | |
| $t_{13}$ 0.001293199 | $t_{23}$ 0.00122497 | | | |
| $t_{14}$ 0.000504773 | $t_{24}$ 0.000425244 | | | |
| PSO | | | | |
| Piston tolerances | Cylinder tolerances | Manufacturing cost | Quality cost | *Total cost* |
| $t_{11}$ 0.016277 | $t_{21}$ 0.016221 | **67.169968** | **5.1012** | **72.271168** |
| $t_{12}$ 0.003723 | $t_{22}$ 0.003779 | | | |
| $t_{13}$ 0.001277 | $t_{23}$ 0.001221 | | | |
| $t_{14}$ 0.000522 | $t_{24}$ 0.000432 | | | |

*Table 6. Near-optimal tolerances & costs for example (based on the EMS criteria)*

| GA | | | | |
|---|---|---|---|---|
| Piston tolerances | Cylinder tolerances | Manufacturing cost | Quality cost | *Total cost* |
| $t_{11}$ 0.015133 | $t_{21}$ 0.01600 | **67.726833** | **4.869800** | **72.596633** |
| $t_{12}$ 0.003712 | $t_{22}$ 0.003793 | | | |
| $t_{13}$ 0.001261 | $t_{23}$ 0.001182 | | | |
| $t_{14}$ 0.000519 | $t_{24}$ 0.000411 | | | |
| DE | | | | |
| Piston tolerances | Cylinder tolerances | Manufacturing cost | Quality cost | *Total cost* |
| $t_{11}$ 0.016042029 | $t_{21}$ 0.016150995 | **67.240821** | **5.204609** | **72.445430** |
| $t_{12}$ 0.003742413 | $t_{22}$ 0.00369906 | | | |
| $t_{13}$ 0.001231184 | $t_{23}$ 0.001297045 | | | |
| $t_{14}$ 0.00052282 | $t_{24}$ 0.000441672 | | | |
| PSO | | | | |
| Piston tolerances | Cylinder tolerances | Manufacturing cost | Quality cost | *Total cost* |
| $t_{11}$ 0.016291 | $t_{21}$ 0.01624 | **67.274875** | **4.971521** | **72.246396** |
| $t_{12}$ 0.003709 | $t_{22}$ 0.00376 | | | |
| $t_{13}$ 0.001291 | $t_{23}$ 0.00124 | | | |
| $t_{14}$ 0.000509 | $t_{24}$ 0.000434 | | | |

## CONCLUSION

The method of synthesizing tolerances simultaneously for both manufacturing cost and quality has been presented utilizing three evolutionary algorithms, namely GA, DE and PSO. This methodology has been demonstrated with the help of a simple linear assembly considering different tolerance stack-up conditions, namely worst case, Spotts' estimated mean shift and RSS criteria. In the present study, the penalty function approach has been adopted for constraint handling for all the algorithms. The results obtained by these algorithms are found to be comparable with those obtained by the STS method. It is also important to note that the solutions obtained by PSO are superior to those of the GA and DE for all the four stack-up conditions.

## REFERENCES

Al-Ansary, M. D., & Deiab, I. M. (1997). Concurrent optimization of design and machining tolerances using the genetic algorithms method. *International Journal of Machine Tools & Manufacture, 37*(12), 1721–1731. doi:10.1016/S0890-6955(97)00033-3

Babu, B. V., & Sastry, K. K. N. (1999). Estimation of heat transfer parameters in a trickle-bed reactor using differential evolution and orthogonal collocation. *Computers & Chemical Engineering, 23*(3), 327–339. doi:10.1016/S0098-1354(98)00277-4

Chase, K. W., & Greenwood, W. H. (1988). Design issues in mechanical tolerance analysis. *Manufacturing Review, 1*(1), 50–59.

Chase, K. W., Greenwood, W. H., Loosli, B. G., & Hauglund, L. F. (1990). Least cost tolerance allocation for mechanical assemblies with automated process selection. *Manufacturing Review, 3*(1), 49–59.

Deb, K. (1995). *Optimization for engineering design: Algorithms and examples*. New Delhi, India: Prentice-Hall.

Deb, K. (1999). An introduction to genetic algorithms. *Sadhana, 24*, 293–315. doi:10.1007/BF02823145

Feng, C., & Kusiak, A. (1997). Robust tolerance design with the integer programming approach. *Journal of Manufacturing Science and Engineering, 119*, 603–610. doi:10.1115/1.2831193

Goldberg, D. E. (1989). *Genetic algorithms in search, optimization and machine learning*. Reading, MA: Addison Wesley.

Jeang, A. (1997). An approach of tolerance design for quality improvement and cost reduction. *International Journal of Production Research, 35*, 1193–1211. doi:10.1080/002075497195272

Joshi, R., & Sanderson, A. C. (1999). Minimal representation multisensor fusion using differential evolution. *IEEE Transactions on Systems, Man, and Cybernetics. Part A, Systems and Humans, 29*(1), 63–76. doi:10.1109/3468.736361

Kennedy, J., & Eberhart, R. C. (1995). Particle swarm optimization. In *Proceedings of the IEEE International Conference on Neutral Networks*, Perth, Australia (pp. 1942-1948).

Kennedy, J., Eberhart, R. C., & Shi, Y. (2001). *Swarm intelligence*. San Francisco, CA: Morgan Kaufman.

Lee, M. H., Han, C., & Chang, K. S. (1999). Dynamic optimization of a continuous polymer reactor using a modified differential evolution algorithm. *Industrial & Engineering Chemistry Research, 38*(12), 4825–4831. doi:10.1021/ie980373x

Lee, W. J., & Woo, T. C. (1989). Optimum selection of discrete tolerances. *ASME Journal of Mechanisms . Transmissions and Automatic Design, 111*(2), 243–252. doi:10.1115/1.3258990

Ostwald, P. F., & Huang, J. (1977). A method of optimal tolerance selection. *ASME Journal of Engineering for Industry, 92*, 677–682.

Raquel, C., & Naval, P. (2005). An efficient use of crowding distance in multiobjective particle swarm optimization. In *Proceedings of the Conference on Genetic and Evolutionary Computation* (pp 259-264).

Sarker, R., Kamruzzaman, J., & Newton, C. (2003). Evolutionary optimization (EvOpt): A brief review and analysis. *International Journal of Computational Intelligence and Applications, 3*(4), 311–330. doi:10.1142/S1469026803001051

Singh, P. K., Jain, P. K., & Jain, S. C. (2003). Simultaneous optimal selection of design and manufacturing tolerances with different stack-up conditions, using genetic algorithms. *International Journal of Production Research, 41*(11), 2411–2429. doi:10.1080/0020754031000087328

Slowik, A., & Bialko, M. (2008, May 25-27). Training of artificial neural networks using differential evolution algorithm. In *Proceedings of the International Conference on Human System Interactions* (pp. 60-65).

Soderberg, R. (1993). Tolerance allocation considering customer and manufacturing objectives. *Advances in Design Automation, 65*(2), 149–157.

Spekhart, F. H. (1972). Calculation of tolerance based on a minimum cost approach. *ASME Journal of Engineering for Industry, 94*, 447–453. doi:10.1115/1.3428175

Spotts, M. F. (1973). Allocation of tolerances to minimize cost of assembly. *ASME Journal of Engineering for Industry, 95*, 762–764. doi:10.1115/1.3438222

Storn, R. (1995). *Differential evolution design of an IIR-filter with requirements for magnitude and group delay* (Tech. Rep. No. TR-95-026). Berkeley, CA: International Computer Science Institute.

Storn, R., & Price, K. (1997). Differential evolution—a simple evolution strategy for a fast optimization. *Dr. Dobb's Journal, 22*(4), 18–21.

Sutherland, G. H., & Roth, B. (1975). Mechanism design: Accounting for manufacturing tolerance and costs in function generating problems. *ASME Journal of Engineering for Industry, 97*, 283–286. doi:10.1115/1.3438551

Taguchi, G. (1989). *Quality engineering in production systems*. New York, NY: McGraw-Hill.

Wang, F.-S., & Jing, C.-H. (1998). Fuzzy-decision-making problems of fuel ethanol production using a genetically engineered yeast. *Industrial & Engineering Chemistry Research, 37*(8), 3434–3443. doi:10.1021/ie970736d

Ye, B., & Salustri, F. A. (2003). Simultaneous tolerance synthesis for manufacturing and quality. *Research in Engineering Design, 14*(2), 98–106.

Zhang, C., & Wang, H. P. (1993). Integrated tolerance optimization with simulated annealing. *International Journal of Advanced Manufacturing Technology, 8*, 167–174. doi:10.1007/BF01749907

Zhang, G. (1996). Simultaneous tolerancing for design and manufacturing. *International Journal of Production Research, 34*, 3361–3382. doi:10.1080/00207549608905095

*This work was previously published in the International Journal of Applied Evolutionary Computation, Volume 2, Issue 2, edited by Wei-Chiang Samuelson Hong, pp. 1-20, copyright 2011 by IGI Publishing (an imprint of IGI Global).*

# Chapter 6
# Parallel Single and Multiple Objectives Genetic Algorithms:
## A Survey

**B. S. P. Mishra**
*KIIT University, India*

**R. Mall**
*Indian Institute of Technology Kharagpur, India*

**S. Dehuri**
*Fakir Mohan University, India*

**A. Ghosh**
*Indian Statistical Institute, India*

## ABSTRACT

*This paper critically reviews the reported research on parallel single and multi-objective genetic algorithms. Many early efforts on single and multi-objective genetic algorithms were introduced to reduce the processing time needed to reach an acceptable solution. However, some parallel single and multi-objective genetic algorithms converged to better solutions as compared to comparable sequential single and multiple objective genetic algorithms. The authors review several representative models for parallelizing single and multi-objective genetic algorithms. Further, some of the issues that have not yet been studied systematically are identified in the context of parallel single and parallel multi-objective genetic algorithms. Finally, some of the potential applications of parallel multi-objective GAs are discussed.*

## 1. INTRODUCTION

Genetic algorithms (GAs) are a class of powerful search techniques that are popularly being used to solve problems in many different disciplines such as business, engineering, and science (Aguirre & Coello, 2002; Al-Somani, 2000; Alander, 1994). Researchers have found GAs to be especially useful for solving problems with large number of parameters whose effects on the problems are not well understood. For many complex problems, GAs find good solutions in reasonable amounts of time. However, GAs usually require large number of expensive function evaluations to be made. Based on the cost of each evaluation GAs may take days, months or even years to find an acceptable solution. Therefore, parallelization of GAs is an attractive proposition in such situation.

Parallel GAs (PGAs) have been found to be particularly easy to implement and at the same

DOI: 10.4018/978-1-4666-3628-6.ch006

time yield substantial gains in performance (Grama, Gupta, & Kumar, 1993). For example, adoption of sequential GA based solution to problems such as classification and association rule mining tasks with very large population sizes and long chromosomal representations may take considerable amount of time. Parallel GAs can provide effective solutions to these problems. PGAs have been observed to yield good results for different classes of problems. However, there are many problems that are highly dominated by computational costs and also many open questions arise in designing appropriate PGAs for these (Alba & Tomasdni, 2002). In particular, the design of PGAs involves making choices like single or multiple population, size of the population in either case, and for multiple population one must decide how many to use. Furthermore the population may remain isolated or they may communicate by exchanging individual or some other information. Communication involves extra cost and additional decision making depending on the pattern of communication, on the number of individuals participating in the communication, and on the frequency of communication. This paper reviews the state-of-the-art models of the PGAs and identifies their pros and cons. Additionally, some of the emerging issues (Cantu-Paz, 1998; Alba & Troya, 2002) are discussed.

So far, we have confined our discussions to the single objective genetic algorithms and its parallel-realization. However, most real world search and optimization problems do involve multiple objectives (Coello et al., 2002). A suitable solution may require making trade-offs (conflicting scenario) among different objectives. A solution that is optimum with respect to one objective may require compromising other objectives. Hence, simultaneous optimization of various objectives considering Pareto- optimal solutions (Coello, 1999) is required.

The ability of GAs to find multiple Pareto optimal solutions in one run makes it a preferred technique for solving multi-objective optimiza-

tion problems. Over the years a large number of multi-objective evolutionary algorithms (MOEAs) have been proposed (Coello, 2000, 2001; Knowles & Corne, 2000; Deb, 2001; Fonseca & Flemming, 1993; Zitzler et al., 2003). MOEAs like Vector Evaluated Genetic Algorithm (VEGA), Multi-Objective Genetic Algorithm (specifically Fonseca MOGA), Niched-Pareto Genetic Algorithm (NPGA), Non-Dominated Sorting Genetic Algorithm-II (NSGA II), Strength Pareto Evolutionary Algorithm (SPEA), Pareto-Archived Evolution Strategy (PAES), etc, are computationally very expensive, because instead of searching for single optimal solution, one generally needs to find the whole front of Pareto optimal solution. For that reason, parallelizing MOGAs (in general) has caught the attention of interest of many researchers.

In the context of parallelization, the main difference between single and multi-objective genetic algorithms seems to be that in the multi-objective case a set of non-dominated solutions is sought rather than a single optimum solution (Soh & Kirley, 2006). This opens up the possibility of having the different processors search for different solutions, rather than each to cooperate to find the overall solution. We discuss several models in parallel multi-objective genetic algorithm including parallel GAs (Alba & Troya, 2001). There are also several specialized parallel multi-objective genetic algorithms (PMOGAs) such as divide range multi-objective genetic algorithms, Parallel NSGA-II, Clustering based parallel MOGAs, etc, which are also addressed in this paper.

The remainder of this paper is organized as follows. In Section 2 a short review of state-of-the-art GAs is presented. Section 3 discusses the PGAs. Section 4 discusses present research issues in PGAs. Section 5 discusses multi-objective genetic algorithms. Section 6 presents the parallel multi-objective genetic algorithms and Section 7 provides few of the applications areas. Finally, we conclude the paper in Section 8.

## 2. GENETIC ALGORITHMS AND THEIR VARIANTS

In the early 1960s several computer scientists independently investigated whether natural evolution could be used as an optimization tool for engineering problems (Aguirre & Coello, 2002; Goldberg, 1989; Back, Fogel, & Michalewicz, 1997). As an outcome of such studies, GAs were first described by John Holland in the 1960s and further developed by Holland and his students and colleagues at the University of Michigan in the 1960s and 1970s. A simple algorithmic form of the GA works as follows:

- Begin
  - Generate an initial population.
  - Evaluate each individual of the population.
  - Repeat
  - Select M individuals.
  - Perform crossover and Mutation with respective probabilities.
  - Evaluate the resulting children.
  - Replacement of the children with parents.
- Until < Stop criterion reached>
- End.

This process is iterated over many generations. After several generations, the result is often in the form of one or more highly fit chromosomes in the population. We say that a population has converged when all the individuals are very much alike and further improvements may only be possible by a favorable mutation (Bäck, 1996; Deb & Goldberg, 1991; Tanese, 1987; Mingjie & Sheng, 2008).

An outgrowth of GAs is Estimation of Distribution Algorithms (EDAs) (Larranga et al., 2002) popularly known as Probabilistic Model Building Genetic Algorithms (PMBGAs). Unlike GA, in an EDA explicit representation of the population is done always and it is replaced with a probability distribution that represents a population member. In GAs new individuals are often created by combining and modifying existing individuals in a stochastic process. Whereas in EDAs, a population may be approximated with a probability distribution and new candidate solutions are obtained by sampling this distribution. This may have several advantages like avoiding premature convergence, less memory space requirement and computational speed up. A few representative EDAs include: 1) Population Based Incremental Learning (PBIL) (Baluja et al., 1994), 2) Compact Genetic Algorithm (cGA) (Pelikan, 1999), 3) Extended Compace Genetic Algorithm (ECGA) (Pelikan, 1999), 4) Bayesian Optimization Algorithm (BOA) (Pelikan et al., 2005). As this paper is focused on Parallel single and multi-objective genetic algorithms therefore, EDAs, parallel version of EDAs and their family is treated as beyond the scope of the focus. However, the inetersted readers can obtain parallel EDAs (PEDAs) from the specilized literatures which are available in proceedings and journals (Mendiburu et al., 2005; Ossa et al., 2004, 2005; Ahn et al., 2004).

Genetic algorithms are not guaranteed to find an optimal solution and their effectiveness is determined largely by the population size $n$. As the population size increases, the GA has a better chance of finding the global solution, on the flip side, the computation cost increases with population size. In contrast, PGAs can find high quality results relatively faster because using parallel machines larger population can be processed in less time. This helps keep the confidence factor high and the response time low, opening up possibilities of applying genetic algorithms in time constrained applications. Additionally PGAs may evolve several different independent solutions that may be recombined at later stages to form better solutions (Pettey & Leuze, 1989).

## 3. PARALLEL GENETIC ALGORITHMS

The basic idea behind most parallel solutions is to divide a large problem into smaller ones and solving each one simultaneously using multiple processors. The hope is that such a divide-and-conquer principle is more efficient than if all the processors work on the whole problem.

There are three different ways to parallelize GA. The first approach in parallelizing GAs is to do a global parallelization. In this class of PGAs, there is a single pragmatic population (just as in a simple GA), but the evaluation of fitness is distributed among several processors (Figure 3). Since in this type of PGA, selection and crossover are carried out in the entire population, it is known as global PGAs. Here the semantics of the operators remain unchanged (Alba et al., 2002; Poli, 1999).

In the second approach, called coarse grained PGAs, a more sophisticated approach is used. The population is divided into a few sub-populations keeping them relatively isolated from each other (Figure 7). This model of parallelization introduces a migration operator to send some individuals from one subpopulation to other. Two models for population structures are used in different implementations of coarse grained PGAs: the island and stepping stone model. The population in the island model is partitioned in to small sub-populations by geographic isolation and individuals can migrate to any other sub-population. In the stepping stone model, the population is partitioned in the same way but migration is restricted to neighboring sub-populations. Sometimes coarse- grained parallel GAs are known as distributed GAs since they are usually implemented in distributed memory Multiple Instructions and Multiple Data Stream(MIMD) computers (Hiroyasu, Kaneko, & Miki, 2000; Hiroyasu, Miki, & Tanimura, 1999; Kaneko, Hiroyasu, & Miki, 2000).

The third approach in parallelizing GAs uses fine grained parallelism (Figure 8). Fine grained parallel GAs partition the population into a large number of very small sub-populations. The ideal case is to have just one individual for every processing element available. This model calls for

massively parallel computers. In the last two approaches, selection and mating occur only within each subpopulation (also called demes). Since the size of the demes is usually smaller than the population used by a serial GA, it is reasonable to expect that the PGA will converge faster. However, when we consider that there is communication between the demes it is no longer clear whether the PGA will converge faster or not. It is important to notice that while the global model did not affect the behavior of the algorithm the last two approaches introduce fundamental changes to the way the GA works. In the subsequent sections, we shall identify these changes and investigate how GAs can be effectively parallelized.

The final method to parallelize GAs uses some combination of the first three methods. We will call this class of algorithms hybrid PGAs. The histogram plot of year wise research publications in PGAs collected from several secondary sources e.g., (DBLP, SCOPUS and many of the URLs) is plotted in Figure 1.

In summary, we can classify the parallel implementation of GAs into three main categories: 1) Global single population master-slave genetic algorithms (GPGAs); 2) Massively parallel genetic algorithms (MPGAs); 3) Distributed genetic algorithms (DGAs).

A dendrogram representation of the categories of PGAs is given in Figure 2.

## 3.1. Global Parallelization

In this model, there is a single population generated by a master processor and the evaluation of the individuals is done by slave processors. This model is also known as master-slave model. The evaluation can be parallelized by assigning a subset of individuals to each of the processors available. There is no communication between the processors during the evaluation because the fitness of each individual is independent of the

*Figure 1. Year wise publication of PGAs*

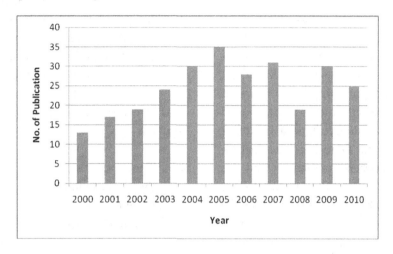

*Figure 2. Classification of PGAs*

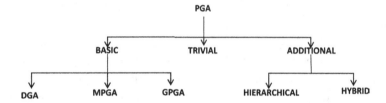

*Figure 3. Steps of Global Parallization*

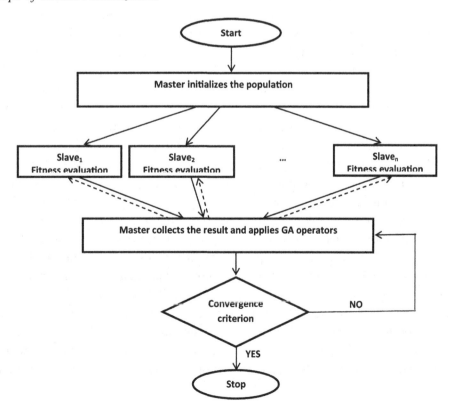

others. Communication only occurs at the start and at the end of the evaluation phase (Cantu-Paz, 1997; Arryo & Conejo, 2002).

On a shared memory multi-processor (Uniform Memory Access Architecture (UMA)), the individuals could be stored in shared memory. Each processor can read the individuals assigned to it and write the evaluation results back without any conflicts. Note that there is some synchronization needed between generations and the processors. In some cases (like in a multi-user environment), it may be necessary to balance the computational load among the processors using a dynamic scheduling algorithm. On a distributed memory computer (Non-Uniform Memory Access Architecture), the population can be stored on one node known as master to simplify the implementation of the genetic operators. Note that anyone node can be designated as the master. The master is responsible for sending the individuals to the other processors (slaves) for evaluation, collecting the results, and applying the genetic operators to produce the next generation. In this case the inter-process communication is required between the master and slaves. A bottleneck in the algorithm is that the slave processors sit idle while the master is doing its work. Figure 3 shows the flow of global parallelization.

A further step in global parallelization is to apply the genetic operators in parallel. First, consider the selection operator. There are several variants of the approach to select individuals for application of genetic operations some require a global statistic (e.g., population average) which could be a serial bottleneck. Fortunately, if we use some form of tournament selection we only need the fitness of a subset of the individuals (usually only two). Let us now consider crossover. It can be applied simultaneously over $n/2$ pairs of individuals. Mutation can be applied to each individual and even to each bit independently of the others. On the other hand, it is not clear whether parallelizing the application of the operators would result on a performance improvement or not. The genetic

operators are very simple and the time spent in communication could easily be longer than the time of performing any computation. This is especially true in distributed memory machines where the overhead on account of each message might be considerable.

These algorithms are important due to several reasons:

- They explore the search space in exactly the same manner as sequential GAs, and therefore the existing design guidelines for simple GAs become directly applicable.
- They are rather easy to implement, which makes them popular with practitioners.
- In many cases, master-slave GAs result in significant improvements to performance.

The execution time of master-slave GAs has two basic components: the time spent in computations and the time required communicating information among processors. In summary, global master-slave PGAs are easy to implement and it can be a very efficient method of parallelization in situations where the evaluation step needs considerable computations. An example of such a situation is rule generation from a database of several gigabytes in data mining. Besides, the method has the advantage of keeping the search capability of GA unaltered, which make all the theory available for simple GAs directly applicable.

Golub and Jakobovic (2000) model, is a GPGA (Figure 4) that uses the shared memory concept. In this model, the master creates a random initial population, evaluates created individuals and starts the slaves. Each slave performs the whole evolution process and returns the final results to master as illustrated in Figure 4. These results may probably fall in a local optimum because there is only one initial population created. So, this model needs modification. In the modified model, the master creates new initial populations randomly for each slave and each slave works on different populations as shown in Figure 5. In this model,

*Figure 4. Golub and Jakobovic Model*

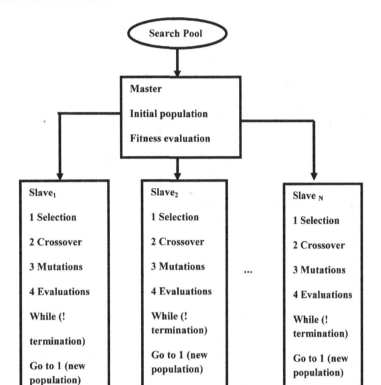

the master creates the population, performs the fitness evaluation and then the slaves starts their operations. One of the drawbacks of this model is that a slave has to wait till the fitness evaluation has been completed by the master. Further, the master has to wait after distributing the population for the slaves till they complete the operation. These disadvantages are overcome in the trigger model.

Trigger model was proposed by Al-somani and Qureshi (2000) (Figure 6). In this model, the master triggers the slaves, and also performs all the works with the slaves instead of being idle. In this model, the master is numbered as the slave 0. The master as well as the slaves independently create random initial populations, evaluate the created individuals, and perform whole evolution

process. Finally they return the final results to the master. This eliminates the time required to generate each population by the master, eliminates the communication overhead and at the same time allows for an exhaustive search of the solution space by the slaves.

The key points of the various global parallelization methods are the followings:

1. The master slave model is easy to implement and also yields good performance improvement.

2. The performance of the master-slave model is determined by two factors: computation time and communication cost. The computation time in a master slave model can be reduced

*Figure 5. Golub and Jakobovic Modified Model*

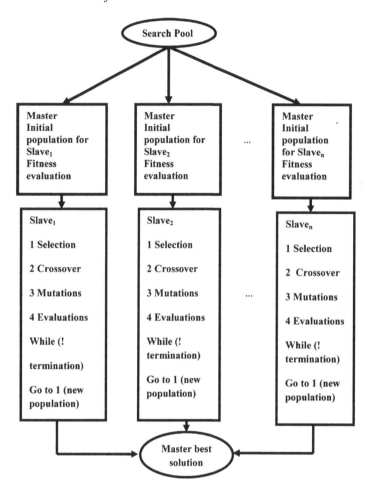

remarkably; hence the communication cost becomes a critical issue.

3.  The main process stops and waits for all evaluations to complete before moving to next generation. The algorithm is therefore said to be synchronous and the model is known as Synchronous Master Slave Model (SMSM).

A synchronous global PGA (Golub & Jakobovic, 2000) carries the same search as a sequential GA, with speed being the only difference. An asynchronous global PGA has different population dynamics. Its results are also more difficult to duplicate. Reasonable speedups can be obtained with up to 16 processors, but further increase prove futile due to the overhead of communica-

tion between the master processor and the slaves. Since the numbers of processors are rather small, different topologies yield almost similar results.

Balancing strategy is one of the important aspects of the master slave model. The number of individuals dispatched to each slave process can be fixed or dynamically determined. In case of fixed strategy, if there are '$m$' number of processors and '$k$' number of population, then we can allocate to each slave '$k/m$' of the population, leading to an even distribution. A fixed strategy is usually less efficient because it often leads to imbalance.

## 3.2. Coarse Grained Parallelization

Coarse grained parallel GAs are possibly the most popular model. Many papers have been published

*Figure 6. Trigger Model*

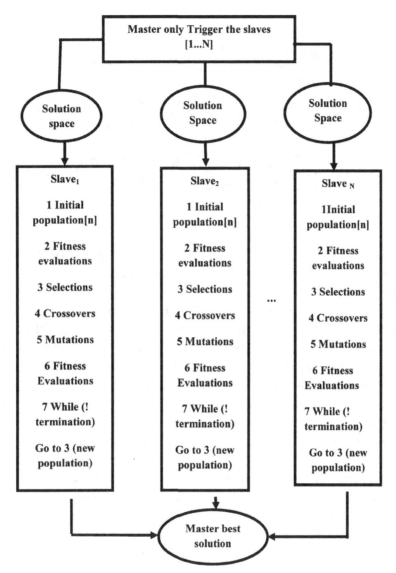

*Figure 7. A schematic coarse-grained PGA*

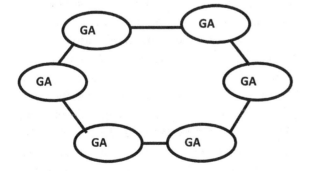

on course-grained parallel GAs (Arryo & Conejo, 2002; Zhi-xin & Gang, 2009; Xu, Ge, & Ming, 2009; Yan, Jumin, & Zhuoshang, 2000). Sometimes these models are known as distributed GAs as they are usually implemented on distributed memory MIMD computers. Since the computation to communication ratio is usually high, they are occasionally called coarse grained GAs. Two important characteristics of this class of algorithms are the use of relatively few large demes and the

*Figure 8. A schematic representation of the fine-grained model*

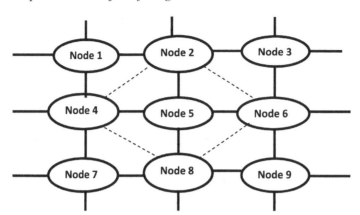

introduction of a migration operator. Some of the early research attempts are summarized below.

One of the pioneering efforts is due to Grosso (1985). He simulated diploid individuals and the population was divided in five demes. The demes exchanged individuals using a fixed migration rate and several rates were experimented. He found that the rate of improvement was greater in the smaller demes than in a single large pragmatic population confirming the views of Sewall Wright (1964). However, when the demes were isolated this rapid rise in the fitness stopped at a lower level as compared to that with the larger population. At intermediate migration rate, the divided population displayed a behavior similar to the pragmatic population with a lower migration rate, the demes had the opportunity to behave independently and explore different regions of the search space. But if the migration rate is too low the migrants might not have a significant effect on the receiving deme. These results point out that there is a critical migration rate below which the performance of the algorithm deteriorates due to the isolation of the demes and above which the partitioned population behaves as a panmatic one.

Tanese (1987) proposed a parallel GA that uses a 4-D hyper-cube topology to communicate individuals from one deme to another. In Tanese's algorithm, migrations occurred at uniform periods of time between neighbor processors along one dimension of the hypercube. The migrants were chosen probabilistically from the best individuals in the subpopulation and they replaced the worst individuals in the receiving deme. She reported that the result of the parallel GA was as good as the sequential GA, even though there was the advantage of near-linear speedup.

Tanese (1989) continued her work making a very exhaustive experimental study on the frequency of migrations and the number of individuals exchanged. She found that migration of too many individuals too frequently or too few individuals very infrequently degraded the performance of the algorithm. However, good quality results were found faster than the sequential GA, even in cases that had no migration at all.

An analysis of the reported results points to a few interesting issues. First migration is controlled by several parameters. These parameters include the topology that defines the connection between the sub-populations, a migration rate that controls how many individuals migrate and a migration interval that affects how often migrations occur. Second, the values for these parameters are chosen empirically rather than based on any analysis. Probably the first attempt to provide some theoretical foundations to the performance of a parallel GA was reported by Pettey and Leuze (1989). They propose a schema theorem for parallel GAs. They showed that the expected number of trials allocated to the schemata can be bounded by an exponential function when randomly selected individuals are broadcast every generation. It can be expected that relatively isolated demes will find different partial solutions to a given problem. Stark Weather et al. (1991) showed that if partial solutions can be combined to form a better solution, then a parallel GA would probably outperform a serial GA. On the other hand, if the recombination of partial solutions results in a less fit individual then the sequential GA might be advantageous.

A traditionally neglected aspect of parallel GAs has been the topology of the interconnection between demes. The topology is an important factor in the performance of the parallel GA because it determines how fast (or how slow) a good solution percolates to other demes. If the topology has a dense connectivity (or a short diameter or both), good solutions will spread fast to all demes and may quickly take over the population. On the other hand, if the topology is sparsely connected (or has a long diameter) solutions will spread slower and the demes will be more isolated from each other permitting different solutions. These solutions may come together at a later time and recombine to form potentially better individuals. Most implementations of coarse grained PGAs use the native topology of the computer available to the researchers. An unconventional approach to migration was recently developed by Marin et al. (1994). They propose a centralized model where the processes that are executing the GAs periodically send their best partial results to a master process. The master process chooses the fittest individuals among those that it receives and broadcasts them to all the nodes. Thus empirically showed that near linear speedups can be obtained with a small number of nodes ($\approx6$) and the authors claims that this approach can scale up to larger workstation networks.

The design of multiple-deme parallel GAs involves difficult and related choices. The main issues are to determine: 1) the size and the number of demes; 2) the topology of the demes; 3) the migration rate of the individuals; 4) the frequency of migration that determines how often migrations occur; 5) the migration policy that determines which individuals migrate and which are replaced in the receiving deme.

The overall process of the above model can be summarized as below:

- Split the population into many sub-populations known as islands.
- Alternate periods of extensive isolated evolution with migration.
- During isolated evolution, each process runs on its island a full blown GA.
- At certain times, few individuals migrate between islands.

The pros and cons of using this model are the following:

- It is uniquely suited for message passing parallel systems.
- It maps well on many topologies such as mesh, ring, and hyper-cube.
- However, more complex design decisions need to be made due to increased number of parameters as well as dynamics of multiple GAs running in parallel.

## 3.3. Fine Grained Parallelization

In fine grained parallel model, the population is divided into many small demes. The demes overlap providing a way to disseminate good solutions across the entire population by following the neighborhood approach. Again selection and mating occur only within a deme (Soh & Kirley, 2006; Li & Kirley, 2002). Manderick et al. (1989) implemented a fine grained PGA with the population distributed on a 2-D grid. Migrations of individuals were within a small neighborhood, and the authors observed that the performance of the algorithm degraded as the size of the neighborhood increased. On the extreme end, if the size of the neighborhood is too big the PGA turns out to be equivalent to a single pragmatic population.

It can therefore be said that though fine-grained algorithms can be implemented both on SIMD and MIMD computers, these are more suitable for massively parallel computers. It can easily parallelize many features of the EA: selection, survival, mating. This model is associated with certain pitfalls like the gain in efficiency is worth only on parallel computers; otherwise it suffers from severe communication overhead.

Decisions concerning the implication of topology, neighborhood size and shape complicate the design and understanding of the dynamics. The performance of the algorithm degrades as the size of the neighborhood increases. At the extreme end, if the size of the neighborhood is big enough, PGA is equivalent to a single pragmatic population. Sharma and De Jong (1996) found that the ratio between the size of the neighborhood and the size of the whole grid are the critical parameter that determines the selection pressure.

## 3.4. Hybrid Parallelization

A few researchers have tried to combine the coarse-grained and fine-grained methods to parallelize GAs. Some of these new hybrid algorithms add an additional degree of complexity to the already complicated scene of PGAs (Zhang, Chen, & Liu, 2007).

One way to hybridize a parallel GA (Figure 9) is to use global parallelization on each of the demes of a coarse-grained GA. Migration occurs between demes as in the coarse grained algorithm but the evaluation of the individuals is handled in parallel. This approach does not introduce new analytic problems and can be useful when working with complex applications with objective functions that need a considerable amount of computation time. This approach has not been used yet in any application, but it does not introduce more complexity into its analysis. Recall that the global

*Figure 9. A schematic representation of hybrid parallelization model*

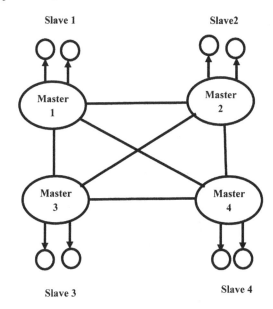

parallelization model has the same properties as a serial GA thus the analysis for this hybrid model will follow the exact same path as the analysis for coarse grained PGAs. Good speedups can be expected from this method when applied to problems that need a long time to be evaluated and for extremely large population.

## 3.5. Virtual Community PGA Model

Tan and Smith (2002) proposed the virtual community PGA model (Figure 10). This model overcomes the disadvantages of the island and cellular model. In case of the above two models the globally best individuals are propagated to the nearest neighbor. The propagation delay ($P_d$) of the globally best individual is proportional to network distance (D) between two processors i.e., $P_d \alpha D$. Delayed migration of best individuals in PGA is an essential deviation from sequential version of GA in which the best individuals are always used to compete with other individuals. In virtual community model, each processor hosts a sub-population just like the island model.

*Figure 10. VC-PGA Model*

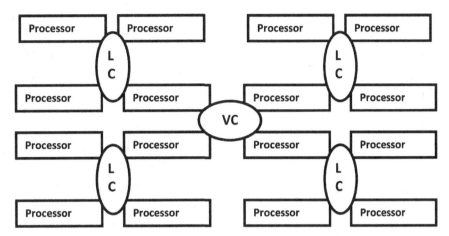

A local community (LC) is formed among neighbors and the local community has a designated master to facilitate exchanges of best individuals within community and with other communities. To facilitate exchange of the best local individuals across the community, a virtual community (VC) can be formed and a virtual master would perform tasks similar to a local community master.

The working of the VC-PGA model consists of the following four steps:

1.  Set up the local and virtual communities in a cluster of workstations. A local community is formed with adjacent processors, and one of processor is elected as its community server. Grouping local community-servers forms a virtual community. Higher-level of virtual communities can be formed if necessary.
2.  Initialize a sub-population of size $p$ on each community member across the network.
3.  On each processor of a local community, run GA for a fixed number of iterations, and send the top $n$ fittest individuals of the local sub-population to the community-server. In the mean time, compare the fitness of any received individual with the best local fitness, and include it in local population if the received has a higher fitness value.
4.  On each community-server, find the best individuals of local community from the received best individuals of community members. Send top $n$ fittest individuals of local community to higher level community server. In the mean time, compare the fitness of any received individual from its virtual community with the best local fitness, and include it to local population if the received has a higher fitness value. Send the best individuals to community members.

Virtual community model gives three advantages over island model: 1) Local sub-populations can get globally fittest individuals; 2) The communication overhead is much less expensive; 3) The evolution surface of solution space is independent from topology of network of workstations.

A few representative PGAs with their categorical label and adopted topology are summarized in Table 1.

## 4. SOME ISSUES WITH PGAS

We have already pointed out that PGAs are effective to solve a number of difficult problems and can be mapped to different kinds of parallel machines. PGAs promise higher speedups and

*Table 1. Summary of a few representative PGAs*

| Name of PGA | Category of Parallelism | Topology |
|---|---|---|
| PGA pack | Global | Any |
| EnGENEer | Global | Any |
| Genitor II | Coarse grained | Ring |
| DGENESIS | Coarse grained | Any |
| GALOPPS | Coarse grained | Any |
| IiGA | Coarse grained | Any |
| ASPARAGOS | Fine grained | Ladder |
| ASPARAGOS96 | Hybrid | Ring |
| CoPDEB | Coarse grain | Full connected |
| Dga | Distributed population | Ring |
| ECO-GA | Fine grain | Grid |
| RPL2 | Coarse grain | Any desired |

improved the search quality of the sequential GAs. In spite of several published research, there are several issues that are not adequately understood. In this section we summarize the important problems and recent work in solving these problems. We focus on coarse grained GAs because of their realistic simulation of the natural processes, better understood than fine grained GAs and are possibly the most popular approach in research community. To start our review of the problem we need to highlight several issues. A formal investigation of the PGAs requires us to decompose the problem into manageable parts that can be studied independently, which we can recombine later (Leon, Miranda, & Segura, 2008; Pettey & Leuze, 1989). A simple first level decomposition divides the study of PGAs into two parts: population sizing and migration. The size of the population is probably the parameter that affects the performance of the GA to a large extent. There is a population sizing theory of serial GAs that is based on statistical decision making theory and gives conservative lower bounds on the population sizes needed to solve problems with a given confidence factor. In a PGA, the population sizing question is very closely related to the island size. That is, how many demes and of

what size does the PGA need to solve a problem with a given confidence? After we determine the number and size of demes, we need to establish how they would communicate. Migration should be the next step in the investigation of PGAs. It is a very complex operator and as we have already pointed out, the migration of individuals across demes is affected by several parameters. To study migration, we have to examine each of its facts independently but in a way that allows for reconstruction of the whole issue again. In other words, we need a second decomposition. A possible decomposition of the migration parameter could be as follows:

- **A Migration Time Scale:** Intuitively migration should occur, after the number of building blocks in each individual is relatively high. Migrating before that is probably a waste of communication resources.
- **Migration Rate:** The number of individuals that should migrate is very closely related with the migration time scale. If individuals are rich in building blocks maybe we can get good results even while migrating just a few.
- **Topology:** What is the best way to connect the demes? If we use a topology with a long diameter, good solutions will take longer to propagate to all the demes. On the other hand, if we use a topology that retards the mixing of partial solutions different species might appear as they may not mix to produce a better solution.

The above three issues are not yet been resolved and are considered to be open areas of research. After going through several research papers that favor some migration intervals, migration rates, or topologies over others, no conclusive results have yet emerged. From the above discussions, the following can be concluded:

- Hybrid models that mix the canonical models.

- Hierarchical models combine the benefits of its components and were found to give better performance than any of them alone.

## 5. MULTI-OBJECTIVE GENETIC ALGORITHMS

Multi-objective optimization methods deal with finding optimal solutions to problems having multiple objectives (Coello et al., 2002; Coello, 1999; Hajela & Yin, 1992; Khan, 2003; Zydallis, 2003). For this type of problems, a solution that is optimum with respect to a single criterion may be highly suboptimal with respect to the other objectives. The principle of a multi-criteria optimization procedure is different from that of a single criterion optimization. In a single criterion the main objective is to find a global optimal solution. However, in a multi-criteria optimization problem, there exists more than one objective function, each of which may have a different individual optimal solution. If there is a sufficient difference in the optimal solutions corresponding to different objectives then we say that the objective functions are conflicting.

Multi-criteria optimization with such conflicting objective functions usually gives rise to a set of optimal solutions, instead of just one optimal solution. These set of optimal solutions are known as Pareto-optimal solutions (Coello, 2001, 2006; Jones, et al., 2002; Deb, 2001, 2004; Murata & Ishibuchi, 1995; Schaffer, 1985; Okuda, Hiroyasu, Miki, & Watanabe, 2002; Valdhuizen & Lamont, 2000; Veldhuizen, 1999; Zitzler, Laumanns, & Bleuler, 2004).

Let us consider a problem having $m$ objectives (say $f_i$, $i = 1, 2,…..,m$ and $m>1$). Any two solutions $U^1$ and $U^2$ (having 't' decision variables each) can have two possibilities -one dominates the other or there is none that dominates the others. A solution $U^1$ is said to dominate the solution $U^2$, if the following conditions hold:

1. The solution $U^1$ is not worse (say the operator < denotes worse and > denotes better) than $U^2$ in all objectives, or $f_i(U^1) \geq f_i(U^2)$ for all $i= 1, 2, 3,……,$m.
2. The solution $U^1$ is strictly better than $U^2$ in at least one of the objectives, or $f_i(U^1) > f_i(U^2)$ for at least one $i$, $i = 1,2,3,..,$m.

If any of the above conditions is violated then the solution $U^1$ does not dominate the solution $U^2$. If $U^1$ dominates the solution $U^2$, then we can also say that $U^2$ is dominated by $U^1$, or is non-dominated by $U^2$, or simply between the two solutions, $U^1$ is the non-dominated solution.

- **Local Pareto-Optimal Set:** If for every member u in a set S, there exist no solution v satisfying ‖u-v‖∞ ≤ ε, where ε is a small positive number, that dominates any member in the set S, then the solutions belonging to the set S constitute a local Pareto-optimal set.
- **Global Pareto-Optimal Set:** If no solutions exist in the search space, which dominates any member in the set S, then the solutions belonging to the set S constitute a global Pareto-optimal set.
- **Difference between Non-Dominated Set and a Pareto-Optimal Set:** A non-dominated set is defined in the context of a sample of the search space (need not be the entire search space). In a sample of search points, solutions that are not dominated (according to the previous definition) by any other solution in the sample space constitute the non-dominated set. A Pareto-optimal set is a non dominated set, when the sample is the entire search space. The location of the Pareto optimal set in the search space is sometimes loosely called the Pareto optimal region.

Multi-criteria optimization algorithms attempt to achieve mainly of the following two goals:

- Guide the search towards the global Pareto-optimal region
- Maintain population diversity in the Pareto-optimal front.

The first task is a natural goal of any optimization algorithm. The second task is unique to multi criteria optimization. Multi-criteria optimization is not a new field of research and application in the context of classical optimization. Figure 11 is a plot of the number of year-wise publications of MOGA collected from various secondary sources (i.e., DBLP, SCOPUS and available URLs).

The weighted sum approach (Jones et al., 2002), $\varepsilon$ -perturbation method (Jones et al., 2002), goal programming (Gao et al., 2000), Tchybeshev method (Leon et al., 2008), min-max method (Leon et al., 2008), and others are popular methods often used in practice (Gao et al., 2000). The core of these algorithms is a classical optimizer, which can at best find a single optimal solution in one simulation. In solving multi-criteria optimization problems, this has to be used many times, and hopefully it would find a different Pareto-optimal solution each time. Moreover, these classical methods have difficulties in solving problems having non-convex search spaces. Genetic algo-

rithms (GAs) are a natural choice for solving multi-criteria optimization problems because of their population-based nature (Jaszkiewicz, 2002; Jin-hua, 2007; Horn, 1997; Deb, 2001; Deb, Agrawal, Pratap, & Meyarivan, 2000; Deb, Pratap, Agarwal, & Meyarivan, 2002; Zitzler, Laumanns, & Thiele, 2001; Lamont et al., 2001; Kita et al., 1996; Zitzler & Thiele, 1998; Corne et al., 2000, 2001; Jaddan, Rajamani, & Rao, 2008; Jiong-liang & Jin-hua, 2008; Juan & Xu Lihong, 2006; Knowles & Corne, 1999; Kumar & Rockett, 2002; Kunzli & Zitzler, 2004; Laumanns, Thiele, Deb, & Zitzler, 2002; Zitzler, Laumanns, & Bleuler, 2004). A number of Pareto-optimal solutions can, in principle, be captured in an EA population, thereby allowing a user to find multiple Pareto-optimal solutions in one simulation. The fundamental difference between a single objective and multi-objective GA is that in the case of a single objective GAs fitness of an individual is defined using only one objective; where as in the second case fitness is defined by incorporating the influence of all the objectives. Other genetic operators like selection and reproduction are similar in both cases. The possibilities of using GAs to solve multi-objective optimization problems were proposed in the seventies. David

*Figure 11. Statistics of the number of publications per year related to MOGA*

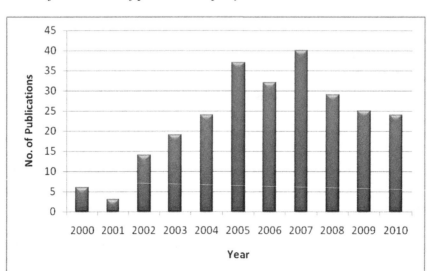

Schaffer was the first to implement Vector Evaluated Genetic Algorithm (VEGA) (Schaffer, 1984). There was lukewarm interest for a decade, but the major popularity of the field began in 1993 following a suggestion by David Goldberg based on the use of the non domination concept and a diversity-preserving mechanism. There are various multi criteria GAs proposed so far, by different authors and good surveys are available in (Deb, 2001; Zitzler et al., 1999, 2001; Lamont et al, 2001, 2002; Das & Dennis, 1997; Horn, Nafpliotis, & Goldberg, 1994; Ishibuchi, Nojima, Narukawa, & Doi, 2006; Mahfoud, 1995; Zheng & Lei, 2008; Zhongxi, Xiaoqing, & Liangming, 2006; Zydallis, Veldhuizen, & Lamont, 1993). A simple algorithmic flow of MOGA is given in the following:

- Begin
  - Perform population initialization (Size $P$)
  - Compute each population member's fitness (w.r.t. $K$ functions)
- Loop
  - Execute GA operators.
  - Compute each population member's fitness (w.r.t. $K$ functions)
  - Conduct selection,
  - Generate Pareto front current ($t$)
  - Update Pareto front known ($t$)
  - Conduct local search (if specified)
  - Generate Pareto front known and Present.
- End

Table 2 presents some of the potential MOGA algorithms. These algorithms are categorized based on generations (i.e. whether 1st generation or 2nd generation). The abbreviated name of the algorithm is given in column 2 and the name of the author with year of publication is given in column 3 of the Table 2. Similarly Table 3 presents classified MOGA algorithms into elitist or non elitist group. Similarly Table 4 summarizes the advantage and disadvantage of the MOGA algorithms.

*Table 2. Representative MOGA*

| Sl. no. | Algorithm | Year | Generation |
|---|---|---|---|
| 1 | VEGA | 1985 Schaffer | 1st |
| 2 | VOES | 1990 Frank Kursawe | 2nd |
| 3 | WBGA | 1993 Hajela and Lin | 2nd |
| 4 | MOGA | Fonesca and Flemming | 1st |
| 5 | NPGA | 1991 Oei et al. | 1st |
| 6 | NPGAIII | 1994 Horn et al. | 1st |
| 7 | NSGA | 1994 Srinivas and Deb | 1st |
| 8 | NSGA 2 | 2000 Deb et al. | 2nd |
| 9 | DPGA | 1995 Osyczka and Kundu | 2nd |
| 10 | NRGA | 2008 Omar Al Jadaan, Lakshmi Rajamani, C.R. Rao | 2nd |
| 11 | TDGA | 1996 Kita et al. | 2nd |
| 12 | SPEA | 1998 Zitzler and Thiele | 2nd |
| 13 | SPEA 2 | 2001 Zitzler, Laumanns and Thiele | 2nd |
| 14 | MOMGA I | 1996 Veldhuizen | 2nd |
| 15 | MOMGA II | 1999 Veldhuizen | 2nd |
| 16 | MOMGA III | 2001 Zydallis et al. | 2nd |
| 17 | PAES | 2000 Knowles and Corne | 2nd |
| 18 | PESA | 2000 David. W. Corne et al. | 2nd |
| 19 | PASE II | 2000 Corne et al. | 2nd |
| 20 | Micro GA | 1989 Krishna Kumar | 1st |
| 21 | Micro GA II | 2000 Coello Toscano | 2nd |
| 22 | RWGA | 1995 Murata and Ishibuchi | 2nd |
| 23 | RDGA | 2003 Lu H and Yen GG | 2nd |
| 24 | MSGA | 1996 Lis and Eiben | 1st |

# 6. PARALLEL MULTI-OBJECTIVE GENETIC ALGORITHMS

MOGA are highly suitable for parallelization as crossover and mutation and in particular the time consuming fitness evaluation can be performed independently on different processors (Zhi-xin & Gang, 2009; Hiroyasu, Miki, & Watanabe, 2000).

*Table 3. Classified MOGA algorithms into Elitist and non Elitist group*

| Algorithm | Fitness | Elitism | Repository |
|---|---|---|---|
| VEGA | Sub population evaluated with different objectives | NO | NO |
| VOES | Weighted average method and in 2:1 ratio | NO | NO |
| WBGA | Weighted average method | NO | NO |
| MOGA | Pareto ranking | NO | NO |
| NPGA | No fitness assignment | NO | NO |
| NPGA2 | No fitness assignment | YES | NO |
| NSGA | Ranking based on non domination sorting | NO | NO |
| NSGA2 | Ranking based on non domination sorting | YES | NO |
| DPGA | Based on its distance from the elite set | YES | YES |
| NRGA | Equal on its non-domination level | YES | NO |
| TDGA | Rank of a solution is assigned as fitness | YES | NO |
| SPEA | External archive of non-dominated solutions | YES | YES |
| SPEA2 | Strength of dominators | YES | YES |
| PAES | Pareto dominance | YES | YES |
| PESA | No fitness assignment | Pure Elitist | YES |
| RWGA | Weighted average of normalized objectives | YES | YES |
| MSGA | Rank method | NO | NO |

*Table 4. Summarizes the advantage and disadvantage of MOGA algorithms*

| Algorithms | Advantage | Disadvantage |
|---|---|---|
| VEGA | Straight forward Implementation | Tend converge of each objective |
| VOES | self adaptive strategy used | Tend converge of each objective |
| WBGA | Extension of single objective GA | not fit for non convex objective function space |
| MOGA | Extension of single objective GA | slow convergence |
| NPGA | simple selection process | Problems for niche size parameter |
| NSGA | efficient for fast convergence | Problems for niche size parameter |
| NSGA 2 | Single parameter N | Crowding distance works in objective space |
| DPGA | no explicit niching method | More complex |
| TDGA | Efficient elitism mechanism | needs a pre-defined annealing schedule |
| SPEA | No parameter for clustering | Complex clustering algorithm |
| SPEA2 | extreme points are preserved | Expensive fitness and density calculation |
| PAES | Random hill climbing strategy | Not a population based approach |
| PESA | computationally efficient | Performance depends on cell size |
| RWGA | Efficient and easy to implement | not fit for non convex objective function space |
| RDGA | Robust to any number of objectives | More difficult to implement |
| MSGA | Similar to the principle of VEGA | no explicit niche- preserving mechanism |

The main problem is the parallelization of the selection operator, where global information is required to determine the relative performance of an individual with respect to all others in the current population. The four-main parallel models include the master-slave, island, diffusion models and DRMOGA model. A classification of PMOGA is shown in Figure 12. The histogram plot of year wise growth of this area is demonstrated in Figure 13, the data is collected from various secondary sources like (e.g., DBLP, SCOPUS, and several URLs).

1.  **Master-Slave Model:** In this model, the objective function evaluations are distributed among slave processors while a master processor executes the other MOGA operations to decrease the overall execution time. The search space exploration is conceptually identical to that of a serial MOGA (Mishra et al., 2010).

2.  **Island Model:** In this model, every processor runs an in-dependent GA, using a separate sub-population. The processors co-operate

*Figure 12. A classification of PMOGA*

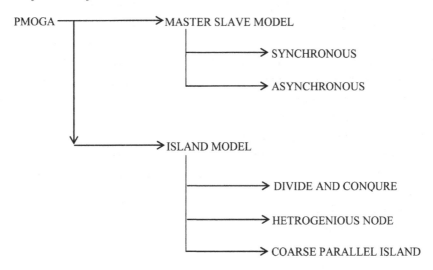

*Figure 13. Statistics of the number of publications per year related to PMOGA*

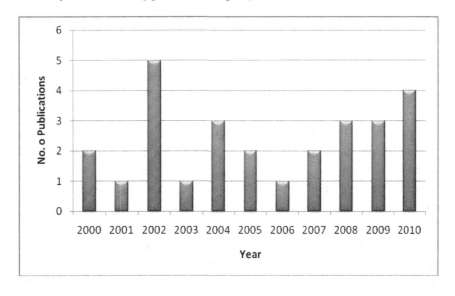

by regularly exchanging migrants (good individuals). The island model is particularly suit-able for computer clusters, as communication is limited (Horii, Miki, Koirumi, & Tsujiuchi, 2002).

3. **Diffusion Model:** Here the individuals are spatially arranged, and mate with other individuals from the local neighborhood. When parallelized, there is a lot of inter-processor communication (as every individuals has to communicate with its neighbors in every iteration), but the communication is only local. Thus this paradigm is particularly suitable for massively parallel computers with an underlying fast local communication network.

4. **DRMOGA Model:** The DRMOGA is a model of genetic algorithm in multi-objective problems for parallel processing. In the DRMOGA, the population of GAs is sorted with respect to the values of the objective function and is divided into sub-populations. In each sub-population, simple GA for multi-objective problems is performed. After some generations, all individuals are gathered and they are sorted again. In this model, the Pareto optimum solutions which are close to each other are collected by one sub population. Therefore, this algorithm increases the calculation efficiency, and the neighborhood search can be performed (Hiroyasu, Miki, & Watanabe, 2000).

The pseudo code of master slave model is described as follows:

1. Randomly generate the population. Randomly generate the population of size P on processor 0

2. Evaluate each population member's fitness
   a. Send P/N population members to each processor from process 0.
   b. Each processor conducts 'k' fitness evaluations for each of the P/N population members.

c. Each processor sends k*P/N fitness values to process 0.

d. Process 0 determines Pareto Front $_{current\,(t)}$, update Pareto Front $_{known}$ and assigns rank if necessary.

3. Perform clustering/ Niching /Crowding on processor 0.

4. Execute evolutionary operators (crossover, mutation) on processor 0.

5. Evaluate the new populations' fitness.
   a. Send P/N population members to each processor from process 0.
   b. Each processor conducts 'k' fitness evaluations for each of the P/N population members.
   c. Each processor sends k*P/N fitness values to process 0.
   d. Process 0 determines Pareto Front $_{current\,(t)}$, update Pareto Front $_{known}$ and assigns rank if necessary.

6. Conduct selection on processor 0.

7. Repeat until termination criteria are met.

8. Conduct local search on processor 0 if specified.

9. Processor 0 generates and presents PF known as the solution.

There are many strategies proposed in literature on parallelizing multi-objective genetic algorithms. They are discussed in detail and summarized in Table 5.

## 6.1. Divide Range Multi-Objective Genetic Algorithm

Divide range multi-objective genetic algorithm (DRMOGA), was proposed by Hiroyasu et al. (2000). In this algorithm population of GAs is sorted with respect to the values of an objective function and divided into sub populations. In each sub- population, simple GA for multi-objective problems is performed. After some generations, all individuals are gathered and they are sorted again with respect to the other objectives. In this model,

*Table 5. Summarizes the advantage and disadvantage of PMOGA algorithms*

| Algorithm | Author | Year | Technique used | Advantage | Disadvantage |
|---|---|---|---|---|---|
| DRMOGA | Hieroyasu et al. | 2000 | Divide-and-conquer | High searching ability of Pareto solutions. | Does not guarantee that sub-populations will remain in their assigned region. |
| MOGADES | Kamiura et al. | 2002 | Divide-and- conquer | It could derive the wide spread Pareto optimal solutions | Using weight parameter a MOP is turned into SOP. |
| Cone Separated NSGA II | Branke et al. | 2004 | Divide-and- conquer | Converges much quicker to the Pareto-optimal front without guidance scheme. | Before shape of the Pareto optimal front is known it is difficult to define the search algorithm. It is difficult to apply on the problems having more than three objectives. |
| Clustering based NSGA II | Streichert et al. | 2005 | Divide-and- conquer | Each sub-population is guaranteed to be non-empty | High communication over head. |
| Multi-Front equitable distribution | Essabri et al. | 2006 | Elitist Technique | Allows each processor to generate a better representing set of the Pareto frontier | Automatic identification of the number of clusters is not done. |
| MROMOGA | Jaimes et.al. | 2007 | Island paradigms with heterogeneous nodes | It improves convergence | Poor distribution at the fine grain level |
| Master slave approach to parallelize NSGA II | Durillo et al. | 2008 | Master Slave Model (Syn) | | Doesn't take advantage of large processor. |
| | | | Master Slave Model (aSyn) | Take the advantage of large processor. | Works well if fitness is computationally expensive. |
| PNSGA | Zhi-xin et al. | 2009 | Based on individual migration & update strategy | Due to migration strategy the convergence is better. | The spread of the solution is worst. |
| SMPGA | Qiu et al. | 2010 | Migration takes place only if it satisfies the migration condition | Spread of the solution is good due to the migration strategy. | Convergence is not so fast. |

(Note: Syn: synchronous, aSyn: asynchronous)

the Pareto optimum solutions which are close to each other are collected by one sub-population. Therefore, this algorithm increases the calculation efficiency and the neighborhood search can be performed. The main goal of this approach is to focus on search effort of the population in different regions of the objective space. However, in this approach it cannot be guaranteed that the subpopulations will remain in their assigned region (Jaimes & Coello, 2007).

The performance of the DRMOGA depends on the true Pareto front. If the true Pareto is like Figure 14(a), then the vertical division would give better result as each processor shares almost equal number of non-dominated solution. When the same problem is divided horizontally, the processor doesn't share the best solution equally as shown in Figure 14(b) as a result the result detoriates.

## 6.2. Cone-Separated NSGA-II

Branke et al. (2004) implemented the concept of "divide-and-conquer", which is more efficient than

*Figure 14. Division of the population in 3 processors with respect to (a) f1 and (b) f2*

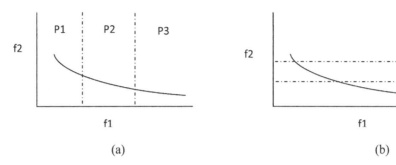

(a)                                        (b)

when all processors work on the entire problem. The first approach in this direction was proposed by Deb et al. (2003). That approach was based on an island model with migration, and used the guided dominance principle (Branke, Kaubler, & Schmeck, 2001) to give different islands (=processors) different search directions. It produced excellent results, in the sense that it converged much quicker to the Pareto-optimal front than without guidance scheme (i.e., when every island searched for the whole Pareto-optimal front).

They compared the algorithms with the number of generations, the respective algorithms takes to converge to the Pareto optimal solutions. They concluded that performance deteriorates with an increasing number of processors, independent of the approach used. Simply running several NSGA-II in parallel performs worst. Migration clearly helped, as the island model performs much better. The cone-separated NSGA-II performed best, confirming their assumption that dividing up the search space and having different populations focus on different areas improves efficiency.

This algorithm has several drawbacks. It may be difficult to define appropriate search directions before the shape of the Pareto-optimal front is known. In case of discontinuous or non-evenly distributed Pareto fronts small or empty subpopulations can be generated. The geometrical subdivision scheme of cone separation becomes rather complicated in the case of more than three objectives (Durillo, Nebro, Luna, & Alba, 2008; Mishra et al., 2011). Furthermore, the approach

works satisfactorily only if the Pareto optimal front is convex.

## 6.3. Clustering Based Parallelization

Streichert, Ulmer, and Zell (2005) decided to search for a suitable subdivision scheme ('divide and conquer' approach, island model was considered) on the search space by means of clustering algorithms. Each *migration_rate* generations, all subpopulations $P_i$ remote (a non-dominated remote population) are gathered, the aggregated Pareto front $P_{local}$ (the local population) is clustered and all individuals are redistributed onto the available processors depending on the cluster centroids.

For clustering, they used a k-means clustering on the current Pareto front, because k Means allows the user to choose the number of clusters according to the number of available processors $k$. In case the size of $P_{local}$ is smaller than $k$, next level Pareto fronts are also used for clustering. They further distinguish between two variants for clustering; first search spaces based clustering and second an objective space clustering. One advantage of the clustering based parallelization scheme is that each subpopulation is guaranteed to be non-empty. They concluded that the standard island MOEA with migration proves to be quite robust and hard to beat. They found that the simple and contiguous structure of the standard test functions allows lateral exploration once a good solution is found.

The main disadvantage of this approach is that repeated gathering of all sub-populations produces a high communication overhead, which is increased with the number of processor (Jaimes & Coello, 2007). In this technique equal number of non-dominated solution is not shared by every processor as shown in Figure 15.

## 6.4. Multi-Front Equitable Distribution

Essabri, Gzara, and Loukil (2006) proposed Multi-front Equitable Distribution (MFED) which is based on an elitist technique. MFED makes evolve several populations (one on each processor). Every population evolves with its own genetic operators to perform exploration of the search space. The main algorithm consists of two kinds of processes, an organizer and several elitist MOEA. There is only one organizer, with the responsibility of collecting the different fronts from other processors, updating the global front and equitably dividing the $n$ first global front between all processors (the organizer and others). After the sharing process, in each processor, the set received from the sharing of the first front replaces its external population and the other sets ($F_2$ to $F_n$) replace its internal population ($P_{tk}$). At the end, the different archives make up the global one. The size of the internal population will be increased so that, this later will

*Figure 15. Chromosomes assigned to different processors*

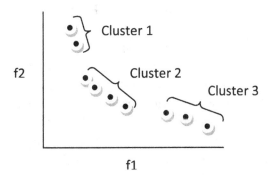

be reduced by clustering to its initial size (Zitler & Thiele, 1999). At the end, the different archives make up the global one. The equitable distribution of the obtained fronts allows each processor to generate a better representing set of the Pareto frontier. However, the fixed number of clusters (on which each front of solutions gathered from different processors must be divided) is arbitrary.

Automatic identification of the number of clusters is not done in this technique. The combination of $n$ number of fronts and then clustering each front independently is an exhaustive task. With the variation of $n$ the result fluctuates. So experimentally one has to find the best $n$ for each problem.

## 6.5. Multiple Resolution Multi-Objective Genetic Algorithms

Multiple resolution multi-objective genetic algorithms (MROMOGA) (Jaimes & Coello, 2007), is based on island paradigm with heterogeneous nodes. This algorithm encodes the solutions using a different resolution in each island. The resolution of each island is increased when it has reached nominal coverage (Figure 16). In this way, the variable decision space is divided into hierarchical levels with well-defined overlaps. The performance assessment of the proposed approach considers both effectiveness and efficiency. To evaluate the effectiveness they adopt well-known metrics traditionally used to evaluate serial MOEAs, namely: success counting, inverted generational distance, spacing, and two set coverage. On the other hand, efficiency was evaluated using the following well-known metrics from parallel computing: speedup, efficiency and serial fraction. The results of the proposed algorithm were compared against those of a parallel version of the NSGA-II (Deb, Agrawal, Pratap, & Meyarivan, 2000). This approach can be considered to be dividing the variable decision space. From the comparative study they concluded that the proposed scheme to divide the decision

*Figure 16. A schematic representation of MRMOGA*

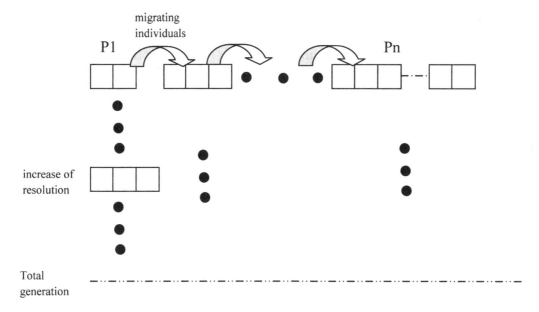

space improves noticeably the convergence of a PMOGA. The main weakness of this approach is the poor distribution at the fine-grain level.

## 6.6. Parallel Genetic Algorithm for Multi-Objective Optimization

Parallel genetic algorithm for multi-objective optimization (PNSGA) was proposed by Zhi-xin and Gang (2009). They introduced individual migration and update strategy to maintain the convergence and diversity of Pareto optimal set. Experimentally they showed the effectiveness of the algorithm PNGA in comparison with NSGA-II (Deb, Pratap, Agarwal, & Meyarivan, 2002), and improved multi-objective particle swarm optimization (MOCLPSO) (Huang, Suganthan, & Liang, 2006).

PNSGA is a coarse parallel island model. It maintains Elite Population (EP) to archive the non-dominated solutions in the entire population. The original population is defined as Searching Population (SP). Independent MOGA is performed in both SP and EP at the same time. To avoid the

algorithm from converging to a local optimal set or premature convergence an individual update strategy is introduced in PNSGA. PNSGA uses a SP to find the optimal solution all over the objective space, and send the new non-dominated individual found at each generation to EP for further optimization. If the number of the individual send from SP to EP is zero, it shows that there is no new non-dominated individual is found at this generation. If the number is zero as long as several generations, it is necessary to update the search populations using the individual update strategy because the algorithm has stopped at a partial optimal.

## 6.7. Selective Migration PGA

Selective migration parallel genetic algorithm (SMPGA) was proposed by Qiu and Ju (2010). It is a modification of PNSGA (Zhi-xin & Gang, 2009). They claimed that the migrating individuals of search population (SP) and elite population (EP) depends on domination relation, can strengthen the convergence but the spread of the solution become worse. So they introduced a migration strategy in the PNSGA and compared the results of proposed SMPGA with NSGA-II, and PNSGA.

# 7. APPLICATIONS

MOGA based algorithms have become increasingly popular in a wide variety of application domains. In order to provide a rough idea of the sort of applications that are being tackled in the current literature, we can classify the applications in three large groups: engineering (Al-Somani, 2000; Pelikan & Goldberg, 2000; Balling, 2003; David et al., 2003), industrial (Huaping, Gu, & Bingyuan, 2006) and scientific (Kaestner et al., 2002; Rosenberg, 1967). The engineering area is most popular due to the fact that engineering problems have well-studied mathematical models. A representative sample of engineering applications is Electrical engineering (Aguirre & Coello, 2002; Zebulum, Pacheco, & Vellasco, 1999), hydraulic engineering (Andersson, 2001; Knarr, Goltz, Lamont, & Huang, 2000; Horn, Nafpliotis, & Goldberg, 1994; Horn, Erickson, & Mayer, 2000), structural engineering (Basseur et al., 2002), aeronautical engineering (Cui, Li, & Fang, 2001; Guangwen et al., 2007), robotics and control (Zhi-xin & Gang, 2009). A representative sample of industrial applications is Design and manufacture, Scheduling, Management. Finally, we have a variety of scientific applications in the field of Chemistry, Physics (Pelikan & Goldberg, 2000), Medicine (Lamont et al., 2001), Computer science (Jingping, Zhirui, & Haifeng, 2007; Kamiura et al., 2002). The strong interest for using MOGAs in so many different disciplines is due to the multi-objective nature of many real-world problems. However, some application domains have received relatively little attention from researchers for example: cellular automata (Lamont et al., 2001), bioinformatics (Miettinen, 1999), and financial applications

(Miettinen, 1999). Srivastava and Kim (2009) have used a genetic algorithm based solution to optimize software testing efficiency by identifying the most critical path clusters in a program, they did it by developing variable length Genetic algorithms that optimize and select the software path clusters which are weighted in accordance with the criticality of the path.

Badarudin et al. (2010) applied genetic algorithm in the agricultural domain to find the optimal shapes for space allocation for optimal plantation and in turn finding the optimal number of trees in a given area. Hobbs and Rodgers (1998) have applied a hybrid GA that is used to improve the layout of a graph according to a number of aesthetic criteria. The GA incorporates spatial and topological information by operating directly with a graph based representation. Yeh, Chang, and Chiu (2004) applied genetic algorithm to the shape optimization of constrained double chamber muffler with extended tubes. They applied GA to conjugate the acoustic performance of sound transmission loss (STL) derived by transfer matrix. Yang, Xianggen, and Zhe (2009) have presented a wide-area intelligent protection system based on abundant power network information by analyzing the practical application of wide area protection and further combining it with the recent development of power network. The system works with main protection system and strengthens the capability of power system relay protection and simplifies the backup protection. This paper also gives the decision-making and working mode of a new intelligent protection including the principle of state correlation wide-area protection and the principle of fault identification based on genetic algorithm. Wu and Qishi (2000) applied genetic algorithm for GIS to provide a strong decision support system for users in searching optimal path, finding the nearest facility and determining the service area. Venkatesan and Narayanasamy (2003) applied the genetic algorithm in the extrusion phase of the metal for mining. They have applied GA and simulated annealing based algorithm to optimize the extrusion die ratio and die cone angle.

Falco, De, Balio, Cioppa, and Tarantina (1996) applied PGA for the design of transonic airfoil due to the high computational load aerodynamics parameter which is tightly correlated with the fitness evaluation. Tang and Lau (2007) applied PGA to solve floor plan optimization problem. They applied parallel genetic based on island model with asynchronous communication migration mechanism. Wang et al. (2005) studied the five parallel models of genetic algorithm for solving the travelling salesman problem. They found two approaches for to be effective for enhancing the performance of PGA: (1) inter-PE information exchange during the evolution progress (e.g., migration of the locally best chromosomes) and (2) tour segmentation and recombination. Belkadi et al. (2006) compared the performance serial and parallel genetic algorithm based on flow scheduling. Levine (1995) has applied an island based PGA developed for the solution of the set partitioning problem. Doorly and Peiro (1997) proposed a multi-agent based supervised parallel distributed genetic algorithm for aerodynamics optimization. Mihaylova and Brandisky (2006) present a genetic algorithm based approach to optimization to problems in electrical engineering. They implemented on a cluster of computers.

Sundar, Umadevi, and Alagarsamy (2010) have applied multi-objective genetic algorithms for optimized resource usage and prioritization of the constraints in the software planning. They have suggested a Multi objective genetic algorithm (MOGA) for minimization of the human resources used. So in turn MOGA has been used to minimize the cost associated, minimize the time involved and to maximize the efficiency by proper usage. Fonesca (1995) has applied multi-objective GA to three realistic problems in optimal controller design and non-linear system identification. Kehinde, Alawode, Jubr, and Komolafe (2010) applied non-dominated sorting algorithm for solv-

ing the environmental/ economic dispatch power system problem. They have used the NSGA-II with convergence accelerator operator for solving the problem. Kayo and Ooka (2009) applied multi-objective genetic algorithm for optimal design of distributed energy system. The proposed method designs the most efficient energy system by optimizing operation of available systems in consideration of optimal machinery capacity in the systems Multi-objective genetic algorithm has been widely used in scheduling of real time jobs in multiprocessor environment. Yoo (2009) proposed the multi-objective genetic algorithm with combination of adaptive weight approach for soft real time task scheduling in homogeneous multiprocessor environment. Later Yoo and Gen (2007) used the multi-objective genetic algorithm for optimization of scheduling of real time task under heterogeneous environment. Miryani and Naghibzadeh (2009) applied multi-objective genetic algorithm for optimization of hard real time scheduling of jobs in heterogeneous systems.

The rule mining problem can be considered as multi-objective problem rather than as a single objective problem. The predictive accuracy and comprehensibility used for evaluating a rule ca n be thought of as different objectives of our classification rule mining. This makes it an optimization problem that is very difficult to solve efficiently. Intuitively, MOGA appears to be the best- available technique for this problem. The following points are motivating factors for proposing parallel processing techniques as a solution to discover the classification rules using MOGA.

1.  As we have mentioned, a rule consequent in a MOGA simply associates all individuals of the population with the same rule consequent. Hence to discover a set of rules with k different predictions we usually have to run the MOGA k times at least once for each rule consequent to be predicted; which can be computation expensive.

2. MOGA itself tends to be slow and as the data size is growing and hence the computation of fitness is very expensive.

There are several interesting ideas which deserve closer attention. These are summarized in the following:

- The transformation of single-objective problems into a multi-objective form often facilitates their solution. For example, some researchers have proposed the handling of the constraints of a problem as objectives, and others have proposed the so-called "multi objectification" by which a single-objective optimization problem is decomposed into several subcomponents considering a multi-objective approach. This procedure has been found to be helpful in removing local optima from a problem and has attracted a lot of attention in the last few years.

- Parameter control is a topic that has been scarcely explored in MOGAs. In this context a question that needs closer attention is the following. Is it possible to design a MOGA that self-adapts its parameters such that the user doesn't have to fine-tune them by hand? Some researchers have proposed a few self-adaptation and online adaptation procedures for MOGAs. But, of late, not much research has been reported on this topic.

- A question that is intriguing researchers: What is the minimum number of fitness function evaluations that are actually required to achieve a minimum desirable performance with an MOGA? Recently, some researchers have proposed the use of black-box optimization techniques normally adopted in engineering to perform an incredibly low number of fitness function evaluations while still producing reasonably good solutions. However, this sort of approach is inherently limited to problems of low dimensionality. So, the question is: are there any other ways of reducing the number of evaluations without sacrificing dimensionality?

- It is still not clear how to deal with problems that have "many" objectives. Some recent studies have shown that traditional Pareto ranking schemes do not behave well in the presence of many objectives (where "many" is normally a number above 3 or 4).

## 8. CONCLUSION

In this paper, we critically surveyed the representative literatures on PGAs. We started by classifying the PGAs work into four categories such as global parallelization, coarse grained and fine grained algorithms, and hybrid approaches. We analyzed the important contributions in each of these categories and identified the issues that affect the design of these algorithms and their implementation on currently available parallel computer environments.

We highlighted that the research in this field is dominated by the description of experimental results and that very little work has been conducted to give an analytical explanation of what is observed. We focused on coarse grained PGAs partly because of their popularity but mainly because of their close resemblance to nature. For this class of algorithms the spatial allocation of resources (i.e., the decision on the number and size of demes) has been solved for extreme cases but the migration issue is still unresolved. Parallelization of GAs is not an intrinsically difficult task, and many implementations are reported in the literature. What we need now are studies that focus on particular aspects of PGAs. We however, are yet to understand what truly affects the performance of the algorithm so we can design faster and more reliable genetic systems.

Finally, we have also surveyed some of the representative state-of-the-art MOGA and PMOGA. We classified them by considering several parameters. We also enlightened some of the basic application areas of MOGA and PMOGA with a central focus on several associated issues. We emphasized on several interesting ideas of parallel multi-objective genetic algorithms which deserve closer attention.

# REFERENCES

Aguirre, A. H., & Coello, C. A. (2002). Design of combinational logic circuits through an evolutionary multiobjective optimization approach. *Artificial Intelligence for Engineering Design, Analysis and Manufacturing*, *16*(1), 39–53.

Ahn, C. W., Goldberg, D. E., & Ramkrishna, R. S. (2004). Multiple deme parallel estimation of distribution algorithms: Basic framework and application. In R. Wyrzkowski, J. Dongarra, M. Paprzycki, & J. Wasniewski (Eds.), *Proceedings of the 5<sup>th</sup> International Conference on Parallel Processing and Applied Mathematics* (LNCS 3019, pp. 544-551)

Al-Somani, T., & Qureshi, K. (2000). *Reliability optimization using genetics algorithms*. Saudi Arabia: King Abdul-Aziz University.

Alander, J. T. (1994). *An indexed bibliography of genetic algorithms: Years 1957-1993*. Vassa, Finland: University of Vassa.

Alawode, K. O., Jubr, I. A., & Komolafe, O. A. (2010). Multiobjective optimal power flow using hybrid evolutionary algorithms. *International Journal of Energy and Power Engineering*, *3*(3), 196–201.

Alba, E., Nebro, A., & Troya, J. (2002). Heterogeneous computing and parallel genetic algorithms. *Journal of Parallel and Distributed Computing*, *62*(9), 1362–1385. doi:10.1006/jpdc.2002.1851

Alba, E., & Tomasdni, M. (2002). Parallelism 'and evolutionary algorithms. *IEEE Transactions on Evolutionary Computation*, *6*(5), 443–461. doi:10.1109/TEVC.2002.800880

Alba, E., & Troya, J. (2001). Synchronous and asynchronous parallel distributed genetic algorithms. *Future Generation Computer Systems*, *17*(4), 451–465. doi:10.1016/S0167-739X(99)00129-6

Alba, E., & Troya, J. M. (2002). Improving flexibility and efficiency by adding parallelism to genetic algorithms. *Statistics and Computing*, *12*(2), 91–114. doi:10.1023/A:1014803900897

Andersson, J. (2001). *Optimization in engineering design- applications to fluid power systems*. Linkoping, Sweden: Linkoping University.

Arryo, J. M., & Conejo, A. J. (2002). A parallel repair GA to solve the unit commitment problem. *IEEE Transactions on Power Systems*, *17*(4), 1216–1224. doi:10.1109/TPWRS.2002.804953

Bäck, T. (1996). *Evolutionary algorithms in theory and practice*. New York, NY: Oxford University Press.

Bäck, T., Fogel, D. B., & Michalewicz, Z. (1997). *Handbook of evolutionary computation*. New York, NY: Oxford University Press. doi:10.1887/0750308958

Badarudin, I. M., Sultan, A. B., Sulaiman, M. N., & Mamat, A. (2010). Shape assignment by genetic algorithm towards designing optimal areas. *International Journal of Computer Science*, *7*(4), 1–7.

Balling, R. (2003). The maximin fitness function; Multiobjective city and regional planning. In C. M. Fonseca, P. J. Fleming, E. Zitzler, L. Thiele, & K. Deb (Eds.), *Proceedings of the Second International Conference on Evolutionary Multi-Criterion Optimization*, Faro, Portugal (LNCS 2632, pp. 1-15).

Baluja, S. (1994). *Population based incremental learning: A method for integrating genetic search based function optimization and competitive learning* (Tech. Rep. No. CMU-CS-94-163). Pittsburgh, PA: Carnegie Mellon University.

Basseur, M., Seynhaeve, F., & Talbi, E. G. (2002). Design of multi-objective evolutionary algorithms: Application to the flow-shop scheduling problem. In *Proceedings of the Congress on Evolutionary Computation*, Honolulu, HI (pp. 1151-1156). Washington, DC: IEEE Computer Society.

Belkadi, K., Gourgand, M., Benyettou, M., & Aribi, A. (2006). Sequential and parallel genetic algorithms for hybrid flow shop scheduling. *Journal of Applied Sciences*, 6(4), 775–778. doi:10.3923/jas.2006.775.778

Branke, J., Kaubler, T., & Schmeck, H. (2001). Guidance in evolutionary multiobjective optimization. *Advances in Engineering Software*, 32(6), 499–508. doi:10.1016/S0965-9978(00)00110-1

Branke, J., Schmeck, H., Deb, K., & Maheshwar, R. S. (2004). Parallelizing multiobjective evolutionary algorithms: Cone separation. In *Proceedings of the Congress on Evolutionary Computation*, Portland, OR (pp. 1952-1957). Washington, DC: IEEE Computer Society.

Cantu-Paz, E. (1997). Designing efficient master-slave parallel genetic algorithms. [University of Illinois at Urbana-Champaign.]. *Urbana (Caracas, Venezuela)*, IL.

Cantu-Paz, E. (1998). A survey of parallel genetic algorithms. *Calculateurs Paralleles*, 10(2), 141–171.

Coello, C. A. (1999). A comprehensive survey of evolutionary-based multiobjective optimization techniques. *International Journal of Knowledge and Information Systems*, 1, 269–308.

Coello, C. A. (2000). Preferences in evolutionary multiobjective optimization: A survey. In []. Washington, DC: IEEE Computer Society.]. *Proceedings of the Congress on Evolutionary Computation*, 1, 30–37.

Coello, C. A. (2001). A short tutorial on evolutionary multiobjective optimization. In E. Zitzler, K. Deb, L. Thiele, C. A. Coello, & D. Corne (Eds.), *Proceedings of the First International Conference on Evolutionary Multi-Criterion Optimization* (LNCS 1993, pp. 21-40).

Coello, C. A. (2006). Evolutionary multi objective optimization: A historical view of the field. *IEEE Computational Intelligence Magazine*, 1(1), 28–36. doi:10.1109/MCI.2006.1597059

Coello, C. A., Veldhuizen, A. D., & Lamont, G. B. (2002). *Evolutionary algorithms for solving multi-objective optimization problems*. Boston, MA: Kluwer Academic.

Corne, D. W., Jerram, N. R., Knowles, J. D., & Oates, M. J. (2001). PESA-II: Regionbased selection in evolutionary multiobjective optimization. In *Proceedings of the Genetic and Evolutionary Computation Conference* (pp. 238-290).

Corne, D. W., Knowles, J. D., & Oates, M. J. (2000). The Pareto envelope-based selection algorithm for multiobjective optimization. In *Proceedings of the Sixth International Conference on Parallel Problem Solving from Nature* (pp. 18-20).

Cui, X., Li, M., & Fang, T. (2001). Study of population diversity of multiobjective evolutionary algorithm based on immune and entropy principles. In *Proceedings of the Congress on Evolutionary Computation* (pp. 1316-1321). Washington, DC: IEEE Computer Society.

Das, I., & Dennis, J. (1997). A closer look at drawbacks of minimizing weighted sums of objectives for Pareto set generation in multi criteria optimization problems. *Structural Optimization, 14*, 63–69. doi:10.1007/BF01197559

David, A., Veldhuizen, V., Zydallis, J. B., & Lamont, G. B. (2003). Considerations in engineering parallel multi objective evolutionary algorithms. *IEEE Transactions on Evolutionary Computation, 7*(2), 144–174. doi:10.1109/TEVC.2003.810751

De, F., Balio, R. D., Cioppa, A. D., & Tarantina, E. (1996). A parallel genetic algorithm for transonic airfoil optimisation. In []. Washington, DC: IEEE Computer Society.]. *Proceedings of the IEEE International Conference Evolutionary Computation, 1*, 429–434.

Deb, K. (2001). *Multi-objective optimization using evolutionary algorithms*. Chichester, UK: John Wiley & Sons.

Deb, K., Agrawal, S., Pratap, A., & Meyarivan, T. (2000). A fast elitist nondominated sorting genetic algorithm for multi-objective optimization: NSGA-II. In *Proceedings of the Sixth International Conference on Parallel Problem Solving from Nature* (pp. 18-20).

Deb, K., & Goldberg, D. E. (1991). *MGA in C: A messy genetic algorithm in C*. Champaign, IL: Illinois Genetic Algorithms Laboratory.

Deb, K., Pratap, A., Agarwal, S., & Meyyarivan, T. (2002). A fast and elitist multiobjective genetic algorithm: NSGA-II. *IEEE Transactions on Evolutionary Computation, 6*(2), 182–197. doi:10.1109/4235.996017

Deb, K., Zope, P., & Jain, A. (2003). Distributed computing of pareto-optimal solutions with evolutionary algorithm. In C. M. Fonseca, P. J. Fleming, E. Zitzler, K. Deb, & L. Thiele (Eds.), *Proceedings of the International Conference on Evolutionary Multi-Criterion Optimization* (LNCS 2632, pp. 534-549).

Doorly, D. J., & Peiro, L. (1997). Supervised parallel genetic algorithms in aerodynamic optimization. In *Proceedings of the 13th AIAA Conference on Computational Fluid Dynamics*.

Durillo, J. J., Nebro, A. J., Luna, F., & Alba, E. (2008). A study of master slave approaches to parallelize NSGA-II. In *Proceedings of the IEEE International Symposium on Parallel and Distributed Processing* (pp. 1-18). Washington, DC: IEEE Computer Society.

Essabri, A., Gzara, M., & Loukil, T. (2006). Parallel multi-objective evolutionary algorithm with multi-front equitable distribution. In *Proceedings of the Fifth International Conference on Grid and Cooperative Computing* (pp. 241-244). Washington, DC: IEEE Computer Society.

Fonseca, C. M. (1995). *Multiobjective genetic algorithms with application to control engineering problems*. Unpublished doctoral dissertation, University of Sheffield, Sheffield, UK.

Fonseca, C. M., & Flemming, P. J. (1993). Genetic algorithms for multiobjective optimization: Formulation, discussion and generalization. In *Proceedings of the 5th International Conference on Genetic Algorithms* (pp. 416-423). Washington, DC: IEEE Computer Society.

Gao, Y., Shi, L., & Yao, P. (2000). Study on multiobjective genetic algorithm. *IEEE*, 646-650.

Goldberg, D. E. (1989). *Genetic algorithms in search, optimization and machine learning*. Reading, MA: Addison-Wesley.

Golub, M., & Jakobovic, D. (2000). A new model of global parallel genetic algorithm. In *Proceedings of the 22nd International Conference on Information Technology Interfaces* (pp. 363-368). Washington, DC: IEEE Computer Society.

Grama, A., Gupta, A., & Kumar, V. (1993). Iso efficiency: Measuring the scalability of parallel algorithms and architectures. *IEEE Parallel and Distributed Technology*, 12-21.

Grosso, P. B. (1985). *Computer simulation of genetic adaptation: Para interaction in multilocus model*. Ann Arbor, MI: University of Michigan.

Guangwen, L., Weiguo, Z., & Jian, L. (2007). The niche genetic algorithm and its application in the optimization of an aircraft control system. *Flight Dynamics*, *25*(3), 79–82.

Hajela, P., & Yin, C. Y. (1992). Genetic search strategies in multicriterion optimal design. *Structural and Multidisciplinary Optimization*, *4*(2), 99–107.

Hiroyasu, T., Kaneko, M., & Miki, M. (2000). A parallel genetic algorithm with distributed environment scheme. In []. Washington, DC: IEEE Computer Society.]. *Proceedings of the International Conference on Parallel and Distributed Processing Techniques and Applications*, *2*, 619–625.

Hiroyasu, T., Miki, M., & Tanimura, Y. (1999). Characteristics of models of parallel genetic algorithms on pc cluster systems. In *Proceedings of the 1st International Workshop on Cluster Computing* (pp. 879-886).

Hiroyasu, T., Miki, M., & Watanabe, S. (2000). The new model of parallel genetic algorithm in multi objective optimization problems - divided range multi objective GA. In []. Washington, DC: IEEE Computer Society.]. *Proceedings of Congress on Evolutionary Computation*, *1*, 333–340.

Hobbs, M., & Rodgers, P. (1998). Representing space: A hybrid genetic algorithm for aesthetic graph layout. In *Proceedings of the Fourth Joint Conference on Frontiers in Evolutionary Algorithms*.

Horii, H., Miki, M., Koirumi, T., & Tsujiuchi, N. (2002). Asynchronous migration of island parallel ga for multi-objective optimization problem. In *Proceedings of the Asia-Pod Conference on Simulated Evolution and Learning*.

Horn, J. (1997). The nature of niching: Genetic algorithms and the evolution of optimal, co-operative populations. [University of Illinois at Urbana-Champaign.]. *Urbana (Caracas, Venezuela)*, IL.

Horn, J., Erickson, M., & Mayer, A. (2000). The niched pareto genetic algorithm applied to the design of groundwater remediation systems. In E. Zitzler, K. Deb, L. Thiele, C. A. Coello, & D. Corne (Eds.), *Proceedings of the First International Conference on Evolutionary Multi-Criterion Optimization* (LNCS 1993, pp. 681-695).

Horn, J., Nafpliotis, N., & Goldberg, D. E. (1994). A niched Pareto genetic algorithm for multi objective optimization. In *Proceedings of the First IEEE World Congress on Computational Intelligence*, Orlando, FL (Vol. 1, pp. 82-87). Washington, DC: IEEE Computer Society.

Huang, V. L., Suganthan, P. N., & Liang, J. J. (2006). Comprehensive learning particle swarm optimizer for solving multiobjective optimization problems. *International Journal of Intelligent Systems*, *21*(2), 209–226. doi:10.1002/int.20128

Huaping, C., Gu, F., & Bingyuan, L. (2006). Application of self-adaptive multi-objective genetic algorithm in flexible job shop scheduling. *Journal of System Simulation*, *18*(18), 2271–2274.

Ishibuchi, H., Nojima, Y., Narukawa, K., & Doi, T. (2006). Incorporation of decision maker's preference into evolutionary multi objective optimization algorithms. In *Proceeding of the Genetic and Evolutionary Impact Conference*, Seattle, WA (Vol. 1, pp. 741-742).

Jaddan, O. A., Rajamani, L., & Rao, C. R. (2008). Non-dominated ranked genetic algorithm for solving multi objective optimization problems: NRGA. *Journal of Theoretical and Applied Information Technology*, 61-67.

Jaimes, A. L., & Coello, C. A. (2007). MRMOGA: Parallel evolutionary multiobjective optimization using multiple resolutions. *Concurrency and Computation, 19*(4), 397–441. doi:10.1002/cpe.1107

Jarosław, M., & Tomasz, W. (2003). A genetic algorithm for motion detection. In *Proceedings of the 9th International Conference on Soft Computing*, Brno, Czech Republic.

Jaszkiewicz, A. (2002). On the performance of multiple-objective genetic local search on the 0/1 knapsack problem-a comparative experiment. *IEEE Transactions on Evolutionary Computation, 6*(4), 402–412. doi:10.1109/TEVC.2002.802873

Jin-hua, Z. (2007). *Multi-objective evolutionary algorithm and its application*. Beijing, China: Science Press.

Jingping, Z., Zhirui, L., & Haifeng, S. (2007). Research on reactive power optimization of distribution network based on the improved crowding niche genetic algorithm. *Relay, 35*(1), 19–22.

Jiong-liang, X., & Jin-hua, Z. (2008). Research on cause for overlapping solutions and on their influence in NSGA- II algorithm. *Computer Engineering and Application, 4*(22), 69–72.

Jones, D. F., Mirrazavi, S. K., & Tamiz, M. (2002). Multiobjective meta-heuristics: An overview of the current state-of-the-art. *European Journal of Operational Research, 137*(1), 1–9. doi:10.1016/S0377-2217(01)00123-0

Juan, C., & Xu Lihong. (2006). A dynamic niche genetic algorithm for multimodal function optimization. *Journal of Tong Ji University, 34*, 684–688.

Kaestner, C. A., Pappa, G. L., & Freitas, A. A. (2002). A multiobjective genetic algorithm for attribute selection. In *Proceedings of the 4th International Conference on Recent Advances in Soft Computing*, Nottingham, UK (pp. 116-121).

Kamiura, J., Hiroyasu, T., Miki, M., Watanabe, S., & Sakoda, T. (2002). MOGADES: Multi-objective genetic algorithm with distributed environment scheme. In *Proceedings of the Second International Workshop on Intelligent Systems Design and Applications* (pp. 143-148).

Kaneko, M., Hiroyasu, T., & Miki, M. (2000). A parallel genetic algorithm with distributed environment scheme. In *Proceedings of the International Conference on Parallel and Distributed Processing Techniques and Applications* (pp. 619-625). Washington, DC: IEEE Computer Society.

Kayo, G., & Ooka, R. (2009). Application multiobjective genetic algorithm for optimal design method distributed energy system. In *Proceedings of the Eleventh International IBPSA Conference*, Glasgow, Scotland (pp. 167-172).

Khan, N. (2003). Bayesian optimization algorithms for multiobjective and hierarchically difficult problems. [University of Illinois at Urbana-Champaign.]. *Urbana (Caracas, Venezuela)*, IL.

Kita, H., Yabumoto, Y., Mori, N., & Nishikawa, Y. (1996). Multi-objective optimization by means of the thermodynamical genetic algorithm. In H.-M. Voigt, W. Ebeling, I. Rechenberg, & H.-P. Schwefel (Eds.), *Proceedings of the International Conference on Evolutionary Computation and the 4th International Conference on Parallel Problem Solving from Nature* (LNCS 1141, pp. 504-5412).

Knarr, M. R., Goltz, M. N., Lamont, G. B., & Huang, J. (2000). Bioremediation of perchlorate-contaminated groundwater using a multi-objective parallel evolutionary algorithm. In *Proceedings of the Congress on Evolutionary Computation* (pp. 1604-1621). Washington, DC: IEEE Computer Society.

Knowles, J., & Corne, D. (1999). The Pareto archived evolution strategy: a new baseline algorithm for Pareto multiobjective optimisation. In *Proceedings of the Congress on Evolutionary Computation* (pp. 6-9). Washington, DC: IEEE Computer Society.

Knowles, J., & Corne, D. (2000). M-PAES: A memetic algorithm for multi-objective optimization. In *Proceedings of the Congress on Evolutionary Computation* (pp. 325-332). Washington, DC: IEEE Computer Society.

Kumar, R., & Rockett, P. (2002). Improved sampling of the Pareto-front in multiobjective genetic optimizations by steady-state evolution: A Pareto converging genetic algorithm. *Evolutionary Computation*, *10*(3), 283–314. doi:10.1162/106365602760234117

Kunzli, S., & Zitzler, E. (2004). Indicator-based selection in multiobjective search. In X. Yao, E. Burke, J. A. Lozano, J. J. Merelo-Guervos, J. A. Bullinaria, J. Rowe et al. (Eds.), *Proceedings of the 8th International Conference on Parallel Problem Solving from Nature*, Birmingham, UK (LNCS 3242, pp. 832-842).

Lamont, G. B., Coello, C. A., & Veldhuizen, A. V. (2002). *Evolutionary algorithms for solving multi-objective problems*. Boston, MA: Kluwer Academic.

Lamont, G. B., & Veldhuizn, D. A. (2001). On measuring multi objective evolutionary algorithm performance. In *Proceedings of the Congress on Evolutionary Computation* (pp. 204-211). Washington, DC: IEEE Computer Society.

Larranga, P., & Lozano, J. A. (Eds.). (2002). *Estimation of distribution algorithms: A new tool for evolutionary computation*. Boston, MA: Kluwer Academic.

Laumanns, M., Thiele, L., Deb, K., & Zitzler, E. (2002). *Combining convergence and diversity in evolutionary multi-objective optimization* (*Vol. 10*). Cambridge, MA: MIT Press.

Leon, C., Miranda, G., & Segura, C. (2008). Parallel hyper heuristic: A self-adaptive island-based model for multi-objective optimization. In *Proceedings of the 10th Annual Conference on Genetic and Evolutionary Computation*, Atlanta, GA (pp. 757-758).

Levine, D. M. (1995). *A parallel genetic algorithm for the set partitioning problem*. Chicago, IL: Illinois Institute of Technology.

Li, X., & Kirley, M. (2002). The effects of varying population density in a fine grained parallel genetic algorithm. In *Proceedings of the IEEE World Congress on Computational Intelligence* (pp. 1709-1714). Washington, DC: IEEE Computer Society.

Mahfoud, S. W. (1995). The nature of niching: Genetic algorithms and the evolution of optimal, cooperative populations. [University of Illinois at Urbana-Champaign.]. *Urbana (Caracas, Venezuela)*, IL.

Manderick, B., & Spiessens, P. (1989). Fine-grained parallel genetic algorithms. In *Proceedings of the Third International Conference on Genetic Algorithms* (pp. 428-433).

Marin, F., Trelles-Salazar, O., & Sandoval, F. (1994). Genetic algorithms on LAN message passing architectures using PVM: Application to the routing problem. In Y. Davidor, H.-P. Schwefel, & R. Manner (Eds.), *Proceedings of the Third Conference on Parallel Problem Solving from Nature* (LNCS 866, pp. 534-543).

Mendiburu, A., Lozano, J. A., & Miguel, J. A. (2005). Parallel implementation of EDAs based on Probabilistic graphical Models. *IEEE Transactions on Evolutionary Computation, 9*(4), 406–423. doi:10.1109/TEVC.2005.850299

Mendiburu, A., Lozano, J. A., Miguel, J. A., Ostra, M., & Ubide, C. (2005). Parallel and multi-objective EDAs to create multi-variate calibration models for quantitative chemical applications. In *Proceeding of the 34th International Conference on Parallel Processing*, Oslo, Norway (pp. 596-603). Washington, DC: IEEE Computer Society.

Miettinen, K. M. (1999). *Nonlinear multi-objective optimization*. Boston, MA: Kluwer Academic.

Mihaylova, P., & Brandisky, K. (2006). Parallel genetic algorithm optimization of die press. In *Proceedings of the 3rd International PhD Seminar on Computational Electromagnetics and Technical Applications* (pp. 155-159).

Mingjie, C., & Sheng, L. (2008). An improved adaptive genetic algorithm and its application in function optimization. *Journal of Harbin Engineering University, 28*, 677–680.

Miryani, M. R., & Naghibzadeh, M. (2009). Hard real-time multiobjective scheduling in heterogeneous systems using genetic algorithm. In *Proceedings of the International Conference on Parallel and Distributed Processing Techniques and Applications*, Las Vegas, NV (pp. 13-16). Washington, DC: IEEE Computer Society.

Mishra, B. S. P., Adday, A. K., Dehuri, S., & Cho, S.-B. (2010). An empirical study on parallel multi-objective genetic algorithms: 0/1 knapsack problem- a case study. In *Proceedings of the 3rd International Conference on Computational Intelligence and Industrial Application*, Wuhan, China.

Mishra, B. S. P., Adday, A. K., Roy, R., & Dehuri, S. (2010). Parallel multi-objective genetic algorithms for associative classification rule mining. In *Proceedings of the International Conference on Communication, Computing & Security*, Odisha, India.

Murata, T., & Ishibuchi, H. (1995). MOGA: Multi-objective genetic algorithms. In []. Washington, DC: IEEE Computer Society.]. *Proceedings of the IEEE International Conference on Evolutionary Computation, 29*, 289–294. doi:10.1109/ICEC.1995.489161

Okuda, T., Hiroyasu, T., Miki, M., & Watanabe, S. (2002). DCMOGA: Distributed cooperation model of multi-objective genetic algorithm. In *Proceedings of the PPSN/SAB Workshop on Multi Objective Problem Solving from Nature II*, Granada, Spain (pp. 155-160).

Ossa, L. D., Gamez, J. A., & Puerta, J. M. (2004). Migration of probability models instead of individual: An alternative when applying the island model to EDAs. In X. Yao, E. Burke, J. A. Lozano, J. J. Merelo-Guervos, J. A. Bullinaria, J. Rowe et al. (Eds.), *Proceedings of the 8th International Conference on Parallel Problem Solving from Nature*, Birminghan, UK (LNCS 3242, pp. 242-252).

Ossa, L. D., Gamez, J. A., & Puerta, J. M. (2005). Improving model combination through local search in parallel univariate EDAs. In *Proceedings of the Congress on Evolutionary Computation*, Edinburgh, UK (pp. 1426-1433). Washington, DC: IEEE Computer Society.

Ossa, L. D., Gamez, J. A., & Puerta, J. M. (2005) Initial approaches to the application of islands based parallel EDAs in continuous domains. In *Proceedings of 34th International Conference on Parallel Processing Workshop*, Oslo, Norway (pp. 580-587). Washington, DC: IEEE Computer Society.

Paliken, M. (2005). *Hierarchical Bayesian optimization algorithm: Towards a new generation of evolutionary algorithms.* New York, NY: Springer.

Pappa, G. L., Freitas, A. A., & Kaestner, C. A. (2002). Attribute selection with a multiobjective genetic algorithm. In *Proceedings of the 16th Brazilian Symposium on Artificial Intelligence* (pp. 280-290).

Pelikan, M., David, G., & Labo, F. (1999). A survey of optimization by building and using probabilistic models. [University of Illinois at Urban-Champaign.]. *Urbana (Caracas, Venezuela)*, IL.

Pelikan, M., & Goldberg, D. (2000). Heirarchical problem solving and the bayesian optimization algorithm. In *Proceedings of the Genetic and Evolutionary Computation Conference* (pp. 267-274).

Pettey, C. C., & Leuze, M. R. (1989). A theoretical investigation of a parallel genetic algorithm. In *Proceedings of the Third International Conference on Genetic Algorithms* (pp. 398-405).

Poli, M. N. (1999). Parallel genetic algorithm taxonomy. In *Proceedings of the Third International Conference on Knowledge-Based Intelligent Information Engineering Systems*, Adelaide, Australia (pp. 88-92).

Qishi, W. (2000). The application of genetic algorithm in GIS network analysis. *International Archives of Photogrammetry and Remo*, *33*, 1184–1191.

Qiu, T., & Ju, G. (2010). A selective migration parallel multi-objective genetic algorithm. In *Proceedings of the Chinese Control and Decision Conference* (pp. 463-467).

Rosenberg, R. S. (1967). *Simulation of genetic populations with biochemical properties.* Ann Arbor, MI: University of Michigan.

Sahiner, B., Chan, H.-P., Petrick, N., Helvie, M. A., & Goodsitt, M. M. (1998). Design of a high-sensitivity classifier based on a genetic algorithm: Application to computer-aided diagnosis. *Physics in Medicine and Biology*, *43*(10), 2853–2871. doi:10.1088/0031-9155/43/10/014

Schaffer, J. D. (1984). *Multiple objective optimization with vector evaluated genetic algorithms.* Nashville, TN: Vanderbilt University.

Schaffer, J. D. (1985). Multiple objective optimization with vector evaluated genetic algorithms. In *Proceedings of the International Conference on Genetic Algorithm and their Applications* (pp. 93-100).

Schwehm, M. (1992). Implementation of genetic algorithms on various interconnection network. In Valero, M., Onate, E., Jane, M., Larriba, J. L., & Suarez, B. (Eds.), *Parallel computing and transputer applications* (pp. 195–203). Amsterdam, The Netherlands: IOS Press.

Sharma, J., & Jong, K. (1996). An analysis of the effects of the neighborhood size and shape on local selection algorithms. In H.-M. Voigt, W. Ebeling, I. Rechenberg, & H.-P. Schwefel (Eds.), *Proceedings of the 4th International Conference on Parallel Problem Solving from Nature* (LNCS 1141, pp. 236-244).

Shaw, K. J., & Flemming, P. J. (1996). Initial study of practical multi-objective genetic algorithms for scheduling the production of chilled ready meals. In *Proceedings of the 2nd International Mendel Conference on Genetic Algorithms*, Brno, Czech Republic (pp. 1-6).

Soh, H., & Kirley, M. (2006, July). MOPGA: Towards a new generation of multi-objective genetic algorithms. In *Proceedings of the IEEE Congress on Evolutionary Computation* (pp. 1702-1710). Washington, DC: IEEE Computer Society.

Srivastav, P. R., & Him, T.-H. (2009). Application of genetic algorithm in software testing. *International Journal of Software Engineering and its Applications, 3*(4), 87-96.

Starkweather, T., Whitley, D., & Mathias, K. (1991). Optimization using distributed genetic algorithms. In H.-P. Schwefel & R. Manner (Eds.), *Proceedings of the First Workshop on Parallel Problem Solving from Nature* (LNCS 496, pp. 176-185).

Streichert, F., Ulmer, H., & Zell, A. (2005). Parallelization of multi-objective evolutionary algorithms using clustering algorithms. In C. A. Coello Coello, A. Hernández Aguirre, & E. Zitzler (Eds.), *Proceedings of Evolutionary Multi-Criterion Optimization* (LNCS 3410, pp. 92-107).

Sundar, D., Umadevi, B., & Alagarsamy, K. (2010). Multi objective genetic algorithm for the optimized resource usage and the prioritization of the constraints in the software project planning. *International Journal of Computers and Applications, 3*(3), 1–4. doi:10.5120/718-1010

Tan, L., Taniar, D., & Smith, K. A. (2002). A new parallel genetic algorithm. In *Proceedings of the International Symposium on Parallel Architectures, Algorithms and Networks* (pp. 378-392). Washington, DC: IEEE Computer Society.

Tanese, R. (1987). Parallel genetic algorithms for a hypercube. In *Proceedings of the Second International Conference on Genetic Algorithms* (pp. 177-183).

Tanese, R. (1989). Distributed genetic algorithms. In *Proceedings of the 3rd International Conference on Genetic Algorithms* (pp. 434-439).

Tang, M., & Lau, R. Y. (2007). A parallel genetic algorithm for floorplan area optimization. In *Proceedings of the 7th International Conference on Intelligent Systems Design and Applications*, Rio, Brazil (pp. 20-24). Washington, DC: IEEE Computer Society.

Thiele, L., & Zitzler, E. (1999). Multiobjective evolutionary algorithms: A comparative case study and the strength pareto approach. *IEEE Transactions on Evolutionary Computation, 3*(4), 257–271. doi:10.1109/4235.797969

Valdhuizen, D. A., & Lamont, G. B. (2000). Multiobjective evolutionary algorithms: Analyzing the state-of-the-art. *Journal of Evolutionary Computation, 8*(2), 125–147. doi:10.1162/106365600568158

Veldhuizen, D. A. (1999). *Multiobjective evolutionary algorithms: Classifications, analyses, and new innovation. Wright-Patterson AFB*. OH: Air Force Institute of Technology.

Venkatesan, R., & Narayanswamy, R. (2003). Application of genetic algorithm and simulated annealing for optimization of extrusion die ratio and die cone angle. In *Proceedings of the 12th International Scientific Conference on Achievements in Mechanical and Material Engineering*, Gliwice, Zakopane (pp. 1001-1006).

Wang, L., Maciejewski, A. A., Siegel, H. J., Roychowdhury, V., & Eldridge, B. (2005). A study of five parallel approaches to genetic algorithm for the travelling salesman problem. *Intelligent Automation and Soft Computing, 11*(4), 217–234.

Wright, S. (1964). Stochastic processes in evolution. *Stochastic Models in Medicine and Biology*, 199-241.

Xie, G., Wang, Q., & Sunden, B. (2008). Application of a genetic algorithm for thermal design of fin-and tube heat exchangers. *Heat Transfer Engineering, 29*(7), 597–607. doi:10.1080/01457630801922337

Xu, L., Ge, Z., & Ming, H. (2009). Research of an improved parallel genetic algorithm with adjustable migration rate. *Journal of Control and Instruments in Chemical Industry, 34*(1).

Yan, L., Jumin, H., & Zhuoshang, J. (2000). A Study of genetic algorithm based on isolation niche technique. *Journal of Systems Engineering, 15*, 86–91.

Yang, W., Xiang-gen, Y., & Zhe, Z. (2009). Wide area intelligent protection system based on genetic algorithm. *Journal of Electrical and Electronics Engineering, 9*(2), 1093–1099.

Yeh, L.-J., Chang, Y.-C., & Chiu, M.-C. (2004). Application of genetic algorithm to the shape optimization of a constrained double-chamber muffler with extended tubes. *Journal of Marine Science and Technology, 12*(3), 189–199.

Yoo, M. (2009). Real-time task scheduling by multiobjective genetic algorithm. *Journal of Systems and Software, 82*(4), 619–628. doi:10.1016/j.jss.2008.08.039

Yoo, M., & Gen, M. (2007). Scheduling algorithm for real-time tasks using multiobjective hybrid genetic algorithm in heterogeneous multiprocessors system. *Computers & Operations Research, 34*(10), 3084–3098. doi:10.1016/j.cor.2005.11.016

Zebulum, R. S., Pacheco, M. A., & Vellasco, M. (1999). A multi-objective optimization methodology applied to the synthesis of low-power operational amplifiers. In *Proceedings of the 13th International Conference in Microelectronics and Packaging*, Curitiba, Brazil (pp. 264-271).

Zhang, D., Chen, Q., & Liu, J. (2007). An improved hybrid genetic algorithm for solving multi-modal function global optimization problem. In *Proceedings of the IEEE International Conference on Automation and Logistics*, Jinan, China (pp. 2486-2490). Washington, DC: IEEE Computer Society.

Zheng, Y., & Lei, D. M. (2008). New progresses and prospect of multi-objective evolutionary algorithm. In *Proceedings of the Seventh International Conference on Machine Learning and Cybernetics*, Kunming, China (pp. 962-968). Washington, DC: IEEE Computer Society.

Zhi-xin, W., & Gang, J. (2009). A parallel genetic algorithm in multi-objective optimization. In *Proceedings of the Control and Decision Conference*, Guilin, China (pp. 3497-3501).

Zhongxi, H., Xiaoqing, C., & Liangming, G. (2006). An improved multi objective evolutionary algorithm base on crowing mechanism. *Journal of National University of Defense Technology, 28*, 18–21.

Zitler, E., & Thiele, L. (1999). Multi-objective evolutionary algorithms: A comparative case study and the strength Pareto approach. *IEEE Transactions on Evolutionary Computation, 3*(4), 257–271. doi:10.1109/4235.797969

Zitzler, E., Laumanns, M., & Bleuler, S. (2004). A tutorial on evolutionary multi objective optimization. In X. Gandibluex, M. Sevaux, K. Sorenson, & V. T'kindt (Eds.), *Metaheuristics for multiobjective optimisation* (Vol. 535, 3-38). Berlin, Germany: Springer-Verlag.

Zitzler, E., Laumanns, M., & Thiele, L. (2001). *SPEA2: Improving the strength Pareto evolutionary algorithm* (Tech. Rep. No. TIK 103). Zurich, Swizerland: Computer Engineering and Networks Lab (TIK).

Zitzler, E., Laumanns, M., & Thiele, L. (2002). SPEA2: Improving the strength Pareto evolutionary algorithm for multi-objective optimization. In *Proceedings of the Evolutionary Methods for Design Optimisation and Control with Applications to Industrial Problems* (pp. 95-100).

Zitzler, E., & Thiele, L. (1998). *An evolutionary algorithm for multiobjective optimization: The strength Pareto approach*. Zurich, Switzerland: Swiss Federal Institute of Technology (ETH).

Zitzler, E., & Thiele, L. (1998). *Multiobjective optimization using evolutionary algorithms-a comparative study*. Berlin, Germany: Springer-Verlag.

Zitzler, E., Thiele, L., Laumanns, M., Fonseca, C. M., & Fonseca, V. G. (1999). Performance assessment of multiobjective optimizers: An analysis and review. *IEEE Transactions on Evolutionary Computation*, *3*(4), 257–271. doi:10.1109/4235.797969

Zydallis, J. (2003). *Building-block multiobjective genetic algorithms: Theory, analysis, and development*. Wright-Patterson AFB, OH: Air Force Institute of Technology

Zydallis, J. B., Veldhuizen, D. A., & Lamont, G. B. (1993). A statistical comparison of multi-objective evolutionary algorithms including the MOMGA-II. In E. Zitzler, L. Thiele, K. Deb, C. A. C. Coello, & D. Corne (Eds.), *Proceedings of the First International Conference on Evolutionary Multi-Criterion Optimization* (LNCS 1993, pp. 226-240).

*This work was previously published in the International Journal of Applied Evolutionary Computation, Volume 2, Issue 2, edited by Wei-Chiang Samuelson Hong, pp. 21-57, copyright 2011 by IGI Publishing (an imprint of IGI Global).*

# Chapter 7
# Experimental Study on Recent Advances in Differential Evolution Algorithm

**G. Jeyakumar**
*Amrita School of Engineering, India*

**C. Shanmugavelayutham**
*Amrita School of Engineering, India*

## ABSTRACT

*The Differential Evolution (DE) is a well known Evolutionary Algorithm (EA), and is popular for its simplicity. Several novelties have been proposed in research to enhance the performance of DE. This paper focuses on demonstrating the performance enhancement of DE by implementing some of the recent ideas in DE's research viz. Dynamic Differential Evolution (dDE), Multiple Trial Vector Differential Evolution (mtvDE), Mixed Variant Differential Evolution (mvDE), Best Trial Vector Differential Evolution (btvDE), Distributed Differential Evolution (diDE) and their combinations. The authors have chosen fourteen variants of DE and six benchmark functions with different modality viz. Unimodal Separable, Unimodal Nonseparable, Multimodal Separable, and Multimodal Nonseparable. On analyzing distributed DE and mixed variant DE, a novel mixed-variant distributed DE is proposed whereby the subpopulations (islands) employ different DE variants to cooperatively solve the given problem. The competitive performance of mixed-variant distributed DE on the chosen problem is also demonstrated. The variants are well compared by their mean objective function values and probability of convergence.*

## INTRODUCTION

Differential Evolution (*DE*), proposed by Storn and Price (1995, 1999), is a simple yet powerful evolutionary algorithm (EA) for global optimization in the continuous search domain (Price, 1999). *DE* has shown superior performance in

both widely used benchmark functions and real-world problems (Price et al., 2005; Vesterstrom & Thomsen, 2004). Like other EAs, *DE* is a population-based stochastic global optimizer employing mutation, recombination and selection operators and is capable of solving reliably nonlinear and multimodal problems. However, it has some unique characteristics that make it different from other members of the EA family. DE

DOI: 10.4018/978-1-4666-3628-6.ch007

uses a differential mutation operation based on the distribution of parent solutions in the current population, coupled with recombination with a predetermined parent to generate a trial vector (offspring) followed by a one-to-one greedy selection scheme between the trial vector and the parent. The algorithmic description of a classical *DE* is depicted in Figure 1.

*Figure 1. Algorithmic description of a classical DE*

```
Population Initialization X(0) ← { x₁(0),..,xNP(0) }
g ←0
Compute { f(x₁(g)),....f(xNP(g)) }
 while the stopping condition is false do
  for i = 1 to NP do
    yᵢ ← generatemutant(X(g))
    zᵢ ← crossover(xᵢ(g), yᵢ)
    if f(zᵢ) < f(xᵢ(g)) then
        xᵢ(g+1) ← zᵢ
    else
        xᵢ(g+1) ← xᵢ(g)
    end if
  end for
  g ← g+1
  Compute{ f(x₁(g)),......f(xNP(g))}
end while
```

Depending on the way the parent solutions are perturbed to generate a trial vector, there exist many trial vector generation strategies and consequently many *DE* variants. With seven commonly used differential mutation strategies (Montes et al., 2006), as listed in Table 1, and two crossover schemes (binomial and exponential), we get fourteen possible variants of *DE* viz. *rand/1/bin, rand/1/exp, best/1/bin, best/1/exp, rand/2/bin, rand/2/exp, best/2/bin, best/2/exp, current-to-rand/1/bin, current-to-rand/1/exp, current-to-best/1/bin, current-to-best/1/exp, rand-to-best/1/bin* and *rand-to-best/1/exp*. So far, no single DE variant has turned out to be best for all problems which is quiet understandable with regard to the No Free Lunch Theorem (David et al., 1997).

The conceptual simplicity, high convergence characteristics and robustness of *DE* has made it one of the popular techniques for real-valued parameter optimization. The algorithmic simplicity of *DE* has attracted many researchers who are actively working on its various aspects. Dynamic differential evolution, adaptive mixing of perturbation techniques, multi-objective optimization,

*Table 1. Differential mutation strategies*

| Nomenclature | Variant |
|---|---|
| rand/1 | $V_{i,c} = X_{r^1_2,c} + F(X_{r^1_2,c} - X_{r^1_2,c})$ |
| best/1 | $V_{i,c} = X_{best,c} + F(X_{r^1_2,c} - X_{r^1_2,c})$ |
| rand/2 | $V_{i,c} = X_{r^1_2,c} + F(X_{r^1_2,c} - X_{r^1_2,c} + X_{r^1_4,c} - X_{r^1_2,c})$ |
| best/2 | $V_{i,c} = X_{best,c} + F(X_{r^1_2,c} - X_{r^1_2,c} + X_{r^1_2,c} - X_{r^1_4,c})$ |
| current-to-rand/1 | $V_{i,c} = X_{i,c} + K(X_{r^1_2,c} - X_{i,c}) + F(X_{r^1_2,c} - X_{r^1_4,c})$ |
| current-to-best/1 | $V_{i,c} = X_{i,c} + K(X_{best,c} - X_{i,c}) + F(X_{r^1_2,c} - X_{r^1_2,c})$ |
| rand-to-best/1 | $V_{i,c} = X_{r^1_2,c} + K(X_{best,c} - X_{r^1_2,c}) + F(X_{r^1_2,c} - X_{r^1_2,c})$ |

high dimensional optimization, diversity enhancement and generation of multiple trial vectors, to cite but a few examples, are some of the recent advances and ideas in DE literature (Chakraborty, 2008). In this paper we demonstrate some of the ideas given in the literature.

The remainder of the paper is organized as follows. First we describe the new ideas, which are focused by us, in DE literature. After a brief review of the related works, details of the design of experiments are presented. We then discuss the simulation results and finally conclude the paper.

## RECENT ADVANCES AND IDEAS IN DE

From the point of view of population updating, DE is static i.e. DE responds to the population progress after a time lag. The whole population in *DE* remains unchanged until it is replaced by a new population. Inevitably, it results in slower convergence. To alleviate this problem, a dynamic version of *DE* called Dynamic Differential Evolution (*dDE*) has been proposed in (Qing, 2006). *dDE* updates the population dynamically and responds to any improvement immediately. The dynamic evolution mechanism in *dDE* updates both the current optimal individual with the new competitive individual (if better than the current optimal) and the non optimal individuals dynamically. Consequently, the trial vectors are always generated using the newly updated population and thus *dDE* always responds to any progress immediately. Owing to the dynamicity in population updation, the creation of every NP trial vectors is considered as one generation of *dDE* in the current work.

To increase the probability of generating fitter trial vector by each parent, multiple trial vectors generation scheme has been proposed (Montes et al., 2007; Storn, 1999). The multiple trial vector differential evolution (*mtvDE*) works as follows. At each generation, each parent vector will create

*nt* trial vectors by repeated *nt* cycles of differential mutation and crossover. After that, a tournament selection between *nt* trial vectors and their corresponding parent vector is carried out and the winner is placed in the new population.

To increase the convergence speed, instead of generating one trial vector, at each generation, and move to the selection process, it is proposed to keep generate trail vectors until the one which is better than the parent vector is found (Storn, 1999) (best trial vector DE – *btvDE*).

In order to balance the strength and weakness of the various trial vector generation strategies, they can be mixed to generate a trial vector (Qin et al., 2009) (mixing of variants -*mvDE*). This may balance the weakness of one by the strength of the other.

Owing to the fact that, unlike the other EAs, the crossover and selection operations in *DE* are local in nature, island based distributed versions of *DE* algorithm becomes a natural extension is parallel framework (Tasoulis et al., 2004; Ntipteni et al., 2006; Weber et al., 2009). For all the above mentioned fourteen *DE* variants we have implemented their equivalent island based *diDE* counterpart whereby the population is partitioned into small subsets (known as islands) each evolving independently but also exchanging (migrating) information among them to co-operatively enhance the efficacy of the *DE* variant. The island based *diDE* is characterized by the following parameter – number of islands *ni*, migration frequency *mf*, number of migrants *nm*, selection policy *sp* that decides what individual migrate, replacement policy *rp* that determines which individual(s) the migrant(s) replace and the migration topology *mt* that decides which islands can send to (or receive from) from the migrants

Little research effort has been devoted to understand these various ideas. In this paper, we extend these ideas to fourteen variants of classical *DE*, performs an empirical performance of the variants on six benchmark problems. A comparative performance analysis between *DE, dDE, mtvDE, mvDE, btvDE* and *diDE* variants and their classical counterparts on the benchmark functions has also been carried out.

The proposed algorithm, namely island based mixed variants distributed differential evolution (*mv-diDE*) employs different DE variants operating on the sub-populations (islands) evolving independently with different mutation-crossover strategies, but also exchanging solutions among them to co-operatively solve the problem at hand. Apart from the above said parameters that characterize the island based *diDE*, the choice of variants to be employed in *mv-diDE* is also crucial. In that respect, the empirical performance analysis of fourteen DE variants has provided the insight towards the choice of DE variants for the proposed *mv-diDE*. Despite the fact that a very limited set of 6 benchmark problems will not guarantee reliable conclusion, the analysis indeed give insights about the implementation issues of the new ideas.

## RELATED WORKS

Menzura-Montes et al. (2006) empirically compared the performance of eight DE variants, involving arithmetic recombination along with binomial and exponential, on unconstrained optimization problems. The study concluded *rand/1/bin, best/1/bin, current-to-rand/1/bin* and *rand/2/dir* as the most competitive variants.

Qing (2006) proposed the dynamic differential evolution in and analyzed the performance of *dDE/best/1* variant on a function minimization problem with 8, 16, 24, 50 and 100 optimization parameters and on a benchmark electromagnetic inverse scattering problem. The study concluded that *dDE* significantly outperforms the classical *DE*.

A recent study by Qing (2008) compared *dDE/rand/1/bin* and *dDE/best/1/bin* against their classical counterparts. The test bed involved around 37 test functions with dimension less than 10 and three application problems with 6, 8, 9, 16 and 24

dimensions. Only the representative results on the test bed have been presented. The work concluded *dDE/best/1/bin* as the most competitive variant among the scrutinized four strategies.

Storn (1999) explored the idea of multiple trial vectors generation for each parent, the trial vectors were generated and compared with parent vector one after another till a better trial vector than its parent vector was found. Once a fitter trial vector was found, the differential mutation and recombination operations end.

Menzura-Montes et al. (2007) used multiple trial vectors generation in DE to solve constrained optimization problems in engineering design. Five trial vectors were produced by each parent using *rand/1/bin* variant. Through a pre-selection mechanism, the best of the trial vectors was identified (based on feasibility or lowest sum of constraint violation) and made to compete against its corresponding parent vector.

Babu and Munawar (2008) compared the performance of ten variants of DE (excluding the *current-to-rand/1/\** and *current-to-best/1/\** variants of our variants suite) to solve the optimal design problem of shell-and-tube heat exchangers. They concluded *best/\*/\** strategies to be better than *rand/\*/\** strategies.

Qin, Huang, and Suganthan, recently (2009), proposed a self adaptive *DE (SaDE)* in which both trial vector generation strategies and their associated control parameter values are gradually self-adapted by learning from past experiences in generating promising solutions. Though this work does not empirically analyze the performance difference between *DE* variants, it indeed stresses the importance of understanding the efficacy of different trial vector generation strategies during different stages of evolution.

Kozlov and Samsonov (2006) proposed a new migration scheme for parallel differential evolution to achieve high speed of convergence on the test problem. The new scheme replaces the oldest members of the population than the random one, in the migration process. The results suggest that the accuracy of the final result of optimization depends on the communication period.

Tasoulis et al. (2004) implemented DE in parallel and experimentally shown that the extent of information exchange among subpopulation assigned to different processor nodes bears a significant impact on the performance of the algorithm.

Ntipteni et al. (2006) implemented a parallel asynchronous differential evolution algorithm. The asynchronous DE algorithm uses a panmictic approach – a unique population is distributed among a cluster of PCs, with master-slave architecture. Different executable programs realize the evolution of each individual of the population; the exchange of information between different individuals is performed through shared text files.

Weber et al. (2009) proposed a novel distributed differential evolution algorithm named Distribute Differential Evolution with Explorative-Exploitative Population Families (*DDE-EEPF*). In *DDE-EEPF* the sub-populations are grouped into two families. This first family of sub-population has the role of exploring the decision space and the second family is for exploitation. The results show that the proposed algorithm is efficient for most of the analyzed problems, and outperforms all the other algorithms considered in this study.

Zaharie and Petcu (2003) describe coarse-gained parallelization of an adaptive differential evolution algorithm. The parallelization is based on the multi-population model, a random connection topology being used, the results showed speedup in execution time and higher probability of convergence.

The scale factor local search differential evolution (SFLSDE) is proposed (Neri & Tirronen, 2009), it is DE based memetic algorithms, with two additional local search algorithms. The SFLSDE performs well in terms of good convergence speed Anderson quality solutions.

A new differential evolution algorithm (JADE) is proposed in Zhang and Sanderson (2009), with a new mutation strategy *DE/Current-to-pbest,* and

adaptive selection of control parameters. Two variants of JADE viz. *rand-JADE* and *nona-JADE* are experimented and compared with other DE variants. Compared to other DE algorithms and PSO, JADE showed competitive results.

Pant et al. (2009) proposed *MDE*, which uses a new mutant vector with self adaptive F (scaling factor). The results showed that the use of random variable having Laplace distribution as a scaling factor F, improves the performance of classical DE, significantly.

Thangaraj et al. (2010) performed a study by proposing five new mutation schemes for basic DE algorithm, the corresponding versions are named as MDE1, MDE2, MDE3, MDE4 and MDE5. The proposed algorithms are validated with a electrical engineering problem dealing with the optimization of directional over-current relay setting.

## DESIGN OF EXPERIMENT

In our experiment we investigate the implementation of *DE, dDE, mtvDE, mvDE, btvDE* and *diDE* algorithms to analyze the performance of fourteen variants on a set of problems with high dimensionality and different features. We have chosen six test functions (Montes et al., 2006; Yao et al., 2003), the details of the functions are presented in the Figure 2. All the test functions have an optimum value at zero except of $f_3$. In order to show the similar result, the description of $f_3$ was adjusted by adding the value 12569.486618164879 (Montes et al. 2006).

The parameters for all the variants are: population size NP = 60 and maximum number of generations = 3000. The moderate population size and number of generations were chosen to demonstrate the efficacy of all the variants in solving the chosen problems. The variants will stop before the number of generations is reached only if the tolerance error (which has been fixed as an error value of 1 x $10^{-12}$) with respect to the

*Figure 2. Description of the benchmark functions*

| |
|---|
| $f_1$ - Schwefel's Problem 2.21 |
| $f_2$ – Schwefel's Problem 1.2 |
| $f_3$ – Generalized Schwefel's Problem 2.26 <br> ; |
| $f_4$ – Generalized Restrigin's Function |
| $f_5$ - Generalized Rosenbrock's Function <br> $f_{Ros}(x) = \sum_{(i=1)}^{2} [100_{(x_i}(+1) \mid x_i \uparrow 2)\uparrow 2] + (x_i \mid 1)\uparrow 2 \mid ; 30 \le x_i) \le 30$ |
| $f_6$ - Generalized Griewank's Function |

global optimum is obtained. Following (Montes et al., 2006; Montes, personal communication), we defined a range for the scaling factor, $F \in [0.3, 0.9]$ and this value is generated anew at each generation for all variants. We use the same value for K as F. In case of *mtvDE*, for all the variants, we set *nt* to be 2 (i.e. 2 trial vectors are produced by each parent vector).

The crossover rate, CR, was tuned for each variant-test function combination. Eleven different values for the CR viz. {0.0, 0.1, 0.2, 0.3, 0.4, 0.5, 0.6, 0.7, 0.8, 0.9 and 1.0} were tested for each variant-test_function combination for *DE* variants. For each combination of variant-test_function-CR value, 50 independent runs were performed. Based on the obtained results, a bootstrap test was conducted in order to determine the confidence interval for the mean objective function value. The CR value corresponding to the best confidence interval, of 95%, was chosen to be used in our experiment. The bootstrap test was conducted separately for *DE*, *dDE* and *mtvDE* variants.

The parameter for all *diDE* and *mv-diDE* variants are: *ni*=4 (the initial population of size 60 is divided into four subpopulations of size 15), *mf*=45 (empirically decided based on previous experiments), *nm*=1, *sp*=best solution, *rp*=random solution (except the best solution) and *mt*=ring

topology. Being a preliminary study, the *diDE* and *mv-diDE* have been implemented as multi-process MPI (Message Passing Interface) applications on a single machine.

As EA's are stochastic in nature, 100 independent runs were performed per variant per test function (by initializing the population for every run with uniform random initialization within the search space). For the sake of performance analysis among the variants, we present the mean objective function values (*MOV*) and the probability of convergence ($P_c$) (Feoktistov, 2006) for each variant-test_function combination.

## RESULTS AND DISCUSSION

### Comparison between DE Variants

The simulation results for the classical DE variants are presented in Tables 2 and 3. The mean object function value of 100 independent runs is measured for each variant-function combination. The results, Table 2, show that the most competitive variants are *rand/1/bin, rand/2/bin, best/2/bin* and *rand-to-best/1/bin*. *best/1/bin* also equally as good as the other competitive variants, except for $f_5$. On the other hand the worst results were

*Table 2. MOV measured for DE variants*

| Variant | $f_1$ | $f_2$ | $f_3$ | $f_4$ | $f_5$ | $f_6$ |
|---|---|---|---|---|---|---|
| rand/1/bin | 0.00 | 0.07 | 0.13 | 0.00 | 21.99 | 0.00 |
| rand/1/exp | 3.76 | 0.31 | 0.10 | 47.93 | 25.48 | 0.05 |
| best/1/bin | 1.96 | 13.27 | 0.00 | 4.33 | 585899.88 | 3.72 |
| best/1/exp | 37.36 | 57.39 | 0.01 | 50.74 | 64543.84 | 5.91 |
| rand/2/bin | 0.06 | 1.64 | 0.22 | 0.00 | 19.01 | 0.00 |
| rand/2/exp | 32.90 | 269.86 | 0.27 | 101.38 | 2741.32 | 0.21 |
| best/2/bin | 0.00 | 0.00 | 0.17 | 0.69 | 2.32 | 0.00 |
| best/2/exp | 0.05 | 0.00 | 0.08 | 80.63 | 1.12 | 0.03 |
| current-to-rand/1/bin | 3.68 | 3210.36 | 0.14 | 37.75 | 52.81 | 0.00 |
| current-to-rand/1/exp | 57.52 | 3110.90 | 0.12 | 235.14 | 199243.32 | 1.21 |
| current-to-best/1/bin | 3.71 | 3444.00 | 0.19 | 37.04 | 56.91 | 0.00 |
| current-to-best/1/exp | 56.67 | 2972.62 | 0.10 | 232.80 | 119685.68 | 1.21 |
| rand-to-best/1/bin | 0.00 | 0.07 | 0.22 | 0.00 | 17.37 | 0.00 |
| rand-to-best/1/exp | 3.38 | 0.20 | 0.12 | 48.09 | 24.54 | 0.05 |

*Table 3. Successful runs and $P_c$(%) for DE variants*

| Variant | $f_1$ | $f_2$ | $f_3$ | $f_4$ | $f_5$ | $f_6$ | nc | $P_c$ (%) |
|---|---|---|---|---|---|---|---|---|
| rand/1/bin | 100 | 73 | 4 | 100 | 100 | 0 | 377 | 62.83 |
| rand/1/exp | 0 | 4 | 7 | 0 | 68 | 0 | 79 | 13.17 |
| best/1/bin | 79 | 86 | 88 | 3 | 1 | 0 | 257 | 42.83 |
| best/1/exp | 0 | 58 | 85 | 0 | 0 | 0 | 143 | 23.83 |
| rand/2/bin | 0 | 0 | 1 | 100 | 100 | 0 | 201 | 33.50 |
| rand/2/exp | 0 | 0 | 2 | 0 | 3 | 0 | 5 | 0.83 |
| best/2/bin | 100 | 100 | 1 | 47 | 100 | 38 | 386 | 64.33 |
| best/2/exp | 1 | 100 | 17 | 0 | 44 | 29 | 191 | 31.83 |
| current-to-rand/1/bin | 0 | 0 | 2 | 0 | 96 | 0 | 98 | 16.33 |
| current-to-rand/1/exp | 0 | 0 | 3 | 0 | 0 | 0 | 3 | 0.50 |
| current-to-best/1/bin | 0 | 0 | 3 | 0 | 96 | 0 | 99 | 16.50 |
| current-to-best/1/exp | 0 | 0 | 5 | 0 | 0 | 0 | 5 | 0.83 |
| rand-to-best/1/bin | 100 | 79 | 0 | 100 | 100 | 0 | 379 | 63.17 |
| rand-to-best/1/exp | 0 | 10 | 6 | 0 | 69 | 0 | 85 | 14.17 |

provided by the variants *best/1/exp, current-to-best/1/exp* and *current-to-rand/1/exp. best/2/exp* is comparatively better than other "exp" variants. The other variants viz. *rand/1/exp, rand/2/exp, rand-to-best/1/exp, current-to-best/1/bin* and *current-to-rand/1/bin* were continuously shown

different performances. It is worth noting that binomial recombination showed a better performance over the exponential recombination. Function $f_5$ was not solved by any variant.

The probability of convergence ($P_c$), the percentage of successful runs to total runs, is calculated for each variant-function combination. This measure identifies variants having higher convergence capability to global optimum. It is calculated as the mean percentage of number of successful runs out of total runs i.e $P_c = (nc / nt)\%$ where $nc$ is total number of successful runs made by each variant for all the functions and $nt$ is total number of runs, in our experiment $nt = 6 * 100 = 600$.

The convergence probability measured for the variants are shown in Table 3. As can be seen from the tables, the competitive variants identified earlier viz. *best/2/bin, rand-to-best/1/bin* and *rand/1/ bin* have higher probability of convergence. The worst performing variants *rand/1/exp, current-to-best/1/exp, current-to-rand/1/exp* and *rand/2/ exp* were found to have the least probability of convergence. It is worth noting that binomial variants have given overall more number of successful runs that that of exponential variants.

## Comparing *DE* and *dDE* Variants

The simulation results for comparing *DE* and *dDE* is presented in Table 4. For the function $f_1$, It is interesting to note that the best and worst

performance were provided by similar set of *DE* and *dDE* variants. Except for three variants showing moderate performance, in all other cases *dDE* performs better than *DE* in terms of *MOV*. The top 4 variants of $f_1$ displayed similar high performance in the case of $f_2$ too and, for $f_2$, all *dDE* variants have outperformed their classical counterparts. The superiority of *dDE* is evident in the case of worst performing variants, in $f_1$ and $f_2$. In case of $f_3$, *dDE* performs better than *DE* in most of the variants. In case of $f_4$, */rand-to-best/1/bin* and */rand/1/ bin* have once again emerged as best performing variants along with */rand/2/bin*. *dDE* variants still maintain an edge over the classical counterparts in performance. Test function $f_5$ was not solved by any variant. However, */best/2/** variants have displayed relatively better performance. Interestingly */best/1/** and */rand/2/exp* variants have also shown poor performance in both the cases (*DE* and *dDE*). In case of $f_6$ also, *dDE* performs better than *DE* in most of the variants. It is worth noting that the *dDE* variants have consistently outperformed the *DE* variants in terms of mean objective function value.

The probability of convergence measured for each variant also presented in Table 4. As can be

*Table 4. MOV and $P_c(\%)$ comparison for DE and dDE variants*

| Variant | $f_1$ | $f_2$ | $f_3$ | $f_4$ | $f_5$ | $f_6$ | $P_c(\%)$ |
|---|---|---|---|---|---|---|---|
| *rand/1/bin* | 0.00/0.00 | 0.07/0.00 | 0.13/0.15 | 0.00/0.00 | 21.99/17.20 | 0.00/0.00 | 62.83/64.67 |
| *rand/1/exp* | 3.76/3.32 | 0.31/0.13 | 0.10/0.11 | 47.93/47.67 | 25.48/41.34 | 0.05/0.05 | 13.17/13.5 |
| *best/1/bin* | 1.96/1.81 | 13.27/0.00 | 0.00/0.00 | 4.33/3.63 | 585899.88/32747.01 | 3.72/2.64 | 42.83/30.33 |
| *best/1/exp* | 37.36/9.40 | 57.39/0.00 | 0.01/4.46 | 50.74/52.06 | 64543.84/449714.63 | 5.91/5.11 | 23.83/29.67 |
| *rand/2/bin* | 0.06/0.05 | 1.64/1.71 | 0.22/0.21 | 0.00/0.00 | 19.01/16.17 | 0.00/0.00 | 33.51/33.67 |
| *rand/2/exp* | 32.90/31.34 | 269.86/233.07 | 0.27/0.23 | 101.38/102.78 | 2741.32/1877.42 | 0.21/0.19 | 0.83/1.33 |
| *best/2/bin* | 0.00/0.00 | 0.00/0.00 | 0.17/0.10 | 0.69/0.65 | 2.32/1.87 | 0.00/0.00 | 64.33/67.33 |
| *best/2/exp* | 0.05/0.04 | 0.00/0.00 | 0.08/0.07 | 80.63/79.78 | 1.12/0.78 | 0.03/0.03 | 31.83/36.33 |
| *current-to-rand/1/bin* | 3.68/3.70 | 3210.36/61.85 | 0.14/0.14 | 37.75/37.49 | 52.81/56.68 | 0.00/0.14 | 16.33/0.83 |
| *current-to-rand/1/exp* | 57.52/52.10 | 3110.90/62.17 | 0.12/0.10 | 235.14/232.59 | 199243.32/254655.74 | 1.21/1.21 | 0.51/0.00 |
| *current-to-best/1/bin* | 3.71/3.77 | 3444.00/61.54 | 0.19/0.11 | 37.04/38.26 | 56.91/56.01 | 0.00/0.00 | 16.51/16.17 |
| *current-to-best/1/exp* | 56.67/51.63 | 2972.62/63.70 | 0.10/0.12 | 232.80/232.94 | 119685.68/271844.82 | 1.21/1.22 | 0.83/1.17 |
| *rand-to-best/1/bin* | 0.00/0.00 | 0.07/0.01 | 0.22/0.13 | 0.00/0.00 | 17.37/15.92 | 0.00/0.00 | 63.17/65.00 |
| *rand-to-best/1/exp* | 3.38/3.48 | 0.20/0.14 | 0.12/0.09 | 48.09/47.40 | 24.54/32.52 | 0.05/0.06 | 14.17/11.67 |

seen from the table, the competitive variants identified earlier viz. */best/2/bin, */rand-to-best/1/bin and */rand/1/bin have higher probability of convergence. The worst performing variants */current-to-best/1/exp, */current-to-rand/1/exp and */rand/2/exp were found to have the least probability of convergence. It is worth noting that dDE variants have higher probability of convergence compared to classical DE variants, irrespective of their recombination type.

## Comparing DE and mtvDE Variants

The simulation results for comparing DE and mtvDE for all the test functions are presented in Table 5. For the function $f_1$, $f_2$ and $f_6$, the best

and worst performance were provided by similar set of DE and mtvDE variants. It is interesting to note that all the mtvDE variants outperform their classical counterpart, except mtvDE/best/1/bin and mtvDE/best/1/exp. In case of $f_3$ the best performance is provided by */best/1/bin and mtvDE/best/1/exp variants, and all the mtvDE variants perform better than the DE variants In case of $f_4$, */rand/1/bin and */rand-to-best/1/bin have once again emerged as best performing variants along with */rand/2/bin. Test function $f_5$ was not solved by any variant. However, */best/2/* and mtvDE/rand/2/bin variants have displayed relatively better performance.

Based on the overall results in 4 and 5 the most competitive variants were */rand-to-best/1/bin,

*Table 5. MOVand $P_c$(%) Comparison for DE and mtvDE variants*

| Variant | $f_1$ | $f_2$ | $f_3$ | $f_4$ | $f_5$ | $f_6$ | $P_c$ (%) |
|---|---|---|---|---|---|---|---|
| rand/1/bin | 0.00/0.00 | 0.07 / 0.00 | 0.13 / 0.07 | 0.00 / 0.00 | 21.99 / 5.77 | 0.00 / 0.00 | 62.83/68.50 |
| rand/1/exp | 3.76/0.92 | 0.31 / 0.00 | 0.10 / 0.21 | 47.93 /10.72 | 25.48 / 6.23 | 0.05 / 0.02 | 13.17/32.50 |
| best/1/bin | 1.96 / 11.99 | 13.27 / 44.32 | 0.00 / 0.00 | 4.33 / 3.73 | 585899.88 / 727417.29 | 3.72 / 4.74 | 42.83/30.67 |
| best/1/exp | 37.36 / 50.54 | 57.39 / 178.88 | 0.01 / 0.00 | 50.74 / 52.49 | 64543.84 / 37552.84 | 5.91 / 13.09 | 23.83/15.50 |
| rand/2/bin | 0.06 / 0.00 | 1.64 / 0.00 | 0.22 / 0.10 | 0.00 / 0.00 | 19.01 / 0.66 | 0.00 / 0.00 | 33.50/68.17 |
| rand/2/exp | 32.90 / 13.28 | 269.86 / 1.47 | 0.27 / 0.10 | 101.38 / 121.26 | 2741.32 / 204.31 | 0.21 / 0.08 | 0.83/1.33 |
| best/2/bin | 0.00 / 0.00 | 0.00 / 0.00 | 0.17 / 0.04 | 0.69 / 1.16 | 2.32 / 0.84 | 0.00 / 0.00 | 64.33/71.00 |
| best/2/exp | 0.05 / 0.00 | 0.00 / 0.00 | 0.08 / 0.02 | 80.63 / 38.98 | 1.12 / 0.84 | 0.03 / 0.02 | 31.83/58.50 |
| current-to-rand/1/bin | 3.68 / 0.59 | 3210.36 / 139.42 | 0.14 / 0.06 | 37.75 / 14.28 | 52.81 / 28.84 | 0.00 / 0.00 | 16.33/17.50 |
| current-to-rand/1/exp | 57.52 / 49.20 | 3110.90 / 227.42 | 0.12 / 0.06 | 235.14 / 207.61 | 199243.32 / 47153.21 | 1.21 / 0.36 | 0.50/0.83 |
| current-to-best/1/bin | 3.71 / 0.23 | 3444.00 / 132.64 | 0.19 / 0.05 | 37.04 / 13.56 | 56.91 / 30.88 | 0.00 / 0.00 | 16.50/18.50 |
| current-to-best/1/exp | 56.67 / 49.68 | 2972.62 / 268.08 | 0.10 / 0.10 | 232.80 / 207.22 | 119685.68 / 41046.61 | 1.21 / 0.38 | 0.83/1.17 |
| rand-to-best/1/bin | 0.00 / 0.00 | 0.07 / 0.00 | 0.22 / 0.06 | 0.00 / 0.00 | 17.37 / 5.68 | 0.00 / 0.00 | 63.17/68.67 |
| rand-to-best/1/exp | 3.38 / 0.97 | 0.20 / 0.00 | 0.12 / 0.07 | 48.09 / 10.80 | 24.54 / 8.00 | 0.05 / 0.03 | 14.16/32.00 |

*/best/2/bin* and */rand/1/bin*. The variants */rand/2/bin* and */best/2/exp* variants also showed good performance consistently. On the other hand, the worst overall performance were consistently displayed by the variants */current-to-best/1/exp* and */current-to-rand/1/exp*. The variants */best/1/bin* and */rand/2/exp* were also displaying poor performance. */best/1/** variants show good performance for multimodal separable function. It is also worth noting that the relatively better performance of *mtvDE* over *DE* in all the test functions may largely be attributed to the increased number of function evaluations available to *mtvDE*. As a matter of fact, when in some representative runs, both *DE* and *mtvDE* were allowed precisely the same number of fitness evaluations, both displayed similar high performance capability.

The convergence probability for both *DE* and *mtvDE* variants were calculated separately and the results are shown in Table 5. As can be seen from the table, the competitive variants identified earlier have higher probability of convergence. The worst performing variants were found to have the least probability of convergence. It is worth noticing that, *mtvDE* variants have higher probability of convergence compared to classical *DE* variants.

## Comparing *DE* and *mvDE* Variants

Next we compared *DE* and *mvDE* variants. As a preliminary study, we mixed every "*bin*" variant with its corresponding "*exp*" variant. The experiment was carried out with two levels of mixing, called as 30:30 mixing and 45:15 mixing. In 30:30 mixing, of given population size 60, 30 trail vectors are generated by a "*bin*" variant and 30 are by its corresponding "*exp*" variants. In 45:15 mixing, 45 trial vectors are generated by "*bin*" variant and 15 by "*exp*" variant. The variants are compared by their *MOV* and *Pc*, the simulation results for *MOV* are presented in Tables 6 and 7. It is worth noticing that in all the cases the *mvDE* variants

*Table 6. MOV Comparison for DE and mvDE variants for $f_1$, $f_2$, $f_3$ and $f_4$*

| Variant | $f_1$ | | | $f_2$ | | | $f_3$ | | | $f_4$ | | |
|---|---|---|---|---|---|---|---|---|---|---|---|---|
| | DE | 30:30 | 45:45 | DE | 30:30 | 45:45 | DE | 30:30 | 45:45 | DE | 30:30 | 45:45 |
| rand/1/bin | 0.00 | 1.56 | 0.11 | 0.07 | 0.00 | 0.00 | 0.13 | 0.16 | 0.15 | 0.00 | 10.94 | 0.00 |
| rand/1/exp | 3.76 | | | 0.31 | | | 0.10 | | | 47.93 | | |
| best/1/bin | 1.96 | 4.37 | 0.68 | 13.27 | 1.83 | 4.37 | 0.00 | 0.03 | 0.15 | 4.33 | 0.68 | 0.95 |
| best/1/exp | 37.36 | | | 57.39 | | | 0.01 | | | 50.74 | | |
| rand/2/bin | 0.06 | 20.33 | 11.09 | 1.64 | 51.92 | 10.36 | 0.22 | 0.23 | 0.26 | 0.00 | 23.14 | 12.03 |
| rand/2/exp | 32.90 | | | 269.86 | | | 0.27 | | | 101.38 | | |
| best/2/bin | 0.00 | 10.50 | 1.20 | 0.00 | 218.59 | 0.12 | 0.17 | 0.11 | 0.09 | 0.69 | 17.83 | 1.78 |
| best/2/exp | 0.05 | | | 0.00 | | | 0.08 | | | 80.63 | | |
| current-to-rand/1/bin | 3.68 | 15.26 | 8.86 | 3210.36 | 4393.22 | 4115.76 | 0.14 | 0.17 | 0.14 | 37.75 | 32.82 | 35.40 |
| current-to-rand/1/exp | 57.52 | | | 3110.90 | | | 0.12 | | | 235.14 | | |
| current-to-best/1/bin | 3.71 | 14.97 | 8.83 | 3444.00 | 4276.26 | 4074.71 | 0.19 | 0.15 | 0.27 | 37.04 | 33.37 | 35.25 |
| current-to-best/1/exp | 56.67 | | | 2972.62 | | | 0.10 | | | 232.80 | | |
| rand-to-best/1/bin | 0.00 | 1.25 | 0.11 | 0.07 | 0.00 | 0.00 | 0.22 | 0.15 | 0.13 | 0.00 | 10.64 | 0.00 |
| rand-to-best/1/exp | 3.38 | | | 0.20 | | | 0.12 | | | 48.09 | | |

*Table 7. MOV Comparison for DE and mvDE variants for $f_5$ and $f_6$*

| Variant | $f_5$ | | | $f_6$ | | |
|---|---|---|---|---|---|---|
| | DE | 30:30 | 45:45 | DE | 30:30 | 45:45 |
| *rand/1/bin* | 21.99 | 7.76 | 5.60 | 0.00 | 0.00 | 0.00 |
| *rand/1/exp* | 25.48 | | | 0.05 | | |
| *best/1/bin* | 585899.88 | 2039.25 | 51.12 | 3.72 | 0.00 | 0.00 |
| *best/1/exp* | 64543.84 | | | 5.91 | | |
| *rand/2/bin* | 19.01 | 36.39 | 135.33 | 0.00 | 0.12 | 0.02 |
| *rand/2/exp* | 2741.32 | | | 0.21 | | |
| *best/2/bin* | 2.32 | 2725.20 | 1.20 | 0.00 | 1.03 | 0.00 |
| *best/2/exp* | 1.12 | | | 0.03 | | |
| *current-to-rand/1/bin* | 52.81 | 565.24 | 151.27 | 0.00 | 0.73 | 0.02 |
| *current-to-rand/1/exp* | 199243.32 | | | 1.21 | | |
| *current-to-best/1/bin* | 56.91 | 411.52 | 134.70 | 0.00 | 0.71 | 0.02 |
| *current-to-best/1/exp* | 119685.68 | | | 1.21 | | |
| *rand-to-best/1/bin* | 17.37 | 9.18 | 6.58 | 0.00 | 0.00 | 0.00 |
| *rand-to-best/1/exp* | 24.54 | | | 0.05 | | |

are performing better than their corresponding "*exp*" variants. On the other hand, only in few cases the *mvDE* variants showed its superiority than its corresponding "*bin*" variants. Comparatively, in 45:15 mixing, the *mvDE* variants are performing better than the case of 30:30 mixing. The *Pc(%)* measured for *DE* and *mvDE* variants are presented in Table 8. It shows the 45:15 mixing gives more number of successful runs than that of 30:30 mixing. In limited number of cases, *mvDE* variants have shown higher probability of convergence than their *DE* counterparts. This analysis can still be extended further by mixing different mutation strategies

## Comparing *DE*, *mtvDE* and Other Combinations

Next in our experiment, we focused more on *mtvDE* variants. It was observed that, they outperform their counterpart at the cost of more number of function evaluations. In case of *DE*, the maximum

number of function evaluations was 1,80,000. On the other hand for *mtvDE*, since at each generation it generates two trial vectors (i.e $nt=2$), the maximum number of function evaluations was 3,60,000.

The number function evaluations performed by *mtvDE* variants are *nt* times of the function evaluations done by their classical DE counterpart variants. It is essential that both *mtvDE* and *DE* are to be allowed precisely the same number of function evaluations (or else the comparison is not fair).

To investigate on this point, we restricted *mtvDE* variants to have maximum of 1,80,000 function evaluations (and hence allowed to take maximum of 1500 generations). Now the *DE* variants with 3000 generations (*DE3000G* Variants) are compared with *mtvDE* variants with 1500 generations (*mtvDE1500G* Variants), by their MOV, in Table 9. The results shows that only for 25% of variant-tes_function combinations the *mtvDE1500G* variants could perform better than

*Table 8. $P_c$(%) Comparison for DE and mvDE variants (1. DE, 2. 30:30 mvDE and 3. 45:15 mvDE)*

| Variant | $f_1$ | | | $f_2$ | | | $f_3$ | | | $f_4$ | | | $f_5$ | | | $f_6$ | | |
|---|---|---|---|---|---|---|---|---|---|---|---|---|---|---|---|---|---|---|
| | 1 | 2 | 3 | 1 | 2 | 3 | 1 | 2 | 3 | 1 | 2 | 3 | 1 | 2 | 3 | 1 | 2 | 3 |
| rand/1/bin | 100 | 0 | 0 | 73 | 98 | 100 | 4 | 4 | 0 | 100 | 0 | 100 | 0 | 0 | 1 | 100 | 88 | 100 |
| rand/1/exp | 0 | | | 4 | | | 7 | | | 0 | | | 0 | | | 68 | | |
| best/1/bin | 79 | 0 | 0 | 86 | 7 | 97 | 88 | 34 | 54 | 3 | 39 | 46 | 0 | 1 | 0 | 1 | 86 | 91 |
| best/1/exp | 0 | | | 58 | | | 85 | | | 0 | | | 0 | | | 0 | | |
| rand/2/bin | 0 | 0 | 0 | 0 | 0 | 0 | 1 | 2 | 1 | 100 | 0 | 0 | 0 | 0 | 0 | 100 | 53 | 5 |
| rand/2/exp | 0 | | | 0 | | | 2 | | | 0 | | | 0 | | | 3 | | |
| best/2/bin | 100 | 0 | 0 | 100 | 0 | 3 | 1 | 6 | 12 | 47 | 0 | 1 | 38 | 0 | 0 | 100 | 0 | 98 |
| best/2/exp | 1 | | | 100 | | | 17 | | | 0 | | | 29 | | | 44 | | |
| current-to-rand/1/bin | 0 | 0 | 0 | 0 | 0 | 0 | 2 | 2 | 8 | 0 | 0 | 0 | 0 | 0 | 0 | 96 | 0 | 7 |
| current-to-rand/1/exp | 0 | | | 0 | | | 3 | | | 0 | | | 0 | | | 0 | | |
| current-to-best/1/bin | 0 | 0 | 0 | 0 | 0 | 0 | 3 | 3 | 3 | 0 | 0 | 0 | 0 | 0 | 0 | 96 | 0 | 14 |
| current-to-best/1/exp | 0 | | | 0 | | | 5 | | | 0 | | | 0 | | | 0 | | |
| rand-to-best/1/bin | 100 | 0 | 0 | 79 | 99 | 100 | 0 | 8 | 4 | 100 | 0 | 100 | 0 | 1 | 2 | 100 | 89 | 100 |
| rand-to-best/1/exp | 0 | | | 10 | | | 6 | | | 0 | | | 0 | | | 69 | | |

their *DE3000G* variants, and also this observation is not pertaining to any particular variant. And hence, it is worth noting that *mtvDE* variants are failing to show their superiority (if it is restricted to maximum of 1,80,000 function evaluations).

To experiment further on *mtvDE*, with the objective of bringing superiority to *mtvDE1500G* variants, we formed few combinations of above discussed advances in DE. The following combinations were experimented:

- *mtv_dDE*: Combining *dDE* and *mtvDE*
- *mtv_mv_dDE*: Combining *dDE*, *mtvDE* and *mvDE*
- *mtv_btv_dDE*: Combining *dDE*, *mtvDE* and *btvDE*
- *mtv_btv_DE*: Combining *DE*, *mtvDE* and *btvDE*

For our further experiments, we set the maximum number of function evaluations to 1,80,000 (and hence the maximum number of generations is to 1500). The comparison between *DE*, *mtv_dDE*, *mtv_mv_dDE*, *mtv_btv_dDE* and *mtv_btv_DE* variants is done by their MOV and $P_c$(%). The results are presented in Tables 10, 11, 12, 13 and 14.

For the unimodal separable function, $f_1$, it is observed from the results, Table 10, that the *mtv_btv_DE* variants are showing superior performance, they are competitive than other variants, in the case of "*exp*" variants, except of *mtv_btv_DE* variants. For the *DE/rand/1/exp*, *DE/best/1/bin* and *DE/best/1/exp* the *mtv_dDE* variants are performing better than their *DE* counterparts. The *mtv_mv_dDE* variants are showing competitive performance than all its "*exp*" counterparts, except of *DE/best/1/exp* and *DE/best/2/exp*. For the unimodal nonseparable, $f_2$, results, Table 11, shows

*Table 9. MOV Comparison for DE and mtvDE1500G variants*

| Variant | $f_1$ | $f_2$ | $f_3$ | $f_4$ | $f_5$ | $f_6$ | $P_c$ (%) |
|---|---|---|---|---|---|---|---|
| *rand/1/bin* | 0.00/ 0.00 | 0.07/ 1.01 | 0.13/ 0.14 | 0.00/ 0.00 | 21.99/ 19.01 | 0.00/ 0.00 | 62.83/ 61.67 |
| *rand/1/exp* | 3.76/ 3.97 | 0.31/ 0.21 | 0.10/ 0.14 | 47.93/ 49.94 | 25.48/ 24.00 | 0.05/ 0.08 | 13.17/ 10.67 |
| *best/1/bin* | 1.96/ 13.05 | 13.27/ 29.69 | 0.00/ 0.00 | 4.33/ 3.80 | 585899.88/ 613734.96 | 3.72/ 4.93 | 42.83/ 20.00 |
| *best/1/exp* | 37.36/ 47.21 | 57.39/ 1537.12 | 0.01/ 0.00 | 50.74/ 51.18 | 64543.84/ 77422.90 | 5.91/ 10.80 | 23.83/ 14.33 |
| *rand/2/bin* | 0.06/ 0.09 | 1.64/ 1.25 | 0.22/ 0.16 | 0.00/ 0.00 | 19.01/ 20.56 | 0.00/ 0.00 | 33.50/ 33.67 |
| *rand/2/exp* | 32.90/ 34.35 | 269.85/ 252.30 | 0.27/ 0.20 | 101.38/ 165.82 | 2741.32/ 8617.88 | 0.21/ 0.21 | 0.83/ 0.67 |
| *best/2/bin* | 0.00/ 0.00 | 0.00/ 0.00 | 0.17/ 0.07 | 0.69/ 23.75 | 2.32/ 4.08 | 0.00/ 0.00 | 64.33/ 54.83 |
| *best/2/exp* | 0.05/ 0.07 | 0.00/ 0.00 | 0.08/ 0.05 | 80.63/ 79.88 | 1.12/ 3.03 | 0.03/ 0.02 | 31.83/ 28.50 |
| *current-to-rand/1/ bin* | 3.68/ 5.86 | 3210.36/ 3446.33 | 0.14/ 0.14 | 37.75/ 38.50 | 52.81/ 65.31 | 0.00/ 0.00 | 16.33/ 16.17 |
| *current-to-rand/1/ exp* | 57.52/ 56.69 | 3110.90/ 2993.30 | 0.12/ 0.12 | 235.14/ 236.10 | 199243.32/ 103651.84 | 1.21/ 1.24 | 0.50/ 1.71 |
| *current-to-best/1/ bin* | 3.71/ 3.79 | 3444.00/ 3340.89 | 0.19/ 0.22 | 37.04/ 38.64 | 56.91/ 57.02 | 0.00/ 0.00 | 16.50/ 16.50 |
| *current-to-best/1/ exp* | 56.67/ 57.94 | 2972.62/ 2935.55 | 0.10/ 0.11 | 232.80/ 233.61 | 119685.68/ 246754.55 | 1.21/ 1.26 | 0.83/ 0.83 |
| *rand-to-best/1/bin* | 0.00/ 0.00 | 0.07/ 0.05 | 0.22/ 0.23 | 0.00/ 0.00 | 17.37/ 19.16 | 0.00/ 0.00 | 63.17/ 62.00 |
| *rand-to-best/1/exp* | 3.38/ 4.12 | 0.20/ 0.17 | 0.12/ 0.10 | 48.09/ 50.19 | 24.54/ 28.80 | 0.05/ 0.05 | 14.17/ 13.33 |

*mtv_btv_DE* variants shows superior performance than *DE* variants in case the cases of *DE/best/1/ bin* and *DE/best/1/exp*. For the arithmetic variants viz., *DE/current-to-rand/1/\** and *DE/current-to-best/1/\**, the *mtv_dDE* and *mtv_btv_dDE* variants have outperformed their *DE* counterparts.

Comparatively *mtv_btv_dDE* variants are showing good results. In most of the cases, the *mtv_mv_dDE* have given competitive performance than their corresponding "*bin*" and "*exp*" variants.

The results are shown in Table 12 for the multimodal separable functions $f_3$ and $f_4$. In the case of $f_3$, the *mtv_dDE* and *mtv_btv_dDE* variants have outperformed their *DE* variants. As in

the case of unimodal functions, for multimodal separable case also the *mtv_mv_dDE* variants are performing better than their corresponding "*bin*" and "*exp*" variants. The similar trend of performance is observed in the case of $f_4$ also.

The results for the multimodal nonseparable functions $f_5$ and $f_6$ are shown in Table 13. In the case of $f_5$, the *mtv_mv_DDE* variants are outperforming only their "*exp*" *DE* counterparts. The *mtv_dDE* variants are outperforming *DE/rand/1/bin*, *DE/ best/1/bin*, *DE/rand/2/bin*, *DE/rand/2/exp*, *DE/ current-to-rand/1/exp* and *DE/current-to-best/1/ bin*. But the superiority of *mtv_mv_dDE* and *mtv_mv_DE* variants is evident only in the cases

*Table 10. MOV Comparison for 1.DE, 2. mtv_dDE, 3.mtv_mv_dDE, 4.mtv_btv_dDE and 5.mtv_btv_DE variants for unimodal seprable function - $f_1$*

| Variant | 1 | 2 | 3 | 4 | 5 |
|---|---|---|---|---|---|
| *rand/1/bin* | 0.00 | 0.00 | 0.03 | 0.01 | 0.16 |
| *rand/1/exp* | 3.76 | 3.68 |  | 2.36 | 0.02 |
| *best/1/bin* | 1.96 | 0.92 | 5.96 | 7.52 | 0.04 |
| *best/1/exp* | 37.36 | 2.67 |  | 1.82 | 0.11 |
| *rand/2/bin* | 0.06 | 0.07 | 0.03 | 0.33 | 1.94 |
| *rand/2/exp* | 32.90 | 33.01 |  | 27.15 | 5.26 |
| *best/2/bin* | 0.00 | 0.00 | 6.82 | 0.05 | 0.13 |
| *best/2/exp* | 0.05 | 0.05 |  | 0.34 | 0.13 |
| *current-to-rand/1/bin* | 3.68 | 5.80 | 14.16 | 7.59 | 12.85 |
| *current-to-rand/1/exp* | 57.52 | 57.75 |  | 52.52 | 44.56 |
| *current-to best/1/bin* | 3.71 | 3.76 | 41.23 | 7.73 | 12.95 |
| *current-to-best/1/exp* | 56.67 | 56.76 |  | 52.41 | 44.77 |
| *rand-to-best/1/bin* | 0.00 | 0.00 | 0.07 | 0.00 | 0.01 |
| *rand-to-best/1/exp* | 3.38 | 3.64 |  | 2.45 | 0.32 |

*Table 11. MOV Comparison for 1.DE, 2. mtv_dDE, 3.mtv_mv_dDE, 4.mtv_btv_dDE and 5.mtv_btv_DE variants for unimodal nonseparable function $f_2$*

| Variant | 1 | 2 | 3 | 4 | 5 |
|---|---|---|---|---|---|
| *rand/1/bin* | 0.07 | 2.36 | 0.00 | 0.14 | 251.74 |
| *rand/1/exp* | 0.31 | 0.22 |  | 0.20 | 22.03 |
| *best/1/bin* | 13.27 | 65.59 | 1.95 | 587.86 | 0.00 |
| *best/1/exp* | 57.39 | 1602.79 |  | 363.99 | 0.00 |
| *rand/2/bin* | 1.64 | 2.60 | 18125.79 | 1.95 | 27973.58 |
| *rand/2/exp* | 269.86 | 280.27 |  | 313.48 | 2688.85 |
| *best/2/bin* | 0.00 | 0.00 | 28.47 | 29.79 | 0.05 |
| *best/2/exp* | 0.00 | 0.00 |  | 0.00 | 0.01 |
| *current-to-rand/1/bin* | 3210.36 | 3268.59 | 977.76 | 123.08 | 2346.85 |
| *current-to-rand/1/exp* | 3110.90 | 2923.59 |  | 118.47 | 2427.42 |
| *current-to-best/1/bin* | 3444.00 | 3342.17 | 958.44 | 126.94 | 2372.56 |
| *current-to-best/1/exp* | 2972.62 | 2931.93 |  | 117.72 | 2475.62 |
| *rand-to-best/1/bin* | 0.07 | 0.05 | 2329.55 | 0.37 | 198.02 |
| *rand-to-best/1/exp* | 0.20 | 0.23 |  | 0.37 | 22.05 |

of limited DE variants. But for $f_6$, classical *DE* variants outperform others, in most of the cases.

All the above observations are reiterated by calculating the probability convergence, presented in Table 14. The standard deviation of the objective function values achieved by *DE, dDE, mtvDE* and *mvDE* variants (for 100 runs) is measured, it is presented in Table 19. Overall, it is observed from

*Table 12. MOV Comparison for 1.DE, 2. mtv_dDE, 3.mtv_mv_dDE, 4.mtv_btv_dDE and 5.mtv_btv_DE variants for multimodal separable functions - $f_3$ and $f_4$*

| $f_3$ | | | | | |
|---|---|---|---|---|---|
| **Variant** | **1** | **2** | **3** | **4** | **5** |
| *rand/1/bin* | 0.13 | 0.13 | 0.10 | 0.16 | 0.78 |
| *rand/1/exp* | 0.10 | 0.09 | | 0.09 | 1.09 |
| *best/1/bin* | 0.00 | 0.00 | 0.00 | 0.00 | 0.10 |
| *best/1/exp* | 0.01 | 0.01 | | 0.00 | 0.06 |
| *rand/2/bin* | 0.22 | 0.19 | 0.11 | 0.17 | 1.30 |
| *rand/2/exp* | 0.27 | 0.18 | | 0.22 | 1.30 |
| *best/2/bin* | 0.17 | 0.08 | 0.01 | 828.59 | 86.75 |
| *best/2/exp* | 0.08 | 0.09 | | 0.08 | 1.46 |
| *current-to-rand/1/bin* | 0.14 | 0.13 | 0.17 | 0.14 | 2.15 |
| *current-to-rand/1/exp* | 0.12 | 0.13 | | 0.15 | 0.75 |
| *current-to-best/1/bin* | 0.19 | 0.17 | 0.13 | 0.10 | 0.78 |
| *current-to-best/1/exp* | 0.10 | 0.12 | | 0.11 | 1.42 |
| *rand-to-best/1/bin* | 0.22 | 0.17 | 0.11 | 0.11 | 1.42 |
| *rand-to-best/1/exp* | 0.12 | 0.09 | | 0.10 | 2.03 |

*Table 13. MOV Comparison for 1.DE, 2. mtv_DDE, 3.mtv_mv_DDE, 4.mtv_btv_DDE and 5.mtv_btv_DE variants for multimodal nonseparable functions - $f_5$ and $f_6$*

| $f_5$ | | | | | |
|---|---|---|---|---|---|
| **V** | **1** | **2** | **3** | **4** | **5** |
| *rand/1/bin* | 21.99 | 16.68 | 16.88 | 17.98 | 23.32 |
| *rand/1/exp* | 25.48 | 47.73 | | 58.99 | 23.32 |
| *best/1/bin* | 585899.88 | 29858.67 | 370.45 | 51698.29 | 2.56 |
| *best/1/exp* | 64543.84 | 115326.34 | | 1600619.62 | 89408.91 |
| *rand/2/bin* | 19.01 | 18.99 | 20.09 | 21.22 | 11500.10 |
| *rand/2/exp* | 2741.32 | 783.62 | | 5296.34 | 2856.21 |
| *best/2/bin* | 2.32 | 2.80 | 78121.75 | 3.17 | 25.83 |
| *best/2/exp* | 1.12 | 2.34 | | 2.82 | 13.25 |
| *current-to-rand/1/bin* | 52.81 | 59.39 | 14016.93 | 59.45 | 89.36 |
| *current-to-rand/1/exp* | 199243.32 | 151042.70 | | 316839.61 | 1684118.68 |
| *current-to-best/1/bin* | 56.91 | 53.91 | 11024.39 | 56.53 | 94.70 |
| *current-to-best/1/exp* | 119685.68 | 247953.23 | | 222417.92 | 353079.70 |
| *rand-to-best/1/bin* | 17.37 | 17.64 | 20.56 | 16.92 | 24.53 |
| *rand-to-best/1/exp* | 24.54 | 63.00 | | 24.91 | 44.13 |

*Table 14. Pc(%) Comparison for 1.DE, 2. mtv_dDE, 3.mtv_mv_dDE, 4.mtv_btv_dDE and 5.mtv_btv_DE variants*

| Sno | Variant | 1 | 2 | 3 | 4 | 5 |
|---|---|---|---|---|---|---|
| 1 | *rand/1/bin* | 62.83 | 64.67 | 52.00 | 52.00 | 33.83 |
| 2 | *rand/1/exp* | 13.17 | 12.00 | | 11.67 | 23.83 |
| 3 | *best/1/bin* | 42.83 | 35.33 | 32.50 | 15.50 | 49.17 |
| 4 | *best/1/exp* | 23.83 | 11.50 | | 16.00 | 39.67 |
| 5 | *rand/2/bin* | 33.50 | 33.83 | 34.50 | 33.67 | 16.33 |
| 6 | *rand/2/exp* | 0.83 | 1.67 | | 16.50 | 4.17 |
| 7 | *best/2/bin* | 64.33 | 58.00 | 24.17 | 29.83 | 29.83 |
| 8 | *best/2/exp* | 31.83 | 32.33 | | 29.17 | 35.17 |
| 9 | *current-to-rand/1/bin* | 16.33 | 16.50 | 0.67 | 0.17 | 0.33 |
| 10 | *current-to-rand/1/exp* | 0.50 | 0.50 | | 0.67 | 0.33 |
| 11 | *current-to-best/1/bin* | 16.50 | 16.50 | 0.83 | 16.50 | 10.33 |
| 12 | *current-to-best/1/exp* | 0.83 | 0.50 | | 0.33 | 0.83 |
| 13 | *rand-to-best/1/bin* | 63.17 | 64.50 | 18.33 | 61.83 | 47.83 |
| 14 | *rand-to-best/1/exp* | 14.17 | 1.83 | | 22.17 | 25.83 |
| | Total | 38.47 | 34.97 | 16.3 | 30.60 | 31.75 |

*Table 15. MOV obtained for DE and diDE variants*

| Variant | $f_1$ | $f_2$ | $f_3$ | $f_4$ | $f_5$ | $f_6$ |
|---|---|---|---|---|---|---|
| | **DE**/ *diDE* | **DE**/ *diDE* | **DE**/ *diDE* | **DE**/ *diDE* | **DE**/ *diDE* | **DE**/ *diDE* |
| *rand/1/bin* | 0.00/ 0.00 | 0.07 / 2.55 | 0.13/ 0.09 | 0.00 / 0.00 | 21.99 / 38.82 | 0.00 / 0.00 |
| *rand/1/exp* | 3.76/ 3.23 | 0.31 / 0.00 | 0.10/ 0.08 | 47.93 / 10.54 | 25.48 / 34.32 | 0.05 / 0.01 |
| *best/1/bin* | 1.96 / 0.04 | 13.27/ 0.00 | 0.00/ 0.00 | 4.33 / 0.90 | 585899.88/ 35.48 | 3.72 / 0.00 |
| *best/1/exp* | 37.36 / 9.68 | 57.39 / 0.00 | 0.01/ 0.00 | 50.74 / 36.39 | 64543.84 / 196.97 | 5.91 / 0.41 |
| *rand/2/bin* | 0.06 / 0.00 | 1.64 / 0.05 | 0.22 / 0.01 | 0.00 / 0.01 | 19.01 / 21.34 | 0.00 / 0.00 |
| *rand/2/exp* | 32.90 / 7.56 | 269.86 / 0.25 | 0.27 / 0.09 | 101.38/ 17.73 | 2741.32 / 25.82 | 0.21 / 0.01 |
| *best/2/bin* | 0.00 / 0.00 | 0.00 / 0.00 | 0.17/ 0.0.4 | 0.69 / 0.63 | 2.32 / 4.05 | 0.00 / 0.00 |
| *best/2/exp* | 0.05 / 0.89 | 0.00 / 0.00 | 0.08/ 0.05 | 80.63 / 29.52 | 1.12 / 6.19 | 0.03 / 0.01 |
| *current-to-rand/1/bin* | 3.68 / 0.64 | 3210.36/ 13.79 | 0.14/ 0.22 | 37.75 / 9.02 | 52.81 / 41.18 | 0.00 / 0.00 |
| *current-to-rand/1/exp* | 57.52 / 20.56 | 3110.90/ 22.20 | 0.12/ 0.23 | 235.14/ 134.19 | 199243.32/ 433.25 | 1.21 / 0..18 |
| *current-to-best/1/bin* | 3.71 / 0.65 | 3444.00/ 13.62 | 0.19/ 0.31 | 37.04 / 9.50 | 56.91 / 40.56 | 0.00 / 0.00 |
| *current-to-best/1/exp* | 56.67 / 20.01 | 2972.62/ 28.07 | 0.10/ 0.22 | 232.80/ 131.13 | 119685.68/ 276.23 | 1.21 / 0.19 |
| *rand-to-best/1/bin* | 0.00 / 0.00 | 0.07 / 0.22 | 0.22/ 0.23 | 0.00 / 0.00 | 17.37 / 27.49 | 0.00 / 0.00 |
| *rand-to-best/1/exp* | 3.38 / 2.84 | 0.20 / 0.02 | 0.12/ 0.04 | 48.09 / 9.98 | 24.54 / 31.52 | 0.05 / 0.01 |

the results in Table 10, 11, 12, 13, 14 and 19 that, comparatively, the *mtv_btv_dDE* and *mtv_btv_DE* are able to outperform their *DE* counterparts.

## Comparing *DE* and *diDE* Variants

The simulation results for the 14 DE variants and their island based *diDE* counterparts are presented in Table 15 and Table 16. As can be seen from the Table 15, the most competitive variants are *rand-to-best/1/bin, best/2/bin* and *rand/1/bin*. The variants *rand/2/bin* and *best/2/exp* also showed good performance consistently. On the other hand

the worst overall performances were consistently displayed by variants *current-to-best/1/exp* and *current-to-rand/1/exp*. The variants *best/1/exp* and *current-to-rand/1/bin* were also displaying poor performance.

Table 15 also shows the performance of island based *diDE* variants on the chosen six benchmark functions. As is clearly evident form the table, in most of the cases *diDE* variants outperformed their serial counterparts. This is evident in the case of worst performing variants also.

Table 16 shows, in most of the cases, *diDE* variants display increased probability of conver-

*Table 16. Number of successful runs and probability of convergence ($P_c$) for DE and diDE variants*

| Variant | DE/*diDE* | | | | | | |
|---|---|---|---|---|---|---|---|
| | $f_1$ | $f_2$ | $f_3$ | $f_4$ | $f_5$ | $f_6$ | Pc (%) |
| *rand/1/bin* | 100/ 100 | 73/ 5 | 4/ 4 | 100/ 100 | 0/ 3 | 100/ 100 | 62.83/52 |
| *rand/1/exp* | 0/ 0 | 4/ 68 | 7/ 55 | 0/ 0 | 0/ 1 | 68/ 70 | 13.17/32.33 |
| *best/1/bin* | 79/ 8 | 86/ 100 | 88/ 75 | 3/ 39 | 0/ 4 | 1/ 100 | 42.83/54.33 |
| *best/1/exp* | 0/ 0 | 58/ 100 | 85/ 82 | 0/ 0 | 0/ 0 | 0/ 2 | 23.83/30.67 |
| *rand/2/bin* | 0/ 5 | 0/ 90 | 1/ 93 | 100/ 100 | 0/ 1 | 100/ 100 | 33.50/64.83 |
| *rand/2/exp* | 0/ 0 | 0/ 5 | 2/ 72 | 0/ 0 | 0/ 0 | 3/ 70 | 0.83/24.5 |
| *best/2/bin* | 100/ 100 | 100/ 100 | 1/ 90 | 47/ 51 | 38/ 18 | 100/ 100 | 64.33/76.55 |
| *best/2/exp* | 1/ 0 | 100/ 100 | 17/ 62 | 0/ 0 | 29/ 13 | 44/ 57 | 31.83/38.67 |
| *current-to-rand/1/bin* | 0/ 0 | 0/ 0 | 2/ 3 | 0/ 0 | 0/ 0 | 96/ 92 | 16.33/15.83 |
| *current-to-rand/1/exp* | 0/ 0 | 0/ 0 | 3/ 24 | 0/ 0 | 0/ 0 | 0/ 0 | 0.5/6.16 |
| *current-to-best/1/bin* | 0/ 0 | 0/ 0 | 3/ 1 | 0/ 0 | 0 /0 | 96/ 100 | 16.50/16.83 |
| *current-to-best/1/exp* | 0/ 0 | 0/ 0 | 5/ 29 | 0/ 0 | 0/ 0 | 0/ 0 | 0.83/6.5 |
| *rand-to-best/1/bin* | 100/ 100 | 79/ 7 | 0/ 1 | 100/ 100 | 0/ 3 | 100/ 100 | 63.16/51.83 |
| *rand-to-best/1/exp* | 0/ 0 | 10/ 86 | 6/ 57 | 0/ 0 | 0/ 0 | 69/ 66 | 14.17/34.83 |

*Table 17. Speedup Measurement*

| Function | Average Execution Time | | Speedup (%) |
|---|---|---|---|
| | *DE* (sec) | *diDE* (sec) | |
| $f_1$ | 0.56 | 0.20 | 64.75% |
| $f_2$ | 1.22 | 0.35 | 71.76% |
| $f_3$ | 1.20 | 0.32 | 73.68% |
| $f_4$ | 1.32 | 0.29 | 77.85% |
| $f_5$ | 0.60 | 0.20 | 66.77% |
| $f_6$ | 1.37 | 0.32 | 76.82% |

gence. The table presents the number of successful runs made by each variant for each function and the probability of convergence. As can be shown from the table, for all the variants their parallel implementation have improved their probability of convergence, except for *DE/rand/1/bin, DE/rand-to-best/1/bin* and *DE/current-to-rand/1/bin*.

Despite the fact that *diDE* variants have been implemented as multi-process MPI applications on a single machine, we have observed improvement in average execution time as well, as shown in Table 17.

*Table 18. MOV and $P_c$ obtained for DE, diDE and mv-diDE Variants*

| Function | Variant | MOV | | | Pc (%) | | |
|---|---|---|---|---|---|---|---|
| | | **DE** | *diDE* | *mv-diDE* | **DE** | *diDE* | *mv-diDE* |
| $f_1$ | *rand/1/bin* | 0.0000 | 0.0000 | 0.0000 | 100 | 100 | 100 |
| | *rand/2/bin* | 0.0559 | 0.0075 | | 0 | 5 | |
| | *best/2/bin* | 0.0000 | 0.0000 | | 100 | 100 | |
| | *rand-to-best/1/bin* | 0.0000 | 0.0000 | | 100 | 100 | |
| $f_2$ | *rand/1/bin* | 0.0729 | 2.5516 | 0.0006 | 73 | 5 | 100 |
| | *rand/2/bin* | 1.6441 | 0.0543 | | 0 | 90 | |
| | *best/2/bin* | 0.0000 | 0.0000 | | 100 | 100 | |
| | *rand-to-best/1/bin* | 0.0691 | 0.2189 | | 79 | 7 | |
| $f_3$ | *rand/1/bin* | 0.1349 | 0.0899 | 0.0194 | 4 | 4 | 86 |
| | *rand/2/bin* | 0.2237 | 0.0085 | | 1 | 93 | |
| | *best/2/bin* | 0.1709 | 0.0386 | | 1 | 90 | |
| | *rand-to-best/1/bin* | 0.2178 | 0.2393 | | 0 | 1 | |
| $f_4$ | *rand/1/bin* | 0.0000 | 0.0000 | 0.0000 | 100 | 100 | 100 |
| | *rand/2/bin* | 0.0000 | 0.0100 | | 100 | 100 | |
| | *best/2/bin* | 0.6940 | 0.6268 | | 47 | 51 | |
| | *rand-to-best/1/bin* | 0.0000 | 0.0000 | | 100 | 100 | |
| $f_5$ | *rand/1/bin* | 21.9868 | 38.8159 | 13.9187 | 0 | 3 | 17 |
| | *rand/2/bin* | 19.0076 | 21.3438 | | 0 | 1 | |
| | *best/2/bin* | 2.3167 | 4.0566 | | 38 | 18 | |
| | *rand-to-best/1/bin* | 17.3714 | 27.4891 | | 0 | 3 | |
| $f_6$ | *rand/1/bin* | 0.0000 | 0.0000 | 0.0000 | 100 | 100 | 100 |
| | *rand/2/bin* | 0.0000 | 0.0000 | | 100 | 100 | |
| | *best/2/bin* | 0.0000 | 0.0000 | | 100 | 100 | |
| | *rand-to-best/1/bin* | 0.0000 | 0.0000 | | 100 | 100 | |

## Comparing *DE, diDE* and *mv-diDE* Variants

Since the variants *rand/1/bin, rand/2/bin, best/2/bin* and *rand-to-best/1/bin* emerged as competitive variants with good performance, we employed these four variants to operate on the four islands to evolve independently but also exchange their solutions. The performance of *mv-diDE* against that of the individual variants and their *diDE* counterparts are shown Table 18. It is observed from the results that the performance of *mv-dDE* is equally competitive with that of the constituent *DE* and *dDE* variants. It is worth noting that reported performance has been achieved with little tuning on the part of both *diDE* and *mv-diDE*. It suggests that the cooperative co-evolution of the variants bringing changes in the exploration and exploitation capabilities of the individual variants. The one could balance its weakness by the strength of the other one.

Next, we analyzed the convergence nature of the *DE, diDE* and *mv-diDE* variants. We measured function error value, which is the difference between the global optimum and the current objective function value, denoted as $f(x)$-$f(x^*)$, for every generation. The Figure 3 shows the graphs for the number of generations Vs the error value ($f(x)$-$f(x^*)$), for a random run for the functions $f_3$ and $f_4$ for the variant *rand/2/bin*. It shows how the variant *rand/2/bin* converges in its *DE, diDE* and *mv-diDE* implementation. As it can be seen from the graph the *mv-diDE* implementation of the variants converges faster than other implementations.

The obtained results show that the variants of *dynamic differential evolution, mixed variant differential evolution, distributed differential evolution* are competitive than their *DE* counterpart variants, with faster convergence. The superiority of *mixed variant distributed differential evolution* variant is still more evident than other variants.

*Table 19. Comparison of Standard Deviation for DE, dDE, mtvDE and mvDE variants*

| $f_1$ | | | | | $f_2$ | | | | | $f_3$ | | | | |
|---|---|---|---|---|---|---|---|---|---|---|---|---|---|---|
| DE | dDE | mtvDE | mvDE 30:30 | mvDE 45:15 | DE | dDE | mtvDE | mvDE 30:30 | mvDE 45:15 | DE | dDE | mtvDE | mvDE 30:30 | mvDE 45:15 |
| 0.00 | 0.00 | 0.00 | 2.11 | 0.03 | 0.42 | 0.01 | 0.00 | 0.00 | 0.00 | 0.13 | 0.01 | 0.12 | 0.14 | 0.16 |
| 2.11 | 2.13 | 1.53 | | | 0.56 | 0.18 | 0.00 | | | 0.13 | 0.02 | 1.55 | | |
| 5.00 | 1.80 | 11.92 | 1.76 | 1.73 | 99.04 | 0.00 | 211.08 | 8.45 | 34.18 | 0.01 | 0.02 | 0.00 | 0.05 | 0.03 |
| 18.26 | 10.37 | 12.95 | | | 337.34 | 0.00 | 160.39 | | | 0.02 | 0.02 | 0.00 | | |
| 0.01 | 0.01 | 0.00 | 1.31 | 1.29 | 2.12 | 1.37 | 0.00 | 32.72 | 6.40 | 0.21 | 0.03 | 0.10 | 0.24 | 0.34 |
| 5.57 | 5.14 | 2.86 | | | 151.06 | 122.03 | 1.14 | | | 0.28 | 0.03 | 0.10 | | |
| 0.00 | 0.00 | 0.00 | 0.95 | 0.25 | 0.00 | 0.00 | 0.00 | 174.94 | 0.15 | 0.20 | 0.02 | 0.06 | 0.12 | 0.11 |
| 0.04 | 0.03 | 0.00 | | | 0.00 | 0.00 | 0.00 | | | 0.18 | 0.02 | 0.03 | | |
| 0.38 | 0.40 | 0.08 | 1.57 | 0.85 | 619.01 | 14.27 | 38.25 | 913.78 | 773.92 | 0.14 | 0.03 | 0.05 | 0.18 | 0.17 |
| 5.16 | 3.81 | 4.66 | | | 1104.15 | 15.55 | 128.52 | | | 0.11 | 0.02 | 0.05 | | |
| 0.41 | 0.36 | 0.03 | 1.66 | 0.88 | 792.04 | 13.17 | 36.37 | 947.81 | 818.87 | 0.20 | 0.02 | 0.12 | 0.20 | 0.87 |
| 5.16 | 4.05 | 5.00 | | | 1023.46 | 14.35 | 134.31 | | | 0.11 | 0.02 | 0.07 | | |
| 0.00 | 0.00 | 0.00 | 1.36 | 0.03 | 0.40 | 0.04 | 0.00 | 0.00 | 0.00 | 0.20 | 0.02 | 0.09 | 0.37 | 0.14 |
| 1.59 | 1.95 | 1.63 | | | 0.35 | 0.23 | 0.00 | | | 0.13 | 0.02 | 0.21 | | |

*Figure 3. Number of Generations Vs the error value (f(x)-f(x*)), for a random run of functions f₃ and f₄ for the variant In Figure 4(a) and 4(b) the convergence speed of mv-diDE implementation of the variant rand/2/bin is shown for the function f₃ and f₄, where the mean error value is measured as the average error values of 100 runs. The superiority of mv-diDE variants is still evident.*

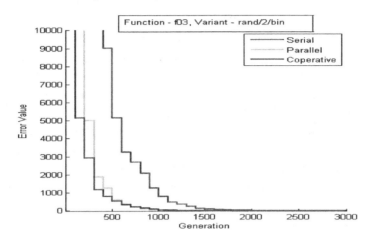

*3 (a)*

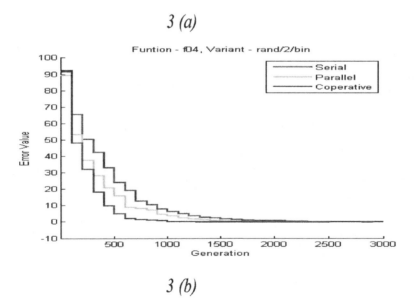

*3 (b)*

## CONCLUSION

In this paper we presented an empirical performance analysis of fourteen variants of *DE* against the recent advances in *DE* viz Dynamic DE, Multiple Trial Vector DE, Mixed Variant DE, Best Trail Vector DE and Distributed DE. The variants were tested on 6 test functions of dimension 30, grouped by their modality and decomposability. The experiments identified */best/2/bin, */rand-to-best/1/bin* and */rand/1/ bin* variants as the most competitive variants in terms of the mean objective function values. The worst performing variants were */current-to-best/1/exp, */current-to-rand/1/exp* and */ rand/2/exp. In fact the calculation of probability

*Figure 4. Number of Generations Vs the mean error value (f(x)-f(x\*)), for 100 runs of functions $f_3$ and $f_4$ for the variant rand/2/bin.*

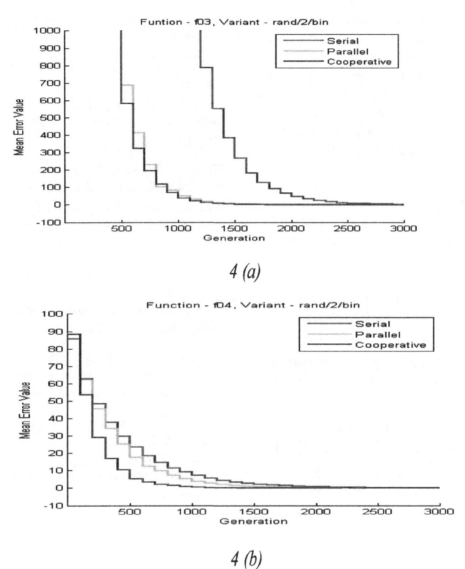

4 (a)

4 (b)

of convergence reiterated the observation about the performance of above said variants. The *dDE* variants have often outperformed *DE* variants and consistently showed superior performance. The *mtvDE* variants also outperformed *DE* variants, but at the cost of more number of function evaluations. Also, we attempted to make *mtvDE* variants to maintain their superiority, even with restricted number of maximum number

of function evaluation, by some possible combinations of the algorithmic superiority of the chosen advances with *mtvDE*. In general, it is observed that the combination of *dDE*, *mtvDE* and *btvDE* shows superior performance than others. The island based *diDE* variants were observed to outperform the serial counterparts in most of the cases. The proposed *mv-diDE* which employs different DE variants in the subpopulations cooperatively evolves to solve the problem in hand. The *DE* variants (*rand/1/bin, rand/2/bin, best/2/bin* and *rand-to-best/1/bin*) with competitive good performance were identified. The *mv-diDE* with the identified 4 variants displays competitive performance against the constituent *DE* and *diDE* variants. Our future work would involve validating above observations by testing the variants on a larger suite of test functions, with more statistical tests.

# REFERENCES

Babu, B. V., & Munawar, S. A. (2001). *Optimal design of shell-and-tube heat exchanges by different strategies of differential evolution (Tech. Rep. No. PILANI -333 031)*. Rajasthan, India: Birla Institute of Technology and Science.

Chakraborty, U. K. (Ed.). (2008). *Advances in differential evolution, studies in computational intelligence series (Vol. 143)*. New York, NY: Springer.

Feoktistov, V. (2006). *Differential evolution in search of solutions*. New York, NY: Springer.

Kozlov, K. N., & Samsonov, A. M. (2006). New migration scheme for parallel differential evolution. In *Proceedings of the Fifth International Conference on Bioinformatics of Genome Regulation and Structure* (pp. 141-144).

Montes, E. M., Coello, C. A. C., Velazquez-Reyes, J., & Muñoz-Davila, L. (2007). Multiple trial vectors in differential evolution for engineering design. *Engineering Optimization, 39*(5), 567–589. doi:10.1080/03052150701364022

Montes, E. M., Velazquez-Reyes, J., & Coello, C. A. C. (2006). A comparative study on differential evolution variants for global optimization. In *Proceedings of the 8th Annual Conference on Genetic and Evolutionary Computation* (pp. 1397-1398).

Neri, F., & Tirronen, V. (2009). Scale factor local search in differential evolution. *Memetic Computation, 1*, 153–171. doi:10.1007/s12293-009-0008-9

Ntipteni, M. S., Valakos, I. M., & Nikolos, I. K. (2006). An asynchronous parallel differential evolution algorithms. In *Proceedings of the International Conference on Design Optimization and Application*.

Pant, M., Thangaraj, R., Abraham, A., & Grosan, C. (2009). Differential evolution with laplace mutation operator. In *Proceedings of the IEEE Congress on Evolutionary Computation* (pp. 2841-2849).

Price, K. V. (1999). An introduction to differential evolution. In Corne, D., Dorigo, M., & Glover, F. (Eds.), *New ideas in optimization* (pp. 79–108). New York, NY: McGraw-Hill.

Price, K. V., Storn, R., & Lampinen, J. A. (2005). *Differential evolution: A practical approach to global optimization*. Berlin, Germany: Springer-Verlag.

Qin, A. K., Huang, V. L., & Suganthan, P. N. (2009). Differential evolution algorithm with stratefy adapdation for global numerical optimization. *IEEE Transactions on Evolutionary Computation, 13*(2), 398–417. doi:10.1109/TEVC.2008.927706

Qing, A. (2006). Dynamic differential evolution strategy and applications in electromagnetic inverse scattering problems. *IEEE Transactions on Geoscience and Remote Sensing, 44*(1).

Qing, A. (2008). A study on base vector for differential evolution. In *Proceedings of the IEEE World Congress on Computational Intelligence and Evolutionary Computation* (pp. 550-556).

Storn, R. (1999). System design by constraint adaptation and differential evolution. *IEEE Transactions on Evolutionary Computation, 3*(1), 22–34. doi:10.1109/4235.752918

Storn, R., & Price, K. (1995). *Differential evolution – a simple and efficient adaptive scheme for global optimization over continuous spaces* (Technical Report TR-95-012). Berkeley, CA: International Computer Science Institute.

Storn, R., & Price, K. (1997). Differential evolution – a simple and efficient heuristic strategy for global optimization and continuous spaces. *Journal of Global Optimization, 11*(4), 341–359. doi:10.1023/A:1008202821328

Tasoulis, D. K., Pavliis, N. G., Plagianakos, V. P., & Vrahatis, M. N. (2004). Parallel differential evolution. In *Proceedings of the IEEE Congress on Evolutionary Computation.*

Thangaraj, R., Pant, M., & Abraham, A. (2010). New mutation schemes for differential evolution algorithm and their application to the optimization of directional over-current relay settings. *Applied Mathematics and Computation, 216*, 532–544. doi:10.1016/j.amc.2010.01.071

Vesterstrom, J., & Thomsen, R. A. (2004). Comparative study of differential evolution particle swarm optimization and evolutionary algorithm on numerical benchmark problems. In. *Proceedings of the IEEE Congress on Evolutionary Computation, 3*, 1980–1987.

Weber, M., Neri, F., & Tirronen, V. (2009). Distributed differential evolution with explorative-exploitative population families. In. *Proceedings of the Genetic Programming and Evolvable Machine, 10*, 343–371. doi:10.1007/s10710-009-9089-y

Wolpert, D. H., & Macreedy, G. (1997). No free lunch theorems for optimization. *IEEE Transactions on Evolutionary Computation, 1*(1), 67–82. doi:10.1109/4235.585893

Yao, X., Liu, Y., Liang, K. H., & Lin, G. (2003). Fast evolutionary algorithms. In Rozenberg, G., Back, T., & Eiben, A. (Eds.), *Advances in evolutionary computing: Theory and applications* (pp. 45–94). New York, NY: Springer.

Zaharie, D., & Petcu, D. (2003). Parallel implementation of multi-population differential evolution. In Grigoras, D., & Nicolau, A. (Eds.), *Concurrent information processing and computing* (pp. 262–269). Amsterdam, The Netherlands: IOS Press.

Zhang, J., & Sanderson, A. C. (2009). JADE: Adaptive differential evolution with optional external archive. *IEEE Transactions on Evolutionary Computation, 13*(5), 945–958. doi:10.1109/TEVC.2009.2014613

*This work was previously published in the International Journal of Applied Evolutionary Computation, Volume 2, Issue 2, edited by Wei-Chiang Samuelson Hong, pp. 58-81, copyright 2011 by IGI Publishing (an imprint of IGI Global).*

# Chapter 8
# The Volatility for Pre and Post Global Financial Crisis:
## An Application of Computational Finance

**Shih-Yung Wei**
*National Yunlin University of Science & Technology, Taiwan*

**Jen-Tseng Chen**
*TransWorld University, Taiwan*

**Jack J. W. Yang**
*National Yunlin University of Science & Technology, Taiwan*

**Wei-Chiang Hong**
*Oriental Institute of Technology, Taiwan*

## ABSTRACT

*The asymmetric volatility, temporary volatility, and permanent volatility of financial asset returns have attracted much interest in recent years. However, a consensus has not yet been reached on the causes of them for both the stocks and markets. This paper researched asymmetric volatility and short-run and long-run volatility through global financial crisis for eight Asian markets. EGARCH and CGARCH models are employed to deal with the daily return to examine the degree of asymmetric volatility (temporary volatility and permanent volatility). The authors find that after global financial crisis asymmetric volatility is lower (expect Hong Kong), and the long-run effect is more than the short-run effect. The empirical results for the short-run show that, after global financial crisis, there is significant decreasing in China and Taiwan but not in Japan; the others are significantly increasing. For the long-run, there is significant decreasing (except Thailand and Korea).*

## 1. INTRODUCTION

The phenomenon of asymmetric volatility refers to a situation when new information often causes price change. When new information is positive, future price volatility is smaller; on the contrary,

when new information is negative, future price volatility is greater (Chelley-Steeley & Steeley, 1996; Hung, 1997; Laopodis, 1997; Yang, 2000).

Asymmetric volatility is firstly observed in stock market research. Black (1976) examines data and firstly finds that current returns have a negative correlation with future volatility. Christie (1982) and Schwert (1990) also find the same results. Based on these studies, it can be assumed

DOI: 10.4018/978-1-4666-3628-6.ch008

that when new information results in the falling of stock prices, then, the financial leverage of companies will be rose; in other words, the risk of holding a stock will be increased, and future returns will be more volatile. On the other hand, when new information causes stock price to be rose, the financial leverage of companies will be decreased, and future returns will be less volatile. This phenomenon is called the leverage effect. However, Sentana and Wadhwani (1992) assume that the phenomenon of asymmetric volatility is due to herding behaviors by traders; while Lo and MacKinlay (1987) consider it as resulting from non-synchronous trading. It is still not conclusive whether asymmetric volatility of stock return values is caused by leverage effects or not.

In the empirical modeling, when dealing with high-frequency financial data, Engle (1982) establishes the ARCH model (autoregressive conditional hetroskedasticity) to solve self-relative and hetroskedasticity problems. Bollerslev (1986) extends it into the GARCH model (generalized ARCH) to describe the phenomenon of volatility clustering of returns. However, the GARCH model cannot distinguish the difference of volatility between positive and negative information (the phenomenon of the violability asymmetries), thus, Nelson (1991) develops the exponential GARCH model (EGARCH) to distinguish this difference; Campbell and Hentschel (1992) distribute the asymmetric volatility by the quadratic GARCH model (QGARCH). Later, Engle and Ng (1993) compare these two models and find that the EGARCH model has a better distribution, and Hafner (1998) proves that, with empirical data, the EGARCH model is better at distributing the volatility of high-frequency data. In addition, the EGARCH model is widely applied to high-frequency data; therefore, this research uses the EGARCH model to discuss the asymmetric volatility of stock returns.

As to the persistence of stock return volatility, Ding and Granger (1996), Ding, Granger, and Engle (1993) and Engle, Granger, and Robins (1986) all proclaim that volatility contains high persistence and it can have long memory behavior or be fractionally integrated. In the volatility model, long memory behavior can be divided into two parts, an approximate unit root and a quick reduction with time. French, Schwert, and Stambaugh (1987), Chou (1988), Pagan and Schwert (1990) and Bollerslev, Engle, and Nelson (1994), extend these two parts into a more complicated academic process, and conclude it to a permanent and transitory volatility. Permanent volatility can be regard as long-run volatility, while transitory volatility can be considered short-run volatility. The distinguishing feature of these two types of volatility is that short-run volatility is faster mean-reverting compared to long-run volatility. Besides, the model of component GARCH has been widely used in the empirical analysis. Christoffersen, Jacobs, and Wang (2008) analyze the volatility of the option by long-run and short-run effects; they find that the biased estimate of the volatility of the option can be decreased. Tobias and Rosenberg (2008) also think the risks at stock markets can be influenced by short-run and long-run volatility, and even if the mean of the risk premium is smaller than the long-run volatility effect, the important factor is that the return of the volatility for size and the book-to-market ratio can be influenced by short-run volatility effect. According to the above, we claim that the volatility of return has long-run and short-run effects. Hence, this research uses the CGARCH model to discuss long-run and short-run effects of volatility.

This paper extends the lemma of heterogeneous expectation made by Hogan and Melvin (1994) and Tse and Tsui (1997), considering that the more the government interferes in the stock market, the more heterogeneous expectations there are; thus, asymmetric volatility is more significant. That is to say, government's interference and the asymmetric volatility should exhibit positive relations. Other researchers like Ding and Granger (1996), Ding, Granger, and Engle (1993), and Engle, Granger, and Robins (1986) all declare that volatility has high constancy, which can divide the volatility into two sections long memory and fractionally integrated. They also discuss about the long-run and short-run effects of volatility after the government's deduction of the price limit policy is carried out.

This paper contains four parts. The second part presents the data and methodology, adopting the EGARCH and CGARCH Analysis to assess which of the eight Asian countries an influence on the daily return asymmetric volatility and the effects of the long-run and short-run on the stock market. The third part presents the empirical results. The fourth part is the summary and conclusions.

## 2. DATA AND METHODOLOGY

### 2.1. Data and Descriptive Statistics

The paper employs daily closing prices for the stock indexes of Hong Kong, Singapore, Japan, Malaysia, Thailand, Korea, China, and Taiwan. The names of the indexes used are shown in Table 1.

The data are retrieved from the Taiwan Economic Journal Data. The principal methodology of this study is applying EGARCH and component GARCH models. Due to the suggestion from Skinner (1989) that a minimum of five hundred observations is necessary to ensure reliable esti-

mation with the EGARCH model. Therefore, the research period of the study extends from June 1, 2006 to December 31, 2010.

Two sub-periods, pre and post the global financial crisis, are compared with each other based on the nature of stock market volatility. The global financial crisis has been in September 15, 2008, the per- global financial crisis period covering from June 1, 2006 to September 14, 2008, and the per- global financial crisis period covering from September 15, 2008 to December 31, 2010.

Figure 1 illustrates the daily stock price movements for eight markets. Evident from the plot, these eight markets almost experience a drastic fall in stock price around September 2008.

The return for each market is calculated as the percent logarithmic difference in the 30-minutes stock index, i.e.,

$$R_t = \ln\left(\frac{P_t}{P_{t-1}}\right) \times 100$$

where $R_t$ and $P_t$ stand for the market return and price for each 30-minutes, respectively. In the continuous compounding factor, return descriptive statistics of two sub-periods and the number of observations are exhibited in Table 2. The skewness statistics ($S$) indicates that all return series are either negatively or positively skewed.

*Table 1. Stock market index and the period of the research*

| Country | The name of stock market | Per- | POST |
|---|---|---|---|
| Hong Kong | Hong Kong-Hang Seng Index | 2006/6/1~2008/9/14 | 2008/9/15~2010/12/31 |
| Singapore | Singapore FTSE Straits Times Index | | |
| Japan | Tokyo Topix Stock Indexes | | |
| Malaysia | Kuala Lumpur-Composite Stock Index | | |
| Thailand | Stock Exch of Thaiidex | | |
| Korea | South Korea-Kospi Index | | |
| China | Shanghai Synthesis Stock Index | | |
| Taiwan | Taiwan Security Exchange Corporation-Weighted Stock Index-Total | | |

*Figure 1. Daily stock index movements in eight markets (2006/6/1~2010/12/31)*

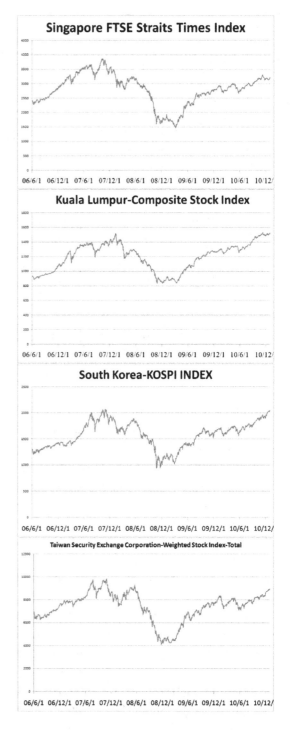

The excess kurtosis statistics ($K$) suggests departure from normality, that is, all series are highly leptokurtic. Hence, the Jarque-Brea statistics ($JB$) rejects the normality for each return series. The unit root test results of Augmented Dickey-Fuller ($ADF$) and Phillips and Perron ($PP$) reveal all the series are stationary. This research uses return series to analyze asymmet-

*Table 2. Descriptive statistics of eight daily stock return series in two sample periods*

| Country | Period | Obs. | μ | σ | S | K | JB | | ADF | | PP | |
|---------|--------|------|-----|-----|------|------|-------|-----|---------|-----|---------|-----|
| Hong Kong | PER- | 566 | 0.035 | 1.758 | -0.089 | 6.881 | 356 | *** | -26.066 | *** | -26.163 | *** |
| | POST- | 571 | 0.031 | 2.294 | 0.161 | 9.665 | 1059 | *** | -24.230 | *** | -24.319 | *** |
| Singapore | PER- | 578 | 0.007 | 1.339 | -0.236 | 4.840 | 87 | *** | -24.044 | *** | -24.082 | *** |
| | POST- | 577 | 0.043 | 1.678 | -0.056 | 7.573 | 503 | *** | -23.501 | *** | -23.521 | *** |
| Japan | PER- | 550 | -0.054 | 1.453 | -0.481 | 4.719 | 89 | *** | -23.060 | *** | -23.294 | *** |
| | POST- | 559 | -0.048 | 1.916 | -0.129 | 10.191 | 1206 | *** | -17.521 | *** | -25.174 | *** |
| Malaysia | PER- | 568 | 0.019 | 1.063 | -1.866 | 17.950 | 5619 | *** | -11.601 | *** | -21.727 | *** |
| | POST- | 567 | 0.068 | 0.837 | -0.073 | 6.601 | 307 | *** | -19.590 | *** | -19.586 | *** |
| Thailand | PER- | 563 | -0.018 | 1.468 | -1.607 | 32.237 | 20295 | *** | -25.959 | *** | -25.956 | *** |
| | POST- | 558 | 0.085 | 1.753 | -0.975 | 9.683 | 1127 | *** | -22.278 | *** | -22.336 | *** |
| Korea | PER- | 564 | 0.020 | 1.392 | -0.393 | 5.257 | 134 | *** | -23.451 | *** | -23.452 | *** |
| | POST- | 578 | 0.057 | 1.834 | -0.663 | 11.216 | 1668 | *** | -23.691 | *** | -23.691 | *** |
| China | PER- | 563 | 0.042 | 2.267 | -0.578 | 4.849 | 111 | *** | -23.904 | *** | -23.943 | *** |
| | POST- | 558 | 0.054 | 1.923 | -0.145 | 5.181 | 113 | *** | -23.203 | *** | -23.204 | *** |
| Taiwan | PER- | 571 | -0.022 | 1.462 | -0.512 | 4.920 | 113 | *** | -24.320 | *** | -24.319 | *** |
| | POST- | 577 | 0.068 | 1.562 | -0.283 | 5.695 | 182 | *** | -21.726 | *** | -21.663 | *** |

Notes:*** denote significance at the.01 level.

ric volatility. The Ljung-Box (*LB*) statistics for 12 lags applied to residuals and squared residuals indicate that significant linear/nonlinear dependence exists. If the Q statistics of Ljung-Box return series is significant, then it will show that in this series the autocorrelation phenomenon is existent; that is to say, if the Ljung-Box of the square of return series Q statistics is significant, then, the variance of the series is existent for the autocorrelation phenomenon, and this means this series contains the heteroskedasticity phenomenon. The tests of $LB(12)$, $LB^2(12)$ and Lagrange multiplier (*LM*) tests shown in Table 3 exhibit that most of the return series and the square of return series all contain the autocorrelation phenomenon, which indicates that these analysis models should take autoregression (AR), conditional hetrocedesticity (CH) into consideration. The autoregressive process is required in describing linear dependent series.

We adopt the Akaike information criterion (AIC) to determine the order of the AR(*p*) and the smallest value of AIC is chosen and as shown in Table 4. Since the mean equation of the GARCH family model can settle autocorrelation series, and its variance equation allows the variance to be decided by the pre-variance and disturbance term, thus, the existence of the conditional hetrocedesticity is acceptable, and adopting the GARCH family models to explain the phenomenon is the best choice.

## 2.2. Asymmetric Volatility Model

The diagnostics of autoregressive conditional heteroskedasticity of high order and volatility clustering suggests that a GARCH-class model would be appropriate. Nevertheless, ordinary GARCH models do not distinguish the differential impacts of good news from bad news on volatility. To examine the asymmetric responses

*Table 3. The test of linear dependent and conditional heteroskedasticity variance*

| Country | Period | LB(12) | | | LB(12)² | | | ARCH LM(6) | | |
|---|---|---|---|---|---|---|---|---|---|---|
| Hong Kong | PER- | 12.572 | 0.401 | | 273.080 | 0.000 | *** | 103.788 | 0.000 | *** |
| | POST- | 25.455 | 0.013 | ** | 505.910 | 0.000 | *** | 149.502 | 0.000 | *** |
| Singapore | PER- | 9.390 | 0.669 | | 137.590 | 0.000 | *** | 71.032 | 0.000 | *** |
| | POST- | 28.018 | 0.005 | *** | 552.660 | 0.000 | *** | 145.378 | 0.000 | *** |
| Japan | PER- | 14.071 | 0.296 | | 107.540 | 0.000 | *** | 43.699 | 0.000 | *** |
| | POST- | 21.796 | 0.040 | ** | 839.140 | 0.000 | *** | 219.265 | 0.000 | *** |
| Malaysia | PER- | 28.244 | 0.005 | *** | 33.431 | 0.000 | *** | 24.440 | 0.000 | *** |
| | POST- | 29.607 | 0.003 | *** | 266.080 | 0.000 | *** | 114.335 | 0.000 | *** |
| Thailand | PER- | 17.483 | 0.132 | | 43.366 | 0.000 | *** | 45.060 | 0.000 | *** |
| | POST- | 31.634 | 0.002 | *** | 316.650 | 0.000 | *** | 94.525 | 0.000 | *** |
| Korea | PER- | 12.220 | 0.428 | | 104.060 | 0.000 | *** | 60.616 | 0.000 | *** |
| | POST- | 9.813 | 0.632 | | 490.080 | 0.000 | *** | 172.709 | 0.000 | *** |
| China | PER- | 21.804 | 0.040 | ** | 26.799 | 0.000 | *** | 13.067 | 0.000 | *** |
| | POST- | 6.323 | 0.899 | | 114.830 | 0.000 | *** | 49.328 | 0.000 | *** |
| Taiwan | PER- | 17.834 | 0.121 | | 121.600 | 0.000 | *** | 52.938 | 0.000 | *** |
| | POST- | 18.839 | 0.092 | * | 154.500 | 0.000 | *** | 60.321 | 0.000 | *** |

Notes: *,** and*** denote significance at the .1, .05 and .01 level, respectively

*Table 4. Values of AIC*

| Country | Period | Value of AIC | | | | | |
|---|---|---|---|---|---|---|---|
| | | AR(1) | AR(2) | AR(3) | AR(4) | AR(5) | AR(6) |
| Hong Kong | PER- | **3.9636** | 3.9668 | 3.9709 | 3.9750 | 3.9782 | 3.9797 |
| | POST- | 4.4951 | 4.4952 | 4.4947 | **4.4665** | 4.4708 | 4.4691 |
| Singapore | PER- | 3.4280 | **3.4272** | 3.4319 | 3.4359 | 3.4353 | 3.4338 |
| | POST- | 3.8792 | 3.8757 | 3.8724 | **3.8575** | 3.8607 | 3.8592 |
| Japan | PER- | 3.5919 | 3.5947 | 3.5908 | 3.5937 | 3.5920 | **3.5842** |
| | POST- | **4.1300** | 4.1347 | 4.1369 | 4.1325 | 4.1311 | 4.1303 |
| Malaysia | PER- | 2.9583 | 2.9610 | **2.9401** | 2.9441 | 2.9489 | 2.9449 |
| | POST- | 2.4393 | 2.4436 | 2.4408 | **2.4107** | 2.4154 | 2.4202 |
| Thailand | PER- | **3.6038** | 3.6053 | 3.6080 | 3.6102 | 3.6056 | 3.6052 |
| | POST- | 3.9599 | 3.9524 | 3.9576 | 3.9523 | 3.9552 | **3.9487** |
| Korea | PER- | 3.5040 | 3.5055 | 3.5090 | 3.5081 | **3.4964** | 3.5000 |
| | POST- | 4.0365 | 4.0371 | 4.0394 | **4.0299** | 4.0348 | 4.0386 |
| China | PER- | 4.4799 | 4.4835 | 4.4825 | 4.4791 | **4.4726** | 4.4752 |
| | POST- | 4.1416 | 4.1427 | 4.1467 | 4.1087 | 4.0816 | **4.0810** |
| Taiwan | PER- | 3.6032 | 3.6071 | 3.5974 | 3.6026 | 3.5997 | **3.5863** |
| | POST- | 3.7067 | 3.7096 | 3.6979 | **3.6808** | 3.6820 | 3.6868 |

Notes: block is the minimum.

of volatility to positive and negative information, the EGARCH model developed by Nelson (1991) is employed. As suggested by Bollerslev, Chou, and Kroner (1992) in using a model as parsimonious as possible, we adopt the EGARCH (1,1) model in this study. The model can be described as Equations (1) to (3),

$$R_t \left| I_{t-1} \sim f\left(\mu_t, \sigma_t^2\right)\right. \tag{1}$$

$$R_t = \beta_0 + \sum_{i=1}^{p} \beta_i R_{t-1} + \varepsilon_t \tag{2}$$

$$\ln\left(\sigma_t^2\right) = \alpha_0 + \alpha_1 \left(\left|z_{t-1}\right| - E\left[\left|z_{t-1}\right|\right] + \delta z_{t-1}\right) + \varphi \ln\left(\sigma_{t-1}^2\right) \tag{3}$$

Equation (1) expresses the conditional return $R$ at time $t$, given the information set $I$ at time $t$-1. With the conditional density function of $f(\cdot)$, $R_t$ has the conditional mean $\mu_t = E(R_t | I_{t-1})$ and conditional variance $\sigma_t^2 = E(\varepsilon_t^2 | I_{t-1})$, where $\varepsilon_t$ represents the information at time $t$, i.e., $\varepsilon_t = R_t - \mu_t$. Equation (2) describes the autoregressive process of order $p$ for the stock returns, with $\sum_{i=1}^{p} \beta_i R_{t-1}$ capturing the autocorrelation.

As described in the previous section, the order of AR($p$) is decided based on the AIC and the selected order for each market in each period is presented in Table 4. The process of conditional variance is expressed by Equation (3), where the logarithm of the conditional variance is modeled as an asymmetric function of last period's standardized information, $z_{t-1}$, and the logarithm of the last period's conditional variance The standardized information, $z_t$, is defined as $\varepsilon_t / \sigma_t^2$ such that a positive $z_t$ implies an unexpected increasing in stock returns whereas a negative $z_t$ implies an unexpected decreasing. Thus, the second term in Equation (3) allows the conditional variance process to respond asymmetrically to rising and falling in stock prices. Specifically,

the term $|z_t| - E|z_{t-1}|$ represents the size effect of the information, that is providing $\alpha_1$ is positive, then, a positive (negative) impact on $ln(\sigma_t^2)$ when the magnitude of $z_{t-1}$ is larger (smaller) than its expected value. The term $\delta z_{t-1}$ on the other hand captures the sign effect; that is, when the coefficient $\delta$ is significantly negative (positive), then negative (positive) information increases volatility more than does positive (negative) information of the same magnitude. In essence, to examine whether the presence of asymmetric volatility is presented, the impact of positive information on $ln(\sigma_t^2)$ is equal to $\alpha_1(1-|\delta|)|z_{t-1}|$ and the impact of a negative information is $\alpha_1(1+|\delta|)|z_{t-1}|$.

Given the data for the return series $R_t$, estimates of the parameters in Equation (2) and Equation (3) (namely $\beta_0$, $\beta_1$, $\alpha_0$, $\alpha_1$, $\delta$, $\psi$) can be derived by maximizing the log-likelihood of the returns over the sample period. Diagnostic tests for appropriateness of the models are performed on the standardized residuals and squared residuals via Ljung-Box test and Lagrange multiplier test. Specifically, the Ljung-Box test is applied to the standardized residuals tests for remaining serial correlation in the mean equation; the Lagrange multiplier test is applied to the squared standardized residuals for checking the specification of the variance equation.

## 3. TEMPORARY AND PERMANENT VOLATILITY MODEL

Engle and Lee (1999) extend the settings in Bollerslev's (1986) GARCH model, regarding the sum for pre residual and variance as the mean-reverting for the conditional variance; moreover, they relax the condition criteria of setting the models as well as the assumption of the long-run volatility's proxy variance as a random variance to develop the component GARCH model. The structure of the volatility model is shown as Equations (4) to (6),

$$h_t = q_t + s_t \tag{4}$$

$$s_t = (\alpha + \beta)s_{t-1} + \alpha\left(\varepsilon_{t-1}{}^2 - h_{t-1}\right) \tag{5}$$

$$q_t = \omega + \rho q_{t-1} + \varphi\left(\varepsilon_{t-1}{}^2 - h_{t-1}\right) \tag{6}$$

$h_t$ is the conditional variance, which consists of the volatility factor of the long-run and short-run; $q_t$ is the volatility factor of the long-run; $s_t$ is the volatility factor of the short-run. In the equation of the volatility factor of the short-run (Equation(5)), it shows $s_t$ subjects the stochastic processes of AR(1), $\varepsilon_{t-1}{}^2$ is the impact of pre-volatility or unexpected term, and $(\alpha+\beta)$ presents the mean-reverting rate of the volatility factor of the short-run, the value would be between 0 and 1.

The conditional variance will recover unconditional variance by the geometry ratio of $(\alpha+\beta)$. If the recovery rate is smaller, the persistent influence on market shocks is less, and after the market takes the shocks messages, the volatility would rapidly respond to any shocks in the market, and the persistent influence caused by the volatility would be decreased. In addition, in the equation of the volatility factor of the long-run (Equation (6)), $q_t$ subjects the stochastic processes of AR(1), $\rho$ can refer to the mean-reverting rate of the volatility factor of the long-run, whose value is also between 0 and 1, and it will converge to $\omega/(1-\rho)$ in the long-run. The Component GARCH model must adapt to stationary and non-negativity statistic conditions. The condition of stationary is $\rho<1$ and $(\alpha+\beta)<1$, at the time the model will exist the estimate of the unconditional variance in a long-run. Since the volatility measure must show non-negativity; therefore, it must satisfy $\rho>(\alpha+\beta)>0$, $\beta>\psi>0$, $\alpha>0$, $\omega>0$; while all the above conditions need to be sufficient but not necessary, so the component of short-run volatility does not need to allow the restraint of non-negativity.

That the CGARCH(1,1) model for Equations (5) and (6) can be written as Equations (7) and (8), respectively.

$$h_t = q_t + \alpha\left(\varepsilon_{t-1}{}^2 - q_{t-1}\right) + \beta\left(h_{t-1} - q_{t-1}\right) \tag{7}$$

$$q_t = \omega + \rho\left(q_{t-1} - \omega\right) + \phi\left(\varepsilon_{t-1}{}^2 - h_{t-1}\right) \tag{8}$$

## 4. EMPIRICAL RESULTS

The main point of studying asymmetric volatility focuses on the comparison of the absolute value of the coefficient $\delta$, and the long-run effects emphasize on the long-run and short-run effects between $\rho$ and $\alpha+\beta$.

### 4.1. Asymmetric Volatility

The maximum likelihood estimates of the EGARCH model is presented in Table 5. As for the conditional variance equations, the majority of the estimated parameters are significant across markets.

The asymmetric volatility exists when volatilities caused by positive information and negative information are in different ranges. When $\delta$ is negative, negative information will increase future volatility more than that of positive information. Likewise, if $\delta$ is positive, positive information will increase the future volatility more than that of negative information. Take the per-period of Singapore for example, the EGARCH(1,1) model estimate of the result would be as follows:

$$\ln\left(\sigma_t{}^2\right) = 0.622 + 0.307\left(|z_{t-1}| - E\left[|z_{t-1}|\right] - 0.133 z_{t-1}\right)$$
$$-0.551\ln\left(\sigma_{t-1}{}^2\right)$$

If the $t$-1 period contains negative information to make $\varepsilon_{t-1}$ become negative, $z_{t-1}=\varepsilon_{t-1}/\sigma_{t-1}{}^2$ should be negative, then $z_{t-1}$ in each unit will make $ln(\sigma_t{}^2)$ in the next period ($t$ period) increase 0.307*(1+0.133), it means 0.348. On the contrary, if there is positive information, each $t$-1 period will contain positive information, then each $z_{t-1}$ will

*Table 5. Maximum likelihood method estimates of the EGARCH model*

$$\ln\left(\sigma_t^2\right) = \alpha_0 + \alpha_1\left(\left|z_{t-1}\right| - E\left[\left|z_{t-1}\right|\right] + \delta z_{t-1}\right) + \varphi\ln\left(\sigma_{t-1}^2\right)$$

| Country | Period | AR(p) | $\alpha_0$ | | $\alpha_1$ | | $\delta$ | | $\psi$ | | $\dfrac{1+\left|\delta\right|}{1-\left|\delta\right|}$ | t value of $\delta$ | |
|---|---|---|---|---|---|---|---|---|---|---|---|---|---|
| Hongkong | PER- | 1 | 2.1423 | | -0.0035 | | -0.0327 | | -0.9335 | | 1.0677 | 0.1922 | |
| | | | (0.0000) | *** | (0.9233) | | (0.2040) | | (0.0000) | *** | | | |
| | POST- | 4 | -0.0780 | | 0.1020 | | -0.0330 | | 0.9913 | | 1.0683 | | |
| | | | (0.0020) | *** | (0.0018) | *** | (0.1363) | | (0.0000) | *** | | | |
| Singapore | PER- | 2 | 0.6216 | | 0.3071 | | -0.1326 | | -0.5505 | | 1.3056 | -27.8390 | *** |
| | | | (0.0018) | *** | (0.0019) | *** | (0.0255) | ** | (0.0013) | *** | | | |
| | POST- | 4 | -0.1275 | | 0.1585 | | -0.0593 | | 0.9926 | | 1.1260 | | |
| | | | (0.0000) | *** | (0.0000) | *** | (0.0071) | *** | (0.0000) | *** | | | |
| Janpan | PER- | 6 | -0.0578 | | 0.0882 | | -0.1287 | | 0.9720 | | 1.2955 | -27.8227 | *** |
| | | | (0.1340) | | (0.0818) | * | (0.0000) | *** | (0.0000) | *** | | | |
| | POST- | 1 | -0.1389 | | 0.1898 | | -0.0864 | | 0.9781 | | 1.1890 | | |
| | | | (0.0001) | *** | (0.0000) | *** | (0.0003) | *** | (0.0000) | *** | | | |
| Malaysia | PER- | 3 | -0.2476 | | 0.2985 | | -0.1185 | | 0.9405 | | 1.2690 | -19.6867 | *** |
| | | | (0.0000) | *** | (0.0001) | *** | (0.0081) | *** | (0.0000) | *** | | | |
| | POST- | 4 | -0.1433 | | 0.1692 | | -0.0783 | | 0.9817 | | 1.1698 | | |
| | | | (0.0000) | *** | (0.0000) | *** | (0.0000) | *** | (0.0000) | *** | | | |
| Thailand | PER- | 1 | -0.0481 | | 0.1403 | | -0.1608 | | 0.8791 | | 1.3833 | -46.6431 | *** |
| | | | (0.3031) | | (0.0500) | * | (0.0023) | *** | (0.0000) | *** | | | |
| | POST- | 6 | -0.1470 | | 0.2187 | | -0.0500 | | 0.9691 | | 1.1053 | | |
| | | | (0.0000) | *** | (0.0000) | *** | (0.0115) | ** | (0.0000) | *** | | | |
| Korea | PER- | 5 | -0.1215 | | 0.1885 | | -0.1533 | | 0.9344 | | 1.3621 | -9.5653 | *** |
| | | | (0.0060) | *** | (0.0009) | *** | (0.0001) | *** | (0.0000) | *** | | | |
| | POST- | 4 | -0.0800 | | 0.1165 | | -0.1360 | | 0.9847 | | 1.3148 | | |
| | | | (0.0000) | *** | (0.0000) | *** | (0.0000) | *** | (0.0000) | *** | | | |
| China | PER- | 5 | -0.0809 | | 0.1637 | | -0.0487 | | 0.9725 | | 1.1024 | -22.7355 | *** |
| | | | (0.0367) | ** | (0.0026) | *** | (0.1443) | | (0.0000) | *** | | | |
| | POST- | 6 | -0.0621 | | 0.1262 | | -0.0127 | | 0.9683 | | 1.0257 | | |
| | | | (0.0022) | *** | (0.0005) | *** | (0.4623) | | (0.0000) | *** | | | |
| Taiwan | PER- | 6 | -0.1238 | | 0.1829 | | -0.0799 | | 0.9662 | | 1.1737 | -15.3659 | *** |
| | | | (0.0022) | *** | (0.0008) | *** | (0.0381) | ** | (0.0000) | *** | | | |
| | POST- | 4 | -0.0778 | | 0.0991 | | -0.0534 | | 0.9984 | | 1.1128 | | |
| | | | (0.0000) | *** | (0.0000) | *** | (0.0003) | *** | (0.0000) | *** | | | |

*continued on following page*

*Table 5. Continued*

| Country | Period | AR(p) | $\alpha_0$ | $\alpha_1$ | $\delta$ | $\psi$ | $\dfrac{1+|\delta|}{1-|\delta|}$ | t value of $\delta$ |
|---|---|---|---|---|---|---|---|---|

Notes: ** and*** denote significance at the .05 and .01 level, respectively.

Numbers in parentheses are p-values.

As the order of AR(p) is different for each event, to save space, the estimates of the conditional mean equations are shown as following.

$$t = \frac{\left|\delta_{post}\right| - \left|\delta_{pre}\right|}{\sqrt{\dfrac{\hat{\sigma}_{post}^{2}}{n_{post}} + \dfrac{\hat{\sigma}_{pre}^{2}}{n_{pre}}}}$$

make $ln(\sigma_t^2)$ in the next period increase 0.307*(1-0.133), which is 0.266. The degree of asymmetry can be measured by $(1+|\delta|)/(1-|\delta|)$ (Koutmos & Saidi, 1995). Because the degree of asymmetry is measured by $(1+|\delta|)/(1-|\delta|)$, a higher absolute value of $\delta$ implies a higher degree of asymmetry, we can simply compare the absolute values of $\delta$ between the two sub-periods to examine whether there is a change in the extent of asymmetry. Thus, while comparing to the positive information, the volatility caused by negative information will be 1.307 times to positive information. When the absolute of $\delta$ increases, the more volatile the asymmetric volatility will be. For eight markets exhibiting asymmetric volatility in both sub-periods, all the absolute values of $\delta$ are much lower in the post-sub-period (expect Hong Kong). The one-tailed *t*-test is therefore utilized to examine whether the absolute values of $\delta$ are significantly lower in the post- rather than in the pre-sub-period (expect Hong Kong).

## 4.2 THE EFFECTS OF TEMPORARY AND PERMANENT

According to the four events, we analyze them by making a comparison of the long-run ($\rho$) and the short-run ($\alpha + \beta$) before and after price limits (Table 6). For example, for the post-period of Singapore, the CGARCH(1,1) model is as follows:

$$h_t = q_t - 0.0476\left(\varepsilon_{t-1}^2 - q_{t-1}\right) - 0.8180\beta\left(h_{t-1} - q_{t-1}\right)$$
$$q_t = \omega + 0.9892\left(q_{t-1} - \omega\right) + 0.0678\left(\varepsilon_{t-1}^2 - h_{t-1}\right)$$

The effect of the long-run is $\rho$=0.99892, and the effect of the long-run is $|\alpha+\beta|$= 0.9124.

When our model is applied to eight markets, we find the long-run effect is more than the short-run effect. And this matches with our model. For the short-run, the empirical results show that after Global Financial Crisis, there are significantly decreasing in China and Taiwan, but not in Japan, the others are significantly increasing. And the long-run, there are significantly decreasing (expect Thailand and Korea).

## 5. SUMMARY AND CONCLUSION

This paper mainly makes EGARCH and CGARCH to test the influences of the volatility for the financial crisis. By examining the daily return series covering the period 2006/6/1 to 2010/12/31 for stock of Hong Kong, Singapore, Japan, Malaysia, Thailand, Korea, China, and Taiwan, we documented the existence of asymmetry volatility, temporary volatility, and permanent volatility for these markets.

For asymmetry volatility, the empirical results of this paper are lower after financial crisis. There are different from Yang and You (2003), in which

*Table 6. Maximum likelihood method estimates of the component EGARCH model*

$$h_t = q_t + \alpha\left(\varepsilon_{t-1}^2 - q_{t-1}\right) + \beta\left(h_{t-1} - q_{t-1}\right)$$

$$q_t = \omega + \rho\left(q_{t-1} - \omega\right) + \phi\left(\varepsilon_{t-1}^2 - h_{t-1}\right)$$

| Country | Period | ω | | ρ | | δ | | α | | β | | |α+βl | t value of |α+βl | | ρ | t value of ρ | |
|---|---|---|---|---|---|---|---|---|---|---|---|---|---|---|---|---|---|
| Hong Kong | PER- | 17.7996 | | 0.9996 | | 0.0058 | | 0.0817 | | 0.8071 | | 0.8889 | 2.7812 | ** | 0.9996 | -36.6970 | *** |
| | | (0.9312) | | (0.0000) | *** | (0.9517) | | (0.3720) | | (0.0000) | *** | | | | | | |
| | POST- | 1.3038 | | 0.9877 | | 0.0352 | | 0.0357 | | -0.9402 | | 0.9045 | | | 0.9877 | | |
| | | (0.0042) | *** | (0.0000) | *** | (0.0201) | ** | (0.0843) | * | (0.0000) | *** | | | | | | |
| Singapore | PER- | 2.3189 | | 0.9933 | | 0.1061 | | 0.0256 | | -0.7087 | | 0.6831 | 5.3523 | *** | 0.9933 | -4.8031 | *** |
| | | (0.1433) | | (0.0000) | *** | (0.0004) | *** | (0.6451) | | (0.3719) | | | | | | | |
| | POST- | 0.8723 | | 0.9892 | | 0.0678 | | -0.0476 | | -0.8160 | | 0.8635 | | | 0.9892 | | |
| | | (0.0313) | ** | (0.0000) | *** | (0.0002) | *** | (0.1262) | | (0.0000) | *** | | | | | | |
| Japan | PER- | 2.6054 | | 0.9903 | | 0.0775 | | -0.0239 | | 0.2395 | | 0.2156 | 0.3206 | | 0.9903 | -21.3314 | *** |
| | | (0.2762) | | (0.0000) | *** | (0.0103) | ** | (0.7396) | | (0.9283) | | | | | | | |
| | POST- | 2.4979 | | 0.9663 | | 0.1686 | | -0.1097 | | -0.1428 | | 0.2526 | | | 0.9663 | | |
| | | (0.0152) | ** | (0.0000) | *** | (0.0000) | *** | (0.0326) | ** | (0.7661) | | | | | | | |
| Malaysia | PER- | 12.4081 | | 0.9999 | | 0.0110 | | 0.1769 | | 0.7438 | | 0.9207 | 11.4718 | *** | 0.9999 | -46.3041 | *** |
| | | (0.5226) | | (0.0000) | *** | (0.4381) | | (0.0002) | *** | (0.0000) | *** | | | | | | |
| | POST- | 0.4696 | | 0.9784 | | 0.0902 | | -0.0107 | | -0.9559 | | 0.9666 | | | 0.9784 | | |
| | | (0.0026) | *** | (0.0000) | *** | (0.0000) | *** | (0.3653) | | (0.0000) | *** | | | | | | |
| Thailand | PER- | 2.0781 | | 0.8956 | | 0.1317 | | 0.0955 | | 0.5169 | | 0.6124 | 10.0583 | *** | 0.8956 | 20.0948 | *** |
| | | (0.0013) | *** | (0.0000) | *** | (0.5461) | | (0.6604) | | (0.4586) | | | | | | | |
| | POST- | 0.7611 | | 0.9961 | | -0.0141 | | 0.0953 | | 0.8271 | | 0.9225 | | | 0.9961 | | |
| | | (0.0424) | ** | (0.0000) | *** | (0.0000) | *** | (0.0000) | *** | (0.0000) | *** | | | | | | |
| Korea | PER- | 2.7644 | | 0.9872 | | 0.1121 | | -0.1279 | | 0.2155 | | 0.0876 | 39.6876 | *** | 0.9872 | 10.6379 | *** |
| | | (0.3049) | | (0.0000) | *** | (0.0002) | *** | (0.0126) | ** | (0.6581) | | | | | | | |
| | POST- | 0.3627 | | 0.9951 | | 0.0085 | | 0.0777 | | 0.8331 | | 0.9108 | | | 0.9951 | | |
| | | (0.3905) | | (0.0000) | *** | (0.0874) | * | (0.0001) | *** | (0.0000) | *** | | | | | | |

*continued on following page*

144

*Table 6. Continued*

| Country | Period | | ω | | ρ | | δ | | α | | β | | \|α+β\| | t value of \|α+β\| | | ρ | t value of ρ | |
|---------|--------|---|---|---|---|---|---|---|---|---|---|---|---------|-------------------|---|---|-------------|---|
| China | PER- | | 17.8545 | | 0.9964 | | 0.0932 | | 0.0143 | | 0.7889 | | 0.8032 | -22.2433 | *** | 0.9964 | -31.8893 | *** |
| | | | (0.7976) | | (0.0000) | *** | (0.0202) | ** | (0.7823) | | (0.2842) | | | | | | | |
| | POST- | | 2.9910 | | 0.9660 | | 0.0629 | | -0.1071 | | 0.0973 | | 0.0098 | | | 0.9660 | | |
| | | *** | (0.0000) | | (0.0000) | *** | (0.0008) | *** | (0.0010) | *** | (0.8125) | | | | | | | |
| Taiwan | FER- | | 6.8518 | | 0.9969 | | 0.0883 | | 0.0471 | | 0.8789 | | 0.9259 | -29.7288 | *** | 0.9969 | -8.9009 | *** |
| | | | (0.8096) | | (0.0000) | *** | (0.1686) | | (0.4837) | | (0.0000) | *** | | | | | | |
| | POST- | | 1.4366 | | 0.9905 | | 0.0652 | | -0.0712 | | 0.5977 | | 0.5265 | | | 0.9905 | | |
| | | ** | (0.0138) | | (0.0000) | *** | (0.0000) | *** | (0.0064) | *** | (0.0226) | ** | | | | | | |

Notes: *, ** and *** denote significance at the .1, .05 and .01 level, respectively.
Numbers in parentheses are p-values.
As the order of AR(p) is different for each event, to save space, the estimates of the conditional mean equations are shown as following. .

$$t = \frac{|value_{post}| - |value_{pre}|}{\sqrt{\dfrac{\hat{\sigma}_{value_{post}}^2}{n_{post}} + \dfrac{\hat{\sigma}_{value_{pre}}^2}{n_{pre}}}}$$

they indicate that the asymmetry volatility will increase after financial crisis. But the phenomenon of asymmetric volatility refers to a situation when new information often causes price change. When new information is positive, future price volatility is smaller; on the contrary, when new information is negative, future price volatility is greater. After global financial crisis, there are high growths in the economic in the Asian countries. The influence of global financial crisis is small.

For temporary and permanent volatility, the paper finds the short-run volatility is lower in China and Taiwan after global financial crisis, the result is similarly to Greenwald and Stein (1991) indicate in their research of the stock market, they proclaim that the deduction of the price limit can reduce volatility in the stock market because the investors can have the opportunity to calm down; therefore, it can make the price decrease so that the price over volatility can be avoided (China and Taiwan have price limit for 10% and 7%, respectively). And the long-run volatility, we find it is smaller after global financial crisis (expect Thailand and Korea). The result seems to indicate that the short-run component captures market skewness risk, while the long-run component captures business cycle risk. Furthermore, short-run volatility is the most important cross-sectional risk factor, even though its average risk premium is smaller than the premium of the long-run component (Tobias & Rosenberg, 2008).

The paper ignores volume and interaction from different markets, even they are some critical factors of the influence of the volatility. It should be taken into account in the future research.

## ACKNOWLEDGMENT

This research was conducted with the support of National Science Council, Taiwan, ROC (NSC 99-2410-H-161-001).

## REFERENCES

Black, F. (1976). Studies in stock price volatility changes. In *Proceedings of the Business Meeting of the Business Economic Statistics Section* (pp. 177-181).

Bollerslev, T. (1986). Generalized autoregressive conditional heteroskedasticity. *Journal of Econometrics*, *31*, 307–327. doi:10.1016/0304-4076(86)90063-1

Bollerslev, T., Chou, R., & Kroner, K. (1992). ARCH modeling in finance: A review of the theory and empirical evidence. *Journal of Econometrics*, *51*, 5–59. doi:10.1016/0304-4076(92)90064-X

Bollerslev, T., Engle, R., & Nelson, D. (1994). ARCH models. In Engle, R., & McFadden, D. (Eds.), *Handbook of metrics* (pp. 2959–3038). Amsterdam, The Netherlands: North Holland Press.

Campbell, J., & Hentschel, L. (1992). No news is good news: An asymmetric model of changing volatility in stock returns. *Journal of Financial Economics*, *31*, 281–318. doi:10.1016/0304-405X(92)90037-X

Chelley-Steeley, P. L., & Steeley, J. M. (1996). Volatility, leverage and firm size: The U.K. evidence. *The Manchester School of Economic and Social Studies*, *64*, 83–103. doi:10.1111/j.1467-9957.1996.tb01456.x

Chou, R. (1988). Volatility persistence and stock valuations: Some empirical evidence using GARCH. *Journal of Applied Econometrics*, *3*, 279–294. doi:10.1002/jae.3950030404

Christie, A. A. (1982). The stochastic behavior of common stock variances: Value, leverage and interest rate effects. *Journal of Financial Economics*, *10*, 407–432. doi:10.1016/0304-405X(82)90018-6

Christoffersen, P., Jacobs, K., & Wang, Y. (2008). Option valuation with long-run and short-run volatility components. *Journal of Financial Economics, 90,* 272–297. doi:10.1016/j.jfineco.2007.12.003

Ding, Z., & Granger, C. W. J. (1996). Modeling volatility persistence of speculative returns: A new approach. *Journal of Econometrics, 73,* 185–215. doi:10.1016/0304-4076(95)01737-2

Ding, Z., Granger, C. W. J., & Engle, R. (1993). A long memory property of stock returns and a new model. *Journal of Empirical Finance, 1,* 83–106. doi:10.1016/0927-5398(93)90006-D

Engle, R. F. (1982). Autoregressive conditional heteroskedasticity with estimates of the variance of United Kingdom inflation. *Econometrica, 50,* 987–1007. doi:10.2307/1912773

Engle, R. F., Granger, C. W. J., & Robins, R. (1986). Wholesale and retail prices: Bivariate modeling with forecast able variances. In Belsey, D., & Kuh, E. (Eds.), *Model reliability.* Cambridge, MA: MIT Press.

Engle, R. F., & Lee, G. (1999). A long-run and short-run component model of stock return volatility. In Engle, R., & White, H. (Eds.), *Cointegration, causality and forecasting.* New York, NY: Oxford University Press.

Engle, R. F., & Ng, V. K. (1993). Measuring and testing the impact of news on volatility. *The Journal of Finance, 48,* 1749–1778. doi:10.2307/2329066

French, K. R., Schwert, W. G., & Stambaugh, R. F. (1987). Expected stock returns and volatility. *The Journal of Finance, 19,* 3–29.

Greenwald, B., & Stein, J. (1991). Transactional risk, market crashes, and the role of circuit breakers. *The Journal of Business, 64,* 443–462. doi:10.1086/296547

Hafner, C. M. (1998). Estimating high-frequency foreign exchange rate volatility with nonparametric ARCH models. *Journal of Statistical Planning and Inference, 68,* 247–269. doi:10.1016/S0378-3758(97)00144-4

Hogan, K. C. Jr, & Melvin, M. T. (1994). Sources of meteor showers and heat waves in the foreign exchange market. *Journal of International Economics, 37,* 239–247. doi:10.1016/0022-1996(94)90047-7

Hung, J. (1997). Intervention strategies and exchange rate volatility: A noise trading perspective. *Journal of International Money and Finance, 16,* 779–793. doi:10.1016/S0261-5606(97)00023-5

Koutmos, G., & Saidi, R. (1995). The leverage effect in individual stocks and the debt to equity ratio. *Journal of Business Finance & Accounting, 22,* 1063–1075. doi:10.1111/j.1468-5957.1995.tb00894.x

Laopodis, N. T. (1997). U.S. dollar asymmetry and exchange rate volatility. *Journal of Applied Business Research, 13,* 1–8.

Lo, A., & MacKinlay, C. (1987). An econometric analysis of nonsynchronous trading. *Journal of Econometrics, 55,* 181–211.

Nelson, D. (1991). Conditional heteroskedasticity in asset returns: A new approach. *Econometrics, 59,* 347–370. doi:10.2307/2938260

Pagan, A. R., & Schwert, G. W. (1990). Alternative models for conditional stock volatility. *Journal of Econometrics, 45,* 267–290. doi:10.1016/0304-4076(90)90101-X

Schwert, W. G. (1990). Stock volatility and the crash of 87. *Review of Financial Studies, 3,* 77–102. doi:10.1093/rfs/3.1.77

Sentana, E., & Wadhwani, S. (1992). Feedback traders and stock return autocorrections: evidence from a century of daily data. *The Economic Journal*, *102*, 415–425. doi:10.2307/2234525

Skinner, D. (1989). Option markets and stock return volatility. *Journal of Financial Economics*, *23*, 61–87. doi:10.1016/0304-405X(89)90005-6

Tobias, A., & Rosenberg, J. (2008). Stock returns and volatility: Pricing the short-run and long-run components of market risk. *The Journal of Finance*, *63*(6), 2997–3030. doi:10.1111/j.1540-6261.2008.01419.x

Tse, Y. K., & Tsui, A. K. C. (1997). Conditional volatility in foreign exchange rates: Evidence from the Malaysian ringgit and Singapore dollar. *Pacific-Basin Finance Journal*, *5*, 345–356. doi:10.1016/S0927-538X(97)00002-4

Yang, J. J. W. (2000). The Leverage effect and herding behaviour in Taiwan's stock market. *Journal of Risk Management*, *2*, 69–86.

Yang, J. J. W., & You, S.-J. (2003). Asymmetric volatility: Pre and post Asian financial crisis. *Journal of Management*, *20*(4), 805–827.

*This work was previously published in the International Journal of Applied Evolutionary Computation, Volume 2, Issue 2, edited by Wei-Chiang Samuelson Hong, pp. 82-95, copyright 2011 by IGI Publishing (an imprint of IGI Global).*

# Chapter 9
# Differential Operators Embedded Artificial Bee Colony Algorithm

**Tarun Kumar Sharma**
*Indian Institute of Technology Roorkee, India*

**Millie Pant**
*Indian Institute of Technology Roorkee, India*

## ABSTRACT

*Artificial Bee Colony (ABC) is one of the most recent nature inspired (NIA) algorithms based on swarming metaphor. Proposed by Karaboga in 2005, ABC has proven to be a robust and efficient algorithm for solving global optimization problems over continuous space. However, it has been observed that the structure of ABC is such that it supports exploration more in comparison to exploitation. In order to maintain a balance between these two antagonist factors, this paper suggests incorporation of differential evolution (DE) operators in the structure of basic ABC algorithm. The proposed algorithm called DE-ABC is validated on a set of 10 benchmark problems and the numerical results are compared with basic DE and basic ABC algorithm. The numerical results indicate that the presence of DE operators help in a significant improvement in the performance of ABC algorithm.*

## 1. INTRODUCTION

In the past few decades several nature inspired algorithms (NIA) have emerged for solving global optimization problems. NIA algorithms may be classified as the ones based on natural evolution, commonly known as Evolutionary Algorithms (EA) and the ones that are based on behavioral pattern displayed by various species, particularly the ones that live in groups (or swarms). Evolutionary Algorithms (EAs) are optimization techniques based on the concept of a population of individuals that evolve and improve their fitness through probabilistic operators like recombination and mutation. These individuals are evaluated and those that perform better are selected to compose the population in the next generation. After several

DOI: 10.4018/978-1-4666-3628-6.ch009

generations these individuals improve their fitness as they explore the solution space for optimal value. Some popular EA are Genetic Algorithms (GA) (Goldberg, 1989; Holland, 1975), Evolutionary Strategies (ES) (Rechenberg, 1994), Evolutionary Programming (EP) (Back & Schwefel, 1996; Back, Hammel, & Schwefel, 1997; Fogel, 1995; Fogel, Owens, & Walsh, 1996), and Differential Evolution (DE) (Storn & Price, 1995, 1997).

The other class of NIA is based on the intelligent behavior exhibited by various species like fish birds, bees, ants, termites etc. The algorithms belonging to this class are also known as swarm algorithms and are modeled on the information sharing mechanism of the species. Some popular algorithms belonging to this class include Particle Swarm Optimization (PSO) (Kennedy & Eberhart, 1995), Ant Colony Optimization (ACO) (Dorigo & Gambardella, 1997), Artificial Bee Colony (ABC) algorithm (Karaboga & Basturk, 2007, 2008; Karaboga, 2005; Basturk & Karaboga, 2006), Bacteria Foraging Algorithm (BFO) (Passino, 2002), and Biogeography Based Algorithm (BBO) (Simon, 2008). A survey of algorithms based on bee swarm algorithms is given by Karaboga and Akay in (2009).

In the present study, the focus is on ABC, which is one of the recently proposed NIA. ABC follows the analogy of the socio-cooperative behavior demonstrated by honey bees in their search for nectar. A brief overview of the working of ABC algorithm is given in section 3.

ABC has been successfully applied for solving a variety of real life and benchmark problems. Its comparison with the contemporary algorithms has shown its competence in dealing with different types of problems (Singh, 2009; Karaboga, 2009; Ponton & Klemes, 1993; Rao, Narasimham, & Ramalingaraju, 2008; Karaboga, Akay, & Ozturk, 2007; Pawar, Rao, & Davim, 2008; Karaboga & Basturk, 2007; Pan, Tasgetiren, Suganthan, & Chua, 2011).

However, like most of the NIA in their basic form, ABC is not completely flawless. As pointed out by Zhu and Kwong (2010), ABC has a structure

which supports *exploration (diversification)* more in comparison to *exploitation (intensification)*. These two antagonist factors should be balanced judiciously for the success of an optimization algorithm. In the present study an attempt is made to include the Differential Evolution (DE) operators in the structure of basic ABC. The rationale is to improve the exploitation capabilities of ABC algorithm. In the proposed algorithm named as Differential Evolution Operators Embedded Artificial Bee Colony (DE-ABC), ABC is used to explore the solution space in search of positions of potential food sources while the DE operators are used to exploit those sources with the hope of finding a better location (or position) of food sources.

The remaining of paper is organized as follow. Section 2 and 3 introduces DE algorithm & ABC algorithm respectively. The proposed DE – ABC algorithm is discussed in section 4. Parameter settings for all the algorithms, the considered benchmark problems and the criteria for the comparison of the algorithms are given in section 5. The simulation results obtained are presented and discussed in section 6. Finally, the paper concludes with section 7.

## 2. DIFFERENTIAL EVOLUTION

Differential evolution (DE) is an Evolutionary Algorithm (EA) proposed by Storn and Price in 1995 and 1997. DE starts with an initial population vector, which is randomly generated when no preliminary knowledge about the solution space is available.

Let $X_{i, G}$, $i = 1, 2 \ldots, NP$ be the solution vector, where $i$ denote the population and G denote the generation to which the population belongs. The initial population should ideally cover the entire parameter space by randomly distributing each parameter of an individual vector with uniform distribution between the prescribed upper and lower parameter bounds $x_j^u$ and $x_j^i$. At each generation G, DE employs mutation and crossover operations to produce a trial vector $U_{i,G}$ for each individual vector $X_{i,G}$, also called target vector, in the current population.

## A. Mutation Operation

For each target vector $X_{i,G}$ at generation G, an associated mutated vector $V_{i,G} = \{v_{1i,G+1}, v_{2i,G+1,...}, v_{ni,G+1}\}$ can usually be generated by using

$$V_{i,G} = X_{r1,G} + F(X_{r2,G} - X_{r3,G}) \qquad (1)$$

where $r_1, r_2, r_3 \in (1,2...,NP)$ are randomly chosen integers, different from each other and also different from the running index i.F is a real and constant factor having value between [0, 2] and controls the amplification of differential variation $(X_{r2,G} - X_{r3,G})$.

## B. Crossover Operation

After the mutation phase, the "binominal" crossover operation is applied to, each pair of the generated mutant vector $V_{i,G}$ and its corresponding target vector $X_{i,G}$ to generate a trial vector: $U_{i,G} = (u_{1i,G+1}, u_{2i,G+1}, ..., u_{ni,G+1})$.

$$U_{j,i,G+1} \begin{cases} V_{j,i} & if \ rand_j(0,1) \leq Cr \ \forall \ j = k \\ X_{j,i} & otherwise \end{cases}$$

$$(2)$$

where $j = 1, 2, ..., n$ (n dimension problem), Cr is a user-specified crossover constant in the range [0,1], $rand_j$ is a randomly chosen integer in the range [0,1] to ensure that the trial vector $U_{i,G}$ will differ from its corresponding target vector $X_{i,G}$ by at least one parameter and $k \in (1,2,...,D)$ is the randomly chosen index.

## C. Selection Operation

If the values of some parameters of a newly generated trial vector exceed the corresponding upper and lower bounds, we randomly and uniformly reinitialize it within the search range. Then the fitness values of all trial vectors are evaluated. After that, a selection operation is performed. The fitness value of each trial vector $f(U_{i,G})$ is compared to that of its corresponding target vector $f(X_{i,G})$ in the current population. If the trial vector has smaller or equal fitness value (for minimization problem) than the corresponding target vector, the trial vector will replace the target vector and enter the population of the next generation. Otherwise, the target vector will remain in the population for the next generation.

## 3. ARTIFICIAL BEE COLONY (ABC) OPTIMIZATION ALGORITHM

ABC, as pointed out in the previous section is one of the most recently defined NIA algorithms. It was proposed by Dervis Karaboga, Erciyes University of Turkey in 2005 (Karaboga & Basturk, 2007). ABC is motivated by the intricate and disciplined behavior displayed by honey bees (Karaboga & Basturk, 2008; Karaboga, 2005: Basturk & Karaboga, 2006). In ABC system, artificial bees fly around in the search space, and some (employed and onlooker bees) choose food sources depending on the experience of themselves and their nest mates, and adjust their positions. Some (scouts) fly and choose the food sources randomly without using experience. If the nectar amount of a new source is higher than that of the previous one in their memory, they memorize the new position and forget the previous one. Thus, ABC system combines local search methods, carried out by employed and onlooker bees, with global search methods, managed by onlookers and scouts, attempting to balance exploration and exploitation process.

In order to introduce the model of forage selection that leads to the emergence of collective intelligence of honey bee swarms, the three essential components: food sources, unemployed foragers and employed foragers are described as:

- **Food Sources:** (A and B in Figure 2): For the sake of simplicity, the "profitability" of a food source can be represented with a single quantity. In our function optimization problem, the position of a food source represents a possible solution to the optimization problem and the nectar amount of a food source corresponds to the quality (fitness) of the associated solution.

- **Unemployed Foragers:** If it is assumed that a bee have no knowledge about the food sources in the search field, bee initializes its search as an unemployed forager. There are two types of them, scouts and onlookers. Their main task is exploring and exploiting food source. At the beginning, there are two choices for the unemployed foragers: (1) it becomes a scout or (2) it becomes a onlooker.

- **Scouts (S in Figure 2):** Randomly search for new food sources without any knowledge around the nest. The percentage of scout bees varies from 5% to 30% according to the information into the nest (Seeley, 1995).

- **Onlookers(R in Figure 2):** The onlookers wait in the nest and search the food source through sharing information of the employed foragers, and there is a greater probability of onlookers choosing more profitable sources.

- **Employed Foragers:** They are associated with a particular food source which they are currently exploiting. They carry with them information about this particular source, the profitability of the source and share this information with a certain probability. After the employed foraging bee loads a portion of nectar from the food source, it returns to the hive and unloads the nectar to the food area in the hive. There are three possible options related to residual amount of nectar for the foraging bee.

- If the nectar amount decreased to a low level or exhausted, foraging bee abandons the food source and become an unemployed bee (UF in Figure 2).

- If there are still sufficient amount of nectar in the food source, it can continue to forage without sharing the food source information with the nest mates (EF2 in Figure 2).

- Or it can go to the dance area to perform waggle dance for informing the nest mates about the food source (EF1 in Figure 3), as is shown in Figure 1.

In this way, the bees finally can construct a relative good solution of the optimization problems.

## Pseudocode of the ABC Algorithm

1. Initialize the population of solutions $X_{i,G}$.
2. Evaluate the population.
3. Cycle=1
4. Repeat

*Figure 1. Waggle dance of honey bees (adapted from Duan, Xing, & Xu, 2009)*

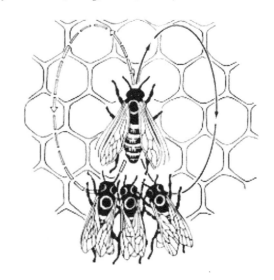

*Figure 2. The behavior of honey bee foraging for nectar (adapted from Duan, Xing, & Xu, 2009)*

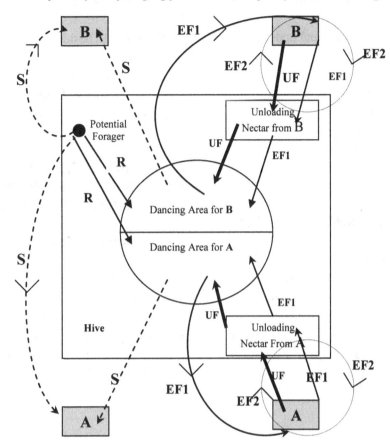

5. Produce new solutions (food source positions) $V_{ij,G}$ in the neighborhood of $X_{ij,G}$ for the employed bees using the equation:

$$V_{ij,G} = X_{ij,G} + \Phi ij(X_{ij,G} - X_{kj,G})$$ (3)

where $k \in \{1,2,...,NP\}$ and $j \in \{1,2,...D\}$ are randomly chosen indexes; $k$ has to be different from $i$; $\Phi ij$ is a random number in the range [-1, 1].

6. Apply the greedy selection process between $X_{ij,G}$ and $V_{ij,G}$.

7. Calculate the probability values $P_i$ for the solutions $X_{ij,G}$ by means of their fitness values using the equation:

$$P_i = fit_i / \sum_{i=1}^{SN} fit_i$$ (4)

In order to calculate the fitness values of solutions the following equation is employed:

$$fit_i = 1/(1 + f_i) \text{ if } f_i \geq 0$$

$$fit_i = 1 + abs(f_i) \text{ if } f_i < 0$$ (5)

Normalize $P_i$ values into [0, 1]

8. Produce the new solutions (new positions) $V_{ij,G}$ for the onlookers from the solutions $X_{ij,G}$, selected depending on $P_i$, and evaluate them.

9. Apply the greedy selection process for the onlookers between $X_{ij,G}$ and $V_{ij,G}$.

10. Determine the abandoned solution (source), if exists, and replace it with a new randomly produced solution $x_i$ for the scout using the equation:

$$X_{ij} = min_j + rand(0,1)*(max_j - min_j) \qquad (6)$$

where $min_j$ and $max_j$ are lower and upper bounds respectively.

11. Memorize the best food source position (solution) achieved so far.
12. Cycle = cycle+1
13. until cycle= Maximum Cycle Number (MCN)

## 4. PROPOSED DE-ABC ALGORITHM

The proposed DE-ABC algorithm starts like the ABC algorithm and the food sources are initialized using the steps given in the previous section. After the completion of an ABC cycle the DE operators are activated using equations (1) and (2). The presence of DE operators helps in exploitation of the food sources. Although at a glance, the structure of DE and ABC looks similar to each other; their working principals are quite different. The proposed DE-ABC preserves the structure of ABC algorithm besides including the DE operators in it. The distribution of population using DE, ABC and DE – ABC algorithms for the Sphere function is shown in Figures 3 through 5 and for the Griekwank function is in Figures 6 through 8.

## 5. PARAMETER SETTINGS, BENCHMARK PROBLEMS AND COMPARISON CRITERIA

### 5.1. Parameter Settings

DE and ABC have certain control parameters that have to be set by the user.

- The population size, which is common to all the algorithms, is taken 10, 50 and 80 for 2, 10 and 20 dimensions respec-

*Figure 3. Sphere population generation using DE for (a) NP = 50 (b) NP = 10 (c) NP = 80*

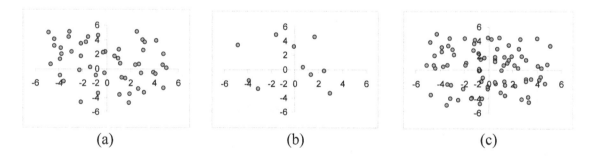

(a)    (b)    (c)

*Figure 4. Sphere population generation using ABC for (a) NP = 50 (b) NP = 10 (c) NP = 80*

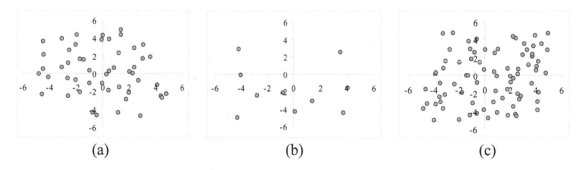

(a)    (b)    (c)

*Figure 5. Sphere population generation using DE – ABC for (a) NP = 50 (b) NP = 10 (c) NP = 80*

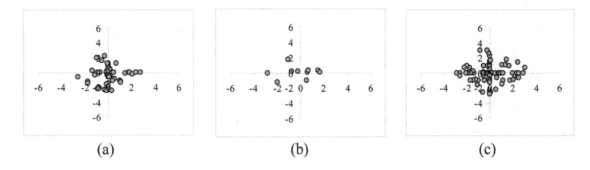

| (a) | (b) | (c) |

*Figure 6. Griekwank population generation using DE for (a) NP = 50 (b) NP = 10 (c) NP = 80*

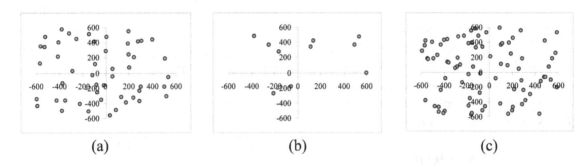

| (a) | (b) | (c) |

*Figure 7. Griekwank population generation using ABC for (a) NP = 50 (b) NP = 10 (c) NP = 80*

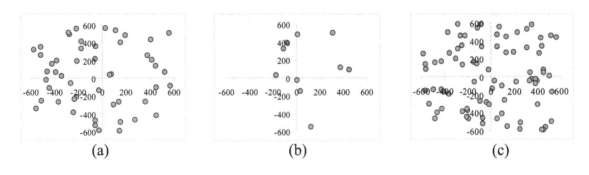

| (a) | (b) | (c) |

*Figure 8. Griekwank population generation using DE – ABC for (a) NP = 50 (b) NP = 10 (c) NP = 80*

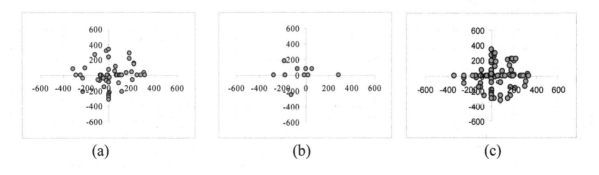

| (a) | (b) | (c) |

tively in all the algorithms for an unbiased comparisons.

- F (scaling factor) & Cr (Crossover rate) are fixed at 0.5 for DE and DE – ABC.
- The percentage of onlooker bees is 50% of the colony, the employed bees are 50% of the colony and the number of scout bees is selected as one for ABC and DE-ABC.
- Random numbers are generated using in-built function *rand( )* in DEVC++.

## 5.2. Benchmark Problems

The proposed DE-ABC algorithm is validated on a set of 4 standard benchmark problems for dimensions 2, 10 and 20 for population size 10, 50 and 80 respectively. Thus a total of 10 cases are considered. Mathematical models of the test problems are given in the Appendix.

## 5.3. Comparison Criteria

The proposed DE-ABC is compared with basic DE and basic ABC algorithm in terms of best and mean fitness function values, standard deviation and average number of function evaluations (NFE). It should be noted here that according to literature in most of the ABC algorithms the stopping criteria is that of the number of cycles (or generations)

however, in the present study we have considered NFE as a stopping criteria.

The tests are repeated for 30 runs and the average number of function evaluations (NFE) is recorded.

The maximum number of function evaluations is set $10^6$ and therefore, a *'no convergence'* (N/C) either indicates that the algorithm got stuck, or the number of function evaluations exceeded NFE max.

In every case, a run was terminated when an accuracy of $| f_{\max} - f_{\min} | < 10^{-4}$ was reached or when the maximum number of function evaluation was reached.

All algorithms i.e. classic DE, ABC, and the proposed DE – ABC are executed on Pentium IV, using DEV C++.

## 6. SIMULATION RESULTS

The simulation results obtained are recorded in Tables 1 through 10. From Tables 1 through 10, which we see that for dimension 2, the proposed DE-ABC gave the best performance although it took higher NFEs in comparison to DE and ABC. However, when we increased the dimension to 10 and 20 we observe that DE-ABC took lesser numbers of NFE in comparison to the other two algorithms.

*Table 1. Simulation results of Sphere ($f_1$) Function*

| Algorithm | NP | D | Best | Mean | SD | NFE |
|---|---|---|---|---|---|---|
| **DE – ABC** | 10 | 2 | 1.41426e-007 | 0.000135839 | 0.000337444 | 366 |
| | 50 | 10 | 1.35181e-006 | 0.000662368 | 0.000867693 | 5890 |
| | 80 | 20 | 6.82436e-006 | 0.000311187 | 0.000411421 | 20600 |
| **DE** | 10 | 2 | 7.97633e-006 | 7.97633e-006 | 1.69407e-021 | 220 |
| | 50 | 10 | 5.39006e-006 | 6.78787e-006 | 1.39781e-006 | 6700 |
| | 80 | 20 | 6.67943e-006 | 8.87211e-006 | 9.12925e-007 | 24040 |
| **ABC** | 10 | 2 | 8.64848e-006 | 8.64848e-006 | 1.69407e-021 | 200 |
| | 50 | 10 | 4.1869e-006 | 5.53121e-006 | 7.00794e-007 | 11280 |
| | 80 | 20 | 3.90216e-006 | 7.2454e-006 | 2.13423e-006 | 23730 |

*Table 2. Simulation results of Ackly's ($f_2$) Function*

| Algorithm | NP | D | Best | Mean | SD | NFE |
|---|---|---|---|---|---|---|
| **DE – ABC** | 10 | 2 | 1.39885e-006 | 0.000126046 | 0.000174626 | 832 |
| | 50 | 10 | 0.000122379 | 0.000435667 | 0.000306346 | 11595 |
| | 80 | 20 | 0.000151835 | 0.00802742 | 0.0185825 | 33856 |
| **DE** | 10 | 2 | 8.97379e-006 | 8.97379e-006 | 0 | 740 |
| | 50 | 10 | 7.58899e-006 | 9.54162e-006 | 7.15395e-007 | 14495 |
| | 80 | 20 | 8.64953e-006 | 9.29829e-006 | 4.8044e-007 | 47416 |
| **ABC** | 10 | 2 | 7.38782e-006 | 8.40324e-006 | 1.24363e-006 | 578 |
| | 50 | 10 | 6.34768e-006 | 9.00233e-006 | 9.62394e-007 | 13117 |
| | 80 | 20 | 6.81165e-006 | 8.42812e-006 | 9.34178e-007 | 36248 |

*Table 3. Simulation results of Restrigin's ($f_3$) Function*

| Algorithm | NP | D | Best | Mean | SD | NFE |
|---|---|---|---|---|---|---|
| **DE – ABC** | 10 | 2 | 2.69931e-006 | 0.253053 | 0.387342 | 815 |
| | 50 | 10 | 4.00232e-006 | 0.000142761 | 8.73691e-005 | 35595 |
| | 80 | 20 | 5.9908e-006 | 0.000996842 | 0.00163558 | 281112 |
| **DE** | 10 | 2 | 3.20153e-006 | 0.0994988 | 0.00298487 | 1005 |
| | 50 | 10 | 6.45279e-006 | 8.42915e-006 | 9.52216e-007 | 36215 |
| | 80 | 20 | 7.39131e-006 | 0.0041725 | 0.00087791 | 340192 |
| **ABC** | 10 | 2 | 2.2923e-006 | 6.31198e-006 | 2.63149e-006 | 462 |
| | 50 | 10 | 1.1587e-006 | 4.19782e-006 | 2.21857e-006 | 35940 |
| | 80 | 20 | 1.55747e-006 | 5.01263e-006 | 2.73504e-006 | 319550 |

*Table 4. Simulation results of Michalewicz ($f_4$) Function*

| Algorithm | NP | D | Best | Mean | SD | NFE |
|---|---|---|---|---|---|---|
| **DE – ABC** | 10 | 2 | -1.8013 | -1.80128 | 3.62225e-005 | 418 |
| | 50 | 10 | -9.66014 | -9.63914 | 0.0588461 | 18445 |
| | 80 | 20 | N/C | N/C | N/C | N/C |
| **DE** | 10 | 2 | -0.960503 | -0.960503 | 1.11022e-016 | 103 |
| | 50 | 10 | -3.12762 | -3.12762 | 0 | 112 |
| | 80 | 20 | -5.25674 | -5.25674 | 8.88178e-016 | 137 |
| **ABC** | 10 | 2 | -0.935911 | -0.935911 | 0 | 100 |
| | 50 | 10 | -3.36116 | -3.36116 | 4.44089e-016 | 107 |
| | 80 | 20 | -5.01121 | -5.01121 | 8.88178e-016 | 132 |

*Table 5. Simulation results of Alpine ($f_5$) Function*

| Algorithm | NP | D | Best | Mean | SD | NFE |
|-----------|-----|-----|------|------|-----|-----|
| *DE – ABC* | 10 | 2 | 9.39029e-007 | 0.000186107 | 0.00047641 | 714 |
| | 50 | 10 | 0.000132767 | 0.00124653 | 0.00175087 | 27435 |
| | 80 | 20 | 0.000139115 | 0.000635562 | 0.000474558 | 54385 |
| *DE* | 10 | 2 | 4.06555e-006 | 4.06555e-006 | 8.47033e-022 | 630 |
| | 50 | 10 | 9.03604e-006 | 9.19599e-006 | 1.95892e-007 | 38920 |
| | 80 | 20 | 7.63127e-006 | 9.19597e-006 | 6.65184e-007 | 71052 |
| *ABC* | 10 | 2 | 9.91257e-006 | 9.91257e-006 | 0 | 290 |
| | 50 | 10 | 8.76647e-006 | 9.6068e-006 | 2.80109e-007 | 35600 |
| | 80 | 20 | 4.13845e-006 | 9.12121e-006 | 1.66714e-006 | 76750 |

*Table 6. Simulation results of Axis ($f_6$) Function*

| Algorithm | NP | D | Best | Mean | SD | NFE |
|-----------|-----|-----|------|------|-----|-----|
| *DE – ABC* | 10 | 2 | 3.21442e-006 | 0.00134908 | 0.00396866 | 379 |
| | 50 | 10 | 1.38415e-005 | 0.00036464 | 0.000580475 | 7085 |
| | 80 | 20 | 6.73907e-005 | 0.000383795 | 0.00029495 | 23088 |
| *DE* | 10 | 2 | 7.63574e-006 | 7.63574e-006 | 1.69407e-021 | 400 |
| | 50 | 10 | 4.58075e-006 | 6.70094e-006 | 2.13832e-006 | 7760 |
| | 80 | 20 | 5.55072e-006 | 7.67583e-006 | 1.19273e-006 | 27512 |
| *ABC* | 10 | 2 | 9.26607e-006 | 9.26607e-006 | 0 | 180 |
| | 50 | 10 | 3.7798e-006 | 8.18618e-006 | 2.20867e-006 | 10670 |
| | 80 | 20 | 3.97282e-006 | 7.46319e-006 | 1.83606e-006 | 24940 |

*Table 7. Simulation results of Zakharov ($f_7$) Function*

| Algorithm | NP | D | Best | Mean | SD | NFE |
|-----------|-----|-----|------|------|-----|-----|
| *DE – ABC* | 10 | 2 | 2.65288e-007 | 1.78716e-005 | 1.91056e-005 | 421 |
| | 50 | 10 | 9.81609e-006 | 0.000252435 | 0.00030021 | 7990 |
| | 80 | 20 | 6.4807e-005 | 0.000593566 | 0.000938498 | 28480 |
| *DE* | 10 | 2 | 5.15121e-006 | 5.15121e-006 | 0 | 480 |
| | 50 | 10 | 3.41773e-006 | 7.22354e-006 | 1.9298e-006 | 8680 |
| | 80 | 20 | 7.14735e-006 | 9.14185e-006 | 8.45823e-007 | 32584 |
| *ABC* | 10 | 2 | 2.0567e-006 | 2.0567e-006 | 0 | 210 |
| | 50 | 10 | 4.72241e-007 | 5.42201e-006 | 2.30606e-006 | 6745 |
| | 80 | 20 | 4.89654e-006 | 7.15085e-006 | 1.71268e-006 | 29771 |

*Table 8. Simulation results of Schawefel's ($f_8$) Function*

| Algorithm | NP | D | Best | Mean | SD | NFE |
|---|---|---|---|---|---|---|
| *DE – ABC* | 10 | 2 | 1.73534e-005 | 0.000226622 | 0.000418352 | 619 |
| | 50 | 10 | 7.0052e-005 | 0.0004471 | 0.000684975 | 10405 |
| | 80 | 20 | 0.000251964 | 0.00236929 | 0.00359792 | 31152 |
| *DE* | 10 | 2 | 5.45714e-006 | 5.45714e-006 | 0 | 670 |
| | 50 | 10 | 7.00576e-006 | 7.00576e-006 | 0 | 12500 |
| | 80 | 20 | 9.7283e-006 | 9.83354e-006 | 5.26196e-008 | 43248 |
| *ABC* | 10 | 2 | 5.32975e-006 | 5.32975e-006 | 8.47033e-022 | 380 |
| | 50 | 10 | | | | |
| | 80 | 20 | 8.03105e-006 | 8.62398e-006 | 7.26188e-007 | 41982 |

*Table 9. Simulation results of Griekwank ($f_9$) Function*

| Algorithm | NP | D | Best | Mean | SD | NFE |
|---|---|---|---|---|---|---|
| *DE – ABC* | 10 | 2 | 4.19473e-007 | 0.00079131 | 0.00193917 | 1561 |
| | 50 | 10 | 7.68649e-006 | 0.00216352 | 0.00615874 | 35165 |
| | 80 | 20 | 2.1205e-005 | 0.000816291 | 0.00131217 | 41056 |
| *DE* | 10 | 2 | 4.81652e-006 | 4.81652e-006 | 0 | 1250 |
| | 50 | 10 | 4.79866e-006 | 8.4106e-006 | 1.56693e-006 | 36780 |
| | 80 | 20 | 7.74183e-006 | 9.03474e-006 | 6.50681e-007 | 44320 |
| *ABC* | 10 | 2 | 7.32681e-007 | 7.32681e-007 | 0 | 1140 |
| | 50 | 10 | 3.17282e-007 | 6.69451e-006 | 3.33404e-006 | 35365 |
| | 80 | 20 | 2.12065e-006 | 5.6188e-006 | 2.9738e-006 | 41062 |

*Table 10. Simulation results of Schawefel's ($f_{10}$) Function*

| Algorithm | NP | D | Best | Mean | SD | NFE |
|---|---|---|---|---|---|---|
| *DE – ABC* | 10 | 2 | 6.26428e-006 | 0.0016042 | 0.00470305 | 1330 |
| | 50 | 10 | 0.000143101 | 0.00269601 | 0.00428292 | 26920 |
| | 80 | 20 | 0.000420069 | 0.00281519 | 0.00285889 | 103728 |
| *DE* | 10 | 2 | 7.26849e-006 | 7.26849e-006 | 0 | 1010 |
| | 50 | 10 | 8.51298e-006 | 8.77891e-006 | 8.86454e-008 | 27705 |
| | 80 | 20 | 8.62295e-006 | 9.10112e-006 | 5.01392e-007 | 138136 |
| *ABC* | 10 | 2 | 9.82577e-006 | 9.82577e-006 | 1.69407e-021 | 1150 |
| | 50 | 10 | N/C | N/C | N/C | N/C |
| | 80 | 20 | N/C | N/C | N/C | N/C |

It can also be noticed that the proposed algorithm do not converge for the Michalewicz Function when NP = 80 & D = 20 and has taken more NFE's compared to DE and ABC algorithms for all combinations of NP and D.

The SD is also noticed 0 (Zero) for DE when NP = 50 and D = 10, similarly for ABC the SD is 0 (zero) when NP = 10 and D = 0, which clearly indicates that DE and ABC are sensitive at these combinations.

Figures 9 through 11 illustrate the summary of the results in a series of 'easy-to-compare' charts. For each dimension the following information is shown; best, mean fitness function value, the standard deviation, and the NFE, The y-axis shows the normalized values of the variable which means equal segments from different dimensions can correspond to entirely different actual values. Therefore, these charts are useful to compare the performance of various algorithms for only the same dimension.

*Figure 9. Results of sphere function*

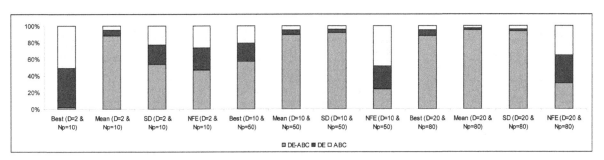

*Figure 10. Results of Ackly's Function*

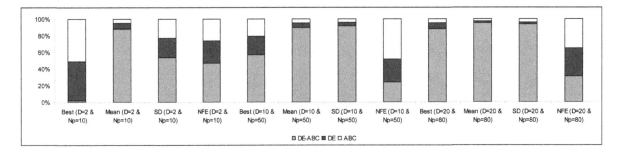

*Figure 11. Results of Restrigin's Function*

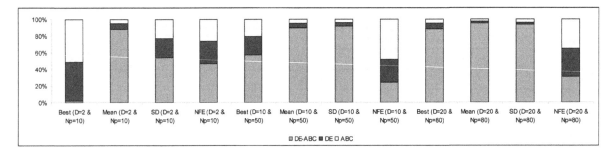

## 7. CONCLUSION

In the present study we proposed an Artificial Bee Colony algorithm embedded with Differential Evolution operators. The algorithm named DE-ABC is validated on a set of ten standard benchmark problems for different dimensions. The numerical results on comparison with basic DE and basic ABC algorithms showed that the proposed DE-ABC algorithm performed better or at par with the other algorithms. However, the problem set considered in the present study is rather narrow and more test problems are needed to make any concrete judgment about the algorithm. Further, the proposed DE-ABC failed to give a solution for a 20 dimension Michalewicz function indicating that it needs further improvement.

## REFERENCES

Bäck, T., Hammel, U., & Schwefel, H.-P. (1997). Evolutionary computation: Comments on the history and current state. *IEEE Transactions on Evoltionary Computing*, *1*(1), 3–17. doi:10.1109/4235.585888

Bäck, T., & Schwefel, H.-P. (1996). Evolutionary computation: An overview. In *Proceedings of the IEEE International Conference on Evolutionary Computation* (pp. 20-29).

Basturk, B., & Karaboga, D. (2006, May 12-14). An artificial bee colony (ABC) algorithm for numeric function optimization. In *Proceedings of the IEEE Swarm Intelligence Symposium*, Indianapolis, IN.

Dorigo, M., & Gambardella, L. M. (1997). Ant colony system: A cooperative learning approach to the traveling salesman problem. *IEEE Transactions on Evolutionary Computation*, *1*(1), 53–66. doi:10.1109/4235.585892

Duan, H., Xing, Z., & Xu, C. (2009). An improved quantum evolutionary algorithm based on artificial bee colony optimization. In Yu, W., & Sanchez, E. N. (Eds.), *Advances in computational intelligence* (pp. 269–278). Berlin, Germany: Springer-Verlag. doi:10.1007/978-3-642-03156-4_27

Fogel, D. (1995). *Evolutionary computation*. Los Alamitos, CA: IEEE Press.

Fogel, L. J., Owens, A. J., & Walsh, M. J. (1996). *Artificial intelligence through simulated evolution*. New York, NY: John Wiley & Sons.

Goldberg, D. E. (1989). *Genetic algorithms in search, optimization, and machine learning*. Reading, MA: Addison-Wesley.

Holland, J. H. (1975). *Adaptation in natural and artificial systems*. Ann Arbor, MI: University of Michigan Press.

Karaboga, D. (2005). *An idea based on honey bee swarm for numerical optimization* (Tech. Rep. No. TR06). Kayseri, Turkey: Erciyes University.

Karaboga, D., & Akay, B. (2009). A survey: Algorithms simulating bee swarm intelligence. *Artificial Intelligence Review*, *31*, 61–85. doi:10.1007/s10462-009-9127-4

Karaboga, D., Akay, B., & Ozturk, C. (2007). Artificial bee colony (ABC) optimization algorithm for training feed-forward neural networks. In V. Torra, Y. Naurkawa, & Y. Yoshida (Eds.), *Proceedings of the 4th International Conference on Modeling Decisions for Artificial Intelligence* (LNCS 4617, pp. 318-329).

Karaboga, D., & Basturk, B. (2007). A powerful and efficient algorithm for numerical function optimization: Artificial bee colony (ABC) algorithm. *Journal of Global Optimization*, *39*(3), 459–471. doi:10.1007/s10898-007-9149-x

Karaboga, D., & Basturk, B. (2007). Artificial bee colony (ABC) optimization algorithm for solving constrained optimization problems. In P. Melin, O. Castillo, L. T. Aguilar, J. Kacprzyk, & W. Pedrycz (Eds.), *Proceedings of the 12th International Conference on Advances in Soft Computing-Foundations of Fuzzy Logic and Soft Computing* (LNCS 4529, pp. 789-798).

Karaboga, D., & Basturk, B. (2008). On the performance of artificial bee colony (ABC) algorithm. *Applied Soft Computing, 8*, 687–697. doi:10.1016/j.asoc.2007.05.007

Karaboga, N. (2009). A new design method based on artificial bee colony algorithm for digital IIR filters. *Journal of the Franklin Institute, 346*, 328–348. doi:10.1016/j.jfranklin.2008.11.003

Kennedy, J., & Eberhart, R. (1995). Particle swarm optimization. In *Proceedings of the IEEE International Conference on Neural Networks*, Perth, Australia (pp. 1942-1948).

Pan, Q.-K., Tasgetiren, M. F., Suganthan, P. N., & Chua, T. J. (2011). A discrete artificial bee colony algorithm for the lot-streaming flow shop scheduling problem. *Information Sciences, 181*(12), 2455–2468. doi:10.1016/j.ins.2009.12.025

Passino, K. M. (2002). Biomimicry of bacterial foraging for distributed optimization and control. *IEEE Control Systems Magazine*, 52–67. doi:10.1109/MCS.2002.1004010

Pawar, P., Rao, R., & Davim, J. (2008). Optimization of process parameters of milling process using particle swarm optimization and artificial bee colony algorithm. In *Proceedings of the International Conference on Advances in Mechanical Engineering*.

Ponton, J. W., & Klemes, J. (1993). Alternatives to neural networks for inferential measurement. *Computers & Chemical Engineering, 17*, 42–47. doi:10.1016/0098-1354(93)80080-7

Rao, R. S., Narasimham, S., & Ramalingaraju, M. (2008). Optimization of distribution network configuration for loss reduction using artificial bee colony algorithm. *International Journal of Electrical Power and Energy Systems Engineering, 1*, 116–122.

Rechenberg, I. (1994). *Evolution strategie.* Stuttgart, Germany: Frommann-Holzboog.

Seeley, T. D. (1995). *The wisdom of the hive.* Boston, MA: Harvard University Press.

Simon, D. (2008). Biogeography-based optimization. *IEEE Transactions on Evolutionary Computation, 12*(6), 702–713. doi:10.1109/TEVC.2008.919004

Singh, A. (2009). An artificial bee colony algorithm for the leaf-constrained minimum spanning tree problem. *Applied Soft Computing, 9*, 625–631. doi:10.1016/j.asoc.2008.09.001

Storn, R., & Price, K. (1995). *DE –a simple and efficient adaptive scheme for global optimization over continuous space* (Tech. Rep. No. TR-95-012). Berkeley, CA: International Computer Science Institute.

Storn, R., & Price, K. (1997). Differential evolution – a simple and efficient heuristic for global optimization over continuous spaces. *Journal of Global Optimization, 11*, 341–359. doi:10.1023/A:1008202821328

Zhu, G., & Kwong, S. (2010). Gbest-guided artificial bee colony algorithm for numerical function optimization. *Applied Mathematics and Computation, 217*(7), 3166–3173. doi:10.1016/j.amc.2010.08.049

# APPENDIX

*Table 11. Mathematical models of test problems*

| Function Name | Definition | S | X* | $f_{min}$ |
|---|---|---|---|---|
| Sphere | $f_1(x) = \sum_{i=1}^{n} x_i^2$ | [-5.12, 5.12] | $f_1(0,...,0)$ | 0 |
| Ackly's | $f_2(x) = $ $-20 * \exp\left(-.2\sqrt{\frac{1}{n}\sum_{i=1}^{n} x_i^2}\right) - \exp\left(\frac{1}{n}\sum_{i=1}^{n}\cos(2\pi x_i)\right) + 20 + e$ | [-32, 32] | $f_2(0,...,0)$ | 0 |
| Restrigin's | $f_3(x) = 10n + \sum_{i=1}^{n}\left(x_i^2 - 10\cos\left(2\pi x_i\right)\right)$ | [-5.12, 5.12] | $f_3(0,...,0)$ | 0 |
| Michalewicz | $f_4(x) = -\sum_{i=1}^{n}\sin(x_i)(\sin(ix_i^2 / \pi))^{2m}$ | [0, $\pi$] | $f_4(n=10)$ | -9.66015 |
| Alpine | $f_5(x) = \sum_{i=1}^{n}\left|x_i \sin(x_i) + 0.1x_i\right|$ | [-10, 10] | $f_5(0,...,0)$ | 0 |
| Axis – Parallel | $f_6(x) = \sum_{i=1}^{n} ix_i^2$ | [-5.12, 5.12] | $f_6(0,...,0)$ | 0 |
| Zakharov | $f_7(x) = \sum_{i=1}^{n} x_i^2 + (\sum_{i=1}^{n} 0.5ix_i)^2 + (\sum_{i=1}^{n} 0.5ix_i)^4$ | [-5, 10] | $f_7(0,...,0)$ | 0 |
| Schawefel's | $f_8(x) = \sum_{i=1}^{n}\left|x_i\right| + \prod_{i=1}^{n}\left|x_i\right|$ | [-10, 10] | $f_8(0,...,0)$ | 0 |
| Griekwank | $f_9(x) = \frac{1}{4000}\sum_{i=1}^{n} x_i^2 - \prod_{i=1}^{n}\cos(\frac{x_i}{\sqrt{i}}) + 1$ | [-600, 600] | $f_9(0,...,0)$ | 0 |
| Schawefel's | $f_{10}(x) = \max_i\left\{\left|x_i\right|, 1 \le i \le n\right\}$ | [-100, 100] | $f_{10}(0,...,0)$ | 0 |

Notes: $f_{min}$ = the minimum of the value of the function: $X^*$ = the minimum: $S$ = the feasible region: and $S \in$ R$^n$, n is dimension of the function.

*This work was previously published in the International Journal of Applied Evolutionary Computation, Volume 2, Issue 3, edited by Wei-Chiang Samuelson Hong, pp. 1-14, copyright 2011 by IGI Publishing (an imprint of IGI Global).*

# Chapter 10
# Appropriate Evolutionary Algorithm for Scheduling in FMS

**B. B. Choudhury**
*IGIT Sarang, India*

**D. Mishra**
*VSS University of Technology, India*

**B. B. Biswal**
*NIT Rourkela, India*

**R. N. Mahapatra**
*Institute of Technical Education and Research, India*

## ABSTRACT

*The diffusion of flexible manufacturing systems (FMS) has not only invigorated production systems, but has also given considerable impetus to relevant analytical fields like scheduling theory and adaptive controls. Depending on the demand of the job there can be variation in batch size. The change in the jobs depends upon the renewal rate. But this does not involve much change in the FMS setup. This paper obtains an optimal schedule of operations to minimize the total processing time in a modular FMS. The FMS setup considered here consists of four numbers of machines to accomplish the desired machining operations. The scheduling deals with optimizing the cost function in terms of machining time. The powers Evolutionary Algorithms, like genetic algorithm (GA) and simulated annealing (SA), can be beneficially utilized for optimization of scheduling FMS. The present work utilizes these powerful approaches and finds out their appropriateness for planning and scheduling of FMS producing variety of parts in batch mode.*

## 1. INTRODUCTION

With the increasing sophistication of production practices there has been a corresponding increase in the importance and profitability of efficient production scheduling. The global nature of the present manufacturing environment has necessitated an improvement in the way companies

DOI: 10.4018/978-1-4666-3628-6.ch010

manufacture their products. This increase in demand has been matched by an increase in theoretical findings. The current state of production scheduling is a mixture of approaches from different areas. The intractability of the problem also lends itself to making the developments widely varied. Since the scheduling problem is not amenable to any particular solution, it is treated as NP-hard problem, and it can be treated as a subset of operational research (Buyurgan,

Saygin, & Kilic, 2004; Moon, Kim, & Gen, 2004; Lee, Kim, & Choi, 2003). Production scheduling concerns the efficient allocation of resources over time for the manufacture of goods. The objective of the present scheduling problem is to find a way to assign and to sequence the activities of these shared resources such that production constraints are satisfied and production costs are minimized. FMS is designed to combine the high efficiency of a transfer line and the flexibility of a job shop to best suit to the batch production of mid-volume and mid-variety products. It may be realized that for an industry it is possible to reach for high flexibility by making innovative technological and organizational efforts. There has been a paradigm shift in manufacturing industries over the years which can be attributed to this idea (Vieira, Herrmann, & Lin, 2003; Lee, Jeong, & Moon, 2002). Flexibility is a property of a system and a system has a definite purpose to carry out. So flexibility is defined with reference to a particular task set (Mandelbaum & Brill, 1989). Manufacturing flexibility may be defined as the ability to cope with changing circumstances or instability caused by the environment (Gupta, 1993; Primrose & Verter, 1996). The intangible parts of flexibility that cannot be quantified in monetary terms are measured by a surrogate value (usually, the scoring method is applied) (Demmel & Askin, 1992; Stam & Kuula, 1991; Son, 1991; Suresh, 1991; Troxler & Blank, 1989; Venk, 1990; Zahir, 1991).

Given the part types and their volume in each batch FMS Scheduling is concerned with the real time operation of the system and the allocation of tools to the machine and allocation of operations to machines and is concerned with the following:

a.  Releasing of part types to the system: Only a subset of the part types constitutes a batch. Releasing rule priorities the part type of the batch leading to their ordered entry to the system.

b.  Assignment of operations of part type to machines: Routing flexibility provides alternate machines for an operation of a part type. Operation assignment rule is used to assign an operation to one amongst the alternate machines available for the purpose.

c.  Dispatching of part types waiting for processing before a machine: At any given point of time several part types wait in the local buffer for their turn to get service in a machine. Dispatching rules are used to prioritize them.

The present work is envisaged to work out the optimal scheduling process for modular FMS setups. The scheduling deals with optimizing the cost function in terms of machining time. The search space includes a number of feasible combinations and out of these; the best fit solution is derived with help of Genetic Algorithm (GA) and Simulated Annealing (SA). In order to accomplish the objective, the methodology is split into the following:

• Detailing the machining processes involved in the manufacture of the parts
• Application of GA and SA for scheduling
• Optimization of scheduling time with alternate assignments within FMS.
• Comparison of results obtained from the scheduling optimization methods and recommending the appropriate one.

## 2. MODEL FORMULATION

### 2.1. Description of the Parts

FMS has the capability to process a large number of part types. However, in the present study, the parts to be processed in the selected setups are so chosen that they are almost similar in their functions with differences in their physical and geometrical properties. The study of the physical properties (design attributes) and manufacturing requirements (manufacturing attributes) of the considered parts put them under one group from group technology viewpoint. The parts are manufactured in batches and depending on the demand, there can be variation in batch size as well as the product renewal rate. The machining requirements are almost same for all the parts. The parts have been chosen keeping in view that they can be manufactured under the set of facilities under consideration without major changes in the setup requirements. The machining requirements for the parts are: 1) facing, 2) turning, 3) drilling, 4) boring, and 5) thread cutting.

The details of machining operations of part-1, part-2 and part-3 (as shown in Figures 1(a) through 1(c) respectively) are given in Tables 1 through 3 respectively.

## 2.2. Description of the Setups

The three setups under consideration consist of four machines (M) to accomplish the desired machining operations viz. facing, turning, drilling, boring and thread cutting as described before, on all the three parts.Setup-1 consists of two numbers of lathes, namely lathe-1($M_1$) and lathe-2 ($M_3$) and two numbers of machining centres, machining centre-1 ($M_2$) and machining centre-2 (M4). In setup-2, a CNC drilling machine replaces the machining centre-2 of setup-1 as machine $M_4$. Rest of the machines in the setup remains unaltered. In setup-3, another CNC drilling machine replaces the machining centre-1 of setup-2 as machine M2. Rest

*Figure 1. (a) Graphical model of part 1, (b) Graphical model of part 2 and (c) Graphical model of part 3*

*Table 1. Processing operations for part-1*

| Sl.No. | Operation | Tool used |
|---|---|---|
| 1 | Facing of face 1 ($F_{11}$) | Facing tool |
| 2 | Turning of φ 75 ($T_{11}$) | Turning tool |
| 3 | Drilling of φ 2.5 ($D_{11}$) | Drills |
| 4 | Step boring of φ 60 and φ 20 ($B_{11}$) | Boring tool |
| 5 | Facing of face 2 ($F_{12}$) | Facing tool |
| 6 | Turning of φ 25 ($T_{12}$) | Turning tool |
| 7 | Thread cutting M30×2.5 ($TH_{11}$) | Threading tool |
| 8 | Drill φ 6, 3 nos. ($D_{12}$) | Drills |

*Table 2. Processing operations for part-2*

| Sl.No. | Operation | Tool used |
|---|---|---|
| 1 | Facing of face 1 (F2₁) | Facing tool |
| 2 | Turning of φ 114 ($T_{21}$) | Turning tool |
| 3 | Drilling of φ 7,4 nos. ($D_{21}$) | Drills |
| 4 | Step boring of φ 76,φ 60 & φ 32 ($B_{21}$) | Boring tool |
| 5 | Facing of face 2 ($F_{22}$) | Facing tool |
| 6 | Turning of φ 72 ($T_{22}$) | Turning tool |
| 7 | Drill φ 5, 2 nos. ($D_{22}$) | Drills |
| 8 | Thread cutting M30×5, 2 nos. ($TH_{21}$) | Threading tool |

*Table 3. Processing operations for part-3*

| Sl.No. | Operation | Tool used |
|---|---|---|
| 1 | Facing of face 1($F_{31}$) | Facing tool |
| 2 | Turning of φ 100 ($T_{31}$) | Turning tool |
| 3 | Drilling of φ 7,4 nos. ($D_{31}$) | Drills |
| 4 | Drilling of φ 5,4 nos. ($D_{32}$) | Drills |
| 5 | Thread cutting M30×5, 4 nos. ($TH_{31}$) | Threading tool |
| 6 | Facing of face 2 ($F_{32}$) | Facing tool |
| 7 | Turning of φ 60 ($T_{32}$) | Turning tool |
| 8 | Drilling of φ 2.5, ($D_{33}$) | Drills |

of the machines in the setup remains the same as in setup-2. Alternate routes have been considered in the setups for all the three parts with machine breakdown and availability fully captured.

The three different alternate routes via which the parts are manufactured in setup-1 are: $R_1 = M_1 \rightarrow M_2 \rightarrow M_3 \rightarrow M_4$, $R_2 = M_3 \rightarrow M_4 \rightarrow M_2$, and $R_3 = M_1 \rightarrow M_4 \rightarrow M_3 \rightarrow M_4$. The operations performed, at all the machines via different routes, for each part in setup-1 are given in Table 4 for part-1, part-2 and part-3 correspondingly. The routes for setup-2 are: $R1 = M1 \rightarrow M2 \rightarrow M3 \rightarrow M_4$, $R_2 = M_3 \rightarrow M_4 \rightarrow M_2 \rightarrow M_3$, and $R_3 = M_1 \rightarrow M_4 \rightarrow M_3 \rightarrow M_4$. The operations performed, at all the machines via different routes, for each part in setup-2 are given in Table 5 for part-1, part-2 and part-3 correspondingly. The routes for setup-3 are: $R_1 = M_1 \rightarrow M_2 \rightarrow M_3 \rightarrow M_4$, $R_2 = M_3 \rightarrow M_4 \rightarrow M_2 \rightarrow M_3$, and $R_3 = M_1 \rightarrow M_2 \rightarrow M_3 \rightarrow M_2$.

The operations performed, at all the machines via different routes, for each part in setup-3 are given in Table 6 for part-1, part-2 and part-3 correspondingly.

## 3. METHODOLOGY

The different approaches made by researchers are mostly theoretical and specific problems are not dealt with. It is also observed that a good number of authors have attempted to relative and logical assessing of manufacturing a system. The present study is aimed at quantification of manufactur-

*Table 4. Machines on routes of setup-1*

| Route1:$M_1(F_{11},T_{11}) \rightarrow M_2(D_{11},B_{11}) \rightarrow M_3(F_{12},T_{12}) \rightarrow M_4(D_{12},TH_{11})$ Route2:$M_3(F_{11},T_{11}) \rightarrow M_4(D_{11},B_{11}) \rightarrow M_2(F_{12},T_{12},D_{12}) \rightarrow M_3(TH_{11})$ Route3:$M_1(F_{11},T_{11}) \rightarrow M_4(D_{11},B_{11}) \rightarrow M_3(F_{12},T_{12}) \rightarrow M_4(D_{12},TH_{11})$ |
| --- |
| Route1:$M_1(F_{21},T_{21}) \rightarrow M_2(D_{21},B_{21}) \rightarrow M_3(F_{22},T_{22}) \rightarrow M_4(D_{22},TH_{21})$ Route2:$M_3(F_{21},T_{21}) \rightarrow M_4(D_{21},B_{21}) \rightarrow M_2(F_{22},T_{22},D_{22}) \rightarrow M_3(TH_{21})$ Route3:$M_1(F_{21},T_{21}) \rightarrow M4(D_{21},B_{21}) \rightarrow M_3(F_{22},T_{22}) \rightarrow M_4(D_{22},TH_{21})$ |
| Route1:$M_1(F_{31},T_{31}) \rightarrow M_2(D_{31},D_{32},TH_{31}) \rightarrow M_3(F_{32},T_{32}) \rightarrow M_4(D_{33},TH_{32})$ Route2:$M_3(F_{31},T_{31}) \rightarrow M_4(D_{31},D_{32},TH_{31}) \rightarrow M_2(F_{32},T_{32},D_{33}) \rightarrow M_3(TH_{32})$ Route3:$M_1(F_{31},T_{31}) \rightarrow M_4(D_{31},D_{32},TH_{31}) \rightarrow M_3(F_{32},T_{32}) \rightarrow M_4(D_{33},TH_{32})$ |

*Table 5. Machines on routes of setup-2*

| Route1:$M_1(F_{11},T_{11}) \rightarrow M_2(D_{11},B_{11}) \rightarrow M_3(F_{12},T_{12},TH_{11}) \rightarrow M_4(D_{12})$ Route2:$M_3(F_{11},T_{11}) \rightarrow M_4(D_{11},B_{11}) \rightarrow M_2(D_{12}) \rightarrow M_3(F_{12},T_{12},TH_{11})$ Route3:$M_1(F_{11},T_{11}) \rightarrow M_2(D_{11},B_{11}) \rightarrow M_3(F_{12},T_{12},TH_{11}) \rightarrow M_2(D_{12})$ |
| --- |
| Route1:$M_1(F_{21},T_{21}) \rightarrow M_2(D_{22},B_{21}) \rightarrow M_3(F_{22},T_{22},TH_{21}) \rightarrow M_4(D_{21})$ Route2:$M_3(F_{21},T_{21}) \rightarrow M_4(D_{21},D_{22}) \rightarrow M_2(B_{21}) \rightarrow M_3(F_{22},T_{22},TH_{21})$ Route3:$M_1(F_{21},T_{21}) \rightarrow M_2(D_{22},B_{21}) \rightarrow M_3(F_{22},T_{22},TH_{21}) \rightarrow M_2(D_{21})$ |
| Route1:$M_1(F_{31},T_{31}) \rightarrow M_2(D_{32},D_{33}) \rightarrow M_3(F_{32},T_{32},TH_{31},TH_{32}) \rightarrow M_4(D_{31})$ Route2:$M_3(F_{31},T_{31},F_{32},T_{32}) \rightarrow M_4(D_{31},D_{32}) \rightarrow M_2(D_{33}) \rightarrow M_3(TH_{31},TH_{32})$ Route3:$M_1(F_{31},T_{31}) \rightarrow M_2(D_{32},D_{33}) \rightarrow M_3(F_{32},T_{32},TH_{31},TH_{32}) \rightarrow M_2(D_{31})$ |

*Table 6. Machines on routes of setup-3*

| Route 1:$M_1(F_{11},T_{11}) \rightarrow M_2(D_{11},B_{11}) \rightarrow M_3(F_{12},T_{12},TH_{11}) \rightarrow M_4(D_{12})$ Route 2:$M_3(F_{11},T_{11}) \rightarrow M_4(D_{11},B_{11}) \rightarrow M_2(F_{12},T_{12},D_{12}) \rightarrow M_3(TH_{11})$ Route 3:$M_1(F_{11},T_{11}) \rightarrow M_2(D_{11},B_{11}) \rightarrow M_3(F_{12},T_{12}) \rightarrow M_2(D_{12},TH_{11})$ |
| --- |
| Route 1:$M_1(F_{21},T_{21}) \rightarrow M_2(D_{22},B_{21}) \rightarrow M_3(F_{22},T_{22},TH_{21}) \rightarrow M_4(D_{21})$ Route 2:$M_3(F_{21},T_{21}) \rightarrow M_4(D_{21},B_{21}) \rightarrow M_2(F_{22},T_{22},D_{22}) \rightarrow M_3(TH_{21})$ Route 3:$M_1(F_{21},T_{21}) \rightarrow M_2(D_{21},B_{21}) \rightarrow M_3(F_{22},T_{22}) \rightarrow M_2(D_{22},TH_{21})$ |
| Route1:$M_1(F_{31},T_{31}) \rightarrow M_2(D_{32},D_{33},TH_{31},TH_{32}) \rightarrow M_3(F_{32},T_{32}) \rightarrow M_4(D_{31})$ Route2:$M_3(F_{31},T_{31}) \rightarrow M_4(D_{31},D_{32},D_{33}) \rightarrow M_2(F_{32},T_{32}) \rightarrow M_3(TH_{31},TH_{32})$ Route3:$M_1(F_{31},T_{31}) \rightarrow M_2(D_{31},D_{32},TH_{31}) \rightarrow M_3(F_{32},T_{32}) \rightarrow M_2(D_{33},TH_{32})$ |

ing systems. Scheduling of FMS as a whole is a complex concept influenced by a large number of components with the machines, the flow pattern of the inventories, the processing operations, the parts and the material handling systems being the major ones. The effects of change in these components can be studied accurately by considering an actual production system. However, in the present study, virtual production environments analogous to actual manufacturing facilities in shop floor have been considered which facilitate better manipulation for the purpose of flexibility study in changed situations. The results of design of experiments give rise to concentrating the study on three numbers of setups, each producing same three numbers of parts through three alternate routes. Selection of setups was carried out in virtual environment using VNC in which three alternate setups were finally selected on the basis of convenience, utility, and operational requirement for producing the three parts. The GA interface interacts with the modules of design process modelling and configuration and prepares the data necessary for the GA-engine. Using the data gathered, the GA-engine searches the near optimal solution among candidates in the population pool. The schedule displayer transforms each candidate solution into a feasible schedule by considering the resource constraints imposed, while the iterative design analyzer is invoked to assess the time span for the schedule. The objective function determines the quality of a schedule. In the first sections, the operators of GA used in this work, namely chromosome encoding, crossover and mutation operators as well as the fitness scaling and selection are addressed in detail. It is important to note that this work focuses on non-interrupted scheduling, where interruption is not allowed when a task is underway. In the second sections, the SA approach for finding out the optimal schedule of operations assignment to machines is carried out. SA is motivated by an analogy to annealing in solids. The algorithm simulates the cooling processes by gradually lowering the temperature of the system until it converges to a steady frozen state. In the present work an attempt has been made to optimize the scheduling of FMS setups using GA and SA.

## 3.1. Simulation of the Setups

The setups have been modeled in QUEST ver. 4.0 a 3D graphics-based Queuing Event Simulation Tool for analyzing the manufacturing process visu-

ally and obtaining useful data for further analysis. The production scenarios, product mixes and failure responses for machine and labour utilization, throughput bottlenecks and inventory evaluation are efficiently explored in this software. The information and statistics generated by the simulation gives useful inputs for studying the behaviour of a manufacturing process and comparing the same with one another. The setups under are modeled using QUEST to study the operation of the entire process, regulating the flow of inventory, determination of material handling time, determination of cycle time and getting a complete picture of scheduling and for plotting of the process charts.

The individual machining times are obtained from modeling the machines and performing virtual operations in VNC ver. 5.0, interactive 3D graphics-based real time simulation software. This enables to improve the quality of CNC part programs, eliminate catastrophic program errors and optimize machining process. The fast and real time simulation eliminates the uncertainty about NC programs. It automatically detects collisions and near misses between tool and fixtures, spindle and workpiece and virtually any part in the work cell. The CNC lathe, CNC machining centre and CNC drilling machine have been retrieved from the library of VNC and have been modified according to the need of the setups for performing the machining simulation. Virtual NC helps to reduce cycle times by more than 40% and avoid CNC machine downtime for dry runs. The outputs of simulation in VNC have been used as inputs to the models in QUEST. The timings (in seconds) for each individual operation (such as $F_{11}$, $T_{11}$, $F_{22}$, $T_{22}$, $D_{11}$, $D_{12}$, etc.) were recorded for different machines on which the operations were actually carried out, from simulation and are presented in Table 7.

In the setups, robots carry out the loading/ unloading operations in various machines for different parts and, the modeling and simulation of these operations are done using another simulation tool IGRIP ver. 5.0, is an interactive 3D

*Table 7. Machining time for different operations*

| | | L-1 | L-2 | C-1 | C-2 | D-1 | D-2 |
|---|---|---|---|---|---|---|---|
| Part 1 | $F_{11}$ | 020 | 030 | × | × | × | × |
| | $F_{12}$ | × | 020 | 020 | × | × | × |
| | $T_{11}$ | 060 | 070 | × | × | × | × |
| | $T_{12}$ | × | 040 | 035 | × | × | × |
| | $D_{11}$ | × | × | 100 | 120 | 090 | 100 |
| | $D_{12}$ | × | × | 070 | 080 | 070 | 090 |
| | $B_{11}$ | × | × | 100 | 120 | 090 | 100 |
| | $TH_{11}$ | × | 080 | 055 | 060 | × | × |
| Part 2 | $F_{21}$ | 030 | 040 | × | × | × | × |
| | $F_{22}$ | × | 60 | 050 | × | × | × |
| | $T_{21}$ | 050 | 060 | × | × | × | × |
| | $T_{22}$ | × | 080 | 070 | × | × | × |
| | $B_{21}$ | × | × | 120 | 140 | 100 | 110 |
| | $D_{21}$ | × | × | 080 | 100 | 070 | 090 |
| | $D_{22}$ | × | × | 075 | 080 | 070 | 090 |
| | $TH_{21}$ | × | 150 | 110 | 120 | × | × |
| Part 3 | $F_{31}$ | 100 | 110 | × | × | × | × |
| | $F_{32}$ | × | 050 | 040 | × | × | × |
| | $T_{31}$ | 080 | 100 | × | × | × | × |
| | $T_{32}$ | × | 180 | 160 | × | × | × |
| | $D_{31}$ | × | × | 120 | 140 | 100 | 120 |
| | $D_{32}$ | × | × | 120 | 140 | 100 | 120 |
| | $D_{33}$ | × | × | 020 | 020 | 020 | 25 |
| | $TH_{31}$ | × | 200 | 180 | 200 | × | × |
| | $TH_{32}$ | × | 040 | 025 | 030 | × | × |

L-1: Lathe-1; L-2: Lathe-2; C-1: Machining Center-1; C-2: Machining Center-2; D-1: Drilling Machine-1; D-2: Drilling Machine-2.

graphics simulation tool for designing, evaluation and offline programming of robotic work cells.

## 3.2. Genetic Algorithm

GA is an adaptive search techniques based on specific mechanisms found in natural evolution. GA begins its search from a randomly generated population of designs that evolve over successive generations (iterations). GA employs three operators to propagate its population from one generation to another to perform its optimization process. The first operator is the "Selection" operator that mimics the principal of "Survival of the Fittest". The second operator is the "Crossover" operator, which mimics mating in biological populations. The crossover operator propagates features of good surviving designs from the current population into the future population, which will have better fitness value on average.

### 3.2.1. Applications of GA

Optimization is the art of selecting the best alternative among a given set of options. In any optimization problem there is an objective function or objective that depends on a set of variables. GA is excellent for all tasks requiring optimization and is highly effective in any situation where many inputs (variables) interact to produce a large number of possible outputs (solutions).

A GA starts with a pool of feasible solutions (population) and a set of biologically inspired operators defined over the population itself. In each and every loop (or) cycle a new population of solutions is created by breeding and mutation, with the fitter solutions being more likely to procreate. According to evolutionary theories, only the most suited elements in a population are likely to survive and generate offspring, transmitting their biological inheritance to the next generation. GAs operate through a simple cycle of stages: creation of a population a strings, evaluation of each string, selection of the best strings, and reproduction to create a new population. Individuals are encoded as strings known as chromosomes (or) strings composed over an alphabet.

After reproduction, the cycle is repeated. New individuals are decoded and the objective function evaluated to give their fitness values. Individuals are selected for mating according to fitness and so the process continues. The average performance of individuals in a population is expected to increase as good individuals are preserved and bred, while less fit members die out. The GA is terminated under a given criteria, for example, a certain number of generations have been completed, a level of fitness has been obtained or a point in the search space has been reached. There are several parameters to fine-tune in a GA, such as population size and mutation frequency. These parameters can be chosen with experience or through experiments. An important factor in selecting the string representation for the search nodes is that all of the search nodes in the search space are represented and the representation is unique. It is also desirable, though not necessary, that the strings are in one-to-one correspondence with the search nodes.

The outline of the technique can be stated as follows:

**Step 1:** Set up initial population of chromosomes at random & assign each of them a fitness value.

**Step 2:** Select two chromosomes based on their fitness value.

**Step 3:** Crossover them to produce an offspring.

**Step 4:** Mutate the offspring.

**Step 5:** Repeat steps 2 to 4 until the number of offsprings equal to that of parent's generation.

**Step 6:** Replace the parent's generation with the offsprings and regard it as the new generation.

**Step 7:** Repeat steps 2 to 6 until either all the chromosomes are same or the maximum iterations are reached.

The last operator is "Mutation", which promotes diversity in population characteristics. The appropriate values of the GA parameters are arrived at, based on the satisfactory performance of trials conducted for this application with different ranges of values. The crossover probability was varied from 0.4 to 0.9 and it was found that the solution was improving faster for a crossover probability of 0.60. Similarly, in the range from 0.001 to 0.010 the mutation probability of 0.005 was found to retain much better solutions than worse solutions.

Population size $(n) = 20$ samples

Crossover probability $(pc) = 0.600$

Mutation probability $(pm) = 0.005$.

## 3.3. Simulated Annealing

SA is motivated by an analogy to annealing in solids. The idea was first given by Metropolis in 1953. The algorithm in his work simulated the cooling of material in a heat bath. This is a process known as annealing. When a solid is heated past melting point and then cool it, the structural properties of the solid depend on the rate of cooling. The algorithm simulates the cooling processes by gradually lowering the temperature of the system until it converges to a steady frozen state. In SA, there is an analogy with thermodynamics, specifically with the way liquids freeze and crystallize or metals cool and anneal. At high temperatures the molecules of a liquid move freely with respect to one another. If the liquid is cooled slowly, thermal mobility is lost. The SA (Noorul, Karthikeyan, & Dinesh, 2003) approach for finding out the optimal schedule of operations assignment to machines is carried out, first by giving the machining time of individual operations at different machines as input.

The initial solution is derived by using the shortest processing time (SPT) rule. The other solutions or moves are derived from the neighborhood. The neighborhood search is conducted by interchanging the elements with its neighborhood. The stopping criterion of the algorithm in this work is the maximum number of iterations. The cooling parameter is taken to be 0.9 and the maximum number of iterations is taken to be 50. The parameters were so chosen for fast convergence to the optimal value. Further, sufficient care is taken care of machine overloading. The SA procedure is depicted in Figure 2. The SA programs for various jobs are run several times by varying the temperature decrement and the cooling range to obtain the optimal scheduling of the FMSs by minimizing the cost function i.e. by minimizing the total machining time for realization of the part. However, the machine setup times are not taken into consideration for minimization of the cost function. Only the machining times are considered for optimal scheduling.

## 4. PROBLEM STATEMENT

The processing times for various operations are obtained from the graphical simulations of the processes at different machines. The processing times are used to describe the combined objective function of the genetic optimization process.

These are termed as intermachine restrictions and intramachine restrictions. For example in setup-1, if the operation $F_{11}$ is carried out in $M_1$, the same operation is not performed by $M_2$, $M_3$ and $M_4$. Further in, the same machine ($M_1$), the other operations like $F_{12}$, $T_{12}$ and $TH_{11}$ cannot be done. The former condition is an example of intermachine restriction and the latter is an example of intramachine restriction. The intermachine restrictions take care of the ease in operation for a machine taking into consideration the part orientation. All possible restrictions for all the three setups are found out and put as the rule base in the GA program. The intermachine restrictions and intramachine restrictions for setup-1, setup-2 and setup-3 are prepared. The GA programs for various setups are run several times by varying the population size and the number of generations to obtain the optimal scheduling of the FMS by minimizing the Combined Objective Function

*Figure 2. The simulated annealing process*

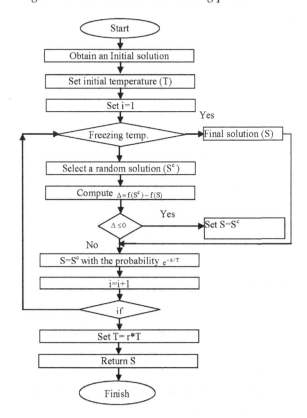

(COF), that is, by minimizing the total machining time for realization of the part. However, for computational convenience, the machine setup times are assumed to be same for all the machines. After every generation of the GA cycle, every individual in the population (i.e. feasible schedule) is evaluated using the COF for minimizing the total penalty cost and maximizing machine utilization. Therefore the objective becomes,

Minimize COF = $(W_1) \times (X_p/MPP) + (W_2) \times (X_q / TE)$, where, $W_1$ = weight factor for customer satisfaction and $W_2$ = weight factor for machine utilization.

$X_p$ = total penalty cost incurred, and

$$X_p = \sum_i (CT_i - DD_i) \times UPC_i \times BS_i$$

where, i = job number, $CT_i$ = completion time of job i, $DD_i$ = due date for job I, $UPC_i$ = unit penalty cost for job I, $BS_i$ = batch size of job I.

MPP = maximum permissible penalty

$X_q$ = total machine down time, and

$$X_q = \sum_j MD_j$$

TE= total elapsed time,

$PT_{ji}$= processing time of $i^{th}$ job with $j^{th}$ machine, where

j= machine number, and

$$MD_j = TE - \sum_i PT_{ji} .$$

In the computation the weight factors $W_1$ and $W_2$ are assumed to be equal and hence, $W_1$ = 0.5 and $W_2$ = 0.5. However, different ratios can be applied to them according to the demand of business situation.

## 5. RESULTS AND CONCLUSION

The proposed approach was coded in MATLAB. The algorithm was run with control parameters obtained from the graphical simulation in QUEST. The proper values of these parameters were determined in a pre-processing phase. Due to the stochastic behavior of the algorithm, and the fact that it does not have a natural termination point, it was decided to run the algorithms for fixed time duration and report the best solution obtained after this time has elapsed. The generated solutions were quantified by the solution quality given in percentage offset from the best known solutions. The optimal schedules and optimized machining times as obtained from the GA and SA runoff programs for setup-1, setup-2, setup-3 respectively and results are presented in the Table 8, Table 9 and Table 10. It is observed from the tables that the total machining time is the lowest in setup-2.

This is due to the fact that the operations such as $F_{11}$, $T_{11}$, $D_{11}$, $B_{11}$, $D_{12}$, $TH_{11}$ are more effectively carried out in the machines they are assigned to in setup-2. The optimization technique adopted in the present work will always produce the optimal value of the cost function as it is based on the principle of survival of fittest. Any type of layout can be implemented as the rule base takes care of the operation sequence. The GA optimization technique depends on the size of operational requirement and the complexity of the part. However, the approaches differ widely from each other with respect to coding, parameters used, the constraints handled and the goals pursued. Despite of these differences, all approaches have in common that the domain knowledge is required in order to produce competitive results.

The present work used two different approaches viz.GA and SA on the same set of problems to determine the optimized schedule in an FMS. The choice of the methods has been made on the basis that most of the previous work reported the use of these two methods in optimizing similar problems and the methods are used independently. The present work uses both these methods to find out the appropriate one for the purpose. The coding of the methods is designed in a manner that yields global optima for the solution. The results show that GA scores over SA in dealing with the FMS scheduling under constraint condition and such behavior of GA against that of SA may be attrib-

uted to the fact that, the intricacies of the problem are well taken care of by the coding methods of GA. A comparison of the total machining time obtained from the GA and that obtained from SA is presented in Figure 2. GA achieves a good efficiency with respect to the total machining time.

*Table 8. Operation assignment and processing time at machines in setup-1*

| Machines | $M_1$ | | $M_2$ | | $M_3$ | | $M_4$ | |
|---|---|---|---|---|---|---|---|---|
| | GA | SA | GA | SA | GA | SA | GA | SA |
| Operation assigned | $F_{11}, T_{11}$ | $F_{31}, F_{32}$ $T_{31}$ | $F_{12}, D_{11,}$ $TH_{11}$ | $D_{31}, D_{32}, D_{33},$ $,TH_{32}$ | $T_{12}$ | $TH_{31}$ | $B_{11}, D_{12}$ | $T_{32}$ |
| Machining time | 80 | 240 | 175 | 268 | 45 | 180 | 157 | 160 |
| % of Machine Utilization | 17.5 | 28.3 | 38.3 | 31.6 | 9.8 | 21.1 | 34.4 | 19 |
| Total Machining Time:457 (GA), Total Machining Time:848 (SA) | | | | | | | | |

*Table 9. Operation assignment and processing time at machines in setup-2*

| Machines | $M_1$ | | $M_2$ | | $M_3$ | | $M_4$ | |
|---|---|---|---|---|---|---|---|---|
| | *GA* | *SA* | *GA* | *SA* | *GA* | *SA* | *GA* | *SA* |
| Operation assigned | $F_{12},$ $T_{12}$ | $F_{11},$ $T_{11,} D_{11}$ | $B_{11},$ $D_{12}$ | $F_{12},$ $T_{12}$ | $F_{11},$ $T_{11}$ | $D_{12},$ $B_{11}$ | $D_{11},$ $TH_{11}$ | $TH_{11}$ |
| Machining time | 42 | 170 | 170 | 53 | 95 | 170 | 180 | 60 |
| % of Machine Utilization | 8.6 | 37.5 | 34.9 | 11.7 | 19.5 | 37.6 | 37 | 13.2 |
| Total Machining Time:487 (GA), Total Machining Time:453 (SA) | | | | | | | | |

*Table 10. Operation assignment and processing time at machines in setup-3*

| Machines | $M_1$ | | $M_2$ | | $M_3$ | | $M_4$ | |
|---|---|---|---|---|---|---|---|---|
| | *GA* | *SA* | *GA* | *SA* | *GA* | *SA* | *GA* | *SA* |
| Operation assigned | $F_{11},$ $T_{11}$ | $F_{21},$ $D_{21}$ | $D_{11},$ $TH_{11}$ | $B_{21}$ | $F_{12},$ $T_{12}$ | $F_{22},$ $TH_{21}$ | $B_{11},$ $D_{12}$ | $T_{21}, T_{22}, D_{22}$ |
| Machining time | 80 | 110 | 155 | 120 | 53 | 160 | 157 | 203 |
| % of Machine Utilization | 18 | 18.5 | 34.8 | 20.2 | 12 | 27 | 35.2 | 34.3 |
| Total Machining Time:445 (GA), Total Machining Time:593 (SA) | | | | | | | | |

## REFERENCES

Buyurgan, N., Saygin, C., & Kilic, S. E. (2004). Tool allocation in flexible manufacturing systems with tool alternatives. *Robotics and Computer-integrated Manufacturing*, *20*(4), 341–349. doi:10.1016/j.rcim.2004.01.001

Choudhury, B. B., Mishra, D., & Biswal, B. B. (2008). Task assignment and scheduling in a constrained manufacturing system using GA. *International Journal of Agile Systems and Management*, *3*(1-2), 127–146.

Demmel, J. G., & Askin, R. G. (1992). A multiple objective decision model for the evaluation of advanced manufacturing system technologies. *Journal of Manufacturing Systems*, *11*, 179–194. doi:10.1016/0278-6125(92)90004-Y

Gupta, D. (1993). On measurement and valuation of manufacturing flexibility. *International Journal of Production Research*, *31*, 2947–2958. doi:10.1080/00207549308956909

Lee, C. S., Kim, S. S., & Choi, J. S. (2003). Operation sequence and tool selection in flexible manufacturing systems under dynamic tool allocation. *Computers in Industry*, *45*(1), 61–73. doi:10.1016/S0360-8352(03)00019-6

Lee, Y. H., Jeong, C. S., & Moon, C. (2002). Advanced planning and scheduling with outsourcing in manufacturing supply chain. *Computers & Industrial Engineering*, *43*(1-2), 351–374. doi:10.1016/S0360-8352(02)00079-7

Mandelbaum, M., & Brill, P. H. (1989). Examples of measurement of flexibility and adaptivity in manufacturing systems. *The Journal of the Operational Research Society*, *40*(6), 603–609.

Moon, C., Kim, J. S., & Gen, M. (2004). Advanced planning and scheduling based on precedence and resource constraints for E-plant chains. *International Journal of Production Research*, *42*(15), 2941–2954. doi:10.1080/00207540410001691956

Noorul, H. S., Karthikeyan, T., & Dinesh, M. (2003). Scheduling decisions in FMS using a heuristic approach. *International Journal of Advanced Manufacturing Technology*, 374–379.

Primrose, P. I., & Verter, V. (1996). Do companies need to measure their production flexibility? *International Journal of Operations & Production Management*, *16*, 4–11. doi:10.1108/01443579610119054

Son, Y. K. (1991). A decision support system for factory automation: A case study. *International Journal of Production Research*, *29*, 1461–1473. doi:10.1080/00207549108948023

Stam, A., & Kuula, M. (1991). Selecting a flexible manufacturing system using multiple criteria analysis. *International Journal of Production Research*, *29*, 803–820. doi:10.1080/00207549108930103

Suresh, N. C. (1991). An extended multi-objective replacement model for flexible automation investments. *International Journal of Production Research*, *28*, 1823–1844. doi:10.1080/00207549108948052

Troxler, J. N., & Blank, J. (1989). A comprehensive methodology for manufacturing system evaluation and comparison. *Journal of Manufacturing Systems*, *8*, 175–183. doi:10.1016/0278-6125(89)90039-3

Venk, S. (1990). Strategic optimization cycle as a competitive tool for economic justification of advanced manufacturing systems. *Journal of Manufacturing Systems*, *9*, 194–205. doi:10.1016/0278-6125(90)90051-I

Vieira, G. E., Herrmann, J. W., & Lin, E. (2003). Rescheduling manufacturing systems: A framework of strategies, policies, and methods. *Journal of Scheduling*, *6*(1), 39–62. doi:10.1023/A:1022235519958

Whitley, D. (2001). An overview of evolutionary algorithms. *Journal of Information and Software Technology*, *43*, 817–831. doi:10.1016/S0950-5849(01)00188-4

Zahir, M. S. (1991). Incorporating the uncertainty of decision judgments in the analytic hierarchy process. *European Journal of Operational Research*, *53*, 206–216. doi:10.1016/0377-2217(91)90135-I

*This work was previously published in the International Journal of Applied Evolutionary Computation, Volume 2, Issue 3, edited by Wei-Chiang Samuelson Hong, pp. 15-26, copyright 2011 by IGI Publishing (an imprint of IGI Global).*

# Chapter 11
# GBF Trained Neuro–Fuzzy Equalizer for Time Varying Channels

**Archana Sarangi**
*Siksha O Anusandhan University, India*

**Siba Prasada Panigrahi**
*Konark Institute of Science & Technology, India*

**Sasmita Kumari Padhy**
*Siksha O Anusandhan University, India*

**Shubhendu Kumar Sarangi**
*Siksha O Anusandhan University, India*

## ABSTRACT

*This paper proposes a neuro-fuzzy filter for equalization of time-varying channels. Additionally, it proposes to tune the equalizer with a hybrid algorithm between Genetic Algorithms (GA) and Bacteria Foraging (BFO), termed as GBF. The major advantage of the method developed in this paper is that all parameters of the neuro-fuzzy network, including the rule base, are tuned simultaneously through the proposed hybrid algorithm of genetic Algorithm and bacteria foraging. The performance of the Neuro-Fuzzy equalizer designed using the proposed approach is compared with Genetic algorithm based equalizers. The results confirm that the methodology used in the paper is much better than existing approaches. The proposed hybrid algorithm also eliminates the limitations of GA based equalizer, i.e. the inherent characteristic of GA, i.e. GAs risk finding a sub-optimal solution.*

## 1. INTRODUCTION

Communication channels medium are often modeled as band limited channel for which the channel impulse response is that of an ideal low pass filter. When a sequence of symbols is transmitted, the low pass filtering of the channel distorts the transmitted symbols over successive time intervals causing symbols spread and overlap with adjacent symbols. This resulting linear distortion is known as inter symbol interference (ISI). In addition non-linear distortion is also caused by cross talk in the channel and use of amplifiers. Adaptive channel equalizers play an important role in recovering digital information from digital communication channels. Preparta (1989) had suggested a simple and attractive scheme for dispersal recovery of digital information based on the Discrete Fourier

DOI: 10.4018/978-1-4666-3628-6.ch011

Transform. Subsequently Gibson et al. (1991) have reported an efficient nonlinear ANN structure for reconstructing digital signals, which have been passed through a dispersive channel and corrupted with additive noise. In a recent publication (Voulgaris & Hadjicostics, 2004) the authors have proposed optimal preprocessing strategies for perfect reconstruction of binary signals from a dispersive communication channels. Touri et al. (2006) have developed deterministic worst-case framework for perfect reconstruction of discrete data information from digital communication channels. Preparta (1989) had suggested a simple and attractive scheme for dispersal recovery of digital information based on the Discrete Fourier Transform. Subsequently Gibson et al. (1991) have reported an efficient nonlinear ANN structure for reconstructing digital signals, which have been passed through a dispersive channel and corrupted with additive noise.

In a recent publication (Voulgaris & Hadjicostics, 2004) the authors have proposed optimal preprocessing strategies for perfect reconstruction of binary signals from a dispersive communication channels. Touri et al. (2006) have developed deterministic worst case frame work for perfect reconstruction of discrete data transmission through a dispersive communication channel. In recent past new adaptive equalizers have been suggested using soft computing tools such as Artificial Neural Network (ANN), PPN and the FLANN (Patra, Pal, Baliarsingh, & Panda, 1999). It has been reported that these methods are best suited for nonlinear and complex channels. Recently, Chebyshev Artificial Neural Network has also been proposed for nonlinear channel equalization (Patra, Poh, Chaudhari, & Das, 2005). The drawback of these methods is that the estimated weights may likely fall to local minima during training. For this reason Genetic Algorithm (GA) has been suggested for training adaptive channel equalizers (Panda, Majhi, Mohanty, Choubey, & Mishra, 2006). The main attraction of GA lies in the fact that it does not rely on Newton-like

gradient-descent methods, and hence there is no need for calculation of derivatives. This makes them less likely to be trapped in local minima. But only two parameters of GA, the crossover and the mutation, help to avoid local minima problem. There are still some situations when the weights in GA optimization are trapped to local minima.

In recent days Bacterial Foraging Optimization (BFO) has been proposed (Passino, 2002) and has been applied for signal recovery (Acharya, Panda, & Lakshmi, 2009; Majhi & Panda, 2010; Guzmán, Delgado, & De Carvalho, 2009; Shoorehdeli, Teshnehlab, & Sedigh, 2009). The BFO is a useful alternative to GA and requires less number of computations. In addition BFO is also derivative free optimization technique. The number of parameters that are used for searching the total solution space are much higher in BFO compared to those in GA. Hence the possibility of avoiding the local minimum is higher in BFO. In this scheme, the foraging (methods for locating, handling and ingesting food) behavior of E. Coli bacteria present in our intestines is mimicked.

In this paper, a hybrid algorithm of GA and BFO (GBF) is used for updating the weights of the proposed neuro-fuzzy filter based adaptive equalizer. The same equalizer is also trained using GA to have a comparative study.

The organization of the paper is as follows: Section 2 discusses proposed system model. Activation functions for the proposed equalizer are discussed in Section3. In Section 4 the BFO and GA based hybrid algorithm is developed to update the equalizer. For performance evaluation, the simulation study is carried out which is dealt in Section 5. Finally conclusion of the paper is outlined in Section 6.

## 2. SYSTEM MODEL

The Neuro-fuzzy model used in this paper uses a multi-layer fuzzy neural network shown in Figure 1. The system has a total of 5 layers as proposed

*Figure 1. Proposed neuro fuzzy equalizer*

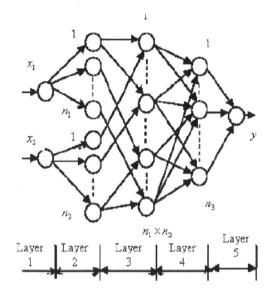

by Lin and Lee (1991) and Farag et al. (1998). Here, a model with 2 inputs and a single output is considered. Accordingly, there are two nodes accounting for two inputs in layer 1 and one output node in layer 5 (the output layer).

The nodes in layers 2 & 4 account for membership functions of fuzzy linguistic input and output variables respectively. The fuzzy sets of two input variables and the lone output consist of $n_1, n_2$ and $n_3$ linguistic terms, respectively. Hence, $n_1 + n_2$ nodes in layer 2 and $n_3$ nodes in layer 4 are included. There are $n_1 \times n_2$ nodes in layer 3 to form a fuzzy rule base for the two linguistic input variables. The links of layers 3 and 4 define preconditions and consequences of rule nodes, respectively. For each rule node, there are two fixed links from input term nodes. Layer 4 links are adjusted in response to varying control situations. By contrast, links of layers 2 and 5, between input-output nodes and their corresponding term nodes, remain fixed and equal to unity. The neuro-fuzzy model can adjust fuzzy rules and their membership functions by modifying links of layer 4 and parameters that represent the gaussian membership functions for each node in layers 2 and 4.

The following notations are used to describe the functions of the nodes in each of the five layers: $L$

- $x_i^{(L)}$ : Input value to the $i^{th}$ node in layer $L$ .
- $y_i^{(L)}$ : Output value from the $i^{th}$ node in layer.

$m_i^{(L)}$ , $\sigma_i^{(L)}$ Centre and width of the Gaussian function of the $i^{th}$ node in layer $L$ .

$w_{ij}$ Weight connecting the output of $j^{th}$ node in layer 3 to the $i^{th}$ node in layer 4.

**Layer 1:** The input layer directly transmits input signals to the next layer.

$$y_1^{(1)} = x_1^{(1)} \tag{1}$$

**Layer 2:** This layer fuzzifies the numerical input by applying Gaussian membership function.

$$x_i^{(2)} = \begin{cases} y_1^{(1)} & i = 1, 2, \cdots n_1 \\ y_2^{(1)} & i = n_1 + 1, \cdots n_1 + n_2 \end{cases} \tag{2}$$

$$y_1^{(2)} = \exp\left[-\left[\frac{x_i^{(2)} - m_i^{(2)}}{\sigma_i^{(2)}}\right]^2\right] \tag{3}$$

$; for \, i = n_1 + 1, .... n_1 + n_2$

**Layer 3:** The links in this layer perform a conjunctive operation in the 'premise' part of the fuzzy rules. Thus, each node has two input values from layer 2.

$$y_i^{(3)} = \prod\left(y_j^{(2)}, y_k^{(2)}\right), for, j = 1, 2, ..... n_1$$
$$k = n_1 + 1, .... n_1 + n_2; i = n_1\left(j - 1\right) + \left(k - n_2\right) \tag{4}$$

Link weights in this layer are also set to unity.

**Layer 4:** The weight $W_{ij}$ for this layer expresses the interconnection strength of the $j^{th}$ rule with the $i^{th}$ output linguistic variable. For each rule, the correct consequent (output linguistic term) is identified by a simple procedure outlined below:

```
        for  j = 1 to n₁ * n₂
for  i = 1, n₃
find  max(Wᵢⱼ)
label its consequent link as  iₘₐₓ
assign              Wᵢⱼ = Wᵢⱼ   for  i = iₘₐₓ
     = 0              otherwise
end
end
```

Each node of this layer performs the disjunction (OR) operation to integrate the fuzzy rules leading to the same output linguistic variable. The output of the nodes in this layer is given by:

$$y_i^{(4)} = \sum_{j=1}^{n_1 * n_2} w_{ij} y_i^{(3)}; for\ i = 1, 2 ... n_3 \qquad (5)$$

**Layer 5:** This layer acts as a defuzzifier and computes the output signal of the neuro-fuzzy network. The center of area defuzzification scheme is used in this model and is given as follows:

$$y_1^{(5)} = \frac{\sum_{j=1}^{n_3} m_j^{(4)} \sigma_j^{(4)} y_j^{(4)}}{\sum_{j=1}^{n_3} \sigma_j^{(4)} y_j^{(4)}} \qquad (6)$$

## 3. OBJECTIVE FUNCTIONS

Although the structure of equalizer is same for both QAM and PSK signal constellations, the activation functions used for these signal constellations are different. The nonlinear activation functions perform the decorrelation of input signal and thus help in equalization (Pandey, 2001). The choice of activation functions, therefore, plays an important role in the performance of the blind equalizers. It has been observed that, the use of different nonlinear functions in different layers gives better results in some channel models (Pandey, 2001). In the present model of complex-valued neural blind equalizers, different nonlinear functions are chosen for hidden and output layer neurons. For the neurons of hidden layer, the activation function $\phi^{(1)}$ is described as:

$$\phi^{(1)}(z) = \phi^{(1)}(z_R) + j\phi^{(1)}(z_I) \qquad (7)$$

where $z_R$ and $z_I$ are the real and imaginary parts of the complex quantity z, and $\phi^{(1)}(.)$ is a nonlinear function. For the neuron of output layer, the activation function is described as:

$$\phi^{(2)}(z) = \phi^{(2)}(z_R) + j\phi^{(2)}(z_I) \qquad (8)$$

where, $\phi^{(2)}(.)$ is another nonlinear function.

With M-ary PSK signals, for the neurons in the hidden layer, following function can be used.

$$\phi^{(1)}(x) = \alpha \tanh(\beta x) \qquad (9)$$

while, $\alpha$ and $\beta$ are two real constants. For the node of the output layer, the activation function is given by

$$\phi^{(2)}(z) = f_1(|z|) . \exp(jf_2(\langle z \rangle))$$
$$= f_1(|z|) . \cos(f_2(\langle z \rangle)) + jf_1(|z|) . \sin(f_2(\langle z \rangle)) \qquad (10)$$

where $|z|$ and $\langle z$ denote the modulus and the angle of a complex quantity z. The function $f_1(.)$ and $f_2(.)$ are defined as

$$f_1\left(|z|\right) = a\tanh\left(b.|z|\right) \qquad (11)$$

$$f_2\left(\langle z\rangle\right) = \langle z - c\sin\left(n\langle z\rangle\right) \qquad (12)$$

where $a$, $b$ and $c$ are real constants and $n$ is the order of PSK signals.

In case of M-ary QAM Signals, for the hidden layer nodes, following function can be used.

$$\phi^{(1)}\left(x\right) = x + d\sin\left(\pi x\right) \qquad (13)$$

Here $d$ is a positive constant. The activation function of (10) is found to be suitable for M-*ary* QAM signals in stationary channels (Pandey, 2001), and has been used in both hidden and output layers. However, these functions are most effective in the output layer because of their saturation characteristics. For nonstationary channels, we define a modified activation function for the output layer, as the function defined in (10) cannot correct the arbitrary phase of the equalizer's output signal in time-varying channels. In case of the output node, the function is defined as

$$\phi^{(2)}\left(z\right) = f\left(z_R\cos\theta\left(n\right) - z_I\sin\theta\left(n\right)\right)$$
$$+ jf\left(z_R\sin\theta\left(n\right) - z_I\cos\theta\left(n\right)\right). \qquad (14)$$

where $z = z_R + jz_I$ is a complex quantity, the function $f(.)$ is defined as $f\left(x\right) = x + d\sin\left(\pi x\right)$, and $d$ is a positive real number. The parameter $\theta\left(n\right)$, introduced in (7), is used for the correction of the phase of the output signal and is updated using the algorithm to be discussed in following section.

## 4. PROPOSED HYBRID GBF

Genetic algorithm and Bacteria Foraging Optimization, population-based search algorithms, maintain a population of structure as key elements in the design and implementation of problem solving algorithms. Each individual in the population is evaluated according to its fitness value. Both algorithms are sufficiently complex to provide powerful adaptive search approaches, and usually can be embedded with heuristics to speed up their search performances for optimization problems.

### 4.1. Genetic Algorithms (GA)

Genetic algorithms start with a set of randomly selected chromosomes as the initial population that encodes a set of possible solutions. In genetic algorithms, variables of a problem are represented as genes in a chromosome, and the chromosomes are evaluated according to their fitness values using some measures of profit or utility that we want to optimize. Recombination typically involves two genetic operators: crossover and mutation. The genetic operators alter the composition of genes to create new chromosomes called offspring. In crossover operator, it generates offspring that inherits genes from both parents with a crossover probability $P_c$. In Mutation operator, it inverts randomly chosen genes in a chromosome with a mutation probability $P_m$. The selection operator is an artificial version of natural selection, a Darwinian survival of the fittest among populations, to create populations from generation to generation, and chromosomes with better fitness values have higher probabilities of being selected at the next generation. After several generations, genetic algorithms can converge to the best solution. Let $P\left(t\right)$ and $C\left(t\right)$ at $t \leftarrow 0$ $C\left(t\right)$ re parents and offspring at generation . A simple genetic algorithm is shown in the following (Gen & Cheng, 1997):

```
Procedure: Simple genetic algorithm
Begin
    t ← 0;
    Initialize P(t);
```

```
Evaluate  P(t);
While (not match the termination
conditions) do
      Recombine  P(t) to yield  C(t);
      Evaluate  C(t);
      Select  P(t+1) form  P(t) and
C(t);
      t ← t+1;
      End;
End;
```

Basically, the one cut point crossover, inversion mutation and $u + \lambda$-ES (evolution strategy) survival (Gen & Cheng, 1997; Merz & Freisleben, 2000) where $u$ is the population size and $\lambda$ is the number of offspring created, can be employed as the operators for resource allocation problem addressed in this paper. However, these operations are not carefully designed for channel equalization problem, the search in the solution space might become inefficient or even random.

Recently, genetic algorithms with local search have also been considered as good alternatives for solving optimization problems. The flow chart of the GA with local search is shown as follows (Kolen & Pesch, 1994; Miller, Potter, Gandham, & Lapena, 1993).

```
Procedure: GA with local search
Begin
      t ← 0 ;
      Initialize  P(t);
      Evaluate  P(t);
      While (not match the termination
conditions) do
      Apply crossover on  P(t) to
generate  c₁(t);
      Apply local search on  c₁(t) to
yield  c₂(t);
      Apply mutation on  c₂(t) to
yield  c₃(t);
```

```
      Apply local search on  c₃(t) to
yield  c₄(t);
      Evaluate
C(t) = {c₁(t),c₂(t),c₃(t),c₄(t)};
      Select  P(t+1) form  P(t) and
C(t);
      t ← t+1;
      End;
End;
```

Where local search can explore the neighborhood in an attempt to enhance the fitness value of the solution in a local manner. It starts from the current solution and repeatedly tries to improve the current solution by local changes. If a better solution is found, then it replaces the current solution and the algorithm searches from the new solution again. These steps are repeated until a criterion is satisfied. It is noted that the local search approach can be well designed by heuristics to ameliorate its search performance. In this paper, we embed heuristics into genetic algorithm as local search approach.

## 4.2. Bacteria Foraging Optimization (BFO)

Natural selection tends to eliminate animals with poor foraging strategies and favor the propagation of genes of those animals that have successful foraging strategies, since they are more likely to enjoy reproductive success. After many generations, poor foraging strategies are either eliminated or shaped into good ones. This activity of foraging led the researchers to use it as optimization process. The *E. coli* bacteria that are present in our intestines also undergo a foraging strategy. The control system of these bacteria that dictates how foraging should proceed can be subdivided into four sections, namely, chemo taxis, swarming, reproduction, and elimination and dispersal.

For initialization, we must choose $P, S, N_c, N_s, N_{re}, N_{ed}, P_{ed}$ and the

$C(i), i = 1, 2, \cdots S$. In case of swarming, we will also have to pick the parameters of the cell-to-cell attractant functions; here we will use the parameters given above. Also, initial values for the $\theta^i, i = 1, 2, \cdots S$ must be chosen. Choosing these to be in areas where an optimum value is likely to exist is a good choice. Alternatively, we may want to simply randomly distribute them across the domain of the optimization problem. The algorithm that models bacterial population chemo taxis, swarming, reproduction, elimination, and dispersal is given here (initially, $j = k = l = 0$). For the algorithm, note that updates to the $\theta^i$ automatically result in updates to $P$. Clearly, we could have added a more sophisticated termination test than simply specifying a maximum number of iterations.

- **Elimination-Dispersal Loop:** $l = l + 1$
- **Reproduction Loop:** $k = k + 1$
- **Chemo Taxis Loop:** $j = j + 1$
  - *For* $i = 1, 2, \cdots S$ take a chemo tactic step for bacterium $i$ as follows.
  - *Compute* $J(i, j, k, l)$ (i.e., add on the cell-to-cell attractant effect to the nutrient concentration).
  - *Let* $J_{last} = J(i, j, k, l)$ to save this value since we may find a better cost via a run.
- **Tumble:** Generate a random vector $\Delta(i) \in R^P$ with each element $\Delta_m(i), m = 1, 2, \cdots, p$, a random number on [-1, 1].
  - *Move:*

$$\theta^i(j+1, k, l) = \theta^i(j, k, l)$$
$$+c(i)\Delta(i)\frac{1}{\sqrt{\Delta^t(i)\Delta(i)}}$$

This results in a step of size $c(i)$ in the direction of the tumble for bacterium $i$.

*Compute* $J(i, j+1, k, l)$ and then let,

$$J(i, j+1, k, l) = J(i, j+1, k, l)$$
$$+J_{cc}\left(\theta^i(j+1, k, l).P(j+1, k, l)\right)$$

*Swim* (note that we use an approximation since we decide swimming behavior of each cell as if the bacteria numb $J_{last} = J(i, j+1, k, l)$ ere $m < N_s$ d $\{1, 2 \cdots i\}$ have moved and $\{i+1, I+2 \cdots s\}$ have not; this is much simpler to simulate than simultaneous decisions about swimming and tumbling by all bacteria at the same time):

- *Let* $m = 0$ (counter for swim length).
- *While* (if have not climbed down too long)
- *Let* $m = m + 1$
- *If* $J(i, j+1, k, l) < J_{last}$ (if doing better),
- *Let*

$$\theta^i(j+1, k, l) = \theta^i(j, k, l)$$
$$+c(i)\Delta(i)\frac{1}{\sqrt{\Delta^t(i)\Delta(i)}}$$

and use this $\theta^i(j+1, k, l)$ to compute new $J(i, j+1, k, l)$ as we did in above step.

- *Else, let* $m = N_s$ this is the end of the while statement.
- *Go to next bacterium* $(i+1)$ if $i \neq S$ (i.e., go to b) to process the next bacterium).
- *If* $j \leq N_c$, go to step 3. In this case, continue chemo taxis, since the life of the bacteria is not over.

## Reproduction

For the given k and l, and for each $i = 1, 2, \cdots S$ let

$$J_{health}^{i} = \sum_{j=1}^{N_c+1} j\left(i, j, k, l\right)$$

be the health of bacterium $i$ (a measure of how many nutrients it got over its lifetime and how successful it was at avoiding noxious substances) Sort bacteria and chemo tactic parameters $c\left(i\right)$ in order of ascending cost $J_{health}$ (higher cost means lower health).

The $S_r$ bacteria with the highest $J_{health}$ values die and the other $S_r$ bacteria with the best values split (and the copies that are made are placed at the same location as their parent).

If $K \leq N_{re}$ go to step 2. In this case, we have not reached the number of specified reproduction steps, so we start the next generation in the chemo tactic loop.

- **Elimination-Dispersal:** for $i = 1, 2, \cdots S$, with probability $P_{ed}$, eliminate and disperse each bacterium (this keeps the number of bacteria in the population constant). To do this, if you eliminate a bacterium, simply disperse one to a random location on the optimization domain.

If $I \leq N_{ed}$ then go to step 1; otherwise end.

### 4.3. Proposed Algorithm

In this paper, we propose to hybridize genetic algorithm and Bacteria Foraging Optimization with heuristics to solve equalization problem. The proposed algorithm has both the advantages of genetic algorithm, the ability to find feasible solutions and to avoid premature convergence, and that of Bacteria Foraging, the ability to conduct fine-tuning in the search space and to find better solutions. Meanwhile, heuristics are embedded into genetic algorithm as local search to improve the search ability. Nomenclature used in the algorithm is outlined as:

- $n$ : Dimension of the search space,
- $N$ : The number of bacteria in the population,
- $N_c$ : Chemotactic steps,
- $N_{re}$ : The number of reproduction steps
- $N_{ed}$ : The number of elimination–dispersal events,
- $P_{ed}$ : Elimination–dispersal with probability,
- $C_i$ : The size of the step taken in the random direction specified by the tumble.

### 5. SIMULATIONS

Training data of 500 points is generated from the plant model, assuming a random input signal " $u_k$ " uniformly distributed in the interval [-1, 1]. The plant is modeled using the neuro-fuzzy network described above. The model has three inputs $u_k, y_{k-1}, y_{k-2}$ and a single output $y_k$. The inputs $u_k, \& y_{k-1}$ are partitioned into five fuzzy linguistic spaces {NL, NS, ZE, PS, PL}. The input $y_{k-2}$ is partitioned into three fuzzy spaces {N, Z, P} and the output yk is partitioned into 11 fuzzy spaces {NVL, NL, NM, NS, NVS, ZE, PVS, PS, PM, PL, PVL}.

The initial centers ($m$) and widths $\left(\sigma\right)$ s of the total 24 membership functions of input-output variables of the fuzzy model and the possible 825 rule combinations are chosen at random. The universe of discourse for all linguistic variables is uniformly chosen to be [-0.5, 0.5]. The input $u$ and output $y$ are scaled so that they do not exceed the limits of universe of discourse. According to the structure of the fuzzy-neural network described above, the number of rules (rule nodes in the third layer) is 5x5x3 = 75. The algorithm described above is used to find the 75 rules and the 48 input-output membership function parameters, $\left(m, \sigma\right)$.

In this section we present the simulation of the proposed models in the time-varying environment.

*Box 1. The GBF Algorithm*

```
Step 1.
Initialize parameters:
```
$n, N, N_c, N_s, N_{re}, N_{ed}, P_{ed}, C_i \left( i = 1, 2, \cdots N \right), \varphi_i,$
```
where,
Step 2.
Elimination-dispersal loop:
```
$l = l + 1$
```
Step 3.
Reproduction loop:
```
$k = k + 1$
```
Step 4.
Chemotaxis loop:
```
$j = j + 1$

**Substep-a.** For $i = 1, 2, \cdots N$, take a chemotactic step for bacterium $i$ as follows.

**Substep-b.** Compute fitness function, $\text{ITSE}(i, j, k, l)$

**Substep-c.** Let $\text{ITSE}_{\text{last}} = \text{ITSE}(i, j, k, l)$ to save this value since we may find a better cost via a run.

Substep-d.

Tumble: generate a random vector $\Delta(i) \in R^n$ with each element $\Delta_m(i), m = 1, 2, \cdots, p,$ a random number on $\left[ -1, 1 \right]$.

**Substep-e.** Move: Let

$$\varphi^x \left( i+1, j\ k \right) = \varphi^x \left( i, j\ k \right) + C_i \frac{\Delta(i)}{\sqrt{\Delta^T(i)\Delta(i)}}$$

This results in a step of size $C(i)$ in the direction of the tumble for bacterium $i$.

**Substep-f.** Compute ITSE $(i, j+1, k, l)$.

**Substep-g.** Swim

```
# Let
```
$m = 0$
```
(counter for swim length)
# While
```
$m < N_s$
```
(if have not climbed down too long).
Let
```
$m = m + 1$

If ITSE $(i, j+1, k, l) <$ ITSE$_{\text{last}}$ (if doing better), let ITSE $(i, j+1, k, l) =$ ITSE$_{\text{last}}$ and let

$$\varphi^x \left( i+1, j\ k \right) = \varphi^x \left( i, j\ k \right) + C_i \frac{\Delta(i)}{\sqrt{\Delta^T(i)\Delta(i)}}$$

and use this $\varphi^x \left( i+1, j\ k \right)$ to compute the new ITSE $(i, j+1, k, l)$ as we did in [substep f].

else, let $m = N_s,$ This is end of while statement.

**Substep-h.** Go to next bacterium $(i, 1)$ if $i \neq N$ (i.e., go to [substep b] to process the next bacterium).

```
Step 5.
If
```
$j < N_c$, go to step 3. In this case, continue chemotaxis, since the life of the bacteria is not over.

*continued on following page*

*Box 1. Continued*

**Step 6.** Reproduction:

Substep-a.

For the given $k$ and $l$, and for each $i = 1, 2, \cdots N$, let

$$ITSE_{health}^{i} = \sum_{j=1}^{N_c+1} ITSE\left(i, j, k, l\right)$$

be the health of the bacterium $i$ (a measure of how many nutrients it got over its lifetime and how successful it was at avoiding noxious substances). Sort bacteria and chemotactic parameters $C_i$ in order of ascending cost $ITSE_{health}$ (higher cost means lower health).

Substep-b.

The $S_r$ bacteria with the highest $ITSE_{health}$ values die and the remaining $S_r$ bacteria with the best values split (this process is performed by the copies that are made are placed at the same location as their parent).

Step 7.

If $k < N_{re}$, go to [step 3]. In this case, we have not reached the number of specified reproduction steps, so we start the next generation of the chemotactic loop.

Step 8.

Elimination-dispersal: For $i = 1, 2, \cdots N$, with probability $P_{ed}$, eliminate and disperse each bacterium, which results in keeping the number of bacteria in the population constant. To do this, if a bacterium is eliminated, simply disperse one to a random location on the optimization domain. If $l < N_{ed}$, then go to [step 2]; otherwise end.

As an example, a time-varying channel used for the simulation is shown in Figure 2. This channel incorporates both, a sudden change and a gradual change in the environment. There is a fixed zero at $z_1 = 0.5$. After 3000 iterations another zero, which is a mobile zero, appears as:

$$z_2\left(n\right) = 1.6 \exp\left(j2\pi / 3\right)$$
$$+ 0.2 \exp\left(j\pi\left(n - 3000\right).10^{-4}\right)$$

The channel suddenly changes after $n = 3000$ and becomes a continuously varying medium.

*Figure 2. Poles & Zeros of non-stationary channel*

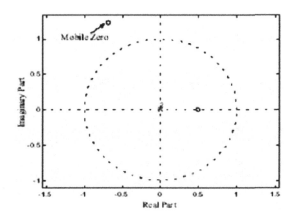

The error probability plots obtained without phase correction in the output of the linear equalizer, GA trained equalizer and the proposed model is shown in Figure 3 for 16-QAM signals. Averaging 50 independent runs we obtained these plots. The Error probability curves obtained from the GA trained equalizer, BFO trained equalizer and the proposed model with external phase correction applied at the output of the equalizer is shown in Figure 4.

From these figures, it can be seen that the use GBF gives lower error than those obtained when GA and BFO at the output of the neuro-fuzzy equalizer. The comparison with the linear equalizer shows that the proposed equalizer with the proposed activation function gives lower error.

## 6. CONCLUSION

In this paper a new method for blind equalization of time-varying channel was derived. The new equalizer is a neuro-fuzzy filter tuned with GBF. The major advantage of the method developed is that all parameters of the neuro-fuzzy network including the rule base are tuned simultaneously. The initial GA populations for simulated problems are randomized, which implies that minimum heuristic control knowledge is used. The neuro-fuzzy approach is implemented for equalization of non-linear channel in absence of supervised learning. The performance of the NFC designed using the proposed approach is compared with other existing approaches. The results confirm that the methodology used in the paper is much better than existing approaches. The proposed models also give lower MSE and SER under time-varying environment. These benefits are, however, obtained at the cost of increased complexity. Proposed hybrid algorithm eliminates the limitations of GA based equalizer, i.e. the inherent characteristic of GA, i.e. GAs risk finding a sub-optimal solution.

*Figure 3. Error Probability for Linear, GA trained and proposed equalizer*

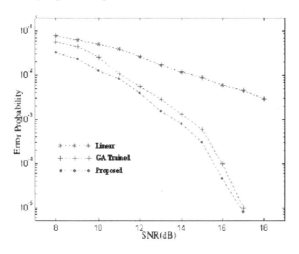

*Figure 4. BER for GA trained, BFO trained and proposed equalizer*

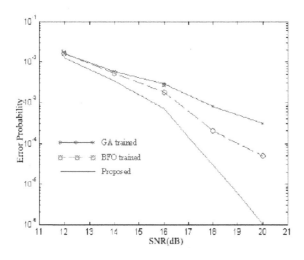

## REFERENCES

Acharya, D. P., Panda, G., & Lakshmi, Y. V. S. (2010). Effects of finite register length on fast ICA, bacterial foraging optimization based ICA and constrained genetic algorithm based ICA algorithm. *Digital Signal Processing*, *20*(3). doi:10.1016/j.dsp.2009.08.012

Arts, E. H. L., & Lenstra, J. K. (1997). *Local search in combinatorial optimization.* New York, NY: John Wiley & Sons.

Dorigo, M., & Caro, G. D. (1999). Ant colony optimization: A new meta-heuristic. In . *Proceedings of the Congress on Evolutionary Computation, 2,* 1470–1477.

Farag, W. A., Quintana, V. H., & Lambert-Torres, G. (1998). A genetic based neuro-fuzzy approach for modeling and control of dynamic systems. *IEEE Transactions on Neural Networks, 9*(5), 756–767. doi:10.1109/72.712150

Gen, M., & Cheng, R. (1997). *Genetic algorithms and engineering design.* New York, NY: John Wiley & Sons.

Gibson, G. J., Siu, S., & Cowan, C. F. N. (1991). The application of nonlinear structures to the reconstruction of binary signals. *IEEE Transactions on Signal Processing, 39*(8), 1877–1884. doi:10.1109/78.91157

Guzmán, M. A., Delgado, A., & De Carvalho, J. (2010). A novel multiobjective optimization algorithm based on bacterial chemotaxis. *Engineering Applications of Artificial Intelligence, 23*(3), 292–301. doi:10.1016/j.engappai.2009.09.010

Kolen, A., & Pesch, E. (1994). Genetic local search in combinatorial optimization. *Discrete Applied Mathematics and Combinatorial Operations Research and Computer Science, 48,* 273–284.

Lee, Z.-J., & Lee, W.-L. (2003). A hybrid search algorithm of ant colony optimization and genetic algorithm applied to weapon–target assignment problems. In J. Liu, Y. Cheung, & H. Yin (Eds.), *Proceedings of the 4th International Conference on Intelligent Data Engineering and Automated Learning* (LNCS 2690, pp. 278-285).

Lee, Z.-J., Su, S.-F., & Lee, C.-Y. (2003). Efficiently solving general weapon–target assignment problem by genetic algorithms with greedy eugenics. *IEEE Transactions on Systems, Man and Cybernetics, Part B,* 113-121.

Lin, C. T., & Lee, C. S. G. (1991). Neural network based fuzzy logic control and decision system. *IEEE Transactions on Computers, 40,* 1320–1336. doi:10.1109/12.106218

Majhi, B., & Panda, G. (2010). Development of efficient identification scheme for nonlinear dynamic systems using swarm intelligence techniques. *Expert Systems with Applications, 37*(1), 556–566. doi:10.1016/j.eswa.2009.05.036

Merz, P., & Freisleben, B. (2000). Fitness landscape analysis and memetic algorithms for quadratic assignment problem. *IEEE Transactions on Evolutionary Computation, 4*(4), 337–352. doi:10.1109/4235.887234

Miller, J., Potter, W., Gandham, R., & Lapena, C. (1993). An evaluation of local improvement operators for genetic algorithms. *IEEE Transactions on Systems, Man, and Cybernetics, 23*(5), 1340–1341. doi:10.1109/21.260665

Panda, G., Majhi, B., Mohanty, D., Choubey, A., & Mishra, S. (2006, January 27-29). Development of novel digital channel equalisers using genetic algorithms. In *Proceedings of the National Conference on Communication,* Delhi, India (pp.117-121).

Pandey, R. (2001). *Blind equalization and signal separation using neural networks.* Unpublished doctoral dissertation, Indian Institute of Technology, Roorkee, India.

Passino, K. M. (2002). Biomimicry of bacterial foraging for distributed optimization and control. *IEEE Control Systems Magazine, 22*(3), 52–67. doi:10.1109/MCS.2002.1004010

Patra, J. C., Pal, R. N., Baliarsingh, R., & Panda, G. (1999). Nonlinear channel equalization for QAM signal constellation using artificial neural network. *IEEE Transactions on Systems, Man, and Cybernetics. Part B, Cybernetics, 29*(2). doi:10.1109/3477.752798

Patra, J. C., Poh, W. B., Chaudhari, N. S., & Das, A. (2005, August). Nonlinear channel equalization with QAM signal using Chebyshev artificial neural network. In *Proceedings of the International Joint Conference on Neural Networks*, Montreal, QC, Canada (pp. 3214-3219).

Preparata, F. (1989). Holographic dispersal and recovery of information. *IEEE Transactions on Information Theory, 35*(5), 1123–1124. doi:10.1109/18.42233

Shoorehdeli, M. A., Teshnehlab, M., & Sedigh, A. K. (2009). Training ANFIS as an identifier with intelligent hybrid stable learning algorithm based on particle swarm optimization and extended kalman filter. *Fuzzy Sets and Systems, 160*(7), 922–948. doi:10.1016/j.fss.2008.09.011

Touri, R., Voulgaris, P. G., & Hadjicostis, C. N. (2006, June). Time varying power limited pre-processing for perfect reconstruction of binary signals. In *Proceedings of the American Control Conference*, Minneapolis, MN (pp. 5722-5727).

Voulgaris, P. G., & Hadjicostics, C. N. (2004). Optimal processing strategies for perfect reconstruction of binary signals under power-constrained transmission. In *Proceedings of the IEEE Conference on Decision and Control*, Atlantis, Bahamas (pp. 4040-4045).

*This work was previously published in the International Journal of Applied Evolutionary Computation, Volume 2, Issue 3, edited by Wei-Chiang Samuelson Hong, pp. 27-38, copyright 2011 by IGI Publishing (an imprint of IGI Global).*

# Chapter 12
# An Evolutionary Functional Link Neural Fuzzy Model for Financial Time Series Forecasting

**S. Chakravarty**
*Regional College of Management Autonomous, India*

**V. Ravikumar Pandi**
*Indian Institute of Technology Delhi, India*

**P. K. Dash**
*Siksha O Anusandhan University, India*

**B. K. Panigrahi**
*Indian Institute of Technology Delhi, India*

## ABSTRACT

*This paper proposes a hybrid model, evolutionary functional link neural fuzzy model (EFLNF), to forecast financial time series where the parameters are optimized by two most efficient evolutionary algorithms: (a) genetic algorithm (GA) and (b) particle swarm optimization (PSO). When the periodicity is just one day, PSO produces a better result than that of GA. But the gap in the performance between them increases as periodicity increases. The convergence speed is also better in case of PSO for one week and one month a head prediction. To testify the superiority of the EFLNF, a number of comparative studies have been made. First, functional link artificial neural network (FLANN) and functional link neural fuzzy (FLNF) were combined with back propagation (BP) learning algorithm. The result shows that FLNF performs better than FLANN. Again, FLNF is compared with EFLNF where the latter outperforms the former irrespective of the periodicity or the learning algorithms with which it has been combined. All models are used to predict the most chaotic financial time series data; BSE Sensex and S&P CNX Nifty stock indices one day, one week and one month in advance.*

DOI: 10.4018/978-1-4666-3628-6.ch012

## 1. INTRODUCTION

The chaotic, volatile and random nature of stock market has remained as main hurdle in forecasting. As an institution, it is not only impacted by macro-economic factors but also political development of a country, strategic planning of corporate houses and above all, mood of individual investors. However, over the years efficient and intelligent models have been developed by researchers to forecast it.

Broadly, there are two types of models for time series forecasting: (1) linear models, e.g. moving average, exponential smoothing, autoregressive moving average (ARMA) and autoregressive integrated moving average (ARIMA); (2) non-linear models, e.g. neural network models, support vector machine, fuzzy system models etc. For better result, researchers have also developed hybrid models integrating both linear and nonlinear models (Valenzuelaa et al., 2007; Khashei, Bijari, & Ardali, 2009). Secondly, hybrid models have also been developed combining non-linear models only and different evolutionary learning algorithms like genetic algorithm (GA) and particle swarm optimization (PSO) technique. A survey of literature will show this clearly.

A local linear wavelet neural network (LL-WNN) (Chen, Yang, & Dong, 2006) is used to predict Box-Jenkins and Mackey glass time series where a hybrid training algorithm of particle swarm optimization and gradient descent method is introduced to train the model. Application of the same model is seen (Chen, Dong, & Zhao, 2005) to predict stock market indices where the parameters are optimized by using estimation of distribution algorithm. A combination of wavelet and Takagi Sugeno Kang (TSK) fuzzy rules based system is applied (Chang, Fan, & Chen, 2007) to predict financial time series data of Taiwan stock market. A fuzzy time series method based on a multiple-period modified equation derived from adaptive expectation model (Cheng, Chen, & Teoh, 2007) is used to forecast, taking the same data set.

Support vector machine (Huang, Nakamori, & Wang, 2004) is used to forecast stock movement direction for NIKKEI 225 index. A least square support vector machine with a mixed kernel where genetic algorithm is used to select input features and another GA used for parameters optimization (Yu, Chen, Wang, & Lai, 2009) to predict S&P 500, DJIA and New York stock exchange. Kim and Han (2000) have applied a hybrid model, combination of artificial neural network (ANN) and GA to predict stock price indices where GA works to reduce the dimension of ANN and determine the connection weights (Kim & Han, 2000). A linear combinatory with adaptive bacterial foraging optimization is used (Majhi, Panda, Majhi, & Sahoo, 2009) to predict stock market indices. A single multiplicative neuron with cooperative random learning particle swarm optimization is applied (Zhao & Yang, 2009) to predict Mackey glass time series. A hybrid forecast method, combination of fuzzy time series and particle swarm optimization technique is used (Kuo et al., 2009) to forecast Taiwan stock exchange.

A fuzzy neural network is used (Yu & Zhang, 2005) to forecast financial time series where genetic algorithm and gradient descent learning algorithm are used alternatively in an iterative manner to adjust the parameters until the error is less than the required value. Slim (2006) has applied neuro fuzzy architecture based on kalman filter to predict financial time series taking Mackey glass time series as experimental data. Fu-yuan (2008b) has adopted a combination of improved PSO algorithm and fuzzy neural network to predict Shanghai stock market indices and genetic fuzzy neural network (Fu-yuan, 2008a) to forecast Shhenzhen stock indices. Kuo has applied neural fuzzy model (Kuo, 2001) to forecast sales data of well known convenience store franchise company in Taiwan where weights are generated by GA. Functional link neural network (FLANN), an improved ANN, is used (Majhi, Shalabi, & Fathi, 2005) to predict S&P 500 stock. Recently, the same FLANN model when combined with recursive least square (RLS) algorithm (Majhi, Panda, & Sahoo, 2009) produces better result in stock market predictions. A review of 100 published articles related to prediction of stock market indices has concluded that neuro-fuzzy hybrid models are most suitable for stock market prediction (Atsalakis & Valavanis, 2009). A functional link based neuro fuzzy network (Chen, Lin, & Lin, 2008) is used for non linear system control (water bath). We propose to apply the same neuro fuzzy network model integrated with evolutionary learning algorithms to forecast stock market indices.

In the proposed model, evolutionary functional link neural fuzzy (EFLNF), GA and PSO have separately been used as learning algorithm and compared. From the available literature, it is mostly seen that GA has been compared with back propagation and found GA to be better one. A comparison of back propagation and genetic algorithm is discussed (Sexton, Dorsey, & Johnson, 1998; Gupta & Sexton, 1999) where GA overcomes many of the limitation of BP and it gives better result to train a feed forward neural network. A comparison is made between GA and BP (Sexton & Gupta, 2000) where they concluded that GA is superior to BP in effectiveness, ease-of-use and efficiency for training neural network. They have taken five chaotic time series problem as the illustrations.

However, in this paper GA and PSO has been compared. We shall see the result in the Section 6 that PSO gives better result than that of GA irrespective of the time series.

This paper is organized in 8 sections. Section 1 focuses on introduction and reviews of literature. The development of the proposed EFLNF model is dealt in section 2 and the architecture of all three models (EFLNF, FLANN and FLNF) is given in subsection A, B and C respectively. Back propagation learning algorithm and the evolutionary algorithms (GA and PSO) are discussed in section 3 and 4. Experimental data sets and inputs needed for the models are analyzed in section 5. Simulation results are presented in section 6. The analyses of results obtained from the models are discussed in section 7. Section 8 presents the conclusion.

## 2. ARCHITECTURE OF PROPOSED MODELS

### A. Functional Link Artificial Neural Network

Amongst the different ANN tools: (MLP, RBF, RNN), MLP neural networks are mostly used by the researchers for its inherent capabilities to approximate any non-linear function to a high degree of accuracy. In spite of this, it has two major limitations 1. Convergence speed is slow and 2. Computational complexity is higher. To overcome these two limitations, we prefer to use a different kind of ANN i.e. functional link artificial neural network (FLANN) i.e. a single neuron and single layer architecture (Majhi, Hasan, & Fathi, 2005; Majhi, Panda, & Sahoo, 2009). Pao, the pioneer of FLANN has shown that this network may be conveniently used for functional approximation and pattern classification with faster convergence rate and lesser computational load. In FLANN, each input of the network undergoes functional expansion through a set of basis functions. Here the functional link generates a set of linearly independent functions. The inputs expanded by a set of linearly independent functions in the functional expansion block cause an increase in input vector dimensionality. This helps FLANN to solve complex classification problems by generating non-linear boundaries.

In this model (Figure 1) fthe functional expansion block comprises of a set of trigonometric functions.

$$\hat{y}_j = \tanh(w_{110} + w_1 x_1 + \dots\dots + w_n x_n) \quad (1)$$

*Figure 1. Structure of FLANN model*

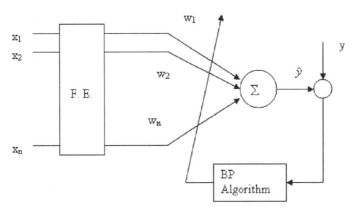

where $X=[x_1, x_2 \dots \dots \dots \dots x_n]$ is the input vector and

$W_j = [w_{j1}, w_{j2} \dots \dots \dots \dots w_{jn}]$ is the weight vector associated with $J^{th}$ output of FLANN. $W_{110}$ is the bios. $\hat{y}_j$ denotes the local output of FLANN structure and consequent part of $j^{th}$ fuzzy rule in our proposed hybrid model.

The matrix of the local out put or 'r' dimensional linear out put may be given as

$$\hat{y} = \left[\hat{y}_1, \hat{y}_2 \dots \dots \dots \dots \hat{y}_r\right] \qquad (2)$$

where r denotes the number of functional link bases which equals the number of fuzzy rules in the hybrid model.

## B. Functional Link Neural Fuzzy Model

In Functional Link Neural Fuzzy (FLNF) model, both Functional Link Artificial Neural Network (FLANN) and Fuzzy Logic System (FLS) are combined to get the advantages from both the tools (Chen, Lin, & Lin, 2008). Fuzzy Logic System is famous for its precision and dealing with uncertainty; whereas neural network is known for learning, adaptation, fault tolerance, parallelism, and generalization. The proposed model uses a functional link neural network to the consequent part of the fuzzy rules. The consequent part of the model is a non-linear combination of input variables. Each fuzzy rule corresponds to a sub-FLANN, comprising a functional link.

In Figure 2 the structure of the model is given. This model uses a fuzzy IF-THEN rule in the following form.

```
Rule j:
IF x₁ is A₁ⱼ and x₂ is A₂ᵢ............. and xᵢ
is Aⱼᵢ.......... and x_N is A_Nⱼ
```
$$\text{THEN } \hat{y}_i = \sum_{k=1}^{M} w_{kj}\varphi_k \quad (3)$$

where xi is the input and $\hat{y}_j$ is the local output variables. Aji is the linguistic term of the precondition part with Gaussian membership function. N is the number of input variables. wkj is the link weight of the local output. $\varphi_k$ is the basis trigonometric function of input variables. M is the number of basis function and rule j is the jth fuzzy rule. Total five layers are present in FLNF model. The operations of nodes in each layer are described below.

## Layer 1

No computations are required in layer 1. Each node in this layer only transmits input values to the next layer.

*Figure 2. Structure of FLNF model*

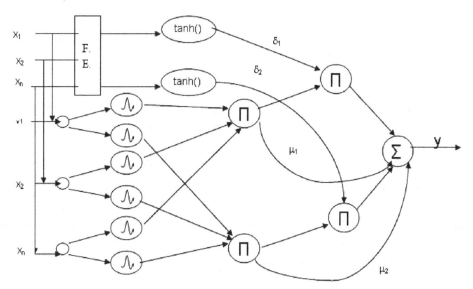

$$O_i^{(1)} = x_i \qquad (4)$$

## Layer 2

Each fuzzy set $A_{ij}$ is described by a Gaussian membership function.

$$O^{(2)}{}_{ij} = (\exp(-(x_{ij} - c_{ij}))^2) / \sigma_{ij}{}^2 \qquad (5)$$

where $c_{ij}$ is the mean and $\sigma_{ij}$ is the variance.

## Layer 3

Layer 3 receives one dimensional membership degrees of the associated rule from the nodes of layer 2. Now the output function of each inference node is

$$\mu_j^{(3)} = \amalg O_{ij}^{(2)} \qquad (6)$$

where $\amalg O_{ij}$ of a rule node represents the firing strength of its corresponding rule.

## Layer 4

Nodes in layer 4 are called consequent nodes. The input to a node in layer 4 is the output from layer 3 and the output collected from FLANN.

$$\delta_j^{(4)} = \mu_j^{(3)} \sum_{k=1}^{M} w_{kj} \varphi_k \qquad (7)$$

where $w_{kj}$ is the link weight of FLANN and $\varphi_k$ is the functional expansion of input variables.

## Layer 5

The output node in layer 5 acts as a defuzzifier which combines all the actions recommended by layer 3 and layer 4.

$$y^{(5)} = \frac{\mu_1 \left( \delta_1 \right) + \mu_2 \left( \delta_2 \right)}{\mu_1 + \mu_2} \qquad (8)$$

where $\delta_1$ and $\delta_2$ are the output of FLANN and $\mu_1$ and $\mu_2$ are the output of layer-3.

Finally, a crisp value is obtained after passing through four stages: Fuzzification, Fuzzy Rule Base, Fuzzy Inference Engine and Defuzzification. This crisp value is considered as the model output.

## C. Evolutionary Functional Link Neural Fuzzy Model

To overcome two major limitations of back propagation learning algorithm, slowness in convergence and its inability to escape local optima, the FLNF model is combined with evolutionary algorithms i.e. GA and PSO which can be termed as evolutionary functional link neural fuzzy model (EFLNF). The parameters of EFLNF model are initialized as well as optimized by the above said algorithms separately for a comparative analysis. In Figure 3 the structure of the proposed model is given.

## 3. BACK PROPAGATION LEARNING ALGORITHM

Both FLANN and FLNF models use a supervised learning algorithm i.e. Delta rule which is well known for its two pass weighted features. In a forward pass, an error is detected; the measured error is then propagated backward through the network while weights are adjusted to reduce the overall

*Figure 3. Structure of EFLNF model*

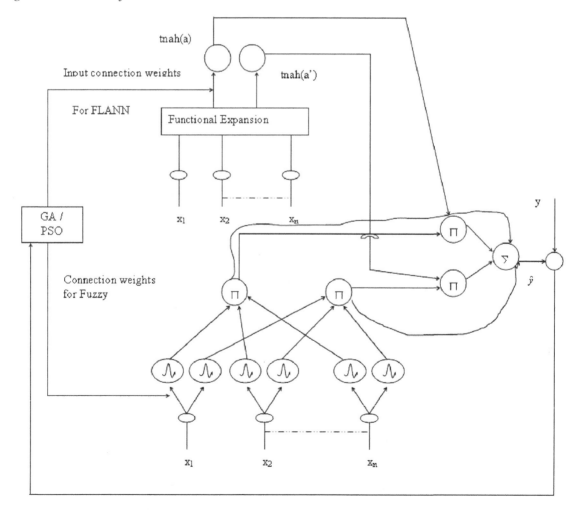

error. The learning process involves determining the minimum of a given error function. The error of the output neuron is

$$E(t) = \frac{1}{2} \sum_{k=1}^{n} [y_k(t) - y_k^d(t)]^2 \qquad (9)$$

where $y_k^d$ denotes target output and

$$y_k = \frac{\mu_1(\delta_1) + \mu_2(\delta_2)}{\mu_1 + \mu_2}$$

is the calculated output of the proposed model.

$$\delta_1 = \tanh(w11*x1 + w21*x2 + \ldots\ldots + w71*x7 + w81*sma + w110) \qquad (10)$$

$$\delta_2 = \tanh(w12*x1 + w22*x2 + \ldots\ldots + w72*x7 + w82*sma + w220) \qquad (11)$$

Through the learning algorithm the weight vector of FLNF model is adjusted such that the error defined in (9) is less than the desired threshold value after a number of training cycles.

In back propagation learning algorithm the weights are adjusted by

$$w(t+1) = w(t) + \Delta w(t) \qquad (12)$$

where

$$\Delta w(t) = \left(-\eta \frac{\partial E(t)}{\partial w(t)}\right)$$

and $\eta$ is the learning rate. In standard back propagation, too low a learning rate makes the network learn very slowly and too high learning rate makes the weight and objective function diverge, leading to no learning at all.

Like that $\dfrac{\partial E}{\partial w_{21}}$ to $\dfrac{\partial E}{\partial w_{71}}$ and $\dfrac{\partial E}{\partial w_{22}}$ to $\dfrac{\partial E}{\partial w_{72}}$ are calculated. $w_{81}$ and $w_{82}$ are the weights of the indicator, sma (simple moving average). Similarly the weights of other indictors are updated.

$w_{110}$ and $w_{220}$ are the biases.

## 4. EVOLUTIONARY LEARNING ALGORITHMS

For the last three decades neural networks have been gaining popularity in solving several business and technical problems. As the parameters or weights in neural network are initially taken by trial and error method, the researchers have commonly used gradient descent technique to train the neural network and finally to optimize them to reduce the overall errors. Since BP converges locally, if these initial weights are located on a local grade, the BP algorithm will likely be trapped in local solution that may or may not be the global solution (Sexton & Gupta, 2000). To overcome this limitation we used evolutionary algorithms (GA and PSO) to initialize as well as optimize the model parameters. Evolutionary algorithm (EA) comes from the idea of applying

*Box 1.*

$$\frac{\partial E}{\partial w_{11}} = \left(\tanh\left(w_{11}*x_1 + w_{21}*x_2 + \ldots\ldots + w_{71}*x_7\right)*o_{11}(i) + \tanh\left(w_{12}*x_1 + \ldots\ldots + w_{72}*x_7\right)*o_{22}(i)\right)/$$
$$\left(o_{11}(i) + o_{22}(i)\right) - ytr(i)*\left(1 - \tanh\left(w_{11}*x_1 + w_{21}*x_2 + \ldots\ldots + w_{71}*x_7\right)^2\right)*x_1*o_{11}(i)/\left(o_{11}(i) + o_{22}(i)\right) \qquad (13)$$

$$\frac{\partial E}{\partial w_{12}} = \left(\tanh\left(w_{11}*x_1 + w_{21}*x_2 + \ldots\ldots + w_{71}*x_7\right)*o_{11}(i) + \tanh\left(w_{12}*x_1 + \ldots\ldots + w_{72}*x_7\right)*o_{22}(i)\right)/$$
$$\left(o_{11}(i) + o_{22}(i)\right) - ytr(i)*\left(1 - \tanh\left(w_{12}*x_1 + w_{22}*x_2 + \ldots\ldots + w_{72}*x_7\right)^2\right)*x_1*o_{22}(i)/\left(o_{11}(i) + o_{22}(i)\right) \qquad (14)$$

*Box 2.*

$$\frac{\partial E}{\partial w_{81}} = \left(\tanh\left(w_{110} + w_{11} * x_1 + ..... + w_{71} * x_7 + w_{81} * sma\right) * o_{11}(i) + \tanh\left(w_{220} + w_{12} * x_1 + ..... + w_{72} * x_7 + w_{82} * sma\right) * o_{22}(i)\right) /$$

$$\left(o_{11}(i) + o_{22}(i)\right) - ytr(i) * \left(1 - \tanh\left(w_{110} + w_{11} * x_1 ....... + w_{71} * x_7 + w_{81} * sma\right)^2\right) * sma * o_{11}(i) / \left(o_{11}(i) + o_{22}(i)\right)$$

(15)

$$\frac{\partial E}{\partial w_{82}} = \left(\tanh\left(w_{110} + w_{11} * x_1 + ..... + w_{71} * x_7 + w_{81} * sma\right) * o_{11}(i) + \tanh\left(w_{220} + w_{12} * x_1 + ..... + w_{72} * x_7 + w_{82} * sma\right) * o_{22}(i)\right) /$$

$$\left(o_{11}(i) + o_{22}(i)\right) - ytr(i) * \left(1 - \tanh\left(w_{220} + w_{12} * x_1 ....... + w_{72} * x_7 + w_{82} * sma\right)^2\right) * sma * o_{22}(i) / \left(o_{11}(i) + o_{22}(i)\right)$$

(16)

*Box 3.*

$$\frac{\partial E}{\partial w_{110}} = \left(\tanh\left(w_{110} + w_{11} * x_1 + ..... + w_{71} * x_7\right) * o_{11}(i) + \tanh\left(w_{220} + w_{12} * x_1 + ..... + w_{72} * x_7\right) * o_{22}(i)\right) / \left(o_{11}(i) + o_{22}(i)\right) - ytr(i) *$$

$$\left(1 - \tanh\left(w_{110} + w_{11} * x_1 ....... + w_{71} * x_7\right)^2\right) * o_{11}(i) / \left(o_{11}(i) + o_{22}(i)\right)$$

(17)

$$\frac{\partial E}{\partial w_{220}} = \left(\tanh\left(w_{110} + w_{11} * x_1 + ..... + w_{71} * x_7\right) * o_{11}(i) + \tanh\left(w_{220} + w_{12} * x_1 + ..... + w_{72} * x_7\right) * o_{22}(i)\right) / \left(o_{11}(i) + o_{22}(i)\right) - ytr(i) *$$

$$\left(1 - \tanh\left(w_{220} + w_{12} * x_1 ....... + w_{72} * x_7\right)^2\right) * o_{22}(i) / \left(o_{11}(i) + o_{22}(i)\right)$$

(18)

the biological principle of natural evolution to artificial systems. EAs are successfully applied to numerous problems from different domains, including optimization, automatic programming, machine learning, economics, operations research, ecology, and population genetics.

## A. Genetic Algorithm

Genetic algorithm introduced by John Holland in the United States in 1970s at University of Michigan, is a particular class of evolutionary algorithms that use techniques inspired by evolutionary biology such as inheritance, mutation, selection, and crossover (also called recombination). Genetic algorithms are typically implemented as a computer simulation in which a population of abstract representations (called chromosomes) of candidate solutions (called individuals) to an optimization problem, evolves toward better solutions. Traditionally, solutions are represented in binary strings of 0s and 1s, but different encodings are also possible. The evolution starts from a population of completely random individuals and occur in generations. In each generation, the fitness of the whole population is evaluated, multiple individuals are stochastically selected from the current population (based on their fitness), and modified (mutated or recombined) to form a new population. The new population is then used in the next iteration of the algorithm.

## Selection

Chromosomes are selected from the population to become parents to crossover. The problem is how to select these chromosomes. There are many methods to select the best chromosomes, for example roulette wheel selection, Boltzman selection, tournament selection, rank selection, steady state selection and many others. Every method has some merits as well as some limitations. Roulette wheel selection is used here to select the chromosomes. Lastly elitism is used to copy the best chromosome (or a few best chromosomes) to new population. Elitism helps in increasing the performance of GA, because it prevents losing the best found solution.

## Crossover

Crossover selects genes from parent chromosomes and creates a new offspring. The simplest way to do this is to choose randomly some crossover point and interchange the value before and after that point.

## Mutation

After crossover mutation takes place. Mutation changes randomly the new offspring. For binary encoding we can switch a few randomly chosen bits from 1 to 0 or 0 to 1. Mutation ensures genetic diversity within population. The parameters used for EFLNF model with GA as the optimization algorithm are given in Table 1.

## B. Particle Swarm Optimization

Particle swarm optimization (PSO) is a population based, self adaptive search optimization technique first introduced by Kennedy and Eberhart (1995). Similar to other population based optimization techniques like GA (genetic algorithm) the PSO starts with the random initialization of a popula-

*Table 1. Parameters used for EFLNF model (GA)*

| Parameters | Values |
| --- | --- |
| Population size P | 30 |
| Maximum No. of generation G | 200 |
| Dimension or No. of variables D | 39 |
| No. of consecutive generation for which no improvement is observed | 25 |
| | 0.0001 |
| Lower bound | 1 |
| Upper bound | 0.8 |
| Crossover rate | 0.08 |
| Mutation rate | |

tion of particles in the search space. The PSO algorithm works on the social behavior of particles in the swarm and finds the global best solution by simply adjusting the trajectory of each individual towards its best location and towards the best particle of the entire population at each generation. The PSO method is becoming very popular due to its simplicity in implementation and its ability to quickly converge to an optimal solution. For a particle moving in a multidimensional search space let $S_i$ denotes the position of the i[th] particle and $v_i$ denotes the velocity at the sampling instant $k$, and the dimension $j$ denotes the number of parameters to be optimized which if too high will result in allowing the particles to fly past good solutions. On the other hand, if $v_{max}$ is too small, particles end up in local solutions only.

As with GA, PSO has premature convergence and thus results in an inaccurate solution. To circumvent this problem, an alternative approach is used to dynamically vary the inertia weight based on the variance of the population fitness. This results in better local and global searching ability of the particles which improves the convergence velocity and better accuracy for stock market indices prediction. The modified velocity and position of each particle at the sampling instant $(k+1)$ can be calculated as

$$v_i(k+1) = \omega_i v_i(k) + c_i rand(\ ) \\ +(pbest_i - s_i(k)) + c_2 rand(\ )(gbest_i - s_i(k))$$

(19)

and

$$S_i(k+1) = S_i(k) + v_i(k+1)$$

(20)

When $c_1$ and $c_2$ are constants known as acceleration co-efficient, rand () is an uniformly distributed random number in the range (0, 1), and $\omega_i$ is the inertia weight for the i[th] particle.

A suitable selection of inertia weight $\omega$ and constants $c_1$ and $c_2$ is crucial in providing a balance between the global and local search in the flying space. The particle velocity at any instant is limited to $v_{max}$.

Since the PSO algorithm depends on the objective function to guide the search, the choice is made as

$$O_i = \frac{1}{NS} \sum_{k=1}^{NS_s} (\hat{y}(t) - y_d(t))^2 \qquad (21)$$

NS= number of samples over which the RMSE is compared and the fitness of the i[th] particle

becomes $F_i = \dfrac{1}{1 + O_i}$ $\qquad (22)$

The inertia weight $\omega_i$ is updated by finding the variance of the population fitness as

$$\sigma^2 = \sum_{i=1}^{M} \left( \frac{F_i - F_{avg}}{F} \right)^2 \qquad (23)$$

$F_{avg}$ = average fitness of the population

$F_i$ = fitness of the i[th] particle

in the population, and

M = total number of particles

If $\sigma$ is found to be large, the population will be a random searching mode, while for small $\sigma$ the solution tends towards a premature convergence and will give the local best position of the particles. To circumvent this problem the inertia weight is changed in the following way:

$$\omega(k) = \lambda \omega(k-1) + (1 - \lambda) \sigma^2 \qquad (25)$$

The forgetting factor $\lambda$ is chosen as 0.9 for faster convergence.

Another alternative will be

$$\omega(k) = \lambda_1 \omega(k-1) + rand(\ )/2 \qquad (26)$$

with $0 \le \lambda_1 \le 0.5$

where rand () is a random number between (0, 1).Besides the influence of the past velocity of a particle on the current velocity is chosen to be random and the inertia weight is adapted randomly depending on the variance of the fitness value of a population. This result is an optimal coordination of local and global searching abilities of the particles. The parameters used for EFLNF model with PSO as a learning algorithm are given in Table 2.

## 5. ANALYSIS OF DATASETS AND INPUT SELECTION

SENSEX and NIFTY are indices of major Stock Market of INDIA i.e. the Bombay Stock Exchange (BSE) and the National Stock Exchange (NSE) respectively. Both the indices are the barometer of the stock exchange. Sensex is based on 30 largest trading companies on the BSE comprising all major sectors such as IT, Cement, Oil and Natural Gas, Bank, Auto etc. The Nifty is an indicator of all the major companies of the NSE. The major difference between two indices is that the later uses 50 stocks and situated in Delhi as compared to 30 stocks used for Sensex and situated in Bombay.

*Box 4.*

$$
\begin{aligned}
F &= \max \left\{ \left| F_i - F_{avg} \right| \right\}, i = 1, 2, \cdots, M \quad if \ \max \left\{ \left| F_i - F_{avg} \right| \right\} > 1 \\
&= 1, \qquad\qquad\qquad\qquad\qquad\qquad if \ \max \left\{ \left| F_i - F_{avg} \right| \right\} < 1
\end{aligned}
\qquad (24)
$$

*Table 2. Parameters used for EFLNF model (PSO)*

| Parameters | Values |
|---|---|
| Population size P | 30 |
| Maximum No. of generation G | 200 |
| Dimension or No. of variables D | 39 |
| No. of consecutive generation for which no improvement is observed | 20 |
| Acceleration co-efficient $C_1$, $C_2$ | 2.1,2.1 |
| Lower bound | 0.001 |
| Upper bound | 1 |

The experimental data for both Sensex and Nifty are obtained from the 1st March 1993 to 23rd July 2009. The total numbers of samples are 4000. Both the data sets are shown in Figure 3 and Figure 4 respectively. The proposed model is used to predict the Sensex and Nifty one day, one week and one month in advance. In our model, input is scaled between 0 and +1 using the standard formula described below.

$$\tilde{X}^i = \frac{X^i - X_{\min}}{X_{\max} - X_{\min}} \qquad (27)$$

where $X^i$ is the current day Closing price, $\tilde{X}^i$ is the scaled price and $X_{\min}$ and $X_{\max}$ are the minimum and maximum of the dataset respectively. Scaling is not mandatory but it will help to improve the performance. Both the datasets are divided into two, one for training and another for testing. The number of samples taken for training and testing are given in Table 3. Five important technical

indicators are taken into consideration along with the daily closing prices of the respective stocks. The used technical indicators and the formula are given in Table 4.

The Mean Absolute Percentage Error (MAPE) and Root Mean Square Error (RMSE) are used to measure the performance of all the models. The MAPE and RMSE are defined as

$$\text{MAPE} = \frac{1}{N} \sum_{i=1}^{N} \left| \frac{y_i - \hat{y}_i}{y_i} \right| \text{X}100 \qquad (28)$$

$$\text{RSME} = \sqrt{\frac{1}{n} \sum_{k=1}^{n} \left( y_k - \hat{y}_k \right)^2} \qquad (29)$$

where $y_i$ is the predicted value and $\hat{y}_i$ is the desired value. N is the total number of test data.

## 6. EXPERIMENTAL RESULTS

## A. FLANN

FLANN model is used to forecast both BSE Sensex and S&P CNX Nifty stock indices (Figure 5) for one day, one week and one month in advance. Here BP is used as a learning algorithm. Figure 6 and Figure 7 show the target Vs predicted during testing of BSE Sensex and S&P CNX Nifty respectively. MAPE obtained from FLANN model for all type of periodicity (one day, one week, one month) are given in Table 5.

*Figure 4. Normalized BSE sensex indices*

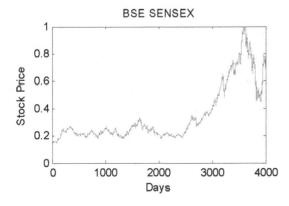

*Table 3. Number of samples*

| Data sets | Date From & To | Total Samples | Training | Testing |
|---|---|---|---|---|
| BSE Sensex | 1st Mar93 to 23rd July09 | 4000 | 1000 | 450 to 500 |
| S&P CNX Nifty | 1st Mar93 to 23rd July09 | 4000 | 1000 | 450 to 500 |

*Table 4. Technical indicators with formula*

| Indicators | Formulae |
|---|---|
| 1.Moving Average | $\dfrac{1}{N}\displaystyle\sum_{i=1}^{N}x_i$ , N=no. of Days, $x_i$=today's price; |
| 2.Exponential Moving Average | (P x A)+(Previous EMA x(1-A)); <br> A=$\dfrac{2}{N+1}$ ; P=Current Price; A=Smoothing factor; N=Time period; |
| 3.High Price Acceleration (HP Acc) | (High Price-High Price N-Periods ago)/(High Price N-Periods ago)x100 |
| 4. Closing Price Acceleration (CP Acc) | (Close Price-Close Price N-Periods ago)/(Close Price N-Periods ago)x100 |
| 5.Accumulation/Distribution Oscillator (ADO) | ((C.P-L.P)-(H.P-C.P))/((H.P-L.P)x(Period's volume)); <br> C.P-Closing price; H.P-Highest price; L.P-lowest Price; |

*Figure 5. Normalized S&P CNX Nifty indices*

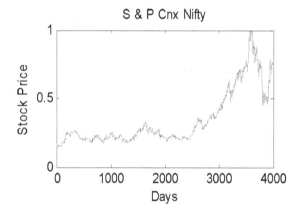

*Figure 7. Target vs predicted of FLANN with BP (one day ahead)*

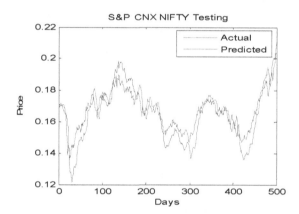

*Figure 6. Target vs predicted of FLANN with BP (one day ahead)*

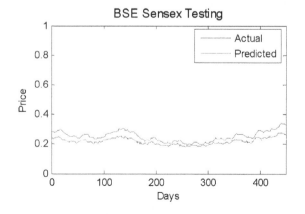

*Table 5. Comparison of MAPE during Testing (FLANN & FLNF)*

| Datasets | Days ahead | FLANN | FLNF |
|---|---|---|---|
| BSE Sensex | 1 | 4.2% | 2.11% |
| S&P CNX Nifty | 1 | 4% | 2.13% |
| BSE Sensex | 7 | 4.9% | 2.8% |
| S&P CNX Nifty | 7 | 4.56% | 2.9% |
| BSE Sensex | 30 | 5.2% | 4.12% |
| S&P CNX Nifty | 30 | 5.1% | 4.0% |

## B. FLNF

The hybrid FLNF model with back propagation learning algorithm is used to forecast both the data sets for all type of periodicity. Figure 8 and Figure 9 show target Vs predicted during testing for one day ahead of S&P CNX Nifty and BSE Sensex respectively. Figure 10 and Figure 11 show target Vs predicted for S&P CNX Nifty for one week and one month in advance. In Figure 12 one month advance prediction for BSE Sensex is given. In Table 5 the comparison of MAPE for FLANN and FLNF model is given. Figure 13 show the convergence speed of FLANN and FLNF models with back propagation learning algorithm.

*Figure 8. Target vs predicted of FLNF with BP (one day ahead)*

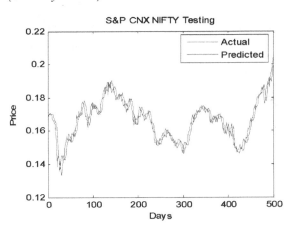

*Figure 9. Target vs predicted of FLNF with BP (one day ahead)*

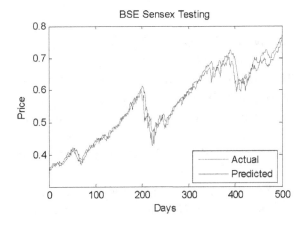

*Figure 10. Target vs predicted of FLNF with BP (one week ahead)*

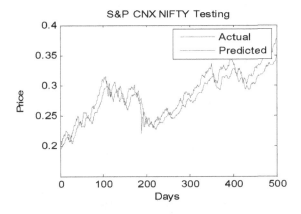

*Figure 11. Target vs predicted of FLNF with BP (one month ahead)*

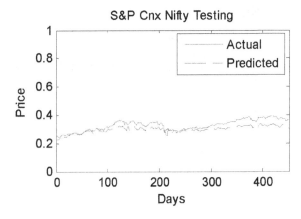

*Figure 12. Target vs predicted of FLNF with BP (one month ahead)*

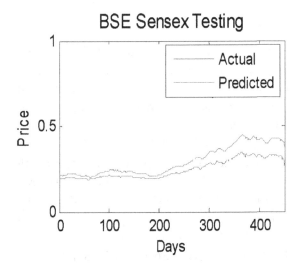

*Figure 13. Convergence speed of FLANN and FLNF models using BP*

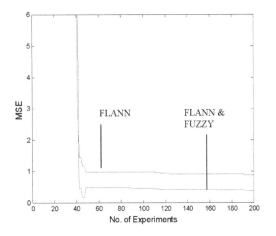

*Figure 15. Target vs predicted EFNF with GA (one week ahead)*

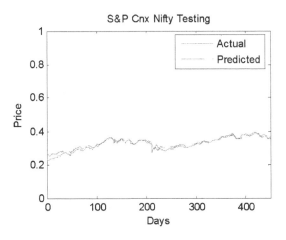

*Figure 14. Target vs predicted EFLNF with GA (one day ahead)*

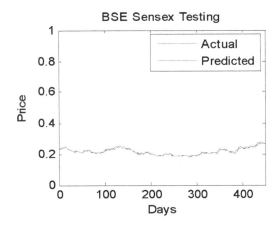

*Figure 16. Target vs predicted EFNF with GA (one month ahead)*

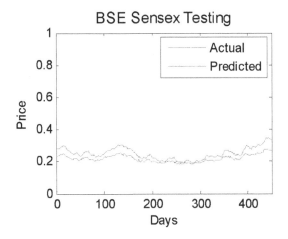

## C. EFLNF

EFLNF model is the evolutionary FLNF model. Here two important global search techniques GA and PSO are separately used to initialize and optimize the parameters of EFLNF model. Figure 14 through Figure 16 show target Vs predicted during testing of EFLNF model with GA for one day, one week and one month in advance for both the data sets. Figure 17 through Figure 19 shows the same with PSO for all type of periodicity. The comparison of MAPE during Testing obtained from EFLNF for both the data sets using GA and PSO are given in Table 6. Figure 20 and Figure 21

show the convergence speed of S&P CNX Nifty for one day and one month in advance respectively.

## 7. ANALYSIS OF RESULTS

This paper used three different models to forecast most chaotic financial time series data i.e. stock market indices for one day, one week and one month in advance. Two important stock indices, BSE Sensex and S&P CNX Nifty are taken as the experimental data. MAPE of BSE Sensex and S&P CNX Nifty during testing for one day in advance, obtained from FLNF with BP are respectively

*Figure 17. Target vs predicted EFNF with PSO (one day ahead)*

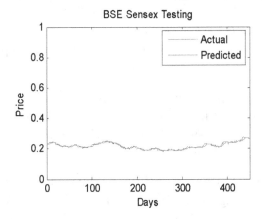

*Table 6. Comparison of MAPE during testing (GA & PSO)*

| Datasets | Days ahead | EFLNF with GA | EFLNF with PSO |
|---|---|---|---|
| BSE Sensex | 1 | 0.43% | 0.31% |
| S&P CNX Nifty | 1 | 0.41% | 0.32% |
| BSE Sensex | **7** | 1.1% | 0.72% |
| S&P CNX Nifty | **7** | 1.0% | 0.75% |
| BSE Sensex | 30 | 1.93% | 0.76% |
| S&P CNX Nifty | 30 | 1.89% | 0.82% |

*Figure 18. Target vs predicted EFNF with PSO (one week ahead)*

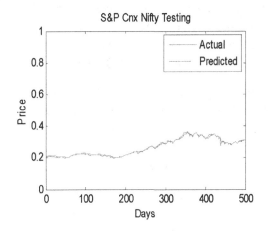

*Figure 20. Convergence speed S&P CNX Nifty (one day a head)*

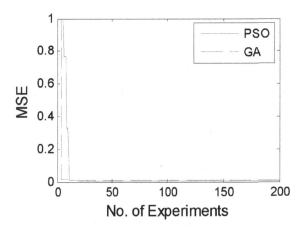

*Figure 19. Target vs predicted EFNF with PSO (one month ahead)*

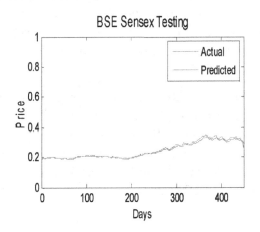

*Figure 21. Convergence speed S&P CNX Nifty (one month a head)*

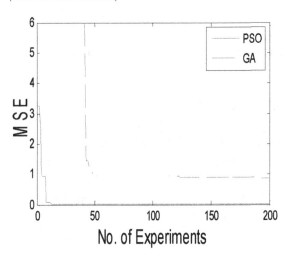

2.11% and 2.13%. The MAPE of EFLNF with GA for the same data sets are respectively 0.43% and 0.41%, whereas with PSO 0.31% and 0.32% for the same (one day ahead) periodicity. From the simulation results it is clearly seen that evolutionary learning algorithms always outperform the traditional back propagation learning algorithm in terms of prediction accuracy as well as the error convergence speed. Secondly, when the prediction is only for one day ahead, PSO gives slightly better prediction accuracy as compared to GA but this accuracy increases while the periodicity increases to one week or one month (Table 6).

## 8. CONCLUSION

Three types of comparisons are made in this paper (1) between FLANN and FLNF model (2) between back propagation and evolutionary learning algorithms (3) between GA and PSO. Our experimental results show that FLNF constantly outperform the single FLANN model. Secondly, though BP is most popular in training neural networks, to overcome two of its important drawbacks (slowness in convergence and its inability to escape local optima) evolutionary algorithms have been applied. Our empirical results show that EFLNF is producing better results as compared to FLNF model. Thirdly when the same EFLNF model is trained by GA and PSO independently, PSO gives comparatively better results and the performance increases when the periodicity increases.

## REFERENCES

Atsalakis, G. S., & Valavanis, K. P. (2009). Surveying stock market forecasting techniques-part 11: Soft computing methods. *Expert Systems with Applications, 36*, 5932–5941. doi:10.1016/j.eswa.2008.07.006

Chang, P.-C., Fan, C.-Y., & Chen, S.-H. (2007). Financial time series data forecasting by Wavelet and TSK fuzzy rule based system. In *Proceedings of the IEEE Fourth International Conference on Fuzzy Systems and knowledge Discovery* (pp. 331-335).

Chen, C.-H., Lin, C.-J., & Lin, C.-T. (2008). A functional-link-based neurofuzzy network for nonlinear system control. *IEEE Transactions on Fuzzy Systems, 16*(5).

Chen, Y., Dong, X., & Zhao, Y. (2005). Stock index modeling using EDA based local linear wavelet neural network. In *Proceedings of the IEEE International Conference on Neural Networks and Brain* (pp. 1646-1650).

Chen, Y., Yang, B., & Dong, J. (2006). Time series prediction using a local linear wavelet neural network. *Neurocomputing, 69*, 449–465. doi:10.1016/j.neucom.2005.02.006

Cheng, C., Chen, T.-L., & Teoh, H. (2007). Multiple-period modified fuzzy time series for forecasting TAIEX. In *Proceedings of the IEEE Fourth International Conference on Fuzzy systems and Knowledge Discovery* (pp. 2-6).

Eberhart, R., & Kennedy, J. (1995). A new optimizer using particle swarm theory. In *Proceedings of the IEEE Sixth International Symposium on Micro Machine and Human Science* (pp. 39-43).

Fu-yuan, H. (2008a). Forecasting stock price using a genetic fuzzy neural network. In *Proceedings of the IEEE International Conference on Computer Science and Information Technology* (pp. 549-552).

Fu-yuan, H. (2008b). Integration of improved particle swarm optimization algorithm and fuzzy neural network for Shanghai stock market prediction. In *Proceedings of the IEEE Workshop on Power Electronics and Intelligent Transportation Systems* (pp. 242-247).

Gupta, J. N. D., & Sexton, R. (1999). Comparing back propagation with a genetic algorithm for neural network training. *Omega*, 679–684. doi:10.1016/S0305-0483(99)00027-4

Huang, W., Nakamori, Y., & Wang, S.-Y. (2004). Forecasting stock movement direction with support vector machine. *Computer and Operation Research, 32*(10).

Khashei, M., Bijari, M., & Ardali, G. A. R. (2009). Improvement of auto-regressive integrated moving average models using fuzzy logic and artificial neural network. *Neurocomputing, 72*, 956–967. doi:10.1016/j.neucom.2008.04.017

Kim, K.-J., & Han, I. (2000). Genetic algorithm approach to feature discretization in artificial neural networks for prediction of stock price index. *Expert Systems with Applications, 19*, 125–132. doi:10.1016/S0957-4174(00)00027-0

Kuo, I.-H., Horng, S.-J., Chen, Y.-H., Run, R.-S., Kao, T.-W., & Chen, R.-J. (2009). Forecasting TAIFEX based on fuzzy time series and particle swarm optimization. *Expert Systems with Applications, 37*(2), 1494–1502. doi:10.1016/j.eswa.2009.06.102

Kuo, R. J. (2001). A sales forecasting system based on fuzzy neural network with initial weights generated by genetic algorithm. *European Journal of Operational Research, 129*, 496–517. doi:10.1016/S0377-2217(99)00463-4

Majhi, B., Shalabi, H., & Fathi, M. (2005). FLANN based forecasting of S&P 500 Index. *Information Technology Journal, 4*(3), 289–292. doi:10.3923/itj.2005.289.292

Majhi, R., Panda, G., Majhi, B., & Sahoo, G. (2009). Efficient prediction of stock market indices using adaptive bacterial foraging optimization (ABFO) and BFO based technique. *Expert Systems with Applications, 36*, 10097–10104. doi:10.1016/j.eswa.2009.01.012

Majhi, R., Panda, G., & Sahoo, G. (2009). Development and performance evaluation of FLANN based model for forecasting of stock market. *Expert Systems with Applications, 36*, 6800–6808. doi:10.1016/j.eswa.2008.08.008

Sexton, R. S., Dorsey, R. E., & Johnson, J. D. (1998). Toward global optimization of neural networks: A comparison of the genetic algorithm and back propagation. *Decision Support Systems, 22*, 171–185. doi:10.1016/S0167-9236(97)00040-7

Sexton, R. S., & Gupta, J. N. D. (2000). Comparative evaluation of genetic algorithm and back propagation for training neural network. *Information Sciences, 129*, 45–59. doi:10.1016/S0020-0255(00)00068-2

Slim, C. (2006). Neuro-fuzzy network based on extended Kalman filtering for financial time series. In *Proceedings of the World Academy of Science, Engineering and Technology Conference* (Vol. 15).

Valenzuelaa, O., Rojasb, I., Pomaresb, H., Herrerab, L. J., Guillenb, A., & Marqueza, L. (2007). Hybridization of intelligent techniques and ARIMA models for time series prediction. *Fuzzy Sets and Systems, 159*, 821–845. doi:10.1016/j.fss.2007.11.003

Yu, L., Chen, H., Wang, S., & Lai, K. K. (2009). Evolving least square support vector machines for stock market trend mining. *IEEE Transactions on Evolutionary Computation, 13*(1).

Yu, L., & Zhang, Y. Q. (2005). Evolutionary fuzzy neural networks for hybrid financial prediction. *IEEE Transactions on Systems, Man, and Cybernetics, 35*(2).

Zhao, L., & Yang, Y. (2009). PSO-based single multiplicative neuron model for time series prediction. *Expert Systems with Applications, 36*, 2805–2812. doi:10.1016/j.eswa.2008.01.061

*This work was previously published in the International Journal of Applied Evolutionary Computation, Volume 2, Issue 3, edited by Wei-Chiang Samuelson Hong, pp. 39-58, copyright 2011 by IGI Publishing (an imprint of IGI Global).*

# Chapter 13

# Firm Size Transmission Effect and Price–Volume Relationship Analysis During Financial Tsunami Periods

**Shih-Yung Wei**
*National Yunlin University of Science & Technology, Taiwan*

**Wei-Chiang Hong**
*Oriental Institute of Technology, Taiwan*

**Kai Wang**
*China University of Technology, Taiwan*

## ABSTRACT

*Investors attend importance to forecast the price of financial assets, thus, the factors affecting the stock price are usually the focus of financial research in the field, in which the most important factors to scholars are firm size transmission effect and price-volume relationship. In this study, the analysis of these two items in the Taiwan stock market is conducted. The results indicate that the firm size transmission effect is almost significant, and the reversal phenomenon also exists. However, before the financial tsunami, the firm size transmission effect does not significantly exist; this result also indirectly proves the directional asymmetry of the market returns, proposed by McQueen, Pinegar, and Thorley (1996). For price and volume relationship, big cap index reveals that volume leads to price before the financial tsunami, and small cap index appears that price leads to volume in 2010.*

## 1. INTRODUCTION

Recently, along with the diverse developments of investment practical applications, investment analysis has become one of the most important topics in financial analysis. On the other hand, the investors take the return of investment seriously, thus, the exploration of the impact factors between the firm size transmission effect and price volume relationship becomes the most important attentions for financial researchers.

Supply and demand of the market simultaneously deciding equilibrium price and quantity is

DOI: 10.4018/978-1-4666-3628-6.ch013

the basic concept of economics. The price analysis of the asset will also consider the message of volume in the same time. Ying (1966) clearly indicates that it isn't a very complete analysis if price or volume is studied separately. Because price and volume are joint products of market mechanism, any complete analysis should take these two variables into account to provide real market conditions and possible responses. Some theories regarding price and volume relationships are proposed. Clark (1973) proposes the mixture of distributions hypothesis, Copeland (1976) provides sequential information arrival model to discuss the price and volume relationships. Both of them claim that price and volume should have positive relationships.

Osborne (1959) is the pioneer to provide empirical study regarding price and volume relationships, in which, he finds that the variance of changes of stock price and the square root of numbers of the transactions are positive proportional. He does not directly explore price and volume relationships, but the results lead to the discussion of price and volume relationships. Previous researches are mainly focused on the same period of price and volume relationships. After the mid-1980s, the causality of price and volume are gradually taken seriously. Most of these discussions claim price and volume relationships are positive proportional, such as Granger and Morgenstern (1963), Godfrey et al. (1964), Ying (1966), Crouch (1970), Clark (1973), Epps and Epps (1976), Epps (1977), Wood et al. (1985), Harris (1987), Karpoff (1987), Jain and Joh (1988), Bessembinder and Seguin (1992), Basci et al. (1996), and Cooper (1999).

However, the price and volume relationships with positive proportional relationships imply that we can make the one of them to predict the other variable. It initiates another study of the causality of price and volume that mainly focuses on the analysis of lead lag relationship between volume and price (or price and volume), such as Jaffe and Westerfield (1985), Harris (1987), Smirlock and

Starks (1985), Eun and Shim (1989), Hamao et al. (1990), Jarrow (1992), Fendenia and Grammatikos (1992), Campbell et al. (1993), Hiemstra and Jones (1994), Theodossiou and Unro (1995), Chiang and Chiang (1996), Brennan et al. (1998), Kumar et al. (1998), Martens and Poon (2001), Wang and Cheng (2004), Baker and Stein (2004), Leigh et al. (2004), Mazouz (2004), How et al. (2005), Cheuk et al. (2006), and Gebka et al. (2006). Some of the scholars conclude that price influences volume, and some conclude that volume influences price, and, of course, some conclude that two way feedback relationships of price and volume. Although the results are different, it supports that the price and volume relationships existed.

Size effect has been first proposed by Banz (1981) and Reingnanum (1981). They indicate that, after making risk-adjusted, small-size-firms have higher return than big-size-firms. The phenomenon will be supported by other scholars via different research methods, such as Brown et al. (1983), Keim (1983), Schultz (1983), Stoll and Whaley (1983), Barry and Brown (1984), Ma and Shaw (1990), Fama and French (1992), and Huang (1997), all their studies verify size effect. Why exists size effect? Many of the researchers attempt to learn different perspectives to propose a variety of explanations. The most famous is the multi-factor model, proposed by Fama and French (1992, 1993, 1995, 1996, 1998) and Lakonishok, Shleifer, and Vishny (1994), that claims the variables of the firm size and the book to market equity have been the prediction variables of the return. He and Ng (1994) conclude that the return of the small stocks portfolio is overvalued in the early period because the sample does not include unlisted, under being merged and acquired companies. Bhardwaj and Brooks (1993) propose dual beats theory which claims that systemic risk in the bull market and bear market is not the same, i.e., the $\beta$ value of small-size-stocks in the bull market is much higher than the bear market; the systematic risk of a large-size-share in the bull market is smaller than it in the bear market. Eventually, it is found that, in fact, the excess return of small-size-stocks has been overstated. Kim and Burnie (2002) make dual beats theory to look size effect and find that small firms with low productivity and high financial leverage of features shares with the excess return of economic expansion, however, there is not outstanding performance in the economic contraction.

Till now, the academic and practice investors still concern about whether such small cap size effect still exists? Firstly, Barber and Lyon (1997) and Horowitz et al. (2000) find that, in the 1980s to the 1990s, the U.S. stock market reveals "reverse" or "not clear relationship" between returns and firm size. Dimson and Marsh (1999) indicate that, in 1955-1988 in UK stock market, the return performance of small cap companies is superior to big cap companies. However, in the next ten years, the small cap stock returns reveal "reverse" or disappeared.

How firm size affects the information transmission? In general, big cap firms have more messages than smaller cap firms, so the new messages of the stock market will be firstly responded in terms of the stock price of big cap firms, and then responded in terms of the stock price of small cap firms, so there exists lead-lag relationship between these two kinds of stock return, i.e., the so-called information transmissiont effect. Lo and MacKinlay (1988, 1990) propose that there exists cross-serial correlation among different portfolios of market value, stock returns of large companies are usually leading to small companies of the stock returns. Admati and Pfleiderer (1988), Foster and Vishwanathan (1990), Kyle (1985), and Wang (1994) conclude that investors with more information of large company stocks can make strategic phased transactions, in order to avoid their private information over-exposure and loss of strength, but due to the low volume of small company stock turnover and low liquidity, transaction information is not easily hidden. Therefore, the phenomenon will be happened that messages of small-company stock will transmit

to large-company stocks. McQueen, Pinegar, and Thorley (1996) prove that directional asymmetry of the market returns is exist, that only when good news occurs in the market, the stock returns of large companies will lead the stock returns of small company, on the contrary, while bad news occurs in the market, the responding speeds of the big companies and small companies are the same. Kanas (2002) studies the UK stock market from January 1955 to December 1994, empirical evidence that there are significant spillover effect of return and spillover effect of volatility among the three largest capital portfolio. Therefore, these above scholars are confirmed information transmission effect exists in the stock market.

In this study, using Granger causality test to investigate price and volume relationship and the firm size transmission effect (in particular, whether there is reverse of firm size transmission effect) of the stock market of the emerging country (Taiwan). This paper contains four parts. Section 1 introduces the results of the past. The data and the employed methodology are described in Section 2. Section 3 reports and compares the empirical results for the four sample period. Concluding remarks and suggestions for future study are presented in section 4.

## 2. DATA SOURCE AND METHODOLOGY

### 2.1. Data Source

In this paper, the firm size transmission effect and price-volume relationship under the various types of firm size in Taiwan stock market will be explored. The various types of firm size include large stock, mid cap, and small cap. Large stock index is referred from Taiwan 50 Index, mid cap index is from Taiwan Mid Cap 100 index. Because Taiwan stock market doesn't have small-cap index, small-cap index should be estimated. Firstly, the sample of the small stocks are taken by listed companies and not been management stock during the study period, i.e., unlisted in the study period, listed after 1 June 2006 (totally 184 firms), and management stock (totally 45 firms) will not be involved. Secondly, the constituent stocks that have been indexed in Taiwan 50 Index and Taiwan Mid Cap 100 index (totally 206 firms) will not be involved. Therefore, small-cap index of the constituent stocks includes 457 firms. To make index with authenticity, we employ the formulation of the TAIEX weighted average index. The base period is set as 30 May 2006, the base index is set as 7000 (the base index does not affect the results). The calculating formulation of the small cap index makes Eq. (1).

$$I_s \equiv \frac{\text{After screening total market value of small cap constituent stocks}}{2{,}000{,}621} *7000$$

(1)

where 2,000,621 (million) is the sample of small cap of total market value on 30 May 2006. The volume of the small-cap index is the total volume of screened small stocks. The employed indices, market capitalization and trading volume on 30 May 2006 is shown in Table 1. Data resources are from the Taiwan Economic Journal Co., Ltd. (TEJ).

Recently, the subprime mortgage occurs suddenly, then, the financial tsunami is detonated, this paper will explore the four periods during this financial crisis. Along with the subprime mortgage crisis in the United States, real estate bubble bursts from 2005 to 2006, and the consistency large broken of global stock markets is also caused on 27 July 2007, furthermore, Lehman Brothers declare bankruptcy on 15 September 2008, eventually, financial tsunami is detonated. Therefore, this study will take these two time points as a basic period, one-year before and after these time points will be another two research periods, the 2010 full year will be the fourth period to explore the changes of the firm size transmission effect and price-volume relationship in the four periods. The data of the four periods are shown in Table 2.

Obtained from the TEJ big cap index of Taiwan (Taiwan 50), medium cap index of Taiwan (Taiwan

*Table 1. Stock market indices*

| Market | Taiwan weighted average index | Tai 50 index | Tai mid-cap 100 index | Tai small-cap index |
|---|---|---|---|---|
| Index | 6846.95 | 5093.61 | 7215.73 | 7000.00 |
| Market value(million) | 16,510,016 | 2,411,291 | 7,886,267 | 2,000,621 |
| Percent of total market value | 100.00% | 14.61% | 47.77% | 12.12% |
| Trade volume(thousand) | 3,405,848 | 862,712 | 967,528 | 877,076 |
| Percent of total trade volume | 100.00% | 25.33% | 28.41% | 25.75% |

*Table 2. The four research periods*

| Periods | Starting date | Ending date | Number of observations. |
|---|---|---|---|
| 1st | 1 June 2006 | 26 July 2007 | 288 |
| 2nd | 27 July 2007 | 14 September 2008 | 284 |
| 3rd | 15 September 2008 | 31 December 2009 | 327 |
| 4th | 1 January 2010 | 31 January 2011 | 251 |

medium 100) and small cap index of Taiwan, the trend of the index and trading volume shown in Figures 1, 2, and 3. Based on Figures 1, 2, and 3, it can be also found that there exists the consistent droppings, in terms of Taiwan's big, medium and small-cap index, on 27 July 2007 and 15 September 2008, respectively, and the universally rising in 2010. This implies that it is suitable and reason-able to divide the research period into four time periods in this paper.

The daily return for each market is calculated as the percent logarithmic difference in the daily stock index, i.e., $R_t = \ln\left(\dfrac{I_t}{I_{t-1}}\right) \times 100$, where $R_t$, $I_t$ and $I_{t-1}$ stand for the stock market return and

*Figure 1. Tai 50 stock index daily movement and trade volume*

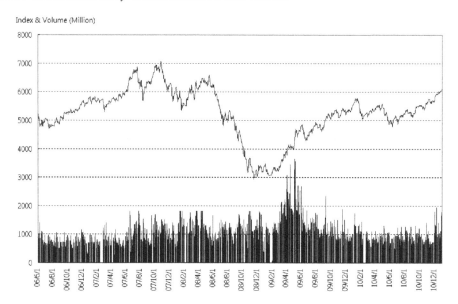

*Figure 2. Tai mid-cap 100 stock index daily movement and trade volume*

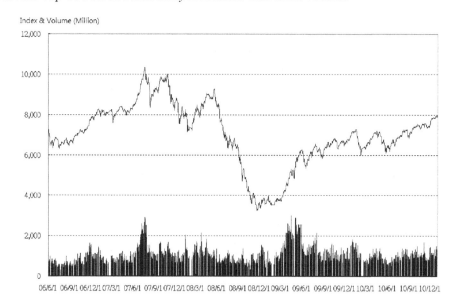

*Figure 3. Tai small-cap stock index daily movement and trade volume*

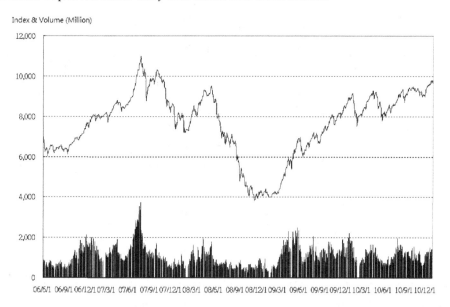

closing index at date $t$ and $t$-1, respectively, ln is continuous compounding factor, return descriptive statistics of four time periods and the number of observations are exhibited in Table 3.

## 2.2. Research Methodology

This paper will investigate firm size transmission effect and price-volume Relationship, the research methodology employs Granger-causality test, spurious regression test, and cointegration test. These research methods are described below.

### 2.2.1. Unit Root Test

Lots of previous studies in time series fields confirm that time series would be stationary. However, each series may individually be non-stationary, and such non-stationary time series would not have stable average values in the long run due to disturbance. Based on a one non-stationary time series, the regression modeling would generate spurious results, the so-called "spurious regression" (Granger & Newbold, 1974). In addition, in this paper, the vector autoregression (VAR) model, proposed by Sims (1980), is employed

to analyze the transmission of market movement across countries. VAR is theoretically required to analyze the stationary time series. Therefore, to convert these non-stationary time series to be stationary ones is important. The unit root test is used to examine the stationary of a time series.

There are three kinds of the unit root test: Dickey-Fuller (DF) unit test (Dickey & Fuller, 1979), Augmented Dickey-Fuller (ADF) unit test (Dickey & Fuller, 1981), and Phillips-Perron (PP) test (Phillips & Perron, 1988). This study employs ADF test and PP test to examine the stationary of time series data.

The ADF test examines the presence of unit root in an autoregression model. The regression model can be written as Eq. (2),

$$r_t = \beta' D_t + (\varphi - 1) r_{t-1} + \sum_{i=1}^{p} \delta_i \Delta r_{t-i} + \varepsilon_t \quad (2)$$

where $r_t$ is the variable of return at time period $t$; $\Delta r_{t-i}$ is the $p$ lagged-differential terms of series; $D_t$ is a vector of deterministic (constant, trend, etc.); and $\varepsilon_t$ is error term. This model can be

*Table 3. Descriptive statistics of nine daily stock return series in four research periods*

| period | series | μ | max | min | σ | S | K | JB | | |
|---|---|---|---|---|---|---|---|---|---|---|
| 1st | Tai 50 index | 0.0934 | 3.0357 | -4.2955 | 1.0981 | -0.5859 | 4.9062 | 60.0808 | 0.0000 | *** |
| | Tai mid-cap 100 index | 0.1185 | 3.6252 | -4.5651 | 1.0881 | -1.0929 | 6.7394 | 225.1267 | 0.0000 | *** |
| | Tai small-cap index | 0.1503 | 3.1395 | -5.0334 | 1.0571 | -1.4789 | 7.7236 | 372.7392 | 0.0000 | *** |
| | Tai 50 volume | 0.1501 | 115.1441 | -108.1695 | 29.5635 | 0.3680 | 4.7287 | 42.3621 | 0.0000 | *** |
| | Tai mid-cap 100 volume | 0.3833 | 67.7857 | -55.5628 | 21.6894 | 0.1367 | 2.9913 | 0.8981 | 0.6382 | |
| | Tai small-cap volume | 0.5018 | 49.2084 | -48.6381 | 17.5052 | -0.1241 | 2.9588 | 0.7599 | 0.6839 | |
| 2nd | Tai 50 index | -0.1282 | 5.7592 | -6.7175 | 1.8855 | -0.1635 | 3.5853 | 5.2815 | 0.0713 | * |
| | Tai mid-cap 100 index | -0.2085 | 5.8887 | -6.8924 | 2.0443 | -0.3637 | 3.3859 | 7.9672 | 0.0186 | ** |
| | Tai small-cap index | -0.2202 | 5.2265 | -6.3866 | 1.8175 | -0.5269 | 3.9027 | 22.6232 | 0.0000 | *** |
| | Tai 50 volume | -0.1088 | 93.0939 | -78.4786 | 26.3544 | 0.3389 | 3.1404 | 5.6291 | 0.0599 | * |
| | Tai mid-cap 100 volume | -0.4295 | 63.4007 | -71.7586 | 20.4258 | 0.1329 | 3.0886 | 0.9218 | 0.6307 | |
| | Tai small-cap volume | -0.6971 | 53.5228 | -45.4833 | 18.3348 | 0.2120 | 2.8171 | 2.5051 | 0.2858 | |
| 3rd | Tai 50 index | 0.0341 | 6.5077 | -6.2869 | 2.0824 | -0.0527 | 4.0856 | 14.0278 | 0.0009 | *** |
| | Tai mid-cap 100 index | 0.0420 | 6.4858 | -6.3694 | 2.3669 | -0.3872 | 3.5949 | 11.2445 | 0.0036 | *** |
| | Tai small-cap index | 0.0968 | 6.0686 | -6.0994 | 2.0092 | -0.5408 | 3.9415 | 24.2499 | 0.0000 | *** |
| | Tai 50 volume | -0.0001 | 86.3484 | -78.8368 | 26.7798 | 0.1561 | 3.8146 | 8.9741 | 0.0113 | ** |
| | Tai mid-cap 100 volume | -0.0082 | 67.2427 | -69.5841 | 22.9261 | 0.0296 | 3.1973 | 0.5005 | 0.7786 | |
| | Tai small-cap volume | 0.2744 | 63.5300 | -60.0235 | 20.7654 | 0.0480 | 3.1197 | 0.2777 | 0.8704 | |
| 4th | Tai 50 index | 0.0607 | 2.9818 | -3.8418 | 1.0223 | -0.4978 | 4.0889 | 26.7563 | 0.0000 | *** |
| | Tai mid-cap 100 index | 0.0768 | 2.9593 | -5.6219 | 1.2132 | -0.9865 | 5.9297 | 153.3517 | 0.0000 | *** |
| | Tai small-cap index | 0.0843 | 3.1713 | -5.2727 | 1.1754 | -1.4197 | 7.2286 | 318.8896 | 0.0000 | *** |
| | Tai 50 volume | 0.2036 | 82.9676 | -79.5579 | 28.0018 | 0.0872 | 3.1731 | 0.7421 | 0.6900 | |
| | Tai mid-cap 100 volume | 0.1512 | 68.5050 | -59.6508 | 21.5660 | 0.2268 | 3.1852 | 2.9499 | 0.2288 | |
| | Tai small-cap volume | 0.0708 | 51.4504 | -54.9441 | 18.5357 | -0.1025 | 3.0703 | 0.5773 | 0.7493 | |
| Notes:*, ** and *** denote significance at the 0.1, 0.05 and 0.01 level, respectively. | | | | | | | | | | |

estimated, and the unit root test is equivalent to test whether $\varphi = 0$.

Phillips and Perron (1988) develop a number of unit root tests that have become popular in the analysis of financial time series. The principal difference between the PP test and the ADF test is the PP test deals with serial correlation and heteroskedasticity in the errors term. Particularly, the ADF test uses a parametric autoregression to approximate the errors of the ARMA structure in the test regression; on the contrary, the PP test ignores any serial correlation in the test regression. The test regression for the PP tests is shown as Eq.(3),

$$\Delta r_t = \beta' D_t + \pi r_{t-1} + \mu_t \qquad (3)$$

where $\mu_t$ is $I(0)$ and may be heteroskedastic. The PP test corrects any serial correlations and heteroskedasticity in the errors term, $\mu_t$, of the test regression by directly modifying the test statistics $\pi = 0$. Thus, this study applies ADF test and PP test to examine the stationary in time series data.

## 2.2.2. Cointegration Test

The study espouses Johansen multivariate maximum likelihood method, proposed by Johansen (1988), by using cointegrated process, to test whether the variables have existed long run equilibrium relationship. The first step uses first order differential in the VAR model, the formula is shown as Eq.(4),

$$R_t = \beta_1 R_{t-1} + \beta_2 R_{t-2} + \cdots + \beta_n R_{t-n} + \varepsilon_t \quad (4)$$

where $R_{t-p}$ is the vector endogenous variable with lag length $p$. Then, the first order differential in the VAR model will be shown as Eq.(5),

$$\Delta R_t = \sum_{j=1}^{p} \pi_j \beta_1 \Delta R_{t-j} + \pi R_{t-p} + \varepsilon_t \quad (5)$$

where $\pi_j$ is the short run adjusting coefficient to explain short run relationship; $\pi$ is long run shock vector that includes long run information in the regression to test the long run equilibrium relationships among variables. The rank of $\pi$ determines the number of cointegrated vector. Generally, $\pi$ has three styles,

1. $rank(\pi) = n$, $\pi$ is full rank, all variables are stationary in the regression $\left(Y_t\right)$
2. $rank(\pi) = 0$, $\pi$ is null rank, no cointegred relationships among variables.
3. $0 < rank(\pi) = r < n$, some cointegrated vector exists among variables with rank $r$

Johansen's (1988) approach applies the rank of $\pi$ to determine the number of cointegrated vector. To examine the rank of a vector, it is necessary to calculate the number of non-zero char-

acteristic roots in the vector. Two statistics are employed to process cointegration test. One is to test trace, i.e., $H_0 : rank\left(\pi\right) \leq r$, the statistics is

$$\lambda_{trace}\left(r\right) = -T \sum_{i=\nu+1}^{p} \ln\left(1 - \hat{\lambda}_i\right)$$

where $T$ is sample size; $\hat{\lambda}_i$ is the estimate of characteristic root. If $H_0$ is not accepted, then, at least $r+1$ long run cointegrated relationships among variables are existed.

The other one is to test maximum eigenvalue, i.e., $H_0 : rank\left(\pi\right) \leq r$, the statistics is

$$\lambda_{max}\left(r, r+1\right) = -T \ln\left(1 - \hat{\lambda}_{\nu+1}\right).$$

If $H_0$ is accepted, then, some cointegrated vector exists among variables with rank $r$. Cointegration test starts from the status of no cointegred relationships among variables, i.e., $r=0$, till the status that cannot reject $H_0$ any more, i.e., some cointegrated vector exists among variables with rank $r$.

## 2.2.3. Granger-Causality Test

Granger (1969) originally defines the lead and lag (causal) relationships between of two variables to verify their predictability. He uses twin factors of VAR to formulate the causal relationships of variables. Thus, two series, $X_t$ and $Y_t$, are defined as Eqs. (6) and (7),

$$X_t = \alpha_0 + \sum_{i=1}^{k} \alpha_{1i} X_{t-1} + \sum_{i=1}^{k} \alpha_{2i} Y_{t-1} + \varepsilon_{1t} \quad (6)$$

$$Y_t = \beta_0 + \sum_{i=1}^{k} \beta_{1i} X_{t-1} + \sum_{i=1}^{k} \beta_{2i} Y_{t-1} + \varepsilon_{2t} \quad (7)$$

The conditions of these four coefficients and corresponding relationships between variables are shown as follows.

a.   $\alpha_{2i} \neq 0 \ and \ \alpha_{1i} = 0$, $Y$ leads $X$ (or $X$ lags $Y$).

b.   $\beta_{1i} \neq 0 \ and \ \beta_{2i} = 0$, $X$ leads $Y$ (or $Y$ lags $X$).

c.   $\alpha_{2i} = 0 \ and \ \beta_{1i} = 0$, both $X$ and $Y$ are independent.

d.   $\alpha_{2i} \neq 0 \ and \ \beta_{1i} \neq 0$, both $X$ and $Y$ are interacted with each other (i.e., feedback relationships).

## 3. EMPIRICAL RESULTS

The study will investigate the lead and lag (causal) relationships in the Taiwan stock market. Firstly, it will conduct unit root test for all series in each research period, and determine the corresponding lag numbers. Secondly, Johansen cointegration test is employed to verify the cointegration phenomenon of all companies in terms of size index and trading volume. Finally, the study will observe causality relation in Taiwan stock market.

### 3.1. Unit Root Test and Lag Numbers Determination

This paper employs two kinds of unit root test, Augmented Dickey-Fuller (ADF) and Phillip-Perron (PP), to ensure all series to avoid spurious regression. The results of ADF, PP unit root test are shown in Table 4. The unit root test results indicate that all series are stationary.

In addition, the lag number, $p$, i.e., the order of autoregression for each research period, could be determined by the AIC (Akaike Information Criterion), the determined lag number for each research period is shown in Table 5.

### 3.2. Johansen Cointegration Test

The unit root test results verify that all series are stationary. Then, it is necessary to conduct the next test, the cointegration relationship test, for each series.

In this study, sample data is divided into four research periods to analyze the long run equilibrium relationship between various types of firm size and price-volume in the stock market. Firstly, based on the AIC criterion (Table 5), the optimal lag number, $p$, for each research period is determined. Secondly, Johansen's Cointegration is used to conduct the test for the number of cointegration vectors. The test results in the four research periods are shown in Tables 6, 7, 8, and 9, respectively. It is clearly to find out that likelihood ratio test statistics and the critical value are significant, i.e., the cointegration phenomenon of all companies in terms of size index and trading volume is existed in the four research periods. Therefore, the existence of long run equilibrium relationship among companies is verified.

### 3.3. Causality Relationship Test

Causality relationship test is employed to analyze whether the relationship between price and volume in the four research periods is two-way feedback relationship or one-way lead-lag causal relationship, furthermore, or the independent relationship without interaction.

In this study, the optimal lag number for each research period is determined based on the smallest AIC value in Table 5. And, the causality relationship test will aim at the price index and trading volume for every kind of firm size. The analysis results for each research period are shown in Tables 10, 11, 12, and 13, respectively. In addition, to facilitate the understandings of the analyzed causality relationship among each firm size, this study provides some pioneering figure to illustrate these transmission effects for four research periods in Figures 4, 5, 6, and 7, respectively.

*Table 4. Unit root analysis*

| period | series | ADF | | PP | | Test critical values | | | LB(12) | | |
|---|---|---|---|---|---|---|---|---|---|---|---|
| 1st | Tai 50 index | -17.2864 | 0.0000 | -17.8305 | 0.0000 | ADF: | 1% level | -3.4530 | 22.5660 | 0.0320 | ** |
| | Tai mid-cap 100 index | -16.1718 | 0.0000 | -16.1789 | 0.0000 | | 5% level | -2.8714 | 12.0450 | 0.4420 | |
| | Tai small-cap index | -16.2866 | 0.0000 | -16.3105 | 0.0000 | | 10% level | -2.5721 | 9.5066 | 0.6590 | |
| | Tai 50 volume | -13.2890 | 0.0000 | -65.3049 | 0.0001 | PP: | 1% level | -3.4530 | 51.8580 | 0.0000 | *** |
| | Tai mid-cap 100 volume | -12.7297 | 0.0000 | -34.8425 | 0.0001 | | 5% level | -2.8714 | 49.5860 | 0.0000 | *** |
| | Tai small-cap volume | -16.8623 | 0.0000 | -26.8316 | 0.0000 | | 10% level | -2.5721 | 38.7350 | 0.0000 | *** |
| 2nd | Tai 50 index | -18.1556 | 0.0000 | -18.3722 | 0.0000 | ADF | 1% level | -3.4537 | 15.2580 | 0.2280 | |
| | Tai mid-cap 100 index | -16.6502 | 0.0000 | -16.6511 | 0.0000 | | 5% level | -2.8717 | 8.5587 | 0.7400 | |
| | Tai small-cap index | -14.5426 | 0.0000 | -14.5722 | 0.0000 | | 10% level | -2.5723 | 16.5510 | 0.1670 | |
| | Tai 50 volume | -14.6424 | 0.0000 | -27.8785 | 0.0000 | PP: | 1% level | -3.4535 | 34.6980 | 0.0010 | *** |
| | Tai mid-cap 100 volume | -13.3561 | 0.0000 | -24.6934 | 0.0000 | | 5% level | -2.8716 | 45.1310 | 0.0000 | *** |
| | Tai small-cap volume | -19.9561 | 0.0000 | -20.9353 | 0.0000 | | 10% level | -2.5722 | 16.8180 | 0.1570 | |
| 3rd | Tai 50 index | -14.9756 | 0.0000 | -14.8926 | 0.0000 | ADF | 1% level | -3.4534 | 17.3260 | 0.1380 | |
| | Tai mid-cap 100 index | -14.9300 | 0.0000 | -14.8618 | 0.0000 | | 5% level | -2.8716 | 14.8370 | 0.2500 | |
| | Tai small-cap index | -14.5303 | 0.0000 | -14.4276 | 0.0000 | | 10% level | -2.5722 | 17.4450 | 0.1340 | |
| | Tai 50 volume | -13.4448 | 0.0000 | -41.3539 | 0.0001 | PP: | 1% level | -3.4534 | 47.5810 | 0.0000 | *** |
| | Tai mid-cap 100 volume | -12.1903 | 0.0000 | -28.5481 | 0.0000 | | 5% level | -2.8716 | 58.2930 | 0.0000 | *** |
| | Tai small-cap volume | -14.8588 | 0.0000 | -24.1173 | 0.0000 | | 10% level | -2.5722 | 28.4050 | 0.0050 | *** |
| 4th | Tai 50 index | -13.3317 | 0.0000 | -15.8141 | 0.0000 | ADF | 1% level | -3.4524 | 15.1540 | 0.2330 | |
| | Tai mid-cap 100 index | -15.9569 | 0.0000 | -15.9608 | 0.0000 | | 5% level | -2.8712 | 13.4860 | 0.3350 | |
| | Tai small-cap index | -15.0973 | 0.0000 | -15.1078 | 0.0000 | | 10% level | -2.5720 | 18.7650 | 0.0940 | * |
| | Tai 50 volume | -12.8847 | 0.0000 | -60.6405 | 0.0001 | PP: | 1% level | -3.4524 | 86.6240 | 0.0000 | *** |
| | Tai mid-cap 100 volume | -12.8631 | 0.0000 | -43.2082 | 0.0001 | | 5% level | -2.8712 | 63.1690 | 0.0000 | *** |
| | Tai small-cap volume | -23.6054 | 0.0000 | -28.2169 | 0.0000 | | 10% level | -2.5720 | 35.6650 | 0.0000 | *** |

Notes:*, ** and *** denote significance at the 0.1, 0.05 and 0.01 level, respectively.

*Table 5. Value of AIC*

| period | 1st research period | 2nd research period | 3rd research period | 4th research period |
|---|---|---|---|---|
| Lag 1 | 31.0539 | 33.2994 | 33.6077 | 30.7847 |
| Lag 2 | 31.0104 | **33.2800** | 33.4897 | **30.6933** |
| Lag 3 | **31.0058** | 33.3078 | 33.2840 | 30.7645 |
| Lag 4 | 31.0086 | 33.3807 | **33.2616** | 30.8215 |
| Lag 5 | 31.0278 | 33.4163 | 33.4521 | 30.9261 |
| Lag 6 | 31.0597 | 33.4917 | 33.5068 | 31.0155 |

Notes: bold words represent the minimum.

*Table 6. Results of Johansen Cointegration of the 1st research period*

| Hypothesized | Eigenvalue | Trace Statistic | 5% Critical Value | Prob.** | Max-Eigen Statistic | 5% Critical Value | Prob.** |
|---|---|---|---|---|---|---|---|
| None * | 0.4219 | 625.3385 | 103.8473 | 0.0001 | 155.6317 | 40.9568 | 0.0000 |
| At most 1 * | 0.3945 | 469.7069 | 76.9728 | 0.0001 | 142.4964 | 34.8059 | 0.0000 |
| At most 2 * | 0.3033 | 327.2105 | 54.0790 | 0.0001 | 102.6268 | 28.5881 | 0.0000 |
| At most 3 * | 0.2739 | 224.5838 | 35.1928 | 0.0000 | 90.9128 | 22.2996 | 0.0000 |
| At most 4 * | 0.2219 | 133.6710 | 20.2618 | 0.0001 | 71.2495 | 15.8921 | 0.0000 |
| At most 5 * | 0.1973 | 62.4215 | 9.1645 | 0.0000 | 62.4215 | 9.1645 | 0.0000 |

*: denote six hypotheses of significant interaction between price and volume in terms of 3 firm sizes.
**: denote significance at the0.05 level.

*Table 7. Results of Johansen Cointegration of the 2nd research period*

| Hypothesized | Eigenvalue | Trace Statistic | 5% Critical Value | Prob.** | Max-Eigen Statistic | 5% Critical Value | Prob.** |
|---|---|---|---|---|---|---|---|
| None * | 0.4639 | 712.6184 | 103.8473 | 0.0001 | 173.9362 | 40.9568 | 0.0001 |
| At most 1 * | 0.4149 | 538.6822 | 76.9728 | 0.0001 | 149.5528 | 34.8059 | 0.0000 |
| At most 2 * | 0.3394 | 389.1294 | 54.0790 | 0.0001 | 115.6874 | 28.5881 | 0.0000 |
| At most 3 * | 0.3290 | 273.4420 | 35.1928 | 0.0000 | 111.3039 | 22.2996 | 0.0000 |
| At most 4 * | 0.2837 | 162.1381 | 20.2618 | 0.0001 | 93.0732 | 15.8921 | 0.0000 |
| At most 5 * | 0.2193 | 69.0649 | 9.1645 | 0.0000 | 69.0649 | 9.1645 | 0.0000 |

*: denote six hypotheses of significant interaction between price and volume in terms of 3 firm sizes.
**: denote significance at the0.05 level.

*Table 8. Results of Johansen Cointegration of the 3rd research period*

| Hypothesized | Eigenvalue | Trace Statistic | 5% Critical Value | Prob.** | Max-Eigen Statistic | 5% Critical Value | Prob.** |
|---|---|---|---|---|---|---|---|
| None * | 0.3590 | 507.3137 | 103.8473 | 0.0000 | 123.6348 | 40.9568 | 0.0000 |
| At most 1 * | 0.3021 | 383.6789 | 76.9728 | 0.0001 | 99.9905 | 34.8059 | 0.0000 |
| At most 2 * | 0.2801 | 283.6885 | 54.0790 | 0.0000 | 91.3479 | 28.5881 | 0.0000 |
| At most 3 * | 0.2467 | 192.3405 | 35.1928 | 0.0000 | 78.7541 | 22.2996 | 0.0000 |
| At most 4 * | 0.2010 | 113.5865 | 20.2618 | 0.0000 | 62.3667 | 15.8921 | 0.0000 |
| At most 5 * | 0.1683 | 51.2198 | 9.1645 | 0.0000 | 51.2198 | 9.1645 | 0.0000 |

*: denote six hypotheses of significant interaction between price and volume in terms of 3 firm sizes.
**: denote significance at the0.05 level.

*Table 9. Results of Johansen Cointegration of the 4th research period*

| Hypothesized | Eigenvalue | Trace Statistic | 5% Critical Value | Prob.** | Max-Eigen Statistic | 5% Critical Value | Prob.** |
|---|---|---|---|---|---|---|---|
| None * | 0.4716 | 734.6943 | 103.8473 | 0.0001 | 186.2465 | 40.9568 | 0.0001 |
| At most 1 * | 0.4205 | 548.4478 | 76.9728 | 0.0001 | 159.3163 | 34.8059 | 0.0001 |
| At most 2 * | 0.3464 | 389.1315 | 54.0790 | 0.0001 | 124.1944 | 28.5881 | 0.0000 |
| At most 3 * | 0.2867 | 264.9371 | 35.1928 | 0.0000 | 98.6663 | 22.2996 | 0.0000 |
| At most 4 * | 0.2521 | 166.2708 | 20.2618 | 0.0001 | 84.8374 | 15.8921 | 0.0000 |
| At most 5 * | 0.2434 | 81.4334 | 9.1645 | 0.0001 | 81.4334 | 9.1645 | 0.0001 |

*: denote six hypotheses of significant interaction between price and volume in terms of 3 firm sizes.
**: denote significance at the0.05 level.

*Table 10. Results of Granger causality of the 1st research period*

| result \ cause | Tai 50 index | Tai mid-cap 100 index | Tai small-cap index | Tai 50 volume | Tai mid-cap 100 volume | Tai small-cap volume |
|---|---|---|---|---|---|---|
| Tai 50 index | | 4.3958 | **7.3657** | 2.0629 | 4.2856 | 3.6690 |
| | | (0.2218) | **(0.0611)** | (0.5595) | (0.2322) | (0.2995) |
| Tai mid-cap 100 index | 0.5089 | | **8.2232** | 0.5148 | 4.3510 | 2.8091 |
| | (0.9169) | | **(0.0416)** | (0.9156) | (0.2260) | (0.4220) |
| Tai small-cap index | 1.2374 | 3.9118 | | 1.0633 | 3.0708 | 1.4207 |
| | (0.7440) | (0.2712) | | (0.7859) | (0.3808) | (0.7007) |
| Tai 50 volume | 1.1250 | 0.7510 | 0.9788 | | 0.4749 | 3.0548 |
| | (0.7710) | (0.8611) | (0.8064) | | (0.9244) | (0.3833) |
| Tai mid-cap 100 volume | 1.1221 | 2.4363 | 0.3178 | 2.0532 | | 3.9352 |
| | (0.7717) | (0.4869) | (0.9566) | (0.5614) | | (0.2685) |
| Tai small-cap volume | 1.5104 | 2.4760 | 4.9821 | 5.1069 | 1.8607 | |
| | (0.6799) | (0.4796) | (0.1731) | (0.1641) | (0.6018) | |
| Notes: bold words represent significant level with 0.1 | | | | | | |

*Table 11. Results of Granger causality of the 2nd research period*

| result \ cause | Tai 50 index | Tai mid-cap 100 index | Tai small-cap index | Tai 50 volume | Tai mid-cap 100 volume | Tai small-cap volume |
|---|---|---|---|---|---|---|
| Tai 50 index | | 3.2066 | 1.8388 | 0.5120 | 1.0065 | 2.8846 |
| | | (0.2012) | (0.3988) | (0.7741) | (0.6046) | (0.2364) |
| Tai mid-cap 100 index | 1.0501 | | 1.6879 | 0.2873 | 0.1402 | 2.6316 |
| | (0.5915) | | (0.4300) | (0.8662) | (0.9323) | (0.2683) |
| Tai small-cap index | 0.4925 | 0.8039 | | 0.5925 | 0.2504 | 2.6081 |
| | (0.7817) | (0.6690) | | (0.7436) | (0.8823) | (0.2714) |
| Tai 50 volume | 3.1202 | 1.2204 | 1.1635 | | 1.1146 | 1.5176 |
| | (0.0712) | (0.5432) | (0.5589) | | (0.5727) | (0.4682) |
| Tai mid-cap 100 volume | 5.0725 | 0.7702 | 0.7631 | 4.7786 | | 2.6847 |
| | (0.0792) | (0.6804) | (0.6828) | (0.0917) | | (0.2612) |
| Tai small-cap volume | 4.6815 | 1.9688 | 0.6888 | 3.6279 | 0.9850 | |
| | (0.0963) | (0.3737) | (0.7086) | (0.0988) | (0.6111) | |
| Notes: bold words represent significant level with 0.1 | | | | | | |

Figures 4 through 7 illustrate that, in each period, the firm size transmission effects in the Taiwan stock market really exist (only the 2nd research period is not significant), and how the impacts from some kind of firm size affect other kind of firm size. The results are similar to Mc-Queen, Pinegar, and Thorley (1996). And, it is also obviously to verify that there exists a reversal phenomenon. Before the financial tsunami, the relationship between price and volume in terms

*Table 12. Results of Granger causality the 3rd research period*

| result \ cause | Tai 50 index | Tai mid-cap 100 index | Tai small-cap index | Tai 50 volume | Tai mid-cap 100 volume | Tai small-cap volume |
|---|---|---|---|---|---|---|
| Tai 50 index | | 5.1612 | 1.8100 | 6.1927 | 5.1970 | 2.6387 |
| | | (0.2712) | (0.7706) | (0.1852) | (0.2677) | (0.6200) |
| Tai mid-cap 100 index | **14.6459** | | 2.9858 | 4.1865 | 3.7759 | 6.4307 |
| | **(0.0055)** | | (0.5602) | (0.3814) | (0.4372) | (0.1692) |
| Tai small-cap index | **11.3241** | 3.1790 | | 2.6347 | 3.9291 | **8.6996** |
| | **(0.0232)** | (0.5283) | | (0.6207) | (0.4157) | **(0.0691)** |
| Tai 50 volume | 4.8885 | 2.2340 | 3.8787 | | 0.0960 | 3.4294 |
| | (0.2989) | (0.6928) | (0.4227) | | (0.9989) | (0.4887) |
| Tai mid-cap 100 volume | 2.3406 | 6.9935 | 2.9522 | **12.0239** | | **17.8144** |
| | (0.6734) | (0.1362) | (0.5659) | **(0.0172)** | | **(0.0013)** |
| Tai small-cap volume | 0.8937 | 2.3452 | 2.0468 | 4.6547 | 3.8238 | |
| | (0.9255) | (0.6725) | (0.7271) | (0.3246) | (0.4304) | |
| Notes: bold words represent significant level with 0.1 | | | | | | |

*Table 13. Results of Granger causality the 4th research period*

| result \ cause | Tai 50 index | Tai mid-cap 100 index | Tai small-cap index | Tai 50 volume | Tai mid-cap 100 volume | Tai small-cap volume |
|---|---|---|---|---|---|---|
| Tai 50 index | | 0.7960 | **9.8174** | 0.7695 | 0.6658 | 1.1892 |
| | | (0.6716) | **(0.0530)** | (0.6806) | (0.7168) | (0.5518) |
| Tai mid-cap 100 index | 0.1529 | | **8.4580** | 0.1539 | 0.1476 | 2.2013 |
| | (0.9264) | | **(0.0626)** | (0.9259) | (0.9288) | (0.3327) |
| Tai small-cap index | 0.0080 | 2.6566 | | 0.8601 | 0.1328 | 3.0600 |
| | (0.9960) | (0.2649) | | (0.6505) | (0.9357) | (0.2165) |
| Tai 50 volume | 0.1371 | 3.9490 | 1.0021 | | 3.1029 | **9.0510** |
| | (0.9338) | (0.1388) | (0.4302) | | (0.2119) | **(0.0108)** |
| Tai mid-cap 100 volume | 1.7129 | 0.4202 | 1.3665 | **14.4957** | | 2.4670 |
| | (0.4247) | (0.8105) | (0.3415) | **(0.0007)** | | (0.2913) |
| Tai small-cap volume | 0.9500 | 1.8827 | **8.8501** | **12.3459** | 1.5381 | |
| | (0.6219) | (0.3901) | **(0.0120)** | **(0.0021)** | (0.4635) | |
| Notes: bold words represent significant level with 0.1 | | | | | | |

of firm size transmission effect, big cap stock index is affected by the volume, that is, volume leads to price. On the contrary, in the overall financial recovery phase, i.e., the fourth research period, small cap stock index affects volume, that is, the volume lags to price.

## 4. SUMMARY AND CONCLUSION

In this paper, we explore the firm size transmission effects and price and volume relationship in Taiwan stock market. The tsunami affect period is divided into four research periods, i.e., before the

*Figure 4. Causality figure of the 1st research period*

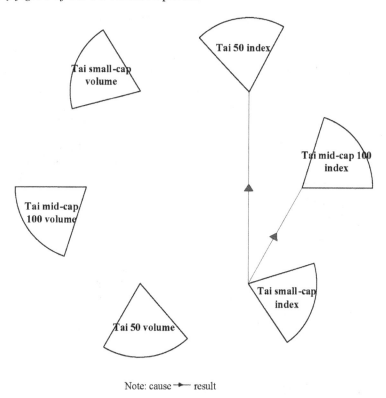

Note: cause → result

*Figure 5. Causality figure of the 2nd research period*

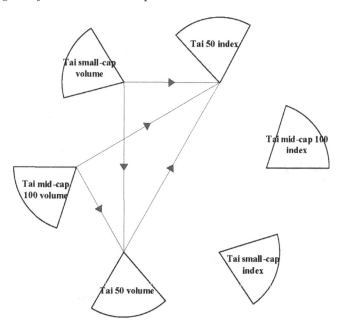

*Figure 6. Causality figure of the 3rd research period*

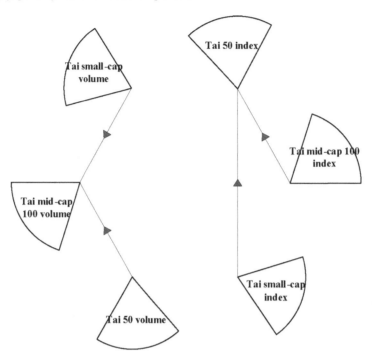

*Figure 7. Causality figure of the 4th research period*

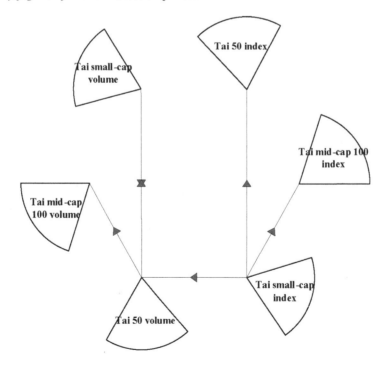

subprime mortgage, after the subprime mortgage and before the financial turmoil, after the financial turmoil, and economic recovery. Research methods include: ADF, PP unit root test, Johansen cointegration, and Granger causality test to analyze sample data.

The empirical results indicate that firm size transmission effects exist in Taiwan stock market, and empirical analysis also show that firm size transmission effects has a reversal situation, which is consistent with Dimson and Marsh's (1999) study. Firm size transmission effects also reveal some reversal phenomenon in Taiwan stock market, because small and medium enterprises are the main stream in Taiwan stock market, especially in the financial tsunami, small cap stock affect not only large cap stock, but also the medium sized stock. However, in the four research periods, the price and volume relationships for small and mid cap stocks are not nearly as significant, only the big cap stock index is affected in volume before the tsunami. In the economic recovery period, small cap index will affect the volumes of other size index; this phenomenon also reveals the fact of Taiwan economic pattern that the small and medium enterprises are the main stream in Taiwan stock market.

# REFERENCES

Admati, A., & Pfleiderer, P. (1988). A theory of intraday trading patters: Volume and price variability. *Review of Financial Studies*, *1*, 3–40. doi:10.1093/rfs/1.1.3

Baker, M., & Stein, J. C. (2004). Market liquidity as a sentiment indicator. *Journal of Financial Markets*, *7*, 271–299. doi:10.1016/j.finmar.2003.11.005

Banz, R. W. (1981). The relationship between return and market value of common stocks. *Journal of Financial Economics*, *9*(1), 3–18. doi:10.1016/0304-405X(81)90018-0

Barber, B. M., & Lyon, J. D. (1997). Firm size, book-to-market ratio, and security returns: A holdout sample of financial firms. *The Journal of Finance*, *50*(2), 875–883. doi:10.2307/2329503

Barry, C. B., & Brown, S. J. (1984). Differential information and the small firm effect. *Journal of Financial Economics*, *13*(2), 283–294. doi:10.1016/0304-405X(84)90026-6

Basci, E., Ozyidirim, S., & Aydogan, K. (1996). A note on price-volume dynamics in an emerging stock market. *Journal of Banking & Finance*, *20*, 389–400. doi:10.1016/0378-4266(95)00003-8

Bessembinder, H., & Seguin, P. J. (1992). Futures-trading activity and stock price volatility. *The Journal of Finance*, *47*, 2015–2134. doi:10.2307/2329008

Bhardwaj, R. K., & Brooks, L. D. (1993). Dual beats from bull and bear markets: Reversal of the size effect. *Journal of Financial Research*, *16*(4), 269–283.

Brennan, M., Chordia, T., & Subrahmanyam, A. (1998). Alternative factor specifications, security characteristics, and the cross-section of expected stock returns. *Journal of Financial Economics*, *49*, 345–373. doi:10.1016/S0304-405X(98)00028-2

Brown, P., Kleidon, A., & Marsh, T. (1983). New evidence on the nature of size-related anomalies in stock prices. *Journal of Financial Economics*, *12*(1), 33–56. doi:10.1016/0304-405X(83)90026-0

Campbell, J. Y., Grossman, S. J., & Wang, J. (1993). Trading volume and serial correlation in stock returns. *The Quarterly Journal of Economics*, *108*, 905–939. doi:10.2307/2118454

Cheuk, M. Y., Fan, D. K., & So, R. W. (2006). Insider trading in Hong Kong: Some stylized facts. *Pacific-Basin Finance Journal*, *14*, 73–90. doi:10.1016/j.pacfin.2005.06.002

Chiang, T. C., & Chiang, J. (1996). Dynamic analysis of stock returns volatility in an integrated international capital market. *Review of Quantitative Finance and Accounting, 6*, 5–17. doi:10.1007/BF00290793

Clark, P. K. (1973). A subordinated stochastic process model with finite variance for speculative prices. *Econometrica, 41*, 135–155. doi:10.2307/1913889

Cooper, M. (1999). Filter rules based on price and volume in individual security overreaction. *Review of Financial Studies, 12*, 901–935. doi:10.1093/rfs/12.4.901

Copeland, T. E. (1976). A model of asset trading under the assumption of sequential information arrival. *The Journal of Finance, 31*, 1149–1168. doi:10.2307/2326280

Crouch, R. L. (1970). A nonlinear test of the random-walk hypothesis. *The American Economic Review, 60*, 199–202.

Dickey, D. A., & Fuller, W. A. (1979). Distribution of estimators for autoregressive time series with a unit root. *Journal of the American Statistical Association, 74*, 427–431. doi:10.2307/2286348

Dickey, D. A., & Fuller, W. A. (1981). Likelihood ratio statistics for autoregressive time series with a unit root. *Econometrica, 49*, 1057–1072. doi:10.2307/1912517

Dimson, E., & Marsh, T. (1999). Murphy's law and market anomalies. *Journal of Portfolio Management, 25*(2), 53–69. doi:10.3905/jpm.1999.319734

Epps, T. W. (1977). Security price changes and transaction volumes: Theory and evidence. *The American Economic Review, 65*, 586–597.

Epps, T. W., & Epps, M. L. (1976). The stochastic dependence of security price changes and transaction volumes: Implications for the mixture of distributions hypothesis. *Econometrica, 44*, 305–321. doi:10.2307/1912726

Eun, C., & Shim, S. (1989). International transmission of stock market movements. *Journal of Financial and Quantitative Analysis, 24*, 241–256. doi:10.2307/2330774

Fama, E. F., & French, K. R. (1992). The cross-section of expected stock returns. *The Journal of Finance, 47*(2), 427–465. doi:10.2307/2329112

Fama, E. F., & French, K. R. (1993). Common risk factors in the returns on stocks and bonds. *Journal of Financial Economics, 33*(1), 3–56. doi:10.1016/0304-405X(93)90023-5

Fama, E. F., & French, K. R. (1995). Size and book-to-market factors in earnings and returns. *The Journal of Finance, 50*(1), 131–155. doi:10.2307/2329241

Fama, E. F., & French, K. R. (1996). Multifactor explanations of asset pricing anomalies. *The Journal of Finance, 51*(1), 55–87. doi:10.2307/2329302

Fama, E. F., & French, K. R. (1998). Value versus growth: The international evidence. *The Journal of Finance, 53*(6), 1975–1999. doi:10.1111/0022-1082.00080

Fendenia, M., & Grammatikos, T. (1992). Options trading and the bid–ask spread of the underlying stocks. *The Journal of Business, 65*, 335–351. doi:10.1086/296574

Foster, F. D., & Vishwanathan, S. (1990). A theory of intraday variations in volume, variance, and trading cost in securities market. *Review of Financial Studies, 3*, 593–624. doi:10.1093/rfs/3.4.593

Gebka, B., Henke, H., & Bohl, M. T. (2006). Institutional trading and stock return autocorrelation: Empirical evidence on polish pension fund investors' behavior. *Global Finance Journal, 16*, 233–244. doi:10.1016/j.gfj.2006.01.007

Godfrey, M. D., Granger, C., & Morgenstern, W. (1964). The random walk hypothesis of stock market behavior. *Kyklos, 17*, 1–30. doi:10.1111/j.1467-6435.1964.tb02458.x

Granger, C., W. J., & Morgenstern, W. (1963). Spectral analysis of New York stock market prices. *Kyklos, 16*, 1–27. doi:10.1111/j.1467-6435.1963.tb00270.x

Granger, C. W. J. (1969). Investigating causal relations by econometric models and cross-spectral. *Econometria, 37*, 424–438. doi:10.2307/1912791

Granger, C. W. J., & Newbold, P. (1974). Superious regressions in econometrics. *Journal of Econometrics, 2*, 111–120. doi:10.1016/0304-4076(74)90034-7

Hamao, Y., Masulis, R. W., & Ng, V. (1990). Correlations in price changes and volatility across international stock markets. *Review of Financial Studies, 3*, 281–307. doi:10.1093/rfs/3.2.281

Harris, L. (1987). Transaction data tests of the mixture of distributions hypothesis. *Journal of Financial and Quantitative Analysis, 22*, 127–139. doi:10.2307/2330708

He, J., & Ng, L. K. (1994). Economic forces, fundamental variables, and equity returns. *The Journal of Business, 67*, 599–609. doi:10.1086/296648

Hiemstra, C., & Jones, J. D. (1994). Testing for linear and nonlinear granger causality in the stock price-volume relation. *The Journal of Finance, 49*, 1639–1664. doi:10.2307/2329266

Horowitz, J. L., Loughran, T., & Savin, N. E. (2000). Three analyses of size premium. *Journal of Empirical Finance, 7*(2), 143–153. doi:10.1016/S0927-5398(00)00008-6

How, J. C. Y., Verhoeven, P., & Huang, C. X. (2005). Information asymmetry surrounding earnings and dividend announcements: An intra-day analysis. *Mathematics and Computers in Simulation, 68*, 463–473. doi:10.1016/j.matcom.2005.02.015

Huang, Y. S. (1997). The size anomaly on the Taiwan stock exchange. *Applied Financial Letters, 4*(1), 7–12.

Jaffe, J., & Westerfield, R. (1985). The weekend effect in common stock returns: The international evidence. *The Journal of Finance, 40*, 433–454. doi:10.2307/2327894

Jain, P., & Joh, G. (1988). The dependence between hourly prices and trading volume. *Journal of Financial and Quantitative Analysis, 23*, 269–284. doi:10.2307/2331067

Jarrow, R. (1992). Market manipulation, bubbles, corners and short squeezes. *Journal of Financial and Quantitative Analysis, 27*, 311–336. doi:10.2307/2331322

Johansen, S. (1988). Statistical analysis of cointegration vectors. *Journal of Economic Dynamics & Control, 12*, 231–254. doi:10.1016/0165-1889(88)90041-3

Kanas, A. (2002). Mean and variance spillover among size-sorted UK equity portfolios. *Applied Economics Letters, 9*, 319–323. doi:10.1080/13504850110065858

Karpoff, J. M. (1987). The relation between price changes and trading volume: A survey. *Journal of Financial and Quantitative Analysis, 22*, 109–126. doi:10.2307/2330874

Keim, D. B. (1983). Size related anomalies and stock return seasonality: Further empirical evidence. *Journal of Financial Economics, 12*(1), 13–32. doi:10.1016/0304-405X(83)90025-9

Kim, M. K., & Burnie, D. A. (2002). The firm size effect and the economic cycle. *Journal of Financial Research*, *25*(1), 111–124. doi:10.1111/1475-6803.00007

Kumar, R., Sarin, A., & Shastri, K. (1998). The impact of options trading on the market quality of the underlying securities: An empirical analysis. *The Journal of Finance*, *53*, 717–732. doi:10.1111/0022-1082.285595

Kyle, A. S. (1985). Continuous auctions and insider trading. *Economertrica*, *53*, 1315–1335. doi:10.2307/1913210

Lakonishok, J., Shleifer, A., & Vishny, R. W. (1994). Contrarian investment, extrapolation and risk. *The Journal of Finance*, *49*(5), 1541–1578. doi:10.2307/2329262

Leign, W., Modani, N., & Hightower, R. (2004). A computational implementation of stock charting: Abrupt volume increase as signal for movement in New York stock exchange composite index. *Decision Support Systems*, *37*, 515–530. doi:10.1016/S0167-9236(03)00084-8

Lo, A. W., & MacKinlay, A. C. (1990). When are contrarian profits due to stock market overreaction. *Review of Financial Studies*, *3*, 175–205. doi:10.1093/rfs/3.2.175

Ma, T., & Shaw, T. Y. (1990). The relationships between market value, P/E ratio, trading volume and the stock return of Taiwan stock exchange. In Rhee, S. G., & Chang, R. (Eds.), *Pacific-Basin capital markets research* (pp. 313–335). Amsterdam, The Netherlands: North-Holland.

Martens, M., & Poon, S. H. (2001). Returns synchronization and daily correlation dynamics between international stock markets. *Journal of Banking & Finance*, *25*, 1805–1827. doi:10.1016/S0378-4266(00)00159-X

Mazouz, K. (2004). The effect of CBOE option listing on the volatility of NYSE traded stocks: A time-varying variance approach. *Journal of Empirical Finance*, *11*, 695–708. doi:10.1016/j.jempfin.2003.09.003

McQueen, G., Pinegar, M., & Thorley, S. (1996). Delayed reaction to good news and the cross-autocorrelation of portfolio returns. *The Journal of Finance*, *51*, 889–920. doi:10.2307/2329226

Osborne, M. F. M. (1959). Brownian motion in the stock market. *Operations Research*, *7*, 145–173. doi:10.1287/opre.7.2.145

Phillips, P. C. B., & Perron, P. (1988). Testing for a unit root in time series regression. *Biometrika*, *75*, 335–346. doi:10.1093/biomet/75.2.335

Reinganum, M. R. (1981). Misspecification of capital asset pricing: Empirical anomalies based on earnings' yields and market values. *Journal of Financial Economics*, *9*(1), 19–46. doi:10.1016/0304-405X(81)90019-2

Schultz, P. (1983). Transactions costs and the small firm effect: A comment. *Journal of Financial Economics*, *12*, 81–88. doi:10.1016/0304-405X(83)90028-4

Sims, C. A. (1980). Macroeconomics and reality. *Econometria*, *48*, 1–48. doi:10.2307/1912017

Smirlock, M., & Starks, L. (1985). A further examination of stock price changes and transactions volume. *Journal of Financial Research*, *8*, 217–225.

Stoll, H. R., & Whaley, R. E. (1983). Transaction costs and the small firm effect. *Journal of Financial Economics*, *12*(1), 57–79. doi:10.1016/0304-405X(83)90027-2

Theodossiou, P., & Unro, L. (1995). Relationship between volatility and expected returns across international stock markets. *Journal of Business Finance & Accounting*, *22*, 289–300. doi:10.1111/j.1468-5957.1995.tb00685.x

Wang, C. Y., & Cheng, N. S. (2004). Extreme volumes and expected stock returns: Evidence from China's stock market. *Pacific-Basin Finance Journal*, *12*, 577–597. doi:10.1016/j.pacfin.2004.04.002

Wang, J. (1994). A model of competitive stock trading volume. *The Journal of Political Economy*, *102*, 127–168. doi:10.1086/261924

Wood, R. A., Mcinish, T. H., & Ord, J. K. (1985). An investigation of transactions data for NYSE stocks. *The Journal of Finance*, *60*, 723–739. doi:10.2307/2327796

Ying, C. C. (1966). Stock market prices and volumes of sales. *Econometrica*, *34*, 676–685. doi:10.2307/1909776

*This work was previously published in the International Journal of Applied Evolutionary Computation, Volume 2, Issue 3, edited by Wei-Chiang Samuelson Hong, pp. 59-78, copyright 2011 by IGI Publishing (an imprint of IGI Global).*

# Chapter 14
# Recursive Learning of Genetic Algorithms with Task Decomposition and Varied Rule Set

**Lei Fang**
*Xi'an Jiaotong-Liverpool University, China*

**Sheng-Uei Guan**
*Xi'an Jiaotong-Liverpool University, China*

**Haofan Zhang**
*Xi'an Jiaotong-Liverpool University, China*

## ABSTRACT

*Rule-based Genetic Algorithms (GAs) have been used in the application of pattern classification (Corcoran & Sen, 1994), but conventional GAs have weaknesses. First, the time spent on learning is long. Moreover, the classification accuracy achieved by a GA is not satisfactory. These drawbacks are due to existing undesirable features embedded in conventional GAs. The number of rules within the chromosome of a GA classifier is usually set and fixed before training and is not problem-dependent. Secondly, conventional approaches train the data in batch without considering whether decomposition solves the problem. Thirdly, when facing large-scale real-world problems, GAs cannot utilise resources efficiently, leading to premature convergence. Based on these observations, this paper develops a novel algorithmic framework that features automatic domain and task decomposition and problem-dependent chromosome length (rule number) selection to resolve these undesirable features. The proposed Recursive Learning of Genetic Algorithm with Task Decomposition and Varied Rule Set (RLGA) method is recursive and trains and evolves a team of learners using the concept of local fitness to decompose the original problem into sub-problems. RLGA performs better than GAs and other related solutions regarding training duration and generalization accuracy according to the experimental results.*

DOI: 10.4018/978-1-4666-3628-6.ch014

## INTRODUCTION

Pattern classification problem plays a major role in various fields of computer science and engineering, such as data mining and image processing has been attracting growing interests. The task of pattern classification is to assign patterns into one out of several predefined classes within which the assigned patterns share some common properties. Assume we have a $c$-class problem in an $n$-dimensional pattern space. And $q$ real vectors $X_i=(x_{i1}\, x_{i2}\, \ldots\, x_{in})\ i = 1,2,\ldots,q$, are given as training patterns from the $c$ classes ($c<<q$). Normally, a GA classifier, for example, will train its chromosomes against a set of training patterns (with known classes) to discover the relationship between the attributes and classes. The discovered rules can be evaluated by classification accuracy or error rate either on the training data or test data. Classification problem has also been widely included among machine learning problems while much research has been done on machine learning techniques by using classification problem as a vehicle.

Many soft computing techniques have been applied to solve the classification problem, including artificial neural networks (ANN) (Guan & Li, 2001; Su, Guan, & Yeo, 2001; Anand, Mehrotra, Mohan, & Ranka, 2002), fuzzy logic (Ishibuchi, Nakashima, & Murata, 2002; Setnes & Roubos, 2002), and evolutionary algorithms (De Jong & Spears, 1991; Zhu & Guan, 2005). Among them, rule-based genetic algorithms (GAs), a member of evolutionary algorithms, is one of the most successful approaches for classification, either supervised or unsupervised (Corcoran & Sen, 1994). There are two main streams of rule-based GAs classifiers (Smith, 1980; De Jong, 1988; Cordón, Herrera, Hoffmann, & Magdalena, 2001). One is the *Pittsburgh* approach, and the other the *Michigan* approach. These names follow the names of the universities at which these approaches were firstly proposed. In the *Pittsburgh (Pitt)* approach, each chromosome is encoded as a complete set of rules. Therefore, one individual chromosome can solve the given classification problem. On the other hand, the *Michigan* approach uses instead the whole population as the solution-set, which means the whole set of chromosomes should work together to solve the classification problem. In this paper, the *Pitt* approach is applied.

Despite of the popularity of GAs, there still exist problems within GAs with reference to solving pattern classification problem. It is usually a time consuming task for GA-based classifiers to evolve a qualified set of solutions. Moreover, the classification accuracy finally achieved by GAs, is not always satisfactory, especially when solving problems in higher dimensions. Time and accuracy are two of the most important metrics that can be used to measure the performance of a pattern classifier. A good pattern classifier should be both efficient in time and effective in accuracy. Besides, GAs also suffer from early convergence such that the evolution process cannot gain further improvement when the solution (population) is still premature.

Conventionally, most GA-based solutions in the literature work in the static mode, where all the parameters of GAs (e.g., rule number, chromosome length in the Pitt approach, population size in the Michigan approach, the attributes, classes and training data, etc.), are determined before the training process starts. However, learning should be an ad hoc process in which all the parameters, especially the rule number, should be determined at run-time according to different classification problems. It is intuitive to see that a larger set of rules may fit for hard problems, on the other hand, a smaller one for simple problems. Therefore, if GA can be equipped with the capability to decide the problem-dependent rule-number parameter, it will be better than its static counterpart.

However, when facing large-scale classification problems, a major drawback of GAs is its inefficiency in utilising genetic resources. For example, when long chromosomes, comprising thousands of rules or with excessively large input size, take part in reproduction procedures, one-point crossover will exchange little information. Therefore, improvement over evolution will be minor and the potential resources are not fully exploited. A common approach to overcome this drawback is to decompose the original task into several subtasks: firstly initialize a set of learners to learn these smaller and simpler subtasks, and then combine the sub-solutions into the final solution. Various task decomposition methods have been proposed. According to their decomposition strategies, these methods can be categorised into four classes: domain decomposition (Guan & Ramanathan, 2004, 2007; Hua Ang, Guan, Tan, & Al Mamun, 2008; Ramanathan & Guan, 2008), input decomposition (Guan & Li, 2001; García-Pedrajas, Hervás-Martíneza, & Muñoz-Pérez, 2002; Guan & Liu, 2002, 2004), class decomposition (Anand et al., 2002; Guan & Li, 2002; Bao, Neo, & Guan, 2007), and hybrid decomposition approach (Tan, Guan, Ramanathan, & Bao, 2009). Most of them are ANN-based approaches (Guan & Li, 2001; Su et al., 2001; Guan & Liu, 2002, 2004; Jenkins & Yuhas, 2002; Hua Ang et al., 2008), while few are GA-based. Among GA-based task decomposition solutions, Potter and De Jong proposed the cooperative co-evolution genetic algorithm (CCGA) (Potter & De Jong, 1998, 2000), featuring input decomposition. Zhu and Guan then revised and adapted CCGA into the enhanced cooperative co-evolution genetic algorithms (ECCGA) (Zhu & Guan, 2008), which gains better performance and can solve classification problems. ECCGA initialises $n$ sub-modules or species for a classification problem with $n$ input dimensions; it then trains each species before integrating them together by a conclusive global evolution. Besides input decomposition, GA with output decomposition has also been proposed. Guan and Zhu designed a GA-based classifier, which applies class decomposition strategy (Guan & Zhu, 2004). This approach partitions a classification problem into several sub-modules according to their output domain. Each module is responsible for solving a fraction of the original

problem, which has the same input vector size but only a sub-set of output vector as the original one. These modules are trained in parallel and independently, while results obtained from them are integrated to form the final solution by resolving conflicts. However, GA-based research on data or domain decomposition has not been done. Moreover, almost all decomposition approaches are imposed manually by human's heuristics rather than being done intelligently and automatically according to specific problem context.

We propose a new GA-based classifier in this paper. The objective is to derive an algorithm that features automatic task- and data-decomposition with ad hoc rule-number provision. We believe the proposed GA solution with the aforementioned features, can avoid the drawbacks of GAs, such as early convergence, so that it outperforms the others.

In this paper, the proposed solution is elaborated in next section. Then, our recursive GA approach for classifier is presented in the following section. The experimental results on benchmark data sets and their analysis are reported in forth section. The Discussion section places our approach in the context further by presenting a brief survey on related work. Last section concludes the paper and presents future work.

## TRADITIONAL GA-BASED CLASSIFIER

Our approach is closely related to canonical GAs. In order to present our approach, a standard rule-based GA classifier will be illustrated first. A typical GA is shown in Figure 1. Such a GA classifier usually contains GA operators, such as selection, crossover, and mutation.

A rule is usually represented as an IF-THEN clause. Such a rule is shown as follows:

$$R_i: \text{IF } (V_{1min} \leq x_1 \leq V_{1max})$$
$$\wedge (V_{2min} \leq x_2 \leq V_{2max}) \cdots \quad (1)$$
$$\wedge (V_{nmin} \leq x_n \leq V_{nmax}) \text{ THEN } y = C$$

*Figure 1. Pseudocode of GA*

```
t=0
initialize P(t)
        //initialize a population of chromosomes randomly
evaluate P(t)
        //evaluate each chromosome from P(t)
        // using a fitness function
while (not terminate-condition) do
        select P'(t) from P(t)
        crossover P'(t)
        mutate P'(t)
         combine P'(t) and P(t) to generate P(t+1)
                    //survival percentage applied
        evaluate P(t+1)
        t=t+1
```

where $n$ is the number of attributes, $(x_1, x_2, …, x_n)$ is the values of the input pattern's attribute set, $y$ is the output class index assigned to the rule, $V_{j\,min}$ and $V_{j\,max}$ are the boundary values for the $j$ th attribute $x_j$ respectively. The encoding mechanism is also depicted in Figure 2.

As shown in Figure 2, each antecedent element represents an attribute, and the consequence element stands for a class. Differing from the rule depicted in equation (2), there are notations, like $Act_j$, denoting whether the attribute $j$ is active or inactive, which is encoded as 1 or 0. By encoding in this way, the rule becomes flexible in its length. Each chromosome $CR_j$ is composed of a number of rules $R_i(i=1,2,…,m)$ by concatenating them together,

$$CR_j = \bigcup_{i=1,m} R_i \quad j = 1, 2, …, p \quad (2)$$

where $m$ denotes the number of rules residing in one chromosome $CR_j$. In most cases, $m$ is set at 30. Moreover, $p$ denotes the population size, i.e., the number of chromosomes processed by one GA. Therefore, one particular chromosome has length of $L$, if encoded in the way introduced above.

$$L = m * |R| \qquad \text{where } |R| = 3 * n + 1 \tag{3}$$

$|R|$ is the length of one rule. A chromosome can be represented by a array with length $L$.

## Fitness Function (Global Fitness)

The fitness of one chromosome shows its ability in classifying patterns. It reflects the success rate achieved while the corresponding rule set is used for classification and is used to select good candidates for reproduction. The fitness is the percentage of patterns that can be accurately classified by the chromosome.

$$f = \frac{C}{N} = \frac{\text{number of patterns correctly classified}}{\text{total number of patterns}}$$
$$(4)$$

Since one chromosome represents one entire rule set, the fitness actually measures the collective performance of all the rules in that chromosome. One task involved is to resolve conflicts among different rules in one single chromosome. Voting mechanism is applied here. The class which obtains highest votes will be the answer of the chromosome. Note that if more than 1 class gets the highest votes, it is then concluded that this

*Figure 2. Encoding mechanism for classification rule*

| Antecedent Gene 1 | | | ... | Antecedent Gene n | | | Consequence Gene |
|---|---|---|---|---|---|---|---|
| $Act_1$ | $V_{1\,min}$ | $V_{1\,max}$ | ... | $Act_n$ | $V_{n\,min}$ | $V_{n\,max}$ | $C$ |

pattern cannot be classified correctly by this rule set. The algorithm to compute the fitness is shown in Figure 3.

## Genetic Operators

## Selection

Roulette wheel selection (Michalewicz, 1996) is used in this project. The probability that a chromosome is selected for mating is given by the chromosome's fitness divided by the sum fitness of all the chromosomes. By doing this, the chromosome with a higher fitness value will have a higher probability to generate offspring compared with chromosomes with lower fitness.

## Crossover and Mutation

Due to the favourable nature of the adopted encoding mechanism, crossover operations can take place anywhere within the length of chromosomes without bringing in inconsistencies. However, mutation should be done carefully because different spot in one chromosome has different constraints. For example, if an activeness element is selected

*Figure 3. Pseudo code for evaluating the global fitness of one chromosome*

---

*hitNumber=0*

*for each pattern {*

  *for each rule in the chromosome{*

  *decode rule antecedents*

  *if all rule antecedents are valid for the instance then*

    *then cast a vote for the class reported in the rule*

  *}*

  *use a voting mechanism to determine the classPredicted*

  *if classPredicted == realClass in the pattern then*

  *hitNumber++;*

*}*

*fitness=hitNumber/totalNumber*

*//totalNumber denote the total number of patterns*

---

for mutation, it will just be toggled. In Figure 4, the crossover and mutation process is presented graphically. Normally, the rate for mutation and crossover are selected at 0.01 and 1.0 (mutaionRate = 0.01 and crossoverRate = 1.0). For reproduction, the survival rate is as 50%, which means half of the chromosomes with lower fitness in one local training session will be discarded and the reproduced chromosomes will cover the vacancies left.

## RECURSIVE GA LEARNING WITH TASK DECOMPOSITION AND VARIED RULE NUMBER

The proposed algorithm is a recursive learning genetic algorithm (RLGA), that features automatic

*Figure 4. The crossover and mutation operations*

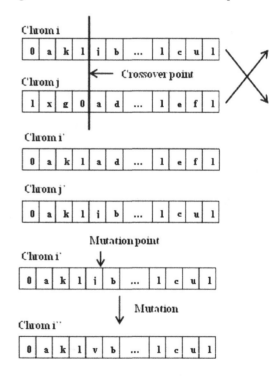

There is no restriction on crossover point, which means every spot in the chromosome can be used as the point. However, different positions in chromosome have different mutation policies. For activeness point, the value will be toggled. For others, a random number in some certain range will be generated to replace the original value.

task and data decomposition with a problem-dependent rule number. Similar to the other task decomposition algorithms, RLGA has two phases: training phase and integration phase. Since the solutions obtained in the RLGA training phase cannot simply be aggregated to produce a good solution to the whole searching space. Therefore, the integration part is required. Training will generate solutions through decomposition processes while integration part will use the generated solutions to form a final solution to solve the given classification problem. These two phases will be introduced in detail in the following two sections.

## Training Phase

The main idea of this algorithm is to automatically decompose the domain at the same time learn with the guidance of local fitness. For each decomposed sub-domain, one trained pseudo-learner will take responsibilities for that searching space. Finally, a collection of pseudo-learners will be integrated to form the solution for the whole domain. In this way, varied numbers of learners will be produced

for different problems. For hard problems, a large number of sub-domains will be separated with the corresponding learners in each sub-domain. To realise automatic task decomposition and problem-dependent rule number features, a new concept called local fitness is introduced. Differing from traditional GA classifiers, our approach does not use the global fitness function illustrated in II-B. Before elaborating the algorithm, the new concept is introduced first.

## Elicitation of Local Fitness and Local Fitness Algorithm

To understand local fitness, the concept of the scopes (ranges) of rule-based chromosomes should be understood at first place. A rule-based chromosome is encoded with an IF-THEN clause. In the premise part, two boundary values of each dimension or attribute are encoded as the checking criteria (refer to equation (2)). In general, the premise part of a rule encloses one sub-searching-space from the whole searching space. Figure 5 shows the relationship between the sub-searching-space

*Figure 5. The range of a chromosome*

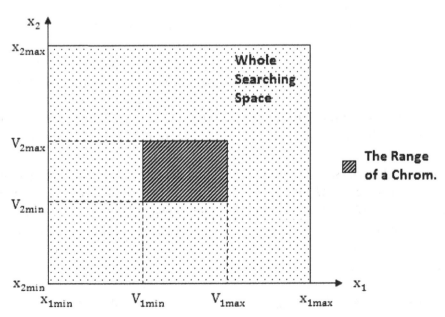

a chromosome encloses and the whole searching space in a two-dimension scenario. According to the diagram, the dark space, enclosed by one typical one-rule chromosome, corresponds to the sub-searching-space, which is much smaller than the whole space. For chromosomes with more than one rule, the sub-domain will be union of the multiple rectangles enclosed by each rule. For simplicity and without losing generality, we only investigate the specific case here, i.e., one-rule chromosome.

Actually, each chromosome has its own unique sub-domain under which it has domain knowledge; furthermore, it is generally unaware of the space outside. Conventionally, a chromosome with fixed 30 rules is usually applied regardless of how complex the task domain's area could be. The potential flaw is obvious here: the whole task domain may not be fully covered or solved by a fixed number, say 30, of rules. Note that this claim is equivalent to – the rule-number of chromosomes, m, required to optimally solve a classification problem, $P$, is a problem dependent parameter.

## Theorem 1

There exist no fixed number M that can be applied to optimally solve any specific classification problem.

## Proof

Apagoge is used.

Assume there exist a fixed rule-number, $M$, which can be used to optimally solve all the existing problems.

For a problem $P$ with $c$-class, where $c > M + 1$, there exists no chromosome with $M$ rule-number that can perfectly (100%) solve the problem, because an $M$-rule chromosome can at most cover $M + 1$ classes (each rule at best covers one unique class's patterns and the complement of them represents the remaining one). As a result, at least one class is left uncovered from the chromosome.

This contradiction contradicts with the premise. Therefore, Theorem 1 is proved.

Having proved the theorem stated above, we can draw a conclusion that a chromosome from a traditional approach is likely not to cover the whole domain entirely. A good solution is to decompose the search domain and map one chromosome to a specific sub-domain problem until the whole search domain is fully covered. However, if the decomposition and the mapping are carried out separately, i.e., firstly, manually and blindly decompose the search domain into n pieces and assign n leaners to learn each sub-domain, which is a prevailing task decomposition approach in the literature, the situation will not be any better. The main reason is that each sub-problem is exactly the same as the original one in almost every aspect except smaller in size. For each sub-problem, the puzzle of producing problem-dependent rule-set chromosomes still remains. Moreover, manual decomposition is no better than blind partitioning, because it may render the classification more complex. Therefore, good decomposition should be done in connection with the good mapping, i.e., a sub-domain should not be decomposed and separated until we find a chromosome which is certain and has profound and accurate knowledge upon that sub-domain. The traditional fitness function serving the purpose of calculating fitness in the global sense cannot be used here, because sub-domain knowledge is the main interest here. Therefore, instead of measuring global performance, an algorithm that focuses on and measures local performance should be designed and applied here to establish the connection between the domain decomposition and mapping. The algorithm and equation that calculate the local fitness of one chromosome are shown in Figure 6. As can be seen from the equation, the metric used here evaluates local performance rather than global.

$$f = \frac{C}{N} = \frac{\text{number of patterns correctly classified}}{\text{total number of applied patterns}}$$

(5)

*Figure 6. Pseudo code for evaluating the local fitness of one chromosome*

```
accurateNumber=0
appliedNumber=0
for each pattern {
  decode rule antecedents
  if all rule antecedents are valid for the instance then
      appliedNum++
      classPredicted=the class reported in the rule
  if classPredicted = = realClass in the pattern then
      accurateNumber++;
}
fitness=accurateNum/appliedNum
```

## The Training Algorithm

The RLGA training algorithm learns the problem through recursively decomposing the domain and meanwhile producing a corresponding solution mapped to that decomposed sub-domain, which successfully establishes the linkage between domain decomposition and learner mapping. The algorithm consists of two sections, global control and decomposition training (D-Train). The D-Train part is responsible for the actual training task. Each time when D-Train method is called, a population of chromosomes with $m$ rules encoded will be initialized; then training follows the same procedure as the canonical GAs classifier (Figure 1), using local fitness instead of global one. Training aims at finding an expert in some sub-search-space, through the use of local fitness. In a D-Train process, a partial pseudo solution will be generated, which is used later to form the final solution. Note the parameter, $m$, or the number of rules each chromosome has, is used here. In this paper, $m$ is set at 1, i.e., each chromosome is encoded with one rule. The Discussion section gives detailed justification over the setting for $m$.

The global control part consists of numerous D-Train processes. During the training phase, the classification task will be recursively solved with the problem domain decomposed and reduced. The global control part will repeatedly call D-Train method to learn the training patterns until all the training patterns are learnt. Note that global control part will mark and remove those learnt patterns from the previous D-Train process and initialize a new D-Train process to learn the remaining training data. Therefore, global control is in charge of the whole training process and maintains the training patterns as well as the pseudo solutions from each D-train process. Finally, all pseudo solutions will be used to form the final solution for the testing phase. The collection of the partial solutions will cover the whole search space when they work together. The detailed algorithms are presented in Figures 7 and 8.

## Stopping Criteria and Coefficients Used

In the D-Train phase, the stopping criterion is a stagnation limit: when the *D-Train* gains no improvement for certain generations, then train-

*Figure 7. Algorithms for the global control of RLGA*

```
1.  Load training patterns from an external file;
    denote the set of patterns as D
2.  Initialize an expert array, denoted as E
3.  Invoke local training method to start weak learner
    training process, P is the population processed in
    local training.
4.  Find the best chromosome obtained from local
    training, denote it as expert, identify the learnt
    patterns from expert and represent them as L
    If |L|>=1 then
        a.  Add expert into the expert array, E
        b.  Remove the L learnt patterns from D
        c.  Re-evaluate P against the updated D
        d.  Initialize a new set of chromosomes to
            replace unsatisfactory chromosomes in P
    Else
        a.  Initialize a new population to replace P
5.  Repeat step 3 and step 4 until all patterns are
    learnt or stagnation occurs, i.e. local training fails
    repetitively to learn any more patterns
```

*Figure 8. Algorithms for the training part of RLGA*

1. Initialize a set of chromosomes with each chromosome encoding $m$ rule. Denote the population as $P$
2. Calculate local fitness for each chromosome in $P$
3. Select good chromosomes from the population according to their fitness
4. Perform crossover and mutation operation on the selected chromosomes to reproduce new individuals
5. Combine the newly reproduced chromosomes with old population, forming a new generation
6. Repeat Step 2 to Step 5 until termination conditions are met

ing stops. While in the global control loop, the termination criteria are that over 2 consecutive *D-Train* processes do not learn any patterns. When this happens, it can be deemed that the remaining problem is unsolvable. The reason is that each D-Train bears similar structure and setting; moreover, each process is independent to each other, i.e., there is no linkage between two consecutive processes. Therefore, they have the same searching power. If one D-Train process does not gain any improvement, we should not expect future ones can.

There are four coefficients involved in the D-train process: rule number per chromosome in D-train, survival rate, crossover rate, and mutation rate. As said in the previous section, each chromosome is encoded as one-rule set. Justification upon this parameter will be given in the Discussion section. The survival rate is 0.5; therefore, half of the population will be replaced in each round. The crossover rate and mutation rate is set at 1 and 0.1 respectively. Due to the usage of local fitness and the fact of short chromosome length (1 rule), the population is easy to converge. Therefore, a relatively large mutation rate is used to ensure population diversity. A detailed discussion on the usage of mutation rate is also deferred to the Discussion section.

## Integration Phase

During the integration phase the solutions generated in the training phase are used to form the final solution. After the training process, an array of experts (chromosomes) is obtained. This array cannot be used to solve the original problem directly. One issue is regarding which expert should be called to solve the problem when a testing pattern is presented, since there are multiple experts in the array. Each chromosome has its own sub-domain; therefore, the scope of each expert can be used to find the right expert from the array, i.e., a pattern should sit within the range of one expert if the expert is assigned to solve that pattern. The integration algorithm is shown in Figure 9.

According to this algorithm, the order of the experts in the array does affect the final answer produced. Because, the *for* loop starts from the front to the rear in the array. Expert in the front will have a higher priority to report answer against the one in the rear, even though both of their ranges cover the input pattern. The reason is elaborated below. In the training phase, the learnt patterns are removed at each round when a *D-Train* process is finished and a corresponding expert is added to the expert array; the later training process is actually conducted without the participation of the previously removed patterns. More precisely, the expert(s) added later if claiming the given test patterns only accidentally covers that space of the patterns because the patterns have been removed in previous round. Therefore, although the expert(s) added later might have some overlapping

*Figure 9. Pseudo code of integration algorithm*

*Pt denotes an input pattern;*
*E denotes the expert array;*
*for each expert e in E*
   *decode rule antecedents of e*
   *if all rule antecedents are valid for the instance then*
      *return classification result reported by the rule*
*return don't know*

in the searching space with some expert(s) added earlier, the later expert(s) is unaware of the pattern's belonging class.

Figure 10 illustrates the rationale behind the integration algorithm further. Assume the white space represents the range of a previously added expert. The patterns within that range are removed (so that the space is empty) when this expert is copied into the expert array. The dark space represents the updated search space with the learnt parts removed. The training continues with a new expert being produced and added. This newly created expert may be trained and generated with its range overlapping with certain ranges from the previous ones due to the coding style in the specified premises. However, the newly expert actually should not be applied to decide anything within these overlapped regions because those parts have already been blanked out. Therefore, the experts in the front are favoured against those sitting in the rear part of the expert array.

## EXPERIMENTAL RESULTS AND ANALYSIS

We have conducted a series of experiments on RLGA via seven benchmark datasets. The detailed information about these datasets is provided in Table 1, which includes the number of instances, attributes, and classes in each data set. The first four of them are taken from the UCI machine learning repository (Blake & Merz, 1998), and they are real-world problems, including cancer, glass, yeast, and wine. The last three data sets are artificially generated data. In the dataset Slant (45°) as shown in Figure 11, there are two classes of patterns symmetrically distributed between the line y = x (with slope 1 and angle 45) in a two-dimensional system. Circle dataset is the case that two classes are distinguished by a circle. The Complex Circles problem (Figure 12) has 5 circles separating the whole search space into two classes. The reasons to use these artificially produced data

*Figure 10. The range of later added expert*

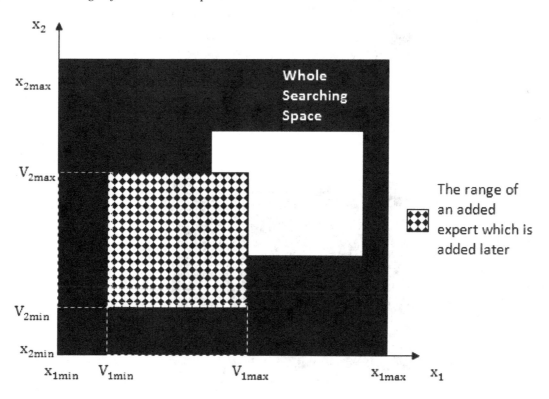

*Table 1. The eight benchmark datasets*

| Data Set | No. of Instances | No. of Attributes | No. of Classes |
|---|---|---|---|
| Cancer | 699 | 9 | 2 |
| Yeast | 1484 | 8 | 10 |
| Glass | 214 | 9 | 6 |
| Wine | 178 | 13 | 3 |
| Slant (45°) | 1000 | 2 | 2 |
| Complex Circles | 1000 | 2 | 2 |
| Two Circles | 1000 | 2 | 2 |

are manifold. For one thing, they can be used to test whether the classifier agent can distinguish data under different separating curves (straight line and curved lines). Secondly, some complex pattern classification problems, with multi-dimension or multi-output-dimension, could be viewed as the integration of multiple two-dimension systems. Therefore, the performance of an agent against simple problems can serve as indicators to their corresponding performance in complex ones.

All data were partitioned into training set and testing set. The training set accounts for 50% of

*Figure 11. Slant(45') dataset*

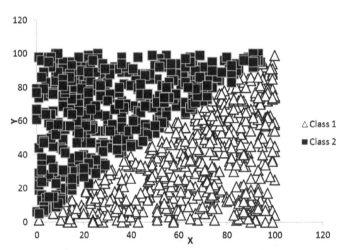

*Figure 12. Complex circles dataset*

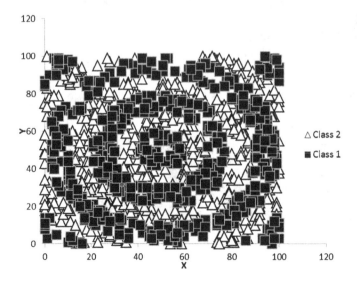

the total instances in each data, and the testing set consist of 50% of patterns. Training data were used to train the classifier, while testing set consists of instances that are unknown to the classifier, therefore can test its generalization performance.

All the experiments were completed on Intel® Core™2 Duo CPU E7500 @ 2.93GHz/2.94GHz PCs with 2.00 GB RAM. The mean values reported were averaged over thirty independent runs. Training time, training classification rate and testing classification rate were measured and compared. The standard deviations (SD) are also reported accordingly.

Overall, three different methods were investigated and compared: Normal GA, Incremental GA on rule-number (IGA-RN), and RLGA. As mentioned earlier, the number of rules within a classifier in traditional GAs is pre-set before training. In many cases, the number is set at 30, which works fine in most cases. To set up a comparison model, the traditional normal GA classifier with a fixed number of rules (30) is still investigated. However, we argue that the number of rules is a problem-dependant parameter. Since RLGA applies different numbers of rules over different problems, the normal GA with the same number of rules should be for comparison. Another approach, IGA-RN, which also features problem-dependent rule-number, is compared with RLGA, in order to see whether RLGA edges other advanced approaches. IGA-RN simply runs in a bottom-up fashion, in which the classifier trains the dataset by increasing the number of rules (for example, from one rule) until stopping criteria are met. The detailed design of IGA-RN is listed in the Appendix.

## 1. Wine

The wine data contains the chemical analysis of 178 wines from three different cultivars in the same region in Italy. The experimental results of the classifier performances are provided in Table 2. According to the table, four classifiers are

*Table 2. Comparison of different approaches of GA on wine data*

| Summary | Normal GA (fixed rule No.) | Normal GA (varied rule No.) |
|---|---|---|
| Training time | 7.50 | 1.88 |
| Ending CR | $0.951 \pm 0.022$ | $0.814 \pm 0.113$ |
| Test CR | $0.875 \pm 0.052$ | $0.756 \pm 0.112$ |
| No. Rules | 30 | 8 |
| Summary | RLGA | IGA-RN |
| Training time | 0.41 (-77.9%) | 29.57 |
| Ending CR | $1 \pm 0.0$ (22.9%) | $0.925 \pm 0.064$ |
| Test CR | $0.928 \pm 0.028$ (22.8%) | $0.792 \pm 0.060$ |
| No. Rules | 7.23 | 58.97 |

examined. Two normal GAs whose rule number is 8, and 30 respectively. The other 2 are RLGA and IGA-RN. Since RLGA has 7.23 rules (average value over 30 independent runs), the normal GA with 8 rules are investigated for comparison. The percentages in the braces are the percentage of the improvements of RLGA over normal GA (with the same number of rules). As can be seen from the data, training time is dramatically decreased, while both training classification rate (CR) and testing CR are significantly improved and the highest among all.

It is also interesting that the number of rules used in RLGA is only about 8 (7.23), which means 8 single rules can handle this problem. However, in the normal GA with 30 rules encoded, lots of unnecessary computations were wasted due to the additional 22 rules. However, normal GA with 8 rules performs poorly in comparison with the other approaches, which on the other hand shows the power of RLGA: using the same and minimal number of rules but evolves the best solution.

The standard deviation of RLGA's training CR and testing CR are 0 and 0.028, which are the smallest among all. This means that RLGA is a reliable and stable approach which performs good jobs consistently.

Figure 13 summarises the data in Table 2. It shows the difference between the IGA-RN and RLGA on wine problem as well as two normal GA approaches' results. In each epoch, RLGA and IGA-RN increments its rule number by one, therefore the rule number is growing as the epoch does. As can be seen from the figure, the initial fitness of RLGA is lower than IGA-RN. However, RLGA improves its fitness within a very short duration and finishes its training process. On contrary, IGA-RN's fitness relatively grows slowly and remains unchanged in the last decades of epochs. This is probably due to that growing rule-set renders inefficiency of utilising genetic resources, which drags down the learning speed.

## 2. Cancer

The cancer problem diagnoses whether a breast cancer is benign or malignant. Table 3 shows the experimental results on the cancer data. As can be seen from the table, RLGA uses only 11.97 rules. Comparing with normal GA of 30 rules, RLGA still excels in both training time and classification rates. Though normal GA with 16 rules is not as good as RLGA, but it is quite close to its counterpart with 30 rules (with difference less than 0.01). This shows that large number of rules can

*Table 3. Comparison of different approaches of GA on cancer data*

| Summary | Normal GA (fixed rule No.) | Normal GA (varied rule No.) |
|---|---|---|
| Training time | 9.129 | 3.785 |
| Ending CR | 0.979 ± 0.003 | 0.969 ± 0.085 |
| Test CR | 0.941 ± 0.009 | 0.931 ± 0.054 |
| No. Rules | 30 | 12 |
| Summary | RLGA | IGA-RN |
| Training time | 0.746 (-80.29%) | 31.733 |
| Ending CR | 1 ± 0.0 (3.17%) | 0.96 ± 0.014 |
| Test CR | 0.947 ± 0.011 (1.67%) | 0.934 ± 0.02 |
| No. Rules | 11.97 | 36.67 |

be considered as unnecessary in some situations. However, IGA-RN ends up with 36.67 rules, and the classification accuracy is not improved much in comparison with RLGA and normal GA, which again indicates IGA-RN suffers from the ever-growing rule set problem. According to Figure 14, the initial fitness of RLGA is lower than IGA-RN. However, RLGA's fitness increases far more quickly than IGA-RN. On the other hand, IGA-RN only gains minor improvements since epoch 7. In other words, incorporated new rules do not function effectively, i.e., IGA-RN does not make full use of the new incoming genetic resources.

*Figure 13. Experimental results of wine data*

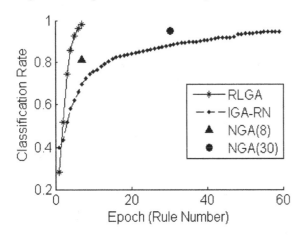

*Figure 14. Experimental results of cancer data*

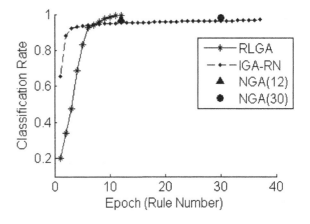

## 3. Glass

The glass dataset contains data of different glass types. The results of chemical analysis of glass splinters plus the refractive index are used to classify a sample to be either float processed or non-float processed building windows, vehicle windows, containers, tableware, or head lamps. Table 4 and Figure 15 report the experiments results on the glass data. RLGA again is the best solution among the listed 4 classifiers. The ending CR is about 2 times over those of normal GAs and IGA-RN. In this problem, 39.93 rules are used by RLGA. IGA-RN also evolves a rule set with a close rule-number 39.6. However, their results achieved are differs significantly, which shows the advantage of RLGA.

## 4. Yeast

The yeast problem predicts the protein localization sites in cells. Table 5 and Figure 16 give the details on the performance comparisons. According to the table, RLGA uses nearly 344 rules, and manages to gain the best performance again. The training and testing CR are dramatically improved when comparing with IGA-RN and normal GA. Notice that the normal GA, which uses the same number of rules (344) as RLGA, does not improve

*Figure 15. Experimental results of glass data*

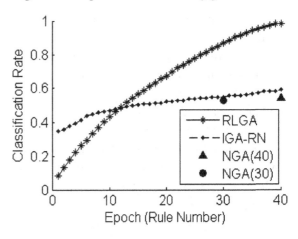

*Table 5. Comparison of different approaches of GA on yeast data*

| Summary | Normal GA (fixed rule No.) | Normal GA (varied rule No.) |
|---|---|---|
| Training time | 30.162 | 475.836 |
| Ending CR | 0.355 ± 0.042 | 0.4 ± 0.038 |
| Test CR | 0.356 ± 0.049 | 0.387 ± 0.042 |
| No. Rules | 30 | 344 |
| Summary | RLGA | IGA-RN |
| Training time | 78.032 (-83.6%) | 219.311 |
| Ending CR | 1 ± 0.0 (149.8%) | 0.387 ± 0.055 |
| Test CR | 0.496 ± 0.02 (-28.12%) | 0.371 ± 0.048 |
| No. Rules | 343.9 | 48.1 |

*Table 4. Comparison of different approaches of GA on glass data*

| Summary | Normal GA (fixed rule No.) | Normal GA (varied rule No.) |
|---|---|---|
| Training time | 5.793 | 8.122 |
| Ending CR | 0.529 ± 0.076 | 0.542 ± 0.078 |
| Test CR | 0.511 ± 0.061 | 0.509 ± 0.072 |
| No. Rules | 30 | 40 |
| Summary | RLGA | IGA-RN |
| Training time | 1.446 (-82.20%) | 14.911 |
| Ending CR | 1 ± 0.0 (84.65%) | 0.540 ± 0.08 |
| Test CR | 0.685 ± 0.057 (34.63%) | 0.470 ± 0.061 |
| No. Rules | 39.93 | 39.6 |

*Figure 16. Experimental results of yeast data*

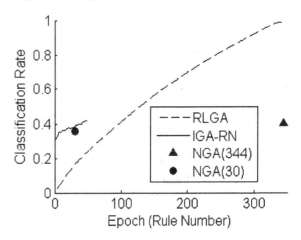

its performance much. However, RLGA makes fully use of the additional rules and produce better solutions overall.

It is worthwhile to take a look at the rule number used here. The average rule-number used by RLGA is 344, which is larger than any other problems analysed here. It is an indicator that yeast problem is a hard problem that large rule set is required to solve the problem. This conclusion is also reflected and justified on the problem itself. Among all the seven investigated problems, yeast problem has the largest pattern set (1484) and also the largest overall input-output dimension (8+10=18). Through this case, we can see that RLGA does produce varied rules according to problem difficulty levels.

## 5. Artificially Created Datasets

There is no exception in terms of the good performance of RLGA in artificially created data. RLGA is always the best candidate in efficiency and effectiveness aspects. The training time is reduced around 80%; however, significant improvements on classification rates are gained. RLGA is not only better than normal GAs, but also its counterpart, IGA-RN. The results on 3 artificially created problems are reported in Table 6.

## DISCUSSION

## Rule Number per Chromosome for D-Training

The number of rules per chromosome was usually set at 30 in most research works; however, one-rule chromosome is used in this paper. The main reason is due to the nature of the RLGA's training. In D-training, the aim is to find an expert in some local region. Using one-rule chromosome will force the training to focus on the one single local region (actually, the number of regions could be zero if the Act value is set at

*Table 6. Comparison of different approaches of GA on artificially created data*

| Slant (45') | NGA (fixed rule) | NGA (varied rule) | RLGA | IGA-RN |
|---|---|---|---|---|
| Training time | 27.802 | 19.53 | 2.04 (-89.55%) | 167.185 |
| Ending CR | 0.937 ± 0.017 | 0.927 ± 0.016 | 1.0 ± 0.0 (7.87%) | 0.959 ± 0.024 |
| Test CR | 0.921 ± 0.014 | 0.918 ± 0.017 | 0.976 ± 0.01 (6.35%) | 0.911 ± 0.028 |
| No. Rules | 30 | 23 | 23 | 85.17 |
| Two Circles | NGA (fixed rule) | NGA (varied rule) | RLGA | IGA-RN |
| Training time | 32.463 | 37.05 | 4.72 (-87.26%) | 142.809 |
| Ending CR | 0.75 ± 0.015 | 0.752 ± 0.012 | 1 ± 0.0 (33.07%) | 0.706 ± 0.046 |
| Test CR | 0.728 ± 0.019 | 0.725 ± 0.018 | 0.949 ± 0.009 (30.84%) | 0.656 ± 0.033 |
| No. Rules | 30 | 43 | 43.47 | 74.13 |
| Complex Circles | NGA (fixed rule) | NGA (varied rule) | RLGA | IGA-RN |
| Training time | 12.435 | 34.28 | 8.171 (-76.16%) | 73.979 |
| Ending CR | 0.571 ± 0.02 | 0.594 ± 0.012 | 1 ± 0.0 (68.36%) | 0.567 ± 0.03 |
| Test CR | 0.579 ± 0.09 | 0.586 ± 0.019 | 0.844 ± 0.023 (44.1%) | 0.548 ± 0.027 |
| No. Rules | 30 | 81 | 81.07 | 46.63 |

0). Another issue is about the speed, the memory and CPU consumption of one-rule chromosomes will be minimal; therefore, a faster algorithm can be expected. More importantly, the learning outcome will not be deteriorated due to the usage of shorter chromosomes. It is obvious that several iterations of short-chromosome learning can achieve the same or better effects of one single long chromosome counterpart, because a long chromosome is simply a concatenation of several one-rules chromosomes. Last but not least, it is interesting to note that with the application of one-rule chromosomes, output partitioning is achieved in RLGA as a side-effect. In each D-train, an expert is finally formulated, whose enclosed and learnt patterns are in turn removed. The patterns removed only belong to one single class. Therefore, the problem is also solved in an output-partitioning manner, i.e., we separate patterns according to their output classes and focus each training session on one-class patterns until all patterns are learnt.

Several experiments have been carried out to show the effect of one-rule chromosome. Four benchmark datasets are used here to examine the effect of various rule numbers. For each benchmark problem with given varied rule number, 20 independent RLGA classifiers with varied rule numbers are initialised and the final results regarding time and accuracy are compared. The rule number is chosen as 1, 30, and the number of output classes of that particular classification problem. For example, rule number 1, 2, 30 are used for Cancer data. According to Figure 17, for almost all problems, RLGAs with one-rule chromosomes produce good solutions in testing classification rates, which is in accordance with our expectation that one-rule chromosome at least does not compromise classification results. Figure 18 shows corresponding training time for each test. It is clear that one-rule chromosome always facilitates fast training. For all the tests, the training time of the classifiers with one-rule chromosomes is the shortest among all.

*Figure 17. Examine number of rules per chromosome against CR*

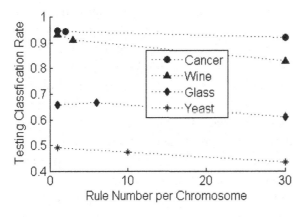

*Figure 18. Examine number of rules per chromosome against training time*

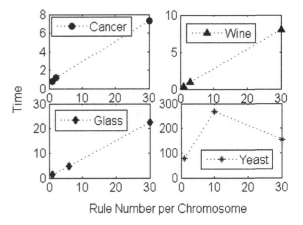

## Search on Optimal Mutation Rate

As discussed, the mutation rate used in this solution is 0.1 rather than 0.01 that is commonly used in traditional GAs training. The reason is that the population in RLGA tends to converge in an early stage. This happens mainly because in each round the population focuses on local performance in some local regions rather than the global performance. The chromosomes in the population easily get trapped and stick into the same local region rather than finding the others, potentially even better solutions. Besides, one-rule chromosome is used, which also makes the population easier to converge. To justify our assumption, several experiments have been done to show that 0.1 is a good parameter for mutation rate in RLGA training. We search the best mutation rate over 4 real-world problems. For each problem, the average testing classification rates over 20 independent runs were recorded as the mutation rates varied from 0 to 1 with step length 0.1. We find that 0.1 is the optimal choice in general in terms of these 4 benchmark tests. The search results are listed in Figure 19. We find that when the mutation rate reaches 0.1, the testing CR is approximately the best. For most of them, the differences between different rates are minor when mutation rate is between 0.1 and 0.9.

*Figure 19. Comparison over different mutation rates against CR*

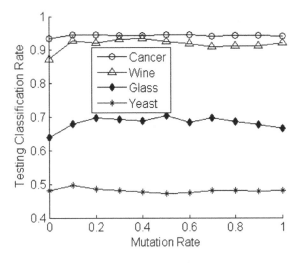

## Observations and Discussion on RLGA

From the experiments on the seven benchmark data sets, we have several remarks on RLGA. First, RLGA is capable of classifying both artificial data sets and real world problems. The performance of RLGA is the best regarding learning time and learning accuracy in comparison with normal GA and IGA-RN. RLGA's performance is even comparable to other sophisticated approaches, including ECCGA (Zhu & Guan, 2008), CCGA (Potter & De Jong, 2000), IGA (Guan & Zhu, 2005) and OIGA (Zhu & Guan, 2005). Table 7 and Table 8

*Table 7. Comparison of various classification methods on yeast*

| Yeast | CCGA | ECCGA | OIGA | RLGA |
|---|---|---|---|---|
| Ending CR | 0.415 | 0.477 | 0.457 | 1.0 |
| Testing CR | 0.391 | 0.435 | 0.414 | 0.496 |

*Table 8. Comparison of various classification methods on glass*

| Glass | CCGA | ECCGA | OIGA | RLGA |
|---|---|---|---|---|
| Ending CR | 0.633 | 0.737 | 0.779 | 1.0 |
| Testing CR | 0.411 | 0.47 | 0.472 | 0.685 |

list several successful classifiers in the literature on Yeast and Glass problem respectively. As we can see from the tables, RLGA achieves both the highest training CR as well as the test CR.

Secondly, equipped with automatic task decomposition and problem-dependent rule number features, RLGA decomposes the problem recursively and produces a problem-dependent rule number as the final solution. The rule number varied from 8 (Wine) to 344 (Yeast), and for each problem, a specific rule number is applied. It is generally believed that the more rules are required, the higher level of classification difficulty the problem has.

Thirdly, RLGA, featuring a top-down problem solver, is generally better than its counterpart, IGA-RN, a bottom-up approach. According to experimental results, IGA-RN usually requires s a larger number of rules; however it does not achieve better performance in general. RLGA makes the training task easier and simpler as training continues by removing learnt patterns. RLGA continues decomposing the learning task and solving the simpler problem. IGA-RN begins its training with one rule, if it finds the problem needs more rules, the rule number will be incremented as need. Because the learnt patterns are not separated from the training data in IGA-RN, the learnt ones and unlearnt are mixed together and the learning task is not made easier. Besides, as the number of rules grows, this approach will need to handle longer chromosomes, which drags down the speed. Moreover, this approach has the risk of rule number explosion, which may trigger system crash due to the limited memory space. The reasons stated above explain why IGA-RN does not perform as expected.

Lastly, the working paradigm of REL-GA is relatively simple when compared with other hybrid or multi-learner algorithms. In those approaches, there will be separated training process: local training and global training, which wastes computation effort. When a global training process identifies a local training region, which requires certain training in global sense, the local training will then take over the task to continue training in that local region in order to produce good solution locally. However, in RLGA, there is no such repeated training process. Once a local region has been trained by a local learner (D-train), the solution obtained from that part can be directly used in the final solution.

There exist also possible improvements that can be made to RLGA. We believe that via certain modification RLGA can be used to solve very complex problems with large input domain. One possible solution is to combine RLGA with OIGA (Guan & Zhu, 2005; Zhu & Guan, 2005). Moreover, RLGA is only applied to solve classification problems currently. However, it can be extended to solve regression problems.

## CONCLUSION

This paper proposed a new GA-based classifier, RLGA, with a unique combination in terms of recursive learning, automatic task and data decomposition, and problem-dependent rule number. Rather than learning the training data in batch, RLGA automatic decomposes the learning data through applying a number of learners to study the partitioned training data. Finally, a specific number of rules will be produced as the final solution looms to solve that specific problem. Through experiments, we found the number of

rules is subject to change according to different problems. This means rule number is a problem-dependent parameter.

By experimenting on different benchmark tests, both real-world classification problems as well as artificially created data, RLGA outperformed normal GA and IGA-RN, another classifier that evolves with a problem-dependent rule number. RLGA spends much less computation time while achieves the best ending and testing CRs, when compared with the others. The improvement shown in these problems are significant, especially for yeast, wine, and glass. Regarding cancer, the improvement is minor; however the computation time is dramatically saved. For all the artificially created data, RLGA is still the best of all.

## REFERENCES

Anand, R., Mehrotra, K., Mohan, C. K., & Ranka, S. (2002). Efficient classification for multiclass problems using modular neural networks. *IEEE Transactions on Neural Networks*, 6(1), 117–124. doi:10.1109/72.363444

Bao, C., Neo, T. N., & Guan, S. U. (2007). Reduced Pattern Training in Pattern Distributor Networks. *Journal of Research and Practice in Information Technology*, 39(4), 273–286.

Blake, C. L., & Merz, C. J. (1998). *UCI repository of machine learning databases*. Retrieved March 14, 2010, from http://archive.ics.uci.edu/ml/

Corcoran, A. L., & Sen, S. (1994). Using real-valued genetic algorithms to evolve rule sets for classification. In *Proceedings of the 1st IEEE Conference on Evolutionary Computation* (Vol. 1, pp. 120-124).

Cordón, O., Herrera, F., Hoffmann, F., & Magdalena, L. (2001). *Evolutionary tuning and learning of fuzzy knowledge bases: Vol. 19 of Advances in Fuzzy Systems - Applications and Theory*. Singapore: World Scientific.

De Jong, K. A. (1988). Learning with genetic algorithms: An overview. *Machine Learning*, *3*(2), 121–138. doi:10.1007/BF00113894

De Jong, K. A., & Spears, W. M. (1991). Learning concept classification rules using genetic algorithms. In *Proceedings of the 12th International Joint Conference on Artificial Intelligence* (Vol. 2). San Francisco, CA: Morgan Kaufmann.

García-Pedrajas, N., Hervás-Martíneza, C., & Muñoz-Pérez, J. (2002). Multi-objective cooperative coevolution of artificial neural networks (multi-objective cooperative networks). *Neural Networks*, *15*(10), 1255–1274. doi:10.1016/S0893-6080(02)00095-3

Guan, S. U., & Li, S. (2001). Incremental learning with respect to new incoming input attributes. *Neural Processing Letters*, *14*(3), 241–260. doi:10.1023/A:1012799113953

Guan, S. U., & Li, S. (2002). Parallel growing and training of neural networks using output parallelism. *IEEE Transactions on Neural Networks*, *13*(3), 542–550. doi:10.1109/TNN.2002.1000123

Guan, S. U., & Liu, J. (2002). Incremental ordered neural network training. *Journal of Intelligent Systems*, *13*(1).

Guan, S. U., & Liu, J. (2004). Incremental neural network training with an increasing input dimension. *Journal of Intelligent Systems*, *12*(3), 137–172.

Guan, S. U., & Ramanathan, K. (2004). Recursive percentage based hybrid pattern (RPHP) training for curve fitting. In *Proceedings of the 2004 IEEE Conference on Cybernetics and Intelligent Systems* (Vol. 1, pp. 445-450).

Guan, S. U., & Ramanathan, K. (2007). Percentage-based Hybrid Pattern Training with Neural Network Specific Crossover. *Journal of Intelligent Systems*, *16*, 1–26. doi:10.1515/JISYS.2007.16.1.1

Guan, S. U., & Zhu, F. (2004). Class decomposition for GA-based classifier agents-a Pitt approach. *IEEE Transactions on Systems, Man, and Cybernetics. Part B, Cybernetics*, *34*(1), 381–392. doi:10.1109/TSMCB.2003.817030

Guan, S. U., & Zhu, F. (2005). An incremental approach to genetic-algorithms-based classification. *IEEE Transactions on Systems, Man, and Cybernetics. Part B, Cybernetics*, *35*(2), 227–239. doi:10.1109/TSMCB.2004.842247

Hua Ang, J., Guan, S. U., Tan, K. C., & Al Mamun, A. (2008). Interference-less neural network training. *Neurocomputing*, *71*(16-18), 3509–3524. doi:10.1016/j.neucom.2007.10.012

Ishibuchi, H., Nakashima, T., & Murata, T. (2002). Performance evaluation of fuzzy classifier systems for multidimensional pattern classification problems. *IEEE Transactions on Systems, Man, and Cybernetics. Part B, Cybernetics*, *29*(5), 601–618. doi:10.1109/3477.790443

Jenkins, R. E., & Yuhas, B. P. (2002). A simplified neural network solution through problem decomposition: The case of the truck backer-upper. *IEEE Transactions on Neural Networks*, *4*(4), 718–720. doi:10.1109/72.238326

Michalewicz, Z. (1996). *Genetic algorithms data structures*. Berlin, Germany: Springer.

Potter, M. A., & De Jong, K. A. (1998). The coevolution of antibodies for concept learning. In *Proceedings of the 5th Parallel Problem Solving from Nature Conference,* Amsterdam, The Netherlands (LNCS 1498, pp. 530-539).

Potter, M. A., & De Jong, K. A. (2000). Cooperative coevolution: An architecture for evolving coadapted subcomponents. *Evolutionary Computation*, *8*(1), 1–29. doi:10.1162/106365600568086

Ramanathan, K., & Guan, S. (2008). Recursive Pattern based Hybrid Supervised Training. *Engineering Evolutionary Intelligent Systems*, *82*, 129–156. doi:10.1007/978-3-540-75396-4_5

Setnes, M., & Roubos, H. (2002). GA-fuzzy modeling and classification: complexity and performance. *IEEE Transactions on Fuzzy Systems, 8*(5), 509–522. doi:10.1109/91.873575

Smith, S. F. (1980). *A learning system based on genetic adaptive algorithms.* Unpublished doctoral dissertation, University of Pittsburgh, Pittsburgh, PA.

Su, L., Guan, S. U., & Yeo, Y. C. (2001). Incremental self-growing neural networks with the changing environment. *Journal of Intelligent Systems, 11*(1), 43–74. doi:10.1515/JISYS.2001.11.1.43

Tan, C. H., Guan, S. U., Ramanathan, K., & Bao, C. (2009). Recursive hybrid decomposition with reduced pattern training. *International Journal of Hybrid Intelligent Systems, 6*(3), 135–146.

Zhu, F., & Guan, S. U. (2005). Ordered incremental training for GA-based classifiers. *Pattern Recognition Letters, 26*(14), 2135–2151. doi:10.1016/j.patrec.2005.04.001

Zhu, F., & Guan, S. U. (2008). Cooperative co-evolution of GA-based classifiers based on input decomposition. *Engineering Applications of Artificial Intelligence, 21*(8), 1360–1369. doi:10.1016/j.engappai.2008.01.009

## APPENDIX

The training algorithm of IGA-RN is listed in Tables 9 and 10. IGA-RN classifier begins training with one rule, and it incrementally increases its chromosomes until no further improvement can be made.

*Table 9. Training algorithm of IGA-RN*

> *epoch=1*
> *initialize $P_{epoch}$ with one-rule length chromosomes*
>   *//initialize a population of chromosomes randomly*
> *Evaluate $P_{epoch}$*
>   *//evaluate each chromosome from P using a fitness function*
>
> *while (stagnation<15) do*
>   *sub-train ($P_{epoch}$)*
>     *if(best CR is not improved)*
>       *stagnation=stagnation+1*
>   *increments $P_{epoch}$, i.e. $P_{epoch} = P_{epoch-1}$*

*Table 10. Sub-train algorithm*

> *t=0*
> *while (not terminate-condition) do*
>       *select P'(t) from P(t)*
>       *crossover P'(t)*
>       *mutate P'(t)*
>       *combine P'(t) and P(t) to generate P(t+1)*
>             *//survival percentage applied*
>       *evaluate P(t+1)*
>       *t=t+1*

How to grow the chromosome, or increment the rule number, is a problem. Through experiments, we found that using the best chromosome from the last generation as the seed and expand that seed by another randomly generated rule is the best solution. The expansion algorithm is shown in Table 11 as well as in Figure 20.

*Table 11. Chromosome expansion algorithm*

$bestChrom = select\ chromosome\ with\ highest\ fitness\ from\ P_{epoch}$
$initialize\ P_{epoch+1}$
$while\ (|P_{epoch}| < populationSize)$
      $clone\ bestChrom'\ from\ bestChrom$
      $expand\ bestChrom'\ by\ one\ rule$
      $store\ bestChrom'\ into\ P_{epoch+1}$
$P_{epoch} = P_{epoch+1}$

*Figure 20. Expansion of chromosomes*

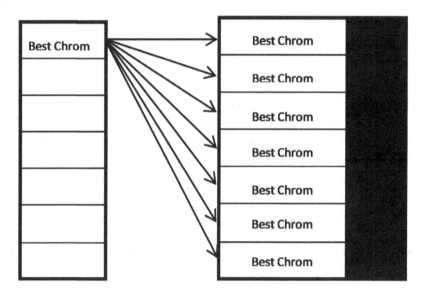

# Chapter 15
# LZW Encoding in Genetic Algorithm

**Worasait Suwannik**
*Kasetsart University, Thailand*

## ABSTRACT

*To solve a problem using Genetic Algorithms (GAs), a solution must be encoded into a binary string. The length of the binary string represents the size of the problem. As the length of the binary string increases, the size of the search space also increases at an exponential rate. To reduce the search space, one approach is to use a compressed encoding chromosome. This paper presents a genetic algorithm, called LZWGA, that uses compressed chromosomes. An LZWGA chromosome must be decompressed using an LZW decompression algorithm before its fitness can be evaluated. By using compressed encoding, the search space is reduced dramatically. For one-million-bit problem, the search space of the original problem is $2^{1000000}$ or about $9.90x10^{301029}$ points. When using a compressed encoding, the search space was reduced to $8.37x10^{166717}$ points. LZWGA can solve one-million-bit OneMax, RoyalRoad, and Trap functions.*

## INTRODUCTION

A Genetic Algorithm (GA) is an algorithm inspired by natural evolution (Mitchell, 1998). To solve a problem using GA, a candidate solution is encoded as a chromosome. Normally, a chromosome is encoded as a fixed length binary string. GA searches in the space of this representation. The length of a chromosome is related to the size of the search space, for $l$-bit chromosomes the search space is $2^l$ points. When $l$ is large, the computational time becomes very long.

There are some approaches to reduce a search space. One approach is to apply a heuristic in an evolution process. For instance, the specific type of crossover is introduced to preserve some constraints can beneficially reduce the search space (Chen & Smith, 1999). The result shows that the proposed crossover can find better solution for a flow shop scheduling problem.

Another approach to reduce the search space is by using compressed encoding. Compressed GA employed compressed encoding chromosome using a format similar to run-length encoding (Suwannik, Kunasol, & Chongstitvatana, 2005). The result shows that Compressed GA uses 805

DOI: 10.4018/978-1-4666-3628-6.ch015

times less fitness evaluations than Simple GA when solving 128-bit OneMax problem. In c²ga, the compressed encoding was combined with compact genetic algorithm (Watchanupaporn, Soonthornphisaj, & Suwannik, 2006). The performance of the c²ga is better than cGA (Harik, Lobo, & Goldberg, 1999) in OneMax and RoyalRoad problems.

To use Compressed GA, an appropriate number of bits of the repetition times (the run length) has to be specified. If the number of bits is too low or too high the effectiveness of compression is suffered. To overcome this problem, Kunasol, Suwannik, and Chongstitvatana (2006) proposed LZWGA. LZWGA uses a compressed encoding that can be decompressed using Lempel-Ziv-Welch (LZW) decompression algorithm. The result shows that LZWGA outperforms Compressed GA for 2048-bit OneMax problem. LZWGA is used to solve one-million-bit OneMax, Royal Road, and Trap problems. The one-million bit problem has an enormous search space. The search space of this problem is $2^{1000000}$ or $9.90 \times 10^{301029}$ points. Solving the problem of this size using any canonical GA is not practical. Using LZWGA, the search space is reduced dramatically. LZWGA can solve one-million-bit OneMax problem in 18 minutes.

This paper summarizes recent researches on LZWGA, which cover various aspects of the algorithm such as selection, crossover, and mutation. This paper is organized as follows. The next section describes LZWGA. The test problems are then explained. The results are reported on selection, crossover, and mutation respectively and a new genetic operator called Shift is described. The final sections provide discussion and conclusions.

## LZWGA

The main difference between LZWGA and Simple GA is that a chromosome is in a compressed format. The LZWGA chromosome has to be decompressed before its fitness can be evaluated. The pseudo code of LZWGA is shown in Figure 1. The algorithm begins by creating the first generation of compressed chromosomes. Before evaluating the fitness of a chromosome, the compressed chromosome is decompressed using LZW Decompression algorithm. The fitness evaluation is performed on the uncompressed chromosome. After that, the new population is created to replace the old population. The algorithm repeats the process of decompression, fitness evaluation, and creating a new population until the termination criterion is met. The algorithm terminates when a solution is found or a maximum generation is reached.

## A. Creating the First Generation

Unlike a canonical GA, a chromosome in LZWGA is encoded as integers. The chromosome in LZWGA is in a compressed format. Each integer is a code for an index of an entry in the dictionary.

*Figure 1. LZWGA pseudo code*

```
Algorithm LZWGA
Z←create_first_generation ()
repeat
        P←decompress(Z)
        evaluate(P)
        Z←create_next_generation(Z)
until is_terminate()
```

A variable $Z$ is the population of compressed chromosome.
A variable $P$ is the population of uncompressed binary chromosomes.

Chromosomes in the first generation are created as a random integer strings with the constraint that the $i^{th}$ integer of a chromosome must not have value greater than $i+1$. The first integer of the chromosome is either 0 or 1 because during the decompression, the dictionary is firstly initialized with 0 and 1.

For example, an LZWGA chromosome that can be successfully decompressed is (1,2,3). The decompression algorithm will output a binary string 111111. A dictionary has the entries ((0,0), (1,1), (2,11) (3,111)). Another valid chromosome is (0,1,2). The decompression algorithm will output a binary string 0101. A dictionary has the entries ((0,0), (1,1), (2,01) (3,10)).

If the $i^{th}$ integer in an LZWGA chromosome is invalid, the dictionary look up in will be failed after the $(i+1)^{th}$ integer is read. An example of an invalid chromosome is (1, 3, 3). Before entering the loop, the input "1" (the $0^{th}$ digit in the chromosome) is read and the algorithm output 1. In the first iteration, the algorithm reads "3" (the $1^{st}$ integer), adds to dictionary the string 11 at the entry 2, and outputs 11. In the second iteration, the algorithm reads "3" (the $2^{nd}$ integer), and fail when trying to execute str("3") (see the pseudo code in Figure 2).

Therefore, in order to generate the value of the $i^{th}$ integer (the first index in the array is 1), a random non-negative integer is modulo with $i+2$.

## B. Decompression

Because the chromosome in LZWGA is compressed, it has to be decompressed before its fitness evaluation. A compressed chromosome is decompressed using LZW decompression algorithm.

The length of the output chromosome is varied. If the length is more than the size of the solution encoding, the excess bits are discarded. After decompression, the decompressed binary string is evaluated. If the length is less than the size of the solution encoding, the chromosome will be evaluated up to the decompressed length. A fitness of a compressed chromosome is equals to the fitness of the decompressed chromosome.

The LZW is a lossless data compression algorithm (Welch, 1984). The compression algorithm starts with a dictionary containing all characters. During the compression, the algorithm dynami-

*Figure 2. LZW Decompress pseudo code*

```
Algorithm LZW Decompress
add 0 and 1 to the dictionary
read one code from input to c
output str(c)
p←c
while input are still left
    read one code from input to c
    if the code c is not in the dictionary
        add str(p)+fc(str(p)) to the dictionary
        output str(p)+fc(str(p))
    else
        add str(p)+fc(str(c)) to the dictionary
        output str(p)
    end if
    p←c
end while

A variable c is used to store a code read from input.
A variable p is the previous value of c.
A function str(code) returns a string associated with code.
A function fc(string) returns the first character in string.
```

cally expands the dictionary and outputs codes that refer to strings in the dictionary. Normally, the number of bits of the code is less than that of the variable length string in the dictionary. Data is compressed when the algorithm replaces the whole string with its code. A nice property of LZW is that the dictionary does not have to be packed with a compressed data. LZW decompression does not require a dictionary because the algorithm can reconstruct the dictionary while processing the compressed data. When using LZW to decompress an English text, the dictionary is initialized with all English characters and symbols. However, in this paper, the output of the decompression algorithm is a binary string. Therefore, the dictionary is initialized with the number 0 and 1. A pseudo code for LZW decompression used in LZWGA is shown in Figure 2.

## C. Creating the Next Generation

LZWGA creates the population of the next generation by selecting, crossing over, and mutating compressed chromosomes. A highly fit chromosome is likely to be selected using any selection methods such as tournament or roulette-wheel selection. Compressed chromosomes can be recombined using single-point, two-point, or uniform crossover. Because each of these crossover methods does not change the position of each integer, it automatically creates valid chromosomes that each integer satisfies the decompression constraint. Therefore, the offspring can be decompressed. Mutation changes an integer in uncompressed chromosome to a random value that satisfied the constraint.

## TEST PROBLEMS

### Standard Benchmark

Standard benchmark in Genetic Algorithms includes OneMax, RoyalRoad, and Trap problems. Each problem models a particular type of opti-

mization problems. The reason that we choose synthetic problems instead of the real problem is because the characteristic of each problem is known. In fact, the characteristic is by designed.

### A. OneMax

OneMax or a bit counting problem is a widely used problem for testing the performance of various genetic algorithms. This problem models an optimization problem which each variable are independent. The problem is formally defined as follows.

$$\text{OneMax}\left(x\right) = \sum_{i=1}^{k} x_i$$

where $x_i$ is the $i^{\text{th}}$ bit of $x$

### B. RoyalRoad

A RoyalRoad functions (Mitchell, Holland, & Forrest, 1994) are defined as:

$$\text{RoyalRoad}\left(x\right) = \sum_{i=1}^{m} \delta_i$$

where

- $k$ is a block size
- $m$ is total block

$\delta_i = \{ k \text{ if } x \in s_i \text{ 0 otherwise}$

For a problem with block size $k$, $s_i$ is a schema that have 1 defined in the range $i \times k$ to $((i+1) \times k) - 1$. All other positions contain a wild card '*'. For example, let $k = 4$.

$s_0 = 1111************$

$s_1 = ****1111********$

$$s_2 = {*}{*}{*}{*}{*}{*}{*}{*}1111{*}{*}{*}{*}$$

$$s_3 = {*}{*}{*}{*}{*}{*}{*}{*}{*}{*}{*}{*}1111$$

The RoyalRoad problem models an optimization problem that some variables depend on other variables.

## C. Trap

A $k$-bit trap functions (Mitchell et al., 1994) are defined as:

$t(b) = \{ k$ ; if $u{=}k$

$k{-}u{-}1$ ; otherwise

where

- $k$ is the block size.
- $b$ is a block in a chromosome $x$.

$u = \sum_{i=1}^{k} b_i$ where $b_i$ is the $i^{th}$ bit of $b$

The trap function are defined as:

$$\text{Trap}_{m \times k}(x) = \sum_{i=1}^{m} t(block(x,i))$$

where

- $m$ is the total block
- $x$ is the chromosome
- $block(x, i)$ return the $i^{th}$ block of $x$

The Trap problem models an optimization problem that some variables depend on other variable and prevents the gradient search.

## Modified Benchmark

LZWGA can find a solution for one-million-bit OneMax, RoyalRoad, and Trap function efficiently. However, those functions have high regularity solution. Chumlamai and Suwannik (2006) proposed new benchmark problems for testing LZWGA and other compressed GA. Those problems are based on standard GA benchmark but the results are created randomly; the solution is not all 1's or all 0's. The proposed benchmarks include RandomMax and RandomRoyalRoad. In this paper, we add RandomTrap to the group of modified benchmarks.

## A. RandomMax

RandomMax is similar to OneMax but the solution is generated randomly before the evolution begins. To evaluate the fitness, we compare each bit in a chromosome with the bit in the same position of the solution. If they are equal, the fitness score is increased by one.

From GA point of view, OneMax and Random-Max have the same difficulty. The fitness curve of solving OneMax and RandomMax are the same. However, LZWGA cannot find a solution for RandomMax problem while it can easily find a solution for OneMax problem.

## B. RandomRoyalRoad

RandomRoyalRoad is similar to RoyalRoad but a solution block is generated randomly before the evolution begins. For example, if a random solution block is 1110. To evaluate the fitness, all bits in a block of an individual should have the same value as the generated block.

## C. RandomTrap

RandomTrap problem is similar to Trap problem but a solution block is generated randomly before the evolution begins. Let $r$ be the randomly generated block. We modified the $u$ function by counting a bit that match with $r$.

$$u = \sum_{i=1}^{k} match(b_i, r_i)$$

where

- $b_i$, $r_i$ is the $i^{th}$ bit of block $b$ and $r$
- $match(b_i, r_i)$ returns 1 if $b_i = r_i$. Otherwise, it returns 0.

## SELECTION

Rotsianglum and Suwannik (2009c) compared three selection operators: tournament, roulette wheel, and rank selection. The test problems are OneMax, RandomMax, RoyalRoad, and Random-RoyalRoad. Tournament selection gives the best result (see Tables 1 through 4).

## CROSSOVER OPERATORS

Crossover operator combines two selected individuals and produces two offspring. In GA, there are several crossover methods such as Single-point, Double-point, and Uniform crossover. Even though LZWGA chromosome is different from GA's, LZWAGA can use the same crossover method as GA.

Numnark and Suwannik (2007, 2008) compared the performance of various crossover methods in LZWGA. Experiments were conducted on one-million-bit OneMax problem and one-million-bit Royal Road problem. The result shows that LZWGA with uniform crossover gives the best performance. After 100 generations, LZWGA with uniform crossover found a solution for OneMax and Royal Road problem with 1.59 and 2.07 times higher fitness than LZWGA with one-point crossover. It found a solution for One-Max and Royal Road problem with 1.61 and 2.59 times higher fitness than LZWGA with two-point crossover. The fitness curve of each crossover method is shown in Figures 3 through 5.

*Table 1. Generation that LZWGA found a solution for OneMax problem*

| Crossover | Selection | | |
|---|---|---|---|
| | Tournament | Roulette Wheel | Rank |
| Uniform | 27 | 97 | 60 |
| One-Point | 28 | 41 | 32 |
| Two-Point | 36 | 55 | 38 |

*Table 2. Generation that LZWGA found a solution for RoyalRoad problem*

| Crossover | Selection | | |
|---|---|---|---|
| | Tournament | Roulette Wheel | Rank |
| Uniform | 28 | 100 | 59 |
| One-Point | 24 | 42 | 34 |
| Two-Point | 28 | 44 | 40 |

*Table 3. Average best fitness when solving RandomMax problem*

| Crossover | Selection | | |
|---|---|---|---|
| | Tournament | Roulette Wheel | Rank |
| Uniform | 623.7 | 589.1 | 596.3 |
| One-Point | 616.4 | 600.8 | 608.0 |
| Two-Point | 608.0 | 595.2 | 598.0 |

*Table 4. Average best fitness when solving RandomRoyalRoad problem*

| Crossover | Selection | | |
|---|---|---|---|
| | Tournament | Roulette Wheel | Rank |
| Uniform | 676.0 | 358.0 | 395.2 |
| One-Point | 418.0 | 619.6 | 594.0 |
| Two-Point | 381.2 | 636.4 | 561.2 |

*Figure 3. Fitness curve of using LZWGA with 1000000-bit OneMax*

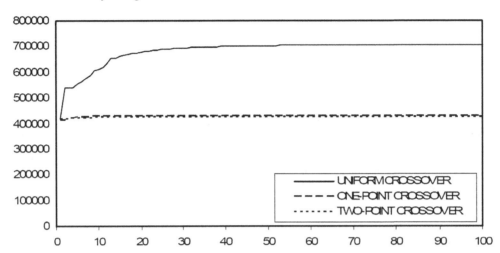

*Figure 4. Fitness curve of using LZWGA with 1000000-bit RoyalRoad, block size 10 bits*

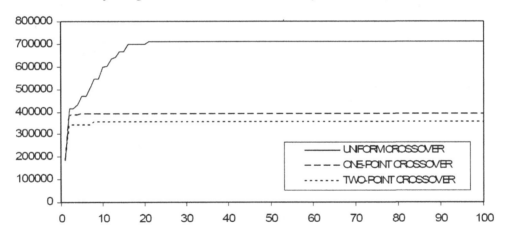

*Figure 5. Fitness curve of using LZWGA with 1000000-bit Royal Road, block size 100 bit*

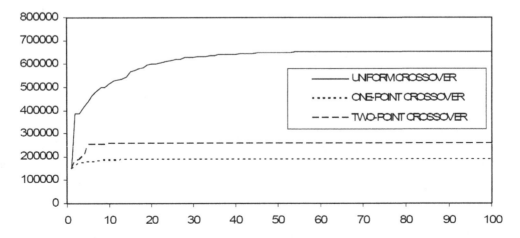

## MUTATION OPERATORS

LZWGA's mutation randomly changes each position in a chromosome to any valid value. The valid value for the $i^{th}$ position in the chromosome is less than $i+2$ (e.g., valid values for the $0^{th}$ position is 0 and 1)

Originally, a mutation rate in LZWGA is equal at every position of an LZWGA chromosome (i.e., the probability that each position will be changed is equal). However, LZWGA has different characteristic from traditional GA. A single change in one position in an LZWGA chromosome may result in several changes in several positions of a GA chromosome. Moreover, a change in different position of an LZWGA chromosome has a different effect on a GA chromosome. Table 5 summarizes an average number of changes in a decompressed chromosome for each mutated position in LZWGA chromosome. A change in the $0^{th}$ and $1^{st}$ positions cause the most changes in a decompressed chromosome. The number of changes decreases at a higher position.

From this observation, a new mutation is proposed. The lower (more to the left) position of LZWGA should have a lower mutation rate than the higher (more to the right) position. An LZWGA chromosome is partitioned into several sub-chromosomes. Every position in the same sub-chromosome has the same mutation rate equals to the following formula.

$$rate(i) = \frac{m}{t - sub(i)}$$

where

- $m$ is the maximum mutation rate
- $t$ is the total sub-chromosomes
- $sub$ is the number of the sub-chromosome of the sub-chromosome of the $i^{th}$ position

For example, a 200-positions LZWGA chromosome, when divided into 10 parts, will have 10 different mutation rates. Each sub-chromosome contains 20 positions.

- The first 20th positions in LZWGA chromosome has a mutation rate equals to $m/(10-0)$, which is the lowest rate.
- The $21^{st}$ to $40^{th}$ positions in LZWGA chromosome has a mutation rate equals to $m/(10-0)$.
- The $41^{st}$ to $60^{th}$ positions in LZWGA chromosome has a mutation rate equals to $m/(10-2)$.
- The last $20^{th}$ positions in LZWGA chromosome has a mutation rate equals to $m+(10-9)$ or $m$, which is the highest mutation rate.

A change in different LZWGA positions is not equal. We compared the performance of LZWGA with an original mutation and with a proposed mutation. We found that the proposed mutation can speed up the search in LZWGA and shorter LZWGA chromosomes.

We conducted an experiment on 10,000 to 1,000,000-bit OneMax problem. The result shows that the proposed mutation method can solve the

*Table 5. Average number of bits in GA chromosome after changing in one position in an LZWGA chromosome*

| Position | Chromosome length | | | | | | |
|---|---|---|---|---|---|---|---|
| | 2 | 3 | 4 | 5 | 6 | 7 | 8 |
| 0 | 1.67 | 2.25 | 2.90 | 3.61 | 4.36 | 5.15 | 5.99 |
| 1 | 1.33 | 2.17 | 2.97 | 3.81 | 4.71 | 5.65 | 6.64 |
| 2 | | 1.39 | 2.12 | 2.85 | 3.62 | 4.42 | 5.26 |
| 3 | | | 1.50 | 2.21 | 2.92 | 3.66 | 4.44 |
| 4 | | | | 1.57 | 2.28 | 2.99 | 3.73 |
| 5 | | | | | 1.64 | 2.35 | 3.06 |
| 6 | | | | | | 1.69 | 2.41 |
| 7 | | | | | | | 1.75 |

problem using shorter compressed chromosome length. Moreover, with equal chromosome length, the proposed mutation method can produce a solution with 64% higher fitness.

## SHIFT OPERATOR

In an experiment of solving RoyalRoad problem, Rotsianglum and Suwannik (2009a) set the LZWGA chromosome length to 47 positions and the solution is the maximum length that the LZWGA chromosome can decompressed, which is 47×48/2 or 1,128 bits. The best solution that LZWGA can find is almost correct. The difference from the real solution is the position of the integers. Therefore, they proposed a shift operator for LZWGA. A shift operator randomly selects a shift position and left-shifts numbers in an LZWGA chromosome with some condition.

The pseudo code of this operator is as follows.

```
r←random(length) // random a number
between 0 and length exclusively
for i = r to length-1
 if a_{i+1} mod (_{i+1}) = 0 and a_{i+1} != 0
 a_i = a_{i+1}-1
 else
 a_i = a_{i+1}
 end
end
```

They tested the shift operator with RoyalRoad and RandomRoyalRoad. The result shows that a shift operator for LZWGA can produce a chromosome that has 33% better fitness.

Note that originally, in the paper, there are two version of the shift operator. The one that we describe in this paper is the one that originally called shift-and-check operator.

To analyze the operator, Rotsianglum and Suwannik (2009b) generated every possible chromosome of the length 4 to 8 and selected each position for shifting. They analyzed the operator using OneMax, RoyalRoad, RandomMax, and RandomRoyalRoad. The result shows that the shift operator can produce a chromosome whose fitness is higher than or equal to the original one with probability greater than 0.5 (Figure 6). Table 6 shows the analysis data in more detail.

As in the variable rate mutation, the unequal effect of changes in various compressed chromosome position to a decompressed chromosome is also exploited in Shift operator. The variable-rate shift operator performs better than the fixed-rate shift (Rotsianglum & Suwannik, 2010). The probability that shifting will occur at the $i^{th}$ position is as follows.

$$p_i = \frac{w_i}{\sum_{j=1}^{n} w_j}$$

where

- $n$ is a chromosome length
- $w_i = n - i + 1$.

## DISCUSSION

LZWGA speeds up search by reducing the size of the search space and reducing the time per generation.

The search space of LZWGA is much smaller than that of GA. However, if the search space is too small, a solution might not exist in this space. For example, if the length of the chromosome is 10 digits, the chromosome cannot be decompressed to one million bit. In general, if we set the LZWGA chromosome length too low, it will not be able to find a solution. On the contrary, if we set the length too high, the search space will become larger and it will likely take longer to solve a problem.

Although LZWGA adds a decompression step before the fitness evaluation, the algorithm can run

*Figure 6. Probability that a chromosome will have fitness higher than or equal to an original chromosome after shifting*

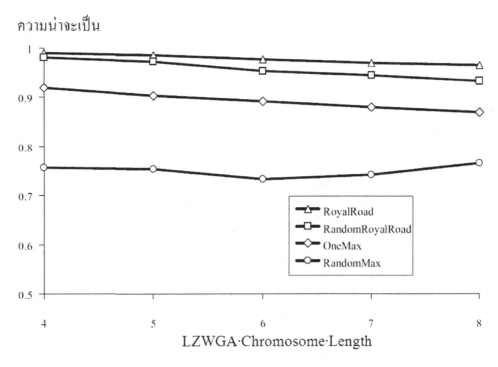

faster than GA in several cases. This is because the decompression step adds only a linear time factor to the complexity of the algorithm. LZW Decompress has the time complexity of $O(n)$, where $n$ is the length of uncompressed string. If the complexity of fitness evaluation for a particular problem is higher than linear, the decompression time will not be a dominant factor. Moreover, in terms of CPU time, a single iteration of LZWGA is much faster than Simple GA. The main factor is the size

of chromosome. For very long chromosomes, it is likely that the computational time is dominated by the access to large size data structure which renders cache memory ineffective. For example, the time spent in creating the next generation in GA with very long chromosome is much longer than in LZWGA with compressed chromosome. Moreover, new types of evolutionary algorithms such as Bayesian Optimization Algorithm (BOA) cannot handle very large problems in short amount

*Table 6. Number of chromosomes that when shifted has the fitness higher than or equal to the original chromosome*

| Length | Total Chromosomes | Problems | | | |
|---|---|---|---|---|---|
| | | OM | RR | RM | RRR |
| 4 | 480 | 441 | 363 | 475 | 471 |
| 5 | 3,600 | 3,252 | 2,715 | 3,548 | 3,497 |
| 6 | 30,240 | 26,928 | 22,174 | 29,540 | 28,825 |
| 7 | 282,240 | 248,157 | 209,327 | 273,577 | 266,326 |
| 8 | 2,903,040 | 2,523,477 | 2,220,282 | 2,802,036 | 2,704,113 |

of time. The limitation of the problem size that the original implementation of BOA can handle is 32767 bits (Pelikan, 1999).

## CONCLUSION

LZWGA bridges two different types of algorithms: evolutionary algorithm and lossless compression algorithm. The future work would investigate combination of lossy compression and genetic algorithms. The higher compression ratio of lossy compression algorithms could reduce the search space even more than the lossless compression encoding GA.

Recent researches in evolution algorithm focus on solving very large scale problem and population modeling (Sastry, Goldberg, & Llorà, 2007; Suwannik & Chongstitvatana, 2008). Currently, we are beginning to investigate the combination of using compressed encoding with population modeling (Watchanupaporn & Suwannik, 2010a, 2010b). The future work is to model dependencies between positions in LZW chromosomes.

## REFERENCES

Chen, S., & Smith, S. (1999). Improving Genetic Algorithms by Search Space Reduction (with Applications to Flow Shop Scheduling). In *Proceedings of the Genetic and Evolutionary Computation Conference (GECCO-99)*. San Francisco, CA: Morgan Kaufmann.

Chumlamai, S., & Suwannik, W. (2007). Benchmark Problems for Compressed Genetic Algorithm. In *Proceedings of the Electrical Engineering Conference (EECON-30)* (pp. 653-656).

Harik, G. R., Lobo, F. G., & Goldberg, D. E. (1999). The compact genetic algorithm. *IEEE Transactions on Evolutionary Computation, 3*(4), 287–297. doi:10.1109/4235.797971

Kunasol, N., Suwannik, W., & Chongstitvatana, P. (2006). Solving One-Million-Bit Problems Using LZWGA. In *Proceedings of International Symposium on Communications and Information Technologies (ISCIT)* (pp. 32-36).

Lobo, F. G., Deb, K., Goldberg, D. E., Harik, G., & Wang, L. (1998). Compressed Introns in a Linkage Learning Genetic Algorithm. In *Proceedings of the 3rd Annual Conference on Genetic Programming,* Madison, WI (pp. 551-558).

Mitchell, M. (1998). *Introduction to Genetic Algorithm*. Cambridge, MA: MIT Press.

Mitchell, M., Holland, J., & Forrest, S. (1994). When Will a Genetic Algorithm Outperform Hill Climbing? *Advances in Neural Information Processing Systems, 6*, 51–58.

Numnark, S., & Suwannik, W. (2007). A Comparison of Crossover Methods in LZWGA. In *Proceedings of the 3rd National Conference on Computing and Information Technology (NCCIT)* (pp. 328-333).

Numnark, S., & Suwannik, W. (2008). Improving the Performance of LZWGA by Using a New Mutation Method. In *Proceedings of the IEEE Conference on Evolutionary Computation (CEC 2008)* (pp. 1862-1865).

Pelikan, M. (1999). *A Simple Implementation of the Bayesian Optimization Algorithm (BOA) in C++ (version 1.0)* (Tech. Rep. No. 99011). Urbana, IL: University of Illinois at Urbana-Champaign.

Rotsianglum, A., & Suwannik, W. (2009a). Shift Operator in LZWGA. In *Proceedings of National Conference on Computing and Information Technology (NCCIT)* (pp. 320-325).

Rotsianglum, A., & Suwannik, W. (2009b, October 28-30). A Performance Analysis of a Shift-and-Check Operator in LZWGA. In *Proceedings of the Electrical Engineering Conference (EECON-32)*.

Rotsianglum, A., & Suwannik, W. (2009c). Comparing the Performance of LZWGA with Various Selection Methods. In *Proceedings of the 2009 National Computer Science and Engineering Conference (NCSEC 2009)* (pp. 198-203).

Rotsianglum, A., & Suwannik, W. (2010). An Improved Shift-and-Check Operator for LZWGA. In *Proceedings of the Joint Conference on Computer Science and Software Engineering (JCSSE)* (pp. 12-16).

Sastry, K., Goldberg, D. E., & Llorà, X. (2007). *Towards billion bit optimization via efficient genetic algorithms* (Tech. Rep. No. 2007007). Urbana, IL: University of Illinois at Urbana-Champaign.

Suwannik, W., & Chongstitvatana, P. (2008). Solving One-Billion-Bit Noisy OneMax Problem using Estimation Distribution Algorithm with Arithmetic Coding. In *Proceedings of IEEE Conference on Evolutionary Computation* (pp. 1203-1206).

Suwannik, W., Kunasol, N., & Chongstitvatana, P. (2005). Compressed Genetic Algorithm. In *Proceedings of Northeastern Computer Science and Engineering Conference* (pp. 203-211).

Watchanupaporn, O., Soonthornphisaj, N., & Suwannik, W. (2006). A Performance Analysis of Compressed Compact Genetic Algorithm. *ECTI-CIT Journal, 2*(2).

Watchanupaporn, O., & Suwannik, W. (2010a). Conditional Probability Mutation in LZWGA. In *Proceedings of the International ACM Conference on Management of Emergent Digital EcoSystems (ACM MEDES)*.

Watchanupaporn, O., & Suwannik, W. (2010b). An Estimation of Distribution Algorithm using the LZW Compression Algorithm. In *Proceedings of the International Conference on Advanced Cognitive Technologies and Applications (IARIA Cognitive)* (pp. 97-102).

Welch, T. A. (1984). A Technique for High-Performance Data Compression. *Computer, 17*(6), 8–19. doi:10.1109/MC.1984.1659158

*This work was previously published in the International Journal of Applied Evolutionary Computation, Volume 2, Issue 4, edited by Wei-Chiang Samuelson Hong, pp. 25-36, copyright 2011 by IGI Publishing (an imprint of IGI Global).*

# Chapter 16

# Usage Profile Generation from Web Usage Data Using Hybrid Biclustering Algorithm

**R. Rathipriya**
*Periyar University, India*

**K. Thangavel**
*Periyar University, India*

**J. Bagyamani**
*Government Arts College, Dharmapuri, India*

## ABSTRACT

*Biclustering has the potential to make significant contributions in the fields of information retrieval, web mining, and so forth. In this paper, the authors analyze the complex association between users and pages of a web site by using a biclustering algorithm. This method automatically identifies the groups of users that show similar browsing patterns under a specific subset of the pages. In this paper, mutation operator from Genetic Algorithms is incorporated into the Binary Particle Swarm Optimization (BPSO) for biclustering of web usage data. This hybridization can increase the diversity of the population and help the particles effectively escape from the local optimum. It detects optimized user profile group according to coherent browsing behavior. Experiments are performed on a benchmark clickstream dataset to test the effectiveness of the proposed algorithm. The results show that the proposed algorithm has higher performance than existing PSO methods. The interpretation of this biclustering results are useful for marketing and sales strategies.*

## 1. INTRODUCTION

With the speedy growth of the World Wide Web (WWW), the study of knowledge discovery in web, modeling and predicting the user's access on a web site has become very important .Web usage mining is a researching area that studies the mining of usage data from the web log files. Its objective is to mine web log files to discover relations among users regarding their browsing interest (Chakraborty & Maka, 2005).

From the business and application point of view, knowledge obtained from the Web usage patterns could be directly applied to efficiently manage activities related to e-Business, e-CRM, e-Services, e-Education, e-Newspapers, e-Gov-

DOI: 10.4018/978-1-4666-3628-6.ch016

ernment, Digital Libraries, and so on (Abhraham & Ramos, 2003). Jespersen, Throhauge, and Bach Pedersen (2002) proposed a hybrid approach for analyzing the visitor click stream sequences.

A user profile (Chen & Shahabi, 2001) is a collection of personal information. The information is stored without adding further description or interpreting this information. It represents cognitive skills, intellectual abilities, intention of browsing, browsing styles, preferences and interactions with the pages of specific web sites. User profiling is the process that refers to construction of user profile via the extraction from a set of data and it is a fundamental task in web personalization.

In Martín-Bautista, Kraft, Vila, Chen, and Cruz (2004) and Martín-Bautista, Vila, and Escobar-Jeria (2008), two types of profiles are proposed. They are simple profiles which are represented by data extracted from the users' interest and the extended profiles containing the additional information about the user such as the age, the language level, location and others. Mobasher, Cooley, and Srivastava (1999) and Mobasher, Dai, Luo, Nakagawa, Sun, and Wiltshire (2000) proposed the web personalization system, which consists of offline tasks related to the mining if usage data and online process of automatic Web page customization based on the knowledge discovered. The LumberJack model proposed by Chi, Rosien, and Heer (2002) builds up user profiles by combining both clustering of user sessions and traditional statistical traffic analysis using k–means algorithm.

Li (2009) has attempted to provide an up-to-date survey of the rapidly growing area of Web session clustering and analyzed the shortcoming of traditional similarity measurement between web sessions. They proposed a framework of Web scssion clustering using sequence alignment in computational biology. Lee and Fu (2008) used hierarchical agglomerative clustering to cluster users' browsing behaviors. In this paper, an improved Two Levels of Prediction Model was presented to achieve higher hit ratio which did not suffer from

the heterogeneity user's behavior. Labroche (2007) proposed a comparison of relational clustering algorithms on web usage data to characterize user access profiles. These methods only rely on numerical values that represents the distance or the dissimilarity between web user sessions to construct web user profiles.

In the literature, in order to obtain the user profiles from web usage data, clustering and association rules (Agrawal, Imielinski, & Swami, 1993) are applied frequently. User profiles derived from the clustering results can be utilized to guide strategies of marketing according to the groups (Krishnapuram, Joshi, & Nasraoui, 2001). The association rules discover associations and correlations among items where the presence of an item or group of them in a transaction implies the presences of other items (Agrawal et al., 1993). Association rules are used to identify the relations among visits of users with a certain navigational pattern to the web site. In Alam, Dobbie, and Riddle (2008), swarm intelligence based PSO-clustering algorithm for the clustering of Web user sessions is proposed, in which author claimed that PSO clustering approach performs better than the benchmark k-means clustering algorithm for clustering Web usage sessions.

In Rambharose and Nikov (2010), various Computational Intelligence (CI) models such as Fuzzy Systems, Genetic Algorithms, Neural Networks, Artificial Immune Systems, Particle Swarm Optimization, Ant Colony Optimization, Bee Colony Optimization and Wasp Colony Optimization for personalization of interactive web systems are reviewed and compared regarding their inception, functions, performance and application to personalization of interactive web systems. But, PSO was credited with good performance as compared to the other methods. In Premalatha and Natarajan (2010), the modification strategies are proposed in PSO using GA. Experiment results are examined with benchmark functions and results show that the proposed hybrid models outperform the standard PSO.

Much research is being done in the area of Web Usage Mining (Martín-Bautista et al., 2004; Pallis, Angelis, & Vakali, 2005) and application of PSO to various fields, based on the goals of the analyst and applications, various algorithms can be applied for cluster analysis. When a clustering method is used for grouping users, it typically partitions users according to their similar browsing interest under all pages. But, it is often the case that some web users' behavior is correlated only on a subset of pages and their behavior is uncorrelated over the rest of the pages of a web site. Therefore, traditional clustering methods failed to identify users groups based on the subset of pages of a website.

To overcome this issue, concept of biclustering (Madeira & Oliveira, 2004) was introduced to identify set of users with correlated browsing pattern under subset of pages. Biclustering attempts to cluster web user and web pages simultaneously based on the users' behavior recorded in the form of click stream data.

The main goal of this paper is to identify pattern based bicluster rather than similar value based bicluster. To achieve this, correlation based merit function is used to capture not only the closeness of values of certain leading indicators but also the closeness of (purchasing, browsing, etc.) patterns exhibited by the users/customers. This type of similarity has a wide range of applications such as E-commerce applications, collaborative filtering, recommendation and marketing. Most of the biclustering algorithms (Chakraborty & Maka, 2005; Banka & Mitra, 2006; Bagyamani, Thangavel, & Rathipri, 2011) in the literature are widely applied to the gene expression data. In web mining area, there is no related work that has been applied biclustering algorithms for discovering the usage profiles from clickstream data using Binary PSO. These usage profiles are generated by using correlation based fitness function and hence it contains group of users whose browsing patterns are highly correlated. In this work, Binary PSO is used as optimization tool to extract the optimized

usage profiles (in terms of optimized biclusters) because of its simplicity and fast convergence.

The paper presents Binary PSO (BPSO) algorithm for biclustering of clickstream. This algorithm is hybrid of BPSO with mutation operator from genetic algorithm. This method detects the highly correlated usage profiles from clickstream data which can be used to improve the web site management and web personalization by providing recommendations.

The paper is organized as follows. Section 2 presents a brief introduction to the biclustering techniques and its applications. Section 3 describes in details the proposed BPSO with genetic mutation based biclustering algorithm for user profiling. The experimental results are presented and discussed in section 4. Section 5 concludes the paper.

## 2. METHODS AND MATERIALS

### 2.1 User Profiles

A user profile is a collection of personal information. If the person knows what he or she is looking for, e.g., when browsing the Web for no specific purpose, knowing the user's additional interests could be used to predict the user's intention for browsing a page of website. Certainly this mode of personalization seems to be of increasing importance in the E-commerce applications.

### 2.2 Biclustering Technique

In data mining, biclustering is defined as the process of simultaneous clustering of rows and column of a data matrix A(U,P) (Figure 1). For user subset U' $\subseteq$ U and page subset P' $\subseteq$ P, A(U',P') denotes the sub-matrix called bicluster of A(U,P). Biclustering algorithms obtain a set of users with the same behavior over a group of pages from web usage data.

*Figure 1. Examples of the different types of biclusters: (a) bicluster with constant rows, (b) bicluster with constant columns, (c) bicluster of additive model on the rows, (d) bicluster of multiplicative model on the rows, (e) bicluster of linear model on the rows, (f) bicluster of linear model (e) with noise, (g) bicluster with order preserved rows, and (h) bicluster with coherent evolution*

| 1 | 1 | 1 | 1 |
|---|---|---|---|
| 2 | 2 | 2 | 2 |
| 5 | 5 | 5 | 5 |
| 3 | 3 | 3 | 3 |

(a)

| 1 | 3 | 7 | 2 |
|---|---|---|---|
| 1 | 3 | 7 | 2 |
| 1 | 3 | 7 | 2 |
| 1 | 3 | 7 | 2 |

(b)

| 1 | 2 | 5 | 0 |
|---|---|---|---|
| 2 | 3 | 6 | 1 |
| 4 | 5 | 8 | 3 |
| 5 | 6 | 9 | 4 |

(c)

| 1 | 3 | 2 | 1 |
|---|---|---|---|
| 2 | 6 | 4 | 2 |
| 3 | 9 | 6 | 3 |
| 5 | 15 | 10 | 5 |

(d)

| 1 | 2 | 3 | 1 |
|---|---|---|---|
| 3 | 4 | 5 | 3 |
| 5 | 7 | 9 | 5 |
| 6 | 9 | 12 | 6 |

(e)

| 1.1 | 1.5 | 2.9 | 0.9 |
|---|---|---|---|
| 3.1 | 4.0 | 4.8 | 3.2 |
| 5.0 | 6.8 | 9.1 | 5.3 |
| 5.9 | 8.9 | 12 | 5.7 |

(f)

| 70 | 13 | 19 | 10 |
|---|---|---|---|
| 53 | 40 | 49 | 35 |
| 40 | 20 | 27 | 15 |
| 90 | 15 | 20 | 12 |

(g)

| ↗ | ↗ | ↘ | ↗ |
|---|---|---|---|
| ↘ | ↘ | ↗ | ↘ |
| → | ↗ | ↘ | ↗ |
| ↘ | ↘ | ↗ | ↘ |

(h)

Madeira and Oliveira (2004) distinguish basically four different categories of biclusters. They are constant biclusters, biclusters with constant values on columns or rows, biclusters with coherent values, and biclusters with coherent evolutions.

## 2.2.1 Coherent Biclusters

Coherent Bicluster is a bicluster with coherent values exhibiting a particular form of covariance between rows and columns. Consider the user access data matrix in Table 1.

If we consider all pages, users 1, 2, and 4 do not seem to behave similarly since their hit count values are uncorrelated under page 2, while users 1 and 2 have an increased hit count value from page 1 to page 2, the hits of user 4 drops from page 1 to page 2. However, these users behave similarly under pages 1, 3, and 4 since all their hit count values increase from page 1 to page 3 and decrease for page 4. This cluster is identified by the biclustering method and it is called as coherent biclusters. In contrast to clustering, a biclustering method produces biclusters, each of which identifies a set of users and a set of pages under which these users behave similarly (Figure 2).

## 2.2.2 Coherent Evolution Bicluster

In this type, biclusters are represented by a set of rows and columns, where the changes of attribute values are common among attribute pairs for all participating rows not in the exact quantity, but only in the fact, that a change happens at all. Some

*Table 1. User access data matrix*

|  | Page1 | Page2 | Page3 | Page4 |
|---|---|---|---|---|
| User 1 | 0 | 5 | 5 | 2 |
| User 2 | 5 | 20 | 9 | 5 |
| User 3 | 10 | 10 | 20 | 6 |
| User 4 | 5 | 0 | 8 | 4 |

*Figure 2. Pattern expressed by the bicluster*

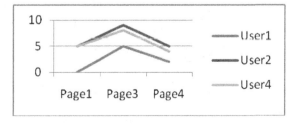

approaches require the change of attribute values to exhibit the same direction (either increasing or decreasing).

## 2.3 Mean Squared Residue Score (MSRS)

One of the most used quality measure for bicluster is Mean Squared Residue or H – Score. Cheng and Church (2000) defined MSR of a bicluster denoted by H (I' J') as

$$H\ (I'\ J')\ = \frac{1}{|I'||J'|} \sum_{i \in I', j \in J'} r(e_{ij})^2$$

where $r(e_{ij}) = e_{ij} - e_{I'j} - e_{iJ'} + e_{I'J'}$

$$e_{I'j} \frac{1}{|I'|} \sum_{i \in I'} e_{ij}$$

$$=, e_{iJ'} = \frac{1}{|J'|} \sum_{j \in J'} e_{ij}$$

and $e_{I'J'} = \frac{1}{|I'||J'|} \sum_{i \in I', j \in J'} e_{ij}$  (1)

## 2.4 Average Correlation Value (ACV)

The ACV measures the average pair-wise correlation between all pairs of users in a bicluster. It is used to evaluate the homogeneity of a bicluster. Matrix $B = (b_{ij})$ has the ACV which is defined by the following function, evaluating a bicluster is the ACV (Bagyamani et al., 2011) defined as

$$ACV = \max \left\{ \begin{array}{c} \dfrac{\sum_i^m = 1 \ \sum_j^m 1 \,|\, c\_row_{ij}\,| - m}{m^2 - m}, \\ \dfrac{\sum_j^n = 1 \ \sum_j^n = 1\,|\,c\_col_{ij}\,| - n}{n^2 - n} \end{array} \right\}$$  (2)

where $c\_row_{ij}$ is the correlation coefficient between rows 'i' and 'j' and $c\_col_{ij}$ is the correlation coefficient between columns 'i' and 'j'.

The correlation between two rows i and j is defined as follows

$$\sum_{i=0}^n (row_i - mean(row_i))$$
$$= \frac{(row_j - mean(row_j))}{(n-1)s_i s_j}$$  (3)

where n is the number of elements in the row and $s_i$ and $s_j$ are the standard deviation of $row_i$ and $row_j$. Similarly $c\_col_{kl}$ is calculated. A high ACV suggests high similarities among the users or pages. ACV can tolerate translation as well as scaling. ACV is robust to noise and works well for non-perfect biclusters, i.e., coherent biclusters. It can be observed that the bicluster with perfect shifting and scaling patterns has an average correlation value of 1 while that the bicluster without these patterns have an average correlation value close to 0. In this work, biclusters with highly correlated users and high volume are preferred.

Table 2 shows a comparison among variance, mean squared residue score and ACV of the biclusters in Figure 1. MSRS change dramatically with the magnitude of the bicluster. It also shows that ACV is more robust for different types of biclusters than the alternatives.

## 2.5 Preprocessing of Clickstream Data

Data Preprocessing is the important stage in the mining process. It is a pre-requisite phase and time consuming process before the data can be mined to obtain useful and interesting patterns. It preprocessed the web usage data, i.e., clickstream data to the data matrix format which is more suitable to apply the biclustering technique. Clickstream is a sequence of Uniform Resource Locators (URLs) browsed by the user within a particular period of time. To discover pattern of group of users with similar interest and motivation for visiting the particular website can be found by biclustering.

Let A(U,P) be an n x m matrix, in which rows represent the users $U=\{u_1, u_2, \ldots, u_n\}$ and the columns represent the pages $P=\{p_1, p_2, \ldots, p_m\}$. The element $a_{ij}$ of A(U,P) represents frequency visit of the $p_j$ of P by user $u_i$ of U during a given period of time.

$$a_{ij} = \begin{cases} Hits(i,j) \ if \ p_j \ is \ visited \ by \ u_i \\ 0, \ otherwise \end{cases} \quad (4)$$

where Hits(i,j) is the frequency of visit of page $p_j$ of P by the user $u_i$ of U

## 2.6 Initial Biclusters

Initial biclusters are generated from preprocessed clickstream data in two ways. They are Two-Way K-Means clustering and Greedy Search Procedure.

### 2.6.1 Two-Way K-Means Clustering

Given a web user access matrix A, let $k_u$ be the number of clusters on user dimension and $k_p$ be the number of clusters on page dimension after K-Means clustering is applied. $C^u$ is the set of user clusters and $C^p$ is the set of page clusters. Let $c_i^u$ be a subset of users and $c_i^u \ C^u$ ($1 \le i \le k_u$). Let $c_j^p$ be a subset of pages and $c_j^p \ C^p$ ($1 \le j \le k_p$). The pair ($c_i^u$, $c_j^p$) denotes a bicluster of A . By combining the results of user dimensional clustering and page dimensional clustering, $k_u \times k_p$ biclusters are obtained. These correlated biclusters are called initial biclusters.

### 2.6.2 Biclustering using Greedy Search Procedure

A greedy algorithm repeatedly executes a search procedure which tries to maximize the size of bicluster obtained from Two-Way K-Means Clustering, based on examining local conditions, with

*Table 2. Comparison among average variance, MSRS and ACV*

| | a | b | C | d | E | f | 9 |
|---|---|---|---|---|---|---|---|
| MSRS | 0 | 0 | 0 | 1.50 | 0.47 | 0.60 | 125.6 |
| ACV | 1 | 1 | 1 | 1 | 1 | 0.98 | 0.9 |

the hope that the outcome will lead to a desired outcome for the global problem. This approach employs simple strategies that are easy to implement and most of the time quite efficient.

In this paper, greedy search procedure is used to improve the quality and volume of the initial biclusters obtained from the Two-Way K-Means clustering of A.

## 2.7 Particle Representation

The algorithm uses particles which represent the binary encoded biclusters of the data set in a vector of length N+M (Figure 3), where N and M are the number of rows (users) and of columns (pages) of the user access matrix, respectively. Each of the first N bits of the binary string is related to the rows, in the order in which the bits appear in the string and in the same way, the remaining M bits are related to the columns. If a bit is set to 1, it means that the relative row or column belongs to the encoded bicluster, otherwise it does not.

*Pseudocode of biclustering uisng greedy search procedure*

```
Step 1: Start with initial bicluster.
Step 2: For each bicluster B (U, P)
i. Collect users and pages not in B.
ii. Add user/page to the bicluster B
sequentially which increase the ACV
of B
iii. Remove user/page from the bi-
cluster B sequentially which increase
the ACV of B
 End for
Step 3. Return optimized biclusters
```

## 2.8 Mutation Operator

In natural evolution, mutation is a random process where one allele of a gene is replaced by another to produce a new genetic structure. In Genetic Algorithms, mutation is randomly applied with low probability, typically in the range 0.001 and 0.01, and modified elements in the chromosomes. In this algorithm, population is the set of binary encoded biclusters. At each generation, binary mutation flips the value of the bit of particle's position at the loci selected to be the mutation point. Generally, mutation is applied uniformly to an entire population of strings, it is possible that a given binary string may be mutated at more than one point. This operation insures diversity in the population over long periods of time and prevents stagnation in the convergence of the optimization technique.

## 2.9 Binary Particle Swarm Optimization with Genetic Mutation

The proposed system is based on population-based heuristic search technique, which can be used to solve combinatorial optimization problems, modeled on the concepts of Cultural and social rules derived from the analysis of the swarm intelligence (PSO) with GA operator such as mutation. In standard PSO the non-oscillatory route can quickly cause a particle to stagnate and also it may prematurely converge on suboptimal solutions that are not even guaranteed to local optimal solution.

In this paper a modification strategy is proposed for the binary particle swarm optimization (BPSO) algorithm and applied for biclustering of clickstream data. This strategy adds reproduction to the particles. Reproduction mechanism is used to avoid the premature convergence of the swarm particles using genetic mutation when they stuck at the local maximum and produce better results.

The particle swarm optimization (PSO) technique is a population-based evolutionary algorithm developed by Kenney and Eberhart in 1995 and Khosla, Kumar, Aggarwal, and Singh (2006). PSO has been developed through simulation of the social behavior of organisms, e.g., fish in a school or birds in a flock. The method is similar to a genetic algorithm, in which particles are initialized within a random population and search for global optimal solutions at each generation. However, PSO is not suitable for optimization problems in a discrete feature space. Hence, Kenney and Eberhart (1997) developed binary PSO (BPSO) to overcome this problem.

The basic elements of BPSO are briefly introduced below:

1.  **Population:** A swarm (population) consists of N particles.

2.  **Particle Position, $x_i$:** Each candidate solution can be represented by a D-dimensional vector; the $i^{th}$ particle can be described as $x_i = (x_{i1}, x_{i2}, \ldots x_{iD})$ where $x_{iD}$ is the position of the $i^{th}$ particle with respect to the $D^{th}$ dimension.

3.  **Particle Velocity, $v_i$:** The velocity of the $i^{th}$ particle is represented by $v_i = (v_{i1}, v_{i2}, \ldots, v_{iD})$, where $v_{iD}$ is the velocity of the $i^{th}$ particle with respect to the $D^{th}$ dimension. In addition, the velocity of a particle is limited within $[Vmin, Vmax]^D$.

4.  **Inertia Weight, w:** The inertia weight is used to control the impact of the previous velocity of a particle on the current velocity. This control parameter affects the trade-off

*Figure 3. Encoded bicluster of length N+M*

| $u_1$ | $u_2$ | $u_3$ | $u_4$ | ........................... | $u_{N-1}$ | $u_N$ | $p_1$ | $p_2$ | ......... | $p_M$ |
|---|---|---|---|---|---|---|---|---|---|---|

between the exploration and exploitation abilities of the particles.

5. **Individual Best, pbest$_i$:** pbest$_i$ is the position of the i$^{th}$ particle with the highest fitness value at a given iteration.

6. **Global Best, gbest:** The best position of all pbest particles is called global best.

7. **Stopping Criteria:** The process is stopped after the maximum allowed number of iterations is reached. Otherwise, the convergence of gbest is met.

The velocity and position update step is responsible for the optimization ability of the BPSO algorithm. The velocity of each particle is updated using the following Equation:

$$v_i(t+1) = w * v_i(t) + c_1 r_1 [pbest(x(t)) - x_i(t)] + c_2 r_2 [g(t) - x_i(t)] \tag{5}$$

A logistic sigmoid transformation function S $(v_i (t + 1))$ is shown in Equation (6) can be used to limit the speed of particle.

$$S(v_i (t+1)) = \frac{1}{1 + e^{v_i(t+1)}} \tag{6}$$

The new position of the particle is obtained using Equation (7) shown below:

$$x_i = \begin{cases} 1, & if \ r_3 < S(v_i(t+1)) \\ 0, & otherwise \end{cases} \tag{7}$$

where $r_3$ is a uniform random number in the range [0, 1].

The index of the particle is represented by i. Thus, $v_i(t)$ is the velocity of particle i at time t and $x_i(t)$ is the position of particle i at time t. The parameters w, $c_1$, and $c_2$ are user supplied coefficients. The values $r_1$ and $r_2$ are random values regenerated for each velocity update. The value pbest(x(t)) is the individual best candidate solution for particle i at time t, and g(t) is the particle's global best candidate solution at time t. w is inertia weight

and $c_1$ and $c_2$ determine the relative influence of the social and cognitive components. Equation (7) is used to update the position of the particle. This process is repeated until the best solution is found or terminate conditions are satisfied.

## 3. USER PROFILING USING BPSO WITH MUTATION BASED BICLUSTERING ALGORITHM

The main goal of this work is to identify the maximal size bicluster constrained to some homogeneity (i.e., ACV) threshold δ. These biclusters have high correlation among users and pages. The following fitness function (Das & Idicula, 2010) is used to extract the high volume bicluster subjected to ACV threshold δ.

max F (I, J) subject to ACV(I,J) ≥ δ . F(I,J) is defined as

$$F(I,J) = \begin{cases} |I| * |J|, & if \ ACV \ (bicluster) \geq \delta \\ 0, & otherwise \end{cases}$$

$$\tag{8}$$

where |I| and |J| are number of rows and columns of bicluster and δ is defined as follows.

Several experimentation was conducted to choose specific constant value for threshold δ because the value of δ is less, then size of the bicluster is very large at same its homogeneity is poor.

In this work, biclustering algorithm is used as pattern discovering tool to extract the coherent browsing pattern which captures the correlation between the users and subset of pages of web site. This is the first step of usage profile generation. Each bicluster is the usage profile. Hence an aggregate usage profile (Mobasher et al., 2000) is determined using the formula:

$$W(p, B) = \frac{\sum_{u \subseteq B} hits(u, p)}{nU} \tag{9}$$

- *hits(u, p)*: Hits of the page p by user u in bicluster B
- **nU:** The number of users in bicluster B

Each of these user profiles describes the typical browsing behavior of a group of users with similar interest about the most visited pages of the web site.

This work proposes hybrid algorithm that enhance the search process by applying mutation operator on stagnated particles. It improves the diversity, and the convergence toward the preferred solution for the biclustering of clickstream data.

Each optimal bicluster is optimal the user profile. Thus, the identified user profiles will be exploited to realize personalization functionalities in the considered web site, such as the dynamical suggestions of links to pages, web site improvement, etc.

## 4. EXPERIMENTAL ANALYSIS AND DISCUSSION

The web log files of msnbc.com web site have been used to evaluate the performance of the proposed

*Algorithm 1. Hybrid BPSO based biclustering algorithm*

```
// Stage 1: Pattern discovery using Hybrid BPSO based Biclustering algorithm
Step 1. Compute k_u user clusters and k_p page clusters from preprocessed click-
stream data.
Step 2. Combine k_u and k_p clusters to form k_u × k_p biclusters called initial bi-
clusters
Step 3. initial particles = initial biclusters
Step 4. Initialize the velocity and position 'x' of each particle
Step 5. Set initial position as pbest and maximum of pbest is set as gbest.
Step 6. Repeat
for each particle in the population
 current fitness =fitness(particle)
 if current fitness > fitness(pbest(particle))
 Update pbest with position of current particle end (if)
end (for)
Update gbest
Update velocity using Equation (5)
Update position using Equation (7)
Apply genetic mutation operator for position
until stopping criteria is met
Step 7. Return gbest as global optimal bicluster
// Stage 2- Pattern Analysis and Generation of Usage Profile
Step 1. Pageset={}
Step 2. For all pages p in global optimal bicluster
i. Calculate the weight of the page p using Equation (10)
ii. If w(p) > θ
pageset= Union(pageset, p)
 end(if)
 end(for)
Step 3. Return the pageset as aggregate user profile.
```

algorithm. The web site includes the page visits of users who visited the "msnbc.com" web site on 28/9/99. The visits are recorded at the level of URL category (for example sports, news and so on) and are recorded in time order. It includes visits to 17 categories. The data is obtained from IIS logs for msnbc.com and news-related portions of msn.com. The client-side data is not available in the web log files.

Each sequence in the dataset corresponds to a user's request for a page. The 17 categories are described in Box 1.

## Example

- 1 1
- 2
- 3 2 2 4 2 2 2

The above is a sequence of visits. Each record is a session. The first row indicates that the user has visited category 1 twice. The second row indicates that a user has visited category 2 once. The third row indicates that the user visited category 3 once, category 2 visited consecutively, then visited category 4 once and finally visited category 2 consecutively three times.

During data filtering process, user sessions with number of visited URL category is less than 5 or greater than 15 are removed (i.e., the these sessions are too short or too long to provide sufficient information for browsing behavior prediction).

From Tables 3 through 5, it can be observed that BPSO in combination with the greedy search method manages to increase the volume of the largest bicluster significantly which is subjected to the homogeneity threshold $\delta$. Moreover, incorporation of the mutation operator in the BPSO, avoids the premature convergence of the swarm particles when they stuck at the local maximum and produce better results than normal BPSO.

Figure 4 clearly shows that hybrid BPSO with Greedy Search Procedure performs better than all other methods described.

*Box 1.*

| Id | Category | Id | Category | Id | Category |
|----|----------|----|----------|----|----------|
| 1 | Frontpage | 7 | Misc | 13 | Summary |
| 2 | News | 8 | Weather | 14 | BBS |
| 3 | Tech | 9 | Health | 15 | Travel |
| 4 | Local | 10 | Living | 16 | Msn-news |
| 5 | Opinion | 11 | Business | 17 | Msn-sports |
| 6 | On-air | 12 | Sports | | |

*Table 3. Characteristic of initial biclusters*

| | Two-Way K-Means Clustering | Biclustering using Greedy Search Procedure |
|----|----|----|
| No. of Biclusters | 120 | 120 |
| Average ACV | 0.5711 | 0.8341 |
| Average Volume | 794.3 | 1899.8 |

*Table 4. Characteristics of global optimal bicluster using HBPSO with greedy search procedure*

| Type of BPSO | No .of user | No. of pages | Optimal Volume | Optimal ACV |
|----|----|----|----|----|
| Hybrid | 1447 | 7 | 10108 | 0.9308 |
| Normal | 1324 | 7 | 9268 | 0.9034 |

*Table 5. Characteristics of global optimal bicluster using hbpso with two way k-means clustering*

| Type of BPSO | No .of user | No. of pages | Optimal Volume | Optimal ACV |
|----|----|----|----|----|
| Hybrid | 1204 | 7 | 8428 | 0.9166 |
| Normal | 1096 | 7 | 7672 | 0.9003 |

The proposed algorithm is used to capture and model the behavioral/ browsing patterns from web usage data and profiles of users interacting with a web site (Tables 6 and 7). Such usage patterns can be used to better understand correlated behavioral characteristics of visitor or user segments. The prediction of user behavior from aggregate usage profiles can be used for web personalization, building proper web site, improving marketing strategy, promotion, product supply, getting marketing information, forecasting market trends, and increasing the competitive strength of enterprises, etc.

## 5. CONCLUSION

A new approach for the discovery of usage profiles from the web usage data based on the biclustering method is presented in this paper. The main contributions of the proposed algorithm are hybrid version of the BPSO algorithm for user profiling, an improved particle initialization procedure in BPSO using Two-Way K-Means and Greedy Search Procedure, and a correlation

*Figure 4. Comparison of Hybrid BPSO and Normal BPSO*

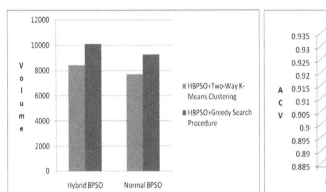
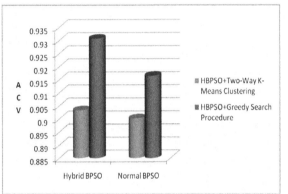

*Table 6. Weight of each pageview in global optimal usage profile*

| Pageview ID | HBPSO with Greedy Search Procedure | BPSO with Greedy Search Procedure | HBPSO with Two Way K-Means | BPSO with Two Way K-Means |
|---|---|---|---|---|
| 2 | 0.1830 | 0.1961 | 0.1951 | 0.2028 |
| 3 | 0.1381 | 0.1450 | # | 0.1553 |
| 6 | 0.1580 | 0.1736 | 0.1675 | # |
| 10 | 0.1122 | 0.1433 | 0.1431 | 0.1512 |
| 11 | 0.1475 | # | 0.1572 | 0.1578 |
| 12 | 0.1428 | 0.1527 | 0.1518 | 0.1532 |
| 14 | 0.1184 | 0.1347 | 0.1327 | 0.1343 |
| 17 | # | 0.0545 | 0.0526 | 0.0454 |

Note: # means that pageview is not presented in that bicluster

*Table 7. Aggregate Usage profile contains following pageviews in various run*

| HBPSO with Greedy Search Procedure | BPSO with Greedy Search Procedure | HBPSO with Two Way K-Means | BPSO with Two Way K-Means |
|---|---|---|---|
| News, Tech, On-air, Living, Business, Sports, Bulletin | News, Tech, On-air, Living, Sports, Bulletin | News, On-air, Living, Business, Sports, Bulletin | News, Tech, Living, Business, Sports, Bulletin |

based fitness function is designed to extract the coherent usage profiles. Moreover, correlation based similarity measure captures pattern based closeness of the users which has wide range of E-Commerce applications like marketing, etc. The results show that hybrid BPSO outperforms the normal BPSO for user profiling. The future works will be focused on the research issues, such as performing experiments over more datasets, broadening comparison and make use of discovered highly correlated usage profiles for web application such as, web recommendation and personalization

## REFERENCES

Abhraham, A., & Ramos, V. (2003). Web Usage Mining Using Artificial Ant Colony Clustering and Linear Genetic Programming. In *Proceedings of the 2003 IEEE Conference on Evolutionary Computation* (pp. 8-12).

Agrawal, R., Imielinski, T., & Swami, A. (1993). Mining association rules between sets of items in large databases. In *Proceedings of the ACM SIGMOD Conference* (pp. 207-216).

Alam, S., Dobbie, G., & Riddle, P. (2008). Particle Swarm Optimization Based Clustering of Web Usage Data. In *Proceedings of the Web Intelligence and Intelligent Agent Technology Conference (WI-IAT '08)* (pp. 451-454).

Bagyamani, J., Thangavel, K., & Rathipriya, R. (2011). Biological Significance of Gene Expression Data using Similarity based Biclustering Algorithm. *International Journal of Biometrics and Bioinformatics*, *4*, 201–216.

Banka, H., & Mitra, S. (2006). Multi-objective Evolutionary biclustering of gene expression data. *Journal of Pattern Recognition*, *39*, 2464–2477. doi:10.1016/j.patcog.2006.03.003

Chakraborty, A., & Maka, H. (2005). Biclustering of Gene Expression Data Using Genetic Algorithm. In *Proceedings of the Conference on Computation Intelligence in Bioinformatics and Computational Biology* (pp. 1-8).

Chen, Y. S., & Shahabi, C. (2001). Automatically improving the accuracy of user profiles with genetic algorithm. In *Proceedings of the IASTED International Conference on Artificial Intelligence and Soft Computing* (pp. 283-288).

Cheng, Y., & Church, G. M. (2000). Biclustering of expression data. In *Proceedings of the 8th International Conference on Intelligent Systems for Molecular Biology* (pp. 93-103).

Chi, E. H., Rosien, A., & Heer, J. (2002). LumberJack: Intelligent Discovery and Analysis of Web User Traffic Composition. In *Proceedings of the ACM-SIGKDD Workshop on Web Mining for Usage Patterns and User Profiles*.

Cooley, R., Mobasher, B., & Srivatsava, J. (1997). Web mining: Information and pattern discovery on the World Wide Web. In *Proceeding of the 9th IEEE International Conference on Tools with Artificial Intelligence* (pp. 558-567).

Das, S., & Idicula, S. M. (2010). Greedy Search-Binary PSO Hybrid for Biclustering Gene Expression Data. *International Journal of Computers and Applications*, *2*(3), 1–5. doi:10.5120/651-908

Jespersen, S. E., Throhauge, J., & Bach Pedersen, T. (2002). A hybrid approach to Web Usage Mining. In *Proceedings of the Data Warehousing and Knowledge Discovery Conference (DaWaK'02)* (LNCS 2454, pp. 73-82).

Kennedy, J., & Eberhart, R. C. (1997). A discrete binary version of the particle swarm algorithm. In *Proceedings of the IEEE International Conference on Systems, Man, and Cybernetics, Computational Cybernetics and Simulation* (Vol. 5, pp. 4104-4108).

Khosla, A., Kumar, S., Aggarwal, K. K., & Singh, J. (2006). A Matlab Implementation of Swarm Intelligence based Methodology for Identification of Optimized Fuzzy Models. In *Swarm Intelligent Systems: Studies in Computational Intelligence* (*Vol. 26*, pp. 175–184). SCI.

Krishnapuram, R., Joshi, A., & Nasraoui, O. (2001). Low-complexity fuzzy relational clusteringalgorithms for Web mining. *IEEE Transactions on Fuzzy Systems*, *9*, 595–607. doi:10.1109/91.940971

Labroche, N. (2007). *Learning web users profiles with relational clustering algorithms*. Menlo Park, CA: Association for the Advancement of Artificial Intelligence.

Lee, C. H., & Fu, Y. H. (2008). Web usage mining based on clustering of browsing features. In *Proceedings of the 8th International Conference on Intelligent Systems Design and Applications* (pp. 281-286).

Li, C. (2009). Research on web session clustering. *Journal of Software*, *4*, 460–468. doi:10.4304/jsw.4.5.460-468

Madeira, S. C., & Oliveira, A. L. (2004). Biclustering algorithms for biological data analysis: A Survey. *IEEE/ACM Transactions on Computational Biology and Bioinformatics*, *1*, 24–45. doi:10.1109/TCBB.2004.2

Martín-Bautista, M. J., Kraft, D. H., Vila, M. A., Chen, J., & Cruz, J. (2004). User profiles and fuzzy logic for Web retrieval issues. *Soft Computing Journal*, *6*(5), 365–372.

Martín-Bautista, M. J., Vila, M. A., & Escobar-Jeria, V. H. (2008). Obtaining user profiles via web usage mining. In *Proceedings of the IADIS European Conference on Data Mining* (pp. 73-76).

Mobasher, B., Cooley, R., & Srivastava, J. (1999). Creating adaptive web sites through usage-based clustering of URLs. In *Proceedings of the IEEE Knowledge and Data Engineering Exchange Workshop (KDEX'99)* (pp. 19-25).

Mobasher, B., Dai, H., Luo, T., Nakagawa, M., Sun, Y., & Wiltshire, J. (2000). Discovery of aggregate usage profiles for web personalization. In *Proceedings of the WebKDD Workshop* (pp. 1-11).

Pallis, G., Angelis, L., & Vakali, A. (2005). Model-based cluster analysis for web users sessions. In *Foundations of Intelligent Systems* (LNCS 3488, pp. 219-227).

Premalatha, K., & Natarajan, A. M. (2010). Hybrid PSO and GA Models for Document Clustering. *International Journal of Advances in Soft Computing and Its Applications*, *2*(3), 597–608.

Rambharose, T., & Nikov, A. (2010). Computational intelligence-based personalization of interactive web systems. *WSEAS Transactions on Information Science and Applications*, *7*, 484–497.

Srivatsava, J., Cooley, R., Deshpande, M., & Tan, P. N. (2000). Web usage mining: discovery and applications of usage patterns from Web data. *ACM SIGKDD: Explorations Newsletter*, *1*, 12–23.

*This work was previously published in the International Journal of Applied Evolutionary Computation, Volume 2, Issue 4, edited by Wei-Chiang Samuelson Hong, pp. 37-49, copyright 2011 by IGI Publishing (an imprint of IGI Global).*

# Chapter 17
# An Effective Hybrid Semi-Parametric Regression Strategy for Rainfall Forecasting Combining Linear and Nonlinear Regression

**Jiansheng Wu**

*Wuhan University of Technology, China & Liuzhou Teachers College, China*

## ABSTRACT

*Rainfall forecasting is an important research topic in disaster prevention and reduction. The characteristic of rainfall involves a rather complex systematic dynamics under the influence of different meteorological factors, including linear and nonlinear pattern. Recently, many approaches to improve forecasting accuracy have been introduced. Artificial neural network (ANN), which performs a nonlinear mapping between inputs and outputs, has played a crucial role in forecasting rainfall data. In this paper, an effective hybrid semi-parametric regression ensemble (SRE) model is presented for rainfall forecasting. In this model, three linear regression models are used to capture rainfall linear characteristics and three nonlinear regression models based on ANN are able to capture rainfall nonlinear characteristics. The semi-parametric regression is used for ensemble model based on the principal component analysis technique. Empirical results reveal that the prediction using the SRE model is generally better than those obtained using other models in terms of the same evaluation measurements. The SRE model proposed in this paper can be used as a promising alternative forecasting tool for rainfall to achieve greater forecasting accuracy and improve prediction quality.*

DOI: 10.4018/978-1-4666-3628-6.ch017

## 1. INTRODUCTION

Rainfall prediction is a challenging task in the climate dynamics and climate prediction theory. Accurate forecasting of rainfall information (including the spatial and temporal distribution of rainfalls) has been one of the most important issues in hydrological research, because it can help prevent casualties and damages caused by natural disasters (Wu, 2009; Lettenmaier & Wood, 1993). In general, rainfall forecasting involves a rather complex nonlinear pattern, for example pressure, temperature, wind speed and its direction, meteorological characteristics of the precipitation area, and so on (Luk, Ball, & Sharma, 2001; Kuligowski & Barros, 1998).

Over the past few decades, most of the research have used traditional statistical methods for rainfall forecasting, such as multiple linear regression, time series methods, and so on (Zwiers & von Storch, 2004). It is extremely difficult to capture the nonlinear characteristic by the traditional statistical methods. At present, although the climate dynamics approach for rainfall forecasting has developed, it is very difficult to describe and establish the forecasting model of rainfall, because the climate dynamic model involve many complex factors of weather and it is very difficult to solve (Druce, 2001).

Recently, artificial neural networks (ANN) techniques have been recognized as more useful than conventional statistical forecasting models. ANN is based on a model of emulating the processing of human neurological system to find out related spatial and temporal characteristics from the historical rainfall patterns (Hong, 2008). They are universal function approximations that can map any non-linear function without understanding the physical laws and any assumptions of traditional statistical approaches required. They have computationally robust, and has the ability to learn and generalize from examples to produce meaningful solutions to problems even when the input data contain errors or are incomplete. So it is widely applied to solve Climate Dynamical Systems problems including rainfall forecasting in comparison to traditional statistical models. French, Krajewski, and Cuykendal (1992) developed the first simulation scheme, whereby synthetically generated rainfall storms were used to both calibrate and validate ANN models. Kuligowski and Barros (1998) have applied an ANN approach for short term rainfall forecasting. Their model used feed-forward neural network (FFNN) architecture with upper atmospheric wind direction and antecedent rainfall data from a rain gauge network to generate a 0-6 h precipitation forecast for a target location. Luk et al. (2001) employed ANN to forecast the short-term rainfall for an urban catchment. Their model used among the ANN configured with different orders of lag and different numbers of spatial inputs. The experimental results shows that the ANN provided the most accurate predictions when an optimum number of spatial inputs was included into the network, and that the network with lower lag consistently produced better performance.

Currently, more hybrid forecasting models have been developed to improve rainfall prediction accuracy. Bowden, Dandy, and Maier (2005a, 2005b) have presented two methodologies, namely partial mutual information (PMI) and self-organizing map (SOM) integrated with a genetic algorithm and general regression neural network. The first method utilizes a dependent measure known as the partial mutual information (PMI) criterion to select significant model inputs. The second method utilizes a self-organizing map (SOM) to remove redundant input variables, and a hybrid genetic algorithm (GA) and general regression neural network (GRNN) to select the inputs that have a significant influence on the model's forecast. The results indicated that the two methods can lead to more parsimonious models with a lower forecasting error than the models developed using the methods from previous studies. Jain and Kumar (2007) have applied Hybrid neural network models for hydrologic time series forecasting. The proposed approach consists of an overall modeling framework, which is a combination of the four time series models of auto-regressive (AR) type and four ANN models. The results obtained in this study suggest that the approach of combining the strengths of the conventional and ANN techniques provides a robust modeling framework capable of capturing the nonlinear nature of the complex time series and thus producing more accurate forecasts. Some recent studies clearly demonstrate that the hybrid model could provide an effective way to improve the forecasting accuracy achieved by either of the models used separately.

Although one can find many applications of developing hybrid models in a variety of areas, such attempts have been limited in the model of rainfall forecasting. There are hybrid pure linear methods or hybrid pure nonlinear methods for rainfall forecasting. The probable reasons for the difficulties in forecasting rainfall are the complexity of atmosphere-ocean interactions and the uncertainty of the relationship between rainfall and hydro-meteorological variables. The characteristic of rainfall involves a rather complex system dynamics under the influence of different meteorological factors. They often contain both linear and nonlinear patterns so that this paper present an effective semi-parametric regression based on linear forecasting model and nonlinear forecasting model.

The rest of the study is organized as follows. In Section 2, linear regression models and nonlinear regression models are described to capture linear and nonlinear characteristics in rainfall system. Section 3 describes the semi-parametric regression ensemble model to integrate the linear and nonlinear output. Section 4 analyzes the results of semi-parametric regression ensemble model for rainfall forecasting incorporating linear and nonlinear regression

to verify the effectiveness and efficiency of the proposed model. The conclusions are contained in Section 5.

## 2. LINEAR AND NONLINEAR REGRESSION METHODS $Y$

### 2.1 Linear Regression

Perhaps the most popular mathematical model for making predictions is the multiple linear regression model in the traditional mathematical method, which use known values of multiple variables to estimate one random variables. There is a continuous random variable called the dependent variable , there are a number of independent variables, $\{x_1, x_2, \cdots x_n\}$. The goal of regression models is to fit a set of data with an equation, the simplest being a linear equation. The linear regression model is given by

$$y = \beta_0 + \beta_1 x_1 + \beta_2 x_2 + \cdots \beta_n x_n \qquad (1)$$

where $\varepsilon$, the "noise" variable, is a normally distributed random variable with mean equal to zero and standard deviation $\sigma$, $\{\beta_1, \beta_2 \cdots, \beta_n\}$ are the values of the coefficients. Unknown parameters values should be estimated by the smallest error sum of squares of the samples.

A frequent problem in modeling is that of use of regression equation to predict the value of a dependent variable when the actual data has a number of variables to choose as independent variables in model. The choice of appropriate variables is very important for a good model. Estimates of regression coefficients are likely to be unstable due to multi-co linearity in models with many independent variables in model. Three types of linear regression models have been made in this paper for parsimony variables, such as stepwise multiple linear (SML) regression (Miller, 1980;

Johnson, 1998), partial least squares (PLS) regression (Helland, 1990; Zhou, Wu, & Qin, 2006) and multi recursive regression (MRR) method (Strang, 2009) to capture the linear characteristics of rainfall system.

## 2.2 Nonlinear Regression Methods

ANN is one of the soft computing of the technologies. They provide an interesting technique that theoretically can approximate any nonlinear continuous function on a compact domain to any designed accuracy. The network learns by adjusting the interconnections among layers. When the network is adequately trained, it is able to learn relevant output for a set of input data. A valuable property of neural network is its generalization, that is a trained neural network is able to provide a correct matching in the form of output data for a set of previously unseen input data. In the practical application, the results of many experiments have shown that the generalization of single neural network is not unique (Hansen & Salamon, 1990). That is, ANN results are not stable. Even for some simple problems, different structures of neural networks (e.g., different number of hidden layers, different hidden nodes and different initial conditions) result in different patterns of network generalization. If carelessly used, it can easily lead to irrelevant information in the system and limit applications of ANN in the rainfall forecasting (Jin, Kuang, Huang, Qin, & Wang, 2004).

Due to the work about bias-variance trade-off of by Bretiman (Yu, Wang, & Lai, 2008), an ANN regression model consisting of diverse models with much disagreement is more likely to have a good generalization (Benediktsson, Sveinsson, Ersoy, & Swain, 1997). In this paper, there are three ANN methods to get nonlinear pattern in rainfall system, such as multi-layer perceptions based on the Levenberg-Marquard algorithms (MLP-NN), the radial basis function network (RBF-NN), and General Regression Neural Network (GR-NN). Interested readers are referred to Mishra, Yadav, Ray, and Kalra (2005) for more details.

## 3. THE BUILDING PROCESS OF THE SEMI-PARAMETRIC REGRESSION MODEL

In recent years, Semi-parametric regression model is the popular regression model which has been widely applied to many fields such as economics, medical science, and so on (Ruppert, Wand, & Carroll, 2008). Semi-parametric regression is an emerging field that represents a fusion between traditional parametric regression analysis and newer nonparametric regression methods. It synthesizes research across several branches of statistics: parametric and nonparametric regression, longitudinal and spatial data analysis, mixed, etc. Semi-parametric regression is a field deeply rooted in applications and its evolution reflects the increasingly large and complex problems that are arising in science and industry.

## 3.1 Semi-Parametric Regression Model

Parametric regression model which realized the pure parametric thinking in curve estimations often does not meet the need in complicated data analysis. The alternatives are highly flexible nonparametric regression techniques, the object of which is to estimate the regression function directly, rather than to estimate parameters. However, in many applications it is necessary to come up with a decision whether a covariate is essential for the understanding of the problem or not. Hence some kinds of parameter testing are required, which cannot be performed in a purely nonparametric setting. An alternative is a semi-parametric regression model with a predictor function consisting of a parametric linear component and a nonparametric component which involves an additional predictor variable. Semi-parametric regression can be of substantial value in the solution of complex scientific problems. The real world is far too complicated for the human mind to comprehend in great detail. Semi-parametric regression models reduce complex data sets to summaries that we can understand. Properly applied, they retain essential features of the data while discarding unimportant details, and hence they aid sound decision-making.

Suppose the data consists of $n$ subjects. For subject $(k = 1, 2, \cdots, n)$, $Y_i$ is the independent variable, $x_i$ is the $m$ vector of clinical covariates and $z_i$ is the $p$ vector of gene expressions within a pathway. We assume an output is included in $x_i$, The output $y_i$ depends on $x_i$ and $z_i$ through the following semi-parametric regression model

$$Y_i = x_i^T \beta + h(z_i) + \varepsilon_i \tag{2}$$

where $\beta$ is a $m$ vector of regression coefficients, $z_i$ is an unknown centered smooth function, and the errors $\varepsilon_i$ are assumed to be independent and follow $N(0, \sigma^2)$. $x_i^T \beta$ is the parametrical part of model for epitaxial forecasting, its objective is to control the independent variable trend. $h(z_i)$ is the non-parametrical part of model for local adjustment so that it is better to fit responses value. So model contains the effects of parametrical part and the effects non-parametrical part. A solution can be obtained by minimizing the sum of squares equation

$$J(h, \beta) = \sum_{i=1}^{n} (y_i - x_i^T \beta - h(z_i))^2 + \lambda \int_a^b [h''(z_i)]^2 dt,$$
$$\lambda \geq 0 \tag{3}$$

where $\lambda$ is a tuning parameter which controls the tradeoff between goodness of fitting and complexity of the model. When $\lambda = 0$, the model interpolates the gene expression data, whereas, when $\lambda = \infty$, the model reduces to a simple linear model without $h(\cdot)$. Based on earlier works (Hall, Kay, & Titterington, 1990; Speckman, 1998), the semi-parametric model involves the following five-step iterative procedures:

1. $\lambda$ is the $n \times n$ positive-definite smoother matrix obtained from univariate cubic spline smoothing, without the parametric terms $x_i^T \beta$. The transformation of an n-vector $z$ to $S_\lambda z$ can be conducted in order of operations.

2. Transform $Y$ to $\tilde{Y} = (I - S_\lambda)Y$, and transform $X$ to $\tilde{X} = (I - S_\lambda)X$. Then calculate the least squares regression of $\tilde{Y}$ on $\tilde{X}$ with $\beta_\lambda$ being the resulting coefficient vector.

$$\beta_\lambda = (\tilde{X}^T \tilde{X})^{-1} \tilde{X}^T (I - S_\lambda) Y \tag{4}$$

3. Compute

$$h = (\tilde{X}^T \tilde{X})^{-1} \tag{5}$$

The output vector $\tilde{Y}$ is then estimated by

$$\tilde{Y} = S_\lambda + \tilde{X}(\tilde{X}^T \tilde{X})^{-1}(I - S_\lambda) \tag{6}$$

4. Select a value for the smoothing parameter $\lambda$ based on the minimize of the generalized cross-validation (GCV) criterion

$$GCV(\lambda) = \frac{n(Y - \hat{Y})^T (Y - \hat{Y})}{(n - tr\, H_\lambda)^2} \tag{7}$$

5. Compute $tr\, H_\lambda$

$$tr\, H_\lambda = tr\, S_\lambda + tr\, (\tilde{X}^T \tilde{X})^{-1} \tilde{X}^T (I - S_\lambda) \tilde{X} \tag{8}$$

The trace of $S_\lambda$ in Equation (8) can be computed by in $0(n)$ operations using algorithms from univariate spline smoothing (Eubank, 2000).

The resulting estimator is often called a partial spline. It is known because this estimator is asymptotically biased for the optimal $\lambda$ choice when the components of $\beta$ depend on $t$. The asymptotic bias can be larger than the standard error.

Correlation between predictors is common in real data analysis.

## 3.2 The Semi-Parametric Regression Ensemble

In weather system, rainfall forecasting problem is far from simple due to high volatility, complexity, irregularity and noisy. In this paper, three linear regression are used to capture rainfall linear characteristics, while three ANN models are capable of capturing nonlinear patterns in weather system. Ensemble the six models may yield a robust method, and more satisfactory forecasting results may be obtained by combining linear regression model and nonlinear regression model.

The forecasting output of linear regression model are $\hat{y}_1$, $\hat{y}_2$ and $\hat{y}_3$, respectively, while $\hat{y}_4$, $\hat{y}_5$ and $\hat{y}_6$ are nonlinear output by three ANN models. In this paper, the PCA technique is used to extract an effective feature from all forecasting output matrix. And then semi-parametric regression ensemble (SRE) is established through the method in Section 3.1

The above-mentioned method can be summed up as follows: firstly, three different linear regression models are used to get linear forecasting output. Secondly, different algorithms training ANN are used to get nonlinear forecasting output. Thirdly, the PCA technique extracts ensemble members from linear and nonlinear forecasting output. Finally, SRE is used to combine the selected individual forecasting results into a semi-parametric ensemble model. The basic flow diagram can be shown in Figure 1.

For the purpose of comparison, we have also built other three ensemble forecasting models:

1.    Simple average(SAL) all the linear forecasting output

*Figure 1. A flow diagram of the proposed semi-parametric ensemble forecasting model*

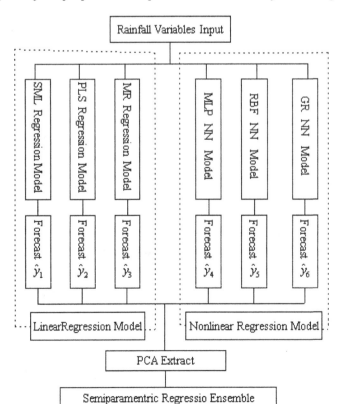

$$\hat{Y}_1 = \hat{y}_1 + \hat{y}_2 + \hat{y}_3 \qquad (9)$$

2.  Simple average (SAN) all the nonlinear forecasting output

$$\hat{Y}_2 = \hat{y}_4 + \hat{y}_5 + \hat{y}_6 \qquad (10)$$

3.  Stepwise regression (SRLN) all the linear and nonlinear forecasting output, the weights of variable can be solved according to Zhou et al. (2006)

$$\hat{Y}_3 = \sum_{i=1}^{6} \omega_i \hat{y}_i + \varepsilon \qquad (11)$$

## 4. EMPIRICAL ANALYSIS

The rainfall data of Guangxi is employed as a case study for development of rainfall forecasting model, which is located in the southwest of China. Due to the southwest monsoon, monsoon trough and tropical cyclones, it has heavy rains typically in summer. Usually, the primary rainy seasons begin in June in Guangxi, which receives an average rainfall of 259 mm, taking up 17.3% of the yearly total amount, June is one of the most concentrate time for precipitation. In this paper, the original daily rainfall data in June is used as the target prediction.

### 4.1 Empirical Data and Selection of Forecasting Factor

Real-time ground rainfall data has been obtained in June from 2003 to 2008 in Guangxi by observing 89 stations, which 144 samples are modelled from June 2003 to June 2007, other 30 samples are tested modelling in June of 2008. Method of modelling is one-step ahead prediction, that is, the forecast is only one sample each time and the

training samples is an additional one each time on the base of the previous training.

Due to the complex terrain of Guangxi and inhomogeneous rainfall, the region has been divided into three regional precipitation based on historical precipitation data by the cluster analysis method to reduce the difficulty of forecasting. Statistics for each district in the average daily precipitation is used as the forecasting object. Figure 2 shows three region maps.

In the first region as an example to show the process of modelling, it is very important to select the appropriate forecasting factors for model, different climatic variability and its effect have been discussed many times in the literature.

In this paper, first of all, the candidate forecasting factors are selected from the numerical forecast products based on 48h forecast field, which includes:

1.  The 17 conventional meteorological elements and physical elements from the T213 numerical products of China Meteorological Administration, the data cover the latitude from $15°$ N to $30°$ N, and longitude from $100°$ E to $120°$ E, with $1° \times 1°$ resolution, altogether there are 336 grid points.

*Figure 2. Group average region map of guangxi rainfall*

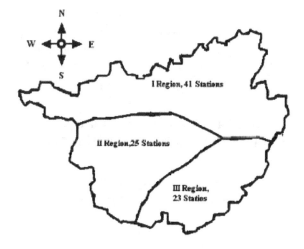

2.  The fine-mesh precipitation data from the East Asia of Japanese Meteorological Agency, the data cover the latitude from $15°$ N to $30°$ N, and longitude from $100°$ E to $120°$ E, with $1.25° \times 1.25°$ resolution, altogether there are 221 grid points.

Secondly, the main forecasting factors are exploited by the correlation coefficients test based on historical precipitation data and the candidate forecasting factors. The correlation coefficients is given by

$$r = \frac{\sum_{i=1}^{144}[(x_i - \frac{1}{144}\sum_{i=1}^{144}x_i)(y_i - \frac{1}{144}\sum_{i=1}^{144}y_i)]}{\sqrt{\sum_{i=1}^{144}[(x_i - \frac{1}{144}\sum_{i=1}^{144}x_i)(y_i - \frac{1}{144}\sum_{i=1}^{144}y_i)]}} \quad (12)$$

where $x_i$ is the value of the candidate forecasting factors, $y_i$ is actual rainfall. If $r \geq 0.33$, pass the $\alpha = 0.05$ significance test.

Finally, the empirical orthogonal function (EOF) technique (Lee, Yeah, Cheng, Chan, & Lee, 2003) is used to integrate the information of forecasting factors from main factors. As comparatively high correlation relationships exist between a large quantity of main factors and the neural network cannot filter factors, it will reduce the ability of having good fitting and prediction. The comprehensive factors can decrease the scale of the modelling and keep it good learning by EOF. We get 6 variables as the predictors by analyzing daily precipitation in the first region. In the second and the third region we get 5 forecasting factors by using the same analytical methods.

## 4.2 The Performance Evaluation and Parameters Setting in the ANN

In order to measure the effectiveness of the proposed method, four types of errors are presented as follows:

*   **Normalized Mean Squared Error (NMSE):**

$$NMSE = \frac{\sum_{i=1}^{n}(y_i - \hat{y}_i)^2}{\sum_{i=1}^{n}(y_i - \overline{y}_i)^2} \quad (13)$$

*   **Pearson Relative Coefficient (PRC):**

$$PRC = \frac{\sum_{i=1}^{n}(y_i - \overline{y}_i)(\hat{y}_i - \overline{\hat{y}}_i)}{\sqrt{\sum_{i=1}^{n}(y_i - \overline{y}_i)^2(\hat{y}_i - \overline{\hat{y}}_i)^2}} \quad (14)$$

*   **The Error Value More than 15mm:**

$$F_1 = \sum_{i=1}^{n}I_i \quad (15)$$

Where $I_i = \begin{cases} 1 & |y_i - \hat{y}_i| > 15 \\ 0 & |y_i - \hat{y}_i| \leq 15 \end{cases}$

*   **The Error Value Less than 5mm:**

$$F_2 = \sum_{i=1}^{n}T_i \quad (16)$$

Where $T_i = \begin{cases} 1 & |y_i - \hat{y}_i| < 5 \\ 0 & |y_i - \hat{y}_i| \geq 5 \end{cases}$

$y_i$ is the original value, $\hat{y}_i$ is the forecast value.

The minimum values of NMSE indicate that the deviations between original values and forecast values are very small. The accurate efficiency of the proposed model is measured as PRC, The higher values of PRC (maximum value is 1) indicate that the forecasting performance of the proposed model is effective, which can capture the average change tendency of the cumulative rainfall data. The effective information of the proposed rainfall forecasting model is measured by Equation 15 and 16. If the Error Value is more than 15mm between the original value and the forecast value, the model predictions don't provide effective information, if the Error Value is less than 5mm, the model predictions provide a piece of very important effective information for the future forecasting.

ANN parameters are set as follows: the number of neurons in the hidden layer is the same number of input factor. The learning rate is 0.9; the momentum factor is 0.7; the iteration times are 1000; the global error is 0.001.

## 4.3 Analysis of the Results

Figures 3 through 5 give graphical representations of the fitting results for the rainfall in all regions

with different models, which are used to fit the rainfall of 144 training samples for comparison. Tables 1 through 3 illustrate the fitting accuracy and efficiency of the model in terms of various evaluation indices for 144 training samples. From the graphs and tables, we can generally see that learning ability of SRE outperforms the other three models under the same network input. The more important factor to measure performance of a method is to check its forecasting ability of testing samples in order for actual rainfall application.

Figures 6 through 8 show the forecasting of testing sample in three regions, respectively, with the different models, which are used to forecast the rainfall of 30 testing samples for comparison. Tables 4 through 6 show the forecasting performance of different models from different perspectives in terms of various evaluation indices. From the graphs and table, we can generally see that the forecasting results are very promising in the rainfall forecasting of all regions under the research

*Figure 3. Fitting results in first region about 144 training samples*

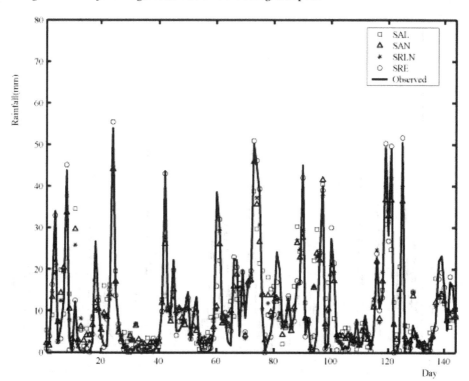

*Figure 4. Fitting results in second region about 144 training samples*

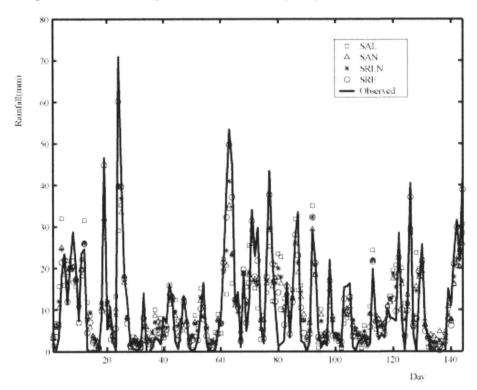

*Figure 5. Fitting results in third region about 144 training samples*

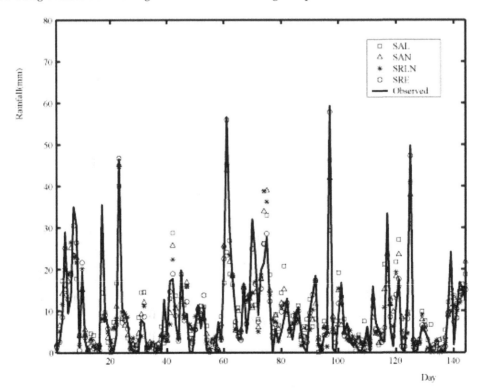

*Table 1. A comparison of fitting result of different models about 144 training samples in the first region*

| Errors | SAL | SAN | SRLN | SRE |
|---|---|---|---|---|
| NMSE | 0.5034 | 0.2537 | 0.2292 | 0.0556 |
| PRC | 0.7057 | 0.8742 | 0.8857 | 0.9718 |
| $F_1$ | 16 | 6 | 6 | 2 |
| $F_1$*100% | 11.11% | 4.17% | 4.17% | 1.39% |
| $F_2$ | 79 | 100 | 95 | 134 |
| $F_2$*100% | 54.86% | 69.44% | 65.97% | 93.06% |

*Table 2. A comparison of fitting result of different models about 144 training samples in the second region*

| Errors | SAL | SAN | SRLN | SRE |
|---|---|---|---|---|
| NMSE | 0.4845 | 0.2864 | 0.2605 | 0.0771 |
| PRC | 0.7197 | 0.8864 | 0.8664 | 0.9679 |
| $F_1$ | 11 | 7 | 7 | 0 |
| $F_1$*100% | 7.64% | 4.86% | 4.86% | 0% |
| $F_2$ | 77 | 87 | 87 | 130 |
| $F_2$*100% | 53.47% | 60.42% | 60.42% | 90.28% |

*Table 3. A comparison of fitting result of different models about 144 training samples in the third region*

| Errors | SAL | SAN | SRLN | SRE |
|---|---|---|---|---|
| NMSE | 0.4604 | 0.3102 | 0.2451 | 0.0748 |
| PRC | 0.7397 | 0.8318 | 0.8703 | 0.9641 |
| $F_1$ | 8 | 4 | 2 | 2 |
| $F_1$*100% | 5.65% | 2.78% | 1.39% | 1.39% |
| $F_2$ | 84 | 98 | 110 | 136 |

where either the measurement of fitting performance is goodness of fit such as NMSE or where the forecasting performance effectiveness is PRC.

Figures 6 through 8 show the comparison for the rainfall of the semi-parametric regression ensemble forecasting results versus the forecast results of simple average all linear forecasting output model, simple average all nonlinear forecasting output model and stepwise regression all the forecasting output including linear and nonlinear. The results indicate that the semi-parametric ensemble forecasting model performs better than the other models presented.

Subsequently, the forecasting performance compares various models in the three regions. From Table 4 in the forecasting of the first region, the differences among the different models are very significant. For example, the NMSE of the SAL model is 0.6180. Similarly, the NMSE of the SAN model is 0.6311 and the NMSE of the SRLE model is 0.4389; however the NMSE of the SRE model reaches 0.2452. In the forecasting of two other regions, the NMSE of the SRE model is also less than three other models, which has obvious advantages over three other models.

*Figure 6. Forecasting results in the first region about 30 testing samples*

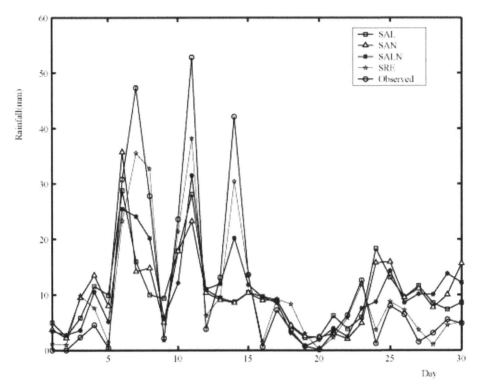

*Figure 7. Forecasting results in the second region about 30 testing samples*

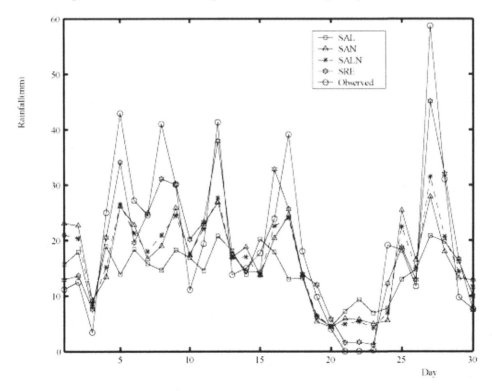

*Figure 8. Forecasting results in the third region about 30 testing samples*

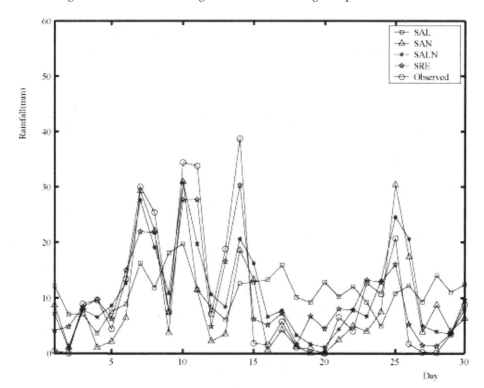

*Table 4. A comparison of forecasting result of different models about 40 testing samples in the first region*

| Errors | SAL | SAN | SRLN | SRE |
|---|---|---|---|---|
| NMSE | 0.6180 | 0.6311 | 0.4389 | 0.2452 |
| PR | 0.6530 | 0.6170 | 0.8784 | 0.9546 |
| $F_1$ | 7 | 6 | 6 | 0 |
| $F_1 * 100\%$ | 23.33% | 20.00% | 20.00% | 0% |
| $F_2$ | 15 | 15 | 15 | 25 |
| $F_2 * 100\%$ | 50.00% | 50.00% | 50.00% | 83.33% |

Similarly, for PRC efficiency index, the proposed SRE model is also deserved to be confident. As shown in Table 4, we can see that the forecasting rainfall values from SRE model have higher correlative relationship with actual rainfall values; As for the testing samples in the first region, the PRC for the SAL model is only 0.6530, for the SAN model it is only 0.6170, and for the SRLN model PRC is 0.8784; while for the SRE forecasting models, the PRC reaches 0.9546. From Tables

5 and 6 in the forecasting of two other regions, it shows that the PRC of SRE model is close to their real values in different models and the SRE model is capable to capture the average change tendency of the daily rainfall data.

In terms of the error value which is more than 15mm or less than 5mm, compared with the other different models presented in this paper, the semi-parametric regression ensemble forecasting model performs the best because it could pro-

*Table 5. A comparison of forecasting result of different models about 40 testing samples in the second region*

| Errors | SAL | SAN | SRLN | SRE |
|---|---|---|---|---|
| NMSE | 0.5963 | 0.5724 | 0.4477 | 0.2050 |
| PR | 0.6471 | 0.7327 | 0.8323 | 0.9304 |
| $F_1$ | 5 | 3 | 4 | 0 |
| $F_1$*100% | 16.67% | 10.00% | 13.33% | 0% |
| $F_2$ | 14 | 13 | 15 | 24 |
| $F_2$*100% | 46.67% | 43.33% | 50.00% | 80.00% |

*Table 6. A comparison of forecasting result of different models about 40 testing samples in the third region*

| Errors | SAL | SAN | SRLN | SRE |
|---|---|---|---|---|
| NMSE | 0.6713 | 0.5176 | 0.3454 | 0.1210 |
| PR | 0.6529 | 0.7208 | 0.8163 | 0.9775 |
| $F_1$ | 4 | 4 | 3 | 0 |
| $F_1$*100% | 13.33% | 13.33% | 10.00% | 0% |
| $F_2$ | 17 | 20 | 21 | 26 |
| $F_2$*100% | 56.67% | 66.67% | 70.00% | 86.67% |

vided more effective information. If the error value is less than 5mm, it is considered to have effective information. From Tables 4 through 6, the effective information for SRE is 93.06% in the first region forecasting, it is 90.28% in the second region forecasting and it is 94.44%. The minimum value of the effective information for the SRE model is 90.28% in the forecasting of all three regions, which the maximum value of the effective information for SAL is 56.67%, the maximum value of the effective information for SAN is 66.67%, and the maximum value of the effective information for SRLN is only 70.00%. Similarly, if the error value is more than 15mm, it is considered to have unreliable information, the SRE model has no unreliable information in the forecasting of all three regions, which the minimum value of unreliable information for the SAL model is 13.33%, the minimum value of unreliable information for the SAN and SRLN models is 10.00%. The empirical results show that the forecasting of SRE model for a meteoro-

logical application has greater forecasting accuracy and could be applied to future forecasting.

From the experiments presented in this study we can draw that the semi-parametric regression ensemble forecasting model is superior to the simple average linear model, the simple average nonlinear model as well as the stepwise linear regression combination with linear and nonlinear methods for the fitting and testing cases of three regions in terms of the different measurement, as can be seen from Tables 1 through 6.

There are three main reasons for this phenomenon. Firstly, the rainfall system contains both complex linear and nonlinear pattern. Neither individual linear nor individual nonlinear regression model can establish the effective model for rainfall forecasting. Secondly, the output of different models has the high correlative relationship, the high noise, nonlinearity and complex factors. If PCA technology don't reduce the dimension of the data and extract the main features, the results of the model is unstable, such as the stepwise linear regression combined linear and nonlinear methods, sometimes it is good, sometimes it is bad. At last, semi-parametric regression ensemble model combine components of linear regression model (parametric partly) and nonlinear regression (nonparametric partly), it keeps the easy interpretability of the linear model and retaining some of the flexibility of the nonlinear model.

## 5. CONCLUSION

A challenging task for a frequent-unanticipated flash flood region is the provision of a quantitative rainfall forecast to avoid life losing and economic loses. The rainfall data of the Guangxi watershed in southwest China shows primary rainy season in the June. Therefore, accurate prediction of daily precipitation is very important for the prevention and mitigation of flood disaster. This study proposes we use a semi-parametric regression ensemble forecasting model that combines the linear regression model and the nonlinear model to predict rainfall based on PCA technology. In terms of the empirical results, we find that different forecasting models for the forecasting samples of three regions of Guangxi on the base of different criteria, the semi-parametric regression ensemble model performs the best.

In the semi-parametric regression ensemble model test samples, the NMSE is the lowest and the PRC is the highest, which indicate that the semi-parametric regression ensemble forecasting model can be used as a viable alternative solution for rainfall forecasting. Moreover the semi-parametric regression ensemble model can provide more effective information for future prediction, and have no unreliable information. These results indicate the semi-parametric regression model based on linear and nonlinear with PCA technology can be used as an alternative tool for rainfall forecasting to obtain greater forecasting accuracy and improve the prediction quality.

## ACKNOWLEDGMENT

The authors would like to express their sincere thanks to the editor and anonymous reviewer's comments and suggestions for the improvement of this paper. This work was supported in part by Program for Excellent Talents in Guangxi Higher Education Institutions, and in part by Natural Science Foundation of Guangxi under Grant No. 2011GXNSFE018006.

## REFERENCES

Benediktsson, J. A., Sveinsson, J. R., Ersoy, O. K., & Swain, P. H. (1997). Parallel consensual neural networks. *IEEE Transactions on Neural Networks*, 8, 54–64. doi:10.1109/72.554191

Bowden, G. J., Dandy, G. C., & Maier, H. R. (2005a). Input determination for neural network models in water resources applications, Part 1. Background and Methodology. *Journal of Hydrology (Amsterdam)*, *301*, 75–92. doi:10.1016/j.jhydrol.2004.06.021

Bowden, G. J., Dandy, G. C., & Maier, H. R. (2005b). Input determination for neural network models in water resources applications, Part 2. Case study: Forecasting salinity in a river. *Journal of Hydrology (Amsterdam)*, *301*, 93–107. doi:10.1016/j.jhydrol.2004.06.020

Box, G. E., & Jenkins, P. G. M. (1976). *Time series analysis: forecasting and control*. San Francisco, CA: Holden-Day.

Druce, D. J. (2001). Insights from a history of seasonal inflow forecasting with a conceptual hydrologic model. *Journal of Hydrology (Amsterdam)*, *249*(1-4), 102–112. doi:10.1016/S0022-1694(01)00415-2

Eubank, R. L. (2000). Spline regression. In Schimek, M. G. (Ed.), *Smoothing and regression approaches, computation, and application*. New York, NY: Wiley.

French, M. N., Krajewski, W. F., & Cuykendal, R. R. (1992). Rainfall forecasting in space and time using a neural network. *Journal of Hydrology (Amsterdam)*, *137*, 1–37. doi:10.1016/0022-1694(92)90046-X

Hall, P., Kay, J. W., & Titterington, D. M. (1990). Asymptotically optimal difference-based estimation of variance in nonparametric regression. *Biometrika*, *77*, 521–528. doi:10.1093/biomet/77.3.521

Ham, F. M., & Kostanic, I. (2001). *Principles of neurocomputing for science and engineering*. New York, NY: McGraw-Hill.

Hansen, L. K., & Salamon, P. (1990). Neural network ensembles. *IEEE Transactions on Pattern Analysis and Machine Intelligence*, *12*(10), 993–1001. doi:10.1109/34.58871

Helland, I. S. (1990). PLS regression and statistical models. *Journal of Statistics*, *179*, 97–114.

Hong, W.-C. (2008). Rainfall forecasting by technological machine learning models. *Applied Mathematics and Computation*, *200*, 41–57. doi:10.1016/j.amc.2007.10.046

Jain, A., & Kumar, A. M. (2007). Hybrid neural network models for hydrologic time series forecasting. *Applied Soft Computing*, *7*, 585–592. doi:10.1016/j.asoc.2006.03.002

Jin, L., Kuang, X. Y., Huang, H., Qin, Z., & Wang, Y. (2004). Study on the over-fitting of the artificial neural network forecasting model. *Acta Meteorologica Sinica*, *62*(1), 62–69.

Johnson, D. (1998). *Applied multivariate methods for data analysts* (1st ed.). Stamford, CT: Thomson Learning.

Kuligowski, R. J., & Barros, A. P. (1998). Experiments in short-term precipitation forecasting using artificial neural networks. *Monthly Weather Review*, *126*(2), 470–482. doi:10.1175/1520-0493(1998)126<0470:EISTPF>2.0.CO;2

Lee, M. A., Yeah, C. D., Cheng, C. H., Chan, J. W., & Lee, K. T. (2003). Empirical orthogonal function analysis of sea surface temperature patterns in Taiwan Strait. *Journal of Marine Science and Technology*, *11*(1), 1–7.

Lettenmaier, D. P., & Wood, E. F. (1993). Hydrology forecasting. In Maidment, D. R. (Ed.), *Handbook of Hydrology*. New York, NY: McGraw-Hill.

Luk, K. C., Ball, J. E., & Sharma, A. (2001). An application of artificial neural networks for rainfall forecasting. *Mathematical and Computer Modelling*, *33*, 683–693. doi:10.1016/S0895-7177(00)00272-7

Miller, R. G. Jr. (1980). *Simultaneous statistical inference* (2nd ed.). New York, NY: Springer.

Mishra, D., Yadav, A., Ray, S., & Kalra, P. K. (2005). Levenberg-Marquardt learning algorithm for integrate-and-fire neuron model. *Neural Information Processing - Letters and Reviews*, *19*(2), 41-51.

Nasseri, M., Asghari, K., & Abedini, M. J. (2008). Optimized scenario for rainfall forecasting using genetic algorithm coupled with artificial neural network. *Expert Systems with Applications*, *35*, 1414–1421. doi:10.1016/j.eswa.2007.08.033

Ruppert, D. M., Wand, P. R., & Carroll, J. (2008). *Semi-parametric regression during 2003-2007*. Retrieved from http://www.uow.edu.au/~mwand/sprpap.pdf

Speckman, P. (1998). Kernel smoothing in partial linear models. *Journal of the Royal Statistical Society. Series B. Methodological*, *50*, 413–436.

Strang, K. D. (2009). Using recursive regression to explore nonlinear relationships and interactions: A tutorial applied to a multicultural education study. *Practical Assessment Research and Evaluation*, *14*(3), 1–13.

Wu, J. S. (2009). A novel nonparametric regression ensemble for rainfall forecasting using particle swarm optimization technique coupled with artificial neural network. In *Advances in Neural Networks – ISNN 2009* (LNCS 5553, pp. 49-58).

Wu, J. S., Jin, L., & Liu, M. Z. (2006). Modeling meteorological prediction using particle swarm optimization and neural network ensemble. In *Advances in Neural Networks – ISNN 2006* (LNCS 3973, pp. 1202-1209).

Yu, L. N., Wang, S. Y., & Lai, K. K. (2008). Neural network-based mean-variance-skewness model for portfolio selection. *Computers & Operations Research*, *35*, 34–46. doi:10.1016/j.cor.2006.02.012

Zhang, G. P., & Berardi, V. L. (2003). Time series forecasting using a hybrid ARIMA and neural network model. *Neurocomputing*, *50*, 159–175. doi:10.1016/S0925-2312(01)00702-0

Zhou, Y. J., Wu, J. S., & Qin, F. J. (2006) Neural network with partial least square prediction model based on SSA and MGF. In *Proceedings of the 6th World Conference on Intelligent Control and Automation*.

Zwiers, F. W., & von Storch, H. (2004). On the role of statistics in climate research. *International Journal of Climatology*, *24*, 665–680. doi:10.1002/joc.1027

*This work was previously published in the International Journal of Applied Evolutionary Computation, Volume 2, Issue 4, edited by Wei-Chiang Samuelson Hong, pp. 50-65, copyright 2011 by IGI Publishing (an imprint of IGI Global).*

# Compilation of References

Abhraham, A., & Ramos, V. (2003). Web Usage Mining Using Artificial Ant Colony Clustering and Linear Genetic Programming. In *Proceedings of the 2003 IEEE Conference on Evolutionary Computation* (pp. 8-12).

Abhyankar, A., Hornak, L. A., & Schuckers, S. (2005). Biorthogonal-wavelets-based iris recognition. *Proceedings of the SPIE Society of Photo Optical Instrumentation Engineers Conference, 5779*, 59–67.

Abhyankar, A., & Schuckers, S. (2009). Iris quality assessment and bi-orthogonal wavelet based encoding for recognition. *Pattern Recognition, 42*, 1878–1894. doi:10.1016/j.patcog.2009.01.004

Acharya, D. P., Panda, G., & Lakshmi, Y. V. S. (2010). Effects of finite register length on fast ICA, bacterial foraging optimization based ICA and constrained genetic algorithm based ICA algorithm. *Digital Signal Processing, 20*(3). doi:10.1016/j.dsp.2009.08.012

Acir, N., Özdamar, O., & Güzeliş, C. (2006). Automatic classification of auditory brainstem responses using SVM-based feature selection algorithm for threshold detection. *Engineering Applications of Artificial Intelligence, 19*, 209–218. doi:10.1016/j.engappai.2005.08.004

Admati, A., & Pfleiderer, P. (1988). A theory of intraday trading patters: Volume and price variability. *Review of Financial Studies, 1*, 3–40. doi:10.1093/rfs/1.1.3

Agrawal, R., Imielinski, T., & Swami, A. (1993). Mining association rules between sets of items in large databases. In *Proceedings of the ACM SIGMOD Conference* (pp. 207-216).

Aguirre, A. H., & Coello, C. A. (2002). Design of combinational logic circuits through an evolutionary multi-objective optimization approach. *Artificial Intelligence for Engineering Design, Analysis and Manufacturing, 16*(1), 39–53.

Ahn, C. W., Goldberg, D. E., & Ramkrishna, R. S. (2004). Multiple deme parallel estimation of distribution algorithms: Basic framework and application. In R. Wyrzkowski, J. Dongarra, M. Paprzycki, & J. Wasniewski (Eds.), *Proceedings of the 5th International Conference on Parallel Processing and Applied Mathematics* (LNCS 3019, pp. 544-551)

Alam, S., Dobbie, G., & Riddle, P. (2008). Particle Swarm Optimization Based Clustering of Web Usage Data. In *Proceedings of the Web Intelligence and Intelligent Agent Technology Conference (WI-IAT '08)* (pp. 451-454).

Alander, J. T. (1994). *An indexed bibliography of genetic algorithms: Years 1957-1993*. Vassa, Finland: University of Vassa.

Al-Ansary, M. D., & Deiab, I. M. (1997). Concurrent optimization of design and machining tolerances using the genetic algorithms method. *International Journal of Machine Tools & Manufacture, 37*(12), 1721–1731. doi:10.1016/S0890-6955(97)00033-3

Alawode, K. O., Jubr, I. A., & Komolafe, O. A. (2010). Multiobjective optimal power flow using hybrid evolutionary algorithms. *International Journal of Energy and Power Engineering, 3*(3), 196–201.

Alba, E., Nebro, A., & Troya, J. (2002). Heterogeneous computing and parallel genetic algorithms. *Journal of Parallel and Distributed Computing, 62*(9), 1362–1385. doi:10.1006/jpdc.2002.1851

Alba, E., & Tomasdni, M. (2002). Parallelism 'and evolutionary algorithms. *IEEE Transactions on Evolutionary Computation*, 6(5), 443–461. doi:10.1109/TEVC.2002.800880

Alba, E., & Troya, J. (2001). Synchronous and asynchronous parallel distributed genetic algorithms. *Future Generation Computer Systems*, 17(4), 451–465. doi:10.1016/S0167-739X(99)00129-6

Alba, E., & Troya, J. M. (2002). Improving flexibility and efficiency by adding parallelism to genetic algorithms. *Statistics and Computing*, 12(2), 91–114. doi:10.1023/A:1014803900897

Allaby, M. (1998). *Dictionary of ecology*. New York: Oxford University Press.

Al-Somani, T., & Qureshi, K. (2000). *Reliability optimization using genetics algorithms*. Saudi Arabia: King Abdul-Aziz University.

Anand, R., Mehrotra, K., Mohan, C. K., & Ranka, S. (2002). Efficient classification for multiclass problems using modular neural networks. *IEEE Transactions on Neural Networks*, 6(1), 117–124. doi:10.1109/72.363444

Andersson, J. (2001). *Optimization in engineering design-applications to fluid power systems*. Linkoping, Sweden: Linkoping University.

Aneja, Y. P., Chandrasekaran, R., & Nair, K. P. K. (2004). Minimal - cost system reliability with discrete choice sets for components. *IEEE Transactions on Reliability*, 53, 71–76. doi:10.1109/TR.2004.824829

Araujo, D. L. A., Lopes, H. S., & Freitas, A. A. (1999). A parallel genetic algorithm for rule discovery in large databases. In *Proceedings of the IEEE Systems, Man and Cybernetics Conference*, Tokyo, (Vol. 3, pp. 940-945).

Arryo, J. M., & Conejo, A. J. (2002). A parallel repair GA to solve the unit commitment problem. *IEEE Transactions on Power Systems*, 17(4), 1216–1224. doi:10.1109/TPWRS.2002.804953

Arts, E. H. L., & Lenstra, J. K. (1997). *Local search in combinatorial optimization*. New York, NY: John Wiley & Sons.

Atsalakis, G. S., & Valavanis, K. P. (2009). Surveying stock market forecasting techniques-part 11: Soft computing methods. *Expert Systems with Applications*, 36, 5932–5941. doi:10.1016/j.eswa.2008.07.006

Babu, B. V., & Munawar, S. A. (2001). *Optimal design of shell-and-tube heat exchanges by different strategies of differential evolution (Tech. Rep. No. PILANI -333 031)*. Rajasthan, India: Birla Institute of Technology and Science.

Babu, B. V., & Sastry, K. K. N. (1999). Estimation of heat transfer parameters in a trickle-bed reactor using differential evolution and orthogonal collocation. *Computers & Chemical Engineering*, 23(3), 327–339. doi:10.1016/S0098-1354(98)00277-4

Bäck, T., & Schwefel, H.-P. (1996). Evolutionary computation: An overview. In *Proceedings of the IEEE International Conference on Evolutionary Computation* (pp. 20-29).

Bäck, T. (1996). *Evolutionary algorithms in theory and practice*. New York, NY: Oxford University Press.

Bäck, T., Fogel, D. B., & Michalewicz, Z. (1997). *Handbook of evolutionary computation*. New York, NY: Oxford University Press. doi:10.1887/0750308958

Bäck, T., Hammel, U., & Schwefel, H.-P. (1997). Evolutionary computation: Comments on the history and current state. *IEEE Transactions on Evoltionary Computing*, 1(1), 3–17. doi:10.1109/4235.585888

Badarudin, I. M., Sultan, A. B., Sulaiman, M. N., & Mamat, A. (2010). Shape assignment by genetic algorithm towards designing optimal areas. *International Journal of Computer Science*, 7(4), 1–7.

Bagyamani, J., Thangavel, K., & Rathipriya, R. (2011). Biological Significance of Gene Expression Data using Similarity based Biclustering Algorithm. *International Journal of Biometrics and Bioinformatics*, 4, 201–216.

Baker, M., & Stein, J. C. (2004). Market liquidity as a sentiment indicator. *Journal of Financial Markets*, 7, 271–299. doi:10.1016/j.finmar.2003.11.005

Balling, R. (2003). The maximin fitness function; Multiobjective city and regional planning. In C. M. Fonseca, P. J. Fleming, E. Zitzler, L. Thiele, & K. Deb (Eds.), *Proceedings of the Second International Conference on Evolutionary Multi-Criterion Optimization*, Faro, Portugal (LNCS 2632, pp. 1-15).

Baluja, S. (1994). *Population based incremental learning: A method for integrating genetic search based function optimization and competitive learning* (Tech. Rep. No. CMU-CS-94-163). Pittsburgh, PA: Carnegie Mellon University.

Banka, H., & Mitra, S. (2006). Multi-objective Evolutionary biclustering of gene expression data. *Journal of Pattern Recognition*, *39*, 2464–2477. doi:10.1016/j.patcog.2006.03.003

Banz, R. W. (1981). The relationship between return and market value of common stocks. *Journal of Financial Economics*, *9*(1), 3–18. doi:10.1016/0304-405X(81)90018-0

Bao, C., Neo, T. N., & Guan, S. U. (2007). Reduced Pattern Training in Pattern Distributor Networks. *Journal of Research and Practice in Information Technology*, *39*(4), 273–286.

Barber, B. M., & Lyon, J. D. (1997). Firm size, book-to-market ratio, and security returns: A holdout sample of financial firms. *The Journal of Finance*, *50*(2), 875–883. doi:10.2307/2329503

Barry, C. B., & Brown, S. J. (1984). Differential information and the small firm effect. *Journal of Financial Economics*, *13*(2), 283–294. doi:10.1016/0304-405X(84)90026-6

Basci, E., Ozyidirim, S., & Aydogan, K. (1996). A note on price-volume dynamics in an emerging stock market. *Journal of Banking & Finance*, *20*, 389–400. doi:10.1016/0378-4266(95)00003-8

Basseur, M., Seynhaeve, F., & Talbi, E. G. (2002). Design of multi-objective evolutionary algorithms: Application to the flow-shop scheduling problem. In *Proceedings of the Congress on Evolutionary Computation*, Honolulu, HI (pp. 1151-1156). Washington, DC: IEEE Computer Society.

Basturk, B., & Karaboga, D. (2006, May 12-14). An artificial bee colony (ABC) algorithm for numeric function optimization. In *Proceedings of the IEEE Swarm Intelligence Symposium*, Indianapolis, IN.

Belhumeur, P., Hespanha, J., & Kriegman, D. (1997). Eigenfaces vs. fisherfaces: Recognition using class specific linear projection. *IEEE Transactions on Pattern Analysis and Machine Intelligence*, *19*(7), 711–720. doi:10.1109/34.598228

Belkadi, K., Gourgand, M., Benyettou, M., & Aribi, A. (2006). Sequential and parallel genetic algorithms for hybrid flow shop scheduling. *Journal of Applied Sciences*, *6*(4), 775–778. doi:10.3923/jas.2006.775.778

Benediktsson, J. A., Sveinsson, J. R., Ersoy, O. K., & Swain, P. H. (1997). Parallel consensual neural networks. *IEEE Transactions on Neural Networks*, *8*, 54–64. doi:10.1109/72.554191

Bessembinder, H., & Seguin, P. J. (1992). Futures-trading activity and stock price volatility. *The Journal of Finance*, *47*, 2015–2134. doi:10.2307/2329008

Bhardwaj, R. K., & Brooks, L. D. (1993). Dual beats from bull and bear markets: Reversal of the size effect. *Journal of Financial Research*, *16*(4), 269–283.

Black, F. (1976). Studies in stock price volatility changes. In *Proceedings of the Business Meeting of the Business Economic Statistics Section* (pp. 177-181).

Blake, C. L., & Merz, C. J. (1998). *UCI repository of machine learning databases*. Retrieved March 14, 2010, from http://archive.ics.uci.edu/ml/

Boles, W. W., & Boashash, B. (1998). A human identification technique using images of the iris and wavelet transform. *IEEE Transactions on Signal Processing*, *46*(4), 1185–1188. doi:10.1109/78.668573

Bollerslev, T. (1986). Generalized autoregressive conditional heteroskedasticity. *Journal of Econometrics*, *31*, 307–327. doi:10.1016/0304-4076(86)90063-1

Bollerslev, T., Chou, R., & Kroner, K. (1992). ARCH modeling in finance: A review of the theory and empirical evidence. *Journal of Econometrics*, *51*, 5–59. doi:10.1016/0304-4076(92)90064-X

Bollerslev, T., Engle, R., & Nelson, D. (1994). ARCH models. In Engle, R., & McFadden, D. (Eds.), *Handbook of metrics* (pp. 2959–3038). Amsterdam, The Netherlands: North Holland Press.

Bowden, G. J., Dandy, G. C., & Maier, H. R. (2005). Input determination for neural network models in water resources applications, Part 1. Background and Methodology. *Journal of Hydrology (Amsterdam)*, *301*, 75–92. doi:10.1016/j.jhydrol.2004.06.021

Bowden, G. J., Dandy, G. C., & Maier, H. R. (2005). Input determination for neural network models in water resources applications, Part 2. Case study: Forecasting salinity in a river. *Journal of Hydrology (Amsterdam)*, *301*, 93–107. doi:10.1016/j.jhydrol.2004.06.020

Box, G. E., & Jenkins, P. G. M. (1976). *Time series analysis: forecasting and control*. San Francisco, CA: Holden-Day.

Branke, J., Schmeck, H., Deb, K., & Maheshwar, R. S. (2004). Parallelizing multiobjective evolutionary algorithms: Cone separation. In *Proceedings of the Congress on Evolutionary Computation*, Portland, OR (pp. 1952-1957). Washington, DC: IEEE Computer Society.

Branke, J., Kaubler, T., & Schmeck, H. (2001). Guidance in evolutionary multiobjective optimization. *Advances in Engineering Software*, *32*(6), 499–508. doi:10.1016/S0965-9978(00)00110-1

Brennan, M., Chordia, T., & Subrahmanyam, A. (1998). Alternative factor specifications, security characteristics, and the cross-section of expected stock returns. *Journal of Financial Economics*, *49*, 345–373. doi:10.1016/S0304-405X(98)00028-2

Brown, P., Kleidon, A., & Marsh, T. (1983). New evidence on the nature of size-related anomalies in stock prices. *Journal of Financial Economics*, *12*(1), 33–56. doi:10.1016/0304-405X(83)90026-0

Buyurgan, N., Saygin, C., & Kilic, S. E. (2004). Tool allocation in flexible manufacturing systems with tool alternatives. *Robotics and Computer-integrated Manufacturing*, *20*(4), 341–349. doi:10.1016/j.rcim.2004.01.001

Campbell, J. Y., Grossman, S. J., & Wang, J. (1993). Trading volume and serial correlation in stock returns. *The Quarterly Journal of Economics*, *108*, 905–939. doi:10.2307/2118454

Campbell, J., & Hentschel, L. (1992). No news is good news: An asymmetric model of changing volatility in stock returns. *Journal of Financial Economics*, *31*, 281–318. doi:10.1016/0304-405X(92)90037-X

Cantu-Paz, E. (1997). Designing efficient master-slave parallel genetic algorithms. [University of Illinois at Urbana-Champaign.]. *Urbana (Caracas, Venezuela)*, IL.

Cantu-Paz, E. (1998). A survey of parallel genetic algorithms. *Calculateurs Paralleles*, *10*(2), 141–171.

Carneiro, S. A. (1994). *Problema de Corte via Algoritmo Genético. Dissertação (Mestrado), Universidade Federal do Espírito Santo*. Brasil: UFES.

CASIA iris database version 3.0, http://www.cbsr.ia.ac.cn/IrisDatabase.htm, (downloaded at 11-December-2008).

Chakraborty, A., & Maka, H. (2005). Biclustering of Gene Expression Data Using Genetic Algorithm. In *Proceedings of the Conference on Computation Intelligence in Bioinformatics and Computational Biology* (pp. 1-8).

Chakraborty, U. K. (Ed.). (2008). *Advances in differential evolution, studies in computational intelligence series* (*Vol. 143*). New York, NY: Springer.

Chandra, A., & Yao, X. (2006). Evolving hybrid ensembles of learning machines for better generalization. *Neurocomputing*, *69*, 686–700. doi:10.1016/j.neucom.2005.12.014

Chang, P.-C., Fan, C.-Y., & Chen, S.-H. (2007). Financial time series data forecasting by Wavelet and TSK fuzzy rule based system. In *Proceedings of the IEEE Fourth International Conference on Fuzzy Systems and knowledge Discovery* (pp. 331-335).

Chase, K. W., & Greenwood, W. H. (1988). Design issues in mechanical tolerance analysis. *Manufacturing Review*, *1*(1), 50–59.

Chase, K. W., Greenwood, W. H., Loosli, B. G., & Hauglund, L. F. (1990). Least cost tolerance allocation for mechanical assemblies with automated process selection. *Manufacturing Review*, *3*(1), 49–59.

Chelley-Steeley, P. L., & Steeley, J. M. (1996). Volatility, leverage and firm size: The U.K. evidence. *The Manchester School of Economic and Social Studies*, *64*, 83–103. doi:10.1111/j.1467-9957.1996.tb01456.x

Chen, S., & Smith, S. (1999). Improving Genetic Algorithms by Search Space Reduction (with Applications to Flow Shop Scheduling). In *Proceedings of the Genetic and Evolutionary Computation Conference (GECCO-99)*. San Francisco, CA: Morgan Kaufmann.

Chen, Y. S., & Shahabi, C. (2001). Automatically improving the accuracy of user profiles with genetic algorithm. In *Proceedings of the IASTED International Conference on Artificial Intelligence and Soft Computing* (pp. 283-288).

Chen, Y., Dong, X., & Zhao, Y. (2005). Stock index modeling using EDA based local linear wavelet neural network. In *Proceedings of the IEEE International Conference on Neural Networks and Brain* (pp. 1646-1650).

Chen, C.-H., Lin, C.-J., & Lin, C.-T. (2008). A functional-link-based neurofuzzy network for nonlinear system control. *IEEE Transactions on Fuzzy Systems*, *16*(5).

Cheng, C., Chen, T.-L., & Teoh, H. (2007). Multiple-period modified fuzzy time series for forecasting TAIEX. In *Proceedings of the IEEE Fourth International Conference on Fuzzy systems and Knowledge Discovery* (pp. 2-6).

Cheng, Y., & Church, G. M. (2000). Biclustering of expression data. In *Proceedings of the 8th International Conference on Intelligent Systems for Molecular Biology* (pp. 93-103).

Chen, Y., Yang, B., & Dong, J. (2006). Time series prediction using a local linear wavelet neural network. *Neurocomputing*, *69*, 449–465. doi:10.1016/j.neucom.2005.02.006

Chern. (1992). On the computational complexity of the reliability redundancy allocation in a series system. *Operations Research Letters, 11*, 309-315.

Cheuk, M. Y., Fan, D. K., & So, R. W. (2006). Insider trading in Hong Kong: Some stylized facts. *Pacific-Basin Finance Journal*, *14*, 73–90. doi:10.1016/j.pacfin.2005.06.002

Chi, E. H., Rosien, A., & Heer, J. (2002). LumberJack: Intelligent Discovery and Analysis of Web User Traffic Composition. In *Proceedings of the ACM-SIGKDD Workshop on Web Mining for Usage Patterns and User Profiles*.

Chiang, T. C., & Chiang, J. (1996). Dynamic analysis of stock returns volatility in an integrated international capital market. *Review of Quantitative Finance and Accounting*, *6*, 5–17. doi:10.1007/BF00290793

Choudhury, B. B., Mishra, D., & Biswal, B. B. (2008). Task assignment and scheduling in a constrained manufacturing system using GA. *International Journal of Agile Systems and Management*, *3*(1-2), 127–146.

Chou, R. (1988). Volatility persistence and stock valuations: Some empirical evidence using GARCH. *Journal of Applied Econometrics*, *3*, 279–294. doi:10.1002/jae.3950030404

Christie, A. A. (1982). The stochastic behavior of common stock variances: Value, leverage and interest rate effects. *Journal of Financial Economics*, *10*, 407–432. doi:10.1016/0304-405X(82)90018-6

Christoffersen, P., Jacobs, K., & Wang, Y. (2008). Option valuation with long-run and short-run volatility components. *Journal of Financial Economics*, *90*, 272–297. doi:10.1016/j.jfineco.2007.12.003

Chuang, L. Y., Chang, H. W., Tu, C. J., & Yang, C. H. (2008). Improved binary PSO for feature selection using gene expression data. *Computational Biology and Chemistry*, *32*, 29–38. doi:10.1016/j.compbiolchem.2007.09.005

Chumlamai, S., & Suwannik, W. (2007). Benchmark Problems for Compressed Genetic Algorithm. In *Proceedings of the Electrical Engineering Conference (EECON-30)* (pp. 653-656).

Clark, P. K. (1973). A subordinated stochastic process model with finite variance for speculative prices. *Econometrica*, *41*, 135–155. doi:10.2307/1913889

Coello, C. A. (2001). A short tutorial on evolutionary multiobjective optimization. In E. Zitzler, K. Deb, L. Thiele, C. A. Coello, & D. Corne (Eds.), *Proceedings of the First International Conference on Evolutionary Multi-Criterion Optimization* (LNCS 1993, pp. 21-40).

Coello, C. A. (1999). A comprehensive survey of evolutionary-based multiobjective optimization techniques. *International Journal of Knowledge and Information Systems*, *1*, 269–308.

Coello, C. A. (2000). Preferences in evolutionary multi-objective optimization: A survey. In []. Washington, DC: IEEE Computer Society.]. *Proceedings of the Congress on Evolutionary Computation, 1*, 30–37.

Coello, C. A. (2006). Evolutionary multi objective optimization: A historical view of the field. *IEEE Computational Intelligence Magazine, 1*(1), 28–36. doi:10.1109/MCI.2006.1597059

Coello, C. A., Veldhuizen, A. D., & Lamont, G. B. (2002). *Evolutionary algorithms for solving multi-objective optimization problems*. Boston, MA: Kluwer Academic.

Cooley, R., Mobasher, B., & Srivatsava, J. (1997). Web mining: Information and pattern discovery on the World Wide Web. In *Proceeding of the 9th IEEE International Conference on Tools with Artificial Intelligence* (pp. 558-567).

Cooper, M. (1999). Filter rules based on price and volume in individual security overreaction. *Review of Financial Studies, 12*, 901–935. doi:10.1093/rfs/12.4.901

Copeland, T. E. (1976). A model of asset trading under the assumption of sequential information arrival. *The Journal of Finance, 31*, 1149–1168. doi:10.2307/2326280

Corcoran, A. L., & Sen, S. (1994). Using real-valued genetic algorithms to evolve rule sets for classification. In *Proceedings of the 1st IEEE Conference on Evolutionary Computation* (Vol. 1, pp. 120-124).

Cordón, O., Herrera, F., Hoffmann, F., & Magdalena, L. (2001). *Evolutionary tuning and learning of fuzzy knowledge bases: Vol. 19 of Advances in Fuzzy Systems - Applications and Theory*. Singapore: World Scientific.

Corne, D. W., Jerram, N. R., Knowles, J. D., & Oates, M. J. (2001). PESA-II: Region based selection in evolutionary multiobjective optimization. In *Proceedings of the Genetic and Evolutionary Computation Conference* (pp. 238-290).

Corne, D. W., Knowles, J. D., & Oates, M. J. (2000). The Pareto envelope-based selection algorithm for multiobjective optimization. In *Proceedings of the Sixth International Conference on Parallel Problem Solving from Nature* (pp. 18-20).

Crouch, R. L. (1970). A nonlinear test of the random-walk hypothesis. *The American Economic Review, 60*, 199–202.

Cui, X., Li, M., & Fang, T. (2001). Study of population diversity of multiobjective evolutionary algorithm based on immune and entropy principles. In *Proceedings of the Congress on Evolutionary Computation* (pp. 1316-1321). Washington, DC: IEEE Computer Society.

Das, I., & Dennis, J. (1997). A closer look at drawbacks of minimizing weighted sums of objectives for Pareto set generation in multi criteria optimization problems. *Structural Optimization, 14*, 63–69. doi:10.1007/BF01197559

Das, S., & Idicula, S. M. (2010). Greedy Search-Binary PSO Hybrid for Biclustering Gene Expression Data. *International Journal of Computers and Applications, 2*(3), 1–5. doi:10.5120/651-908

Daugman, J. G. (1993). High confidence visual recognition of persons by a test of statistical independence. *IEEE Transactions on Pattern Analysis and Machine Intelligence, 15*(11), 1148–1161. doi:10.1109/34.244676

Daugman, J. G. (2004). How iris recognition works. *IEEE Transaction on Circuits Systems and Video Technology, 14*(1), 21–30. doi:10.1109/TCSVT.2003.818350

David, A., Veldhuizen, V., Zydallis, J. B., & Lamont, G. B. (2003). Considerations in engineering parallel multi objective evolutionary algorithms. *IEEE Transactions on Evolutionary Computation, 7*(2), 144–174. doi:10.1109/TEVC.2003.810751

De Jong, K. A., & Spears, W. M. (1991). Learning concept classification rules using genetic algorithms. In *Proceedings of the 12th International Joint Conference on Artificial Intelligence* (Vol. 2). San Francisco, CA: Morgan Kaufmann.

De Jong, K. A. (1988). Learning with genetic algorithms: An overview. *Machine Learning, 3*(2), 121–138. doi:10.1007/BF00113894

De Jong, K. A., Spears, W. M., & Gordon, D. F. (1993). Using genetic algorithms for concept learning. *Machine Learning, 13*, 161–188. doi:10.1023/A:1022617912649

Deb, K., Agrawal, S., Pratap, A., & Meyarivan, T. (2000). A fast elitist nondominated sorting genetic algorithm for multi-objective optimization: NSGA-II. In *Proceedings of the Sixth International Conference on Parallel Problem Solving from Nature* (pp. 18-20).

Deb, K., Zope, P., & Jain, A. (2003). Distributed computing of pareto-optimal solutions with evolutionary algorithm. In C. M. Fonseca, P. J. Fleming, E. Zitzler, K. Deb, & L. Thiele (Eds.), *Proceedings of the International Conference on Evolutionary Multi-Criterion Optimization* (LNCS 2632, pp. 534-549).

Deb, K. (1995). *Optimization for engineering design: Algorithms and examples.* New Delhi, India: Prentice-Hall.

Deb, K. (1999). An introduction to genetic algorithms. *Sadhana, 24,* 293–315. doi:10.1007/BF02823145

Deb, K. (2001). *Multi-objective optimization using evolutionary algorithms.* Chichester, UK: John Wiley & Sons.

Deb, K., & Goldberg, D. E. (1991). *MGA in C: A messy genetic algorithm in C.* Champaign, IL: Illinois Genetic Algorithms Laboratory.

Deb, K., Pratap, A., Agarwal, S., & Meyyarivan, T. (2002). A fast and elitist multiobjective genetic algorithm: NSGA-II. *IEEE Transactions on Evolutionary Computation, 6*(2), 182–197. doi:10.1109/4235.996017

De, F., Balio, R. D., Cioppa, A. D., & Tarantina, E. (1996). A parallel genetic algorithm for transonic airfoil optimisation. In [). Washington, DC: IEEE Computer Society.]. *Proceedings of the IEEE International Conference Evolutionary Computation, 1,* 429–434.

Dehuri, S., & Mall, R. (2006). Predictive and Comprehensible Rule Discovery Using A Multi-Objective Genetic Algorithm. *Knowledge-Based Systems, 19,* 413–421. doi:.doi:10.1016/j.knosys.2006.03.004

Delac, K., Grgis, M., & Grgic, S. (2007). Image compression effect in face recognition systems. *Face Recognition, 75-92.*

Demmel, J. G., & Askin, R. G. (1992). A multiple objective decision model for the evaluation of advanced manufacturing system technologies. *Journal of Manufacturing Systems, 11,* 179–194. doi:10.1016/0278-6125(92)90004-Y

Dickey, D. A., & Fuller, W. A. (1979). Distribution of estimators for autoregressive time series with a unit root. *Journal of the American Statistical Association, 74,* 427–431. doi:10.2307/2286348

Dickey, D. A., & Fuller, W. A. (1981). Likelihood ratio statistics for autoregressive time series with a unit root. *Econometrica, 49,* 1057–1072. doi:10.2307/1912517

Dimson, E., & Marsh, T. (1999). Murphy's law and market anomalies. *Journal of Portfolio Management, 25*(2), 53–69. doi:10.3905/jpm.1999.319734

Ding, Z., & Granger, C. W. J. (1996). Modeling volatility persistence of speculative returns: A new approach. *Journal of Econometrics, 73,* 185–215. doi:10.1016/0304-4076(95)01737-2

Ding, Z., Granger, C. W. J., & Engle, R. (1993). A long memory property of stock returns and a new model. *Journal of Empirical Finance, 1,* 83–106. doi:10.1016/0927-5398(93)90006-D

Domingos, P., & Hulten, G. (2000). Mining high-speed data streams. In *Proceedings of KDD* (pp. 71-80).

Doorly, D. J., & Peiro, L. (1997). Supervised parallel genetic algorithms in aerodynamic optimization. In *Proceedings of the 13th AIAA Conference on Computational Fluid Dynamics.*

Dorigo, M., & Caro, G. D. (1999). Ant colony optimization: a new meta-heuristic. *Congress on Evolutionary Computation* (pp. 1470-1477).

Dorigo, M., Maniezzo, V., & Colorni, A. (1996). The Ant: System Optimization by colony of cooperating Agents. *IEEE Transactions on Systems, man and cybernetics, part B, 26,* 1-13.

Dorigo, M., & Caro, G. D. (1999). Ant colony optimization: A new meta-heuristic. In. *Proceedings of the Congress on Evolutionary Computation, 2,* 1470–1477.

Dorigo, M., & Gambardella, L. M. (1997). Ant colony system: A cooperative learning approach to the traveling salesman problem. *IEEE Transactions on Evolutionary Computation, 1*(1), 53–66. doi:10.1109/4235.585892

Dréo, J., Petrowski, A., Siarry, P., & Taillard, E. (2003). Métaheuristiques pour l'optimisation difficile, *Eyrolles,* 356.

Druce, D. J. (2001). Insights from a history of seasonal inflow forecasting with a conceptual hydrologic model. *Journal of Hydrology (Amsterdam), 249*(1-4), 102–112. doi:10.1016/S0022-1694(01)00415-2

Duan, H., Xing, Z., & Xu, C. (2009). An improved quantum evolutionary algorithm based on artificial bee colony optimization. In Yu, W., & Sanchez, E. N. (Eds.), *Advances in computational intelligence* (pp. 269–278). Berlin, Germany: Springer-Verlag. doi:10.1007/978-3-642-03156-4_27

Durillo, J. J., Nebro, A. J., Luna, F., & Alba, E. (2008). A study of master slave approaches to parallelize NSGA-II. In *Proceedings of the IEEE International Symposium on Parallel and Distributed Processing* (pp. 1-18). Washington, DC: IEEE Computer Society.

Dyckhoff, H. (1990). A typology of cutting and packing problems. *European Journal of Operational Research*, *44*, 145–159. doi:10.1016/0377-2217(90)90350-K

Eberhart, R., & Kennedy, J. (1995). A new optimizer using particle swarm theory. In *Proceedings of the IEEE Sixth International Symposium on Micro Machine and Human Science* (pp. 39-43).

Elegbede, A. O. C., Chu, C., Adjallah, K. H., & Yalaoui, F. (2003). Reliability Allocation through cost minimization. *IEEE Transactions on Reliability*, *52*(1), 106–111. doi:10.1109/TR.2002.807242

Engle, R. F. (1982). Autoregressive conditional heteroskedasticity with estimates of the variance of United Kingdom inflation. *Econometrica*, *50*, 987–1007. doi:10.2307/1912773

Engle, R. F., Granger, C. W. J., & Robins, R. (1986). Wholesale and retail prices: Bivariate modeling with forecast able variances. In Belsey, D., & Kuh, E. (Eds.), *Model reliability*. Cambridge, MA: MIT Press.

Engle, R. F., & Lee, G. (1999). A long-run and short-run component model of stock return volatility. In Engle, R., & White, H. (Eds.), *Cointegration, causality and forecasting*. New York, NY: Oxford University Press.

Engle, R. F., & Ng, V. K. (1993). Measuring and testing the impact of news on volatility. *The Journal of Finance*, *48*, 1749–1778. doi:10.2307/2329066

Epps, T. W. (1977). Security price changes and transaction volumes: Theory and evidence. *The American Economic Review*, *65*, 586–597.

Epps, T. W., & Epps, M. L. (1976). The stochastic dependence of security price changes and transaction volumes: Implications for the mixture of distributions hypothesis. *Econometrica*, *44*, 305–321. doi:10.2307/1912726

Er, M., Chen, W., & Wu, S. (2005). High-speed face recognition based on discrete cosine transform and RBF neural networks. *IEEE Transactions on Neural Networks*, *16*, 679–691. doi:10.1109/TNN.2005.844909

Essabri, A., Gzara, M., & Loukil, T. (2006). Parallel multi-objective evolutionary algorithm with multi-front equitable distribution. In *Proceedings of the Fifth International Conference on Grid and Cooperative Computing* (pp. 241-244). Washington, DC: IEEE Computer Society.

Eubank, R. L. (2000). Spline regression. In Schimek, M. G. (Ed.), *Smoothing and regression approaches, computation, and application*. New York, NY: Wiley.

Eun, C., & Shim, S. (1989). International transmission of stock market movements. *Journal of Financial and Quantitative Analysis*, *24*, 241–256. doi:10.2307/2330774

Fama, E. F., & French, K. R. (1992). The cross-section of expected stock returns. *The Journal of Finance*, *47*(2), 427–465. doi:10.2307/2329112

Fama, E. F., & French, K. R. (1993). Common risk factors in the returns on stocks and bonds. *Journal of Financial Economics*, *33*(1), 3–56. doi:10.1016/0304-405X(93)90023-5

Fama, E. F., & French, K. R. (1995). Size and book-to-market factors in earnings and returns. *The Journal of Finance*, *50*(1), 131–155. doi:10.2307/2329241

Fama, E. F., & French, K. R. (1996). Multifactor explanations of asset pricing anomalies. *The Journal of Finance*, *51*(1), 55–87. doi:10.2307/2329302

Fama, E. F., & French, K. R. (1998). Value versus growth: The international evidence. *The Journal of Finance*, *53*(6), 1975–1999. doi:10.1111/0022-1082.00080

Farag, W. A., Quintana, V. H., & Lambert-Torres, G. (1998). A genetic based neuro-fuzzy approach for modeling and control of dynamic systems. *IEEE Transactions on Neural Networks*, *9*(5), 756–767. doi:10.1109/72.712150

Fendenia, M., & Grammatikos, T. (1992). Options trading and the bid–ask spread of the underlying stocks. *The Journal of Business*, *65*, 335–351. doi:10.1086/296574

Feng, C., & Kusiak, A. (1997). Robust tolerance design with the integer programming approach. *Journal of Manufacturing Science and Engineering*, *119*, 603–610. doi:10.1115/1.2831193

Feoktistov, V. (2006). *Differential evolution in search of solutions*. New York, NY: Springer.

Foerster, H., & Wascher, G. (2000). Pattern reduction in one-dimensional cutting-stock problems. *International Journal of Production Research*, *38*, 1657–1676. doi:10.1080/002075400188780

Fogel, D. (1995). *Evolutionary computation*. Los Alamitos, CA: IEEE Press.

Fogel, L. J., Owens, A. J., & Walsh, M. J. (1996). *Artificial intelligence through simulated evolution*. New York, NY: John Wiley & Sons.

Fonseca, C. M. (1995). *Multiobjective genetic algorithms with application to control engineering problems*. Unpublished doctoral dissertation, University of Sheffield, Sheffield, UK.

Fonseca, C. M., & Flemming, P. J. (1993). Genetic algorithms for multiobjective optimization: Formulation, discussion and generalization. In *Proceedings of the 5th International Conference on Genetic Algorithms* (pp. 416-423). Washington, DC: IEEE Computer Society.

Foster, F. D., & Vishwanathan, S. (1990). A theory of intraday variations in volume, variance, and trading cost in securities market. *Review of Financial Studies*, *3*, 593–624. doi:10.1093/rfs/3.4.593

French, K. R., Schwert, W. G., & Stambaugh, R. F. (1987). Expected stock returns and volatility. *The Journal of Finance*, *19*, 3–29.

French, M. N., Krajewski, W. F., & Cuykendal, R. R. (1992). Rainfall forecasting in space and time using a neural network. *Journal of Hydrology (Amsterdam)*, *137*, 1–37. doi:10.1016/0022-1694(92)90046-X

Freund, Y., & Schapire, R. E. (1996). Experiments with a New Boosting Algorithm. In *Proceeding of 13ᵗʰ international Conference on Machine Learning* (pp. 148-156).

Freund, Y., & Schapire, R. E. (1995). *A Decision-theoretic Generalization of On-line Learning and an Application to Boosting (Tech. Rep.)*. Murray Hill, NJ: AT&T Bell Laboratories.

Fu-yuan, H. (2008). Forecasting stock price using a genetic fuzzy neural network. In *Proceedings of the IEEE International Conference on Computer Science and Information Technology* (pp. 549-552).

Fu-yuan, H. (2008). Integration of improved particle swarm optimization algorithm and fuzzy neural network for Shanghai stock market prediction. In *Proceedings of the IEEE Workshop on Power Electronics and Intelligent Transportation Systems* (pp. 242-247).

Gao, Y., Shi, L., & Yao, P. (2000). Study on multi-objective genetic algorithm. *IEEE*, 646-650.

Gao, J., Ding, B., Fan, W., Han, J., & Yu, P. S. (2008). *Classifying Data Streams with Skewed Class Distributions and Concept Drifts. IEEE Internet Computing, Special Issue on Data Stream Management* (pp. 37–49). IEEEIC.

García-Pedrajas, N., Hervás-Martíneza, C., & Muñoz-Pérez, J. (2002). Multi-objective cooperative coevolution of artificial neural networks (multi-objective cooperative networks). *Neural Networks*, *15*(10), 1255–1274. doi:10.1016/S0893-6080(02)00095-3

Gau, T., & Wascher, G. (1995). CUTGEN1: A Problem Generator for the Standard One-dimensional Cutting Stock Problem. *European Journal of Operational Research*, *84*, 572–579. doi:10.1016/0377-2217(95)00023-J

Gebka, B., Henke, H., & Bohl, M. T. (2006). Institutional trading and stock return autocorrelation: Empirical evidence on polish pension fund investors' behavior. *Global Finance Journal*, *16*, 233–244. doi:10.1016/j.gfj.2006.01.007

Gen, M., & Cheng, R. (1997). *Genetic algorithms and engineering design*. New York, NY: John Wiley & Sons.

Gibson, G. J., Siu, S., & Cowan, C. F. N. (1991). The application of nonlinear structures to the reconstruction of binary signals. *IEEE Transactions on Signal Processing*, *39*(8), 1877–1884. doi:10.1109/78.91157

Gilmore, P. C., & Gomory, R. E. (1961). A linear programming approach to the cutting stock problem. *Operations Research*, *9*, 849–859. doi:10.1287/opre.9.6.849

Gilmore, P. C., & Gomory, R. E. (1963). A linear programming approach to the cutting stock problem. *Operations Research, 11*, 863–888. doi:10.1287/opre.11.6.863

Godfrey, M. D., Granger, C., & Morgenstern, W. (1964). The random walk hypothesis of stock market behavior. *Kyklos, 17*, 1–30. doi:10.1111/j.1467-6435.1964.tb02458.x

Goldberg, D. E. (1989). *Genetic algorithms in search, optimization and machine learning*. Reading, MA: Addison Wesley.

Golfeto, R. R., Moretti, A. C., & SallesNeto, L. L. (2007). Algoritmo genético simbiótico aplicado ao problema de corte unidimensional. In *Anais do XXXIX Simpósio Brasileiro de Pesquisa Operacional*.

Golfeto, R. R., Moretti, A. C., & Salles Neto, L. L. (2009). A Genetic Symbiotic Algorithm Applied to the Cutting Stock Problem with Multiple Objectives. *Advanced Modeling and Optimization, 11*, 473–501.

Golfeto, R. R., Moretti, A. C., & Salles Neto, L. L. (2009). *A Genetic Symbiotic Algorithm Applied To The One-Dimensional Cutting Stock Problem*. Pesquisa Operacional.

Golub, M., & Jakobovic, D. (2000). A new model of global parallel genetic algorithm. In *Proceedings of the 22nd International Conference on Information Technology Interfaces* (pp. 363-368). Washington, DC: IEEE Computer Society.

Grama, A., Gupta, A., & Kumar, V. (1993). Isoefficiency: Measuring the scalability of parallel algorithms and architectures. *IEEE Parallel and Distributed Technology*, 12-21.

Granger, C. W. J. (1969). Investigating causal relations by econometric models and cross-spectral. *Econometria, 37*, 424–438. doi:10.2307/1912791

Granger, C. W. J., & Newbold, P. (1974). Superious regressions in econometrics. *Journal of Econometrics, 2*, 111–120. doi:10.1016/0304-4076(74)90034-7

Granger, C., W. J., & Morgenstern, W. (1963). Spectral analysis of New York stock market prices. *Kyklos, 16*, 1–27. doi:10.1111/j.1467-6435.1963.tb00270.x

Greene, D. P., & Smith, S. F. (1993). Competition-based induction of decision models from examples. *Machine Learning, 13*, 229–257. doi:10.1023/A:1022622013558

Greenwald, B., & Stein, J. (1991). Transactional risk, market crashes, and the role of circuit breakers. *The Journal of Business, 64*, 443–462. doi:10.1086/296547

Grosso, P. B. (1985). *Computer simulation of genetic adaptation: Para interaction in multilocus model*. Ann Arbor, MI: University of Michigan.

Guan, S. U., & Ramanathan, K. (2004). Recursive percentage based hybrid pattern (RPHP) training for curve fitting. In *Proceedings of the 2004 IEEE Conference on Cybernetics and Intelligent Systems* (Vol. 1, pp. 445-450).

Guan, S. U., & ZhuCollard, F. (2005). An incremental approach to genetic-algorithms based classification. Systems. *Man and Cybernetics, Part B, IEEE Transactions, 35*(2), 227-239.

Guangwen, L., Weiguo, Z., & Jian, L. (2007). The niche genetic algorithm and its application in the optimization of an aircraft control system. *Flight Dynamics, 25*(3), 79–82.

Guan, S. U., & Li, S. (2001). Incremental learning with respect to new incoming input attributes. *Neural Processing Letters, 14*(3), 241–260. doi:10.1023/A:1012799113953

Guan, S. U., & Li, S. (2002). Parallel growing and training of neural networks using output parallelism. *IEEE Transactions on Neural Networks, 13*(3), 542–550. doi:10.1109/TNN.2002.1000123

Guan, S. U., & Liu, J. (2002). Incremental ordered neural network training. *Journal of Intelligent Systems, 13*(1).

Guan, S. U., & Liu, J. (2004). Incremental neural network training with an increasing input dimension. *Journal of Intelligent Systems, 12*(3), 137–172.

Guan, S. U., & Ramanathan, K. (2007). Percentage-based Hybrid Pattern Training with Neural Network Specific Crossover. *Journal of Intelligent Systems, 16*, 1–26. doi:10.1515/JISYS.2007.16.1.1

Guan, S. U., & Zhu, F. (2004). Class decomposition for GA-based classifier agents-a Pitt approach. *IEEE Transactions on Systems, Man, and Cybernetics. Part B, Cybernetics, 34*(1), 381–392. doi:10.1109/TSMCB.2003.817030

Guan, S. U., & Zhu, F. (2005). An incremental approach to genetic-algorithms-based classification. *IEEE Transactions on Systems, Man, and Cybernetics. Part B, Cybernetics, 35*(2), 227–239. doi:10.1109/TSMCB.2004.842247

Gupta, D. (1993). On measurement and valuation of manufacturing flexibility. *International Journal of Production Research, 31*, 2947–2958. doi:10.1080/00207549308956909

Gupta, J. N. D., & Sexton, R. (1999). Comparing back propagation with a genetic algorithm for neural network training. *Omega*, 679–684. doi:10.1016/S0305-0483(99)00027-4

Guyon, I., & Elissee, A. (2003). An introduction to variable and feature selection. *Journal of Machine Learning Research, 3*, 1157–1182. doi:10.1162/153244303322753616

Guzmán, M. A., Delgado, A., & De Carvalho, J. (2010). A novel multiobjective optimization algorithm based on bacterial chemotaxis. *Engineering Applications of Artificial Intelligence, 23*(3), 292–301. doi:10.1016/j.engappai.2009.09.010

Haessler, R. (1975). Controlling cutting pattern changes in one-dimensional trim problems. *Operations Research, 23*, 483–493. doi:10.1287/opre.23.3.483

Hafner, C. M. (1998). Estimating high-frequency foreign exchange rate volatility with nonparametric ARCH models. *Journal of Statistical Planning and Inference, 68*, 247–269. doi:10.1016/S0378-3758(97)00144-4

Hajela, P., & Yin, C. Y. (1992). Genetic search strategies in multicriterion optimal design. *Structural and Multidisciplinary Optimization, 4*(2), 99–107.

Hall, P., Kay, J. W., & Titterington, D. M. (1990). Asymptotically optimal difference-based estimation of variance in nonparametric regression. *Biometrika, 77*, 521–528. doi:10.1093/biomet/77.3.521

Hamao, Y., Masulis, R. W., & Ng, V. (1990). Correlations in price changes and volatility across international stock markets. *Review of Financial Studies, 3*, 281–307. doi:10.1093/rfs/3.2.281

Ham, F. M., & Kostanic, I. (2001). *Principles of neurocomputing for science and engineering*. New York, NY: McGraw-Hill.

Hansen, L. K., & Salamon, P. (1990). Neural network ensembles. *IEEE Transactions on Pattern Analysis and Machine Intelligence, 12*(10), 993–1001. doi:10.1109/34.58871

Harik, G. R., Lobo, F. G., & Goldberg, D. E. (1999). The compact genetic algorithm. *IEEE Transactions on Evolutionary Computation, 3*(4), 287–297. doi:10.1109/4235.797971

Harris, L. (1987). Transaction data tests of the mixture of distributions hypothesis. *Journal of Financial and Quantitative Analysis, 22*, 127–139. doi:10.2307/2330708

He, J., & Ng, L. K. (1994). Economic forces, fundamental variables, and equity returns. *The Journal of Business, 67*, 599–609. doi:10.1086/296648

Helland, I. S. (1990). PLS regression and statistical models. *Journal of Statistics, 179*, 97–114.

Hiemstra, C., & Jones, J. D. (1994). Testing for linear and nonlinear granger causality in the stock price-volume relation. *The Journal of Finance, 49*, 1639–1664. doi:10.2307/2329266

Hiroyasu, T., Miki, M., & Tanimura, Y. (1999). Characteristics of models of parallel genetic algorithms on pc cluster systems. In *Proceedings of the 1st International Workshop on Cluster Computing* (pp. 879-886).

Hiroyasu, T., Kaneko, M., & Miki, M. (2000). A parallel genetic algorithm with distributed environment scheme. In []. Washington, DC: IEEE Computer Society.]. *Proceedings of the International Conference on Parallel and Distributed Processing Techniques and Applications, 2*, 619–625.

Hiroyasu, T., Miki, M., & Watanabe, S. (2000). The new model of parallel genetic algorithm in multi objective optimization problems - divided range multi objective GA. In []. Washington, DC: IEEE Computer Society.]. *Proceedings of Congress on Evolutionary Computation, 1*, 333–340.

Hobbs, M., & Rodgers, P. (1998). Representing space: A hybrid genetic algorithm for aesthetic graph layout. In *Proceedings of the Fourth Joint Conference on Frontiers in Evolutionary Algorithms.*

Hogan, K. C. Jr, & Melvin, M. T. (1994). Sources of meteor showers and heat waves in the foreign exchange market. *Journal of International Economics, 37*, 239–247. doi:10.1016/0022-1996(94)90047-7

Holland, J. H. (1962). Outline for a logical theory of adaptive systems. *Journal of the ACM, 3,* 297–314. doi:10.1145/321127.321128

Holland, J. H. (1975). *Adaptation in natural and artificial systems.* Ann Arbor, MI: University of Michigan Press.

Hong, W.-C. (2008). Rainfall forecasting by technological machine learning models. *Applied Mathematics and Computation, 200,* 41–57. doi:10.1016/j.amc.2007.10.046

Horii, H., Miki, M., Koirumi, T., & Tsujiuchi, N. (2002). Asynchronous migration of island parallel ga for multi-objective optimization problem. In *Proceedings of the Asia-Pod Conference on Simulated Evolution and Learning.*

Horn, J., Erickson, M., & Mayer, A. (2000). The niched pareto genetic algorithm applied to the design of ground-water remediation systems. In E. Zitzler, K. Deb, L. Thiele, C. A. Coello, & D. Corne (Eds.), *Proceedings of the First International Conference on Evolutionary Multi-Criterion Optimization* (LNCS 1993, pp. 681-695).

Horn, J., Nafpliotis, N., & Goldberg, D. E. (1994). A niched Pareto genetic algorithm for multi objective optimization. In *Proceedings of the First IEEE World Congress on Computational Intelligence,* Orlando, FL (Vol. 1, pp. 82-87). Washington, DC: IEEE Computer Society.

Horn, J. (1997). The nature of niching: Genetic algorithms and the evolution of optimal, cooperative populations. [University of Illinois at Urbana-Champaign.]. *Urbana (Caracas, Venezuela),* IL.

Horowitz, J. L., Loughran, T., & Savin, N. E. (2000). Three analyses of size premium. *Journal of Empirical Finance, 7*(2), 143–153. doi:10.1016/S0927-5398(00)00008-6

How, J. C. Y., Verhoeven, P., & Huang, C. X. (2005). Information asymmetry surrounding earnings and dividend announcements: An intra-day analysis. *Mathematics and Computers in Simulation, 68,* 463–473. doi:10.1016/j.matcom.2005.02.015

Hua Ang, J., Guan, S. U., Tan, K. C., & Al Mamun, A. (2008). Interference-less neural network training. *Neurocomputing, 71*(16-18), 3509–3524. doi:10.1016/j.neucom.2007.10.012

Huang, W., Nakamori, Y., & Wang, S.-Y. (2004). Forecasting stock movement direction with support vector machine. *Computer and Operation Research, 32*(10).

Huang, C., & Dun, J. (2008). A distributed PSO–SVM hybrid system with feature selection and parameter optimization. *Applied Soft Computing, 8,* 1381–1391. doi:10.1016/j.asoc.2007.10.007

Huang, V. L., Suganthan, P. N., & Liang, J. J. (2006). Comprehensive learning particle swarm optimizer for solving multiobjective optimization problems. *International Journal of Intelligent Systems, 21*(2), 209–226. doi:10.1002/int.20128

Huang, Y. S. (1997). The size anomaly on the Taiwan stock exchange. *Applied Financial Letters, 4*(1), 7–12.

Huaping, C., Gu, F., & Bingyuan, L. (2006). Application of self-adaptive multi-objective genetic algorithm in flexible job shop scheduling. *Journal of System Simulation, 18*(18), 2271–2274.

Hulten, G., Spencer, L., & Domingos, P. (2001). Mining time-changing data streams. In *Proceedings of KDD* (pp. 97-106). New York: ACM.

Hung, J. (1997). Intervention strategies and exchange rate volatility: A noise trading perspective. *Journal of International Money and Finance, 16,* 779–793. doi:10.1016/S0261-5606(97)00023-5

Ishibuchi, H., Nojima, Y., Narukawa, K., & Doi, T. (2006). Incorporation of decision maker's preference into evolutionary multi objective optimization algorithms. In *Proceeding of the Genetic and Evolutionary Impact Conference,* Seattle, WA (Vol. 1, pp. 741-742).

Ishibuchi, H., Nakashima, T., & Murata, T. (2002). Performance evaluation of fuzzy classifier systems for multidimensional pattern classification problems. *IEEE Transactions on Systems, Man, and Cybernetics. Part B, Cybernetics, 29*(5), 601–618. doi:10.1109/3477.790443

Jaddan, O. A., Rajamani, L., & Rao, C. R. (2008). Non-dominated ranked genetic algorithm for solving multi objective optimization problems: NRGA. *Journal of Theoretical and Applied Information Technology,* 61-67.

Jaffe, J., & Westerfield, R. (1985). The weekend effect in common stock returns: The international evidence. *The Journal of Finance, 40,* 433–454. doi:10.2307/2327894

Jaimes, A. L., & Coello, C. A. (2007). MRMOGA: Parallel evolutionary multiobjective optimization using multiple resolutions. *Concurrency and Computation, 19*(4), 397–441. doi:10.1002/cpe.1107

Jain, A., & Kumar, A. M. (2007). Hybrid neural network models for hydrologic time series forecasting. *Applied Soft Computing, 7*, 585–592. doi:10.1016/j.asoc.2006.03.002

Jain, P., & Joh, G. (1988). The dependence between hourly prices and trading volume. *Journal of Financial and Quantitative Analysis, 23*, 269–284. doi:10.2307/2331067

Janikow, C. J. (1993). A knowledge-intensive genetic algorithm for supervised learning. *Machine Learning, 13*, 189–228. doi:10.1023/A:1022669929488

Jarosław, M., & Tomasz, W. (2003). A genetic algorithm for motion detection. In *Proceedings of the 9th International Conference on Soft Computing*, Brno, Czech Republic.

Jarrow, R. (1992). Market manipulation, bubbles, corners and short squeezes. *Journal of Financial and Quantitative Analysis, 27*, 311–336. doi:10.2307/2331322

Jaszkiewicz, A. (2002). On the performance of multiple-objective genetic local search on the 0/1 knapsack problem-a comparative experiment. *IEEE Transactions on Evolutionary Computation, 6*(4), 402–412. doi:10.1109/TEVC.2002.802873

Jeang, A. (1997). An approach of tolerance design for quality improvement and cost reduction. *International Journal of Production Research, 35*, 1193–1211. doi:10.1080/002075497195272

Jenkins, R. E., & Yuhas, B. P. (2002). A simplified neural network solution through problem decomposition: The case of the truck backer-upper. *IEEE Transactions on Neural Networks, 4*(4), 718–720. doi:10.1109/72.238326

Jespersen, S. E., Throhauge, J., & Bach Pedersen, T. (2002). A hybrid approach to Web Usage Mining. In *Proceedings of the Data Warehousing and Knowledge Discovery Conference (DaWaK'02)* (LNCS 2454, pp. 73-82).

Jingping, Z., Zhirui, L., & Haifeng, S. (2007). Research on reactive power optimization of distribution network based on the improved crowding niche genetic algorithm. *Relay, 35*(1), 19–22.

Jing, X., & Wong, H., & Zhang, David. (2005). A Fourier-LDA approach for image recognition. *Pattern Recognition, 38*, 453–457. doi:10.1016/j.patcog.2003.09.020

Jing, X., & Wong, H., & Zhang, David. (2006). Face recognition based on discriminant fractional Fourier feature extraction. *Pattern Recognition Letters, 27*, 1465–1471. doi:10.1016/j.patrec.2006.02.020

Jin-hua, Z. (2007). *Multi-objective evolutionary algorithm and its application*. Beijing, China: Science Press.

Jin, L., Kuang, X. Y., Huang, H., Qin, Z., & Wang, Y. (2004). Study on the over-fitting of the artificial neural network forecasting model. *Acta Meteorologica Sinica, 62*(1), 62–69.

Jiong-liang, X., & Jin-hua, Z. (2008). Research on cause for overlapping solutions and on their influence in NSGA-II algorithm. *Computer Engineering and Application, 4*(22), 69–72.

Johansen, S. (1988). Statistical analysis of cointegration vectors. *Journal of Economic Dynamics & Control, 12*, 231–254. doi:10.1016/0165-1889(88)90041-3

John, G. H., & Langley, P. (1995). Estimating continuous distributions in Bayesian classifiers. In *Proceedings of the Eleventh Conference on Uncertainty in Artificial Intelligence* (pp. 338-345). San Francisco: Morgan Kaufmann Publishers.

Johnson, D. (1998). *Applied multivariate methods for data analysts* (1st ed.). Stamford, CT: Thomson Learning.

Jones, D. F., Mirrazavi, S. K., & Tamiz, M. (2002). Multiobjective meta-heuristics: An overview of the current state-of-the-art. *European Journal of Operational Research, 137*(1), 1–9. doi:10.1016/S0377-2217(01)00123-0

Joshi, R., & Sanderson, A. C. (1999). Minimal representation multisensor fusion using differential evolution. *IEEE Transactions on Systems, Man, and Cybernetics. Part A, Systems and Humans, 29*(1), 63–76. doi:10.1109/3468.736361

Juan, C., & Xu Lihong. (2006). A dynamic niche genetic algorithm for multimodal function optimization. *Journal of Tong Ji University, 34*, 684–688.

Kaestner, C. A., Pappa, G. L., & Freitas, A. A. (2002). A multiobjective genetic algorithm for attribute selection. In *Proceedings of the 4th International Conference on Recent Advances in Soft Computing*, Nottingham, UK (pp. 116-121).

Kamiura, J., Hiroyasu, T., Miki, M., Watanabe, S., & Sakoda, T. (2002). MOGADES: Multi-objective genetic algorithm with distributed environment scheme. In *Proceedings of the Second International Workshop on Intelligent Systems Design and Applications* (pp. 143-148).

Kanan, H. R., & Faez, K. (2008). GA-based optimal selection of PZMI features for face recognition. *Applied Mathematics and Computation*, *205*, 706–715. doi:10.1016/j.amc.2008.05.114

Kanan, H. R., & Faez, K. (2008). An improved feature selection method based on ant colony optimization (ACO) evaluated on face recognition system. *Applied Mathematics and Computation*, *205*, 716–725. doi:10.1016/j.amc.2008.05.115

Kanas, A. (2002). Mean and variance spillover among size-sorted UK equity portfolios. *Applied Economics Letters*, *9*, 319–323. doi:10.1080/13504850110065858

Kaneko, M., Hiroyasu, T., & Miki, M. (2000). A parallel genetic algorithm with distributed environment scheme. In *Proceedings of the International Conference on Parallel and Distributed Processing Techniques and Applications* (pp. 619-625). Washington, DC: IEEE Computer Society.

Kantorovich, L. V. (1960). Mathematical Methods of Organizing and Planning Production. *Management Science*, *6*, 366–422. doi:10.1287/mnsc.6.4.366

Karaboga, D. (2005). *An idea based on honey bee swarm for numerical optimization* (Tech. Rep. No. TR06). Kayseri, Turkey: Erciyes University.

Karaboga, D., & Basturk, B. (2007). Artificial bee colony (ABC) optimization algorithm for solving constrained optimization problems. In P. Melin, O. Castillo, L. T. Aguilar, J. Kacprzyk, & W. Pedrycz (Eds.), *Proceedings of the 12th International Conference on Advances in Soft Computing-Foundations of Fuzzy Logic and Soft Computing* (LNCS 4529, pp. 789-798).

Karaboga, D., Akay, B., & Ozturk, C. (2007). Artificial bee colony (ABC) optimization algorithm for training feed-forward neural networks. In V. Torra, Y. Naurkawa, & Y. Yoshida (Eds.), *Proceedings of the 4th International Conference on Modeling Decisions for Artificial Intelligence* (LNCS 4617, pp. 318-329).

Karaboga, D., & Akay, B. (2009). A survey: Algorithms simulating bee swarm intelligence. *Artificial Intelligence Review*, *31*, 61–85. doi:10.1007/s10462-009-9127-4

Karaboga, D., & Basturk, B. (2007). A powerful and efficient algorithm for numerical function optimization: Artificial bee colony (ABC) algorithm. *Journal of Global Optimization*, *39*(3), 459–471. doi:10.1007/s10898-007-9149-x

Karaboga, D., & Basturk, B. (2008). On the performance of artificial bee colony (ABC) algorithm. *Applied Soft Computing*, *8*, 687–697. doi:10.1016/j.asoc.2007.05.007

Karaboga, N. (2009). A new design method based on artificial bee colony algorithm for digital IIR filters. *Journal of the Franklin Institute*, *346*, 328–348. doi:10.1016/j.jfranklin.2008.11.003

Karpoff, J. M. (1987). The relation between price changes and trading volume: A survey. *Journal of Financial and Quantitative Analysis*, *22*, 109–126. doi:10.2307/2330874

Kayo, G., & Ooka, R. (2009). Application multiobjective genetic algorithm for optimal design method distributed energy system. In *Proceedings of the Eleventh International IBPSA Conference*, Glasgow, Scotland (pp. 167-172).

Keim, D. B. (1983). Size related anomalies and stock return seasonality: Further empirical evidence. *Journal of Financial Economics*, *12*(1), 13–32. doi:10.1016/0304-405X(83)90025-9

Kennedy, J., & Eberhart, R. (1995). Particle swarm optimization. In *Proceedings of the IEEE International Conference on Neural Networks*, Perth, Australia (pp. 1942-1948).

Kennedy, J., & Eberhart, R. C. (1995). Particle swarm optimization. In *Proceedings of the IEEE International Conference on Neutral Networks*, Perth, Australia (pp. 1942-1948).

Kennedy, J., & Eberhart, R. C. (1997). A discrete binary version of the particle swarm algorithm. *IEEE International Conference on Computational Cybernatics and Simulation: Vol. 5* (pp. 4104-4108).

Kennedy, J., Eberhart, R. C., & Shi, Y. (2001). *Swarm intelligence*. San Francisco, CA: Morgan Kaufman.

Kenneth, A. D. J., & Spears, W. M. (1991). Learning concept classification rules using genetic algorithms. In *Proceedings of the 12th international joint conference on Artificial intelligence*, Sydney, New South Wales, Australia (pp. 651-656).

Khan, N. (2003). Bayesian optimization algorithms for multiobjective and hierarchically difficult problems. [University of Illinois at Urbana-Champaign.]. *Urbana (Caracas, Venezuela)*, IL.

Khashei, M., Bijari, M., & Ardali, G. A. R. (2009). Improvement of auto-regressive integrated moving average models using fuzzy logic and artificial neural network. *Neurocomputing*, *72*, 956–967. doi:10.1016/j.neucom.2008.04.017

Khosla, A., Kumar, S., Aggarwal, K. K., & Singh, J. (2006). A Matlab Implementation of Swarm Intelligence based Methodology for Identification of Optimized Fuzzy Models. In *Swarm Intelligent Systems: Studies in Computational Intelligence* (*Vol. 26*, pp. 175–184). SCI.

Kim, K.-J., & Han, I. (2000). Genetic algorithm approach to feature discretization in artificial neural networks for prediction of stock price index. *Expert Systems with Applications*, *19*, 125–132. doi:10.1016/S0957-4174(00)00027-0

Kim, M. K., & Burnie, D. A. (2002). The firm size effect and the economic cycle. *Journal of Financial Research*, *25*(1), 111–124. doi:10.1111/1475-6803.00007

Kira, K., & Rendell, L. (1992). A practical approach to feature selection. *Proceedings of Ninth International Conference on Machine Learning* (pp. 249–256).

Kita, H., Yabumoto, Y., Mori, N., & Nishikawa, Y. (1996). Multi-objective optimization by means of the thermodynamical genetic algorithm. In H.-M. Voigt, W. Ebeling, I. Rechenberg, & H.-P. Schwefel (Eds.), *Proceedings of the International Conference on Evolutionary Computation and the 4th International Conference on Parallel Problem Solving from Nature* (LNCS 1141, pp. 504-5412).

Knarr, M. R., Goltz, M. N., Lamont, G. B., & Huang, J. (2000). Bioremediation of perchlorate-contaminated groundwater using a multi-objective parallel evolutionary algorithm. In *Proceedings of the Congress on Evolutionary Computation* (pp. 1604-1621). Washington, DC: IEEE Computer Society.

Knowles, J., & Corne, D. (1999). The Pareto archived evolution strategy: a new baseline algorithm for Pareto multiobjective optimisation. In *Proceedings of the Congress on Evolutionary Computation* (pp. 6-9). Washington, DC: IEEE Computer Society.

Knowles, J., & Corne, D. (2000). M-PAES: A memetic algorithm for multi-objective optimization. In *Proceedings of the Congress on Evolutionary Computation* (pp. 325-332). Washington, DC: IEEE Computer Society.

Kolen, A., & Pesch, E. (1994). Genetic local search in combinatorial optimization. *Discrete Applied Mathematics and Combinatorial Operations Research and Computer Science*, *48*, 273–284.

Koutmos, G., & Saidi, R. (1995). The leverage effect in individual stocks and the debt to equity ratio. *Journal of Business Finance & Accounting*, *22*, 1063–1075. doi:10.1111/j.1468-5957.1995.tb00894.x

Kozlov, K. N., & Samsonov, A. M. (2006). New migration scheme for parallel differential evolution. In *Proceedings of the Fifth International Conference on Bioinformatics of Genome Regulation and Structure* (pp. 141-144).

Krishnapuram, R., Joshi, A., & Nasraoui, O. (2001). Low-complexity fuzzy relational clustering algorithms for Web mining. *IEEE Transactions on Fuzzy Systems*, *9*, 595–607. doi:10.1109/91.940971

Kuligowski, R. J., & Barros, A. P. (1998). Experiments in short-term precipitation forecasting using artificial neural networks. *Monthly Weather Review*, *126*(2), 470–482. doi:10.1175/1520-0493(1998)126<0470:EISTPF>2.0.CO;2

Kumar, R., & Rockett, P. (2002). Improved sampling of the Pareto-front in multiobjective genetic optimizations by steady-state evolution: A Pareto converging genetic algorithm. *Evolutionary Computation*, *10*(3), 283–314. doi:10.1162/106365602760234117

Kumar, R., Sarin, A., & Shastri, K. (1998). The impact of options trading on the market quality of the underlying securities: An empirical analysis. *The Journal of Finance, 53*, 717–732. doi:10.1111/0022-1082.285595

Kunasol, N., Suwannik, W., & Chongstitvatana, P. (2006). Solving One-Million-Bit Problems Using LZWGA. In *Proceedings of International Symposium on Communications and Information Technologies (ISCIT)* (pp. 32-36).

Kunzli, S., & Zitzler, E. (2004). Indicator-based selection in multiobjective search. In X. Yao, E. Burke, J. A. Lozano, J. J. Merelo-Guervos, J. A. Bullinaria, J. Rowe et al. (Eds.), *Proceedings of the 8th International Conference on Parallel Problem Solving from Nature*, Birmingham, UK (LNCS 3242, pp. 832-842).

Kuo, I.-H., Horng, S.-J., Chen, Y.-H., Run, R.-S., Kao, T.-W., & Chen, R.-J. (2009). Forecasting TAIFEX based on fuzzy time series and particle swarm optimization. *Expert Systems with Applications, 37*(2), 1494–1502. doi:10.1016/j.eswa.2009.06.102

Kuo, R. J. (2001). A sales forecasting system based on fuzzy neural network with initial weights generated by genetic algorithm. *European Journal of Operational Research, 129*, 496–517. doi:10.1016/S0377-2217(99)00463-4

Kuo, W., & Prasad, V. R. (2000). An annotated overview of system reliability optimization. *IEEE Transactions on Reliability, 49*, 176–187. doi:10.1109/24.877336

Kuo, W., Prasad, V. R., Tilman, F. A., & Hwang, C. L. (2001). *Optimal Reliability Design: Fundamentals and Applications*. Cambridge, UK: Cambridge University Press.

Kwedlo, W., & Kretowski, M. (1998). Discovery of Decision Rules from Databases: An Evolutionary Approach Principles of Data Mining and Knowledge Discovery, *Second European Symposium*, PKDD '98, Nantes, France, September 23-26, 1998.

Kyle, A. S. (1985). Continuous auctions and insider trading. *Economertrica, 53*, 1315–1335. doi:10.2307/1913210

Labroche, N. (2007). *Learning web users profiles with relational clustering algorithms*. Menlo Park, CA: Association for the Advancement of Artificial Intelligence.

Lakonishok, J., Shleifer, A., & Vishny, R. W. (1994). Contrarian investment, extrapolation and risk. *The Journal of Finance, 49*(5), 1541–1578. doi:10.2307/2329262

Lamont, G. B., & Veldhuizn, D. A. (2001). On measuring multi-objective evolutionary algorithm performance. In *Proceedings of the Congress on Evolutionary Computation* (pp. 204-211). Washington, DC: IEEE Computer Society.

Lamont, G. B., Coello, C. A., & Veldhuizen, A. V. (2002). *Evolutionary algorithms for solving multi-objective problems*. Boston, MA: Kluwer Academic.

Laopodis, N. T. (1997). U.S. dollar asymmetry and exchange rate volatility. *Journal of Applied Business Research, 13*, 1–8.

Larranga, P., & Lozano, J. A. (Eds.). (2002). *Estimation of distribution algorithms: A new tool for evolutionary computation*. Boston, MA: Kluwer Academic.

Laumanns, M., Thiele, L., Deb, K., & Zitzler, E. (2002). *Combining convergence and diversity in evolutionary multi-objective optimization (Vol. 10)*. Cambridge, MA: MIT Press.

Lee, C. H., & Fu, Y. H. (2008). Web usage mining based on clustering of browsing features. In *Proceedings of the 8th International Conference on Intelligent Systems Design and Applications* (pp. 281-286).

Lee, Z.-J., & Lee, W.-L. (2003). A hybrid search algorithm of ant colony optimization and genetic algorithm applied to weapon–target assignment problems. In J. Liu, Y. Cheung, & H. Yin (Eds.), *Proceedings of the 4th International Conference on Intelligent Data Engineering and Automated Learning* (LNCS 2690, pp. 278-285).

Lee, Z.-J., Su, S.-F., & Lee, C.-Y. (2003). Efficiently solving general weapon–target assignment problem by genetic algorithms with greedy eugenics. *IEEE Transactions on Systems, Man and Cybernetics, Part B*, 113-121.

Lee, C. S., Kim, S. S., & Choi, J. S. (2003). Operation sequence and tool selection in flexible manufacturing systems under dynamic tool allocation. *Computers in Industry, 45*(1), 61–73. doi:10.1016/S0360-8352(03)00019-6

Lee, M. A., Yeah, C. D., Cheng, C. H., Chan, J. W., & Lee, K. T. (2003). Empirical orthogonal function analysis of sea surface temperature patterns in Taiwan Strait. *Journal of Marine Science and Technology, 11*(1), 1–7.

Lee, M. H., Han, C., & Chang, K. S. (1999). Dynamic optimization of a continuous polymer reactor using a modified differential evolution algorithm. *Industrial & Engineering Chemistry Research*, *38*(12), 4825–4831. doi:10.1021/ie980373x

Lee, W. J., & Woo, T. C. (1989). Optimum selection of discrete tolerances. *ASME Journal of Mechanisms. Transmissions and Automatic Design*, *111*(2), 243–252. doi:10.1115/1.3258990

Lee, Y. H., Jeong, C. S., & Moon, C. (2002). Advanced planning and scheduling with outsourcing in manufacturing supply chain. *Computers & Industrial Engineering*, *43*(1-2), 351–374. doi:10.1016/S0360-8352(02)00079-7

Leign, W., Modani, N., & Hightower, R. (2004). A computational implementation of stock charting: Abrupt volume increase as signal for movement in New York stock exchange composite index. *Decision Support Systems*, *37*, 515–530. doi:10.1016/S0167-9236(03)00084-8

Leon, C., Miranda, G., & Segura, C. (2008). Parallel hyper heuristic: A self-adaptive island-based model for multi-objective optimization. In *Proceedings of the 10th Annual Conference on Genetic and Evolutionary Computation*, Atlanta, GA (pp. 757-758).

Lettenmaier, D. P., & Wood, E. F. (1993). Hydrology forecasting. In Maidment, D. R. (Ed.), *Handbook of Hydrology*. New York, NY: McGraw-Hill.

Levine, D. M. (1995). *A parallel genetic algorithm for the set partitioning problem*. Chicago, IL: Illinois Institute of Technology.

Li, X., & Kirley, M. (2002). The effects of varying population density in a fine grained parallel genetic algorithm. In *Proceedings of the IEEE World Congress on Computational Intelligence* (pp. 1709-1714). Washington, DC: IEEE Computer Society.

Liang, Y.-C., & Smith, A. E. (2004). Ant colony optimization algorithm for the redundancy allocation problem (RAP). *IEEE Transactions on Reliability*, *53*(3), 471–23. doi:10.1109/TR.2004.832816

Li, C. (2009). Research on web session clustering. *Journal of Software*, *4*, 460–468. doi:10.4304/jsw.4.5.460-468

Lin, C. T., & Lee, C. S. G. (1991). Neural network based fuzzy logic control and decision system. *IEEE Transactions on Computers*, *40*, 1320–1336. doi:10.1109/12.106218

Lo, A. W., & MacKinlay, A. C. (1990). When are contrarian profits due to stock market overreaction. *Review of Financial Studies*, *3*, 175–205. doi:10.1093/rfs/3.2.175

Lo, A., & MacKinlay, C. (1987). An econometric analysis of nonsynchronous trading. *Journal of Econometrics*, *55*, 181–211.

Lobo, F. G., Deb, K., Goldberg, D. E., Harik, G., & Wang, L. (1998). Compressed Introns in a Linkage Learning Genetic Algorithm. In *Proceedings of the 3rd Annual Conference on Genetic Programming*, Madison, WI (pp. 551-558).

Luk, K. C., Ball, J. E., & Sharma, A. (2001). An application of artificial neural networks for rainfall forecasting. *Mathematical and Computer Modelling*, *33*, 683–693. doi:10.1016/S0895-7177(00)00272-7

Madeira, S. C., & Oliveira, A. L. (2004). Biclustering algorithms for biological data analysis: A Survey. *IEEE/ACM Transactions on Computational Biology and Bioinformatics*, *1*, 24–45. doi:10.1109/TCBB.2004.2

Mahfoud, S. W. (1995). The nature of niching: Genetic algorithms and the evolution of optimal, cooperative populations. [University of Illinois at Urbana-Champaign.]. *Urbana (Caracas, Venezuela)*, IL.

Majhi, B., & Panda, G. (2010). Development of efficient identification scheme for nonlinear dynamic systems using swarm intelligence techniques. *Expert Systems with Applications*, *37*(1), 556–566. doi:10.1016/j.eswa.2009.05.036

Majhi, B., Shalabi, H., & Fathi, M. (2005). FLANN based forecasting of S&P 500 Index. *Information Technology Journal*, *4*(3), 289–292. doi:10.3923/itj.2005.289.292

Majhi, R., Panda, G., Majhi, B., & Sahoo, G. (2009). Efficient prediction of stock market indices using adaptive bacterial foraging optimization (ABFO) and BFO based technique. *Expert Systems with Applications*, *36*, 10097–10104. doi:10.1016/j.eswa.2009.01.012

Majhi, R., Panda, G., & Sahoo, G. (2009). Development and performance evaluation of FLANN based model for forecasting of stock market. *Expert Systems with Applications*, *36*, 6800–6808. doi:10.1016/j.eswa.2008.08.008

Ma, L., Tan, T., Wang, Y., & Zhang, D. (1997). Personal identification based on iris texture analysis. *IEEE Transactions on Pattern Analysis and Machine Intelligence, 25*(12), 1519–1533.

Mandelbaum, M., & Brill, P. H. (1989). Examples of measurement of flexibility and adaptivity in manufacturing systems. *The Journal of the Operational Research Society, 40*(6), 603–609.

Manderick, B., & Spiessens, P. (1989). Fine-grained parallel genetic algorithms. In *Proceedings of the Third International Conference on Genetic Algorithms* (pp. 428-433).

Marin, F., Trelles-Salazar, O., & Sandoval, F. (1994). Genetic algorithms on LAN message passing architectures using PVM: Application to the routing problem. In Y. Davidor, H.-P. Schwefel, & R. Manner (Eds.), *Proceedings of the Third Conference on Parallel Problem Solving from Nature* (LNCS 866, pp. 534-543).

Martens, M., & Poon, S. H. (2001). Returns synchronization and daily correlation dynamics between international stock markets. *Journal of Banking & Finance, 25*, 1805–1827. doi:10.1016/S0378-4266(00)00159-X

Martin, A., Doddington, G., Kamm, T., Ordowski, M., & Przybocki, M. (1997) The DET curve in assessment of detection task performance. *In Proceedings of the European Conference on Speech Communication and Technology* (pp. 1895–1898).

Martín-Bautista, M. J., Vila, M. A., & Escobar-Jeria, V. H. (2008). Obtaining user profiles via web usage mining. In *Proceedings of the IADIS European Conference on Data Mining* (pp. 73-76).

Martín-Bautista, M. J., Kraft, D. H., Vila, M. A., Chen, J., & Cruz, J. (2004). User profiles and fuzzy logic for Web retrieval issues. *Soft Computing Journal, 6*(5), 365–372.

Masek, L. (2003). Recognition of human iris patterns for biometric identification. Bachelor of Engineering Thesis, University of Western Australia, Perth, Australia.

Ma, T., & Shaw, T. Y. (1990). The relationships between market value, P/E ratio, trading volume and the stock return of Taiwan stock exchange. In Rhee, S. G., & Chang, R. (Eds.), *Pacific-Basin capital markets research* (pp. 313–335). Amsterdam, The Netherlands: North-Holland.

Mazouz, K. (2004). The effect of CBOE option listing on the volatility of NYSE traded stocks: A time-varying variance approach. *Journal of Empirical Finance, 11*, 695–708. doi:10.1016/j.jempfin.2003.09.003

McQueen, G., Pinegar, M., & Thorley, S. (1996). Delayed reaction to good news and the cross-autocorrelation of portfolio returns. *The Journal of Finance, 51*, 889–920. doi:10.2307/2329226

Mendiburu, A., Lozano, J. A., Miguel, J. A., Ostra, M., & Ubide, C. (2005). Parallel and multi-objective EDAs to create multi-variate calibration models for quantitative chemical applications. In *Proceeding of the 34<sup>th</sup> International Conference on Parallel Processing*, Oslo, Norway (pp. 596-603). Washington, DC: IEEE Computer Society.

Mendiburu, A., Lozano, J. A., & Miguel, J. A. (2005). Parallel implementation of EDAs based on Probabilistic graphical Models. *IEEE Transactions on Evolutionary Computation, 9*(4), 406–423. doi:10.1109/TEVC.2005.850299

Merz, P., & Freisleben, B. (2000). Fitness landscape analysis and memetic algorithms for quadratic assignment problem. *IEEE Transactions on Evolutionary Computation, 4*(4), 337–352. doi:10.1109/4235.887234

Meziane, R., Massim, Y., Zeblah, A., Ghoraf, A., & Rahli, R. (2005). Reliability optimization using ant colony algorithm under performance and cost constraints. *Electric Power Systems Research, 76*(1-3), 1–6. doi:10.1016/j.epsr.2005.02.008

Michalewicz, Z. (1996). *Genetic algorithms data structures*. Berlin, Germany: Springer.

Miettinen, K. M. (1999). *Nonlinear multiobjective optimization*. Boston, MA: Kluwer Academic.

Mihaylova, P., & Brandisky, K. (2006). Parallel genetic algorithm optimization of die press. In *Proceedings of the 3rd International PhD Seminar on Computational Electromagnetics and Technical Applications* (pp. 155-159).

Miller, J., Potter, W., Gandham, R., & Lapena, C. (1993). An evaluation of local improvement operators for genetic algorithms. *IEEE Transactions on Systems, Man, and Cybernetics, 23*(5), 1340–1341. doi:10.1109/21.260665

Miller, R. G. Jr. (1980). *Simultaneous statistical inference* (2nd ed.). New York, NY: Springer.

Mingjie, C., & Sheng, L. (2008). An improved adaptive genetic algorithm and its application in function optimization. *Journal of Harbin Engineering University*, 28, 677–680.

Min, T.-H., & Park, R.-H. (2009). Eyelid and eyelash detection method in the normalized iris image using the parabolic Hough model and Otsu;s thresholding method. *Pattern Recognition Letters*, 30, 1138–1143. doi:10.1016/j.patrec.2009.03.017

Miryani, M. R., & Naghibzadeh, M. (2009). Hard real-time multiobjective scheduling in heterogeneous systems using genetic algorithm. In *Proceedings of the International Conference on Parallel and Distributed Processing Techniques and Applications*, Las Vegas, NV (pp. 13-16). Washington, DC: IEEE Computer Society.

Mishra, B. S. P., Adday, A. K., Dehuri, S., & Cho, S.-B. (2010). An empirical study on parallel multi-objective genetic algorithms: 0/1 knapsack problem- a case study. In *Proceedings of the 3rd International Conference on Computational Intelligence and Industrial Application*, Wuhan, China.

Mishra, B. S. P., Adday, A. K., Roy, R., & Dehuri, S. (2010). Parallel multi-objective genetic algorithms for associative classification rule mining. In *Proceedings of the International Conference on Communication, Computing & Security*, Odisha, India.

Mishra, D., Yadav, A., Ray, S., & Kalra, P. K. (2005). Levenberg-Marquardt learning algorithm for integrate-and-fire neuron model. *Neural Information Processing - Letters and Reviews, 19*(2), 41-51.

Misra, K. (1986). On optimal reliability design: a review. *System Science, 12*, 5–30.

Mitchell, M. (1998). *Introduction to Genetic Algorithm*. Cambridge, MA: MIT Press.

Mitchell, M., Holland, J., & Forrest, S. (1994). When Will a Genetic Algorithm Outperform Hill Climbing? *Advances in Neural Information Processing Systems, 6*, 51–58.

Mobasher, B., Cooley, R., & Srivastava, J. (1999). Creating adaptive web sites through usage-based clustering of URLs. In *Proceedings of the IEEE Knowledge and Data Engineering Exchange Workshop (KDEX'99)* (pp. 19-25).

Mobasher, B., Dai, H., Luo, T., Nakagawa, M., Sun, Y., & Wiltshire, J. (2000). Discovery of aggregate usage profiles for web personalization. In *Proceedings of the WebKDD Workshop* (pp. 1-11).

Montes, E. M., Velazquez-Reyes, J., & Coello, C. A. C. (2006). A comparative study on differential evolution variants for global optimization. In *Proceedings of the 8th Annual Conference on Genetic and Evolutionary Computation* (pp. 1397-1398).

Montes, E. M., Coello, C. A. C., Velazquez-Reyes, J., & Muñoz-Davila, L. (2007). Multiple trial vectors in differential evolution for engineering design. *Engineering Optimization, 39*(5), 567–589. doi:10.1080/03052150701364022

Moon, C., Kim, J. S., & Gen, M. (2004). Advanced planning and scheduling based on precedence and resource constraints for E-plant chains. *International Journal of Production Research, 42*(15), 2941–2954. doi:10.1080/00207540410001691956

Murata, T., & Ishibuchi, H. (1995). MOGA: Multi-objective genetic algorithms. In []. Washington, DC: IEEE Computer Society.]. *Proceedings of the IEEE International Conference on Evolutionary Computation, 29*, 289–294. doi:10.1109/ICEC.1995.489161

Nahas, N., & Nourelfath, M. (2005). Ant system for reliability optimization of series system with multiple choice and budget constraints. *Reliability Engineering & System Safety, 87*(1), 1–12. doi:10.1016/j.ress.2004.02.007

Nahas, N., Nourelfath, M., & Ait-Kadi, D. (2007). Coupling ant colony and the degraded ceiling algorithm for the redundancy allocation problem of series parallel systems. *Reliability Engineering & System Safety, 92*(2), 211–222. doi:10.1016/j.ress.2005.12.002

Nasseri, M., Asghari, K., & Abedini, M. J. (2008). Optimized scenario for rainfall forecasting using genetic algorithm coupled with artificial neural network. *Expert Systems with Applications, 35*, 1414–1421. doi:10.1016/j.eswa.2007.08.033

Nelson, D. (1991). Conditional heteroskedasticity in asset returns: A new approach. *Econometrics, 59*, 347–370. doi:10.2307/2938260

Neri, F., & Tirronen, V. (2009). Scale factor local search in differential evolution. *Memetic Computation, 1*, 153–171. doi:10.1007/s12293-009-0008-9

Noorul, H. S., Karthikeyan, T., & Dinesh, M. (2003). Scheduling decisions in FMS using a heuristic approach. *International Journal of Advanced Manufacturing Technology*, 374–379.

Ntipteni, M. S., Valakos, I. M., & Nikolos, I. K. (2006). An asynchronous parallel differential evolution algorithms. In *Proceedings of the International Conference on Design Optimization and Application*.

Numnark, S., & Suwannik, W. (2007). A Comparison of Crossover Methods in LZWGA. In *Proceedings of the 3rd National Conference on Computing and Information Technology (NCCIT)* (pp. 328-333).

Numnark, S., & Suwannik, W. (2008). Improving the Performance of LZWGA by Using a New Mutation Method. In *Proceedings of the IEEE Conference on Evolutionary Computation (CEC 2008)* (pp. 1862-1865).

Okuda, T., Hiroyasu, T., Miki, M., & Watanabe, S. (2002). DCMOGA: Distributed cooperation model of multi-objective genetic algorithm. In *Proceedings of the PPSN/SAB Workshop on Multi Objective Problem Solving from Nature II*, Granada, Spain (pp. 155-160).

Osborne, M. F. M. (1959). Brownian motion in the stock market. *Operations Research, 7*, 145–173. doi:10.1287/opre.7.2.145

Ossa, L. D., Gamez, J. A., & Puerta, J. M. (2004). Migration of probability models instead of individual: An alternative when applying the island model to EDAs. In X. Yao, E. Burke, J. A. Lozano, J. J. Merelo-Guervos, J. A. Bullinaria, J. Rowe et al. (Eds.), *Proceedings of the 8th International Conference on Parallel Problem Solving from Nature*, Birminghan, UK (LNCS 3242, pp. 242-252).

Ossa, L. D., Gamez, J. A., & Puerta, J. M. (2005) Initial approaches to the application of islands based parallel EDAs in continuous domains. In *Proceedings of 34th International Conference on Parallel Processing Workshop*, Oslo, Norway (pp. 580-587). Washington, DC: IEEE Computer Society.

Ossa, L. D., Gamez, J. A., & Puerta, J. M. (2005). Improving model combination through local search in parallel univariate EDAs. In *Proceedings of the Congress on Evolutionary Computation*, Edinburgh, UK (pp. 1426-1433). Washington, DC: IEEE Computer Society.

Ostwald, P. F., & Huang, J. (1977). A method of optimal tolerance selection. *ASME Journal of Engineering for Industry, 92*, 677–682.

Pagan, A. R., & Schwert, G. W. (1990). Alternative models for conditional stock volatility. *Journal of Econometrics, 45*, 267–290. doi:10.1016/0304-4076(90)90101-X

Paliken, M. (2005). *Hierarchical Bayesian optimization algorithm: Towards a new generation of evolutionary algorithms*. New York, NY: Springer.

Pallis, G., Angelis, L., & Vakali, A. (2005). Model-based cluster analysis for web users sessions. In *Foundations of Intelligent Systems* (LNCS 3488, pp. 219-227).

Panda, G., Majhi, B., Mohanty, D., Choubey, A., & Mishra, S. (2006, January 27-29). Development of novel digital channel equalisers using genetic algorithms. In *Proceedings of the National Conference on Communication*, Delhi, India (pp.117-121).

Pandey, R. (2001). *Blind equalization and signal separation using neural networks*. Unpublished doctoral dissertation, Indian Institute of Technology, Roorkee, India.

Pan, Q.-K., Tasgetiren, M. F., Suganthan, P. N., & Chua, T. J. (2011). A discrete artificial bee colony algorithm for the lot-streaming flow shop scheduling problem. *Information Sciences, 181*(12), 2455–2468. doi:10.1016/j.ins.2009.12.025

Pant, M., Thangaraj, R., Abraham, A., & Grosan, C. (2009). Differential evolution with laplace mutation operator. In *Proceedings of the IEEE Congress on Evolutionary Computation* (pp. 2841-2849).

Pappa, G. L., Freitas, A. A., & Kaestner, C. A. (2002). Attribute selection with a multiobjective genetic algorithm. In *Proceedings of the 16th Brazilian Symposium on Artificial Intelligence* (pp. 280-290).

Passino, K. M. (2002). Biomimicry of bacterial foraging for distributed optimization and control. *IEEE Control Systems Magazine, 22*(3), 52–67. doi:10.1109/MCS.2002.1004010

Patra, J. C., Poh, W. B., Chaudhari, N. S., & Das, A. (2005, August). Nonlinear channel equalization with QAM signal using Chebyshev artificial neural network. In *Proceedings of the International Joint Conference on Neural Networks*, Montreal, QC, Canada (pp. 3214-3219).

Patra, J. C., Pal, R. N., Baliarsingh, R., & Panda, G. (1999). Nonlinear channel equalization for QAM signal constellation using artificial neural network. *IEEE Transactions on Systems, Man, and Cybernetics. Part B, Cybernetics*, *29*(2). doi:10.1109/3477.752798

Pawar, P., Rao, R., & Davim, J. (2008). Optimization of process parameters of milling process using particle swarm optimization and artificial bee colony algorithm. In *Proceedings of the International Conference on Advances in Mechanical Engineering.*

Pelikan, M. (1999). *A Simple Implementation of the Bayesian Optimization Algorithm (BOA) in C++ (version 1.0)* (Tech. Rep. No. 99011). Urbana, IL: University of Illinois at Urbana-Champaign.

Pelikan, M., & Goldberg, D. (2000). Heirarchical problem solving and the bayesian optimization algorithm. In *Proceedings of the Genetic and Evolutionary Computation Conference* (pp. 267-274).

Pelikan, M., David, G., & Labo, F. (1999). A survey of optimization by building and using probabilistic models. [University of Illinois at Urban-Champaign.]. *Urbana (Caracas, Venezuela)*, IL.

Pettey, C. C., & Leuze, M. R. (1989). A theoretical investigation of a parallel genetic algorithm. In *Proceedings of the Third International Conference on Genetic Algorithms* (pp. 398-405).

Phillips, P. C. B., & Perron, P. (1988). Testing for a unit root in time series regression. *Biometrika*, *75*, 335–346. doi:10.1093/biomet/75.2.335

Poli, M. N. (1999). Parallel genetic algorithm taxonomy. In *Proceedings of the Third International Conference on Knowledge-Based Intelligent Information Engineering Systems*, Adelaide, Australia (pp. 88-92).

Polikar, R., Upda, L., Upda, S. S., & Honavar, V. (2001). Learn++: an incremental learning algorithm for supervised neural networks. *IEEE Transactions on Systems, Man, and Cybernetics*, *31*(4), 497–508. doi:10.1109/5326.983933

Ponton, J. W., & Klemes, J. (1993). Alternatives to neural networks for inferential measurement. *Computers & Chemical Engineering*, *17*, 42–47. doi:10.1016/0098-1354(93)80080-7

Potter, M. A., & De Jong, K. A. (1998). The coevolution of antibodies for concept learning. In *Proceedings of the 5th Parallel Problem Solving from Nature Conference*, Amsterdam, The Netherlands (LNCS 1498, pp. 530-539).

Potter, M. A., & De Jong, K. A. (2000). Cooperative coevolution: An architecture for evolving coadapted subcomponents. *Evolutionary Computation*, *8*(1), 1–29. doi:10.1162/106365600568086

Premalatha, K., & Natarajan, A. M. (2010). Hybrid PSO and GA Models for Document Clustering. *International Journal of Advances in Soft Computing and Its Applications*, *2*(3), 597–608.

Preparata, F. (1989). Holographic dispersal and recovery of information. *IEEE Transactions on Information Theory*, *35*(5), 1123–1124. doi:10.1109/18.42233

Price, K. V. (1999). An introduction to differential evolution. In Corne, D., Dorigo, M., & Glover, F. (Eds.), *New ideas in optimization* (pp. 79–108). New York, NY: McGraw-Hill.

Price, K. V., Storn, R., & Lampinen, J. A. (2005). *Differential evolution: A practical approach to global optimization*. Berlin, Germany: Springer-Verlag.

Primrose, P. I., & Verter, V. (1996). Do companies need to measure their production flexibility? *International Journal of Operations & Production Management*, *16*, 4–11. doi:10.1108/01443579610119054

Pudil, P., Novovicova, J., & Kittler, J. (1994). Floating search methods in feature selection. *Pattern Recognition Letters*, *15*, 1119–1125. doi:10.1016/0167-8655(94)90127-9

Qin, A. K., Huang, V. L., & Suganthan, P. N. (2009). Differential evolution algorithm with stratefy adapdation for global numerical optimization. *IEEE Transactions on Evolutionary Computation*, *13*(2), 398–417. doi:10.1109/TEVC.2008.927706

Qing, A. (2008). A study on base vector for differential evolution. In *Proceedings of the IEEE World Congress on Computational Intelligence and Evolutionary Computation* (pp. 550-556).

Qing, A. (2006). Dynamic differential evolution strategy and applications in electromagnetic inverse scattering problems. *IEEE Transactions on Geoscience and Remote Sensing, 44*(1).

Qishi, W. (2000). The application of genetic algorithm in GIS network analysis. *International Archives of Photogrammetry and Remo, 33*, 1184–1191.

Qiu, T., & Ju, G. (2010). A selective migration parallel multi-objective genetic algorithm. In *Proceedings of the Chinese Control and Decision Conference* (pp. 463-467).

Ramanathan, K., & Guan, S. (2008). Recursive Pattern based Hybrid Supervised Training. *Engineering Evolutionary Intelligent Systems, 82*, 129–156. doi:10.1007/978-3-540-75396-4_5

Rambharose, T., & Nikov, A. (2010). Computational intelligence-based personalization of interactive web systems. *WSEAS Transactions on Information Science and Applications, 7*, 484–497.

Rao, R. S., Narasimham, S., & Ramalingaraju, M. (2008). Optimization of distribution network configuration for loss reduction using artificial bee colony algorithm. *International Journal of Electrical Power and Energy Systems Engineering, 1*, 116–122.

Raquel, C., & Naval, P. (2005). An efficient use of crowding distance in multiobjective particle swarm optimization. In *Proceedings of the Conference on Genetic and Evolutionary Computation* (pp 259-264).

Rechenberg, I. (1994). *Evolution strategie*. Stuttgart, Germany: Frommann-Holzboog.

Reinganum, M. R. (1981). Misspecification of capital asset pricing: Empirical anomalies based on earnings' yields and market values. *Journal of Financial Economics, 9*(1), 19–46. doi:10.1016/0304-405X(81)90019 2

Ribeiro, C. C., Martins, S. L., & Rosseti, I. (2007). Metaheuristics for optimization problems in computer communications. *Computer Communications, 30*, 656–669. doi:10.1016/j.comcom.2006.08.027

Rivera, R. (2004). Scalable Parallel Genetic Algorithms. *Artificial Intelligence Review, 16*, 153–168. doi:10.1023/A:1011614231837

Rosenberg, R. S. (1967). *Simulation of genetic populations with biochemical properties*. Ann Arbor, MI: University of Michigan.

Rotsianglum, A., & Suwannik, W. (2009). Shift Operator in LZWGA. In *Proceedings of National Conference on Computing and Information Technology (NCCIT)* (pp. 320-325).

Rotsianglum, A., & Suwannik, W. (2009b, October 28-30). A Performance Analysis of a Shift-and-Check Operator in LZWGA. In *Proceedings of the Electrical Engineering Conference (EECON-32)*.

Rotsianglum, A., & Suwannik, W. (2009). Comparing the Performance of LZWGA with Various Selection Methods. In *Proceedings of the 2009 National Computer Science and Engineering Conference (NCSEC 2009)* (pp. 198-203).

Rotsianglum, A., & Suwannik, W. (2010). An Improved Shift-and-Check Operator for LZWGA. In *Proceedings of the Joint Conference on Computer Science and Software Engineering (JCSSE)* (pp. 12-16).

Ruppert, D. M., Wand, P. R., & Carroll, J. (2008). *Semiparametric regression during 2003-2007*. Retrieved from http://www.uow.edu.au/~mwand/sprpap.pdf

Sahiner, B., Chan, H.-P., Petrick, N., Helvie, M. A., & Goodsitt, M. M. (1998). Design of a high-sensitivity classifier based on a genetic algorithm: Application to computer-aided diagnosis. *Physics in Medicine and Biology, 43*(10), 2853–2871. doi:10.1088/0031-9155/43/10/014

Salles Neto, L. L., & Moretti, A. C. (2005). Modelo não-linear para minimizar o número de objetos processados e o setup num problema de corte unidimensional. In *Anais do XXXVII Simpósio Brasileiro de Pesquisa Operacional* (pp. 1679-1688).

Samrout, M., Kouta, R., Yalaoui, F., Châtelet, E., & Chebbo, N. (2007). Parameters setting of the ant colony algorithm applied in preventive maintenance optimization. *Journal of Intelligent Manufacturing, 18*(6), 663–677. doi:10.1007/s10845-007-0039-3

Samrout, M., Yalaoui, F., Châtelet, E., & Chebbo, N. (2005). New methods to minimize the preventive maintenance cost of series-parallel systems using ant colony optimization. *Reliability Engineering & System Safety*, *89*(3), 346–354. doi:10.1016/j.ress.2004.09.005

Sarker, R., Kamruzzaman, J., & Newton, C. (2003). Evolutionary optimization (EvOpt): A brief review and analysis. *International Journal of Computational Intelligence and Applications*, *3*(4), 311–330. doi:10.1142/S1469026803001051

Sastry, K., Goldberg, D. E., & Llorà, X. (2007). *Towards billion bit optimization via efficient genetic algorithms* (Tech. Rep. No. 2007007). Urbana, IL: University of Illinois at Urbana-Champaign.

Schaffer, J. D. (1985). Multiple objective optimization with vector evaluated genetic algorithms. In *Proceedings of the International Conference on Genetic Algorithm and their Applications* (pp. 93-100).

Schapire, R. E., & Singer, Y. (1998). Improved Boosting Algorithms Using Confidence-rated Predictions. In *Proceedings of the 11th Annual Conference on Computational Learning Theory* (pp. 80-91).

Schultz, P. (1983). Transactions costs and the small firm effect: A comment. *Journal of Financial Economics*, *12*, 81–88. doi:10.1016/0304-405X(83)90028-4

Schwehm, M. (1992). Implementation of genetic algorithms on various interconnection network. In Valero, M., Onate, E., Jane, M., Larriba, J. L., & Suarez, B. (Eds.), *Parallel computing and transputer applications* (pp. 195–203). Amsterdam, The Netherlands: IOS Press.

Schwert, W. G. (1990). Stock volatility and the crash of 87. *Review of Financial Studies*, *3*, 77–102. doi:10.1093/rfs/3.1.77

Seeley, T. D. (1995). *The wisdom of the hive*. Boston, MA: Harvard University Press.

Sentana, E., & Wadhwani, S. (1992). Feedback traders and stock return autocorrections: evidence from a century of daily data. *The Economic Journal*, *102*, 415–425. doi:10.2307/2234525

Setnes, M., & Roubos, H. (2002). GA-fuzzy modeling and classification: complexity and performance. *IEEE Transactions on Fuzzy Systems*, *8*(5), 509–522. doi:10.1109/91.873575

Sexton, R. S., Dorsey, R. E., & Johnson, J. D. (1998). Toward global optimization of neural networks: A comparison of the genetic algorithm and back propagation. *Decision Support Systems*, *22*, 171–185. doi:10.1016/S0167-9236(97)00040-7

Sexton, R. S., & Gupta, J. N. D. (2000). Comparative evaluation of genetic algorithm and back propagation for training neural network. *Information Sciences*, *129*, 45–59. doi:10.1016/S0020-0255(00)00068-2

Sharma, J., & Jong, K. (1996). An analysis of the effects of the neighborhood size and shape on local selection algorithms. In H.-M. Voigt, W. Ebeling, I. Rechenberg, & H.-P. Schwefel (Eds.), *Proceedings of the 4th International Conference on Parallel Problem Solving from Nature* (LNCS 1141, pp. 236-244).

Shaw, K. J., & Flemming, P. J. (1996). Initial study of practical multi-objective genetic algorithms for scheduling the production of chilled ready meals. In *Proceedings of the 2nd International Mendel Conference on Genetic Algorithms*, Brno, Czech Republic (pp. 1-6).

Shen, l., & Zhen, J. (2009). Gabor wavelet selection and SVM classification for object recognition, *ACTA Automatica Sinica*, *35(4)*, *350-355.*

Shi, X.-J., & Lei, H. (2008). A Genetic Algorithm-Based Approach for Classification Rule Discovery. *International Conference on Information Management, Innovation Management and Industrial Engineering*, *1*, 175-178.

Shi, Y., & Eberhart, R. C. (1998). A modified particle swarm optimizer. *IEEE International Conference on Evolutionary Computation* (pp. 69-73).

Shoorehdeli, M. A., Teshnehlab, M., & Sedigh, A. K. (2009). Training ANFIS as an identifier with intelligent hybrid stable learning algorithm based on particle swarm optimization and extended kalman filter. *Fuzzy Sets and Systems*, *160*(7), 922–948. doi:10.1016/j.fss.2008.09.011

Siedlecki, W., & Sklansky, J. (1989). A note on genetic algorithm for large-scale feature selection. *Pattern Recognition Letters*, *10*, 335–347. doi:10.1016/0167-8655(89)90037-8

Simon, D. (2008). Biogeography-based optimization. *IEEE Transactions on Evolutionary Computation*, *12*(6), 702–713. doi:10.1109/TEVC.2008.919004

Sims, C. A. (1980). Macroeconomics and reality. *Econometria*, *48*, 1–48. doi:10.2307/1912017

Singh, A. (2009). An artificial bee colony algorithm for the leaf-constrained minimum spanning tree problem. *Applied Soft Computing*, *9*, 625–631. doi:10.1016/j.asoc.2008.09.001

Singh, P. K., Jain, P. K., & Jain, S. C. (2003). Simultaneous optimal selection of design and manufacturing tolerances with different stack-up conditions, using genetic algorithms. *International Journal of Production Research*, *41*(11), 2411–2429. doi:10.1080/0020754031000087328

Skinner, D. (1989). Option markets and stock return volatility. *Journal of Financial Economics*, *23*, 61–87. doi:10.1016/0304-405X(89)90005-6

Slim, C. (2006). Neuro-fuzzy network based on extended Kalman filtering for financial time series. In *Proceedings of the World Academy of Science, Engineering and Technology Conference* (Vol. 15).

Slowik, A., & Bialko, M. (2008, May 25-27). Training of artificial neural networks using differential evolution algorithm. In *Proceedings of the International Conference on Human System Interactions* (pp. 60-65).

Smirlock, M., & Starks, L. (1985). A further examination of stock price changes and transactions volume. *Journal of Financial Research*, *8*, 217–225.

Smith, S. F. (1980). *A learning system based on genetic adaptive algorithms*. Unpublished doctoral dissertation, University of Pittsburgh, Pittsburgh, PA.

Soderberg, R. (1993). Tolerance allocation considering customer and manufacturing objectives. *Advances in Design Automation*, *65*(2), 149–157.

Soh, H., & Kirley, M. (2006, July). MOPGA: Towards a new generation of multi-objective genetic algorithms. In *Proceedings of the IEEE Congress on Evolutionary Computation* (pp. 1702-1710). Washington, DC: IEEE Computer Society.

Son, Y. K. (1991). A decision support system for factory automation: A case study. *International Journal of Production Research*, *29*, 1461–1473. doi:10.1080/00207549108948023

Speckman, P. (1998). Kernel smoothing in partial linear models. *Journal of the Royal Statistical Society. Series B. Methodological*, *50*, 413–436.

Spekhart, F. H. (1972). Calculation of tolerance based on a minimum cost approach. *ASME Journal of Engineering for Industry*, *94*, 447–453. doi:10.1115/1.3428175

Spotts, M. F. (1973). Allocation of tolerances to minimize cost of assembly. *ASME Journal of Engineering for Industry*, *95*, 762–764. doi:10.1115/1.3438222

Srivastav, P. R., & Him, T.-H. (2009). Application of genetic algorithm in software testing. *International Journal of Software Engineering and its Applications*, *3*(4), 87-96.

Srivatsava, J., Cooley, R., Deshpande, M., & Tan, P. N. (2000). Web usage mining: discovery and applications of usage patterns from Web data. *ACM SIGKDD: Explorations Newsletter*, *1*, 12–23.

Stam, A., & Kuula, M. (1991). Selecting a flexible manufacturing system using multiple criteria analysis. *International Journal of Production Research*, *29*, 803–820. doi:10.1080/00207549108930103

Starkweather, T., Whitley, D., & Mathias, K. (1991). Optimization using distributed genetic algorithms. In H.-P. Schwefel & R. Manner (Eds.), *Proceedings of the First Workshop on Parallel Problem Solving from Nature* (LNCS 496, pp. 176-185).

Stearns, S. (1976). On selecting features for pattern classifiers. *Proceedings of Third International Conference of Pattern Recognition* (pp. 71–75).

Stoll, H. R., & Whaley, R. E. (1983). Transaction costs and the small firm effect. *Journal of Financial Economics*, *12*(1), 57–79. doi:10.1016/0304-405X(83)90027-2

Storn, R. (1995). *Differential evolution design of an IIR-filter with requirements for magnitude and group delay* (Tech. Rep. No. TR-95-026). Berkeley, CA: International Computer Science Institute.

Storn, R., & Price, K. (1995). *Differential evolution – a simple and efficient adaptive scheme for global optimization over continuous spaces* (Technical Report TR-95-012). Berkeley, CA: International Computer Science Institute.

Storn, R. (1999). System design by constraint adaptation and differential evolution. *IEEE Transactions on Evolutionary Computation, 3*(1), 22–34. doi:10.1109/4235.752918

Storn, R., & Price, K. (1997). Differential evolution – a simple and efficient heuristic for global optimization over continuous spaces. *Journal of Global Optimization, 11,* 341–359. doi:10.1023/A:1008202821328

Strang, K. D. (2009). Using recursive regression to explore nonlinear relationships and interactions: A tutorial applied to a multicultural education study. *Practical Assessment Research and Evaluation, 14*(3), 1–13.

Streichert, F., Ulmer, H., & Zell, A. (2005). Parallelization of multi-objective evolutionary algorithms using clustering algorithms. In C. A. Coello Coello, A. Hernández Aguirre, & E. Zitzler (Eds.), *Proceedings of Evolutionary Multi-Criterion Optimization* (LNCS 3410, pp. 92-107).

Su, L., Guan, S. U., & Yeo, Y. C. (2001). Incremental self-growing neural networks with the changing environment. *Journal of Intelligent Systems, 11*(1), 43–74. doi:10.1515/JISYS.2001.11.1.43

Sun, Z., Bebis, G., & Miller, R. (2003) Boosting object detection using feature selection, *IEEE International Conference on Advanced Video and Signal Based Surveillance* (pp. 290–296).

Sundar, D., Umadevi, B., & Alagarsamy, K. (2010). Multi objective genetic algorithm for the optimized resource usage and the prioritization of the constraints in the software project planning. *International Journal of Computers and Applications, 3*(3), 1–4. doi:10.5120/718-1010

Suresh, N. C. (1991). An extended multi-objective replacement model for flexible automation investments. *International Journal of Production Research, 28,* 1823–1844. doi:10.1080/00207549108948052

Sutherland, G. H., & Roth, B. (1975). Mechanism design: Accounting for manufacturing tolerance and costs in function generating problems. *ASME Journal of Engineering for Industry, 97,* 283–286. doi:10.1115/1.3438551

Suwannik, W., & Chongstitvatana, P. (2008). Solving One-Billion-Bit Noisy OneMax Problem using Estimation Distribution Algorithm with Arithmetic Coding. In *Proceedings of IEEE Conference on Evolutionary Computation* (pp. 1203-1206).

Suwannik, W., Kunasol, N., & Chongstitvatana, P. (2005). Compressed Genetic Algorithm. In *Proceedings of Northeastern Computer Science and Engineering Conference* (pp. 203-211).

Taguchi, G. (1989). *Quality engineering in production systems.* New York, NY: McGraw-Hill.

Tan, L., Taniar, D., & Smith, K. A. (2002). A new parallel genetic algorithm. In *Proceedings of the International Symposium on Parallel Architectures, Algorithms and Networks* (pp. 378-392). Washington, DC: IEEE Computer Society.

Tan, C. H., Guan, S. U., Ramanathan, K., & Bao, C. (2009). Recursive hybrid decomposition with reduced pattern training. *International Journal of Hybrid Intelligent Systems, 6*(3), 135–146.

Tanese, R. (1987). Parallel genetic algorithms for a hypercube. In *Proceedings of the Second International Conference on Genetic Algorithms* (pp. 177-183).

Tanese, R. (1989). Distributed genetic algorithms. In *Proceedings of the 3rd International Conference on Genetic Algorithms* (pp. 434-439).

Tang, M., & Lau, R. Y. (2007). A parallel genetic algorithm for floorplan area optimization. In *Proceedings of the 7th International Conference on Intelligent Systems Design and Applications,* Rio, Brazil (pp. 20-24). Washington, DC: IEEE Computer Society.

Tasoulis, D. K., Pavliis, N. G., Plagianakos, V. P., & Vrahatis, M. N. (2004). Parallel differential evolution. In *Proceedings of the IEEE Congress on Evolutionary Computation.*

Thangaraj, R., Pant, M., & Abraham, A. (2010). New mutation schemes for differential evolution algorithm and their application to the optimization of directional over-current relay settings. *Applied Mathematics and Computation, 216*, 532–544. doi:10.1016/j.amc.2010.01.071

Theodossiou, P., & Unro, L. (1995). Relationship between volatility and expected returns across international stock markets. *Journal of Business Finance & Accounting, 22*, 289–300. doi:10.1111/j.1468-5957.1995.tb00685.x

Thiele, L., & Zitzler, E. (1999). Multiobjective evolutionary algorithms: A comparative case study and the strength pareto approach. *IEEE Transactions on Evolutionary Computation, 3*(4), 257–271. doi:10.1109/4235.797969

Tillman, F. A., Hwang, C. L., & Kuo, W. (1980). *Optimization of systems reliability*. New York: Marcel Dekker.

Tobias, A., & Rosenberg, J. (2008). Stock returns and volatility: Pricing the short-run and long-run components of market risk. *The Journal of Finance, 63*(6), 2997–3030. doi:10.1111/j.1540-6261.2008.01419.x

Toh, K. A., Kim, J., & Lee, S. (2008). Maximizing area under ROC curve for biometric scores fusion. *Pattern Recognition, 41*(11), 3373–3392. doi:10.1016/j.patcog.2008.04.002

Toh, K. A., Kim, J., & Lee, S. (2008). Biometric scores fusion based on total error rate minimization. *Pattern Recognition, 41*, 1066–1082. doi:10.1016/j.patcog.2007.07.020

Touri, R., Voulgaris, P. G., & Hadjicostis, C. N. (2006, June). Time varying power limited preprocessing for perfect reconstruction of binary signals. In *Proceedings of the American Control Conference*, Minneapolis, MN (pp. 5722-5727).

Treptow, A., & Zell, A. (2004). Combining adaboost learning and evolutionary search to select features for real-time object detection. *IEEE congress on Evolutionary Computation, 2*, 2107-2113.

Troxler, J. N., & Blank, J. (1989). A comprehensive methodology for manufacturing system evaluation and comparison. *Journal of Manufacturing Systems, 8*, 175–183. doi:10.1016/0278-6125(89)90039-3

Tse, Y. K., & Tsui, A. K. C. (1997). Conditional volatility in foreign exchange rates: Evidence from the Malaysian ringgit and Singapore dollar. *Pacific-Basin Finance Journal, 5*, 345–356. doi:10.1016/S0927-538X(97)00002-4

Turk, M., & Pentland, A. (1991). Eigenfaces for recognition. *Journal of Cognitive Neuroscience, 3*(1), 71–86. doi:10.1162/jocn.1991.3.1.71

Tzafestas, S. G. (1980). Optimization of system reliability: A survey of problems and techniques. *International Journal of Systems Science, 11*, 455–486. doi:10.1080/00207728008967030

Valdhuizen, D. A., & Lamont, G. B. (2000). Multiobjective evolutionary algorithms: Analyzing the state-of-the-art. *Journal of Evolutionary Computation, 8*(2), 125–147. doi:10.1162/106365600568158

Valenzuelaa, O., Rojasb, I., Pomaresb, H., Herrerab, L. J., Guillenb, A., & Marqueza, L. (2007). Hybridization of intelligent techniques and ARIMA models for time series prediction. *Fuzzy Sets and Systems, 159*, 821–845. doi:10.1016/j.fss.2007.11.003

Veldhuizen, D. A. (1999). *Multiobjective evolutionary algorithms: Classifications, analyses, and new innovation. Wright-Patterson AFB*. OH: Air Force Institute of Technology.

Venkatesan, R., & Narayanswamy, R. (2003). Application of genetic algorithm and simulated annealing for optimization of extrusion die ratio and die cone angle. In *Proceedings of the 12th International Scientific Conference on Achievements in Mechanical and Material Engineering*, Gliwice, Zakopane (pp. 1001-1006).

Venk, S. (1990). Strategic optimization cycle as a competitive tool for economic justification of advanced manufacturing systems. *Journal of Manufacturing Systems, 9*, 194–205. doi:10.1016/0278-6125(90)90051-I

Vesterstrom, J., & Thomsen, R. A. (2004). Comparative study of differential evolution particle swarm optimization and evolutionary algorithm on numerical benchmark problems. In. *Proceedings of the IEEE Congress on Evolutionary Computation, 3*, 1980–1987.

Vieira, G. E., Herrmann, J. W., & Lin, E. (2003). Rescheduling manufacturing systems: A framework of strategies, policies, and methods. *Journal of Scheduling, 6*(1), 39–62. doi:10.1023/A:1022235519958

Viola, P., & Jones, M. (2001). Rapid object detection using a boosted cascade of simple features. *Proceedings of IEEE Computer Society Conference on Computer Vision and Pattern Recognition, 1*, 511–518.

Voulgaris, P. G., & Hadjicostis, C. N. (2004). Optimal processing strategies for perfect reconstruction of binary signals under power-constrained transmission. In *Proceedings of the IEEE Conference on Decision and Control*, Atlantis, Bahamas (pp. 4040-4045).

Wall, M. (1996). *A C++ Library of Genetic Algorithm Components*. Boston: Mechanical Engineering Department Massachusetts Institute of Technology.

Wang, C. Y., & Cheng, N. S. (2004). Extreme volumes and expected stock returns: Evidence from China's stock market. *Pacific-Basin Finance Journal, 12*, 577–597. doi:10.1016/j.pacfin.2004.04.002

Wang, F.-S., & Jing, C.-H. (1998). Fuzzy-decision-making problems of fuel ethanol production using a genetically engineered yeast. *Industrial & Engineering Chemistry Research, 37*(8), 3434–3443. doi:10.1021/ie970736d

Wang, J. (1994). A model of competitive stock trading volume. *The Journal of Political Economy, 102*, 127–168. doi:10.1086/261924

Wang, L., Maciejewski, A. A., Siegel, H. J., Roychowdhury, V., & Eldridge, B. (2005). A study of five parallel approaches to genetic algorithm for the travelling salesman problem. *Intelligent Automation and Soft Computing, 11*(4), 217–234.

Wäscher, G., Haubner, H., & Schumann, H. (2007). An improved typology of cutting and packing problems. *European Journal of Operational Research, 183*, 1109–1130. doi:10.1016/j.ejor.2005.12.047

Watchanupaporn, O., & Suwannik, W. (2010). Conditional Probability Mutation in LZWGA. In *Proceedings of the International ACM Conference on Management of Emergent Digital EcoSystems (ACM MEDES)*.

Watchanupaporn, O., & Suwannik, W. (2010). An Estimation of Distribution Algorithm using the LZW Compression Algorithm. In *Proceedings of the International Conference on Advanced Cognitive Technologies and Applications (IARIA Cognitive)* (pp. 97-102).

Watchanupaporn, O., Soonthornphisaj, N., & Suwannik, W. (2006). A Performance Analysis of Compressed Compact Genetic Algorithm. *ECTI-CIT Journal, 2*(2).

Weber, M., Neri, F., & Tirronen, V. (2009). Distributed differential evolution with explorative-exploitative population families. In *Proceedings of the Genetic Programming and Evolvable Machine, 10*, 343–371. doi:10.1007/s10710-009-9089-y

Welch, T. A. (1984). A Technique for High-Performance Data Compression. *Computer, 17*(6), 8–19. doi:10.1109/MC.1984.1659158

Whitley, D. (2001). An overview of evolutionary algorithms. *Journal of Information and Software Technology, 43*, 817–831. doi:10.1016/S0950-5849(01)00188-4

Wiskott, L., Fellous, J., Kruger, N., & Malsburg, C. (1994). Estimating attributes: analysis and extension of relief. *Proceedings of European Conference on Machine Learning* (pp. 171–182).

Wolpert, D. H., & Macreedy, G. (1997). No free lunch theorems for optimization. *IEEE Transactions on Evolutionary Computation, 1*(1), 67–82. doi:10.1109/4235.585893

Wood, R. A., Mcinish, T. H., & Ord, J. K. (1985). An investigation of transactions data for NYSE stocks. *The Journal of Finance, 60*, 723–739. doi:10.2307/2327796

Wright, S. (1964). Stochastic processes in evolution. *Stochastic Models in Medicine and Biology*, 199-241.

Wu, J. S. (2009). A novel nonparametric regression ensemble for rainfall forecasting using particle swarm optimization technique coupled with artificial neural network. In *Advances in Neural Networks – ISNN 2009* (LNCS 5553, pp. 49-58).

Wu, J. S., Jin, L., & Liu, M. Z. (2006). Modeling meteorological prediction using particle swarm optimization and neural network ensemble. In *Advances in Neural Networks – ISNN 2006* (LNCS 3973, pp. 1202-1209).

Xie, G., Wang, Q., & Sunden, B. (2008). Application of a genetic algorithm for thermal design of fin-and tube heat exchangers. *Heat Transfer Engineering, 29*(7), 597–607. doi:10.1080/01457630801922337

Xu, L., Ge, Z., & Ming, H. (2009). Research of an improved parallel genetic algorithm with adjustable migration rate. *Journal of Control and Instruments in Chemical Industry, 34*(1).

Yalaoui, A., Chu, C., & Châtelet, E. (2004). Allocation de fiabilité et de redondance. *Journal européen des systèmes automatisés, 38*(1-2), 85-102.

Yalaoui, A., Châtelet, E., & Chu, C. (2005). A new dynamic programming method for reliability and redundancy allocation in parallel-series system. *IEEE Transactions on Reliability, (2)*: 254–261. doi:10.1109/TR.2005.847270

Yalaoui, A., Chu, C., & Châtelet, E. (2005). Reliability allocation problem in a series-parallel system. *Reliability Engineering & System Safety, 90*, 55–61. doi:10.1016/j. ress.2004.10.007

Yalaoui, A., Chu, C., & Châtelet, E. (2005). Series-parallel systems design: Reliability Allocation. *Journal of Decision Systems, 14*(4), 473–487. doi:10.3166/jds.14.473-487

Yang, L., Dwi, H. W., Ioerger, T., & Yen, J. (2001). An Entropy-based Adaptive Genetic Algorithm for Learning Classification Rules. In *Proceedings of the 2001 Congress on Evolutionary Computation* (pp. 790-796).

Yang, J. J. W. (2000). The Leverage effect and herding behaviour in Taiwan's stock market. *Journal of Risk Management, 2*, 69–86.

Yang, J. J. W., & You, S.-J. (2003). Asymmetric volatility: Pre and post Asian financial crisis. *Journal of Management, 20*(4), 805–827.

Yang, W., Xiang-gen, Y., & Zhe, Z. (2009). Wide area intelligent protection system based on genetic algorithm. *Journal of Electrical and Electronics Engineering, 9*(2), 1093–1099.

Yan, L., Jumin, H., & Zhuoshang, J. (2000). A Study of genetic algorithm based on isolation niche technique. *Journal of Systems Engineering, 15*, 86–91.

Yao, P. Li, Jun., Ye, X., Zhuang, Z., & Li, B. (2006). Iris recognition using modified log-gabor filters. *Proceedings of the 18th International Conference on Pattern Recognition Vol. 4* (pp. 461-464).

Yao, X., Liu, Y., Liang, K. H., & Lin, G. (2003). Fast evolutionary algorithms. In Rozenberg, G., Back, T., & Eiben, A. (Eds.), *Advances in evolutionary computing: Theory and applications* (pp. 45–94). New York, NY: Springer.

Ye, B., & Salustri, F. A. (2003). Simultaneous tolerance synthesis for manufacturing and quality. *Research in Engineering Design, 14*(2), 98–106.

Yeh, L.-J., Chang, Y.-C., & Chiu, M.-C. (2004). Application of genetic algorithm to the shape optimization of a constrained double-chamber muffler with extended tubes. *Journal of Marine Science and Technology, 12*(3), 189–199.

Ying, C. C. (1966). Stock market prices and volumes of sales. *Econometrica, 34*, 676–685. doi:10.2307/1909776

Yoo, M. (2009). Real-time task scheduling by multiobjective genetic algorithm. *Journal of Systems and Software, 82*(4), 619–628. doi:10.1016/j.jss.2008.08.039

Yoo, M., & Gen, M. (2007). Scheduling algorithm for real-time tasks using multiobjective hybrid genetic algorithm in heterogeneous multiprocessors system. *Computers & Operations Research, 34*(10), 3084–3098. doi:10.1016/j. cor.2005.11.016

Yu, T. L., Goldberg, D. E., & Sastry, K. (2003). Optimal sampling and speed-up for genetic algorithms on the sampled onemax problem. In *Proceedings of the Genetic and Evolutionary Computation Conference (GECCO 2003)* (pp. 1554-1565).

Yu, L. N., Wang, S. Y., & Lai, K. K. (2008). Neural network-based mean-variance-skewness model for portfolio selection. *Computers & Operations Research, 35*, 34–46. doi:10.1016/j.cor.2006.02.012

Yu, L., Chen, H., Wang, S., & Lai, K. K. (2009). Evolving least square support vector machines for stock market trend mining. *IEEE Transactions on Evolutionary Computation, 13*(1).

Yu, L., & Zhang, Y. Q. (2005). Evolutionary fuzzy neural networks for hybrid financial prediction. *IEEE Transactions on Systems, Man, and Cybernetics, 35*(2).

Zaharie, D., & Petcu, D. (2003). Parallel implementation of multi-population differential evolution. In Grigoras, D., & Nicolau, A. (Eds.), *Concurrent information processing and computing* (pp. 262–269). Amsterdam, The Netherlands: IOS Press.

Zahir, M. S. (1991). Incorporating the uncertainty of decision judgments in the analytic hierarchy process. *European Journal of Operational Research, 53*, 206–216. doi:10.1016/0377-2217(91)90135-I

Zeblah, A., Châtelet, E., Samrout, M., Yalaoui, F., & Massim, Y. (2009). Series-parallel power system optimization using a harmony search algorithm. *International Journal Power Energy Conversion, 1*, 15–30. doi:10.1504/IJPEC.2009.023474

Zebulum, R. S., Pacheco, M. A., & Vellasco, M. (1999). A multi-objective optimization methodology applied to the synthesis of low-power operational amplifiers. In *Proceedings of the 13th International Conference in Microelectronics and Packaging*, Curitiba, Brazil (pp. 264-271).

Zhang, D., Chen, Q., & Liu, J. (2007). An improved hybrid genetic algorithm for solving multi-modal function global optimization problem. In *Proceedings of the IEEE International Conference on Automation and Logistics*, Jinan, China (pp. 2486-2490). Washington, DC: IEEE Computer Society.

Zhang, S., & Maruf Hossain, M. Rafiul Hassan, Md., Bailey, J., & Ramamohanarao, K. (2006). Feature weighted SVMs using receiver operating characteristics. *Proceedings of the Sixth SIAM International Conference on Data Mining* (pp. 487-508).

Zhang, C., & Wang, H. P. (1993). Integrated tolerance optimization with simulated annealing. *International Journal of Advanced Manufacturing Technology, 8*, 167–174. doi:10.1007/BF01749907

Zhang, G. (1996). Simultaneous tolerancing for design and manufacturing. *International Journal of Production Research, 34*, 3361–3382. doi:10.1080/00207549608905095

Zhang, G. P., & Berardi, V. L. (2003). Time series forecasting using a hybrid ARIMA and neural network model. *Neurocomputing, 50*, 159–175. doi:10.1016/S0925-2312(01)00702-0

Zhang, J., & Sanderson, A. C. (2009). JADE: Adaptive differential evolution with optional external archive. *IEEE Transactions on Evolutionary Computation, 13*(5), 945–958. doi:10.1109/TEVC.2009.2014613

Zhao, J. H., Liu, Z., & Daou, M. T. (2007). Reliability optimization using multiobjective ant colony system approaches. *Reliability Engineering & System Safety, 92*(1), 109–222. doi:10.1016/j.ress.2005.12.001

Zhao, L., & Yang, Y. (2009). PSO-based single multiplicative neuron model for time series prediction. *Expert Systems with Applications, 36*, 2805–2812. doi:10.1016/j.eswa.2008.01.061

Zheng, Y., & Lei, D. M. (2008). New progresses and prospect of multi-objective evolutionary algorithm. In *Proceedings of the Seventh International Conference on Machine Learning and Cybernetics*, Kunming, China (pp. 962-968). Washington, DC: IEEE Computer Society.

Zhi-xin, W., & Gang, J. (2009). A parallel genetic algorithm in multi-objective optimization. In *Proceedings of the Control and Decision Conference*, Guilin, China (pp. 3497-3501).

Zhongxi, H., Xiaoqing, C., & Liangming, G. (2006). An improved multi objective evolutionary algorithm base on crowing mechanism. *Journal of National University of Defense Technology, 28*, 18–21.

Zhou, Y. J., Wu, J. S., & Qin, F. J. (2006) Neural network with partial least square prediction model based on SSA and MGF. In *Proceedings of the 6th World Conference on Intelligent Control and Automation.*

Zhu, F., & Guan, S. U. (2005). Ordered incremental training for GA-based classifiers. *Pattern Recognition Letters, 26*(14), 2135–2151. doi:10.1016/j.patrec.2005.04.001

Zhu, F., & Guan, S. U. (2008). Cooperative co-evolution of GA-based classifiers based on input decomposition. *Engineering Applications of Artificial Intelligence, 21*(8), 1360–1369. doi:10.1016/j.engappai.2008.01.009

Zhu, G., & Kwong, S. (2010). Gbest-guided artificial bee colony algorithm for numerical function optimization. *Applied Mathematics and Computation, 217*(7), 3166–3173. doi:10.1016/j.amc.2010.08.049

Zitler, E., & Thiele, L. (1999). Multi-objective evolutionary algorithms: A comparative case study and the strength Pareto approach. *IEEE Transactions on Evolutionary Computation, 3*(4), 257–271. doi:10.1109/4235.797969

Zitzler, E., & Thiele, L. (1998). *An evolutionary algorithm for multiobjective optimization: The strength Pareto approach.* Zurich, Switzerland: Swiss Federal Institute of Technology (ETH).

Zitzler, E., Laumanns, M., & Bleuler, S. (2004). A tutorial on evolutionary multi objective optimization. In X. Gandibluex, M. Sevaux, K. Sorenson, & V. T'kindt (Eds.), *Metaheuristics for multiobjective optimisation* (Vol. 535, 3-38). Berlin, Germany: Springer-Verlag.

Zitzler, E., Laumanns, M., & Thiele, L. (2001). *SPEA2: Improving the strength Pareto evolutionary algorithm* (Tech. Rep. No. TIK 103). Zurich, Swizerland: Computer Engineering and Networks Lab (TIK).

Zitzler, E., & Thiele, L. (1998). *Multiobjective optimization using evolutionary algorithms-a comparative study.* Berlin, Germany: Springer-Verlag.

Zitzler, E., Thiele, L., Laumanns, M., Fonseca, C. M., & Fonseca, V. G. (1999). Performance assessment of multiobjective optimizers: An analysis and review. *IEEE Transactions on Evolutionary Computation, 3*(4), 257–271. doi:10.1109/4235.797969

Zwiers, F. W., & von Storch, H. (2004). On the role of statistics in climate research. *International Journal of Climatology, 24*, 665–680. doi:10.1002/joc.1027

Zydallis, J. (2003). *Building-block multiobjective genetic algorithms: Theory, analysis, and development.* Wright-Patterson AFB, OH: Air Force Institute of Technology

Zydallis, J. B., Veldhuizen, D. A., & Lamont, G. B. (1993). A statistical comparison of multiobjective evolutionary algorithms including the MOMGA-II. In E. Zitzler, L. Thiele, K. Deb, C. A. C. Coello, & D. Corne (Eds.), *Proceedings of the First International Conference on Evolutionary Multi-Criterion Optimization* (LNCS 1993, pp. 226-240).

# About the Contributors

**Wei-Chiang Samuelson Hong** is an Associate Professor in the Department of Information Management at the Oriental Institute of Technology, Taiwan. His research interests mainly include computational intelligence (neural networks and evolutionary computation), and application of forecasting technology (ARIMA, support vector regression, and chaos theory), and tourism competitiveness evaluation and management. Dr. Hong's articles have been published in *Applied Mathematics and Computation*, *Applied Mathematical Modelling*, *Applied Soft Computing*, *Control and Cybernetics*, *Current Issues in Tourism*, *Decision Support Systems*, *Electric Power Systems Research*, *Energy*, *Energies*, *Energy Conversion and Management*, *Energy Policy*, *Hydrological Processes*, *IEEE Transactions on Fuzzy Systems*, *International Journal of Advanced Manufacturing Technology*, *International Journal of Electrical Power & Energy Systems*, *Journal of Combinatorial Optimization*, *Journal of Systems and Software*, *Journal of Systems Engineering and Electronics*, *Mathematical Problems in Engineering*, *Neural Computing and Applications*, *Neurocomputing*, and *Water Resources Management*, among others. Dr. Hong is currently on the editorial board of several journals, including *International Journal of Applied Evolutionary Computation*, *Neurocomputing*, *Applied Soft Computing*, *Mathematical Problems in Engineering*, and *Energy Sources Part B: Economics, Planning, and Policy*. Dr. Hong presently teaches courses in the areas of forecasting methodologies and applications, hybridizing evolutionary algorithms, and conducts research in the areas of prediction modeling, simulation and optimization, artificial neural network, and novel forecasting development. Dr. Hong serves as the program committee of various international conferences including premium ones such as IEEE CEC, IEEE CIS, IEEE ICNSC, IEEE SMC, IEEE CASE, IEEE SMCia, etc. In May 2012, his paper had been evaluated as *"Top Cited Article 2007-2011"* by Elsevier Publisher (Netherlands). In Sep. 2012, once again, his paper had been indexed in ISI Essential Science Indicator database as *Highly Cited Papers*, in the meanwhile, he also had been awarded as the *Model Teacher Award* by Taiwan Private Education Association. Dr. Hong is a senior member of IIE and IEEE. He is indexed in the list of Who's Who in the World (25th-29th Editions), Who's Who in Asia (2nd Edition), and Who's Who in Science and Engineering (10th and 11th Editions).

* * *

**J. Bagyamani**, working as associate professor and head, department of computer science, Government Arts College, Dharmapuri and currently pursuing her PhD in the department of computer science, Periyar University, Salem as a Teacher fellow under UGC XI Plan FIP Scheme. She has published 6 papers in reputable international journals and received two best paper awards in International Conferences. Her areas of interest are data mining, biclustering of gene expression data using heuristic and meta-heuristic techniques and web mining.

**Farah Belmecheri** obtained her engineering degree in Information System Engineering from the University of Boumerdes (Algeria) in 2005, her master's degree in Systems Optimization and safety from the University of Technology of Troyes (UTT, France) in 2007. She is currently Ph.D. thesis in Systems Optimization and safety in the University of Technology of Troyes (UTT, France). Her research topic focuses on the transportation problems, operations research, analysis and optimization of vehicle routing problem and on optimization problems in general.

**Julliany Sales Brandão** is graduated in Computer Science from Universidade Estadual de Santa Cruz – UESC (2006). Master in Computational Modeling by Universidade do Estado do Rio de Janeiro – UERJ (2009). Is Information Technology Analyst for CEFET/RJ. And today, is finishing her Ph.D. in Computer Science at Universidade Federal Fluminense - UFF. His research interests include Combinatorial Optimization / Operational Research and Systems Analysis, in particular: Network Optimization and Stock Cutting and Packing Problems, Linear Programming, Integer, Nonlinear and Metaheuristics.

**Eric Châtelet** is Professor at Troyes University of Technology (UTT, France) from 1999. He received his PhD (1991) in Theoretical Physics (Cosmic rays physics) from Bordeaux I University, France, and has worked in Cosmic Rays and Neutrinos Physics until 1994. He was Director of studies of the UTT (2001-2004) and Director of academic programs (2005-2006). He was co-manager (2006-2007) of the national program of the National Agency of the Research in Global Security (UTT is in charge of the program management). He is vice-director of the Charles Delaunay Institute (ICD) from 2009, grouping the whole research teams of the UTT, and he is the head of the UMR CNRS "Sciences and Technologies for Risk Management" from January 2010. Its research is focused on stochastic modelling and optimization for maintenance and reliability, the performance analysis of complex systems and security analysis.

**Jen-Tseng Chen** is a lecturer at the Department & Institute of Business Administration, TransWorld University, Taiwan. He has a good command of statistic and time series and has already succeeded in having two article published in a national science journal.

**Alessandra Martins Coelho** Received the Data Processing Technology degree by Centro de Ensino Superior de Juiz de Fora, Brazil, in 1998. In 2000 received the B.Sc. degree in Informatics (Special Program of the Pedagogic formation) by Centro Federal de Educação Tecnológica do Paraná, Brazil. In same year received degree Especialization in Agricultural Informatic's by Universidade Federal de Lavras, Brazil. In 2006 he received the Master degree in Modelling and Computational Mathematics by Centro Federal de Educação Tecnológica de Minas Gerais, Brazil. Nowadays is Administrative Assistant in Instituto Federal de Educação, Ciência e Tecnologia do Sudeste de Minas, campus Rio Pomba, and is PhD student in Computational Modelling by Instituto Politécnico - Universidade do Estado do Rio de Janeiro, Brazil .His research interests include Combinatorial Optimization, Operational Research, Systems Analysis, Metaheuristics and Imaging Processing Ouvir.

**Satchidananda Dehuri** is working as a Reader and Head in P.G. Department of Information and Communication Technology, Fakir Mohan University, Vyasa Vihar, Balasore, Odisha. He received his M.Sc. degree in Mathematics from Sambalpur University, Odisha in 1998, and the M.Tech. and Ph.D. degrees in Computer Science from Utkal University, Vani Vihar, Odisha in 2001 and 2006, respectively.

He completed his Post Doctoral Research in Soft Computing Laboratory, Yonsei University, Seoul, Korea under the BOYSCAST Fellowship Program of DST, Govt. of India. He was at the Center for Theoretical Studies, Indian Institute of Technology Kharagpur as a Visiting Scholar in 2002. During May-June 2006 he was a Visiting Scientist at the Center for Soft Computing Research, Indian Statistical Institute, Kolkata. He got a prestigious Young Scientist Award from Orissa Bigyan Academy, Department of Science and Technology, Govt. of Orissa in Engineering and Technology. His research interests include Evolutionary Computation, Neural Networks, Pattern Recognition, Data Warehousing and Mining, Object Oriented Programming and its Applications and Bioinformatics. He has already published about 80 research papers in referred journals and conferences, has published two text books for undergraduate students and edited six books, and is acting as an editorial member of various journals.

**Lei Fang** received his BS degree in computer science from the University of Liverpool and Xi'an Jiaotong-Liverpool University in 2010. Currently, he is a SICSA funded student working towards his PhD degree at St. Andrews University. His research interests include machine learning, mission management and adaptation for sensor swarms, and process algebra.

**Liau Heng Fui** received the B.Eng in Electrical and Electronics Engineering from the University of Nottingham Malaysia Campus in 2006. He is currently pursuing his PhD in the same university under Professor Dr Dino Isa. His main interest is in face recognition, iris recognition, pattern recognition and machine learning.

**Ashish Ghosh** is a Professor of the Indian Statistical Institute, Kolkata, India. He received the B.E. degree in Electronics and Telecommunication from the Jadavpur University, Kolkata, in 1987, and the M.Tech. and Ph.D. degrees in Computer Science from the Indian Statistical Institute, Kolkata, in 1989 and 1993, respectively. He received the prestigious and most coveted *Young Scientists* award in Engineering Sciences from the Indian National Science Academy in 1995; and in Computer Science from the Indian Science Congress Association in 1992. He has been selected as an *Associate* of the Indian Academy of Sciences, Bangalore, in 1997. He visited the Osaka Prefecture University, Japan, with a Post-doctoral fellowship during October 1995 to March 1997, and Hannan University, Japan as a *Visiting Faculty* during September to October, 1997 and September to October, 2004. He has also visited Hannan University, Japan, as *Visiting Professor* with a fellowship from Japan Society for Promotion of Sciences (JSPS) during February to April, 2005. During May 1999 he was at the Institute of Automation, Chinese Academy of Sciences, Beijing, with CIMPA (France) fellowship. He was at the German National Research Center for Information Technology, Germany, with a German Government (DFG) Fellowship during January to April, 2000, and at Aachen University, Germany in September 2010 with an European Commission Fellowship. During October to December, 2003 he was a *Visiting Professor* at the University of California, Los Angeles, and during December 2006 to January 2007 he was at the Computer Science Department of Yonsei University, South Korea. His visits to University of Trento and University of Palermo (Italy) during May to June 2004, March to April 2006, May to June 2007, 2008, 2009 and 2010 were in connection with collaborative international projects. He also visited various Universities/Academic Institutes and delivered lectures in different countries including Poland and The Netherlands. His research interests include *Pattern Recognition and Machine Learning, Data Mining, Image Analysis, Remotely Sensed Image Analysis, Soft Computing, Fuzzy Sets and Uncertainty Analysis,*

*Neural Networks, Evolutionary Computation and Bioinformatics*. He has already published more than 120 research papers in internationally reputed journals and referred conferences, has edited seven books and is acting as a member of the editorial board of various international journals. He is a member of the founding team that established a *National Center for Soft Computing Research* at the Indian Statistical Institute, Kolkata, in 2004, with funding from the Department of Science and Technology (DST), Government of India, and at present is the In-Charge of the Center.

**Sheng-Uei Guan** received his MS and PhD from the University of North Carolina at Chapel Hill. He is currently a professor and head of the computer science and software engineering department at Xi'an Jiaotong-Liverpool University. Before joining XJTLU, he was a professor and chair in intelligent systems at Brunel University, UK. Prof. Guan has worked in a prestigious R&D organization for several years, serving as a design engineer, project leader, and manager. After leaving the industry, he joined Yuan-Ze University in Taiwan for three and half years. He served as deputy director for the Computing Center and the chairman for the department of information and communication technology. Later he joined the electrical and computer engineering department at National University of Singapore as an associate professor.

**Dino Isa** received the BSEE (Hons) degree in electrical engineering from the University of Tennessee, Knoxville, in 1986 and the PhD degree from the University of Nottingham, University Park, Nottingham, England, in 1991. He was with Motorola Seremban as the engineering section head and then moved to Crystal Clear Technology in 1996 as the chief technology officer prior to joining the University of Nottingham in 2001. He is the Professor of Intelligent Systems at the Department of Electrical and Electronic Engineering, Faculty of Engineering, University of Nottingham, Malaysia Campus. His current interest is in applying the support vector machine in various domains in order to further understand its mechanisms.

**G.Jeyakumar** received his B.Sc degree in Mathematics in 1994 and M.C.A degree (under the faculty of Engineering) in 1998 from Bharathidasan University, Tamil Nadu, India. He is currently an Assistant Professor (Selection Grade) in the department of Computer Science and Engineering, Amrita School of Engineering, Amrita Vishwa Vidyapeetham University, Tamil Nadu, India since 2000. His research interest include evolutionary algorithm, differential evolution, parallelization of differential evolution and its applications.

**Luiz Leduino de Salles Neto** graduated in Mathematics from University of Campinas (1998), Master in Mathematics University of Campinas (2000), Ph.D. in Applied Mathematics from University of Campinas (2005) and post-doctoral studies at Universidad de Sevilla, España. He is currently assistant professor at the Federal University of São Paulo. He has experience in applied mathematics and Cutting and Packing Problem.

**Rajib Mall** obtained his professional degrees Bachelor's, Master's, and Ph.D, all from Indian Institute of Science, Bangalore. He is working as a faculty in the Department of Computer Science and Engineering at IIT, Kharagpur for the last 17 years. He has published about 150 refereed journal and conference papers.

**Bhabani Shankar Prasad Mishra** is working as an Asst. Professor in School of Computer Science, KIIT University, Bhubaneswar, Odisha. He received his B-Tech degree in Computer Science from Biju Pattanaik Technical University, Odisha in 2003. He received his M-Tech degree in Computer Science from KIIT University, Odisha in 2005. Currently he is pursuing his PhD. His research interest includes Evolutionary Computation, Parallel processing, and Data Mining. He has published many papers in referred journals and conferences.

**Raju Nedunchezhian** is currently working as the Vice-Principal of Kalaignar Karunanidhi Institute of Technology, Coimbatore, TamilNadu, India. Previously, he served as Research Coordinator of the Institute and Head of Computer Science and Engineering Department (PG) at Sri Ramakrishna Engineering College, Coimbatore. He has more than 17 years of experience in research and teaching. He obtained his BE(Computer Science and Engineering) degree in the year 1991, ME(Computer Science and Engineering) degree in the year 1997 and PhD(Computer Science and Engineering) in the year 2007. He has guided numerous UG, PG and M.Phil projects and organized a few sponsored conferences and workshops funded by private and government agencies. Currently, he is guiding many PhD scholars of the Anna University, Coimbatore, and the Bharathiar University. His research interests include knowledge discovery and data mining, Soft Computing, distributed computing, and database security. He has published many research papers in national/international conferences and journals. He is a Life member of Advanced Computing and Communication Society and ISTE.

**André Vieira Pinto** is currently attending college in Information Systems at Universidade Federal do Estado do Rio de Janeiro (UNIRIO). Has a computer technician degree by CEFET/RJ. Fluent in English and with great interest in the language. His research interests include Operational Research, Computer Networking, Database and Web Development.

**R. Rathipriya**, is working as assistant professor in Periyar University, Salem, India. She received her bachelor of science and master of science degrees in computer science from the Periyar University. Currently, she is pursuing her PhD in Bharathiyar University, India. Her research interests are in several areas of data mining, web mining, optimization techniques (in particular, optimization of biclusters in web mining area), and bio-Informatics. K. Thangavel, is presently the professor and head, department of computer science Periyar University, Salem. He has completed his PhD in Gandhigram Rural University. His areas of interest are data mining, image processing, mobile computing and rough set theory and optimization techniques. He is reviewer of reputable journals. He has received Young Scientist Award 2009 from Tamilnadu State Council for Science and Technology.

**Worasait Suwannik** received a PhD degree in computer engineering from Chulalongkorn University. At present, he is an assistant professor at Kasetsart University, Bangkok, Thailand. His research interest includes compressed genetic algorithm and GPU programming.

**C. Shunmuga Velayutham** received the B.Sc degree in Physics from Manonmaniam Sundaranar University, Tamilnadu, India, in 1998, M.Sc degree in Electronics and Ph.D. degree in Neuro-Fuzzy Systems from Dayalbagh Educational Institute, Uttar Pradesh, India in 2000 and 2005 respectively. Currently, he is an Assistant Professor (Selection Grade) in the Department of Computer Science & Engineering, Amrita Vishwa Vidyapeetham, Tamilnadu, India since 2005. His research encompasses theoretical investigation and application potential (esp. in computer vision) of evolutionary-computation.

**João Flávio Vieira de Vasconcellos** is graduated in Mechanical Engineering from Federal University of Santa Catarina (1989), Master in Mechanical Engineering from Mechanical Engineering from Federal University of Santa Catarina (1993) and Ph.D. in Mechanical Engineering from Mechanical Engineering from Federal University of Santa Catarina (1999) and post-doctoral studies at James Cook University of North Queensland, Australia. He is currently assistant professor at the Rio de Janeiro State University and head of the Department of Mechanical Engineering and Energy at the Polytechnic Institute, UERJ. He has experience in Mechanical Engineering with emphasis on Variational principles and numerical methods, mainly in the following topics: scientific computing, finite volume, computational fluid dynamics, Voronoi diagrams.

**Periasamy Vivekanandan** is currently working as Assistant Professor, Department of Computer Science and Engineering, Park College of Engineering and Technology, Coimbatore, Tamilnadu, India. He obtained his B.E (Computer Science and Engineering) from Bharathiar University, Coimbatore, India and his MTech (Distributed Computing Systems) from Pondicherry University, Pondicherry, India. He is also a research scholar of Anna University, Coimbatore, India. His research interests include knowledge discovery and data mining, Soft Computing and distributed computing. He is a life member of ISTE.

**Shih Yung Wei** is a doctoral student at the Department of Finance, National Yunlin University of Science and Technology, Taiwan. He has jointly contributed to scientific papers presented at two conferences in Taiwan and in other countries, and has already succeeded in having seven article published in a national science journal.

**Alice Yalaoui** obtained her Engineering degree in Industrial Engineering and her master's degree in Systems Optimization and safety in 2001 from the University of Technology of Troyes (France) 2001, and her Ph.D. degree in Systems Optimization and safety from the Troyes University of Technology (UTT) in 2004. She is currently associated professor at the OSI-ICD laboratory and at the UMR CNRS "Sciences and Technologies for Risk Management", at the Troyes University of Technology. Her research topic focuses on the reliability optimization, system design, Bin packing problems, operations research, modeling and simulation.

**Farouk Yalaoui** obtained his Engineering degree in Industrial Engineering from the Polytechnics School of Algiers (Algeria) in 1995, his master's degree in Industrial System Engineering from Polytechnics Institute of Lorraine (Nancy, France) in 1997, his Ph.D. degree in Production Management from the Troyes University of Technology (UTT) in 2000 and followed by a Habilitation à diriger les recherches (Dr. Hab) from Compiegne University of Technology (UTT) in 2006. He is currently a full Professor at Troyes University of Technology, France, where he is head of Master programme of UTT and head of Production management and Filed 2 of OSI-ICD team (FRE CNRS, UTT). His research topic focuses on the scheduling problems, system design, operations research, modeling, analysis and optimization of logistic and production systems, reliability and maintenance optimization and on optimization problems in general. He is author or co-author of more than 150 contributions, publications or communications with one book, three book chapters and 35 articles in journals such as IIE Transactions, European Journal of Operational research, International Journal of Production Economics, IEEE Transactions on Reliability, Reliability Engineering and System Safety, Computer & Operations research, Journal of Intelligent Manufacturing. He also published more than 110 papers in conference proceedings.

**Jack J. W. Yang** is a professor at the Department of Finance, National Yunlin University of Science and Technology, Taiwan. Professor Yang has participated with scientific research in more than 45 conferences-inside the country and abroad and has approximately 15 articles published in national science journal.

**Haofan Zhang** is an undergraduate student of the computer science and software engineering department at Xi'an Jiaotong-Liverpool University, P.R. China. He is enrolled in a program leading to an undergraduate degree in information and computing sciences.

# Index